EMPIRE, ENSLAVEMENT
AND FREEDOM
IN THE CARIBBEAN

Empire, ENSLAVEMENT AND FREEDOM IN THE CARIBBEAN

MICHAEL CRATON

Ian Randle Publishers
Kingston

James Currey Publishers
Oxford

Markus Wiener Publishers
Princeton

© Michael Craton 1997

First Published in Jamaica, 1997 by
Ian Randle Publishers
206 Old Hope Road
Kingston 6, Jamaica

ISBN   976-8123-07-9 cloth
       976-8123-08-7 paper

A catalogue record for this book is available from the
National Library of Jamaica

First Published in the United Kingdom, 1997 by
James Currey Publishers
73 Botley Road
Oxford OX2 0BS

ISBN   0-85255-741-8 cloth
       0-85255-742-6 paper

British Cataloguing in Publication Data
Craton, Michael
Empire, enslavement and freedom in the Caribbean
1. Slavery – Caribbean Area – History   2. Caribbean Area – History
I. Title
972.9'03

First Published in the United States of America, 1997 by
Markus Wiener Publishers
114 Jefferson Road
Princeton, NJ 08540

ISBN   1-55876-158-6 cloth
       1-55876-159-4 paper

Library of Congress Cataloging-in-Publication Data
available upon request

Cover and book design by Robert Harris

Set in Janson 10.5/14 x 27

Printed and bound in the U.S.A. by
Data Reproductions Corporation

Cover painting: 'Crop Time', by Albert Huie, 1955

Contents

PART THREE
Transformations and Continuities

Preface

These essays are drawn from the output of almost 40 years' study of the history of the West Indies. The collection is not meant to constitute a complete or final round-up on attaining the normal age of retirement, let alone a kind of *festschrift* to myself. Rather, it is an attempt to integrate, around three broad themes, those shorter pieces which have punctuated the writing, filled in gaps and extended the range of the several books on the region I have produced since 1962. Far more important than representing the process of my own maturing, these books and the essays collated here were written during a period when West Indian historiography and West Indian countries themselves were being hugely transformed.

In vital respects, my involvement with the Caribbean and its history has been conditioned by a close association with the Bahamas and its people, dating back to 1956, long before the achievement of black majority rule and political independence. One year out of university, without a teaching qualification, and so ignorant of the region as to confuse the Bahamas with Bermuda and Barbados, I was appointed to teach history at the Government High School in Nassau, after an interview conducted at the London offices of the Crown Agents for the Colonies by the school's headmaster, a white expatriate and old-fashioned colonialist.

In the year of the UK's Suez debacle, now widely regarded as the last knell of British imperialism, I was broadly on the side of the Egyptian nationalists, but self-centredly regarded my departure for the Bahamas as a disengagement from such issues, rather than as a recruitment as one of the tiniest outlying cogs of the UK's imperial machine. Late colonial realities, however, quickly brought me to my senses. Although (as my contract required) I did not become involved in politics, I resisted the headmaster's advice to join the right (that is, white and expatriate) clubs, and made most of my friends on the other side of the hill, among my black colleagues, the parents of my pupils, and the black Bahamian and Barbadian sportsmen of the cricket league.

At school I was increasingly disgruntled to find my teaching locked into a syllabus that seemed back to front; concentrating on the history of the UK and of the British Empire as viewed from Downing Street, with only a cursory imperialist glance at the West Indies, and virtually nothing on the Bahamas and Bahamians themselves. One of the chief impediments, symptom as well as cause, was the absence of a definitive history of the Bahamas. So in the holidays and spare time of my last two years at GHS, and without any encouragement from the authorities, I wrote one. This, thanks to the enterprising local representative of the publisher Collins, was brought out late in 1962.

Although *A History of the Bahamas* was sufficiently censorious of the white Bay Street oligarchy to make it more comfortable for me to have left the Bahamas before it appeared, the book contained unenlightened views, then still widely held by Bahamians of every shade, about British imperialism, slavery and the African heritage. Even when revised in 1968 and 1986 it remained essentially an old-style narrative history of political events and prominent people. The historical and ideological flaws of this first work were gradually made apparent by three years of graduate study at McMaster University in Canada, and even more by a growing acquaintance with the West Indies at large, their history and historians.

Almost predictably, I chose the study of a British imperial institution in the West Indies, the Vice Admiralty Courts, for my doctoral dissertation topic (1965-68). Then through a lucky set of chances I moved on without a pause to write the tercentenary history of a Jamaican sugar planation, Worthy Park, in collaboration with a friend made at McMaster, James Walvin. This was made possible both by the generous sponsorship of one of Worthy Park's owners, George Clarke, and through the recommendation of a distinguished Jamaican historian, Douglas Hall, who had been asked to take on the commission but was too busy to do so.

James Walvin and I were given remarkably free rein by the Clarkes, and we strove to be impartial and write of the slaves and modern labourers as well as the estate's successive white owners. But this did not prevent some Jamaican academics asking why two white Englishmen had been chosen to write Worthy Park's history, and prejudging the book as biased in favour of Jamaica's white oppressors. Even Douglas Hall, in a good-natured review, categorised *A Jamaican Plantation* as 'the tale of the good ship Worthy Park', essentially a celebratory business history, drawn almost entirely from the owners' ledgers and official colonial records, and thus inevitably skewed.

This moral hardly needed to be driven home. Reading and pondering on Worthy Park's extensive slave records, and becoming ever more familiar with the work of radical and revisionary historians of the Atlantic slave trade, slavery and abolitionism (notably Eric Williams, Philip Curtin and Elsa Goveia), led me first to write a comprehensive short history of British slavery (*Sinews of Empire*, 1974) and then, nailing my colours to the mast, to retell the story of Worthy Park and its people from the point of view mainly of the underclass, in *Searching for the Invisible Man* (1978). The modest success of the first as a paperback with West Indian students was a nice recompense for a complete sundering of friendly relations and the loss of further sponsorship which followed the (somewhat delayed) digestion of the second by the Worthy Park whites and other members of the Jamaican planter class.

Apart from its determination to explore the interrelationship of all elements in slave society – whites and free coloureds as well as slaves – and of the continuities between slave and modern plantation societies, *Searching for the Invisible Man* signalled a growing interest in slave demography and its relationship to the lives slaves made for themselves. This included women as well as men, despite the unfortunate implication of the title. During and after writing the book, I was involved with the growing band of scholars engaged in studies of slave health, family organisation and religion, and became especially interested in the resistance of slaves – along with that of their Amerindian and African predecessors, and their Afro-American and East Indian-West Indian successors – to the dominant socioeconomic system. This interest climaxed in the publication of *Testing the Chains: Resistance to Slavery in the British West Indies* (1982), which was dedicated to the Guyanese socialist martyr historian, Walter Rodney.

In 1983, after more than two decades, I returned, full circle, to re-evaluate Bahamian history, in the light of a now entrenched commitment to telling the story from the point of view of the colonial periphery rather than the imperial metropole, and of the ordinary people rather than the élite. I was now also committed to the multi-disciplinary and cliometric techniques of the so-called New Social History. With the help in the first phase of three admirable graduate students from the University of Waterloo and the full collaboration of a former doctoral supervisee, Gail Saunders (who had the inestimable attribute of being the founding director of the Bahamas Archives), a first volume of *Islanders in the Stream: A History of the Bahamian*

People was published to coincide with the Columbus Quincentennial in October 1992. This volume covered the period up to the end of formal slavery. Delayed as much by the heartening proliferation of Bahamian and British West Indian scholarship as by other commitments and the almost glacial procedures of its academic publisher, the second volume, telling of the Bahamian people's long transition out of slavery and class oppression, their achievement of majority rule and independence, and their first decades as a nation, should appear at about the same time as the present book.

Monumental at least in size, *Islanders in the Stream* may well prove to be the last of my major monographs. But this and the other books published since 1962 somewhat unfairly focus attention on a limited range of the themes touched on over a long career. The books themselves are mainly out of print, but the articles written in between are even more fugitive and reclusive. They are hidden away in a variety of journals, conference proceedings, *festschrifts*, multi-authored commissioned collections, and encyclopedias. It is difficult enough for the author to keep track of what he has written and where it was published, even sometimes to lay his hand on a copy. That for even the most assiduous reader to be familiar with the whole range is almost impossible was recently borne out by the writer of a critique who, while claiming to be 'an avid reader' of my works, castigated me for neglecting certain aspects of a topic which I had in fact fully considered in several published articles, if not in my books.

At the very least, the following 'occasional' pieces augment and reinforce, if not refine, the subjects of my books. Some venture off in further directions, although only essays 1, 2 and 7 travel any distance beyond the bounds of the history of the Caribbean since the arrival of the Europeans and their African slaves. Although numerous (and voluminous) enough, they do not constitute a complete emptying of the barrel, particularly in relation to Bahamian material. Several essays in this collection (notably 11, 12, 19 and 21) involve the Bahamas and its people, the history of which (and whom) has been so important in initiating and rounding out my career as a professional writer-historian. But the wider Caribbean focus of the volume, even more than space considerations, consigns many specifically Bahamian articles already published, and several more planned, to a further specialised collection. This I trust will appear (God and the demigods of the publishing world willing) at least somewhat in advance of my obituaries.

It is for critics to judge what is original, idiosyncratic, or derivative in the following collection. I fear that there will be less of the first category than of the second and third, although I hope that the range and particular combination of topics is at least distinctive. We all, more or less, owe debts to all other scholars whom we have ever read, heard, or talked with, even those who have stimulated us into contradiction. Borrowings are particularly likely to have been unconscious in a person like myself, a jackdaw in respect of historical data and ideas, with (for an historian) a notably poor memory and note-taking technique.

Besides those historians in unrelated fields and scholars in cognate disciplines whose lateral influence, although imponderable, may be profound, I would like to pay special tribute to certain individual scholars (or, in most cases, to their books), and to meetings attended, which have been consciously and directly beneficial. Richard Pares remains for me the greatest historian who has turned his attention to the West Indies; but almost equally inspirational, in different ways, have been C. L. R. James, Eric Williams, Elsa Goveia, Walter Rodney, Charles Verlinden, David Brion Davis, Francisco Moreno Fraginals, Richard Sheridan, Nigel Bolland and Hilary Beckles. Inspiring more contradiction than agreement have been Orlando Patterson and Eugene Genovese. Methodologically I have learned immensely from Philip Curtin, Barry Higman, Jan Vansina, Oscar Zanetti, David Eltis and Stanley Engerman. Across the disciplines, the following have been notably influential: Peter J. Wilson, Sidney Mintz, Arnold Sio, Roger Abrahams, Kenneth Kiple and Richard Price. More generally, the annual meetings of the Association of Caribbean Historians have been potent refuelling stops every year since 1970, while of innumerable special conferences attended I would single out that on slavery issues organised by Eugene Genovese and Stanley Engerman at Rochester in 1974, the Waterloo slavery conference of 1979, the meeting in honour of Herbert Aptheker at Stanford in 1982, the Eric Williams symposium at Bellagio in 1984, and that on the theme 'Large Questions in Small Places' presided over by Charles Joyner at Carolina Coastal College in 1988.

Other institutions and individuals have provided equally valued support and stimulation. Foremost is the History Department at Waterloo which has been my intellectual base since 1966, with special thanks among my colleagues to David Davies, Leonard Guelke, John New, Stanley Johannesen, James Walker and David Wright. I have been lucky in my collaborators, not just those whose names are linked with mine on title pages – James Walvin, David Wright, Gary Greenland and Gail Saunders – but several generations of graduate students who have contributed in ways not always formally acknowledged. Archives and their staffs have always been kind to me, above all those of the Bahamas and Jamaica; and for many years I was

equally fortunate with libraries, especially those of the Royal Commonwealth Society (till it was dispersed) and the University of London (while
it still allowed free access and borrowing privileges to London graduates).
I am also deeply grateful for the 'once in a lifetime' benefits of a residency
at the Rockefeller Center at Bellagio in 1987.

Last, it is fitting and fair that most credit and thanks for this personal
collection of essays goes to my nearest and dearest. Like all my writings, I
offer the book to my chief sustainers and hopes for the future, my wife Pat
and the children, Lorna, Amanda and Darius; less for the few original
thoughts it may contain than for the chance that it may retain for their later
lives echoes of a voice they wish to remember. The work is formally
dedicated, though, to my parents, Morris and Edith Craton, who died in
1946 and 1973. They made me what I am; and only now am I rediscovering
them in myself.

JANUARY 1997

Introduction

This collection cannot claim to be a comprehensive text, but its pieces have been selected and edited with the aim of covering important themes as widely as possible, minimising overlaps and disguising seams. It therefore hopes to provide something close to a supplementary overview for students, as well as a survey of the author's own special contributions to West Indian scholarship for the comparative few to whom this may be of interest.

Although the majority of the essays, reflecting their author's area of concentration, focus on the British West Indies, efforts have been made to select pieces that roam farther abroad or include examples and arguments of more widespread application. This principle especially applies to the choice of the three major thematic units into which the collection is divided, each of which is of general relevance in the history of the region, if not more widely still. The remainder of this introduction will accordingly delineate these general topics, using the individual pieces mainly by way of illustration, rather than describing them systematically. Each essay, however, is briefly introduced where it occurs in the text.

The six essays in Part I range most widely of all, not just in coming to grips with such general concepts as imperialism and colonialism, but spatially and temporally too. The first piece sets the tone by arguing that the development of the West Indies as plantation colonies was but the culmination of a process dating back to classical times, whereby territorial and military expansion and the takeover and exploitation of native peoples were related to the profit motive and the evolution of ever more sophisticated forms of agriculture, processing, commerce and finance.

This may be labelled a form of economic determinism, and even Marxist in many of its assumptions and the use of terms. The same holds true of other essays later in the collection. But as true believers have always detected, I have never been more than – in my own words – a wishy-washy

Marxist. In common with most of my generation I have found many of Marx's concepts and categories useful, even beguiling, as a grammar or language of explanation and communication. This includes Mark's definition of capital, the relationship between capital and class, class relations, and the dialectic. Yet long before the collapse of communism relegated its primary author from his godlike status and changed our views of history's ends, I had found the grand structures of Marx's analysis modified out of recognition by 'Neo-Marxists', or undermined altogether by historical actualities.

It was difficult enough to fit Marx's definitions of slavery, plantations and peasantries into what I observed in the history of the West Indies. But an even greater problem was the reconciliation of the actual development of slavery and plantations with Marx's programmatic and essentially Eurocentric version of global history. Even Eric Williams – far more of a Marxist historian than his socialist critics, or even himself, recognised – although he had valuable things to say about the nature of African slavery, of racism, imperialism and neo-colonialism, was locked into a world view as constricted by his European education as it was by his status as a colonial subject of African extraction (not to mention his quite colossal ego).

Not that this collection plays down the importance of the West Indies or of West Indian chattel slavery in the development of modern world history. On the contrary, in the second essay and other places there are strong statements to the effect that a kind of imperialism of scholarship consequent upon the modern growth of the USA has unfairly marginalised the history of the Caribbean. Marx himself is much to blame, his view of plantations and plantation slavery conditioned by his familiarity with the cotton plantations of the US South at the time of the Civil War and the industrialisation of the North, and by his almost complete ignorance of the West Indies (by then a comparative backwater, except for Cuba). Eric Williams, on the other hand, allowed his antagonism towards the USA to underplay if not ignore the way that the West Indies and North America were indissolubly related, even when the West Indies were the most prized of European colonies. Further, *Capitalism and Slavery* suggests, at least by implication, that it was both Caribbean slavery and the process of abolition and emancipation initiated in the British Empire that were normative throughout the hemisphere, including the USA; an exaggeration that is one of the reasons Williams' most famous work, the Little Red Book of history studies in the Caribbean during the 1960s and 1970s, has had so little resonance in US slavery scholarship.

If giving the history of the West Indies a truer global perspective, and in the process helping the student reader to come to terms with the two writers most influencing modern West Indian historiography, are the grandest aspirations of the first part of this collection, there are at least four other notable subthemes that, if not entirely revisionary, may be equally useful.

As their almost identical titles announce, the two most famous general histories of the Caribbean, by Eric Williams and Juan Bosch, begin with Christopher Columbus and end with Fidel Castro; and studies of the British West Indies even more narrowly tend to run only from the coming of the English to the achievement of political independence, focusing on the colonists, their imperial masters and their anglo-creole slaves. In principle at least this collection is not so narrowly constrained. Unfortunately, there is no separate essay on the pre-Columbian Amerindians (a study of the Lucayans being saved for the planned collection of essays on the Bahamas); but the last essay in Part I does attempt some generalisations about the responses of European colonists and indigenous peoples to each other, and the inevitable mutation and subversion of even the most resistant and resourceful of the latter, through a study of the Black Caribs of St Vincent from the first quarter of the seventeenth century to the end of the eighteenth century.

Likewise, there is no separate essay on the pre-English phase in the history of Caribbean colonisation. Yet from the first essay it is stressed that the arrival of the English was far from being an entirely new dispensation. The period of Spanish hegemony in the Caribbean not only saw the introduction of the sugar plantation system and laid the ground rules for treating native Amerindians, African slaves and the miscegenating runways called maroons; it also saw the non-Iberians initiate phases of plunder and clandestine trade that provided capital for the establishment of their own plantations and set up a lasting pattern of commerce, in which the Spanish colonies, no longer a serious military threat, were a glittering economic prize.

From then on, though, the non-Iberian powers were bitter competitors and rivals of each other. Competition for land and the trade in plantation produce, supplies and African slaves, coupled with aggressively exclusionist economic policies, led to a series of mercantilist wars between the European imperial powers, involving the Caribbean in naval and amphibious conflicts for more than a third of the years between 1652 and 1815. Essential agents in the process of transition from buccaneering to settled plantations, controlled channels of trade and formal mercantilist wars were the imperial Vice Admiralty Courts, the subject of the fifth essay in Part I.

Vice Admiralty Courts were responsible for the profitable business of adjudicating seized enemy cargoes during wartime, for enforcing the national laws of trade and, as an ancillary function, the trying of pirates as international criminals. Because of these imperialist purposes, the rise and decline of the British Caribbean Vice Admiralty Courts in numbers and volume of business neatly illustrate Britain's intermittent rise to imperial hegemony in the Caribbean, and the consequent transition from the First (mercantalist) Empire to the Second Empire of free trade and *laissez faire*. Moreover, as the fifth essay argues, since the Vice Admiralty Courts exercised national policies and served national and sectional interests through legal precepts far from universally accepted, they were classic illustrations of the principle that international law in practice was no more than an index of the capability of a stronger power to lord it over a weaker.

A similar positivist conclusion is argued in the third and fourth essays for the laws which the plantocracies of the British Caribbean framed for themselves in order to control the allocation of the land and the persons of their slaves. Whatever the origins of the plantocratic personnel – and these essays illustrate the wide range of original types from which they were drawn – what defined their class (as perhaps all ruling classes) was their ability to enact and enforce laws essentially in their own interest. In respect of land laws and the laws concerning property in general, these had roots in those principles and practices which had created the British metropolitan landed aristocracy and bourgeoisie. There was inevitable conflict over the definition of crown and private land, but the lasting and in due course crucial issue was whether or not West Indian chattel slavery could be reconciled with British common law in respect of individual rights.

This controversy rose to a climax, of course, in the debates that raged in the metropole after 1787 and led successively to the ending of the British slave trade in 1807 and the freeing of British slaves between 1834 and 1838, which are fully dealt with in Parts II and III. But what the last essay of Part I does illustrate is the way that the moral and legal issues of treating subject natives and transported slaves had already been the subject of heated debate in the imperial parliament about the respective rights of Black Caribs and white would-be planters in St Vincent after the takeover of the so-called Neutral Islands in 1763. As shown, the defence of native and slave rights related not just to the ideals of the Rights of Man emerging from the nascent Enlightenment, but to the considerably older controversy over whether unacculturated natives were noble savages or natural slaves. It was part, indeed, of that timeless controversy over the nature and justice of the enslavement of some humans by others, which David Brion Davis has memorably described as 'The Problem of Slavery in Western Culture'.

The legal and moral issues concerning slavery touched on in Part I act as a prelude to the essential matter of Part II of the collection. Except for the first essay, on the African background, it concentrates on the nature of Caribbean slavery itself. The central sequence of six essays (8-13), indeed, can be regarded as a survey of the subject more comprehensive, detailed and up-to-date, if rather less systematic, than that in my 1974 book *Sinews of Empire*. The analysis of Caribbean slavery in Part II, however, depends on at least four salient features that are still sufficiently problematic to require preliminary discussion here: a distinctive definition of Slave Society; the processual concept of creolisation; the extensive use made of cliometrics; and the stance taken in respect of the debate over slave resistance and accommodation.

Even before writing *Sinews of Empire* I adopted the definition of slave society first propounded by Elsa Goveia in 1965; that is, 'the whole social fabric of communities based on slavery, including masters and all freedmen as well as slaves'. This definition has had the worthy effect of devaluing traditional accounts which either described colonial society to exclude non-whites altogether, or judged the social behaviour of non-whites solely by white European norms, so that they emerged, at best, as an apeish subspecies. Elsa Goveia's definition was also a clarion call to a generation of scholars who wished to turn West Indian studies around so that the history of the region and its people would be seen from a Caribbean not a European perspective.

While giving a truer picture of social relationships and cultural interchange, Goveia's concept of slave society does run the danger of obscuring the degrees to which whites, free coloureds and slaves did in fact have and retain their separate social identities. This is particularly true, at opposite ends of the scale, for those white plantation and slave-owners who were partly or wholly absentees living in the metropole, and those slaves (or aspects of slave life) which obdurately retained African elements never to be incorporated into the colonial social matrix.

Perhaps exaggerating the implications of Elsa Goveia's formulation, we have also tended to set up the rural slave plantation as the truest model for slave society at large. This has, of course, to be modified to take account of urban social life, and to include the undoubtedly significant coexistence of other non-plantation slaves (such as mariners, logcutters and salt-rakers), of poor or transient whites (including officials, soldiers and sailors), of Sephardic Jewish merchants and other foreigners, runaway slaves and, at least in the mainland colonies, of native Amerindians.

The indispensable concept for describing and understanding the complex Caribbean mix and mixing process is that of creolisation. By this we mean not just the steady increase in the proportion of those actually born in the colonies and the concommitant increase in their influence on the culture, but, even more importantly, the syncretic process itself, whereby native and imported persons and cultures were dynamically melded in the crucible of the environment, to produce in time a distinctive new (that is, creole) culture. First articulated by one of Elsa Goveia's students, a black Barbadian poet-historian, Edward Kamau Brathwaite, this concept had the positive merit of countering Orlando Patterson's contention that Caribbean slavery (like all slavery, by definition) was no more than a form of social death, and the even bleaker view of the Trinidad-born East Indian, Vidia Naipaul, that 'nothing was created in the West Indies'.

Yet the concept of creolisation has its own problems. As Kamau Brathwaite's own work demonstrates, it does not apply similarly to whites as to blacks, having more relevance to the latter; and it seems to have little relevance at all to East Indians and other migrants to the Caribbean after slavery ended. Creolisation is surely real, and it has special value as a mode of analysing and presenting; but it is a continuous process without a singular end, almost infinitely varied in pace and form, although it does have its modern ideals in mottos like the Jamaican 'Out of Many One People', or in the designation of creole dialects as authentic regional languages.

Third, no one can deny that cliometrics, particularly the use of demographic statistics, have been an essential part of the revolutionary change towards seeing West Indian history from the inside outwards, and from the perspective of the mass of the people rather than that of their masters. Personally I would be content to have my work in West Indian social history evaluated largely from my use of cliometrics, especially in respect of those few methods I have pioneered (some in this collection, more in *Searching for the Invisible Man*). However, it is important to be sensitive to the fact that the raw data on which cliometrics depend almost inevitably derive from white officials, owners and plantation managers, and to recognise that statistical averages are essentially depersonalising.

It is exciting to resurrect individuals and reconstruct aspects of their lives and family connections from ancient ledgers, and satisfying to learn more about the average fertility, mortality and health patterns of West Indian slaves than anyone previously knew (including the slaves themselves). We can make educated inferences about slaves' daily lives and relationships from these materials, and even about slaves' ideas and ideology from their actions. But beyond this, in the virtual absence of any material directly derived from slaves, we must do what we can to fill in the picture with the help (despite their white provenance) of the few realistic paintings and drawings that have survived, such rare journals as the Jamaican, Thomas Thistlewood's, of planters', soldiers' and governors' letters sent back to Britain, of court cases, or, most poignant of all, of the evidence taken in uncovering slave plots.

For, as at least four of the essays in this collection attest, much of the recent analysis of the behaviour of slaves in West Indian slave society has hinged on the ways in which – indeed, the degree to which – they resisted the slavery system. Initially bowled over by Herbert Aptheker's dictum that 'history is the story of resistance, not acquiescence' (which on reflection simply seemed to be another way of saying that 'since only resistance is important, we'll ignore all other types of subjects' behaviour'), I have since been at pains to qualify what constitutes true resistance. Perhaps in extending the concept so far beyond overt and armed resistance to include all ways in which slaves were able to fashion 'lives of their own' I have gone too far, to the very verge, as one critic claimed, of calling accommodation resistance.

On this matter of interpretation readers will, of course, make their own conclusion. Yet all should acknowledge that to continue to see slaves as merely reactive objects rather than having a subjective input into their own condition is to deny them their distinctive ideology. All peoples, almost by definition, have an ideology, and my belief is that the ideology possessed by West Indian slaves was not so much one of mere survival, or even of simple resistance, as one of aspiring towards the kind of lifestyle achieved by the most fortunate of them after emancipation; that of free peasants, working for others only when and as much as they wished to. This is very much in tune with those many scholars (mostly Marxists or quasi-Marxists) who have in recent years characterised slaves as proto-peasants or proto-proletarians (if not also proto-consumers), among whom I signal my own enrolment with the 1979 essay 'Proto-Peasant Revolts?' included in Part III of this collection.

In Marxist terms, this type of interpretation involves the historical dialectic between counterposed classes. Yet if there is one prevailing theme throughout this collection (and my work at large) it is another type of apposition or counterpoint; what has been labelled by Nigel Bolland and Eric Foner the perennial dialectic between change and continuity. This is clearly apparent already in the treatment of the development of plantations in Part I and of slave resistance in Part II. But it is an especially strong feature of the treatment of the transitions between the age of slavery and the modern era which preoccupy most of the essays in Part III.

All the essays in this book, indeed, reflect the way in which Caribbean scholarship in general has changed over the last few decades, and the directions in which it is currently pointing. The examination and analysis of slavery itself, although a subject far from mined out, largely gave way to the heated debate over how and why slavery came to an end, initiated, but notably not engaged in, by Eric Williams. This, in turn, has been succeeded by a rising wave of interest in the post-slavery period, including the question of the degree to which labour and class relations did, and did not, change as a consequence of slave emancipation.

Leading on naturally from the matter dealt with in Part II, the first four essays in Part III examine the ways (or the degree to which) slave resistance contributed to the slaves' emancipation, and argue that post-emancipation unrest illustrated both the continuance of forms of exploitation and oppression and the ways in which they were resisted by the ex-slave underclasses. Attempting to detail and explain this apparent continuum proceeds on two levels in the following three essays. These can lay claim to being among the most original contributions of the present collection, if only because they do not directly derive from or closely relate to larger works, although some might claim that together they are long enough almost to constitute a book in themselves.

The first of the three, despite being the shortest essay of all, lays out one of the most complex of equations: the relationship of changes in the system of plantation labour to technological change. A simple portmanteau explanation is proposed, but more for the sake of argument than with real conviction, given the existence of so many other contingent factors. The resolution of these is the essential purpose of the other two essays in the trio; one covering the British Caribbean from 1780 to 1890, and the other applying the same principles, as far as possible, to the Caribbean at large. Essential themes are the continuing will to maintain mastery and the ingenuity in sustaining their predominance on the part of the white planter class, and the continuing will to seek a life of their own choice on the part of the black underclass – slaves whom Sidney Mintz and Nigel Bolland first labelled proto-peasants and proto-proletarians becoming after emancipation, for the most part, the uneasy but distinctly Caribbean category termed by Richard Frucht 'part-peasants: part-proletarians'.

The final essay sounds from its metaphorical title as if it intends to put the cap on the collection with a simple *jeu d'esprit*. Yet it has a serious purpose. Reaching back to provide defining examples, it helps to bring the present volume together. It also makes the practical suggestion about the way ahead for Caribbean historiography. More importantly, though, the essay is an attempt to lead readers, especially the young, towards recognising the role of history in defining regional, island and personal identities. It has a special relevance perhaps to the present collection, as well as a personal resonance, even poignancy, for its author. It intentionally celebrates the richness of the history and culture of the Caribbean, constitutes a plea for those lucky enough to have been born and bred there to recognise and revalue their heritage, and is intended to signify the author's own good fortune to have spent a long and not unprofitable career getting to know and recording the history of the region and its people. It rounds off a collection which itself must seem something of a summing up, if not quite a final professional signing-off.

Acknowledgements

1. The Historical Roots of the Plantation Model. *Slavery and Abolition*, Vol. 5, No. 3, December 1984, 189-221.
2. The West Indies and North America. Jacob E. Cooke *et al.* (eds), *Encyclopedia of the North American Colonies*, 3 vols, New York, Macmillan and Scribners, 1993, I, 221-231.
3. The Planters' World in the British West Indies. Bernard Bailyn and Philip Morgan (eds), *Strangers Within the Realm: Cultural Margins of the First British Empire*, Chapel Hill, University of North Carolina Press, 1991, 314-362.
4. Property and Propriety: Land Tenure and Slave Property in the creation of a British West Indian Plantocracy, 1612-1740. Susan Staves and John Brewer (eds), *Early Modern Conceptions of Property*, London and New York, Routledge, 1995, 497-529.
5. Caribbean Vice Admiralty Courts and British Imperialism. *Caribbean Studies*, 2, July 1971, 5-20.
6. Planters, British Imperial Policy and the Black Caribs of St Vincent. Robert Paquette and Stanley Engerman (eds), *Parts Beyond the Seas: The Lesser Antilles in the Age of European Expansion*, Gainesville, Florida Universities Press, 1996, 71-85.
7. The African Background of American Slavery. Randall M. Miller and John David Smith (eds), *Dictionary of Afro-American Slavery*, Westport, CT, Greenwood Press, 1988, 10-23.
8. Slavery and Slave Society in the British Caribbean. Seymour Drescher and Stanley Engerman (eds) *Encyclopedia of Slavery*, New York, Garland Press, 1998.
9. Jamaican Slavery. Eugene Genovese and Stanley Engerman (eds), *Race and Slavery in the Western Hemisphere: Quantitative Studies*, Princeton, Princeton University Press, 1975, 249-284.

10. The Rope and the Cutlass: Slave Resistance in Plantation America. *Indian Historical Review*, XVIII, 1994, 1-19.

11. Hobbesian or Panglossian? The Two Extremes of Slave Conditions in the British West Indies, 1783-1834. *William and Mary Quarterly*, 35, 1978, 226-256.

12. Changing Patterns of Slave Family in the British West Indies. *Journal of Interdisciplinary History*, 10, Summer 1979, 1-35.

13. Slave Culture, Resistance and Emancipation in the British West Indies. James Walvin (ed.), *Slavery and British Society, 1776-1846*, London, Macmillan, 1982, 100-122.

14. Proto-Peasant Revolts? The Late Slave Rebellions in the British West Indies, 1816-32. *Past and Present*, 85, November 1979, 99-125.

15. What and Who, to Whom and What: The Significance of Slave Resistance in the British West Indies. Stanley Engerman and Barbara Solow (eds), *Caribbean Slavery and British Capitalism: The Legacy of Eric Williams*, Cambridge University Press, 1987, 259-282.

16. Continuity Not Change: Late Slavery and Post-emancipation Resistance in the British West Indies. *Slavery and Abolition*, Vol. 7, No. 1, Fall 1988, 144-170.

17. Changing Sugar Technology and the Labour Nexus: The Search for a Unified Field Theory. *Nieuwe Westindische Gids*, Spring 1990, 135-142.

18. Reshuffling the Pack: The Transition from Slavery to other forms of Labour in the British Caribbean, 1780-1890. *Nieuwe Westindische Gids*, 68, 1-2, 1994, 23-75; *Estudos Afro-Asiaticus* (Rio de Janeiro), 28, October 1995, 31-83 (in Portuguese).

19. Transition to Free Wage Labour in the British Caribbean, 1780-1890. *Slavery and Abolition*, Vol. 13, No. 2, August 1992, 37-67; *Estudos Afro-Asiaticus* (Rio de Janiero), 22, September 1992, 5-32 (in Portuguese).

20. A Recipe for the Perfect Calalu: Island and Regional Identity in the West Indies. Hilary Beckles (ed.), *Inside Slavery: Process and Legacy in the Caribbean Experience*, Barbados, Canoe Press, 1996, 120-140.

PART ONE

Colonisation
and
Imperialism

1

The Historical Roots
of the Plantation Model

Introduction: This essay was to have been delivered as the first paper in the first session of a major conference on slavery organised by Vera Rubin in New York in 1984, but it fell by the wayside through a misunderstanding when the meeting was rescheduled. Because of its non-delivery at the conference it failed to benefit from the constructive criticisms that would have been expected there. Published shortly afterwards in unamended form in *Slavery and Abolition*, it came under fire for seemingly slighting previous scholarship in the field, notably that of the great Charles Verlinden. The article has been revised for this publication to the extent that the author agrees the criticisms were justified. But it should be pointed out that the main purpose of the essay was not simply to describe the gradual westward shift of sugar production and plantations in general, but to trace the roots, continuities and slow evolution of the plantation model *per se*, and to summarise the interrelationship of geographical and political factors, technology, distribution, markets, capital formations, ownership and, above all, the institution of chattel slavery (mainly African), which were not nearly so well covered in the established literature. In this version, advantage is taken of the important work on the historical geography of the cane sugar industry by J. H. Galloway, published in 1989, although plantations producing crops other than sugar – notably cotton and coffee – are also considered.

Classic Marxism, reinforced by the influential work of Eric Williams, assumes that the true plantation was an artifact of the modern world. Essentially land –, capital – and labour-intensive, it is thought to have been incompatible with feudal modes, means and relations of production. Its genesis is therefore assumed to have been related to the westward expansion of Europe, the concomitant rise of bourgeois capitalism, and the development of Negro slavery following the unlocking of the West African coast.[1] This essay, on the contrary, will build on the work of the great non-Marxist historian of colonisation, Charles Verlinden, to show that not only was the

1

plantation slow to evolve, exhibiting changes of scale rather than fundamental transformations, but that it antedated European expansion into the
Atlantic sphere by at least 350 years. The plantation was undoubtedly
related to European colonisation of a sort from the beginning, but the initial
stages of plantation development occurred outside the ambit of European
feudalism proper and largely independent of it, and the initial area of
colonial plantation activity was the Mediterranean not the Atlantic.[2]

After defining the classic plantation and distinguishing it from classic
feudalism, we will test the assumptions outlined above from the historical
evidence. Because the earliest important plantations, in Old and New
World alike, grew sugar, and because of the bias in earlier scholarship, we
will concentrate on the history of sugar production, though with side
glances at other large-scale agricultural enterprises.[3] As far as possible, in
each phase of plantation development the same features will be analysed;
to compare and contrast, but also to show, wherever relevant, how one
enterprise related – and often led – to another. These features include the
form of ownership and its authorisation, whether individual, hereditary or
corporate; the relationship between owner-planters and the state, and the
degree to which the law reflected the will of the owner-planter class; the
methods of raising capital for land, technology and labour; the means of
acquiring land and, where relevant, authority over indigenous people; the
nature of the labour force and the degree of servility imposed; the agricultural and processing operations involved; the distribution and sale of
produce and the generation and deployment of profits; the relations between ownership, management and labour, whether or not these related to
ethnic and cultural as well as class differences; and, lastly, the relations
between colonial planters – whether or not organised as a local plantocracy
– and metropolitan or imperial authorities.

The central intention is to prove that the plantation model was not the
product of Europe alone over a couple of centuries, but of the Mediterranean world in general over something like a millennium. In the development of plantations there was a progression analogous to the maturation of
an oak. But it was only in the scale and intensity, location and directions of
flow of their operations that plantations in Brazil in 1550, Barbados in 1650,
mainland North America between 1750 and 1850 – even plantations after
slavery ended – differed significantly from those, say, in Madeira in 1450,
Sicily in 1350, Cyprus in 1250, or Palestine in 1150. The roots of the
plantation model were deep indeed, and almost as ramified as the branches
of the tree above, resulting from a commingling of the traditions, structures,

energies and actual peoples of Rome, Byzantium and Islam, the Jewish diaspora, medieval Christian Europe, the Italian city-states of Genoa, Pisa and Venice, and the vast pagan hinterlands of Asia and Africa.

The plantation is a system of large-scale agriculture for export, generally involving the production of tropical crops in a colonial situation. Plantations tend towards monoculture, with produce exported in a raw or, at most, semi-processed condition. Plantations require large areas of suitable available land, fertile and well-watered, but with either a low-density original population or an indigenous people easily converted into a resident work-force. For plantations are labour-intensive, at least during planting and harvesting seasons, and they require a large, locationally rooted and constrained, if not actually servile, work-force. In the absence of an adequate indigenous population, plantations require the means to import suitable labourers who, if available easily and cheaply enough, and sufficiently constrained, will be worked virtually to death, with little or no concern for self-propagation.

Because of the necessarily exploitative conditions of plantation labour, imported labourers are ideally chattel slaves, or at least quasi-slaves. The local colonial polity will also, ideally, be plantocratic; that is, reflect the will of the planter class. Occasionally, plantation owners will be resident and act as their own managers, but more commonly they are absentees, engaged in the business of shipping, refining and marketing, or living a leisured life on their profits, while leaving the harsh realities of primary production, labour exploitation and tropical climate to an intermediate managerial class. Almost inevitably, though, both owners and their salaried employees are of a different ethnicity from the mass of the plantation labour force – be it native or imported.

The success of plantations depends upon the availability of suitable technology, and the means to export and distribute the product profitably. This predicates a certain level of industrialisation, the control of shipping and land transportation routes, and at least a rudimentary mechanism of credit and exchange. The need for capital, for land, labour, processing technology and shipping, and the profit motive itself, determine that the ownership of plantations will be capitalistic. The forms of ownership differ; including not only individuals but families, family businesses, religious orders, municipal corporations, companies, city-states, or even nation-states in the person of the monarch or royal family. In any case, plantations require a considerable degree of state endorsement, in the granting of lands, charters, a legal mandate, monopolies and other forms of economic protection. This produces a binding tension between colonial plantocracies and imperial or metropolitan authority, though at times the plantation system – that is, the whole nexus of production, processing and marketing – becomes important enough almost to control the larger political economy, not vice versa, creating what might be termed an imperial, rather than purely local, plantocracy.

Plantation development has always been facilitated where chattel slavery has been institutionalised, but slavery has never been a *sine qua non*. Plantations existed before, and outside, the institution of chattel slavery, and have easily survived the abolition of formal slavery. Modern plantation theorists, indeed, argue that the plantation economy has been strong enough also to survive all phases of formal imperialism, having perpetuated an almost irreversible dependency upon the tropical regions of the world. For the West Indies at least, the Plantation Economy School – alias New World Group – has maintained that this insidious neocolonialism has stemmed from a kind of political and psychological inertia, reinforced by a set of conditions and constraints that determine that tropical ex-colonies remain primary agricultural producers and industrially underdeveloped. These include the continued command by plantations of a disproportionate amount of flat, fertile land, the concomitant control of the labour force through the shortage of land and markets for peasant produce and competition for wages because of relative overpopulation, as well as the perpetuation of capitalistic and absentee control by the retention of shipping, refining, marketing and banking as metropolitan monopolies.[4]

By definition, the classic plantation, as outlined above, was incompatible with classic feudalism, though this is not to say that either model was ever found in its purest form, or that the two systems were not bound to interrelate in areas and periods of crossover and change. To emphasise the essential and crucial contrast, before going on to examine the ways in which the two systems, and others, interrelated, one cannot do better than to quote the definition of feudalism given in the 15th Edition of the *Encyclopedia Britannica* (1979); 'In its specific, technical meaning', Feudalism was

> a social system of rights and duties based on land tenure and personal relationships in which land (and to a much lesser degree other sources of income) is held in fief by vassals from lords to whom they owe specific services and with whom they are bound by personal loyalty. In a broad sense, the term denotes 'feudal society', a form of civilisation that flourishes especially in a closed agricultural economy and has certain general characteristics besides the mere presence of lands, vassals and fiefs. In such a society, those who fulfill official duties, whether civil or military, do so not for the sake

of an abstract notion of 'the state' or of public service but because of personal and freely accepted links with their overlord, receiving remuneration in the form of fiefs, which they hold hereditarily. Because various public functions are closely associated with the fief rather than with the person who holds it, public authority becomes fragmented and decentralized. Another aspect of feudalism is the manorial or seigneurial system in which landlords exercise over the unfree peasantry a wide variety of police, judicial, fiscal and other rights.[5]

In some ways, but not all, Roman latifundia, and their Byzantine equivalents, were structural prototypes of later plantations, just as in some ways, but not all, the productive aspects of plantations were anticipated by the Arabs and Egyptians as they brought the cultivation of sugar westward from the Indian subcontinent to the shores of the Mediterranean Sea.

The development of the Roman *latifundia* – great privately owned landed estates growing wheat, vines and olives with the labour of slaves – accompanied the early territorial expansion of the Roman republic after the first Punic War, particularly in central and southern Italy and the adjacent island of Sicily. These great agricultural enterprises were, in a sense, colonial, though contiguous rather than – Sicily notwithstanding – overseas. They were created by a fortunate class of improving landlords, spurred by the almost insatiable demands of a growing metropolis for agricultural staples, and freed from the costs of competitive wage labour by the availability of perhaps 2 million enslaved war captives. In an area of relative underdevelopment, lands were easily consolidated, and the process accelerated as peasants were recruited into the army or, dispossessed, migrated to swell the plebian population of the city of Rome.

The more one learns of the nature and organisation of Roman *latifundia*, the more one is struck by parallels with later plantations. The socioeconomic structure was headed by a stratum of new-rich *latifundistas* who, like Cato, used their wealth partly to enter and influence the ruling class in Rome itself, with a middling class of citizen managers, and a mass of labourers drawn from many different non-Italian ethnicities. The wheat, wine and olive-oil produced required limited technology, but a complex machinery of distribution and sale. The owners – despite Marx's own puzzling remarks on Cato[6] – were more landed aristocrats than capitalists, but there was at least a proto-capitalist infrastructure, in the business of buying and speculating in land and slaves, manufacturing and providing tools, clothing and foodstuff, shipping and marketing the produce, and the quite sophisticated methods of banking, credit and even insurance.

But *latifundia* were properly the by-product of Roman imperial expansion and the flow of war captives which accompanied it, rather than themselves the driving force of that imperialism. They were not necessarily situated on overseas colonies (where tribute was the more normal form of exploitation) and they did not grow tropical crops for export. Instead, they were originally located in the peninsular heartland of the Roman Empire, growing staples for home consumption. Moreover, the slave-owning *latifundistas* never constituted a true plantocracy, their powers being curtailed by rival interests and a government concerned by the threat they posed to 'republican virtues', backed by an army which consisted of citizen-peasants, many of whom had themselves been dispossessed.

Thus the proto-plantation system of the *latifundium*, far from controlling the Roman Empire, never became the dominant agricultural system. Nor did it survive the Roman Empire save, to a limited degree, in the East. As the Roman Empire of the West declined, the flow of enslavable war captives dried up, and the increasing cost of labour are into profits. Later, trade was disrupted and the *latifundia* themselves were threatened with slave revolt and sack by pirates and barbarian marauders. Embattled estates fell into the hands of creditors and were broken up, with the descendants of slaves becoming progressively more like peasants, though still hereditarily tied to the land. With the breakdown of effective central government and the increased threat of barbarian incursions, the class of absentee *latifundistas* virtually disappeared, and only those landlords who could provide security for their tenants – that is, military protection in return for rent and services – were likely to survive. Thus the scene was set in western Europe, not for the consolidation of a plantation economy and the creation of a plantocratic class, but for what we have come to know as the feudal system.[7]

Only in the Eastern Empire, where the Byzantine emperors were able to re-conquer and control Asia Minor and Syria for several hundred years, did *latifundia* continue and expand, with plutocratic landlords able to appropriate, consolidate and improve captured farmlands, under the umbrella of military rule, dispossessing or depressing the status of the inhabitants and introducing a supplementary labour force of enslaved captives. In the Byzantine economy, the huge metropolis of Constantinople played much the same role as Rome in the earlier epoch, as market, trade and banking centre, as well as administrative and cultural capital – the glittering focus of power and conspicuous consumption that drew successful landlords like a magnet.[8]

Romans never grew the sugar cane, or even knew it, merely importing small quantities of processed sugar from the Orient as a mysterious and costly spice. It was the Arabs, within a hundred years of the original Mohammedan conquests, who brought the cultivation and processing of sugar inexorably westward. Between 800 and 1000 AD, almost as an index of the expansion of Islam and the luxurious prosperity that flowed from military power, the production of sugar spread from Mesopotamia to Egypt, Palestine, Syria, Cyprus, Crete, Sicily, North Africa and southern Spain, spilling over into the southernmost provinces of the Byzantine Empire. Thanks to a relatively sophisticated network of trade, processed sugar became a common commodity throughout the Mediterranean, even penetrating into the darkest recesses of western Europe – though still so expensive as to be regarded as having mainly medicinal value.[9]

Since the demand for sugar was seemingly open-ended, its profits were compellingly high. Yet while the sugar cane will grow like a weed in the right conditions of soil and climate, its conversion into a profitable market commodity almost determines the emergence of some, if not all, aspects of a plantation system. Planted canes take 18 months to mature, and even re-growths (ratoons) require a year, yet once ready, canes must be harvested at a high but steady rate over a comparatively short period, requiring to be processed within a few days of cutting. The few months of the crop, coupled with a similar period of back-breaking toil in the planting season, determine the need for a hard-driven and comparatively large, if seasonal, labour force which, especially if sugar production competes with other crops and modes of production, ideally consists of slaves. The size of the unit of production is decided by the efficiency of the mill used for crushing the cane stalks, and the boiling house used to crystallise the resulting juice. But the cost of plant and the lack of a continuous flow of income require the pre-existence of capital and credit, which tend to make sugar-growing landlords more or less subject to bankers or moneylenders. Sugar-planting landlords are similarly dependent on carriers, refiners, merchants and shippers to distribute their product and, if possible, to optimise their profits.

The somewhat hazy accounts of sugar production under Islam suggest that nowhere were all the elements necessary for a true plantation system found together, at least before 1000 AD. The largest areas of production were those where a sufficiency of fertile, well-watered or irrigable land was coupled with the availability of a servile work-force. What is often cited as the earliest instance of a plantation economy, southern Mesopotamia in the eighth and ninth centuries, was significantly found where there were huge resources of fertile reclaimable land, and the possibility of importing in large numbers, those persons whom the Arabs regarded as natural slaves, the black African *Zanj*. Though they were more famous for rice and other cereals than for sugar, for a century these 'proto-plantations' in the Tigris-Euphrates delta provided great wealth for a class of 'proto-capitalist' absentees in the city of Basra. The epochal revolt of the *Zanj* between 869 and 883 AD, however, convinced Islamic rulers of the unwisdom of allowing such large numbers of foreign slaves to remain virtually uncontrolled, and has led the Mesopotamian case to be described as an exceptional failed experiment in most subsequent accounts.[10]

Clearly, the problems of control (more than any religious scruples about the employment of slaves) decided that the normal and preferred labour system employed in Islamic sugar production was the compulsory labour of indigenous peasants – a form of corvée. This reduced productivity even more than did the relatively rude technology – which usually consisted of a single horizontal mill powered by oxen or men, and a modest-sized boiling house. Comparison with later West Indian plantations suggests that most Islamic factories were capable of producing no more than a dozen tons of sugar a year, which implies a unit of no more than a few acres in canes and a work-force numbered in tens, not hundreds.[11] Nowhere could such a scale of production have amounted to a plantation monoculture, let alone lead to the creation of a true plantocracy.

Two areas of Islam may have been partial exceptions: Morocco and Egypt. Archaeological research by Paul Berthier in the Sous and neighbouring valleys leading from the High Atlas towards the Atlantic has corroborated literary evidence that western Morocco had a sugar industry dating from before 900 AD, which reached peaks between the eleventh and twelfth centuries and again around 1550, before fading away altogether. Moroccan sugar production seems to have been a royal monopoly, with mills powered by water drawn from the High Atlas by aqueducts, and boiling houses fuelled from the forests which then covered the lower slopes. From inconclusive evidence, it also appears that the labour force consisted of black African slaves.[12]

Egypt, the area which between 1000 and 1350 AD produced as much sugar for export as the rest of Islam together, had even greater potential for developing a planation system, and probably came closest to it. The lower Nile valley and delta enjoyed an ideal climate and rich alluvial soils, the landlord class was able to command a large population of native *fellahin*, augmented by Nubian slaves, and production was further advanced by technical improvements such as the vertical two-roller mill and water-power, by excellent waterway transportation, and by the refining and mercantile services provided by Alexandria, the largest and richest of all Mediterranean commercial centres.[13] These relatively favourable conditions, however, only lasted until the later fourteenth century, when a combination of technological stagnation, labour shortages, and harassment and corruption on the part of the Sultanate, quite apart from increasing difficulties in the export trade, led to a marked decline in the Egyptian sugar industry.

Not coincidentally, Alexandria, during its golden centuries, contained the largest and most prosperous of all Jewish communities. For, as David Brion Davis has pointed out, 'from the ninth to the twelfth century Jews played a central role in the expansion of Mediterranean commerce and in pioneering long-distance trade'.[14] During this period, the Jews played an indispensable, if uncomfortable, intermediate role between otherwise incompatible centres of Islam, Byzantium and western Europe. They were tolerated for their energy and expertise, for their almost familial networks, and for the relatively flexible code which permitted them to engage in forms of commercial activity made difficult for Christians and Muslims by religious proscriptions. In every centre of commercial development, from Baghdad to Cordova, Constantinople to Barcelona, Jewish communities were pre-eminent in industry, banking, shipping and trade, including, to a degree that remains controversial, the trade in slaves. Jews were especially involved in the spread of sugar production, owning mills, boiling houses and refineries, first in Egypt and later in Cyprus, Sicily, North Africa and Spain.[15]

The pioneering success of the dispersed Mediterranean Jews aroused the jealousy and animosity of Italian city-states, Christian kingdoms and revivalist Muslims alike, and this in turn accounted for the failure of the Jews to become completely dominant in late medieval and early modern commerce. Yet Jewish history has always been a creative dialectic between enterprise and oppression, and it is significant that the waves of anti-Jewish persecution, which rose to a climax in the fifteenth and sixteenth centuries, did not prevent the vital later contributions to European commerce of the *marrano* converts, or the seminal contributions of Sephardic exiles to the development of plantations in the New World, under the protection of, successively, Portugal, Holland, England and France.[16]

Despite even earlier parallels and influences, the first true plantations can convincingly be held to have stemmed from the first true European colonial enterprise overseas, the catalytic confrontation of peoples and cultures which westerners call the Crusades. When Pope Urban II initiated the process at Clermont in November 1095, he invoked merely the prospect of expiation, sweetened by heavenly reward and earthly plunder. Few of the original crusaders intended to stay in the Holy Land. Yet they represented energies and forces beyond their ken – including relative overpopulation, a tentative economic expansionism, even the faint stirrings of a renaissance spirit – and finding themselves in contact with, if not fully in control of, a wondrous new world, they established a presence that lasted 200 years and changed western Europe for ever.[17]

In the crusading states, the feudal system for the first time confronted a fully established economy, and not least among the symbolic wonders discovered was the sugar cane, which Fulk of Chartres referred to as 'this unsuspected and inestimable present from Heaven'.[18] The lands of *Outremer* were fertile, but underdeveloped, or decayed from centuries of conflict. There were large areas suitable for the Mediterranean staples already well-known to the 'Franks' – wheat, olives and wines – but also the well-established cultivation of crops known only through expensive importations. These included silk, cotton, rice, dates and, above all, sugar, which the crusaders found growing prolifically in the flat plains surrounding the ports which became their longest-held strongholds in the Holy Land – especially Acre, Tyre and Sidon – and also on the shores of Galilee and in the Jordan Valley, over which they were to exercise a more tenuous control.

The indigenous population of the conquered parts of Palestine and Syria, though not densely settled, continued to outnumber the conquerors. Even after 250,000 Frankish colonists were introduced, the newcomers depended upon the natives' labour and skills in order to exploit local resources. Yet it could not be a simple feudal takeover, with the superimposition of a ruling class and administration like the Norman conquest of the British Isles. Classic feudal modes were upset by the complex new environment. A permanent fighting establishment was necessary, and much of the land was nominally carved up into royal domains, and seigneuries held by feudal barons, knights and religious orders. But the overlord class did not rule directly, or even reside on its lands. Unlike feudal Europe, cities predominated, peopled by absentee military landlords, a Frankish middle-class of men-at-arms and clerical bureaucrats, enclaves of Italian merchants and Jews, and a polyglot class of indigenous artisans, shopkeepers and servile labourers.[19]

Outside the cities, and under the protection of strategically placed castles, traditional agriculture was carried on by virtually land-owning peasants, drawn from a bewildering range of religions and cultures, living in clannish villages (*casalia*) under Frankish or local bailiffs (*dragomen*), native headmen (*raises*), or even indigenous sheikhs with incongruous feudal titles. The average peasant family farm was quite substantial – about 200 acres – providing a considerable surplus of produce for local markets. But the holdings of headmen and sheikhs could be far larger, producing crops suitable for export markets and requiring a considerable servile labour force.[20]

Money played a far larger part in the economy of the crusader states than it did in western Europe at that time. A great deal of reliable coin was in circulation, not just to serve a vigorous trading system, but for taxes and rents. There was also considerable sale of lands, even speculation. Though the relatively limited percentage of demesne lands meant that the demand for corvée labour was low, peasants were taxed approximately a third of their produce, with the indirect system of control meaning that these levies were commonly commuted into rent. For their part, the crusader landlords were increasingly content to enjoy an urban lifestyle unmatched in western Europe, made possible not only by incomes derived from rents on lands and such traditional seigneurial monopolies as the control of mills and irrigation works, but by luxurious foods and material goods, locally produced or brought in from a network of trade that included, if intermittently, Islamic cities, especially Damascus.[21]

All in all, though it was said that the indigenous inhabitants of *Outre-mer* felt less oppressed by the Christian crusaders than they had recently been by Arabs, Turks and Egyptians, it was upon their backs, under the stimulus of a crude and militaristic colonisation, that the traditional economy of Palestine and Syria regained some, if not all, of the vitality it had once enjoyed under Rome and Byzantium.[22] Moreover, there were also more 'progressive' forces at work in the crusader states which helped to bring the indigenous agriculture closer to a true plantation economy. The Cistercians, who in the marginal areas of western Europe were pioneer landlords, working with gangs of lay brothers or even paid employees rather than feudal serfs, refused to participate in the crusader enterprise 'because of the invasion of the pagans and the difficulties of the climate'.[23] But their place was even more effectively taken by the military orders, the Hospitallers, Templars and Teutonic Knights.[24]

As guardians of the Holy Places and protectors of pilgrims, the military orders claimed a presence in the Holy Land even before the First Crusade and showed a special adaptability to Levantine ways. Once the Crusades began, their indispensability as fighting forces gave them much leverage, and they became the greatest landowners in *Outre-mer*.[25] Yet they notably dissociated themselves from crusader politics, and they managed their lands less like fiefs than as proto-capitalist enterprise. All the knightly orders were busy buyers and sellers of land, and the Templars were famous as bankers, money-lenders, even mortgagors. The most powerful of all, the Hospitallers, were particularly astute in gaining control of water sources for power and irrigation, and also, as Riley-Smith has said, 'had a general policy towards all their estates that in the long run led them to encourage their tenants to exchange services for rents'.[26]

Yet the primary function of the religious orders was to serve God not Mammon. Even the Templars and Hospitallers aimed not to accumulate surplus wealth, but to deploy profits towards godly ends – caring for pilgrims and the sick, as well as carrying the fight to the Infidel. It was the far more materialistic agents of the Italian city-states who went furthest beyond feudal bounds and Christian duty in exploiting the potential of *Outre-mer*. The sea-girt republic of Venice had long been involved in the Levant, having almost a European monopoly of the trade of Alexandria and being a far from junior partner in the economy of Byzantium. However, it was the emergent cities of Pisa and Genoa, Venice's rivals, which first saw the opportunity that the Crusades offered to maximise profits by getting closer to – even control of – eastern trade. In return for invaluable aid in provisioning and conveying the crusading armies, and in providing naval support in the reduction of the coastal cities which were the first crusader objectives, the Pisans and Genoese exacted important concessions: extra-territorial enclaves, tax exemptions, trade monopolies and, in due course, grants of land outside the cities' walls. Only later, once the crusader states had become established athwart the north-south axis of trade and promised to become an entrepot to rival, even threaten, Alexandria, did the Venetians follow suit.[27]

The very first grant of privileges was made by Count Bohemond to the Genoese at Antioch on July 14, 1098. As Charles Verlinden says, this was, significantly, 'not an agricultural domain given to a noble in return for knight service, but the concession of an urban district to an allied state'.[28] Moreover, as the Italian city-states were communally rewarded for their help in reducing the coastal cities further south – above all, Acre and Tyre – their interests quickly expanded, from being merely privileged traders into owning and developing the fabulously rich agricultural hinterland. It was at this stage that wealthy 'consular' families – the ruling class of the

Italian city republics – began to be individually involved. Such a case was that of the Embriaci, given lands around Tyre by the Genoese state in repayment of debts incurred in earlier overseas ventures, in a manner which Verlinden calls 'the first example of a connexion between the public debt and a colonial concession'.[29]

It was in exploiting the fertile coastline of *Outre-mer* that the late-coming Venetians soon predominated, doubtless building on their experience in colonising the rich agricultural mainland adjacent to Venice itself. By 1125 in the seigneuries of Tyre alone, the Venetians held 21 villages and a third of 51 more, out of a total of 140, becoming relatively harsh exactors of labour from their tenants.[30] Similar developments were occurring around Acre, where chroniclers described mile-long fields of *canamella* in the valley of the sluggish Na'aman River, serving a huge refinery in the city itself. For this was the prime sugar-producing region of the Holy Land, and quite clearly the Venetians were leading the way in optimising production by consolidating cane-growing lands. At the same time, they were busy building mills and boiling houses, and were engaged in perennial battles with the Hospitallers and others to control water sources.[31]

To the novel experience of producing tropical staples for themselves – which included cotton and silk as well as sugar – the Venetians and the other Italians added the advantages of a near monopoly over the shipping, refining and marketing of the produce in Europe. The new surge of long-distance trade and the actual colonisation of the Levant were accompanied by important developments in banking and business methods; more sophisticated forms of contract, credit and accountancy, involving partners, factors, commission agents, letters of credit, bills of exchange. In all these, Pisa, Genoa and Venice were the European pioneers between the twelfth and fourteenth centuries, though in many cases they were following Islamic models, even adapting Arabic words.[32]

The strength and limitations of the Italian city-states in the Levant were symbolised by the establishment, first by Genoa in the mid-thirteenth century, of a gold currency standard. That it was possible signalised the new scope of Italian commerce; that it was necessary illustrated the fragility of existing credit machinery for long-distance trade and long-term transactions.[33] Similarly, the first European involvement in quasi-plantation production in the crusader states demonstrated both the potential of such enterprises, and the insurmountable problems under existing conditions.

The work of Meron Benvenisti and others has stressed that the ruins still traceable in the former crusader states include powerful evidence of economic activity, as well as the more splendid and famous crusader castles.[34] Perhaps the most evocative ruins of all are those of the Tawahin-a-Sukkar, the sugar mills and boiling house near biblical Jericho, which date from at least 1116. This factory complex was water-powered (using an aqueduct first built by Herod the Great) and the wheel-pits in the extant mill ruins are 30 feet long, 10 feet wide and 6 feet deep. This indicates a potential annual production of several hundred tons - well above average for any-where in the world before the advent of steam. Yet the very size and location of the Tawahin-a-sukkar suggest that they were exceptional. Found so far from the coast, in a comparatively arid area that was often a battlefield, they were probably rarely run at full capacity. The fact that they were owned and operated as a monopoly by the Patriarch of Jerusalem also suggests that they retarded rather than speeded the growth of sugar plantations nearby. Indeed, even the Patriarch's own surrounding lands were as noted for the production of dates and bananas as for sugar.[35]

The coastal plains of Palestine and Syria were far more favourably placed, and there the trend towards monocultural production, under con-solidated capitalistic ownership, with the canefields economically clustered round mills and boiling houses as units of production, was clearly more advanced. But progress was hamstrung even there, by the continuing power of feudal magnates, by the continued dependence upon indigenous peasant labour rather than slaves, and, above all, by continuous political uncertainty.

The achievements of medieval Europe in so rapidly adapting to the wonderful new conditions they found in Palestine and Syria were remark-able. Within little more than half a century the newcomers had changed from being merely military crusaders, to ruling an overseas colony and at least restoring its former economy. By joining up with the crusading enterprise, the emergent mercantile capitalists of the Italian city-states had gone farther and established at least a tentative model of a true plantation system. Yet the crusader states failed, and even the Venetian, Genoese and Pisan efforts seem in retrospect both precocious and premature.

The Italians showed even greater adaptability than their Frankish allies, but they were not yet powerful or secure enough entirely to overthrow feudal modes of landholding and labour, or to dispense with the need for a defence establishment. Despite the activities of consular families such as the Genoese Embriaci, and occasional grants to associations of individuals such as that to the Pisan *Societas Vermiliorum* in 1188,[36] the exploitation of the Levantine coastline remained, of necessity, a city-state rather than plantocratic, or even corporate, enterprise. The full development of the plantation model was inherent – perhaps inevitable – by 1150 AD. But the seedling planted in the crusading states would have to be transplanted. After the crushing victory of Saladin at Hittin in 1187, the crusaders were almost thrown out of the Holy Land, and although a series of further crusades recovered and even extended the coastal settlements, these were never again secure, being finally abandoned in 1291 AD.[37]

In significant contrast with Pope Urban II's message to the Council of Clermont 200 years earlier, in 1306 the Venetian Marino Sanuto wrote an appeal for a new crusade addressed to Pope Clement V and the greatest kings of Europe which included as one of its salient arguments the potential benefit to royal treasures from taxes on sugar.[38] At much the same time, the Florentine Francisco Pegolotti listed 15 different types of sugar among the 288 'spices' which constituted Europe's trade with the East.[39] A crusade to recover the Holy Land was now out of the question, but those familiar with the possible profits of sugar production were eager to discover alternative, and if possible superior, sites for sugar plantations, which would, at the least, make Europe less dependent upon trade with Islam. The century and a half after the fall of Acre in 1291, indeed, saw the spread of European-owned sugar plantations westward throughout the Mediterranean, wherever the climate, political and socioeconomic conditions were suitable – particularly in Cyprus, Crete, Sicily, Andalucia and the Algarve.

As with the Holy Land in the crusader period, these territories had all been recovered from the Muslims, who had in each of them established at least a crude system of sugar production. Once again, European feudalism was modified by the exigencies of the new environments, and wherever a permanent state of military readiness was less necessary than in the crusader states, proto-capitalist forces had time and room to develop – building on experience and remedying the deficiencies in the agricultural and commercial system found in Palestine and Syria. Bourgeois bankers, merchants and absentee owners became increasingly the norm, and the Italian city-states consequently remained closely associated with the emergent plantations – establishing in some cases an embryonic type of corporate colonialism. Yet the emergence of stronger, more centralised kingships – first in Sicily and, later, Spain and Portugal – coupled with the intensification of conflict between Cross and Crescent in the fifteenth century, signalised the decline of the city-state and led to the more generalised dissemination of capitalist techniques.

Above all, the switch from the Levant to the Mediterranean islands and Iberian mainland simplified the problems of finding sufficient and suitable labour. In the Holy Land, because the indigenous population was too sparse, and too many of them were Christians, it had proved impossible either to overthrow the prevailing system of peasant labour or to substitute slavery. Yet in the new areas, reconquered Muslim peasants could be reduced to virtual slaves, and also augmented both by Muslim captives and by a steadily growing trade in Slavic and African slaves. Somewhat paradoxically, it was the catastrophic depopulation caused by the Black Death (1347-55) – which on the European mainland and in England gave so much relative power to surviving feudal serfs, that they advanced towards peasants status – that accelerated the process of plantation building. The death of between a third and a half of native populations provided ample chances for planters to consolidate landholdings, while at the same time providing incentive to increase the trade in slaves – a process of capitalistic intensification that was psychologically abetted by the selfish cynicism that naturally accompanied such a demographic disaster.

One of the most important developments in the techniques of plantation-style colonisation occurred not in a sugar island, but in Chios, famous as almost the sole source of the world's supply of mastic – a yellow tree resin used in the manufacture of varnish, cement and liqueurs. Chios was captured by the Genoese in 1346, but the enterprise was largely funded not by the state but by a consortium of merchants, who outfitted 29 galleys at a cost of 200,000 livres. In return, they were granted a *mahona* – the right to administer the island economically and fiscally for 20 years, or until the debt was paid off. Very similar concessions were to be granted by the Iberian monarchs in the development of the Atlantic islands, where, not coincidentally, Genoese interests continued to be heavily involved. More generally, moreover, the *mahona* was the forerunner of corporations and companies chartered for consolidation purposes by the northern European powers.[40]

An island colony that did grow sugar but did not progress was Rhodes. It was taken over as a base by the Knights Hospitaller after they left the Holy Land – after a brief sojourn under the Lusignans in Cyprus – and as far as possible it was used as an entrepot as well as quasi-plantation. For the first time, the Knights were completely free of secular control. Yet Rhodes was too close to the coast of Anatolia and, being regarded as a military threat and affront to Islam, was itself constantly under threat of attack. Much the same held true for Malta, to which the Knights Hospitaller transferred once they were expelled from Rhodes by the Turks in 1530. Agriculture, including the growing of sugar, flourished, but at the cost of a permanent, and increasingly reactionary, military establishment.[41]

The most immediate legatee of the crusader experiment, however, the island of Cyprus, followed a much more linear progress. The island had been captured from Islam by the Byzantines, who took over the Arabic canefields as part of the assimilative process that included the cultivation of sugar in Crete, the Morea and southern Anatolia.[42] Conquered almost accidentally by Richard Lionheart on the Third Crusade (1189), Cyprus was sold to the French crusader Guy de Lusignan, who established a monarchic dynasty that lasted for exactly 300 years. For 23 years after 1268, the Lusignans were also Kings of Jerusalem, but when Acre fell in 1291, King Henry II fell back on Cyprus, along with a raggle-taggle cross-section of those involved in the Holy Land: feudal aristocrats, clerics, Italian merchants, indigenous Christian artisans, even Arabic slaves.[43]

Cyprus proved rather less vulnerable to attack than the Levantine coast or the smaller islands, and the fertile, well-watered yet comparatively under-developed southern plains of the island were ideally suited for growing sugar cane. All types of magnate became involved; the Lusignan Kings themselves, the Bishop of Limassol, the Knights Hospitaller, the Catalan family of Ferrer and, most efficiently of all, the Venetian family business of the Cornaros. For the first time, sugar growing was truly – if only locally – monocultural, with large canefields, water-powered mills, boiling pans and machinery imported from Italy and Alexandria, and local refineries producing loaf and powdered sugar.[44]

The power of the Lusignans fluctuated, but generally declined as capitalist forces mounted and Cyprus became virtually a colonial territory – with not only Genoa and Venice but also Mameluke Egypt competing for control. For 90 years after 1373, the Genoese dominated the island from Famagusta, and at the nadir of Lusignan fortunes, Cyprus became a tributary of the Egyptians. In a last spurt of energy in 1464, King James II allied with the Mamelukes and the Venetians to throw out the Genoese. Meanwhile, however, like many late medieval kings, the Lusignans had become debtors to the emergent capitalist class, having first mortgaged and then lost some of their finest demesne lands to Italian bankers. At the spearhead of this process were the Venetian Cornaros, who to an exceptionally exploitive spirit and unmatched commercial and banking connections in the metropolis, added dynastic ambitions that promised almost supreme local power. As was to happen so often later to lesser aristocrats, a marriage between the last Lusignan king and a Cornaro heiress proved merely a final capitulation. When James II died in 1473, it was his widow, Queen Catherine Cornaro, who first filled the administration with

Venetians and then negotiated the sale of Cyprus to the Venetian republic. This heralded a final century of Christian colonialism, during which family businesses increasingly exploited the island's resources under the protection of Venetian arms, until Cyprus finally fell to the Ottoman Turks in 1571.[45]

In certain respects, the history of Cyprus was foreshadowed by that of Crete. Captured from the Byzantines by Boniface of Montserrat in 1204, it was sold to the Venetians 20 years later. For 20 years, Crete was the most important Italian colony, with the Venetians establishing rural *casalia*, worked by indigenous Greek serfs called *parici* and imported slaves. Sugar became one of the most important exports, thanks to privileges accorded to such mercantile families as the Zenoni and the Zancharoli, though Venice retained some vestiges of feudal tenure by requiring military service from Venetian proprietors and native Greek nobles alike.[46]

A rather different development branched out in the largest of all Mediterranean islands, Sicily, which by 1450 was temporarily the greatest sugar producer in the world. Here the most important formative influence was that of the brilliantly anachronistic Emperor Frederick II (1208-50), called by his contemporaries *Stupor Mundi*.[47] The sugar introduced into Sicily by the Saracens had been exported to Africa as early as the ninth century, and was regarded as so important that Sicily's Christians sent samples to the Normans in 1016 as an inducement to reconquer the island. It was not until the reigns of Roger II and William II between 1130 and 1172 that the great sugar-growing area around Palermo was revived, in true feudal fashion, through the agency of the Benedictines and the cathedral authorities of Monreale. Frederick II immediately grasped the value of sugar production, but determined that its development would strengthen not undermine royal authority. Though far-sighted, he was not a proto-capitalist and was only relatively enlightened – a forerunner of Ferdinand of Aragon and the Emperor Charles V, who also ruled in Sicily.

Frederick II saw the benefits of Muslim learning and techniques, and of limited religious toleration. But he expelled the Saracens from Sicily, and also suppressed the municipalities as being inimical to feudalism and royal power. Frederick II's expulsion of Saracenic artisans and labourers, and his determination to retain the royal monopoly, initially retarded the Sicilian sugar industry. But he also sent to the Holy Land for replacement experts in planting and processing, and encouraged the involvement of Jewish and mainland Italian merchants as long as they remained under state control. The more serious problems of labour was solved by the depression of the forcibly converted Muslims into a helot class and, as throughout the Mediterranean, by the intensification of the slave trade – against which the pragmatic Frederick II and his Aragonese successors had no scruples, religious or otherwise.[48]

Direct royal rule, and direct royal involvement in the sugar industry, declined once the kings of Sicily ceased to be resident, and consequently the island became more an overseas colony – successively of the Aragonese, Hapsburg and Bourbon monarchs. Mercantile elements grew in relative power, while remaining in symbiotic relationship with a proto-plantocracy of landed aristocrats – who preferred to live in the cities or even abroad rather than on their actual estates. Yet the liberties of the merchants remained as dependent as the titles of the Sicilian nobility upon royal patronage, and the concomitant (and even more important) mandate of the monarchic state legal code. Sicilian law allowed for the compulsory purchase of land suitable for cane growing, for the taking of water from whatever source, and for binding labourers to the sugar industry. A decree of Charles V ordained that 'debtors for rent of sugar factories should not be molested by judicial process during those months specially devoted to the harvesting' – a similar provision allowing that labourers should not be arrested during the crop season.[49]

As a result of Sicily's special conditions, the cultivation of sugar expanded hugely in the fifteenth century and remained on a high plateau for most of the sixteenth century. Though Sicily is about as far north as sugar cane has ever been grown on a large scale – which meant that its productivity was low because of retarded growth in the winter months – it did have the advantage of proximity to European markets, particularly those in the expanding Italian sweetmeats and sweet wines industries. Moreover, the trend towards refining in the metropolis, was not so necessary in Sicily, where sugar refineries continued to flourish in the main cities, close to canefields and markets alike.[50]

In the fifteenth century, sugar cultivation spread around almost the entire Sicilian coastline. The plain of Palermo, though, remained the heartland of the Sicilian industry, and in most respects came closer than anywhere else in the Mediterranean sphere to achieving an optimal plantation system. It was not a coincidence that the state university of Palermo as early as 1415 studied and advised on techniques of irrigation, planting and milling, or that it is a Palermitan, Pietro Speciale, who is often – if controversially – credited with the invention of the vertical three-roller mill, which remained the most efficient known until the introduction of steam power, as early as 1449.[51] Visitors from northern Europe noted with wonder how the Conco D'oro Plain was like one great canefield regularly dotted with *trapetti*, how the whole economy was geared to the cycle of the cane – particularly the crop season from November to March – and how a whole hierarchy of labourers with special functions was found on each plantation unit; the sturdy male cane-cutters and younger cane-choppers, female sackers and sack-washers, youngsters to fuel the fires, and reliable older hands to tend the boiling pans.[52] Competition from the Americas was to destroy the Sicilian sugar industry quite suddenly after 1580, but it was, ironically, largely the transfer of Sicilian techniques into more favourably situated and more easily exploited areas that was to bring this about.

Much of what has been said about Sicily could be repeated for the almost forgotten sugar production of mainland Spain and Portugal, which was in any case to be related to the Sicilian industry through the rule of the House of Aragon. The Omayyad sultans of Cordova had been famous for sugar cultivation – perhaps following Moroccan models – and in their last phase gained from a curious association with opportunistic Genoese merchants.[53] But it was a result of the Reconquest that Iberian mainland production developed most rapidly, in the fourteenth and fifteenth centuries. The reconquest of Portugal was completed by 1300, and within a century, the Algarve was noted for producing sugar using the labour of forcibly con-verted *moriscos* – soon to be augmented by black African slaves.[54] Similarly, the gradual reconquest of eastern and southern Spain was accompanied by the spread of trade (including, paradoxically, that between Catholic Cata-lonia and the Muslim *Maghrib*),[55] and by the adoption and development of Arabic agriculture. Sugar was grown on the coast south of Valencia and between Almeria and Malaga, and inland around Seville, though it was only one of a rich variety of semi-tropical crops, including rice, dates and citrus fruits. Although Noel Deerr's calculation that by 1475 there were some 100,000 acres of canefields in Spain, producing about 60,000 tons of sugar a year, may be an exaggeration, it is pretty certain that Spain's total production was not topped by the Atlantic islands until 1500, or by the new World before 1600.[56]

The beneficiaries of this plenitude were mainly the centralising but still feudal monarchy, and an aggressive class of aristocratic *conquistadores*, treating their *morisco* subjects as serfs, and adopting without much modera-tion the institution of actual slavery they encountered.[57] In an age of revivalist bigotry, the *conquistadores'* pragmatism did not extend to the Jews, who were discouraged, subjected to the Inquisition, and finally expelled in

1492. Yet there were some overtly capitalistic tendencies even in conservative Spain. As Charles Verlinden has stressed, Genoese and Venetian influences were vital in the development of Iberian commerce and colonisation.[58] But what is most remarkable is the early involvement of north European merchant capital. As early as 1383, for example, the merchants of Ravensburg had interests in Barcelona, and among much other produce were by 1408 shipping Spanish sugar via Bruges up the Rhine and across to England. Suggesting an even more precocious development, the Ravensburg merchants by 1460 had acquired control of a large sugar plantation at Gandía, south of Valencia, which remained under the ostensible ownership of one Hugo de Cardona, being managed by a local Spaniard named Santafé. This web of non-feudal and foreign investment only came to light as the result of a court case following the abrogation of Cardona's title — with the surprising outcome that the Crown recognised the rights of the Ravensburg merchants, and continued to protect their interests for at least another generation.[59]

Clearly, the factors limiting the development of true plantations between the expulsion of the crusaders from the Holy Land and the opening up of the Atlantic trade triangle included not only the degree of capitalist involvement, but also the problem of sufficient and suitable labour. In Cyprus, many of the skilled artisans were originally refugees from the Holy Land; the problem of finding labourers was much more difficult. Some were described as *serfs du pays* — indigenous Saracens reduced to virtual slavery, or Byzantine Greeks treated only marginally better. Yet these were necessarily augmented by actual slaves, at first Arabic captives from the Holy Land, but increasingly Slavs (even Orthodox Christians), with a trickle of African blacks. Slavery had always existed in Cyprus — being actually expanded under Islam — but now it multiplied.[60]

The key event had been the diversion of the Fourth Crusade to capture Constantinople at the behest of the Venetians in 1204. This infamy was followed by the establishment of Venetian and Genoese factories on the Black Sea, through which flowed, along with other items of trade, a motley host of Bulgarian, Russian, Tartar, Alan and Circassian slaves. To these were added a rising flow of slaves resulting from Turkish conquests in central Anatolia, Thrace and the Balkans, a trade in which the Venetians and Genoese busily engaged, though the captors were Muslim and the captives mainly Christian.[61]

By Charles Verlinden's assessment, the Mediterranean islands were already true slave societies when the Black Death struck in 1347 — even

Majorca, for example, having as high a proportion of slaves in the population as did the southern United States in 1865, some 36 per cent.[62] But the process was undoubtedly speeded by the catastrophic depopulation of the mid-fourteenth century, only slowing again with the fall of Constantinople in 1453. In 1364, Italian clerical authorities, despite an earlier ban on the enslavement of Christians, allowed the unlimited importation of slaves as long as they were not baptised Roman Catholics, and around 1420 at least 1,000 slaves a year were sold in Venice alone.[63]

The campaigns of the Ottoman Turks and the fall of Constantinople changed the nature of the Mediterranean slave trade rather than drying it up. European access to the Black Sea was curtailed, and Turkish captives were now diverted mainly to Islamic markets; but the Christian slavetraders thereupon turned more attention to sub-Saharan Africa. At first, the chief sources were the overland caravans that arrived on the shores of Libya. But after about 1440, the trade was facilitated by the Portuguese acquisition of posts on the north-western African coast, particularly Arguin Island.[64] As a result, the proportion of *sclavi nigri* in the Mediterranean rapidly increased, until by the later fifteenth century, for example, the servile labour force of the Aragonese Kingdom of Naples (including Sicily) was 83 per cent black. This has led Charles Verlinden, with his usual forthrightness, to claim that 'the Mediterranean had developed an "American" form of slavery several decades before America was discovered'.[65]

What was to lead to the pre-eminence of American plantations, beginning with Brazil, was the intensification made possible through even better conditions of climate and soils, and the greater availability of exploitable land and labour, once the special problems of colonisation, long-term capitalisation and long-distance transportation had been finally solved. Yet, relatively speaking, even these conditions were discovered and exploited, and the problems of colonisation and trade more or less solved, before 1492, in the Atlantic islands – Madeira, the Canaries, Azores, Cape Verdes and Sao Tomé – the development of which can be said to have been as much a culmination of the crucial Mediterranean phase of plantation evolution, as a bridge to the final New World phase.[66]

Madeira, which is in the latitude of southern Morocco and Palestine, was first colonised by the Portuguese in 1420 as part of the expansion towards south and west that began with the capture of Ceuta in 1415. Uninhabited and with adequate rainfall only above the 4,000-foot contour, Madeira was ideal for plantations only once sufficient labour had been imported and the problem of irrigation solved. As patron and lord proprietor (*donatário*),

Prince Henry initiated colonisation by outfitting the first ships and subinfeuding the islands as *capitanias* to three ambitious sailor-squires in his personal household. These captains were to subdivide the colony into *sesmarias* – large estates based on peninsular models that could be held hereditarily in perpetuity, or sold to others, provided they were in cultivation within five years of the grant.[67]

Recruitment was difficult, and most of the original grantees – like the Normans long before or most West Indian planters later – were scarcely 'gentle-born', acquiring aristocratic pretensions merely by virtue of holding the land. Within a dozen years, though, the Madeiran colonists had cleared the lower forests and constructed the first *levadas*, the contoured irrigation channels based on Mediterranean models which are still a feature of the islands, using Guanche (Berber) slaves seized in forays against the nearby Canary Islands.[68] At first only wheat was grown, but sugar was introduced by Prince Henry around 1435, from either the Algarve or Sicily, with the aid of Genoese merchants and shippers. Though the Canary Islands were repeatedly scoured for fresh slaves, the Guanches inconsiderately died out within a generation. But their numbers were increasingly made up after *feitorias* were established on the African coast by imports of African slaves, who then became the necessary 'sinews' of a flourishing sugar economy. By 1455, Cadamosto reported that Madeira produced some 300,000 *arrobas* (about 4,800 tons) of sugar a year, and by the end of the century there were 120 factories in operation. One planter alone, Juan Esmeralda, was said to produce 20,000 *arrobas* of sugar a year, from an estate of several thousand acres and the labour of 500 slaves. To a degree that concerned the Portuguese government, much Madeiran sugar was carried direct to foreign ports in foreign vessels – a third to Flanders, a sixth to Venice, an eighth to Genoa and a sixteenth to England. Non-Portuguese investors were also directly involved in the Madeiran industry, including the Welsers of Augsburg and the enterprising merchants of Ravensburg. The upwardly mobile *sesmaristas*, however, remained dominant, and an important new element in the Portuguese ruling class.[69]

After the demise of the Guanches, it was the Spaniards who were to colonise the Canary Islands, on the authority of a grant from Pope Clement VI more than a century earlier. In due course they developed an export-oriented agriculture to rival that of Madeira, with 29 sugar mills reported in 1526. African slaves were important, but much of the sugar cane was grown by share-cropping peasants imported from the poorer parts of Spain, at the rate of 15-20 per factory unit – the origin of the *colono* system used by the Spaniards centuries later in Cuba and Puerto Rico.[70] Despite Spanish protectionism, foreign investment was by no means absent – the Welsers, for example, owning four plantations in Palma as early as 1500. Also like Madeira, and far more than the Iberian peninsula itself, the Canary Islands became the focus of interest of traders from the emergent maritime countries of northern Europe, such as Nicholas Thorne of Bristol in 1526, or John Hawkins the elder of Plymouth in the 1530s, whose more famous son was to use the islands as a stepping stone for England's entry into the Triangle Trade in 1562.[71]

Long before the development of the Canary Islands, however, the south-thrusting Portuguese had colonised three other Atlantic archipelagos. The uninhabited Azores were settled from 1439 mainly by Madeirans, including the son of one of the original capitans. Some sugar was grown from the beginning, but the islands were too hilly, isolated and cool to compete strongly. Instead of plantations, the characteristic colonial settlement became the chartered, semi-autonomous municipally (*vila*), and the chief crops wheat and woad, grown by peasants imported from the poorest and most populous provinces of mainland Portugal.[72]

The Cape Verde Islands, similarly uninhabited when first discovered in 1455, were likewise not ideal for sugar production, being, in contrast, too hot and dry. Yet they were to constitute a significant link in the chain of plantation colonisation. Even more than Madeira, they were a joint Portuguese-Italian enterprise. One of the original captains was the Genoese Antonio da Noli, who first sighted the islands while sailing in Prince Henry's employ and began the settlement of Santiago in 1462. Colonists were hard to find, and the first settlers included Flemings, *marrano* Jews and reprieved convicts. But the nearest Cape Verde Island is less than 300 miles from the coast of Senegal, and slaves were so easily obtained that they soon outnumbered the Europeans. Sugar was introduced from Madeira with the aid of the Genoese, and muscovado and cane brandy (*aquardente*) produced for export. Cotton, however, proved far more suitable to climate and soil and, remarkably, a local cotton textile industry developed, suing largely African expertise and for export not to the metropolis but to the Guinea coast – slaves, next to gold, being the most acceptable commodity in exchange.[73]

Santiago thus became a flourishing entrepot for trade in slaves for the other Portuguese island colonies, despite the fact that it technically contravened the monopoly of Guinea trade granted by the Portuguese crown to Fernao Gomes in 1469. With a weak imperial presence, Santiago thus set the model for colonies with an at least partial autonomous local economy. It probably also set the final model for transatlantic plantation slave societies. At the apex were the small elite of Portuguese white plantation and factory owners, with a lesser elite of white merchants, managers and artisans. The mass of the population were black African slaves; but, as a result of the shortage of Portuguese women and the necessarily easy-going mores of the illicit slavetraders on the Guinea coast, there was from the early years a sizeable group of free mulattos. Because of their isolation and the absence of a strong imperial government, the local whites formed a homogeneous class, a virtual plantocracy, though still nominally loyal to the Portuguese crown, from whom they expected – so often in vain – both military and economic protection.

Perhaps the islands off the African coast with the most potential as pure plantation colonies, though, were São Tomé and neighbouring Príncipe and Annobón.[75] Situated on the Equator in the Gulf of Guinea, where north and south winds and currents converge, they were a natural turning-point for ships from Europe. With abundant rain and harnessable streams, rich soils and much flat land – especially on the north side of Sao Tomé – they were, surprisingly, uninhabited, while at the same time close to an almost unlimited source of black slave labour. Sao Tomé, however, was so far beyond the orbit of Europe that the method of exploitation was bound to be even less feudal and nationalistic, and more capitalistic, than that of the nearer Atlantic islands.

First discovered by the Portuguese in 1470, São Tomé was granted by King John II in 1485 not to a lord proprietor from the royal family, as in the case of the other islands, but to a non-royal donatário-captain (João de Paiva, succeeded by Alvaro de Caminho in 1493) – who would be responsible for all the costs of settlement but would consequently reap the lion's share of the profits. The presumption of the island's suitability for sugar was so strong that the right to a quarter of the income from sugar was specially reserved to the crown in the original grant. Accompanying the donatário-captain was an elite of white settlers, mainly from Madeira, who were granted estates in *sesmaria*, and also a corps of experts in sugar growing, processing and shipping who included Genoese and Sicilians as well as Portuguese. Obtaining sufficient lesser settlers was far more difficult, and the second donatário-captain was authorised to recruit actual criminals, and carry out 2,000 Jewish children whose parents had recently fled to Portugal from a pogrom in Castile. To provide the main force, however, Paiva and his successors were specifically permitted to trade in

Congolese slaves – a concession that was made easier because the nearby coast was south of the monopoly granted to Fernão Gomes, and also beyond the bounds of Christendom and Islam alike, so that all Africans acquired might be presumed to be *bozales*, that is, unequivocally enslaveable pagans.[76]

Paiva failed in his colonisation efforts, but within a decade land was cleared and planted, and many water-powered *engenhos* built. Even before Columbus returned from his second discovery voyage, São Tomé muscovado was on sale in Antwerp. At the peak of their production some 40 years later, Sao Tomé and its neighbours were responsible for at least a third of the sugar produced in the Portuguese islands.[77] Three factors, however, militated against the continuing success of São Tomé as a plantation colony. More than any other Portuguese possession, it proved a graveyard for Europeans. After the rounding of the Cape of Good Hope and the opening up of Angola it became merely a stopping place on the route to the South and East, no longer a terminus. Finally, after Cabral's almost accidental discovery of South America on the way to the East in 1500, it was found that the north-east coast of Brazil not only had almost unlimited potential for plantations, but was actually closer to Europe than was São Tomé.[78]

Brazil, after a slow start, was developed much on the pattern of the Portuguese islands; and once the 'South Atlantic Triangle' was firmly established and the Congo-Angola hinterland tapped for slaves, it became for a period, the richest of all plantation colonies. The process of consolidation is sometimes said to have occurred despite, rather than because of the union of the Iberian crowns between 1580 and 1640.[79] But what is often forgotten is that it was Spain in Española as much as Portugal in Brazil, which pioneered sugar plantations in the New World setting – an achievement overshadowed by the Spanish predilection for other types of colonial exploitation, and by the far greater success in the Caribbean sphere of Spain's competitors.

Eric Williams, in one of his less known works,[80] has shown how virtually every aspect of the later New World plantation economy and society was foreshadowed in Española before 1550, although he ignored the way in which all these features had Atlantic island and Mediterranean roots. Christopher Columbus himself symbolised this transition. A Genoese who was married to the daughter of one of the original Madeiran captains, he had carried Madeiran sugar to Genoa as early as 1477.[81] On his first voyage of discovery, Columbus commented how similar were the indigenous Tainos of the Antilles to the Canary Island Guanches, not only physically but also in their suitability for enslavement. On his second voyage, he carried out sugar cane from the Canary Islands and compared growing conditions in Española with what he had observed in Andalucia and Sicily – having already made sure that his *capitulaciones* from the crown allowed him to authorise planting and the building of mills, as well as the granting of land and the employment of natives as labourers. Sugar was first processed into syrup in 1503, the first *trapiche* (mill) introduced in 1516, and by 1535 Oviedo reported that there were 20 sugar factories in Española – mainly in the river valleys west of Santo Domingo, where, significantly, the largest mill on the optimum site was owned by Diego Columbus.[82]

The Tainos died out as rapidly as the Guanches had done, but at the behest of the Jeronymite friars (who had also offered loans for the establishment of *trapiches*), the Tainos were soon replaced by a rising tide of African slaves, purchased mainly from the Portuguese. The first arrived as early as 1505, and within 30 years Oviedo claimed that there were so many blacks in Española 'as a result of the sugar factories, that the land seems an effigy or an image of Ethiopia itself'.[83]

It is all too easy to list the reasons for the Spanish failure to develop a dominant plantation system in the Americas. Spanish plantations were retarded by the preference for mines and *haciendas*, by the perpetuation of feudal modes, the lack of easy access to African slaves and actual inhibitions against enslavement, by reactionary royal policies of Castilianisation, narrow monopoly and trade exclusivity, and, above all, by a dearth of capital. But the case is relative not absolute. By the time of the union of the Iberian crowns, sugar plantations had spread to the rest of the Greater Antilles and to the Spanish Main. There may have been 150 Spanish plantations, growing 7,500 tons of sugar a year from the labour of 10,000 slaves – totals not yet exceeded by Portuguese Brazil, and which were to be slowly trebled over the following two centuries.[84]

To a certain extent, the Spanish plantation system developed of its own volition, with the emergent creole plantocracy notoriously paying mere lip service to unpopular imperial edicts, trading with foreigners whenever it suited them, and developing a customary social system that often contradicted the nominally humane official slave code. Yet, as in Sicily, the Spanish crown did do more than it is credited with to encourage plantations and endorse their social code. Under Ferdinand and Isabella, and even more under Charles V, the crown granted extensive proprietary rights to the original discoverers and conquistadores, encouraged the importation of Africans once the Amerindians began to decline and, later, authorised the *asiento* system of obtaining slaves from foreign traders. The crown also authorised the immigration of specialist artisans, including converted Jews and non-Castilians, granted protection in suits for debt in regard to sugar plantations, and issued licences for investment by non-Spanish subjects of the Hapsburg Empire, including Italians, Flemings and Germans. It was merely that Spanish monarchs, to an unrealistic degree, wanted the empire to remain strictly mercantilist and under close imperial, indeed royal, control – policies that were even more narrowing once Hapsburgs no longer ruled in Madrid, the Netherlands achieved independence, and the misalliance with Portugal came to an end.[85]

Brazil developed under far looser imperial reins. King Manuel I granted a charter for one of the *donatários* to establish a sugar factory as early as 1516. But while land was cheap and plentiful, capital and labour were short. It was not until 1526 that Brazilian sugar was first exported, and the first known *engenho* dates only from 1533. By 1620, however, there were some 275 *engenhos* in Brazil – nearly all in the five north-eastern provinces – producing perhaps 15,000 tons of sugar a year.[86] Although there were still some Amerindian labourers, the majority were already African slaves – perhaps 100,000 having already been imported from Guinea, Sao Tomé, the Congo and Mozambique.[87] An even more remarkable transformation, however, was the emergence of a mill-owning class, the *señors de engenho*, the richest of whom – such as João de Paus, who owned 18 mills – being said to live in 'an almost oriental pomp' beyond the reach of the *donatários* themselves.[88]

Very few *señors de engenho* were initially wealthy, however, and the need to share costs and risks had led to the comparatively inefficient system of cane-farming. Typically, a mill was served by the cane produced from between five and ten *partidas*, sub-divisions worked by share-cropping Portuguese (or free mulatto) *lavradores*, each of whom owned about 20 slaves and a half-a-dozen oxen. The mill-owner's share was normally two-fifths of the cane or a third of the sugar produced. Each *partida* was divided into 20-40 cane-pieces of about 400 square yards, each of which would keep the mill supplied for about a day. The average production was between 25 and 35 cart-loads of cane per *tarifa* – about 9 tons – which would be expected to produce in due course some 30 *arrobas* – or 960 pounds – of crystalline white, soft muscovado and semi-liquid *panela* sugar. This suggests an annual production from an average mill of well under 100 tons of sugar – a system and level of production that was only really profitable when international sugar prices were very high. In less favourable times when the mill-owners' profits were small, the *lavradores* lived no better than peasants, and the life of slaves was harsh indeed.[89]

The seventeenth century, however, was the 'golden age' of sugar profits, when the demand for the product far outran the supply, while the cost of supplies and slaves remained relatively low and the land cost almost nothing. The potential of Brazilian sugar plantations, measured by the conspicuous wealth of the *señors de engenho*, acted like a magnet to aggressive foreigners, particularly the Dutch, whose West India Company was specifically formed in 1621 with a takeover in mind. Even more attractive was the prospect of optimising sugar production, for it was quite clear that the wealthiest of all *señors de engenho* were those few who owned several contiguous mills and controlled all phases of production, including growing their own cane. João de Paus, for example, was said to own 10,000 slaves and 5,000 oxen himself.[90]

By 1630, the Dutch controlled almost the entire north-eastern coast of Brazil and in Pernambuco established an efficient sugar plantation colony. Many of the mills had been destroyed in the fighting, but this aided in the reorganisation and optimisation achieved under Count Maurice of Nassau. The debts of plantation owners under Dutch protection were cancelled, state loans made for repairs and new machinery, and supplies and provisions allowed in free of duty. Capital was sought throughout the United Provinces and in other countries, and Jews were more openly encouraged than under the Portuguese – many for the first time becoming plantation and slave owners as well as merchants. In general, estates were reorganised as units of production, with fields and factories under single ownership. They were also consolidated towards optimal size – a typical unit producing some 150 tons of sugar a year from 200 acres of canes, by the labour of about one slave per acre. Above all, the Dutch, with state support and through the agency of the federally organised West India Company, were able to provide a far better network of shipping and distribution, and a larger and steadier (and thus even cheaper) flow of slaves through their capture of all the Portuguese *feitorias* on the West African coast – including, for a time, São Tomé and Luanda in Angola.[91]

The Dutch, however, were expelled from North-Eastern Brazil – and from Portuguese Africa south of the Equator – by a virtual Luso-Brazilian war of independence between 1645 and 1654. Hard hit by declining sugar prices, though aided by a greatly increased flow of slaves, Brazilian sugar plantations reverted to their easy-going ways, so that while there were said to be 528 *engenhos* in 1711, their average production for export may have been as low as 30 tons of sugar a year.[92] For their part, the Dutch carried their commercial acumen and new-won expertise, along with their un-matched resources of capital, shipping and distribution, to four plantation colonies of their own on the Guyanese coast, and to the Caribbean islands of the Lesser Antilles, where the French and English had already estab-lished a foothold against the Spanish and Caribs.[93]

In a single decade after 1640, the Dutch helped transform the chief English West Indian colony, Barbados, by introducing the 'method of Pernambuco' – which probably included an embryonic slave code as well as methods of field husbandry, milling and processing – and by offering loans and credit, a reliable supply of slaves, machinery and provisions, and access to the refineries and distribution networks of the Netherlands. By 1680 – after England had fought three maritime wars against the Dutch in order to achieve economic independence and establish a watertight mer-cantilist system of its own – the tiny island of Barbados had become an almost perfect sugar planation monoculture – with sugar products repre-senting over 90 per cent of exports by value, heavily dependent upon imports even of food, and with the black slave population outnumbering the whites by nearly three to one. On an island only 166 square miles in extent (less than half the size of Sao Tomé or the largest of the Cape Verde, Canary, Azores or Madeira Islands), there were said to be 1,000 windmills and some 350 contiguous sugar plantations, averaging 150 acres in size and each producing perhaps 75 tons of sugar a year, from the labour of 100 slaves.[94]

This startling local transformation is often referred to – with typical anglocentricity as *The* Sugar Revolution. What we hope this essay has shown is that it was in fact no revolution at all. The plantation system that was established in Barbados between 1640 and 1680 was not qualitatively new. It differed from its forerunners only in its scale and intensity, and it was not even, by any means, a culmination of the process. Though no area was ever as monoculturally dedicated to sugar, English Jamaica and French Saint Domingue were to outstrip it by far long before slavery ended and steam power introduced, after which, Spanish-American Cuba was to move the plantation model into another – and even then not final – dimension.[95]

Indeed, it could be maintained that the most important change that followed from the development of Barbados and Jamaica between 1650 and 1750 – and the parallel developments in the mainland English colonies – was little more than a semantic one. A hitherto unnoticed transition – awaiting a full etymological investigation – was the way in which the transference described in this paper were accompanied by the narrowing down of the meaning of the very word 'plantation' in the English Language – from being simply a synonym for overseas colonisation of all types, coined in Ireland under the Tudors, to meaning only that extremely profitable, and therefore preferred, type of colonial exploitation here defined and described as the classic plantation model.[96]

This essay has suggested that it is more useful to trace the evolution of plantations throughout the world than to look for sudden transformations, going so far as to argue that New World plantations differed only in scale and intensity from those which developed in the Mediterranean sphere during the European Middle Ages. Critics will doubtless claim that this approach is disingenuous, and that scale and intensity are in fact all-important. The crucial transition, they would maintain, was that complex process which transformed the narrow European economy into a World System.[97] This predicates a critical watershed inextricably related to the growth and development of bourgeois capitalism and negro slavery. These, it is claimed, set in progress processes of capital accumulation and redistribution which contributed to the Industrial Revolution and, in turn, as capital flowed back, reinforced and brought to full flower the plantation system – with steam power, central factories, and 'coolie' labourers and 'wage slaves' rather than chattel slaves – in the later nineteenth and twentieth centuries.

In contrast, it is hoped that this essay shown that there was no such critical or revolutionary watershed; that plantations evolved slowly and unevenly, with the definitional elements established far earlier than previously supposed, and remaining essentially unchanged; and, moreover, that existing analyses, including the Marxist, are damagingly Eurocentric.[98] Plantations were, by definition, labour intensive, but chattel slavery – especially Negro slavery – was by no means an inevitable feature. At most, slavery was an accidental concomitant during the middle phases of plantation intensification, with Negro slaves coming to predominate largely through geographical accident. In their formative years, plantations used other forms of intensive labour, including peasant sharecropping or feudal serfdom, and in their final and most intensive phases, forms of indentured servitude or wage slavery, rather than chattel slavery.

Precocious, or immature, capitalist formations exploited plantations in tandem with feudalism in the years of European colonial expansion, and in due course feudalism faded in favour of bourgeois capitalism as the dominant mode. Yet pre- or extra-capitalist, quasi-feudal modes remained vital and remarkably persistent, even after the ending of formal slavery. The role of the crown, in conjunction with the church, was at least initially indispensable; in apportioning land and native peoples, in granting monopolies, including the trade in slaves, and in sanctioning plantocratic laws. Yet even more insidious was the way in which plantation ownership perpetuated, or more commonly reconstituted, a planter aristocracy; be they Portuguese adventurers turned *senors de engenho*, English *nouveau riche* absentees buying up land at home and seats in Parliament, or North American resident planters promoting the myths of Southern Honour and Civilisation.

Above all, though following the lead of Charles Verlinden, we must deflect the notion that the classic plantation model emerged out of purely European developments. European colonialism of a sort provided the catalyst for critical changes in scale and intensity from the time of the First Crusade onwards. But the components which were melded were as much Muslim and Jewish, Asiatic and African, as purely European. Moreover, the crucible for changes was initially the Mediterranean, rather than the Atlantic sphere.

2

The West Indies and North America

Introduction: If the later predominance of American plantations and transatlantic slavery have teleologically tended to obscure prototypical equivalents in the Mediterranean, so has the modern predominance of the USA tended to obscure the relatively greater significance on the larger world scene of the Caribbean, Central and South America for at least the first three centuries of European expansionism. Similarly, if American historians have not hegemonically quite excluded the Caribbean (and Latin America) from consideration, the natural focus of their interest and studies has tended to compartmentalise North American, Caribbean and South American Studies and to result in some rather glib comparisons and contrasts, as well as to downplay the continuous interconnections between all three areas. The following short essay, written for the *Encyclopedia of the North American Colonies*, edited by Jacob Cooke and others and published in 1993, was intended to remedy these tendencies, at least in respect of the West Indies during the American colonial period. But it is still worth noting that in a three-volume work, totalling more than 3,000 pages, my contribution was limited by the editors to a mere nine pages; albeit with a useful map and a bibliography (of 38 items) almost twice as long as originally requested.

Antechamber to the New World for the European expansionists led by Spain, the West Indies were the focus of Spanish imperial interest only until larger and richer territories were discovered in Central and South America. Once other Europeans challenged the Spaniards and colonised the more northerly parts of the Americas, however – and to an even greater degree, once slave plantations were established – the West Indies assumed huge importance. The Caribbean became the cockpit of European rivalries as French, English and Dutch developed island plantations while they were creating settlement colonies on the North American mainland and establishing trading stations for slaves in West Africa.

The close and reciprocal relationship between the mainland and the islands – subsequently obscured by the relative decline of the West Indies and the enormous expansion of the USA in the nineteenth century – can best be delineated in three main stages: (1) the role of the West Indies in the early phases of North American settlement and the establishment of trading patterns in the North Atlantic; (2) the indispensable connections between the North American mainland and Caribbean islands (and with Africa) at a time when European imperialism preferred plantation to settlement colonies; and (3) the part played by the West Indies during the early phases of commercial and territorial expansion by the USA, down to the establishment of the southern border at the Rio Grande in 1845 and the creation of the Canadian confederation in 1867.

EARLY SETTLEMENT AND TRADE

Spain

Once the Spanish pioneers had established their base in Española (Hispaniola), the rapid depletion of local gold resources and the disastrous decline of the native population led Spaniards to fan outward to the neighbouring islands and mainland in all directions, including north-west. The priority of Columbus' claim and the consequent allocation of the western half of the unknown world to Spain by the Spanish Pope Alexander VI had unwittingly given the Spaniards access to territory 75 times as large as Spain. The combined factors of the hugeness of this expanse and limited available manpower naturally led to a concentration on areas suitable for Spanish-type estates, with large malleable populations and, above all, large new sources of gold and silver; that is, to Mexico and Peru. Despite their teleological importance in the history of the USA, the Caribbean-based exploratory probes into the hinterland north of the Rio Grande by Juan Ponce de León, Pánfilo de Narváez and Hernando de Soto were disappointing failures, as discouraging of permanent settlement as were the Spaniards' experiences in the Carib-defended islands of the Lesser Antilles and the disease-ridden tropical forests of the Spanish Main.

The later-coming powers of France, England and Holland never seriously threatened the centres of the Spanish American Empire, being able to claim and settle only those areas neglected by Spain, which they then developed in ways that were unsuitable and uncongenial to the Spanish imperial economy. The early rivalry with Spain and the location of some of the first settlements were to an extent conditioned by the Reformation: for nearly a century French, Dutch and English *corsarios luteranos* ('Lutheran corsairs', as they were called by the Spaniards) carried out their depredations under the colour of a Protestant crusade, while some of the early non-Iberian settlements were refuges for religious dissidents in the second phase of the Reformation.

A more important and lasting factor for the challenge to Spain (and Portugal, which Spain was united between 1580 and 1640) was the emergence of state mercantilism among the non-Iberian powers. Learning from Spain's inability to move quickly or completely enough out of medieval to modern ways, France, Holland and England each set their sights on pre-eminence in the world's collective balance of trade and accumulation of bullion, each government striving to expand both its overseas markets and its colonial production through the grant of monopolies to favoured companies and individuals. The enthusiastic pursuit of exclusionary wealth and power led these nations from collaboration against Spain into a rising crescendo of wars among themselves, in time relegating Spain to the role of minor player, its empire more a commercial prize than a military threat.

France

Chronologically, it was France – a predominantly Catholic power – that led the challenge to Pope Alexander VI's division of the world between Portugal and Spain. Although at the fighting edge of expansion were Calvinist Huguenots supported by the minister Gaspard de Coligny, the French enterprise drew from a wide spectrum of national support, and it attempted settlements as far apart as the Saint Lawrence (1535-42) and Rio de Janeiro (1555-60). The Huguenots Jen Ribault and René de Laudonnière were the most adventurous of all, attempting settlement athwart the lifeline of the Spanish American Empire, at the Florida Strait (1562-65).

All the initial French efforts failed; and that in Florida, along with the other activities of the 'Lutheran corsairs', provoked drastic counter-measures organised by Pedro Menéndez de Avilés. Besides the eradication of the French settlements with exemplary savagery, these included the setting up of a system of convoys and *guarda costas* to protect Spanish trade and harass the traders of other nations; the creation of a chain of Caribbean fortress ports; and the delimitation of the northern frontier by the establishment of fortified posts centred on Saint Augustine, Florida.

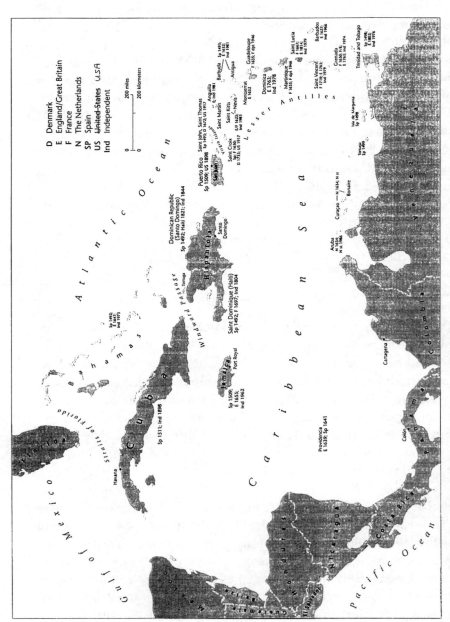

Colonial Possessions in the Caribbean

It was only after the conclusion of its civil wars of religion, with the suppression of the Huguenots and the making of peace with Spain in 1598, that France re-entered the arena, with the first permanent settlements in Canada and the Caribbean. These tended to be fragmented enterprises of different French regions and Atlantic ports until 1664, when the French controller general, Jean Baptiste Colbert, attempted to weld them into a coherent imperial policy under the control of the royal Compagnie des Indes Occidentales. This policy visualised settlements and plantations dedicated to the economic advantage of the metropole through the development of fur trading, fisheries, tropical staple production and a West African trade to provide slave labour, without any local self-determination and with minimal interconnections on the periphery. As with Spain's colonial policy, royal authority remained paramount, and the Catholic church became closely involved, mainly through the activities of missionary friars.

The gradual success of the French colonies, though, was largely self-generated, with considerable cross-recruitment in personnel and some intercolonial commerce in fish, cereals and lumber. Moreover, once the explorers Louis Jolliet and René-Robert Cavalier de La Salle had penetrated from the Saint Lawrence to the mouth of the Mississippi – during the period from 1673 to 1682 – and the French had expanded from the small islands of Martinique and Guadeloupe to take over from Spain and establish plantations in the western half of Española, there was at least the potential, around 1700, of an integrated empire that would give France hegemony in North America. That French supremacy was never achieved was due, in the simplest terms, to the economic and geopolitical advantages enjoyed by Holland and Britain, to their more rational or pragmatic imperial policies, and – to 1763 at least – to the narrow superiority of the British military and naval forces.

Holland

The conception of an effectively integrated imperial system of the North Atlantic – in which the interrelationship of North American and West Indian colonies and the tapping of West Africa for slaves were almost as vital as the connections with the European metropole – was as much the work of the Dutch as the English. Although England's greater resources of people and Holland's early preference for a worldwide empire of commerce, as much as England's victory in three Anglo-Dutch naval wars between 1652 and 1674, gave England a predominance that ended only with the American War of Independence.

With the energies generated from its successful war of independence from Spain, the Calvinist, capitalist, mercantilist, republican and federal Netherlands pursued an overseas empire in the same areas and in similar ways. But the Dutch had even more vigour than the English, whose initial expansion was complicated and delayed by the conflict between a centralising monarchy and an emergent bourgeoisie, not resolved until after the civil wars.

At first the Dutch and English enterprise overlapped and reinforced each other. Not only did freebooters from both nations (as well as French *flibustiers*) combine against Spain and Portugal, but Henry Hudson worked alternately for English and Dutch (providing the latter with their title to New Netherland); the Pilgrim fathers found refuge and financial support in Holland before they departed for Massachusetts; and Dutch finance, expertise and maritime resources were vital in the establishment of West Indian colonies, especially Barbados. The first settlement of that island was largely the work of the Anglo-Dutch Courteen company (based in Leyden and London). Its development as a sugar monoculture depended on emulating Dutch models in Pernambuco, Brazil; on obtaining capital, machinery and slaves from Dutch merchants; and on shipping sugar to European markets in Dutch vessels. At the same time, the Dutch were heavily involved in the financing, shipping and European sales of Virginian tobacco.

By the 1640s, the Dutch American empire was centred on sugar plantations in North-East Brazil and the Guianas, supplied with slaves from fortified factories in Guinea, and with at least the potential of provisions and lumber from the mainland colony of New Netherland. To these possessions the Dutch added islands in the Caribbean not already taken by the English and French, which if too small for profitable plantations would be ideal as trading posts. The very similarity of Dutch and English ventures, however, meant that rivalry and conflict were inevitable, which, when coupled with the continued enmity of the Catholic powers, meant that Holland was overextended.

The Dutch were expelled from Brazil (and Angola) by the Luso-Brazilians, and as a result of the exclusionist English Navigation Acts of 1651 and the consequent Anglo-Dutch wars – reluctantly initiated by the Commonwealth under Oliver Cromwell but continued by the more cynical Charles II – they were forced to concede the North American component of their Atlantic empire, New Netherland, in exchange for Surinam. Over the same period, Holland lost its primacy in West Africa and gave up the Virgin Islands and Tobago – subsequently shared among the English, Danes and sundry minor European powers – retaining in the West Indies only the islands of Curaçao, Aruba and Bonaire off the coast of Spanish Venezuela and the islets of Statia (Saint Eustatius), Saba and Saint Martin in the North-East Antilles, which were to serve as important neutral entrepots in the subsequent Anglo-French wars.

Similar minor victims of England's dominance in the late seventeenth and early eighteenth centuries were several Baltic powers. Sweden for a time had colonies or forts on Saint Barthélemy, the Delaware River and the Gold Coast of Africa before being restricted to its tiny West Indian colony. Denmark never had a North American mainland colony to add to the Faeroes, Iceland and Greenland, but it possessed the important Virgin Islands of Saint Thomas, Saint John and Saint Croix, which it supplied with slaves from its own posts in Guinea. The German Brandenburgers and the subjects of the grand duke of Courland tried but failed to establish a similar system, involving small slave plantations in Tobago.

England

Though English colonisation was initiated unsystematically by individuals, companies and the state, and the method of developing colonies was likewise tripartite, involving chartered companies, quasi-feudal proprietors and the Crown, it was at first an undifferentiated operation, finding suitable locations by chance and succeeding through sore trials and many errors. Those who read history backwards can trace policies and institutions to their flimsiest taproots and claim that all later developments were destined; but it was a half century before the various parts of the mainland and the West Indies became clearly differentiated in purpose and personnel. Not until its second century would England's American empire resolve itself into a rational imperial system; and even then it retained pragmatic variations, unevenly and inefficiently run and, in the end, impermanent.

The protean English colonial promoter, Walter Raleigh, besides being long involved in the 'plantation' of Ireland and innumerable privateering ventures, was successively concerned in the Newfoundland fisheries and mining projects in Labrador, the settlement of the huge coastline he christened Virginia, and visionary schemes to discover El Dorado and take over the Spanish Main with the help of the natives. Despite Raleigh's failures, each of his enterprises had its successors during the reigns of the first two Stuarts. Mixed fortunes in Amazonia and the Guianas (not given up until 1664) led to more permanent success on the generally less population, healthier and more defensible small islands of the Lesser Antilles. Such success included Thomas Warner's descent upon Saint Kitts in 1624 and the settlement of Barbados by the Courteens and the proprietary James Hay, Earl of Carlisle, in competition between 1625 and 1627, leading to an expansion into Nevis, Antigua and Montserrat from 1628 to 1632. The quest for gold mines in Labrador was likewise given up in favour of a fairly effective claim to control the fishing of the Newfoundland and New England banks; while Virginia was parcelled into more manageable swaths, and the first permanent settlements were established, after terrible difficulties, by a company on the Chesapeake (1607-25) and by groups of Puritan refugees in Massachusetts (1620-30).

The perspective of early English colonisation is clearer when it is remembered that tiny Bermuda had more settlers than Virginia until 1620 and that the white population of the English West Indies kept pace with the mainland colonies for another 50 years. Bermuda, indeed, was almost the linchpin in these initial phases, retaining vital connections with all mainland colonies and being involved in the settlement, supply and trade of the colonies in the West Indies before settling into lesser but still-important roles of shipbuilding, intercolonial trade, privateering and the provision of salt for the cod fisheries from the Turks and the Caicos Islands.

The close interaction between all early enterprises and their gradual diversification, however, is epitomised by the history of the failed English colony on the island of Providencia off the coast of Nicaragua (1630-41). Organised by a joint stock company in which Puritans such as the Earl of Warwick and John Pym were prominent, the Providence Island Colony was promoted as a godly (if profit-oriented) venture and, for this reason, obtained vital support from Puritan adventurers in New England and Bermuda. Plantations and trade with the Indians were initiated; but since Providencia was on the direct route of the Spanish silver convoys from the Isthmus, the Spaniards – probably correctly – saw it chiefly as a base for privateers and expelled the English at a second attempt. Had it survived, the Providence Island colony might well have developed as a sugar colony about the size and with the importance of Nevis; for the original smallholdings were already being consolidated and cultivated by a work-force of black slaves as numerous as the white settlers. But the very fact that most of the slaves had been stolen from the Spaniards' ships or plantations added force to Spanish opposition.

PLANTATION ECONOMIES

The draconian extinction of the Providence Island colony fuelled the feelings of revenge against the Spaniards that contributed to the takeover of Jamaica during the Cromwellian Interregnum (1655). But a more general factor was the success of the sugar revolution in the Lesser Antilles, which began in Barbados in the 1640s and spread to the English Leeward Islands in the 1660s. As the Dutch had demonstrated, sugar was so valuable a commodity (producing five times the value of provisions per acre) that monoculture was inevitable wherever the land was suitable. But sugar plantations were highly capital-, land- and labour-intensive, leading to the squeezing out of smallholders, the creation of an oligarchic plantocracy, and the substitution for white indentured labourers of a huge slave work-force – provided first by a series of monopolistic companies, of which the Royal African Company (1672) was the last and greatest, and then, after 1698, by legally sanctioned independent slave traders. Jamaica was seen at first as a location for displaced small settlers but was quickly monopolised by would-be planters. Between 1730 and 1770 it displaced Barbados as 'the jewel in the English Crown' – with 800 sugar plantations and a slave work-force eventually outnumbering all whites by ten to one.

One inevitable result of the establishment of plantation colonies was the phasing out of the international anti-Spanish brotherhood of the bucca-neers – symbolised in most books by the destruction of their main base, Port Royal, Jamaica, by the earthquake of 1692. In fact, the buccaneers had already been outlawed – declared to be pirates or international sea robbers rather than loosely commissioned privateers – as a result of those treaties by which the Spanish had acknowledged the rights of the English, French and Dutch to the colonies they had already effectively settled and planted. Expelled from their second main base on the island of Tortuga off northern Hispaniola in the 1690s, the desperate remnant of the buccaneers set themselves up in the Bahamas and North Carolina, taking advantage of the inefficiency of the proprietary government.

As Marcus Rediker has shown, the actual heyday of the pirates was the short period of peace and of colonial and commercial expansion after the end of Queen Anne's War with the French in 1713, beginning with the demobilisation of the imperial navies and ending with the establishment of effective royal government in the Bahamas and Carolinas around 1725. Piracy continued a dreaded hazard for legitimate trade in the Caribbean for at least another century, although the activities of naval patrols and colonial admiralty courts (particularly the British) restricted the pirates to fugitive crews of unromantic desperados, lurking in the remoter and least policed harbours of southern Cuba and the Spanish Main.

Meanwhile, motive forces similar to those which established sugar plantations in the Caribbean had led to the first settlement of South Carolina by ambitious Barbadian planters with their slaves in 1670 (initially under a Bermudian governor), opening up a long-lasting connection. Slaves became increasingly available to the mainland colonies through the development of the African trade to the West Indies, and plantations rapidly expanded from the Chesapeake southward. Nonetheless, the very different commodities grown on mainland plantations (tobacco, cotton and rice, brought in from South America, the West Indies and Africa respectively), the different climate, and the much greater opportunities for smallholding settlers determined that no mainland colony would ever develop either the degree of monoculture or the overwhelming proportion of slaves found in the West Indies, except in a few localities such as the South Carolina low country and the Georgia Sea Islands.

Some black slaves were imported into all mainland colonies because they became so freely available, but the socioeconomic divergence of New England and the middle colonies from the colonies of the plantation sphere, especially the West Indies, was inevitable. This, and the reciprocal relationship between north-eastern colonies and the West Indies, was encapsulated by John Winthrop of Massachusetts as early as 1647:

> It pleased the Lord to open to us a trade with Barbados and other islands in the West Indies, which as it proved gainful, so the commodities we had in exchange there for our cattle and provisions, as sugar, cotton, tobacco and indigo, were a good help to discharge our engagements in England.

Richard Pares, in *Yankees and Creoles* goes so far as to claim that without reciprocal trade 'the sugar colonies could not have existed and the North American colonies could not have developed'. Once the English had established their monopoly of the coastline from Florida to Maine and their constellation of sugar colonies in the West Indies, it was realised that:

> The colonies north of the Mason-Dixon line had few staples of any value in the European markets but a permanent surplus of food and lumber; the West Indies, just the contrary; and the hybrid colonies from Maryland to Carolina produced both staple crops and a less important surplus of other kinds of food.

Unlike the French West Indian colonies, which could depend for supplies on a metropolitan country that was not only overwhelming agricultural but also several times the size of Great Britain, the English sugar islands became dependent on the wide range of essential supplies that could be delivered from North America in sufficient quantities and far more cheaply than those carried across the Atlantic.

From Boston and the many smaller ports of New England, and from New York, Baltimore and Philadelphia, came dried and salted fish; pickled beef and pork; lard, butter and cheese; peas, beans and onions; corn, flour and bread; cattle, horses, hogs, sheep and poultry; oak and pine boards; 'shook' (that is, broken-down) barrels; iron hoops, bricks and leather. The southern ports of Wilmington, Charleston and Savannah exported mainly rice and dry vegetables, pine tar and all kinds of lumber – especially pine boards, staves and shingles. In all, by 1770, 63 per cent of all New England's dried fish was exported to the West Indies. From the middle (or 'bread') colonies some 400,000 pounds (180,000 kilograms) of wheat, flour and bread were shipped to the West Indies each year, half of which came from Pennsylvania and almost a third from New York. Only 19 per cent of the rice produced by the mainland plantations went to the West Indies, but this amounted to more than 140,000 hundredweight per year.

To an extent, the North American shippers took payment in cash and in credits that were good in England for redressing the imbalance of their trade with the metropolis. But the majority of their exports to the West Indies were paid for in West Indian produce. Sugar, cotton, indigo and later coffee were taken for North American and European markets, but the most favoured commodity was the sugar by-product molasses, the raw material for rum production. By 1770 there were at least 25 sugar refineries and 127 rum distilleries in the middle and New England colonies, of which Boston boasted seven of the former and 36 of the latter. The cities of Newport (Rhode Island), Philadelphia and New York accounted for many of the rest of both.

By 1700 hundreds of vessels of from 15 to 150 tons (9-135 metric tons) were engaged in a commerce that was as often speculative and opportunistic as it was regular and by arrangement, amounting in combination to at least a quarter of the value of Britain's transatlantic traffic. This pattern of trade, with mainland vessels normally sailing out by the eastern Antilles or through the Windward Passage (through the Bahamas and between Cuba and Hispanola), westward through the Caribbean, and back by the Straits of Florida, was an ever-increasing though minimally recognised component of a North Atlantic network of British imperial trade.

The North American-West Indian trade constituted a fourth side to what British historians have commonly misnamed the North Atlantic triangle, consisting of the traffic to and from Britain, Africa and the West Indies. The pattern of trade was in fact more of a cat's cradle once the North Americans developed their own trade with West Africa (confusingly also termed the North Atlantic triangle by some American scholars), in which slaves for the mainland, British West Indian and foreign markets were purchased largely with North American rum – a disreputable traffic in which Rhode Island merchants predominated.

The mercantile connections between the Thirteen Colonies and the West Indies involved some interchange among people – Lawrence Washington sailing to Barbados for his health (accompanied by his half-brother George) and Alexander Hamilton travelling from Nevis to New York for his education are two famous examples. But, in general, North Americans were committed to making a life on the mainland, while the ideal of every white West Indian seems to have been to become a planter and then an absentee in England. West Indians opting to migrate to the Thirteen Colonies were even rarer than North American absentees living in England. This demographic feature was consonant with the growing incompatibility of British imperial policy and the North American economy once the French threat on the mainland declined and the ever-expanding North America-West Indies trade pressed on the large but finite opportunities offered by the British West Indies.

The burgeoning success of trade between the British Thirteen Colonies and the West Indies contrasted with the comparative failure of the commercial connection between the French colonies in Canada and the Antilles. The French ministry of the navy from Colbert's day up to the mid-eighteenth century made great efforts to develop this trade. Canada was to export timber, barrel staves, flour, peas and salted fish – they also tried to ship horses but few of them survived the voyage – with the ships returning with cargoes of sugar, molasses and a potent form of rum called *guildive*. Unfortunately, everything that Canada could supply, New England could provide at far lower cost, thanks to lower costs of production, a much shorter voyage, a longer shipping season and lower insurance rates. Besides, Canada, with its minuscule population, was a limited market for sugar products. Consequently, Canadian ships all too often had to return to Quebec in ballast. Some French merchants trading to Quebec had much the same problem; their captains had to return by way of Saint Domingue (Haiti) or Martinique to get a return cargo that made the voyage worthwhile.

Besides these commercial considerations there was the even more potent question of relative military and naval power. The French role in North

America and the West Indies was challenged and contained in the wars that ended in 1713 and 1748, but a far more important conflict was the so-called Seven Years' War, which ended in 1763. This was a widespread (even worldwide) struggle, with land fighting undertaken by the British against the French and their Indian allies from the Saint Lawrence to the Ohio-Mississippi frontier. But the critical confrontations were increasingly naval, so that much hinged on Britain's conquests of Louisbourg in 1759 and Havana in 1762. Britain had not even had a permanent naval force in the Caribbean before 1740; but after 1763, though it gave back Havana and did not develop Louisbourg as a naval station, it possessed a strong network of naval bases in the west – with Antigua and Jamaica dominating the eastern and central Caribbean, Bermuda in the mid-Atlantic and Halifax, Nova Scotia (held since 1713), serving not only as a base from which to defend the Saint Lawrence and northern mainland but also as an invaluable refuge from the Caribbean summer and hurricane seasons.

Up until the end of the Seven Years' War, the Anglo-Americans had, broadly, been prepared to accept such restrictive legislation as the Molasses Act of 1733 for the benefits of naval and military protection, particularly as long as their more or less clandestine trade with the foreign West Indies continued to be only loosely policed by Britain. The Treaty of Paris in 1763 formalised the French exclusion from the North American mainland; but far from capitalising on wartime successes by retaining all conquered colonies, Britain actually seems to have encouraged the prosperity of those French and Spanish colonies, the trade of which so attracted the Americans. The French did give up the underdeveloped 'neutral islands' of Dominica, Saint Vincent, Grenada and Tobago; but because the powerful British West India lobby feared over-production within its protected system, the French were allowed to retain Martinique and Guadeloupe, as well as to develop Saint Domingue, already poised to become the most profitable and pro-ductive slave-plantation colony in history.

Even more significant was the settlement made with Spain, which regained both Cuba and Louisiana while giving up East and West Florida to Britain. Following some relaxation of Spanish mercantilism, Cuba began to exhibit its potential as a plantation colony, while regarding Louisiana almost as a dependency of Havana. For the Americans, however, both Louisiana and Cuba offered prospects for at least commercial expansion, already encouraged by the extension of the mainland colonies into the Florida peninsula and panhandle, which at that time reached almost to the Mississippi.

New British sugar plantations were developed in the ceded islands of the Lesser Antilles, and some relaxation of mercantilism occurred with the Free Port Acts after 1765. Despite this, the restrictions on North American trade with the West Indies through the ever expanding code of Navigation Laws – and their implementation by a revitalised customs service and colonial vice-admiralty courts – contributed almost as much as taxation without representation, British attempts to close off the western frontier, occupation by the military, and the imbalance of colonials into a war for independence.

Quite apart from the probably specious argument that Britain was not absolutely wholehearted in retaining political control over the Thirteen Colonies because of the greater valuation it placed on the West Indies, the American War of Independence had a West Indian dimension in at least two respects. The timely arrival of Admiral François Joseph Paul de Grasse with the French West Indian fleet ensured the surrender of General Charles Cornwallis at Yorktown in 1781, essentially ending the war on land. Conversely, George Rodney's defeat of the same French admiral off Guadeloupe in the following year completely redressed the balance of the naval war, enabling Britain to sustain its imperial system in the West Indies for a further generation.

ANGLO-AMERICA AND THE BORDERLANDS AFTER 1783

Although the American War of Independence is usually cited as one of the first causes of the decline of the British West Indian plantation colonies, connections between the West Indies as a whole and those parts of North America that remained colonial dependencies continued to be of vital importance to both. Although the British North American colonies of Newfoundland, Nova Scotia, New Brunswick and Lower Canada were unable to make up the shortfall in trade caused by the exclusion of American traders from the West Indies, the attempt to do so provided a boost for their infant economies. Over the same period, the gradual expansion of the USA towards the Rio Grande was as much conditioned by changes in the European imperial system and by revolutionary changes in the Caribbean and the rest of Latin America as by forces generated within the new republic.

In 1800 Spain contracted to sell Louisiana back to the French, but Napoleon's grandiose plans to revive the French Caribbean Empire by the reconquest of Saint Domingue and the development of Louisiana were scotched by the catastrophic defeat of General Charles Victor Emmanuel Leclerc by the Haitian blacks and yellow fever, which led to the declaration of Haitian independence in 1804. In 1803 the USA was able to purchase Louisiana from the French (a tacit bargain in return for ending trade with Haiti), just as Napoleon was about to turn to the takeover of Spain itself.

The French invasion of Spain in 1808 not only encouraged the now isolated *criollos* of Hispanic America in their quest for independence but also made Spain, as Britain's new ally, the natural antagonist of the USA. The idealist anti-colonialism of the Americans was severely qualified both by their ambitions to take over the adjacent Spanish territories and by the desire to compete with the British in monopolising the huge potential Latin American markets under the cloak of support for the independence movements there. Such concerns contributed to the assertion by Congress that Florida could never be transferred except to the USA, the outbreak of war with Britain and Spain in 1812, the acquisition of Florida from Spain in 1821, and the extension of the no-transfer principle throughout the western hemisphere by the Monroe Doctrine of 1823.

Contrary to the mythology that was grown around that famous dictum, it was originally made in conjunction with the British with the tacit approval of the French. As late as 1850 British trade to Latin America remained twice that of the USA, with political influence in proportion. Though the British, French, Dutch and Danish colonies in the region steadily declined, from the ending of the slave trade in 1807 to the emancipation of the slaves between 1834 and 1863, the Americans were effectively unable to penetrate them economically during the rest of the nineteenth century, let alone prise them free from their imperial masters.

Nor were US ambitions concerning the Hispanic territories easily or quickly fulfilled. As early as 1807, Thomas Jefferson had suggested to James Madison that after the destined acquisition of the Floridas, the south-western boundary of the USA might be pushed back as the reward for helping the Mexicans achieve their independence, while Cuba might naturally come under American economic if not political sway. Despite American help for Hidalgo and Iturbide, British and even French competition, as well as Mexican national pride and distrust, kept the USA at bay and determined that the coastline from the Mississippi to the Rio Grande and the huge interior province of Texas would become one of the United States only through a process of steady infiltration, shady dealing and an indirect war. In the Caribbean, though Santo Domingo eventually became independent (without notable help from the USA) in 1865, Cuba and Puerto Rico remained Spanish colonies for another three decades. Indeed, many proud nationalists in the former resisted a destiny manifested by a gradual monopolisation of trade and by a rising tide of American investment under the paradoxical banner of *la lealissima colonia*.

Few Maritimers in British North America would have continued to express loyalism in such grandiloquent terms. The imperial connection was of limited direct value once the structure of British mercantilism had been dismantled – first by the opening of West Indian ports during the last French war and, more slowly, once international rivalries over the Caribbean no longer threatened war, by the gradual abrogation of the Navigation Acts. Yet during the ensuing age of free trade, the general West Indian connection did grow in importance for the British maritime colonies. Maritimers now traded their fish, provisions and lumber, along with some manufactures, to British and foreign West Indies alike, taking in return unrefined sugar, molasses and tobacco for processing and distribution. Moreover, the growing sophistication and volume of transactions between British North American ports and the West Indies, along with the imbalance of visible trade, was already laying the basis for the involvement in West Indian banking and insurance. This special relationship between the British Maritime colonies and the West Indies, and the fear (somewhat exaggerated it must be admitted) of losing the primacy and of being economically diluted through a federated Canada, contributed to the Maritimers' initial reluctance to engage in the plans for Canadian confederation in the 1860s.

BIBLIOGRAPHY

No single work comprehensively covers this huge geographical area and historical span. The literature from which more detailed information must be sought is immense, and the relevant works vary greatly in approach, sharpness of focus and quality. Important gaps also remain, to frustrate explorations or encourage new research and writing. The following is a selection of the best and most recent relevant works, most of which include valuable specialist bibliographies.

Charles M. Andrews, *The Colonial Period of American History*, 4 vols, New Haven, CT, 1934-38.

Kenneth R. Andrews, *Trade, Plunder, and Settlement: Maritime Enterprise and the Genesis of the British Empire, 1480-1630*, Cambridge, UK, 1984.

Van Cleaf Bachman, *Peltries or Plantations: The Economic Policies of the Dutch West India Company in New Netherland, 1623-1639*, Baltimore, MD, 1969.

Jacques A. Barbier and Allan J. Kuethe (eds), *The North American Role in the Spanish Imperial Economy, 1760-1819*, Manchester, UK, 1984.

Robin Blackburn, *The Overthrow of Colonial Slavery, 1776-1848*, London, 1988.

J. F. Bosher, *The Canada Merchants, 1713-1763*, Oxford, 1987.

Charles R. Boxer, *The Dutch Seaborne Empire, 1600-1800*, New York, 1965.

Lester J. Cappon *et al.* (eds), *Atlas of Early American History: The Revolutionary Era, 1760-1790*, Princeton, NJ, 1976.

Selwyn H. H. Carrington, *The British West Indies in the American Revolution*, Dordrecht, The Netherlands, 1988.

Philip D. Curtin, *The Atlantic Slave Trade: A Census*, Madison, WI, 1969.

Kenneth G. Davies, The *North Atlantic World in the Seventeenth Century*, Minneapolis, MN, 1974.

Ralph Davis, *The Rise of the Atlantic Economies*, Ithaca, NY, 1973.

W. J. Eccles, *France in America*, new ed., Toronto, ON, 1990.

David Eltis, *Economic Growth and the Ending of the Transatlantic Slave Trade*, New York, 1987.

Lawrence Henry Gipson, *The British Empire Before the American Revolution*, 13 vols, New York, 1948-68.

Marcel Giraud, *A History of French Louisiana, Vol. 1, The Reign of Louis XIV, 1698-1715*, Baton Rouge, LA, 1974.

Harold A. Innis, *The Cod Fisheries: The History of an International Economy*, rev. ed., Toronto, ON, 1954.

Franklin W. Knight, *The Caribbean: Genesis of a Fragmented Nationalism*, 2nd ed., Oxford, 1990.

Peggy K. Liss, *Atlantic Empires: The Network of Trade and Revolution, 1713-1826*, Baltimore, MD, 1983.

John Robert McNeill, *Atlantic Empires of France and Spain: Louisbourg and Havana, 1700-1763*, Chapel Hill, NC, 1985.

David H. Makinson, *Barbados: A Study of North American-West Indian Relations, 1739-1789*, The Hague, 1964.

Jacques Mathieu, *Le commerce entre la Nouvelle France et les Antilles au XVIIIe siècle*, Paris, 1981.

Donald W. Meinig, *The Shaping of America: A Geographical Perspective on Five Hundred Years of History, Vol. 1, Atlantic America, 1492-1800*, New Haven, CT, 1986.

Stewart L. Mims, *Colbert's West India Policy*, New Haven, CT, 1912.

Arthur Percival Newton, *The Colonising Activities of the English Puritans: The Last Phase of the Elizabethan Struggle with Spain*, New Haven, CT, 1914.

_____ *The European Nations in the West Indies, 1493-1688*, London, 1933.

Richard Pares, *Merchants and Planters*, Cambridge, UK, 1960.

_____ *War and Trade in the West Indies 1739-1763*, Oxford, 1936.

_____ *Yankees and Creoles: The Trade Between North America and the West Indies Before the American Revolution*, London, 1956.

C. Northcote Parkinson (ed.), *The Trade Winds: A Study of British Overseas Trade During the French Wars, 1793-1815*, London, 1948.

Jacob M. Price, *Capital and Credit in British Overseas Trade: The View from the Chesapeake, 1700-1776*, Cambridge, MA, 1980.

Marcus Rediker, *Between the Devil and the Deep Blue Sea: Merchant Seamen, Pirates, and the Anglo-American Maritime World, 1700-1750*, Cambridge, UK, 1987.

Ian K. Steele, *The English Atlantic, 1675-1740*, New York, 1986.

N. M. Miller Surrey, *The Commerce of Louisiana During the French Regime, 1699-1763*, New York, 1916; repr. 1968.

Charlton W. Tebeau, *A History of Florida*, Miami, FL, 1971.

Gary M. Walton and James F. Shepherd, *The Economic Rise of Early America*, Cambridge, UK, 1979.

Eric E. Williams, *Capitalism and Slavery*, London, 1964.

3

The Planters' World in
the British West Indies

Introduction: This extract is perhaps the most original section of a chapter solicited by Bernard Bailyn and Philip Morgan in 1987 for a book on the establishment of British colonies and culture on the American periphery, which was published in 1991. Although initially feeling that a study of planters and their culture was no more than a diversion from a greater concern for West Indian slaves and the slavery system in general (about which Philip Morgan himself wrote an excellent chapter in the Bailyn-Morgan book), and from a growing interest in post-slavery adjustments, the author was inspired by this return to the roots of British colonialism to undertake the more technical and detailed study of the establishment of the British West Indian plantocracy. This is given in full as the subsequent essay in the present collection.

The initial English venturers to the Caribbean were a kind of Protestant *conquistadores*, a product both of the European Renaissance and of the Reformation. Their epitome was perhaps Sir Henry Colt, who in 1631, finding the rigours of planting in St Kitts little to his liking, opted instead to attack the Spaniards: 'For rest we will nott, until we have doone some thinges worthy of ourselves, or dye in the attempt.'[1] Fittingly, no more of Colt is heard thereafter. For the future belonged to those more earthbound planters whom he left behind in the infant colony of St Kitts. Such strenuous settlers, and the society of each successively successful island plantation, were profoundly influenced by two salient sequential changes: the formal institution of colonial government and the creation of a monocultural plantation economy dependent on the labour of African slaves. Together, these changes compelled the emergence of a distinctive local type of white planter ruling class, a plantocracy.

Yet this evolutionary process itself was influenced by at least four models, ideals, or paradigms of social behaviour originating in the mother country and its expanding periphery, commingling, conflicting and fading before the imperatives of local politics and the harsh socioeconomic realities of the sugar plantation, but retaining traces everywhere and remaining strong on the ever-expanding colonial margins beyond the settled plantations. These paradigms were the maritime, the military, the aristocratic (or feudal-seigneurial) and the traditional household-familial.

England's colonisation of tropical islands symbolically began with the hurricane wreck of Sir George Somers's ship *Sea Venture* on Bermuda in 1609, which occasioned Shakespeare's profound meditation on the nature of colonies and colonial societies in *The Tempest* (1611). As an avid reader of Renaissance authors who was personally acquainted with noble and gentlemanly would-be colonisers such as Southampton, Pembroke, Delaware and Sir Dudley Digges, Shakespeare naturally described colonisation as a fit pursuit for aristocratic adventures. But it was also essentially a maritime activity. As Frank Kermode has pointed out, the key words in *The Tempest* include 'nature', 'noble', 'vile', and 'virtue'. Yet the overwhelming element is the sea.

> The most remarkable changes are rung on the word 'sea' and its compounds. The sea, the voyages it supports, and the wrecks it causes, are types of the action of grace and providence. Hence the 'sea-change' and the 'sea-sorrow'. Hence the description of the sea as never surfeited, as incensed, as invulnerable, as apparently cruel, as revealing guilt, as a force which swallows but casts again, which threatens but is merciful.

Just as Shakespeare's *Tempest* is not only a deeply Renaissance work but also the quintessential product of English maritime activity and involvement on the eve of colonisation, so English colonisation in the Caribbean began and remained closely involved with the all-encompassing sea, with its language and metaphors and its societies of captains and crews. The first English venturers into the Caribbean were those whom the Spaniards called 'Lutheran corsairs', such as Sir John Hawkins, Drake, Raleigh or Robert Rich, Earl of Warwick – the last of whom profitably combined privateering ventures against the Spaniards with the promotion of Puritan plantations in Bermuda and Providence Island at least partially worked by captured Negro slaves. The lineal descendants of the Elizabethan and Jacobean seadogs were the buccaneers, the greatest of whom, Henry Morgan, once peace was made with Spain, transferred his plunder into a Jamaican plantation named after his Welsh birthplace, was knighted by Charles II, and became moderately respectable as lieutenant governor of Jamaica and vice-admiralty judge – a significantly transitional figure.[3]

The sea remained the common Caribbean element, the essential medium of communication, a symbol of distance, isolation and danger but also of escape. The sea not only linked the islands with the metropole, the cousin colonies of the North American seaboard and the heartland-homeland of the African slaves, but was also the means of communicating between Caribbean colonies, even, for lack of roads, between different parts of individual islands – with distances measured in time taken rather than nautical miles, because of the prevailing winds and currents and the vagaries of the weather. A high proportion of all West Indian plantations were within sight of the sea, and planters kept spyglasses on hand and a regular lookout and maintained a permanent weather eye. Colonial newspapers too were largely shipping gazettes, with even the sparse and delayed news of the outside world advertised as brought in by the latest-arriving vessel.

The south-westward-setting trade winds that brought provisions, slaves, news and new white recruits, and carried away plantation produce and home-returning whites, also turned the sugarcane windmills – themselves often likened in Barbados and Antigua to ships dotted across a green sea of sugar canes. The trade winds also brought rain and less welcome storms, and, for four months each year, the dread threat of a tropical hurricane. In the early years of settlement in the Leeward Islands the equally dreaded Caribs came in by sea in their swift canoes (especially when the moon was full), and during the dozen imperial wars that punctuated the years between 1652 and 1815, a distant sail anxiously espied might variously betoken famine-averting succour, naval or military relief, the onset of an enemy blockade, or the descent of an invading army. For isolated coastal settlements as for legitimate traders sailing along, pirates remained a peacetime hazard too, into the nineteenth century. A literally marginal category of desperados, pirates were a reproach to plantocratic notions of law and order: polyglot, multiracial, virtually classless groups of international outlaws, including runaway white bondsmen and black slaves, lurking from bases in the least developed, most productive fringes of the Caribbean. Such marginal freemasonries, such undeveloped margins, were among the chosen destinations of those many fugitive bondsmen who took flight by sea.[4]

Not unnaturally, most West Indian planters, and their slaves, knew the sea almost as well as the land. Edward Long in 1774 listed some 25 words in common plantation parlance that had a maritime derivation.[5] It is highly likely that the gang system used on slave plantations had a maritime provenance. In Belize and Providence Island, and doubtless other places too, working gangs, or even any group of male slaves met together, were referred to as 'crews'. The slave name Boatswain, common throughout the West Indies, usually betokened not a slave mariner, but a trusted slave gang leader. Similarly, at least one loyalist planter in the Bahamas referred to his slaves as 'the people', the term used by seventeenth- and eighteenth-century captains for their crews. Conjuring up the surrounding element and the model of life on board ship, with its watches and working parties under the command of 'bo'suns', as well as more poignantly symbolising a longing for the outside world in one of the most scattered, impoverished and isolated colonies are the remarkably accurate drawings of sailing vessels still found scratched into the plaster of the ruins of plantation houses in the islands of the Bahamas.

The fading feudal tradition that a landholder and his retainers formed a local military unit, ultimately linked to the sovereign through a chain of command and fealty, was revived on this colonial periphery, given fresh impetus in the English Civil Wars, and retained in the form of the parish-based colonial militias. As much soldiers as sailors, Elizabethan Protestant hidalgos like Humphrey Gilbert, Drake, Raleigh, Thomas Gates, Thomas Dale, first in Ireland, then in North America, the Spanish Main and the Caribbean, were eager to carve a new patrimony and carry the Word with the sword, wresting the land from its Catholic usurpers or its pagan inhabitants. Once settlements were actually made, moreover, the need for military defence remained as important as it had ever been on the fringes of the Roman Empire or the marches of Europe in the Middle Ages.

That doughty Lincolnshire warrior, John Smith (whose title of captain was surely amphibious and who had, significantly, fought and earned a coat of arms in Transylvania against the Turk), was a key figure in the earliest history of Virginia. His Caribbean equivalent was Captain Thomas Warner, the founder of St Kitts: Suffolk squire (and neighbour of John Winthrop), soldier, sailor and settler, who was knighted for his loyalty, persistence and success by James I. Like Raleigh and Drake as well as Smith himself, Warner saw the value of treating with friendly and useful Indians but an equal necessity of resorting to the sword to cut down unfriendly, 'treacherous', or inconvenient natives. When Warner decided to slaughter his Carib ally Tigreman and his followers as they lay in their hammocks after a feat, John Hilton approvingly claimed that 'he acted like a wise man and a solider'.[6] For more than 30 years thereafter, the English militias in the Leewards kept a nightly watch 'in the trenches' against Carib attacks (doubled at times of full moon) and carried out periodic punitive raids on the neighbouring Carib Islands. The symbolic climax of this phase, though by no means its conclusion, was the personal combat in which Edward Warner, the English commander of the Antigua militia campaigning in Dominica, slew his own half-brother, Thomas 'Indian' Warner (Sir Thomas's half-caste son), who on a visit to London had been rather casually appointed viceroy of Dominica by Charles II.[7]

The early militias of the Lesser Antilles took sides during the English Civil Wars, though they rarely, if ever, came to blows. With marginally more resolution, they sailed under their local commanders, Lord Willoughby of Parham and the two Christopher Codringtons, father and son, to capture or recapture islands (and mainland Surinam) during the Anglo-Dutch and first Anglo-French wars. The most important military enterprise in the early years, however, was the amphibious operation involving discharged veterans of the Civil Wars and recruits from Barbados and the Leewards that led to the takeover of Jamaica by Admiral Penn and General Venables in 1655.[8] Although the original plan was far more grandiose and the local opposition in Jamaica was derisory – with the invading regiments settled in separate districts called 'quarters' and the ordinary soldiers set to planting subsistence crops simply to avoid starvation – yet the surviving officers of the expeditionary force who remained as planters always referred to themselves as 'the conquerors of Jamaica', thus legitimising their land-holding and ranks by right of conquest. In so doing, the founders of English Jamaica were at least instinctively expressing the political philosophy of the Royalist James Harrington, whose *Oceana* was published within a year of the takeover of Jamaica: 'As he [Hobbes] said of the law, that without this sword it is but paper, so he might have thought of this sword, that without an hand it is but cold iron. The hand which holdeth this sword is the militia of a nation.'[9]

Even more than in the mainland colonies, in all British West Indian colonies the militia remained an essential part of the sociopolitical fabric. All free white males between the ages of 16 and 60 were enrolled into regiments based on each parish, under the command of officers whose ranks were in almost exact proportion to their standing as landed proprietors. For much of the slavery period, the local planters were proudly known by their militia ranks. The founder of the Price fortune in Jamaica, for example, was first known simply as Lieutenant Francis Price, presumably from the rank he had held at the time of the conquest of 1655. But later, as a successful planter and member of the Assembly, he was promoted to captain and then major in the Saint John's militia regiment. His son Charles (1678-1730) was colonel and commander of the parochial regiment, and his grandson Sir Charles (1708-72) was not only speaker of the Jamaican Assembly and a baronet but as a major general was the senior officer of the militia forces of one of Jamaica's three shires.[10]

At the apex of the colonial militia structure was the king's deputy, the governor, who was general and commander in chief of the local militia but also, in a remarkably high proportion of cases, a man with actual military experience. For the often beleaguered West Indian colonies the thesis of Stephen Saunders Webb that English colonies in America were essentially military outposts – an extension of models forged on the Scottish and Welsh borders and in Ireland – is truer than for the Thirteen Colonies.[11] But the military paradigm became weaker as the colonies became more securely established and defence and warfare more the concern of professional garrison troops and naval ships on station. The chief sociopolitical purpose of the militia, though, remained an important one: not the external military defence of the colony, but the function of an internal police force against rebellious white bondsmen, black slaves and militant runaways. As Richard Ligon recognised as early as 1647, the parish-based militia of Barbados was the visible and audible instrument of plantocratic power: 'They [the slaves] are held in such awe and slavery, as they are fearful to appear in any daring act; and seeing the mustering of our men, and hearing their Gun-shot, (than which nothing is more terrible to them) their spirits are subjugated to so low a condition, as they dare not look up to any bold attempt.'[12]

Militias continued to be mustered in times of war – first with white bondsmen, then coloured and black freedmen, and finally even reliable slaves employed in subordinate roles under the pressures of need (though on the rare occasions they were used in campaigns the militias scarcely distinguished themselves). Even when summoned at times of threatened Carib attacks or slave uprisings or called upon to leave their native parishes to fight maroons (as in Jamaica in the 1730s), the white rank and file and even the officers were notoriously reluctant to serve. Colonial whites, moreover, were conspicuously unwilling to obey governors whose qualifications were too obviously based upon irrelevant military service or whose attitudes were too militaristic. The most extreme case of this was the occasion of 1710 when the whites of Antigua were so incensed with their governor, the Virginia-born Daniel Parke – allegedly appointed because he had been the officer who first brought the news of the victory of Blenheim to London in 1704 – that they shot him and hacked his body to pieces on the steps of Government House. For the planters, however, the militia and their ranks within it remained vital components of the internal structure of law and order as long as slavery lasted.[13]

The first English colonies in the Americas were founded at a time when the Stuart kings were attempting to resuscitate quasi-feudal concepts of aristocracy, sociopolitical relations and royal administration. Even more than in England itself, and completely contrary to New England, vestiges of such aristocratic and royalist structures, styles and attitudes survived among the planter class of the British West Indies, despite the religious and political turmoil of the Civil Wars and the rising tide of bourgeois capitalism – almost certainly as a defensive response to the harsh realities of the West Indian climate, the plantation economy and the fact that the overwhelming majority of the population consisted of African or Afro-Caribbean slaves.

The first English island colony, Bermuda, though ostensibly run by a chartered company for 69 years, exhibited the initial tendency to provide colonies with marchland extensions of English institutions and populate them with tenants and bondsmen, on almost feudal lines. The planters were noblemen and privileged gentry granted strips of land from sea to sea across the narrow islands, which they either worked with landless bondsmen or (if, as was usual, they remained at home) on which they placed tenants who paid them rent in a share of crops. There was a political superstructure of governor, council and elective assembly even before the crown assumed direct control in 1684, but the basic unit of local government and daily life was parochial. In 1616, Bermuda was divided into six 'tribes' (a term of obscure derivation recognised by 1679 as being exactly synonymous with parishes), each with its church, glebe and common land, its militia unit, and its local justices of the peace, elective vestry and parochial officers drawn from the substantial landowners and long leasehold tenants.[14] Helped by the absence of an indigenous population and the presence of a remarkably large number of white settlers (more numerous than those in Virginia before 1625 and outnumbering the black inhabitants up to 1700), Bermuda by 1684, in the words of Henry C. Wilkinson, possessed all the English trappings of 'counsellors, bailiffs, sheriffs, marshals, courts of law, grand juries, petty juries, justices of the peace, inquests, the militia system, trained bands, churchwardens, sidesmen, glebe, common land' while at the same time, like seventeenth- and eighteenth-century England, it was dominated by a class of local landed proprietors.[15]

Although the most common response of would-be colonisers with or without titles of nobility or influence at court, was to seek a royal charter for a company, a more telling Stuart solution to the problem of authorising and controlling new colonies was the granting of quasi-feudal proprietor-ships. Thus Barbados, the Leewards and the other Caribbee Islands were granted (in patents that confusingly overlapped because of an ignorance of Caribbean geography) to two royal favourites, the earls of Carlisle and Pembroke, whose prerogatives were often in conflict with individuals and companies that had founded the actual settlements.[16] Significantly, the form of the first proprietary grants (including that of Carolina and the Bahamas to Sir Robert Heath in 1629) was that of a feudal tenancy in chief, subject to the ceremony of homage and the paying of a 'peppercorn' rent, 'after the manner of the County Palatine of Durham' – strongly suggesting the conception of such colonies as borderlands, calling for the special delegation of prerogatives by the monarch and special ties and duties, including military service in return for land, imposed on all subfeudatories.

Equally significantly, alter grants (such as the Carolina patent of 1663 and that adding the Bahamas in 1670) were made by the monarch 'in free socage, after the custom of our manor of East Greenwich in the County of Kent'. This indicated a far freer form of tenancy, in which land was held by the proprietors and their subtenants in permanent leasehold, subject only to its development and the payment of an annual quitrent, and able to be bought and sold and bequeathed hereditarily. Barbadian, Leeward Island, and Jamaican planters naturally wanted more – absolute freehold in their land – and were, indeed, in favour of royal over proprietary govern-ment to the degree that it would both facilitate access to undeveloped land and organise, regularise and validate their tenures. The earliest tenures in Barbados (as in most West Indian colonies) were of yeoman size and type, but the early development of freehold in real estate aided the consolidation of land into sugar plantations and the emergence of a sugar planter class in the later 1640s.

Elsewhere, quitrents and the nominal obligation to develop patented lands remained in place in most colonies a century after the crown assumed direct control. But, in general, the early establishment of freehold tenure and the ready availability of undeveloped crown land in new colonies to potential planters with political influence or financial means facilitated the creation and perpetuation of a native class of landed gentry even more tightly tied to the aristocratic system than were their English counterparts. The importance of tenure, possession and inheritance also helps to explain why West Indian planters were so scrupulous and litigious when it came to matters of real estate and why, of all the structure of courts established on the English model, it was the colonial courts of chancery that were the best organised and busiest of all.

The biographies and family histories of successful West Indian planters illustrate both the disparate range of classes from which they sprang (and thus how West Indian plantations were a machine for creating wealth and aiding upward mobility) and the way in which they gravitated towards an aristocratic norm or ideal, derived from feudal culture, in their attitudes and behaviour. At one end of the scale were the genuine aristocrats like the Codringtons, feudal magnates of Gloucestershire, whose ancestor had carried the royal standard at the battle of Poitiers (1356). Christopher Codrington the elder (1640-98) built up one of the richest estates in Barbados during sugar's earliest and most profitable years, was a councillor at twenty-six and deputy governor at twenty-nine. Later, as governor-general of the Leewards he assembled the largest set of holdings in Antigua and acquired the entire island of Barbuda through his privileged access to the patenting process, though many of his lands lay undeveloped for years despite the requirements of the law. As military commander of the expedition that recaptured St Kitts in 1690, he even sought to augment his personal empire by taking over the best lands in the French section of the island, though this was thwarted by the terms of the Treaty of Ryswick (1697). The younger Christopher Codrington (1668-1710), brought up in England, an Oxford scholar and socialite, followed in his father's footsteps as colonial governor-general and military commander during Queen Anne's War (similarly capturing French St Kitts and invading Guadeloupe). The richest and most splendid of all early West Indian grandees, on his premature death in 1710 (three years before the Treaty of Utrecht gave the whole of St Kitts to the English) he bequeathed his magnificent library to his alma mater and left his two Barbadian plantations, with their slaves, to the Society for the Propagation of the Gospel for the establishment of a theological and medical college and a school for white Barbadian youths.[17]

The elegant Georgian buildings of Codrington College (completed between 1721 and 1738), now housing the theology faculty of the University of the West Indies, remain the most conspicuous relic of the golden, or aristocratic, phase of Barbadian sugar plantations. The two Christopher Codringtons, however, were quite exceptional in their aristocratic provenance, their lordly disdain for bourgeois convention, and their style of *nobless oblige*. Rival planters complained that they bent the law to their own advantage — not just the restrictions on the allocation of crown lands, which all planters ignored as best they could, but also the Acts of Trade, which forbade commerce with the Dutch and French in nearby islands. For their part, the Codringtons tended to be dismissive of self-made planters and their legislative pretensions and were openly contemptuous of low-born landless whites. Conversely, though, like true aristocrats, they were able to leap the intervening classes and form bonds of mutual respect with at least some of their numerous African slaves. In an oft-quoted passage, Christopher Codrington, the young in 1701 recalled his father's special relationship with the Coromantees, whom most planters regarded as the most obdurate, troublesome and rebellious of slaves:

> They are not only the best and most faithful of our slaves but are really all born Heroes ... There never was a raskal or coward of the nation, intrepid to the last degree, not a man of them but will stand to be cut to pieces without a sigh or groan, grateful and obedient to a kind master, but implacably revengeful when ill-treated. My Father, who had studied the genius and temper of all kinds of negroes 45 years with a very nice observation, would say, Noe man deserved a Corramante that would not treat him like a Friend rather than a Slave.[18]

In many ways a more typical, perhaps even the quintessential, early West Indian planter was James Drax (1602-75), one of the chief characters (if not heroes) of Richard Ligon's *History of Barbados* (1657). Drax had sailed with the first settlers under John Powell in 1627, an adventurer of obscure, probably yeoman background, with £300 in company stock. Within a year he had cleared enough ground to grow and send a cargo of tobacco to England. With the proceeds he purchased 40 white indentured servants, diversifying into cotton once the tobacco market failed with the help of Arawak Amerindians from the Orinoco. Around 1640, he visited Pernambuco to learn the techniques of sugar planting from the Portuguese and Dutch, forging valuable trading and credit links with Dutch and Sephardic Jewish merchants based in Amsterdam. Opting for the Dutch system of consolidated factory-based farming units rather than the Portuguese-Brazilian system of *senhors de engenho* and cane farming, sharecropping *lavradores*, Drax imported large numbers of slaves from 1644 and erected the first windmill in Barbados.[19]

Selfishly keeping his expertise from his neighbours as long as he could, James Drax, along with his kinsman William Hilliard, was one of the first two Barbadian sugar planters, and soon the richest. By 1647 he was writing that he would not transfer to England unless he could purchase an estate worth £10,000 a year. Although in principle approving the Royalist Governor Lord Willoughby's declaration of legislative independence in 1651 and opposed to the Navigation Act of the same year and the Anglo-Dutch War that followed it, Drax was identified as a Commonwealth supporter by his Cavalier rivals and fined 80,000 pounds of sugar in 1650. A colonel of militia and assemblyman before his temporary eclipse, he really came into his own with the Cromwellian ascendancy, becoming a councillor and commissioner of roads in 1653 and sent off with almost royal pomp on his first return to England (after 27 years) in 1654. On a subsequent visit in 1658, he was knighted by Cromwell himself.[20]

Yet James Drax was an equivocal Puritan and in Barbados lived in almost baronial style. His plantation house, Drax Hall, though much altered, is one of the principal Barbadian monuments to the old plantocracy, and his splendid style of life and hospitality are exemplified by the 50 lines that Ligon takes mouthwateringly to describe the menu of a typical dinner at Drax Hall around 1647.[21] James Drax was also one of the first and most notable of upwardly mobile West Indian planter dynasts. He married the daughter of James Hay, first Earl of Carlisle, by Lucy Percy, one of the ladies-in-waiting to Queen Henrietta Maria; and his own daughter, Frances, married the younger Christopher Codrington. Despite his Cromwellian knighthood, James Drax comfortably survived the Restoration, dividing his time between Barbados and England, where he was one of the prominent members of the prototype committee of West Indian merchants and planters that met informally at the Jamaica Coffee House in Saint Michael's Walk near the Exchange in London. His fortune continued to grow with the help of new interests in Jamaica, but, unlike his son-in-law, he was not a notable Barbadian benefactor. His son, Colonel Henry Drax, who died in Middlesex, England, in 1682, though, left £2,000 in his will for the establishment of a 'free school and college' in Bridgetown, Barbados.[22]

Richard Sheridan has shown how similar conditions led to the creation of a local aristocracy out of those who settled Antigua before 1680, with the Willoughbys and Codringtons illustrating fortunes transferred or extended from Barbados and families like the Martins and Tudways replicating the history of the Draxes from an Antiguan base.[23] But the way in which West Indian sugar plantations not only generated increasing wealth up to at least 1775 but also created a kind of native aristocracy, imitative of European patterns but uniquely West Indian, is epitomised in the history of the Price family, the Jamaican (as opposed to the absentee) phase of which climaxed in the career of the first St Charles Price (1708-72).

Despite the myths contributed to *Burke's Peerage* by a pious descendant, the Welsh origins of the family were as obscure as Henry Morgan's, and probably not dissimilar – impoverished minor gentry. The founder of the Jamaican fortune, Francis, was possibly one of the few officers recruited by General Venables from among the less successful Barbadian smallholders in 1655. Within 20 years of the conquest of Jamaica, Francis Price had painstakingly graduated to the ownership of a 175-acre sugar plantation, worked by about 30 white servants and black slaves, in Guanaboa Vale, not far from the capital, Spanish Town, and the coast. Francis Price, though, also owned the 840 prime acres of Lluidas Vale in the undeveloped centre of Jamaica, which his son Charles turned into the sugar estate called Worthy Park, one of the richest and longest-lived of all such Jamaica operations.[24]

From this nucleus, Charles's son and namesake, the third-generation head of the Jamaican Prices, became the greatest of all contemporary magnates, owning in his prime about 26,000 acres and some 1,300 slaves, located in 11 of Jamaica's 15 parishes. This bloated (indeed, overambitious) patrimony came partly from canny dynastic marriages and successful speculations during Jamaica's most expansive era but mainly through Charles Price's unashamed manipulation of the plantocratic spoils system, which rewarded political power with landed wealth in due proportion. Educated at Eton and Oxford, he returned to Jamaica in 1730 to forge a political alliance with the long-serving (and therefore proplanter) Governor Edward Trelawny (1738-52), during the phase of expansion that followed the signing of peace with the Jamaican maroons. Charles Price's power base was challenged by Edward Trelawny's successor, Admiral Charles Knowles, who formed a Tory, town, merchant, or progovernment faction and symbolically shifted Jamaica's capital from the planters' stronghold, Spanish Town, to the mercantile centre, Kingston, 13 miles away. Behaving much like English Whig landed magnates, with whom they enjoyed many useful connections, Charles Price, his cousin Rose Fuller (brother of the Jamaican agent in London) and Richard Beckford (the brother of Alderman William Beckford, the friend of William Pitt the elder) headed the country and planter clique that engineered the recall of Knowles and the triumphal retransfer of the Jamaican capital from Kingston to Spanish Town. A few years later this victory was reinforced by the defeat of Governor Edward Lyttelton over a question of the Assembly's privileges, his recall to England, and his replacement by Lieutenant-Governor, Roger Hope Elletson, a Jamaican native.

Thereafter, as Jamaica reached the peak of its sugar prosperity and importance after the Seven Years' Wars, Sir Charles Price (created a baronet during the regime of Governor Sir William Trelawny, Edward Trelawny's naval cousin) was the most notable member of that fortunate elite that, while passing local legislation nakedly in its own interest, negotiated successfully for protective imperial sugar duties and naval protection while still indulging in Whiggish rhetoric and loyal addresses in support of the North Americans' stance against the Stamp Act and later imperial enactments and actions. For his leadership in this political juggling game, Sir Charles Price was grandly dubbed 'The Patriot' by his fellow planters – an echo of the nickname that William Pitt had held while in opposition in England.[25]

Besides building up his personal landholdings, Sir Charles Price tried to ensure their development by promoting public acts to push roads into the Jamaican interior as well as a private act to build an aqueduct in Lluidas Vale that doubled the efficiency of Worthy Park, and another to grant himself the monopoly of tolls between Spanish Town and the coast. With such widespread holdings, so many political interests and a distaste for the sordid details of plantation management, he did not spend much time on any of his sugar estates, being almost an internal Jamaican absentee. The legislative and socialising season was spent at his grand house in Spanish Town (which occupied a whole city block) while the hot summer months were mainly passed at a mansion called the Decoy, 2,000 feet up in the hills of St Mary parish. Though constructed entirely of wood, this country retreat, surrounded by a park in which grazed imported fallow deer, was the nearest Jamaican equivalent to an English country house. Edward long in 1774 described it as being

> well finished, and has in front a very fine piece of water, which in winter is commonly stocked with wild-duck and teal. Behind it is a very elegant garden disposed in walks, which are shaded with the cocoanut, cabbage, and sand-box trees. The flower and kitchen-garden are filled with the most beautiful and useful variety which Europe, or this climate, produces. It is decorated, besides, with some pretty buildings; of which the principal is an octagonal saloon, richly ornamented on the inside with lustres, and mirrors empaneled. At the termination of another walk is a grand triumphal arch, from which the prospect extends over the fine cultivated vale of Bagnals quite to the Northside Sea. Clumps of graceful cabbage-trees are dispersed in different parts, to enliven the scene; and thousands of plantane and other fruit-trees occupy a vast tract, that environs this agreeable retreat, not many years ago a gloomy wilderness.[26]

At the Decoy, separated from all but his domestic slaves (and also in his last years insulated from the imminent collapse of his overblown empire), Sir Charles Price could well indulge the style and tastes of a *grand signeur*. He kept a famous open house, especially to visitors from England, and according to the admiring Edward Long was a notable benefactor who pursued a lifelong interest in theology and Latin. His most famous act of *noblesse oblige* was to manumit each year on his birthday a slave whose behaviour had been characterised by exceptional industry and fidelity.[27] When Sir Charles Price died, his virtues were extolled by his son (and successor as speaker of the Jamaican Assembly) on an ornate marble tombstone (erected at the Decoy but later transferred to the parish church at Spanish Town), fittingly, if incongruously, couched in the language of Livy.[28]

A fourth and final paradigm that pertained to the plantocratic lifestyle, congenially related to the ideal of a quasi-feudal aristocracy and bound to fade (as in England itself) under the influence of capitalistic materialism, was that of the patriarchal family household. As Peter Laslett above all others has shown, this notion was still so prevalent in all ranks of English society at the time the first colonies were founded in the Americas that one can talk of a homogeneous social system rather than a true class system (while stopping short of Laslett's own claim that it was a 'one-class society').[29] From the sovereign downward, the titled nobility were grand patriarchs, with virtually no private family life, heads of great households consisting of servants of different ranks living in intimate proximity with each other. They exercised almost absolute authority and dispensed both justice and bounty. Even at the gentry and yeoman levels, households were not the close-knit nuclear family units that the Industrial Revolution made the norm, but larger functional groups of persons not necessarily related by blood. Domestic servitude was such a common feature of life that it was not necessarily demeaning (giving opportunities for upward and outward mobility through formal adoption or marriage), with young family members quite casually interchanged as servants from one patriarchal household to another of similar rank. Even in the commercial life of the towns, the system of apprenticeship widened the size and circumference of household units, with the master of the household and shop either tyrannical or kind, and the bound apprentices sleeping 'under the counter' – just as rural servants traditionally slept in any available corner of the baronial hall.

Such a system of family households was naturally carried into the colonies, reinforced where the viability of the early settlements was determined by the need for medium-sized households with a good proportion of working hands, and tending to prevail wherever later plantations continued to approximate to English rural estates. This was particularly true of Barbados, where the first units were no larger than yeoman holdings (averaging 25 acres in 1640) and plantations never grew to an enormous size (an average of 125 acres in 1700). Colonel Henry Drax, James' son, for example, giving careful instructions to his plantation manger in the 1670s, wrote of 'all the members of my family, black and white', and this letter was quoted in full in a best-selling manual of plantation management published by William Belgrove as late as 1755.[30] The purpose of patriarchal authority in the slave plantation context, and the limits of patriarchal benevolence, however, are clearly revealed when Henry Drax's instructions are read in their entirety. 'You must never punish either to satisfy your own anger or passion,' he wrote, but to use the punishment either to 'reclaim the malefactor or to terrify others from committing the like fault.' Punishments, moreover, were not confined to moral misdemeanours: indeed, were less concerned with strictly moral misdeeds than with industrial misbehaviour and inefficiency. Head sugar boilers, for example, were to be especially monitored (since their efficiency had a crucial bearing on profitability) and upon their 'neglect to be severely punished'. And while Drax recognised that slaves often pillaged food crops to augment their diet and acknowledged that if slaves stole 'for the belly, it is the more excusable', he added, 'But if at any time they are taken stealing, sugar molasses or rum, which is our money and the final product of all our endeavours . . . they must be severely handled being no punishment too terrible on such an occasion as doth not deprive the party of either life or limb.'[31]

Despite the example of the Portuguese *casa grande*, which the early Barbadian planters must have encountered, even admired, in Brazil, the idea of a cohesive extended family household was bound to fade under the conditions essential to the optimal operation of a sugar plantation. The sheer size of the population units in the labour-intensive Dutch or English system of sugar production made the concept of an all-embracing family household increasingly difficult to sustain. Further, a more naked capitalism reduced the labourer to a mere cog in an industrial machine, depersonalised, and soon a mere commodity to be bought and sold. And finally, the immense cultural differences between white European masters and black African slaves made the creation of a social rather than purely functional economic matrix virtually impossible. What sustained the Latin conception of the easygoing multiracial ambiance of the *casa grande* (in the Spanish and, to a certain extent, French Caribbean colonies as well as in Central and South America) was not just a lower level or capitalistic exploitation, but a longer juridical and Christian tradition of socioeconomic integration. Roman law quite effectively integrated masters and slaves into a common socioeconomic system, and the marriage of canon and Roman civil law, which characterised the legal systems of the Catholic imperialists, actually reinforced the master-slave matrix by giving it a godly mandate. All this required was that the *bozal* (that is, pagan and uncivilised) African slave be Christianised as part of the civilising process, that is, taught the proper dutiful behaviour of the good Christian slave, while the slave's owner, in theory at least, was expected to play the part of a good Christian master and patriarch.

Just as the patriarchal household rested on biblical precedents, so Christian observance was an essential feature of the ideal quasi-feudal household. For English planters this was relatively easy to sustain when the majority of their labourers were white indentured servants accustomed to the parish-based society of rural England, but more difficult when the servants were Irish or Scottish Catholics, and almost impossible once the work-force consisted of much larger numbers of black African *bozales*. Indeed, most planters believed that, in order to maintain that all blacks were slaves and that all slaves were chattel, it was best to prevent all slaves and blacks from becoming Christians. Thus the first English colonial laws that defined slaves as chattel made an almost explicit distinction between 'slaves' (that is, blacks) and 'Christians' (meaning whites). This crucial divide was manifest in Henry Drax's instructions during the 1670s: 'all the whites in the family [that is, plantation household]' being 'called to hear morning and evening prayers' on pain of being denied their week's food ration, while the black slaves were presumably left to their own religious observances'.[32]

The degree to which black slaves becoming Christian were any less slaves remained a plantocratic debating point as long as slavery lasted, running in delicate counterpoint to the argument (picked up, no doubt, from Catholic planters) that Christianising one's slaves might have a useful socialising function.[33] The experimental crucible for these debates was not the plantation as a whole, but the narrower ambit of the 'great house', where the domestic slaves not only lived in familiar intimacy with their masters but were the most acculturated of plantation slaves. A significant irony was that in such great houses, with the black housekeepers, hordes of coloured domestics, and their raging social and sexual intrigues, the resident owner-master was normally an observant Christian in reverse proportion to the degree he behaved like a patriarchal *senhor de engenho* in his *casa grande*. Thus while elements of the traditional aristocratic family household were sustained, the realities of West Indian plantation life determined that these would either survive in a narrower context or a (literally) bastardised form or would become, as in England, part of 'the world we have lost'.

4

Property and Propriety

Land Tenure and Slave Property in the Creation of a British West Indian Plantocracy, 1612-1740

Introduction: This essay was commissioned for a cross disciplinary symposium on early modern conceptions of property organised by John Brewer and Susan Staves at the Clark Library of the UCLA in 1990, which was part of an even grander three-year, three-tier project on consumption and culture in the seventeenth and eighteenth centuries. Eventually published by Routledge in 1995 as the 24th of 27 chapters in the third (conceptions of property) volume of the Clark Library series, at an understandably high price, the essay unfortunately suffered a sort of grandiose entombment as far as those more narrowly interested in the history of the Caribbean were concerned – providing ample motive for its re-publication here. Nonetheless, although it stands well enough on its own as a short technical analysis of the origins of British West Indian plantocracy, it does fit into the study of general property concepts for which it was originally written, arguing (among other things) that while plantocratic landholding practices both took advantage of and pragmatically extended the basic precepts and developing concepts of British property law, the ownership of property in slaves was always problematic, given the evolution of ideas of liberty and the development of alternative systems of labour extraction in the metropole.

Sine Justicia Magna Regna nil aliud sunt quam Magna Latrocinia:
The best Common-wealths, without the due current of Law and Justice, are no other than open Robberies.

> (Augustine, quoted by John Jennings, Clerk of the Barbadian
> Assembly, in his preface to the acts, 1654)

Law is as the Soul in Government, that giveth it Life and Form, and is certainly the last Guard, as well of the King's Prerogative, as of the Peoples Darlings, Liberty and Property.

> (William Rawlin, in 'Epistle dedicatory' to Laws of Barbados, 1699)

... this brief Narrative is an Instance and undeniable Proof, that *Liberty* and *Property* are the great Motives that induce Subjects to be faithful, or fight for the Glory of their Prince; and that an Encroachment on these is a sure Sign of a Sickly State, that is on the Decline, and hasting to be lost.

(Charles Leslie, *A New Account of Jamaica* [1739], p. 83)

However diverse were the motives, aims and beliefs of those who founded the earliest English colonies overseas, all concurred in the convenient myth that they were occupying extensions of sovereign territory, and that this allowed them to implant an English society and institutions which had already demonstrated an effective adaptability throughout the British Isles, the Celtic natives notwithstanding. For the settlers and their patrons alike, the forms of land grant and tenure, and the creation of a system of law and order to guarantee them and settle disputes, were of critical importance in establishing an effective socioeconomic structure. For the settlers, the reconstitution of local government on the English model – including its pragmatic dichotomy between appointed and unpaid gentlemen JPs and juries of male freeholders – was more or less taken for granted. But the creation of an autonomous elective assembly with rights similar to those of the English House of Commons was regarded as most vital of all, not so much to ensure that socioeconomic and political standing would continue to be measured by the holding of land, as to guarantee that local statute laws would reflect local needs, conditions and priorities.

Such concerns applied to all the North American settlement colonies, but they had special force when and where labour-intensive plantations became established, above all in the Caribbean. In place of the problems of dealing with inimical indigenes (being initially uninhibited or lightly peopled) these colonies soon had to face the legal, political and socioeconomic problems posed by the fact that black African slaves and their descendants, a steadily increasing number of them of mixed race and nominally free, constituted an overwhelming majority of each colony's population. As much as the need for a protective economic system, and for military and naval protection from enemies within and without, the sustaining of the foundation myth that English overseas colonies were transplanted fragments of English people and their institutions, particularly in relation to the holding of land, self-legislation and the definition of property in persons, therefore helps to explain both the peculiar development of the British West Indian colonies and why they remained loyal to the British Crown even as the mainland colonies fought for their independence.

Given that all English settlement colonies overseas were basically transplantations of English society and English systems of law, courts and representative institutions, four main variables determined the slight but growing variations between the colonies, and their deviations from the original English model. These were the different terms, principles and rules under which the colonies were granted; the different initial and later social composition of each settlement; the turbulent political events and changes that occurred in the metropolis over the foundation period, particularly the conflict between the Stuart kings and Parliament, the Commonwealth era, the restoration, the 'Glorious Revolution' and the Hanoverian Settlement; and the local factors, mainly geographical, that led to important socioeconomic readjustments.

English overseas colonisation began at a critical phase in the transition from the medieval to the modern world, speeding that transition in the process. As far as land tenure and social status in England were concerned, the principle that no land was held but of a lord had faded as completely as that of absolute serfdom. Gradually, feudal services had been commuted, even the lowliest tenants had come more secure in their tenancies and land might more easily be bought, sold and passed on through inheritance. But vestiges of feudalism remained deeply ingrained – in the continuing importance of the manorial unit, in the legal forms of tenure, and in the continuing concepts that there was no such thing as absolute freehold, and that all land was held ultimately of the sovereign. Overseas colonisation, on the one hand, offered the conditions of freer land and looser tenures such as had resulted from the demographic disaster of the Black Death in the fourteenth century, and the opportunities for speculation and upward social mobility for an emergent bourgeoisie that had first been offered by the secularisation of church lands at the Reformation. But on the other hand, it also encouraged a backward-looking Anglo-Scottish monarchy, and its client aristocracy, to revert to a version of the tenurial feudalism that had characterised the extension of royal authority, from southern England to the north and west, and across the narrow sea to the Irish Pale, and from the Scottish lowlands into the highlands and islands.

Such a dichotomy or ambivalence can be traced in the different forms of early colonial charter. Whether they were ambitious courtiers like Gilbert or George's companies of adventurers such as those who founded Virgina, Bermuda, Raleigh, or Providence, or groups of religious and political dissidents like the Pilgrim Fathers, all applicants were prepared to accept royal suzerainty in return for a share of the royal basis for their own viceregal privileges and subordinate tenure. Yet the preferred wording of the royal grants in respect of the tenure was that already hallowed in English practice: 'In free and common socage as of our manor of East Greenwich in the County of Kent.' Contrary to the assertion by Charles M. Andrews that this had nothing to do specifically with either East Greenwich or the County of Kent as such, its preference in the American colonies over alternative forms (such as of the king's manors of Windsor or Hampton Court in England, or of Carregrotion, Trim, or Limerick in Ireland) surely was a calculated reference to the type of late medieval tenurial system found, among other places, in Kent, along with a hint of the peculiar 'liberties, franchises and immunities' associated with the ancient Kentish custom of gavelkind. Not only did 'free and common socage' in the Kentish manner indicate that the land was free of all liabilities other than a nominal quit-rent, but it could be freely bought, sold and inherited, and might not even be subject to 'fines' and 'reliefs' when changing hands. Moreover, by inference, the form of tenure might be argued to favour the kind of 'partible inheritance' more suitable than primogeniture to areas of much available land, since Kentish gavelkind, among other things, allowed lands 'to descend to all the sons and heirs of the nearest degree together.'[1]

The 'East Greenwich' formula left the grant of lands in the hands of the charter grantees, who could, as in England, use the land for themselves like a feudal demesne, assign it in common to the settlers, sub-grant it to individuals on leases of various kinds, or alienate it by grant, sale, or bequest, either in 'fee simple' or in 'fee tail' (that is, entail). The range of land tenures in the charter colonies was thus from the beginning much like those in England, with virtual freeholds being at least as common. The alternative extreme, however, was a reversion to a type of purely feudal land grant found throughout Norman England and lingering on in the northern and western marches, the virtually autonomous tenancy-in-chief granted to favoured individuals, retained, in the formula 'in capite, as of the county palatine and bishopric of Durham'.[2] Such a seignorial and viceregal grant, with its military flavour so suitable in theory to vast colonial marshlands, was especially congenial to the first two Stuart kings, with their Scottish background, reactionary political views and importunate favourites, and to aristocratic courtiers eager to establish an anachronistic overseas feudal estate, or to profit from the hugh tracts of land claimed by the Crown with little or no expense or even effort on their own part.

Elements of the feudal seignory were strong in the Elizabethan grants to Gilbert and Raleigh, and the propriety system actually reached its fullest development – in a progressively less obviously feudalistic form – after the Restoration; in the grants to Lords Fairfax, Berkeley and Carteret, the eight proprietors of Carolina, William Penn, James Oglethorpe and the Georgia trustees.[3] But the Durham palatinate model was essentially an early Stuart device found in the grants on Long Island, Newfoundland, the American mainland and in the Lesser Antilles to Stirling, Calvert, Carlisle, Montgomery-Pembroke, Health and Kirke (1621-37).[4] In the West Indies, geographical ignorance led to the overlapping grants of the 'Caribbees' to Lords Carlisle and Pembroke, decreed in favour of the former in 1629.[5] Yet while the Carlisle patent provided for many settlers a convenient authorisaiton and legal protection for grants of land, in return for the proprietor's right to appoint officials and collect quit-rents, it conflicted from the beginning with the interests of independent commercial colonial promoters and settlers with practical access and prior claims to land, who resented the impositions and pretensions of aristocratic absentees and their local delegates – and pretty soon came to refer direct crown rule to proprietorial exploitation.

This outcome was conditioned and complicated by the intertwining of colonial affairs with the political, social and economic turmoil in the metropole from 1629 to 1689, or 1715. At the most generic level this represented a dynamic phase in the evolution of 'possessive individualism', the development of commercial capitalism, and the emergence to predominance of a capitalistic bourgeois class –in England uniquely reinforced from the aristocracy and nobility as well as from below.[6] To the extent that these trends facilitated the development of colonial economies and strengthened representative colonial assemblies, they were welcomed by at least the dominant settlers in the colonies. Yet, almost paradoxically, the parliamentary and Cromwellian interregnum in England saw the institution of a more aggressive imperialism far from congenial to individual, and individualistic, colonies; an assertion of the imperialistic function of the English Parliament, the imposition of protectionist economic policies initially targeting the Dutch, and the initiation of ideological and expansionist wars embroiling colonies in conflicts with Spain and France as well as Holland.

By and large, the colonials welcomed the Stuart Restoration for the opportunities for reconciliation and renegotiation which it offered, and for the prospect of legitimising a maturing socioeconomic order. But ambivalence and conflict continued as long as the Stuarts ruled, only gradually resolving themselves, as a peripheral result of the institution of 'constitutional monarch' with the accession of William and Mary, Anne and the

Hanoverians, by the provision of more effective systems of economic, naval and military protection, and, above all, by the initiation of the quarter-century of 'Walpole's Peace' between 1713 and 1739.[7]

The early evolution of the English West Indian colonies under the influences of the external factors considered above and the considerable variations in local conditions, is best illustrated through a brief sequential account of developments in the three salient early colonies: Bermuda from 1612 to 684, Barbados from 1625 to about 1700, and Jamaica from 1655 to 1740. (Figure 1)

Claimed in competition with Spain in 1609, uninhabited Bermuda was first granted as a subordinate part of Virginia to a syndicate of 19 London-based investors in 1612.[8] These 'adventurers' sponsored the first shiploads of settlers, some 500 in all, who were distributed over the most fertile central parts of the mini-archipelago. Loosely organised into 'tribes' names for the chief investors, the first inhabitants were set to build fortifications and work the land in common, under the almost absolute authority of a sort of lieutenant-governor chosen by the adventurers. The most notable achievement of this phase was the first survey of the island, made by the remarkable Richard Norwood – indicating the need to know precisely the shape and extent of the land before it could be properly apportioned and developed.[9]

The apparent potential of Bermuda as distinct from Virginia, and the need for a more formal organisation along with more capital, led to the formation of the separate Bermuda or Somers Island Company in 1615. Although Bermudian land provided the main equity for the shareholders, this was almost quintessentially a bourgeois commercial enterprise, run by absentee proprietors much like the 'undertakers' in the Irish 'plantations'. Of the 118 original shareholders, by Henry Wilkinson's computation, five were noblemen (of whom the adventurous puritan Earl of Warwick was much the most influential), 18 knights (including the ubiquitous Thomas Smith and puritan lobbyist Edwin Sandys), 14 'gentlemen' and the remainder almost all City merchants. No fewer than 21 of the non-noble shareholders were at some time Members of Parliament.[10]

By the 1615 charter, local authority was delegated to a governor and his chosen council, who were to promulgate laws consonant with English law and establish common law courts like those in England. There was also a presumption that local government would be an amalgam of quasi-manorial and parochial custom on the evolving English model. By Norwood's second survey, Bermuda was divided into eight tribes (analogous to English par-

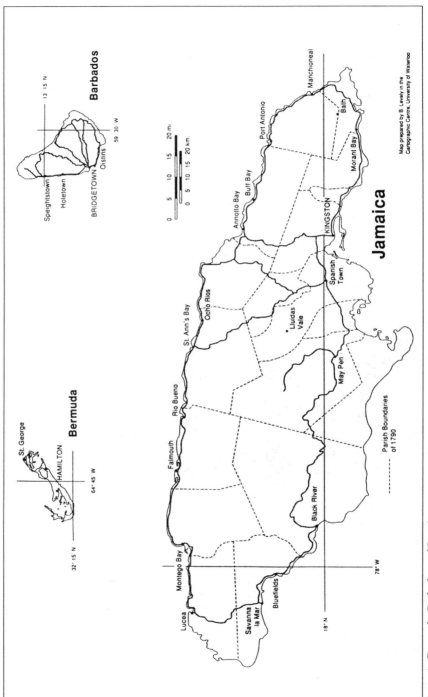

Figure 1: Bermuda, Barbados and Jamaica

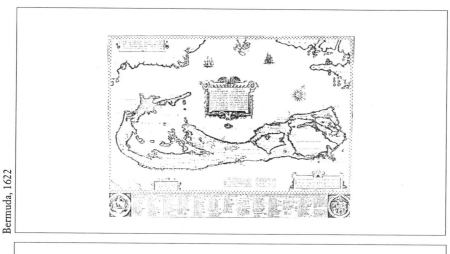

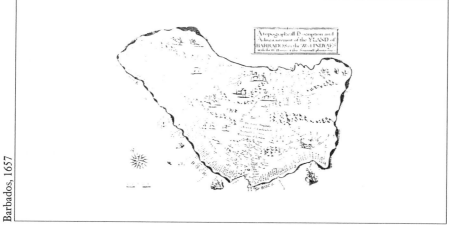

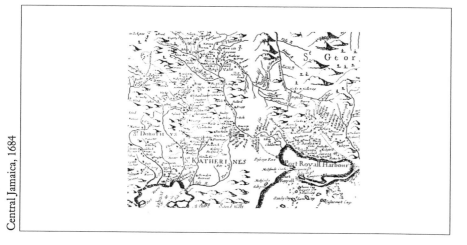

ishes, though not declared to be such until 1679),[11] each made up of some 50 narrow lots stretching from sea to sea of about 20 acres apiece and including a glebe for a church and its minister – with the eastern quarter of the colony reserved to the Company to raise the general running expenses. Lands were allocated to each shareholder according to his investment, at £12 10s per unit, with a limit of 15 to each. The grants were in 'free socage', but in fact were close to absolute freeholds since quit-rents were never exacted during the Company period, and there was an active and complex trade in shares – that is, in Bermudian land – from the beginning.[12]

Few of the original shareholders ever visited the colony, however, their holdings being mainly managed by younger family members or other resident agents, leased, or, of course of time, sold, to the more successful landless settlers. Initially, the majority of the inhabitants were indentured servants, sharecroppers, or tenants on short leases. But the small size of the holdings, the limited amount of total land, and the failure of Bermuda to establish a lasting plantation system while at the same time acquiring a considerable number of slaves, meant that though there was considerable early upward mobility and the creation of a marked social hierarchy based on land and the control of labour, this was relatively soon fixed in the founding families. Wilkinson, with his unrivalled awareness of the genealogical roots of Bermudian class-division, noted that while by the mid-seventeenth century there were no more than a half dozen persons besides the Governor titled 'Esquire', there were at least ten times that number warranting the gentlemanly prefix 'Mister', bearing virtually all the surnames dominant in later Bermudian history. The remainder of the whites were yeomanly 'goodmen' or simply servants, while slaves already constituted more than a quarter of the population.[13]

The Bermudian Assembly proudly dates itself from 1620, just one year after that of Virginia. It was first called by Governor Nathaniel Butler, who also instituted the courts of petty sessions in the separate tribes, presided over by bailiffs much like English local JPs.[14] The earliest Bermudian Assembly, with two elected burgesses from each of the tribes, met in the main church in combined session with the governor and council, like that of Virginia. Though the very first acts passed did include measures in the burgesses' own interest, such as the preservation of boundary marks and the control of indentured servants, the assembly was clearly intended to be little more than a rubber stamp for the governor's policies. But with the evolution of a local landowning class increasingly concerned with questions of social control and at odds with an absentee company felt to be exploitive, the elective assembly became gradually more assertive.

Tensions heightened during the English Civil Wars on religious as well as sociopolitical grounds. The Company was responsible for appointing ministers as well as governors, and the puritan influence in its council insured that these tended to be of a Nonconformist persuasion. Such latitude was unimportant before Bermudian local government became fixed on the parochial mode and before the Laudian reforms in England forced parish clergy into greater conformity. But the developing conflict in England was reflected in Bermuda by the growing division between Independent preachers and their congregations, who rejected most secular obligations, and those landowners who favoured a regular parochial system as the basis of their own sociopolitical position – through the vestries, the militia, the petty sessions courts and representation in the assembly.

The chief Independents were exiled to Eleuthera between 1647 and 1649, and when news of the execution of Charles 1 reached Bermuda, Royalist landowners from 'the country' and the militia which they monopolised took over the government and proclaimed King Charles 11.[15] Although the Commonwealth reasserted its authority in the 1650's and most of the Independents returned, the Restoration saw a steady increase in the power of the chief inhabitants through the assembly and a concomitant decline in the power and authority of the Company, which culminated in the takeover of the colony by the Crown in 1684. However, this process produced a local slaveholding landowning class under imperial auspices which differed in crucial respects from that which evolved in Barbados and Jamaica. The Somers Island Company faded for economic as much as for political reasons, for tiny Bermuda, after some years of legislated parity in the production of tobacco, inevitably failed as a plantation colony in competition with Virginia once that colony (freed of company control in 1625) began to utilise its huge potential. Those Bermudians who had come to monopolise the land – many of them through purchase from the shareholders of a declining company – reinforced their power through turning to the maritime activities for which Bermuda was far more suited: shipbuilding, whaling, salt-raking in the Turks and Caicos Islands, trading and privateering. They became, in fact, more a modest bourgeois oligarchy, though with a vested interest in the imperial system nonetheless.[16]

Barbados, like Bermuda, was uninhabited when the English arrived, and while also a very small island, had the advantage of being immensely fertile once its dense tropical woodlands were cleared. First claimed for the English Crown in 1625, it was initially settled in competition by shiploads of servants and would be smallholders financed by the anglo-Dutch entrepreneur Sir William Courteen and his associates, and by other adventurers authorised by James Hay, Earl of Carlisle, under the terms of a proprietary patent granted in 1627 – including a syndicate of London merchants awarded a block of 10,000 acres, a tenth of the island.[17] In order to counter the courtly influence of the proprietorial dispute, which confused development for over 50 years and has clouded much subsequent scholarship, should really be regarded as no more than one element in a three-sided conflict between quasi-feudal absentee magnates and mercantile investors over who owned the island, and between both of these and the actual settlers, who needed protection and capital, but wanted tax-free land of their own and political self-determination. Similarly, the confused political history of the colony's first 40 years, which most earlier writers saw simply in terms of an extension of the conflict in England between 'Roundheads' and 'Cavaliers', should rather be seen mainly in local terms: as a function of the socioeconomic and therefore political revolution that was a consequence of the shift from smallholding growing tobacco and cotton largely with white indentured servants, to large plantations producing sugar with the labour of African slaves.[18]

Like the Bermudian adventurers, the initial investors in Barbados clearly expected to develop the colony as an overseas estate worked by dependent labourers. But the overlapping claims of the two main principals and the convenience of making sub-leases or even selling land rather than developing it directly through managers, coupled with the will to ownership and ingenuity of the settlers, meant that the governors whom the rival proprietors appointed were unable either to inhibit an active market in land from the beginning, or to deflect the demand for a legislative assembly representing all landholders.

Carlisle's charter promised that the Barbadian settlers would be 'as free as they who were born in England'. and also 'freely, quietly and peaceably, to have and possess all the liberties, franchises and privileges of this kingdom, and to use and enjoy them as liege people of England'. In the context of Stuart England in 1628 this scarcely guaranteed them either freehold tenure or true representative government. The charter, however, did more specifically authorise Carlisle (or his deputy) to enact laws 'with the Consent, Assent and Approbation of the freeholders . . . or the greater part of them thereunto be called'.[19]

The situation clearly hinged on the settlers' claim to be freeholders, and the attitude of the proprietor can clearly be traced in Carlisle's Instructions to his governors. In 1634, Governor Henry Hawley was instructed to make no grants save in leasehold for a maximum of seven years' term, renewable, and in no case for longer than the grantee's lifetime. Besides quit-rents, all lessees were to pay dues to the governor and tithes to the clergy, and lands were to be forfeited for the neglect of any of these terms, the neglect of cultivation, or the failure to provide an indentured servant for every 10 acres granted. Carlisle further instructed Hawley in 1636 to order all landholders to take out new patents, to pay 'fines' on taking over bought or inherited land, and to pay an annual tax of 'the fifth part of ye peoples Labours' – amounting typically to 20 pounds of clean cotton for each man, woman or male child living on the land. This was the substance of the settlers' later claim that the Proprietors had exerted a 'Transcendente Authoritie' which had subjected them 'to slavery worse than villany'.[20]

Deteriorating political conditions in England, the death of the first Lord Carlisle, and the reality of conditions in distant Barbados, however, ensured that Governor Hawley was neither willing nor able to impose quasi-feudal land tenures. When the second Lord Carlisle appointed the more pliant Henry Huncks in his place, Hawley moved to obtain the support of the puritan Earl of Warwick (who had personally bought out Pembroke's interest in Barbados), summoned the first Barbadian Assembly (1639), and had it elect him governor on the promise of a more liberal land policy and self-legislation. As an earnest of this, Hawley had the assembly pass an Act 'for settling the estates and titles of the inhabitants', and set up an Alienation Court, charged with the function of settling land disputes.[21]

The authority of Carlisle and the king was still enough to reinstate Huncks for a year or so, but the political conflagration in England allowed Barbados to develop along its own lines at the same time as the most enterprising and best-funded planters were learning the cultivation and processing of sugar from the Dutch. Vincent T. Harlow entitled the second chapter of his *History of Barbados* on the period 1641-1650 'Barbados as an independent state', though the title of the second chapter of Richard Dunn's *Sugar and Slaves* might be a better alternative: 'Barbados: the rise of the planter class'.[22]

A crucial figure throughout this period was the neutralist Governor Philip Bell, a former governor of Bermuda. Officially appointed by Carlisle although with the approbation of Lord Warwick and the Committee of Trade and Plantations, Bell established the Anglican Church, but also decreed the cessation of proprietary dues, completed the organisation of parish government and the system of courts, chose a council representing the most substantial islanders, regularised the assembly and granted it the power of initiating legislation. Among the crucial pieces of legislation passed during Bell's tenure was that which reaffirmed Hawley's land grant act and added the proviso that 'those who were in quiet possession of land granted to them by former governors or by virtue of conveyance or other acts in law, should be confirmed in it either in part or in whole, or it should otherwise descend, or be confirmed to their heirs forever'. As to the civil war in England, Bell reported of the Barbadians in 1645 that

> it pleased god so to unite all their minds and harts together, that every parish declared themselves resolutely for the maintenance of their peace and present government; and to admitt of noe alterationes or new commissiones from either side . . . for against the kinge we are resolved never to be, and without the freindeshipe of the parliament and free trade of London ships we are not able to subsist.[23]

During the 1640s, many new planters settled in Barbados; not just displaced Royalists as the older books averred, but also more or less a political gentry on the make, most with sound mercantile connections, such as John and Peter Colleton, Thomas Kendall, Thomas Modyford, Daniel Searle, Humphrey Walrond and Lord Willoughby of Parham. In the island, they joined already well-established planters such as Christopher Codrington, James Drax, James Holdip and John Yeamans in the competitive rush to control land, labour and local political power. This is the phase of which Richard Ligon (who accompanied Thomas Modyford to Barbados in 1647) gave such an invaluable account in his *True and Exact History of the Island of Barbados*, published in 1657. Ligon described an island in which almost all land was already patented, though not yet all cleared, where the acreage in smallholdings growing tobacco and cotton was fast being outstripped by large sugar estates, and black slaves already outnumbered white indentured servants (and were thought even more likely to rebel). In other respects, it was virtually a 'Little England' in the Tropics. 'They Govern there by the Lawes of England, for all Criminall, Civill, Martiall, Eccleslasticall and Maritime affairs,' wrote Ligon.

> This law is administered by a Governour, and ten of his Councill, for Courts of ordinary Justice, in Civill causes, which divide the land in four Circuits; Justices of the Peace, Constables, Churchwardens and Tithing-men: five sessions a year, for tryall of Criminall causes, and all Appeals from inferiour Courts, in Civill causes. And when the Governour pleases to call an Assembly, for the supream Court of all, for the last Appeales, for the making of new Lawes, and abolishing old, according to occasion, in the nature of the Parliament of *England*, and accordingly consists of the governour, as Supream, his Councill, in nature of the Peers, and two Burgesses chosen by every Parish for the rest. The island is divided into eleven Parishes. No Tithes paid to the

Minister, but a yearly allowance of a pound of Tobacco, upon an acre of every man's land, besides certain Church-duties, of Mariages, Christenings and Burials.[24]

When King Charles 1 was executed, Lord Willoughby assumed the governorship on the authority of the exiled Charles 11, and the Barbadian legislature declared for the king against the Parliament in England. But the essential issue was not royalism but Barbadian independence against a metropolitan legislature claiming imperial powers, including the right to forbid colonies trading where they wished. This seemed particularly to threaten the commerce with the Dutch, on whom the development of the Barbadian sugar industry had depended, as well as the general right of the Barbadian plantocracy to enact laws controlling their land and labour. As the English Parliament passed the Navigation Act against the Dutch, and the parliamentary authorities declared an embargo on Barbadian trade and organised an expedition under Sir George Ayscue to reduce rebellious colonies in the West Indies, Willoughby, with the support of his council and assembly, issued on February 18, 1651, the remarkable document usually called the Barbadian Declaration of Independence. Anticipating the more celebrated American Declaration by 125 years, it proclaimed self-legislation as the birthright of all freeborn Englishmen, implied the principle of no taxation without representation, and accused the Westminister Parliament of usurpation.[25]

Though the Barbadians were not eager to fight, Ayscue was not strong enough to risk a pitched battle on land and merely blockaded Barbados for three months. Pragmatic moderates, notably Thomas Modyford, effected a deal and Willoughby surrendered under generous terms on January 11, 1652. The Articles of Surrender guaranteed liberty of conscience and the Barbadian constitution, including the right of the assembly to approve all taxation. An amnesty was declared, and the restitution of all goods of Barbadians seized in England promised. The embargo was lifted and free trade with all Barbadians seized in England promised. The embargo was lifted and free trade with all friendly nations pledged – though this was compromised by the Anglo-Dutch War and the terms of the Navigation Act.[26]

Between March 1652 and July 1654, George Ayscue and his successor as governor, Daniel Searle, saw through the Barbadian legislature no fewer than 102 acts which, collected by John Jennings the clerk of the Barbadian Assembly and printed in London, are the earliest surviving set of Barbadian laws – almost the foundation code of the Barbadian plantocracy.[27] Of the eight acts signed by Ayscue, by far the most important was that which declared the Carlisly patent void, while guaranteeing quiet possession to all landowners holding patents from previous governors, legal conveyances, or tenure by legislative acts. Despite the terms of the amnesty, one of Ayscue's acts specifically expelled Lord Willoughby from Barbados, an action gaining legislative approval presumably because Willoughby claimed the leasehold of Carlisle's proprietary rights to the island. Except for the act affirming the subscription of Barbados to the English parliamentary document called the Engagement, these were the only acts relating directly to the recent political strife.

The 94 acts signed by Governor Searle not only confirmed the status quo in Barbados but entrenched the planters' power in respect of their concerns about land and the control of labour. One act reaffirmed the parochial system of local government, while two others established that ranks in the militia would be strictly geared to socioeconomic standing. Field officers were to hold at least 100 acres of land, captains 50, lieutenants 25, and ensigns 15 – though exceptions were, interestingly, made for 'substantial and confiding Merchants and Store-house keepers' in Bridgetown. The freemen aged sixteen to sixty, whether they held property or not. The military purpose of the militia was not stated, but the many laws concerning the regulation and policing of 'Negroes', and the even greater number relating to 'Servants', strongly suggest that it was as much for the control of the labouring population as a defence against foreign enemies.[28] As far as land was concerned, acts were passed against encroachment on boundaries through the cutting down of trees, for the proper registration of title deeds, for the facilitation of transfers through sale and bequest, and for the more efficient management of the property of married women. Besides this, the Chancery court, where many land cases were adjudged, was reconstituted, and an act concerning powers of attorney facilitated the increasing number of property transactions that were being made outside the island.[29]

Fittingly, the Interregnum saw the increase of the power of the Barbadian planters through their local parliament, and their political gains and growing wealth through sugar production enabled them to override and actually profit from the adjustments which followed the Stuart Restoration in 1660. Predictably, Lord Willoughby was reinstated by Charles 11 as governor and granted compensation for the remaining seven years of his lease from Lord Carlisle, but the Barbadian plantocracy was quite able to negotiate favourable terms with the new regime. The basis of this agreement was that the king would assume the proprietorship of Barbados himself, but confirm all land tenures and the rights of the assembly in return for a permanent revenue for his administration of the island. Originally appointed in April 1661, but delayed by the negotiations which allowed him to keep his personal proprietorship of Surinam, Governor Willoughby arrived in Barbados in August 1663. Immediately he met with the council and assembly in plenary session and obtained the permanent grant of 4½ per cent duty on all exports, on the understanding that the king had purchased all proprietary rights, that all proprietary dues were immediately cancelled, and that all existing land titles were good 'in spite of existing defects, in free and common socage of the Crown, on payment of a yearly grain of Indian corn, if demanded' – that is, in virtually absolute freehold, without even the obligation of an annual quit-rent. As soon as the agreement was signed and sealed, Willoughby set sail for the other 'Caribbee Isles' to make identical arrangements.[30]

That the planters of the Lesser Antilles soon quarrelled with the misappropriation of the 4½ per cent duty – a tedious wrangle that continued for almost two centuries – indicated their growing pretensions and congenital dislike of direct taxation, rather than a general dissatisfaction with the principle of Crown Colony rule under the Old Representative System. A study of the first major compilation of Barbadian laws after that by Jennings in 1654, made by William Rawlin in 1699, shows that the plantocracy had not only retained the basic principles of the earlier code, but considerably extended and greatly refined it as the apparatus of their socioeconomic and political power. This was particularly notable in the comprehensive Act for the Conveyance of Estates, originally enacted in 1661 as part of the Restoration Settlement, and other acts regarding land and real estate, in the comprehensive Act for Governing Negroes dating from 1688, and other acts relating to slaves and servants, which, as we shall see, all set models for the other plantation colonies.[31]

This structure of plantocratic laws accurately reflected the completion of the complex socioeconomic and political revolution that began, or was speeded, once Barbados switched to the monucultural production of sugar on large quasi-industrial estates. As Richard S. Dunn has best shown, this was a process which, among other things, saw the total number of landholdings fall from 5,000 in 1650 to 3,000 in 1680, the number of estates over 200 acres rise from 50 to 150, and the percentage of the total land area represented by large estates rise from 40 to 80 per cent. The same 30-year period saw the percentage of Negro slaves in the total population rise from under 50 to over 70 per cent, and an even greater decline in the absolute number of white indentured servants than in the number of white small-holders. By 1680, from figures sent back to England by Governor Atkins, the top 175 planters (less than 7 per cent of all property owners) not only owned 53 per cent of the land and 54 per cent of the slaves and white servants, but also monopolised all the public offices.[32] These factors to-gether accounted for the fact that while Barbados had become economically 'saturated' and socially fixed, and remained one of the most densely popu-lated areas of the world, it steadily exported its surplus white population throughout the rest of plantation America – ineffectually or temporarily to Surinam and St Lucia, more effectively to the Leeward Islands, Virginia and South Carolina, but most notably of all, to what was to become by far the most important British sugar colony, Jamaica.[33]

Twenty-five times larger than Barbados, and 400 times the size of Bermuda, Jamaica was the first British colony acquired by conquest as a result of state policy. Seized by an expedition under Admiral Penn and General Venables in 1655 as a kind of consolation prize after the failure to capture Santo Domingo, the large undeveloped island was not cleared of the Spanish until the year of Charles 11's restoration. Taken over by the Crown from its Cromwellian founders in the fact of Spanish opposition, it was presumably thought too rich or difficult a possession to award to favourite courtiers or mercantile syndicates, and therefore developed as a state enterprise, without the burdens and complications of proprietary or company ownership. Their gratitude for protection of the Crown, and habitual (if disingenuous) expressions of loyalty, though, did not prevent the founding settlers and their descendants claiming special privileges by an imagined right of conquest, and vigorously opposing the Crown's representatives in a successful quest to establish a plantocracy at least as powerful as that of Barbados.[34]

The actual conquest of Jamaica was a raggle-taggle affair. The invading forces, some 5,000 Cromwellian veterans augmented by 2,000 eager but untrained surplus poor whites from Barbados and the Leewards, greatly outnumbered the total population of the island. But unused to the terrain, inadequately supplied and sickly, they were beleaguered in three regimental 'quarters' of southern Jamaica, roaming the woods for wild cattle and desperately growing provisions under the command of their officers. Those who survived and stayed, however, augmented by a trickle of recruits in the first five years, formed the founding nucleus of Jamaican planters – with most of the officers (whom the last Cromwellian governor termed, with some exaggeration, 'men of good Familys' exiled by Cromwell for jealousy)[35] being the first landholders, and most of the labour provided by the other ranks of the disbanded army.

The first formal land grants were made and an embryonic civil government established by the transitional governor, Edward D'Oyley (1657–1661), a more normal structure was put in place by Lord Windsor, the first fully civilian governor (though he stayed less than three months, in 1662), and a prototypical plantocratic system initiated by the Barbadian 'planter-governor', Thomas Modyford, between 1664 and 1671. D'Oyley was instructed to ensure that a large area of the island be reserved as a royal demesne, which implied at least a two-tier system of land allocation, and was also empowered to set up courts and pass laws 'not repugnant' to those of England, with the help of a council of 12, elected by the army officers, chief planters and other substantial white inhabitants.

Governor Windsor, though he found only 3,000 whites and 500 blacks settled in Jamaica, carried a commission and instructions that were much more detailed and precise. Besides a council, he was empowered to call an assembly, 'according to the Custome of our Plantacions, to make Lawes and uppon Eminent Necessityes to leavy Moneys, as shall be most conduceable to the Honour and Advantage of our Crown and the good and wellfare of our Subjects, provided they be not repugnant to any of our Lawes of England', and that such laws 'shall be in force for two yeares and noe longer unless they shall be approved and continued by us'. This body first met in January 1664, during the regime of Windsor's Deputy-Governor, Charles Lyttelton, with five members from Jamaica's only two towns, and one each from 15 sparsely settled and scattered country districts, passing laws which included one dividing the island into 15 'precincts' or parishes, as well as others concerning the raising of revenue.[36]

As to the allocation of land, Windsor's instructions retained traces of the Stuarts' predilection for feudal forms. The Governor was authorised to confirm all existing land tenures, but 400,000 acres was to be set aside, one-fourth in each of the four quarters of Jamaica, as a royal demesne 'as for a Mark of our Soveraignty in and over' the island. Lord Windsor himself, as a kind of tenant-in-chief was granted 50,000 acres, with the authority to allot land in free and common socage at a rent which he and his Council should decide. Much more important than this was the provision for headright land to new settlers, who were promised 30 acres for every man, woman and child, free, indentured and slave, whom they brought to the island.[37]

Thomas Modyford, who arrived in Jamaica in July 1664 with the first half of about 1,700 displaced Barbadian small planters and their servants, was both the developer and chief beneficiary of this new system. The previous scheme with a separate royal demesne was scrapped in favour of crown land grants under quit-rent tenure for all persons who would plant within five years, giving all planters the chance to patent virtually freehold land in proportion to the number of persons in their 'family' of actual relatives and dependent labourers. A land registry was established on the Barbadian model, and a pre-emptive rush began which within a decade saw nearly all the four chief members of the Modyford clan patented at least 21,218 acres throughout Jamaica, of which Sir Thomas and his son claimed over 9,000. In order to forestall complaints, the governor pointed out to the Council of Trade and Plantations that since in addition to his actual family, he owned 400 slaves and servants, he was legally entitled to 12,000 acres.[38]

The freewheeling Modyford also encouraged the freebooters (at least until Charles 11 signed the Treaty of Madrid with Spain in 1670), and was directly involved in the trade in slaves – both through the chartered Royal African Company and by unlicensed 'interlopers'. The former activity, of which Henry Morgan, later Lieutenant-Governor and Vice-Admiralty judge, was the most famous exponent, generated considerable wealth for lateral transfer into Jamaican plantations, while the latter provided a growing, if scarcely cheap, work force for the labour-intensive production of sugar.[39]

A typical early 'planter' ran cattle and grew cocoa, cotton, tobacco and indigo as well as some sugar, all on a modest scale, with the labour of the few white servants and black slaves he could afford. But with land being readily available and almost free, and while the price of sugar remained high and the cost of slaves, 'utensils', and borrowing money relatively low, the graduation towards owning a sizeable sugar plantation – the essential generator of socioeconomic and political power – could be as short as a singly lifetime. The process was also, of course, expedited at every stage by better than average access to capital resources, whether through buccaneering, direct involvement in trade, good mercantile connections, or canny dynastic alliances. In truly exceptional cases, such as that of Henry Morgan, even an indentured servant might become a rich plantocrat, if hardly and long-lived, clever or rapacious, and lucky enough.[40]

Modyford's efforts to attract new and substantial settlers as well as capital to Jamaica were moderately successful, so that by 1673 there were said to be 17,000 persons in Jamaica (a quarter of the population of Barbados), of whom 4,000 were white men, 2,000 white women, 1,700 white children and 9,500 black slaves. There were approximately 500 estates, some of them huge, though no more than 150 were sugar plantations, with 44 planters holding 1,000 or more acres and 16 holding 2,000 or more.[41] During his regime, Governor Modyford firmly established the parochial system of local government, though some of the parishes, up to four times the size of Barbados, were almost unpeopled, and it was a century or more before all had parish churches and parsons. Modyford also almost completed the structure of the island's courts.[42] By his commission he was empowered to select his own council rather than have it elected as formerly, while at the same time he moved to make the assembly more truly representative of the planter class throughout the island – though with some representation for the mercantile element in the towns. Although council and assembly were thus nominally separated, Modyford's choice of the most substantial of his fellow planters for his council ensured that there was little tension between the two bodies, only minor differences between 'town' and 'country' interests in the assembly, and that the laws passed were essentially plantocratic. This is boarne out by the earliest extant compilation of Jamaican laws, made by Charles Harper in 1684, which demonstrated almost exact parallels with Barbados.[43]

The full evolution of a Jamaican plantocracy was not achieved, though, without a protracted and complex constitutional struggle with the imperial government, lasting until 1728, just as the full extension of the Jamaican sugar plantation system was delayed by setbacks, natural disasters and the resolute opposition of the maroons, who controlled the mountainous and forested interiors of the island until the end of the 1730s.[44]

As in all the American colonies, the constitutional conflict concerned the relative rights of the Crown and imperial Parliament on the one hand, and the colonists and their representative assembly on the other. In the Jamaican case the principles debated mainly revolved around the status of conquered colonies rather than those peacefully settled; but in reality, as in Barbados the conflict came down to a simple trade-off between the allocation of a permanent revenue to the administration and the granting of the right of virtual self-legislation to the colonial assembly.

The lordly and contemptuous non-planter, Governor Vaughan, was disgusted by the pretensions of the Jamaican assembly encouraged by Governors Modyford and Lynch, and his successor Lord Carlisle (no relation to the former proprietor of the Caribbees) arrived in Jamaica in

1678 not only with a list of approved nominees for the council and a draft of ready-made Jamaican laws, but with instructions to relegate the assembly to the status of the Irish parliament, as constituted by the terms of Poyning's Law. The issue was soon joined, with Samuel Long, Speaker of the Assembly (grandfather of the great planter-historian Edward Long), and William Beeston (later a popular planter-governor and first of the great absentee planter lobbyists) vigorously putting the plantocratic case. This was that as freeborn and voluntary settlers they had carried with them all their rights and privileges as Englishmen, including the common law, and all statutes in operation when they migrated. From these claims it followed that in the absence of colonial representation in an imperial parliament, they owed allegiance to the monarch through his governor, but had the right to legislate for themselves, especially in regard to Jamaica's special conditions and needs. In addition, they claimed special rights in Jamaica by virtue of being 'the conquerors of the land'.[45]

On the contrary, the imperial lawyers argued (as was maintained by the landmark Jamaican case of *Blankard v. Galdy* in 1694) that,

> where the English people gained territory by discovery and settlement 'all the Laws in Force in England, are in force there'; but in the case of a conquered country such as Jamaica, the laws of England were not operative 'until declared so by the Conqueror and his Successor . . . In such cases where the Laws are rejected or silent, the conquered Country shall be governed according to the Rule of Natural Equity'.[46]

By the most extreme interpretation, this implied not only that the Jamaican colonists had no automatic right to representative government or even the common law, but that they might be ruled directly by the Crown. Nor was the reference to 'natural Equity' an unintentional pun, for it was no accident that the colonial courts of Chancery – so vital for the adjudication of real estate – almost everywhere consisted of the colonial governor and his council sitting as judges.[47]

Yet the extreme imperial position had no more chance of asserting itself than had the Stuarts the likelihood of winning their long-running battles with their Parliaments at home. What gave the Jamaican assembly the whip-hand in the contest was the inability of the imperial government to back up its constitutional demands with financial allocations, and the utter dependence of the governors on the assembly for raising and granting the revenue necessary for running the colonial administration. In 1678, Carlisle was forced to agree to the amendments made by the assembly to his laws and pass them for the normal two years, in return for a two years' revenue grant; and when in 1681 the assembly first departed from the custom of short-term acts to approve a seven years' grant of revenue, the chief island laws were reciprocally confirmed for a seven-year term. Two years later, still during the second term of the proplanter Governor Lynch, when the assembly generously decided to grant revenue for 21 years, the principal laws (including the previous batch) were confirmed for a similar period. Finally, in 1728, during the temporary regime of the planter President of the Council, John Ayscough, the assembly voted the administration a permanent revenue, in return for a grant of all the rights, privileges and immunities already enjoyed by the legislatures of the 'non-conquered' colonies.[48]

These were in fact critical years for Jamaica in every respect. In the 1690s, an earthquake totally destroyed Port Royal, an epidemic of lethal malaria swept the island and a French invasion devastated the eastern settlements. By 1700, the white population had actually fallen below 2,000, and though it made great strides in the years of European peace following Queen Anne's War, the extension of the plantations was hampered by the depredations of the maroons. These descendants of the 'Spanish Negroes' who had resisted the original English incursion had been greatly augmented by runaway slaves, of whom the 'Coromantees', already expert musketeers in their native Ashanti, were the most formidable opponents. Sporadic but bloody wars throughout the 1730s – in which white casualties greatly outnumbered those of the maroons and, uniquely in the annals of war, the wounded were outnumbered by the dead – placed a huge strain on the parochial militia system and the Jamaican treasury.[49]

But sheer numbers, and the inexorable capitalist dynamic of the plantation system (for by 1740, Jamaica contained 10,000 whites and 100,000 slaves, and there were some 400 sugar plantations)[50] eventually told. In 1738 and 1739, the two chief maroon communities were persuaded to sign peace treaties with the regime. Although ostensibly made between equal belligerents, with the maroons becoming allies of the regime, granted lands in perpetuity and promised a large degree of political autonomy, these were in fact trickily unequal agreements, ensuring that the maroons would gradually be subsumed within the plantocratic system, and lose their independent polity and way of life. Perhaps the best (or worse) example of this process was the way in which the maroon heroine Nanny and her clan were treated by the regime. The warrior chieftainess and her followers were allocated land on the forested slopes of the Blue Mountains, but the form of the grant was that of a normal colonial patent. Nanny and her household

– who may have had pre-1655 or even Amerindian antecedents – were fictitiously said to have 'transported themselves and their slaves into our said Island', and to be therefore eligible for land at the usual rate of 30 acres a head. By this formula not only was Nanny seemingly made a recipient of the bounty of the Crown but, more subtly, the idea was conveyed that Jamaica had had no native inhabitants when 'conquered' by the English.[51]

As John Austin and other distinguished positivist theorists have argued, a prevailing system of law can be said to serve and define, that is, to signify, the dominant elements in the social order. If law is not quite simply the will of the sovereign, a society is its law.[52] What then, briefly, was the corpus of law which signified the British West Indian plantocracies once they had established themselves, especially in the key respects of property in land and the control of labour?

In the case of land, the West Indian planters inherited a rich and useful array of customs, common laws and statutes from the mother country, which required minimal adaptation, augmentation and refinement in the colonies. In respect of imposing harsh working conditions on servants and other employees, requiring at least commuted services from tenants with less than freeholds, and imposing a general requirement to work on all landless men by the threat of vagrancy, they also had ample models from the metropole. Only in their pressing need to define the necessary Negro labourers as chattel slaves (while at the same time attempting to police and punish them as if they were persons) were the British West Indian planters forced into inventing new law, or at least to borrowing from ancient times and other legal traditions – in a way that was in due course to be regarded as anachronistic, as well as oppressive and illogical, by all but the planters themselves.[53]

As we have already suggested, throughout the American colonies the method of land grant and tenure, labour and military obligations, the systems of local government, and even household structure, owed much to English feudal and manorial traditions. Yet even before any English persons settled overseas, these traditions had already been greatly modified, in respect of the growth of individual property rights, the extension of practical freehold tenure, a freeing of restrictions on the purchase, sale and inheritance of all real estate, and a steady, if still incomplete, loosening of the bonds that tied individuals to one master, to one locality, or to a permanent rank in the social order. Thus, according to different local conditions, colonial settlers could use English law and custom selectively:

either to sustain or revert to an earlier system, or to hasten the process of change already begun.

The essential difference between old and new world was expressed in the inscription on a colonial token (perhaps intentionally advertising colonisation) dated 1647: 'In Virginia land free and labour scarce; in England land scarce and labour plenty.'[54] But for the plantation and island colonies this motto had different implications than for these settlements farther north. For the northern mainland colonies, conditions invited the formation of a society of small farmers, ruggedly independent, close-family oriented and relatively democratic, socially static but geographically mobile. Such a people naturally adhered to a system of land law favouring the traditions of partible inheritance and the rejection of all binding forms of tenancy, having a particular disinclination for sharecropping arrangements. The common law was valued for the ways in which it defended individual property rights against quasi-feudal magnates, corporations, or even the crown itself, and local statute law developed this individualistic trend.[55]

Early island and southern mainland conditions favoured lands worked in common, and binding tenancies, but this was soon followed by the creation of small plantations strongly rooted in the English rural seignorial family-household tradition – that 'World We Have Lost' of which Peter Laslett writes.[56] The subsequent establishment of larger, more labour-intensive sugar plantations, the 'saturation' of the islands initially settled and the extension of the plantation system from island to island, provided chances of rapid upward mobility for a fortunate few. But it also widened social divisions, first by the depression of white 'servants' from fictional family members into a virtual helot class and then by the substitution for them of black slaves, regarded by the white landowners as outside the social order altogether.

The wealth which sugar could generate – far greater than the profits which could be derived from an English country estate – and the successful sugar planters' almost inevitable connections with merchants and bankers, determined that they became a bourgeois ruling class. But there were aristocratic counter-attractions and influences. Not only did the sugar plantation system fix a planter's fortune in a particular unit (or set of units) of land, but, however meanly born, he inherited the tradition that he was no more than a capitalist entrepreneur unless he and his family were linearly rooted in the land they owned. This explains why West Indian planters always favoured single over partible inheritance, preferred primogeniture, but (given the great mortality of the colonies) were quite prepared to accept female heirs, gave more rights to widows than was common in England, and were far more inclined to entail their estates than were North Americans. They were also, in a more exaggerated way than their English equivalents, active marriage-brokers and dynasts, and, as a notable species of nouveaux riches, ingenious inventors of fictitious genealogies.[57]

In all the above respects, West Indian planters simply had to follow established English legal customs and precedents in their useful variation, or adopt existing English statutes. This explains the concern of the early colonists to assert that they carried with them English legal custom, the common law, and English statutes operative before their own legislatures came into being, as well as their concurrence with the imperial authorities in having an English system of common law courts established from the very beginning. Even some colonial statutes, such as those dealing with the organisaiton of the local courts, show little or no differences in principle from English models. Other colonial acts, however, did show substantial deviations from the beginning, and once the plantocracies established themselves in each colony, the laws they enacted became even more nakedly self-serving, whether or not they risked running foul of the principle of non-repugnancy to English laws.

The essential founding acts for the West Indian plantocracies were those which set up the system of courts and asserted the principles on which they followed English models and practice, those which enumerated the English laws which continued to apply in the colonies and why they did so, and, the critical third stage, those which guaranteed and justified the practice of self-legislation in return for granting a permanent revenue to the Crown.[58] Before this process was completed, colonial statutes, as befitted their mixed provenance, illustrated the different or mutual interests of the Crown through the governor and council, or the settlers represented in the assembly.

Thus acts encouraging settlement by generous land grants and guarding landholdings against misappropriation, encroachment and trespass, giving freeholders authority within the parochial system, and guaranteeing labour by fixing the terms of indenture and policing the servants and slaves, were interleaved with those aimed at ensuring the efficient collection of quit-rents by the Crown, and imposing upon often reluctant planters and their servants the obligations of building and maintaining roads and bridges and serving in the militia.[59]

Yet once the plantocracies were entrenched, colonial acts, first subtly then ever more boldly, were framed in the interests of the ruling class. Even such acts as those laying down the principles of the conveyancing of real estate which essentially followed English practice had tacked to them clauses which liberally served special local conditions and needs. Such a case were the Barbadian Conveyancing Acts of 1661, 1669 and 1670, which included clauses to protect landholdings called in question as a result of the Interregnum, to facilitate deeds contracted outside Barbados, to safeguard the interests of widows, and to establish the generous principle that valid title resided in all lands held in quiet possession for a mere five years.[60]

Once crown land was almost entirely distributed, or its allocation had fallen firmly under the control of the local ruling class, laws naturally placed less emphasis on the encouragement of new settlers, and became more concerned with discouraging land speculation, absenteeism and the non-development of patented land, and with guaranteeing a sufficient proportion of white servants to manage estates and police the slaves. Quit-rent acts had always been notoriously ineffectual, but they now became concerned less with the raising of revenue than with the resumption of undeveloped lands by the Crown. This was both to augment the reservoir of patentable lands for the more active and successful local planters, and to prevent undeveloped land from falling into the hands of squatting small-holders or, even worse, becoming refuges for runaway slaves and bands of maroons. Similarly, the Deficiency Laws, which required a certain proportion of white servants in relation to the number of slaves on pain of fines for non-observance, though almost as ineffectual as the quit-rent acts in their main objective, had several clear plantocratic purposes: not just to provide more effective controls against the slave majority, but to enlarge that class of lesser whites without which the planters had no pretensions to dominate a colonial society from which they had excluded black slaves by law.[61]

Such local legislation was aimed in part against the increasing menace of planter absenteeism, although on this issue the local laws were bound to be ambivalent. From the beginning, colonial legislation had fulfilled the need to facilitate transactions in real estate from abroad, and the metropolitan business involved in trading, making advances, loans and, above all, mortgages. Subsequent acts seeking to penalise planters who forsook the West Indies for English estates or closer involvement in metropolitan commerce, ran uncomfortably counter to these. But in due course, even the local legislatures were bound to acknowledge that much of the tide of absenteeism was involuntary or, in the situation, inevitable, and were therefore moved to pass laws that tried to slow the process by protecting absentee as well as resident planters against proceedings for debt, bankruptcy and foreclosure. Naturally, some of these enactments invoked the criticism of English lawyers representing countervailing interests, as did the acts passed in all the plantation colonies arbitrarily, if almost certainly ineffectually, decreeing a limit – normally 10 per cent on the interest chargeable on West Indian accounts.[62]

One type of enactment very much in the planters' favour on which metropolitan lawyers did comment positively was that which accompanied the issuing of land grant patents with a procedure for formal surveys, and which regularised, recorded and registered property deeds and all dealings in real estate. All of the plantation colonies had a formal registry with a salaried registrar at least a century before such existed in England itself. As Charles Harper described the Jamaican system in 1684, incoming settlers

> take an Order from the Governor for so much [land]: This Order is directed to a legal, sworn Surveyor, and by him returned to the Clerk of the Pattents, who by direction of the King's Attorney, draws the Pattent and affixes the Plat on it; this at Sealing day is Sealed, and afterwards enrolled in the Office of Enrolments; for all which the Surveyor and his Clerk have as in the Act for fees.

'Nor are Purchasers here incumbred with bad Titles', proudly noted Harper, the clerk of the Jamaican Assembly, in another work in the same year, 'for that Register (so much wished for in England) is here established where all Conveyances being acknowledged are to be enroll'd within three months, if the Cognisers inhabit here'.[63]

Other local acts, however, were far more bluntly selfish, even evoking negative comments from lawyers in an England where similar interests were similarly served, and the normal practice was to turn a blind eye to colonial legislation where metropolitan interests and susceptibilities were not directly infringed. Some of the most blatant cases were private acts, such as those passed on behalf of individual Jamaican planters, ostensibly for the improvement of communications and the economy at large. These, for example, allowed individual planters to circumvent restrictions on the size of landholdings, to have aqueducts built across less powerful neighbours' lands, to have roads built at the public expense simply to serve their own inland estates, or even to erect tollgates, wharves or markets for their private emolument.[64]

Of the many general acts which blatantly signified the planters' interests, one kind was perhaps the most significant and aroused most widespread comment throughout the American colonies, as well as in England. This was the set of acts passed in several West Indian colonies declaring that Negro slaves were not just chattel property but should be regarded for legal purposes as real estate. The reason for this was that while estates could be entailed and kept in being through the normal processes of bequest, slaves as chattel property could not be entailed and might easily be sold apart from the estate for which they were the essential labour force – for example, in cases of intestacy, female inheritance or wardship. The effect of the acts was to fix the slave populations on the land which depended upon them, except in the cases where the planters specifically decreed otherwise – although a rider was added in the Barbados case at least, that the act did not prevent slaves being still regarded as chattels in cases of debt.[65]

Several of the slaves-as-real-estate laws did remain in operation into slavery's last years. This not only pointed up the plantocratic imperative to reify the slave work force and treat slaves as legal pawns, and the necessity of self-legislation in order to do so. It also illustrated the essential illogicality and contradictions inherent in the West Indian slave system, not least the willingness of the imperial authorities – including the Crown lawyers – to allow slavery to exist in the colonies although long fallen into disuse, or outlawed, at home. In other words, the corpus of slave laws was not only essential to the British West Indian plantocratic structure, it was also that structure's foundational weakness.

In the absence of clear documentation and contemporary discussion, no one is now able to know with certainty what were the immediate models of the British West Indian slave laws. The very first British slave laws have disappeared, some no doubt destroyed because the planters did not want such a close scrutiny as might reveal a rooting in outmoded English forms of bondage, or, perhaps even more 'repugnant', in the Roman civil law and foreign slave codes, namely those of the Spanish, Portuguese, or Dutch. Besides this, perhaps as a consequence, West Indian planters passed slave laws only to the degree that they were absolutely necessary, preferring the far more effective, and less easily questioned, operation of pragmatic custom. Nonetheless, a whole corpus of slave laws was passed in due course in each colony, and a careful analysis, in particular of the more ingenuous preambles, does disclose a derivation both from Roman civil law principles and those of ancient English serfdom.[66]

Medieval English practice was, indeed, generally agreeable to the early West Indian settlers in trying to attach labourers to their new plantations. Bermudian tenants, as we have seen, commonly worked much like the freer types of manorial bondsmen, for half-shares or less. Hilary Beckles too has cogently argued that Barbadian white servants were not only less free (and worse treated) than any English farm labourers at that time, but that their obligation to labour (if not, strictly, their persons) was a marketable commodity.[67] In the case of the least free of all white labourers in the West Indies, that is, those 'rebel' Irish and Scots rounded up in Cromwell's wars, the later victims of Monmouth's Rebellion, and those unfortunates 'Barbadoed' from English jails, the principles of the generic European law of slavery dating from Roman times were already implicitly applied, that is, that captives in war and criminals could be virtually treated as chattel slaves.

In another respect, however, Roman law principles sometimes worked to the benefit of persons whom the earliest English settlers attempted to enslave, that is, the Amerindian natives. English settlers quite readily enslaved Amerindians whom they could plausibly regard as war captives, or even transgressors against the law of nature, although they generally found it most convenient to ship them to a different colony – such as happened to the captives in King Philip's war who were transported to Bermuda and Barbados in the 1670s. Those Amerindians, however, who could claim to be free natives of the soil and thus subjects of the English king or state, persons not already slaves elsewhere, or guilty of either unnatural practices or defeat in war (admittedly a fulsome list of provisos), were, by the same generic principles, not subject to enslavement. These, rather than the general unsuitability of Amerindians as praedial labourers, were the reasons why certain Arawaks enslaved by Barbadian planters were freed on the orders of the English Council of State in a famous case in 1656.[68]

No such provisions could free those 500,000 Africans carried to the British West Indies before 1740, whose servile labour was so vital to the sugar plantations. 'Whereas the Privileges of England are So universally Extensive as not to admit of the Least thing called Slavery', wrote a Bermudian lawyer ignorant of grammar as of logic, but certain of what he wanted, in 1730:

> Occasioned the making of such Laws for the preservation of every Individual Subject in his or their Lives, Estates and Indisputable Rights and properties; But here in his majesties Colonies and plantations in America the cases and Circumstances of things are wonderfully altered, for the very kindred nay sometimes even the Parents of these unfortunate Creatures (upon the coasts of Affrica) Expose their own Issue to perpetual Bondage and Slavery by Selling them unto your majesties Settlements in America and consequently purchased by the Inhabitants thereof, they being for the Brutishness of their Nature no otherwise valued or Esteemed amongst us than as our goods and Chattels or other personal Estates.[69]

Given such unashamed self-interest in a colony that had many slaves but few lawyers and fewer plantations, it is not surprising to discover the tortuous ingenuity and effort that went into the creation of the slave codes in the true sugar colonies: to define property in slaves, permanently to fix them, their progeny and descendants in their status and location, to guard against their will to run away, rebel, or commit acts of theft or violence, as far as possible to prevent them having property, family or a culture truly their own, and only incidentally, late in the process, and under pressure from outside philanthropists, showing any concern to ensure that they had minimal standards of food and clothing, were protected against the most savage types of oppression, and were promised the benefits of the masters' religion.[70]

The British West Indian planters never constituted a single homogeneous type. Quite apart from inevitable differences of character, health and luck, they varied, more or less, in respect to social background, initial access to money and political influence, the extent of land and local political power acquired, dynastic history and, perhaps most critical of all, the degree of commitment to the islands which were the source of their wealth. Nor were the plantocracies established in different West Indian colonies ever identical, varying according to the context and terms of their foundation, the size, climate, topography and soils of each island, and, above all, the speed and completeness of the achievement of a sugar monoculture. This made for a clear distinction between the neat, complete, well-ordered and comparatively modest Barbadian model, and the much richer, more expensive and flamboyant, but never quite finished, Jamaican model – not to mention the plantocratic variations developed in the islands taken over in 1763, and the colonies acquired in the very last French wars, which are outside the scope of this essay.[71] Yet all British West Indian planters and the plantocracies they constructed were involved in the same basic enterprise in the same global contexts, copied and learned from each other, and gravitated towards a socioeconomic and political ideal form and style. Most important, they all depended for their evolution as a class upon the effective exploitation of undeveloped tropical land and black slave labour. Thus, following up on the evidence and arguments already deployed, it should be possible in conclusion to propose some rounding generalisations and, in particular, to decide whether the British West Indian planters did in fact create a distinctive, fully formed and lasting class.

The essential plantocratic ideology was quasi-aristocratic, a set of altitudes, a culture, drawn from the possession of land and the control over its work-force. It derived from the mother country, although only a minority of the founding planters were 'to the manor born'. There was, in fact, a spectrum of original planter types; from those of noble families who also had initial wealth through those with 'gentle' antecedents but no inherited money, and those with new money but of obscure social origin, to almost completely self-made men (and women) to whom the plantations themselves were the sole fount of wealth and status. Dynastic engineering, however, was a necessary concomitant to the preservation and extension of socioeconomic power, and an increasingly tight and homogeneous network of families evolved among the owners of estates, as land, money and title intermarried.

Although a thorough typology of early British West Indian planters is a worthy project still to be undertaken, it is probably permissible to propose four or five basic categories, with the most dynamic and significant individuals being those who combined several, if not all, of the different typological characteristics, and who, by choice or lack of it, committed themselves to making the West Indies their home.

Foremost of West Indian 'planters' were those noble adventurers and courtiers who became involved in the plantations as a natural extension of their privileged position in the ambit of the Crown. Even if, like Lord Willoughby of Parham, they became directly involved in the colonies, they were more interested in proprietorships than in single plantations (although they might own many), and took it for granted that they were natural candidates to be the king's viceroys.

In the second rank were those gentlemen of squirearchical background like the Codringtons, Modyfords, Stapletons, Warners and Colletons, who committed themselves to the colonies in order to rescue or augment their family fortunes. These filled the upper ranks of the colonial administrations, as much by their gentlemanly training as by natural right, but, having extensive holdings and expansive ideas, were rarely involved in the day-to-day management of individual estates, or permanently committed to a single island.[72]

A third important category were those planters, like the Noells, Poveys, Draxes, Lascelles and Beckfords, who brought investment capital, good mercantile connections and perhaps lobbying influence, rather than title and gentle birth, to become further enriched through the development of the plantations. While some family members might be directly involved in plantation affairs, the ownership of plantations was best managed from

England, and the interests of England-based planters were rarely limited to a single colony.[73]

The majority of the resident planters were recruited from a fourth category: persons of questionably gentle, yeoman, or more obscure social provenance, who made their start and fortunes in the islands – however much they or their descendants tended to exaggerate the distinction of their social origins. Some, like the Pinneys or the Morgans, began as servants, petty traders, or privateers; others, like the Prices, Barretts, Dawkinses, Barhams, or Tharps, were survivors of those who claimed to be the first 'conquerors' of Jamaica. But nearly all were essentially self-made men, beginning as tenants and graduating to smallholders, pen-keepers and perhaps modest sugar producers, and thus laying the groundwork for their descendants to become major sugar producers and slave-owners, with, in the most successful cases, a whole network of estates. Such persons and families, like those whose names dot Richard Ford's 1674 map of Barbados or Bochart and Knollis's Jamaican map of 1684, tended to confine their interests to a single island, although in the earliest years they might, like Cary Helyar, Henry Morgan and perhaps Francis Price, have moved from Barbados to Jamaica, seeking to improve their chances with the general extension of the plantation system.[74]

To this category of upwardly mobile planters should also be added a final formative type, that of the would-be planters at any stage of the process. There was hardly a white person on the socioeconomic ladder who did not strive to climb, rung by rung, into the planter class; from the meanest indentured servant once his time had expired, through the Scots bookkeepers and managers under scarcely less onerous contracts, to the privileged but land-poor overseers and attorneys. Such aspirants included even the collateral members of the upper reaches of white society, the doctors, lawyers, clergymen-teachers and merchants in town. The aspirations, the occupational investment, of all such persons – who, of course, always outnumbered the actual planters – was an important invisible support of the plantocratic system.[75]

As has been suggested already, perhaps the most significant of all early planters was the 'planter-governor', Thomas Modyford (1620-1679), who not only combined in himself several of the types of early planters, but was one of the most influential founders of the plantocratic system, in both Barbados and Jamaica.[76] Thomas Modyford's outstanding career and achievements, although, even his very popularity with his fellow planters, showed up and anticipated the essential flaws in the plantocratic system.

To Barbadian and Jamaican planters alike, Modyford rejoiced in the title of the Planter-Governor, but it proved difficult for him to wear both hats at the same time, and impossible for later governors even to claim such interchangeable headgear. All planters, in fact, were torn between irreconcilable opposites. First of these was that while they were dependent on the Crown as the ultimate source of land and the provider of protection, they were yet compelled by their interests to set up an assembly which was bound to confront any assertions of imperial authority. Thus they were forced into the absurdity of claiming to be a landed aristocracy and professing loyalty to the Crown, while at the same time indulging in republican rhetoric.

Secondly, while the planters were drawn towards an aristocratic lifestyle and ethos by the imperatives of landownership and the control of labour, and affected a spirit of *noblesse oblige*, they were at the same time driven by the commercial profit motive, and by the perceived necessity to regard slaves as less than human beings. Some English noblemen, unlike the French, were able to reconcile the contradictions between landowning and commerce, but few were able to bridge the gap between the conditions of English rural life and the crude realities of slave plantation production; conversely, few persons with the kind of background or temperament that made it possible to exploit Negroes as chattel labourers in the cause of profit, could effectively make the transition to English country gentleman.

Moreover, the very transition to Jamaica which Modyford spearheaded was part of a steady process of economic extension and intensification. Just as the slave sugar plantation first supplanted the quasi-manorial system of smallholdings in Barbados, so the expansion of sugar production to other islands and the quest for efficiencies of scale under increased competition made for a more crudely exploitative system, and progressively widened the gap between the gentlemanly ideal of landowning and the management of independent labour and the harsh industrial reality of the fully developed slave plantation system. Modyford himself was praised for being the 'most considerable' Jamaican planter and 'the ablest and most upright' judge in the white men's court, but was not notable for humanity when it came to managing slaves. Jamaica, in fact, had the character of a crude frontier area from the beginning, compared with settled Barbados, where even the great early sugar magnate, Henry Drax, could still refer to his servants and slaves as his 'family' in 1670. But the process of intensification in the search for efficiency led to an increasingly standard level of practice – best represented perhaps in the widely circulated *Essay on Plantership* by the Antiguan planter Samuel Martin (1750), in which sugar production was no more than an industrial business, and slaves regarded as little more than animate industrial machines.[77]

The response of most planters who found the stink of the sugar factory and the realities of Negro slavery too oppressive was to distance themselves as far as possible from the sordid source of their wealth. Besides, there were other motives which encouraged planters to become absentees. From the earliest times, the planters who succeeded most, and most rapidly, were those who retained good metropolitan mercantile connections, and under the later conditions of expansion and intensification, as the history of the Pinney family fortune conclusively illustrates, it became as vital to have a strong metropolitan base as to have efficient managers on the spot.[78] Many families, such as the Jamaican Barretts, had different branches of a large family in England and Jamaica and nearly all male members of absentee planter families spent at least part of their adult lives directly managing their West Indian plantations. But contrary to most accounts, there were at least as many resident planters whose fortunes evaporated through bad mercantile connections and extravagant dissipation as there were absentee planters milking their distant estates in order to keep up a pretentious lifestyle in England. In course of time, moreover, as plantation profits declined, fewer owners of West Indian property retained any option but to stay in England and attempt to diversify their fortunes, leaving their plantations and slaves in the hands of peripatetic bookkeepers, hard-grafting managers and attorneys.[79]

Barbados was relatively less affected by the absentee problem than was Jamaica. Since Barbadian plantations were modest-sized, relatively few Barbadian planters, like the majority of the landowners of Bermuda, were ever wealthy enough to become absentees. But many families were also encouraged to stay by the very conditions that allowed Barbados to become known as 'the civilised island' or 'Little England'; a comparatively large white population well-distributed throughout the island; a comprehensive and effective system of law and order; small, well-organised parishes with a full complement of parsons; and an adequate system of local schools.[80] Perhaps a quarter of Barbadian plantations were absentee-owned in 1700, but this increased to no more than a third by the end of the eighteenth century. For Jamaica, that proportion had already been exceeded by 1740, and by 1800 it was almost two-thirds. Even Edward Long, the most eloquent proponent of an ideal resident Jamaican plantocracy, and owner of one of the richest plantations in Clarendon parish, spent the years 1769-1813, the greater part of his long life, living in England off the income from his estate and from the fruits of his absentee tenure of the judgeship of the Jamaican Vice-Admiralty court.[81]

Even more than Charles Leslie's substantial account of 1740, Edward Long's three-volume *History of Jamaica* (1774) illustrates the contradictions between plantocratic loyalism and 'republican' independentism, between the ideal of a white society and the cruder realities, between pride in the English legal heritage and the planters' demand to make laws for themselves, and between the need for royal authority in the granting of land the planters' will to have its subsequent disposal entirely in their own hands. But both books, even less intentionally, reveal that the most critical contradiction of all – and ultimately the chief impediment to the forming of a lasting plantocracy – concerned the legal questions surrounding the planters' claim to hold property in their slaves.[82]

To make Negroes into chattels when Britons no longer could be slaves was probably the most compelling reason for the British West Indian planters to have independent legislatures of their own, since (as Lord Mansfield was to decree in 1772) 'so high an act of dominion' required nothing less than a 'positive law'.[83] There was something of an irony in the fact that the rights of property had become a sacred principle of English jurisprudence in parallel with the gradual process whereby property in persons, or even in a person's labour, had become outlawed. Yet the undeniable fading out of slavery in English custom and common law was an embarrassment when at the same time the West Indian planters wanted the benefit of all those English laws and customs which guaranteed the rights of possession and transmission of real estate in general. In addition, the planters had ever to tread carefully, that the principles on which they justified slavery in their statutes – derived without acknowledgement mainly from ancient principles of Roman law – were not held to be repugnant to current English law, and thus disallowed.

The chief contradictions in British West Indian slave laws, however, were internal to the laws themselves. The basic laws defined slaves as property – whether chattel or real estate – yet the slave codes included many other laws which treated slaves as persons, not things, particularly in respect of committing crimes. Even if these were not intrinsically illogical and inoperable (for how could a thing commit a crime any more than it could own property, let alone be brought to court as a person to stand normal trial?), the laws compounded the situation by proposing systems of punishment so flexible and relativistic as to make a mockery of absolute justice. One polar example was that on the one side a white person could never be punished with the normal penalties for murder for killing a slave, while on the other a slave might be put to death in barbaric fashion for even offering violence to a white. Even more ridiculous perhaps was the sliding scale of punishment in the laws concerning slave marronage (running away). A free white person harbouring a runaway would be severely fined, whereas a white indentured servant would be physically punished and serve extra time, and a free black person lose his freedom or even be put to death. The runaway slave, however, being valuable property, would simply be given corporal punishment, albeit of a savage kind (including, in some islands, the loss of a foot for repeated offences). A slave who died during 'justified punishment', was not the victim of murder, and if one was killed while running away or resisting arrest, the owner received monetary compensation from the colonial treasury.[84]

Even had there been far more resident whites in the British West Indies, they could not have created a true society while the corpus of social laws was so untuned to natural justice or equity, and where the majority of people were treated as chattels, even if a sentient type. In course of time, the white plantocracy would be forced to accept, albeit unconsciously, that they were merely the dominant component in a creolised 'slave society', including free coloured persons as well as the black slave majority, in which customary practice was at least as determinant as formal laws.[85] But such problems were merely inherent in Barbados in 1680 or Jamaica in 1740, when the plantocracies were only just established and asserting their rule, and the sugar plantation system as a whole had not yet reaches its apogee. The basic injustices, as well as the intrinsic contradictions of the slave system at large, were inevitably and irresistibly only to surface once sugar plantations and sugar plantocracies started to decline, and the age of Enlightenment promoted the ending of slavery on rational economic as well as humanistic grounds. At this time, the last defenders of the old plantocratic ideology were to be driven back into the tortured logic and scarcely concealed private agonies discernible in the works of Bryan Edwards, Elie Moreau de St Méry and Thomas Jefferson.[86]

5

Caribbean Vice Admiralty Courts and British Imperialism

Introduction: Like many first published scholarly articles, this one was derived from the author's doctoral dissertation (McMaster 1968). That it is a tyro work is, however, insufficient reason for the continued slighting of its subject. The article's insistence that neglect of the Caribbean Vice Admiralty Courts reflects the subsequent decline of the British West Indian colonies and the triumphant emergence of the USA and the hegemonic dominance of its historiography may have been overstated, but it still has some force. Inherent within the article, moreover, are two even more important general principles: that the British imperial administration was always essentially pragmatic, shaped by needs, and that (as argued by positivistic legal theorists, the ostensibly international law administered by the Admiralty Courts represented no more nor less than the will and power of the chief interested party to enforce it.

The later decline of the West Indies and the growing importance of the USA have obscured the predominance of the Caribbean in the British imperial scheme throughout the eighteenth century, and exaggerated the effects of the American secession upon the British Empire as a whole. Notable victims of this teleological process of rewriting history to emphasise the victors have been the Caribbean Vice Admiralty Courts, hitherto almost ignored by American scholars, although they were different in function, more numerous and far busier than those of the mainland colonies, Carl Ubbelohde, for example, wrote an excellent study of the Vice Admiralty Courts in relation to the American War of Independence without mentioning the 23 Courts of the Caribbean.[1] Even the great colonial historian Charles M. Andrews knew so much of the North American Courts yet so little of the Caribbean Courts that he presumed the two types were alike. Andrews asserted that all Courts were probably two-thirds occupied in ordinary Instance and Navigation Act cases,[2] when in fact in the Caribbean Courts, prize cases seem to have outnumbered all others by ten to one, and the volume of business in Jamaica alone probably outran that of all the mainland Courts added together.[3]

Rationalisation not revolution, we would maintain, was the dominant theme of the British Empire during the later eighteenth century. Despite the magnifying effects of the bicentenary celebrations (1975-83), we would argue for a further devaluation of the American War of Independence,[4] seeing it as little more than an important symptom of underlying changes. When we do look beneath the surface, for revolutionary trends in the nature of capital, in imperial administration and policy and the relative importance of formal and informal colonies, the American War of Independence and the loss of the Thirteen Colonies were far less important to the empire than the gradual professionalisation of English administration, the Industrial Revolution, the switch to free trade and informal imperialism, the renewal of interest in the East and the Pacific, and the crescendo of involvement in the Spanish American Empire. Without intending to be perverse, we would maintain that even the slave revolution in Haiti after 1789 had more direct effect upon the British *imperium* than the American secession: by arousing a colonial *grand peur* over the threat of revolutionary infection among British Negroes, by encouraging the desire for the destruction or takeover of sugar-producing rivals, and by signalising the breakdown of the French Empire in the Caribbean and thus upsetting a century-long mercantilist balance of power. Certainly William Pitt was aware of the danger or importance of Haiti to the British Empire, for he sent a far larger expeditionary force to the Caribbean in 1793 than had originally been planned for the rebellious North American colonies. Why should the spoils of history always go to the victors?

In the light of the foregoing contentions, it is perhaps justified to look at the Vice Admiralty Courts of the Caribbean from the points of view of the empire as a whole and their own sphere of operations rather than from a North American viewpoint, and perhaps this approach will shed oblique illumination on the nature of the mainland Courts as well.

Vice Admiralty Courts – like most institutions – arose from needs; their systematisation was a later refinement. Vice Admiralty Courts in the Caribbean were practically coeval with British West Indian colonisation. Wherever colonies were established, Vice Admiralty Courts almost invariably followed, to fulfil the necessary functions of trying pirates, adjudicating prizes and settling ordinary maritime disputes. While deriving their authority from the governors' Admiralty Commissions, they appeared to arise spontaneously to satisfy local needs, and were shaped more by local conditions than by a servile imitation of metropolitan forms. Yet, as haphazard colonies burgeoned into a formal empire, Vice Admiralty Courts were increasingly used as tribunals for the trial of infringements of the Acts of Trade that bound the Empire together; and, during the wars that were the almost inevitable consequence of mercantilist exclusivism, the Courts, by the adjudication of prizes, acted as agents of imperial naval policy.

The process of imperial formalisation that characterised the period between the Restoration and the end of the Seven Years' War required an increased degree of precision and uniformity in the colonial Vice Admiralty Courts, and a greater measure of metropolitan control. This process of formalisation in turn required a clearer distinction between the various functions of the Courts. In 1697, 11 American Vice Admiralty Courts – five being in the West Indies – were uniformly authorised as part of the fundamental imperial organisation of 1696, and by 1763, the functions of the colonial Vice Admiralty Courts had been made distinct, at least in theory. The paradox that the Courts were national tribunals enforcing national statutes as well as the Law of Nations had thereby, to a certain extent, been resolved. The power to try pirates and other high seas felons had been transferred to separate, and separately commissioned, courts of oyer and terminer called Courts of Admiralty Sessions. Prizes were now strictly defined as only those ships and cargoes seized in wartime, and their adjudication had been delegated to special Prize Courts, commissioned only after the outbreak of war. The trial of infringements of the Acts of Trade and Revenue, although they remained nominally a branch of Instance, or ordinary maritime, jurisdiction, with cases commonly interleaved in the records of the Courts, came increasingly to be regarded as separate from the settlement of ordinary maritime disputes.[5]

Besides the division of jurisdiction, certain other principles of uniformity had been established by 1763. The courts were uniformly authorised: by standing commissions for the trial of pirates, by special commissions for Prize Courts on the outbreak of war, and by fresh commissions for Instance Courts upon the appointment of each new governor. Personnel and procedures were understood to be modelled on those of the High Court of Admiralty,[6] the printed forms and precedents of which were increasingly used; and not only were the officers similar from Court to Court, but the control of patronage gradually passed from colonial governors to the metropolitan authorities, particularly to the Lords Commissioner of the Admiralty. Metropolitan control was further augmented by the gradual evolution of a system of appeals from Vice Admiralty Court decisions: to the Privy Council, the High Court of Admiralty and in wartime, to the Court of Prize Appeals.[7]

As far as personnel and procedures were concerned, it was not necessary for the Vice Admiralty Court system to change much from 1763 to 1815.[8] Yet certain inadequacies became increasingly apparent, particularly in the operation of the Courts as agents of the British mercantile system, not all of which were remedied before the end of the Napoleonic Wars ushered in the decline of mercantilism itself. The basic deficiency was that Vice Admiralty Court officials were not salaried, and relied upon fees for their emoluments. In normal times, business was insufficient to provide adequate rewards,[9] and the result was that judges and other officials were usually either inactive or extortionate; and, since colonial posts were rarely lucrative enough to attract highly qualified personnel from the metropolis, the Courts were customarily staffed with local men not only unqualified but also strongly under the influence of local interests.[10] The chances therefore of strictly enforcing an imperial mercantile system were doubly reduced, since colonial judges had neither the competence nor the incentives to support metropolitan authority against local interests. These deficiencies were exacerbated by the delays in the transmission of commissions, orders and fresh precedents and the resulting obscurities inevitable in an age of sailing ships, endemic warfare and an overworked imperial bureaucracy.

Only in their functions as Prize Courts did the Caribbean Vice Admiralty Courts flourish, and thus it was as agents of imperial naval policy that they were most effective. The Seven Years' War and the American and Maritime War saw an enormous increase in British naval and privateering activity in the Caribbean, and the Vice Admiralty Courts prospered in adjudicating the influx of seizures.[11] Not only did the income of the judges and the other officials multiply through the increase in fees, but the Courts also granted great popularity in promptly condemning seizures made by local privateers and in helping to reduce the threat of enemy warships. As a result of the flurry of activity in wartime, the Courts were also relatively active in Instance jurisdiction, including the application of the Laws of Trade to the extent they continued to be applied during wartime. But wars were short lived, and there was not time for the temporary prosperity of the Vice Admiralty Courts to result in the raising of the standards of their personnel.

Besides this, the number of Prize Courts tended actually to outrun their need, so that the inevitable cutback on the coming of peace was unduly magnified. Attempts on the part of the Courts in peacetime to compensate for the loss of prize business by undue zeal in the prosecution of Navigation Act cases rapidly dissipated the stock of popularity garnered during the preceding war.

From the metropolitan point of view, the failure of the Caribbean Vice Admiralty Courts to enforce the mercantilist side of British imperial policy was not a serious fault before the American War of Independence, while the whole system of British mercantilism revolved around the sugar plantation colonies and smuggling was not such a serious problem or temptation in the West Indies as it was in North America. Even after 1783, the imperial bureaucracy was not so much concerned with the interpretation of past error as with confronting the threat to its existing system of a new and competing power, the USA. In other words, far from destroying British mercantilism, the American War merely constituted a successful attempt by the Thirteen Colonies to be released from its statutory bonds, and for the remainder of the Empire the end of the war saw an actual tightening of the system.

In some ways, 1783 came to represent to the loyal West Indian colonists what 1763 had represented to the Americans. As a result of the successful rearguard action of the bureaucratic mercantilists, the Americans were now regarded just like other aliens in commercial matters, despite the value of the reciprocal North American trade to the British West Indians. Moreover, the period between 1783 and 1793 also saw serious attempts by the imperial authorities to apply the Laws of Trade in the Caribbean with greater efficiency than ever before, through the Royal Navy, the Customs service and the Vice Admiralty Courts.[12] Success was limited, however, not only because the Vice Admiralty Courts were little stronger than before, the reform of the customs service was less than complete, and very few naval officers were prepared to do their duty and enforce the Laws of Trade;[13] but also because the local planters and merchants evaded the regulations wherever they could and, through the colonial legislatures and their agents in England, redoubled their opposition to laws from which they derived no obvious benefit. Evasions of the Orders-in-Council and Navigation Acts of 1783-88 became as flagrant as had the evasions of mercantilism in North America in the decade before 1775; and the most outspoken of the memorials of complaint, that of the Assembly of Jamaica in 1789, echoed the very arguments used by the Americans against the navy, the customs service and the Vice Admiralty Courts before the outbreak of the War of Independence.[14]

Neither the imperial system or mercantilism nor the colonial opposition to it had been fully realised before the last and longest of the wars against the French began in 1793.[15] With the renewed spate of seizures, Prize Courts revived like desert flowers after rain, and the conditions of prosperity and popularity continued for a generation.[16] As Prize Courts, the Caribbean Vice Admiralty Courts reached a peak of perspicuity in unravelling the complex subterfuges employed by enemies and neutrals in running the British blockade, and were admirably speedy in their operations.[17] But the experience of previous wars, in which appeals had been extremely rare,[18] and the reliance of the officers upon fees, had led the Courts to regard themselves as little more than machinery for the condemnation of vessels brought before them. In previous wars, condemnations had occasionally provoked diplomatic crises and had even contributed to the belligerency of neutrals and the formation of the Armed Neutrality of 1780;[19] but these condemnations had generally resulted from well-justified seizures made deliberately by Royal Navy vessels and privateers carefully instructed by the Admiralty, after long provocation and following a calculated policy to risk war. The Caribbean Vice Admiralty Courts were faithful servants of such a system, but in the last French wars proved themselves inadequate as agents of a more flexible imperial policy.

The new status of the USA as a neutral alien and the most active and ingenious carrier of belligerent cargoes, proved a serious embarrassment to the British government. For most of the period of the last French wars, Britain was not ready to provoke war against the Americans; and the summary condemnation of some 300 vessels seized as the result of one Order-in-Council in 1793, despite its reversal early in 1794, provided a diplomatic crisis and pointed up the need for the reform of the Courts.[20] Yet American and British reasons for wishing reform were subtly different. In a sense, the Vice Admiralty Courts had become the scapegoats of British policy. American abuse centred on them, but their chief fault lay not in their actions – in which they had little latitude – but in their unresponsiveness to shifts in policy. This may explain why nothing was undertaken in the way of reforming the Caribbean Vice Admiralty Courts for seven more years, although the treaty negotiators made specific promises to John Jay in 1794.[21]

The Prize Commission set up by Jay's Treaty, which sat until 1798, and the related improvement in appeals procedure, helped to loosen the diplomatic tension, though the real reason for the Anglo-American détente was the moderation of British seizures policy. In the late 1790s, however, American complaints were vigorously renewed as British policy led to more American seizures and condemnations; but it was not so much these complaints themselves as the appointment of the reforming Sir William Scott (later Lord Stowell) as Judge of the High Court of Admiralty in 1798 that led to practical reform.

The aim of the reforms passed under the auspices of Lord Grenville, at the urging of Sir William Scott, was not the satisfaction of the Americans as such, but rather a greater degree of responsiveness on the part of the Vice Admiralty Courts to British Orders-in-Council, Admiralty Instructions to Royal Navy vessels and privateers, and to shifts in the law of contraband, blockade and neutral rights as developed by decisions made in the High Court of Admiralty and the Court of Prize Appeals. The reforms were sweeping but incomplete. [22] The number of Prize Courts was reduced from nine to two in 1801, and did not rise above six for the remainder of the war. Judges were salaried and pensioned for the first time and highly qualified men were chosen to fill vacancies; they were sent out with almost absolute power over their subordinates, and with orders to emulate the practice of the High Court of Admiralty more closely than ever before. Above all, accurate records were to be kept and transmitted to London. Absenteeism and sinecurism were reduced, and patronage passed practically from the Lords Commissioner of the Admiralty to the Judge of the High Court of Admiralty, who not only kept a tight rein on the Vice Admiralty judges, but also retained strong links with the chief policy-makers in the imperial government.

In the period of the French Wars after the truce of Amiens, the Caribbean Prize Courts were almost completely responsive to the fluctuations of British policy. Deviations from the model of the High Court of Admiralty became rarer, and West Indian judges responded more readily to changes in instructions form the Admiralty, Treasury and Board of Customs, and to modifications in the law as developed in the cases tried before the High Court of Admiralty and the courts of Appeal. To the cynical it might appear that the imperial government, through the Admiralty, not only commissioned and instructed the captors, but the courts which tried their captures as well; not only set up the courts which tried the captures, but also had an important part in passing the laws by which they were tried. This was not entirely so, for at every stage the authorities took the Opinions of the Law Officers to the Crown, and every attempt was made to make the provisions of Acts, Orders, Commissions and Instructions consistent with 'The Law of Nations and Treaties', and, more specifically, to ensure that the directions to the Prize Courts concentrated on the organisational functions of the Courts and left them as independent as possible. Moreover, justified complaints against decisions made in the Vice Admiralty Courts received inexorable, if delayed, redress in the Courts of Appeal, although most of the criticism of the actions of the Vice Admiralty Courts was henceforth concentrated on the system of which the Courts were now an integral part, not on the peripheral Courts themselves.[23]

As had happened in previous wars, the volume of non-prize business tended to increase during the last French Wars as a natural function of the increased activity and prosperity of the Vice Admiralty Courts. Besides this, the takeover of French, Dutch and Spanish colonies which followed the achievement of absolute British naval hegemony resulted in the establishment of several new Instance Courts, which might have been expected to have helped to enforce the British imperial code.[24] Yet these new Instance Courts, like those Vice Admiralty Courts which had been denied prize jurisdiction in the reforms of 1801-85, suffered from many of the old deficiencies. Only the Prize Courts had salaried judges, and the officials of the Instance Courts continued to rely on fees. After the first surge of business the Courts tended to decline, and even those which managed to attract optimistic personnel with adequate qualifications faded into desuetude, encouraged in their decline by the traditional opposition of local merchants and planters to any form of regulation unprofitable to themselves. Even the Prize Courts aroused opposition, for although most of the judges were salaried, those who had been appointed before the reforms were not. Nor were salaries paid to subordinate officials in any Courts. Although more firmly than ever under the control of their judges, these were allowed in practice an extremely free hand in the levying of fees. Despite increasing complaints from the officers of the Royal Navy, Vice Admiralty Court fees were not uniformly regulated before the end of the wars in 1815.[25]

The effectiveness of the Caribbean Vice Admiralty Courts as agents of the British imperial system after 1801, however, was determined not so much my intrinsic deficiencies in their operation —which, indeed, had been largely eradicated —as by changes which occurred in the system itself. Once British naval hegemony had been established and enemy colonies had fallen into British possession, the flow of prize vessels dried up to a trickle that was only replenished as neutral powers were successively goaded into war.[26] After 1809, even the Prize Courts were threatened with extinction for lack of business, a danger that was fortuitously averted only by the American declaration of war in 1812. Besides, the establishment of almost complete control by Great Britain over the islands of the Caribbean was not accompanied by the increase in Instance business which the Vice Admiralty Courts might have expected, but by a gradual untying of the British mercantilist bonds, particularly in relation to trade with the Spanish American colonies.

Mercantilism had always been flexible where relaxations could be shown to be advantageous to the metropolis, and now that Britain was commercially dominant and had rich possessions in the East as well as the West Indies, 'free trade' was much more attractive than a system of exclusivism based almost solely on the protection of West Indian sugar. During the latter years of the Napoleonic War the system of free trade with the Spanish colonies which had begun even before the establishment of the first British free ports in 1766, was greatly extended, both by the creation of new free ports and by the huge extension of the system of licenses.[27] With the independence of the richest of the old French colonies, Hispaniola (which enjoyed special trading concessions with Great Britain by the Maitland Convention of 1798) and by the additional opening of ports by colonial governors to relieve wartime shortages, the system of Caribbean free trade was almost complete. The operations of the Instance Courts, moreover, were so complicated that prosecutions under the Acts of Trade were made difficult to the verge of impossibility.

Prize business, after the last spurt of 1812-14, came to an abrupt end in 1815. Thereafter, mercantilist business also declined so completely that within 20 years the Vice Admiralty Courts had reverted to a status less significant than at any time since their foundation. Practically speaking, they remained simply occasional tribunals for the settlement of ordinary maritime disputes.[28] Mercantilist business had faded away; piracy had likewise almost disappeared, and the Courts of Admiralty Sessions met even less frequently than the Instance Courts. The Vice Admiralty Courts remained potential Prize Courts, but during the era of free trade war seemed an extremely remote prospect; and indeed, war in which Britain was involved did not even touch the hems of the Caribbean for 99 years after the Treaty of Vienna.

Yet the fading away of the Caribbean Vice Admiralty Courts after 1815, and even their failings during their years of activity, should not disguise the fact that they arose and developed largely in response to imperial needs, both naval and mercantilist. They were indispensable to the British imperial system, if only in the sense that without their completely efficient operation the system could not be completely realised. The fact that, for a multitude of reasons, the Courts achieved a large measure of success only in supporting naval policy, and generally failed in supporting the British mercantile system, does not deny their value. Their successes, while limited, were real enough, and their failure was no greater than that of the Empire itself.

If, then, the Caribbean Vice Admiralty Courts were an important component of the British imperial machine, and consequently shared in the fluctuating fortunes of the Empire as a whole, is it not possible, in conclusion, to seek in the limited compass of the history of the Courts some tentative solutions to the wider problems which exercise British imperial historians? What, for example, was the essence of the change that occurred in the nature of the British Empire between 1763 and 1815, and what separated the 'Old' from the 'New' Empire? How, above all, can we resolve the apparent paradox that increased formalisation and professionalism was accompanied by the physical truncation of the Empire by the secession of the Thirteen Colonies?

Our purpose should be threefold: to decide whether, and in which ways, British colonies reflected the mother country; to show ways in which ideas and their application changed with changes in the mother country; and to show how, in their microcosmic way, the Vice Admiralty Courts of the Caribbean provide evidence of these changes in practice.

Throughout the historiography of imperialism there seem to have been two main theories of empire which struggle for dominance. One sees an empire as simply an accretion of colonies that constitutes an extension of the mother country and its population, however haphazardly the colonies were acquired or however varied were the drives of the original colonists. The other sees an empire consisting, properly, only of components complementary to, and generally dependent upon, the mother country. In the legal sphere, the difference is detectable in two attitudes: that which regards the law as something which a colonist carries with him as his birthright, absolute and immutable; and that which sees the law as a flexible instrument, adaptable to the special conditions and needs of the colonial context. As far as the Vice Admiralty Courts were concerned, there was a difference between those who saw them simply as convenient tribunals for the settlement of maritime disputes, and those who saw their potential as instruments of imperial organisation and control.

Of the two interpretations, the first tends to be that which is held by proud colonists; the second, that which is maintained by studious imperialists. Even in the seventeenth century, the imperial theorists were inclined to emphasise the benefits of the colonies to the mother country rather than to glorify the achievements of the pioneer colonists; but it was an eighteenth century refinement that colonies could be justified solely on the grounds that they provided raw materials, markets and employment for artisans and seamen, not to mention gold for metropolitan merchants and glory for imperial statesmen.

This point of view had two bases: the commercial expansion that made Britain the predominant maritime power in the world; and the social and economic change that provided a powerful voice for commerce in the imperial Parliament, achieved by subtle changes both in parliamentary personnel and in the economic interests of the traditional parliamentary class. Together, these factors explain the evolution of the British mercantile system and the decided preference for plantation colonies which it involved. They also explain how it came about that the Vice Admiralty Courts were transformed, at the end of the seventeenth century, into vital instruments of the application of the British mercantile system.

In the unabashed preference of imperial statesmen for plantation colonies and their disinterest in colonies that were so similar to the mother country and so sophisticated that they were potential rivals, conflict with the Thirteen Colonies was already latent by the beginning of the eighteenth century. But it was the great acceleration in all imperial processes that occurred after 1760 or 1763 that made secession virtually inevitable. Around the middle of the eighteenth century, and manifested, for example, in the careers of George Grenville and Lord Shelburne, disciples of the elder Pitt, there began an increased rationalisation of the whole system of government. Starting with a reorganisation of the departments of state and of their relationships with King and Parliament, it spilled over into a reorganisation of the organs of imperial control.[30] These changes, aimed at augmenting an imperial system already dedicated almost entirely to the exploitation of the sugar colonies, were seen by the Thirteen Colonies as being not only irrelevant but positively baneful.

The rationalisation and reform of the Vice Admiralty Courts in the 1760s was much less complete than that, for example, of the customs service both because the Courts were subordinate to the High Court of Admiralty and therefore could not be reformed directly, and also because they claimed to administer an international law that was not easily susceptible to national fiat. Yet changes were made, in the shift of patronage, in the standardisation of the Courts and the creation of consolidated Courts for North America, that helped to add to the grievances of the Thirteen Colonies.[31]

The underlying causes of the increased imperial rationalisation that occurred after the accession of George III or the signing of the Treaty of Paris are by no means clear; but it is significant that at the same time Britain was imperceptibly undergoing economic as well as political changes. Largely through the release of new capital – which may or may not have originated chiefly, as Eric Williams maintains, from the sugar industry and the international slave trade[32] – industrialisation accelerated, producing in its turn a more aggressive commercialism. These mutations were undoubtedly reflected in the arguments for 'trade not dominion' shown in the writings of Lord Shelburne and his circle, and in the increased interest in the richer markets and new raw materials of Latin America and the East, which was reflected in the creation of the free ports in the Caribbean and the attacks upon the monopoly of the East India Company. This embryonic 'free trade' movement, first emphasised in modern historiography by the late Vincent T. Harlow,[33] was not accompanied by the pacifism that characterised its derivative during the middle decades of the nineteenth century. Indeed, there appears to have been a decided readiness to accept commercial war as a natural concomitant of widened commerce and in this – as in the enforcement of the old mercantilism – the Vice Admiralty Courts played a vital role.

Changes in imperial theory and practice usually attributed to the American War of Independence can nearly all be traced to the years before 1775, or shown to have grown up independently after 1783; and in this light the secessionary war appears far less traumatic to the Empire than is often depicted.[34] Although the secessation was probably inevitable once the majority of the Thirteen Colonies were seen to be 'plantations' no longer, the breakaway was by no means disastrous to a rational empire. The change in the political status of the Americans in 1783 meant dearer provisions for the British West Indies in peacetime, the embarrassing presence of a resourceful additional blockade-runner during wartime, and of a rival for Latin American trade once the fundamental changes in imperial policy and practice. Albeit involuntarily, bureaucratic economies, for which many had clamoured, had been effected; yet economic dependence, as Lord Sheffield predicted, continued long after the achievement of formal political independence.[35] In some ways, indeed, the achievement of independence by Haiti and Hispanic America were more important to the development of the British Empire, for the former did much to deprive the old protective system of its purpose and the latter opened up huge new markets for British industry and capital, while at the same time the East was demonstrating the value of new products, or old ones produced in a 'free' economy.

The result of these discoveries was the obsolescence of the old mercantile system, and with its decay the Caribbean lost its focal importance in the British imperial scheme. Similarly, the Vice Admiralty Courts declined greatly in usefulness and importance, although they did enjoy a final surge of activity during the last French Wars and were, somewhat incompletely, reformed under the influence of Sir William Scott.

There is considerable irony in the fact that the Vice Admiralty Courts only achieved a large measure of reform, rationalisation and responsiveness to imperial control after the need for them had really passed. They had in fact come full circle after barely touching at their goal. Originating in the seventeenth century in response to needs to settle the ordinary maritime problems and disputes occurring from time-to-time in young colonies, they were again, by the middle of the nineteenth century, little more than shadowy relics, exercising the same occasional jurisdiction. A student of the Courts in 1870 would have seen little to remind him of the tremendous blaze of activity that had characterised the 'First' British Empire, and in which the Courts had played such an indispensable role. The evidence was already mouldering in the archives.

Just as many American historians find it difficult to consider that an Empire could survive the secession of the Thirteen Colonies, so most British imperial historians have hitherto thought that the ending of the Old Colonial System meant a halt to British imperialism, or at least the beginning of a Great Imperial Hiatus. Yet the dormancy of the Vice Admiralty Courts, as well as the tragic decline of the sugar plantation colonies, should not lead us to compound the error of thinking that imperialism died with the onset of the free trade era. We would maintain that the history of the British Empire from its beginning shows us that the drive towards commercial empire was always at least as strong as the desire for formal colonies; and we believe, with Fieldhouse, Robinson and Gallagher,[36] that the mid-nineteenth century is just as valid a period for imperial studies as those more familiar periods which preceded and followed it. The history of the British Empire is a coat of many colours, but a seamless garment nonetheless.

6

Planters, British Imperial Policy and the Black Caribs of St Vincent

Introduction: In its present abbreviated form this essay examines and makes some moral points about the ways in which imperialist forces in due course subverted even the most obdurate indigenous Caribbean people. As originally delivered at a conference on the Lesser Antilles held at Hamilton College 1990, however, it was far more ambitious. Subtitled 'An Exercise in Historiographical Triangulation', it not only contrasted (as to an extent here) the responses of imperialist British and French, transported Africans and indigenous Island Caribs to each other, but attempted to show how differently the contact and transformation processes have been viewed by historians (Caribbean as well as metropolitan), by anthropologists and by the modern Black Caribs (alias Garifuna) themselves. Had this version been published here, it would have been the closest that the present collection came to acknowledging the post-modernist contention that all history writing is relativistic, revealing little more than the mindset and the culture of the writer.

When the British took over St Vincent under the terms of the Treaty of Paris in 1763, the colonisers, led by Sir William Young, the First Commissioner for the Sale of Lands in the Ceded Islands, assumed all the European attitudes towards the indigenous inhabitants of the Antilles developed since 1492, while adding refinements of their own. Without acknowledgement (and in fact claiming that their own version was infinitely more benign than that of the Spaniards), they echoed the sentiments of Columbus and his successors that good natives submitted to authority and had thereby the chance of redemption through being assimilated into European culture, whereas the obdurate were irredeemable savages fit to be enslaved if not extirpated.[1]

The resistant Caribs of the Lesser Antilles were the Europeans' classic bad Indians, characterised first by the Spaniards as brutal savages and idolatrous anthropophagi, who knew no civilised arts and failed to cultivate the islands where they lived, and whose enslavement was therefore authorised by a Spanish royal decree in 1503.[2] The situation became more complicated when the non-Iberian powers challenged the Spaniards for a foothold in the Caribbean and the Spanish Main, and the Caribs were found to be useful if equivocal allies for the newcoming Europeans. On the mainland, Caribs cooperated with the Dutch against the Spaniards, and in the islands during the 1660s they cleverly favoured the French against the English in order to obtain virtual recognition from both that the islands between Dominica and Trinidad (and especially Dominica and St Vincent) belonged to them.[3]

Although French and English never hesitated to make treaties with the Caribs when it suited them (and to ignore them when it did not), such transactions actually aided the French infiltration into the Windward Islands, while they convinced the English that the Caribs were wily and treacherous enemies of their own expansion. Meanwhile, diplomacy concerning the Caribbean was undertaken in Europe with little concern for the Caribs, and certainly with no participation by them. As late as the Treaty of Aix-la-Chapelle (1748), the French and the British agreed to regard the islands of Dominica, St Lucia, St Vincent and Tobago as 'neutral', although in fact all had considerable numbers of French colonists, living in somewhat parlous amity with the local Caribs. When the Treaty of Paris was signed in 1763, St Lucia (now with far more French than Caribs) was assigned to France, and the other islands, plus Grenada, to Britain, with no provision made for the native inhabitants.

The situation in St Vincent, regarded as the most promising of the Ceded Islands, was now highly complex, although this did not prevent the new colonists from treating the natives with simplistic pragmatism on long-established principles. The French authorities in 1700 had divided the island longitudinally, with the French colonists settled on the hillier Caribbean half, interspersed with a minority of semi-assimilated Caribs, and the more fertile windward Atlantic side assigned exclusively to the far less friendly Carib majority. These 'wild' Windward Cribs, because of prolonged miscegenation with shipwrecked and runaway African slaves, were referred to as Black Caribs, whereas the more acculturated friendlies (who were, ironically, said to be the purer descendants of the natives once regarded as implacable enemies by the Europeans) were styled the Red or

Yellow Caribs. Although there remained more Caribs of different sorts in the island than in the rest of the Antilles together, some of the Vincentian *Kalinago* had migrated (or remigrated) to the Orinoco basin to join their *Kalinago* cousins over the last century – although whether under French or Black Carib pressure remains unclear.

The evident purposes of Sir William Young and his fellow land commissioners after 1763 were to extend British plantations into the underdeveloped windward side of St Vincent, and to justify this extension, and in this they were, of course, backed to the hilt by the new white colonists. To emphasise the African origins of the Windward Caribs was, of course, to stress that even if they were not actually runaway slaves, they were no more indigenous than the Europeans, and therefore more enslavable than native subjects in international law – quite apart from being, perhaps, 'natural slaves' simply because they were of African provenance. The fact that the Caribs did not optimally cultivate the lands they occupied made them seem *ipso facto* inferior to the Europeans: they possessed land which they did not deserve, and were therefore fit to be reduced to marginal peasants or mere labourers, or to be expelled. To stress the Caribs' obduracy and refusal to accept British suzerainty, as well as their barbarity, was clearly to the colonists' advantage. Yet somewhat paradoxically too, any claim by the Caribs to be a true independent nation might be advantageous to the colonial regime, which could then persuade the imperial government to treat them as a foreign enemy.

These motives clearly informed the reports of Young and his fellow land commissioners to the imperial authorities and even more the accompanying representations by the Vincentian planters, and they were encapsulated in the exculpatory *Account of the Black Charaibs of St Vincent* published by Sir William Young's son and namesake (from his father's notes) in 1795. It was this version, moreover, which was most influential in shaping traditional historiography up to the mid-twentieth century.[4]

In one of their first reports to the imperial government, dated April 11, 1767, Sir William Young the elder and his fellow commissioners pointed out that the Black Caribs controlled the best parts of the island, cultivating only a few scattered spots 'whilst large tracts through which they are scattered remained in wood, useless and unoccupied'. The purpose of the commissioners was to survey and dispose of such lands 'in a manner beneficial to his Majesty and the colony', despite the fact that 'the present situation of these wild and lawless savages was dangerous to his Majesty's subjects already settled in their neighbourhood, and a great impediment to the future population and culture of an island, which they (the commissioners and colonists) conceived to be the best of any ceded to the Crown by the late peace'.[5]

After a token hypocrisy that the extirpation of the Vincentian Caribs would be consistent neither 'with royal clemency, nor indeed the common rights of mankind', Young posed the problem of what to do with them 'without endangering the peace of the colony, and in a manner productive of their own happiness, as well as the future improvement of the country', before going on to give his slanted ethnohistorical account. There were, he claimed, no more than 2,000 Vincentian Caribs in all (an understatement by perhaps 80 per cent), of whom the Yellow descendants of the original inhabitants were no more than a tiny minority. The remainder were all said to be descended from a single cargo of Guinea slaves destined for Barbados, wrecked on St Vincent 'about a century ago' (that is, around 1667).

The few Yellow Caribs who had not been exterminated by the blacks were said to be 'innocent and timid', living among the Europeans for safety and mixing at all with their black enemies. The Black Caribs (whom Young interestingly says were distinguished by having foreheads flattened in infancy – an Amerindian not an African practice) were said to be, with the exception of the few, associated with the French,

> an idle, ignorant and savage people, subject to no law or discipline, and scarcely acknowledging subordination to any chief. The speak a jargon of their own, which, added to an extreme jealousy of their liberty, a distrust of those they converse with, and a little affected cunning, make it very difficult to discourse or reason with them. [6]

The Black Caribs generally went about naked, the men armed with cutlasses and fowling guns in good order. They lived with their families in thatched huts dispersed in the woods, so little given to industry that although St Vincent was as fertile as anywhere on earth, they grew no more than, along with the plentiful fish and game, they needed for subsistence. They had first settled on the mountainous leeward side, where the sea was calmer for their canoes. But the French from Martinique, who by 1763 numbered 4,000-5,000, had 'insinuated themselves' among them and elbowed them out towards the windward half of the island.

The commissioners by 1767 had settled title to almost the entire leeward side, among the French, Yellow Caribs and some British settlers, and this area was already exporting three times as much produce as the much larger island of Dominica. Now, however, the commissioners wanted to open up the windward side to would-be sugar planters, who promised to make

St Vincent second only to Jamaica among British sugar colonies. The occupation of this side of the island, argued Young, was also imperative as a safeguard against the French, who could reach it more easily from St Lucia, 8 leagues to the south, than could British forces stationed on the leeward side of St Vincent. An equal concern was the ease with which the Black Caribs could presently communicate with the French – who were no more distant than a night's paddling by canoe.

The proposal by the commissioners was to push a road through the windward side of St Vincent and to carry out a survey of all cultivable lands, under the protection of the colonial garrison. The surveyed lands were to be offered for sale to planters at a minimum price of £10 per acre. The Black Caribs on such lands were to be reassigned tracts in the interior and recompensed at a rate of £13 4s per acre in gold coin (although only for lands they had planted). They were to be allowed up to five years to wind up their affairs, to clear fresh grounds and build new houses. If unwilling to construct their own houses, the planters would build houses for them and the cost would be deducted from the compensation paid for the appropriated lands. The Caribs were to be exempt from paying quit rents on their new lands, which were to be inalienable to whites, and for which they would hold certificates of title. Despite his opinion about the Caribs' unreliability, Sir William Young was confident that he was sufficiently skilled to achieve these changes by negotiations with the Carib leaders.

The imperial government authorised the commissioners' proposals entirely, while adding some subtle details. The reallocation of lands could apply to all Caribs throughout the island, although the 'native Caribbs' were to be settled in areas distinct from the 'free negroes' if that was their wish. No allocations and reallocations were to occur before the Caribs had been informed, the land title certificates were to be assigned to 'the principal persons among them', and the absolute property of the lands allotted to them was to be 'assured to them and their children, in such a manner as shall be found most to their satisfaction, and most agreeable to their customs'. This, however, was to be subject to their continued fidelity to the Crown, and the grants were to be accompanied by a careful census of all Carib families holding the, 'in order that their declarations of fidelity to the King may be received, as they shall from time-to-time come in for that purpose.[7]

This enforced subjection and their proposed removal into virtual native reserves was utterly rejected by the majority of Caribs, who were further infuriated when a colonial patrol vessel sank four of their canoes in the strait between St Vincent and St Lucia. The work of the surveyors and road-builders was brought to a halt by armed Carib bands, and when Sir William Young arranged a parlay with 40 of their chiefs led by Chatoyer at Morne Garou in 1771, he professed to be 'greatly surprised to find them in a fixed resolution not to consent to our settling any part of the country claimed by them'. The Carib chieftains asserted their independence and refused to acknowledge that they were subject to either the King of Britain or the King of France, although Young claimed that 'at the same time they confessed a great partiality for the French, and declared they had been ordered by the governor of Martinico not to give up any land; and that he had promised to protect them'.[7]

An accompanying memorial from Richard Maitland, the agent for St Vincent, Richard Ottley, the President of the Council, and several prominent planters, spoke in even stronger terms, for the first time advocating the removal of the Black Caribs from St Vincent altogether. Besides refusing either to develop or to quit two-thirds of the island's most fertile lands, the Caribs contributed nothing to the island's treasury and were a negative factor in its defence. Not only were a majority of them ignorant of the English Language, they continued to carry on a dangerous intercourse with the French, many of them becoming nominal Catholics. However, the memorial added,

> the policy of the French not permitting them to teach these savages any thing more of religion than answered the purpose of prejudice, there subsists among them the utmost barbarity, which is not only practiced by them upon each other, without any other punishment than what may arise from retaliation, but they, after encouraging our slaves to run away, have (upon their refusal to work for them, or to go off to the French islands to be sold) cruelly murdered them.[8]

Apparently unaware of any inconsistency, the memorialists combined their accusations of lawless barbarity and treachery with an acknowledgement of quite sophisticated diplomacy. Besides going to the nub of the question by rejecting the sovereignty of the British King, the chiefs assembled under their spokesman Chatoyer at Morne Garou comported themselves 'as an embassy from one state to another'. In their negotiations, moreover, the Carib chiefs seemed to be fully aware of the current crisis between Britain, Spain and France over the question of the distant Falkland Islands, and were cleverly seeking to take advantage of it.[9]

The solution proposed by the colonists was quite as wily and treacherous as any behaviour of which they could accuse their enemies. 'Should the black Caribbs be once removed from the island', they wrote, we conceive we then shall be able to put the yellow Caribbs, or aborigines, upon a footing as advantageous to St Vincent as the free negroes in Jamaica are upon to that island; for the French, considering the Yellow Caribbs too insignificant to do them either good or harm, have left them free from the prejudices they have instilled into the others, by which they are however fit objects for our service, as well as for our humanity and care: being inferior in number to the whites already settled in the island, we shall be under no apprehensions of danger from them.

As to exiling the Black Caribs, giving them the semblance of choice might be politic. But nearby St Lucia, with which they had such close contacts, was, perhaps fortunately, already closed to them since the French governor, their ostensible protector, had refused to receive them. Instead, wrote the Vincentian plantocrats, 'we conceive that the removing them to that part of the world from whence their ancestors came, would as much correspond with their own inclinations, as with the clemency of his Majesty's purposes'.[10] By this they meant Africa, going on to specify 'any unoccupied tract of 10,000 acres' on the African mainland, ideally with rivers running through it and close to the sea for the Caribs fishing, or the island referred to as St Matthew, said to be about the size of St Vincent and off the African coast at latitude 2 degrees, 31 minutes (seemingly the Portuguese island of Principe).

The imperial authorities endorsed the need to reduce the recalcitrant Caribs to the extent of ordering two regiments of regular troops from North America to St Vincent in March 1772 with the cooperation of the Royal Navy. But they kept their options open as to what to do with the Caribs once their submission had been obtained. Whether the Caribs submitted to persuasion or force, the ideal was said to be to retain them on the island under similar terms as had been agreed with the Jamaican Maroons. For this purpose a copy of the Jamaican Maroon Treaty was sent to Governor Leyborne. However, contingency plans were made, in conjunction with the Admiralty, to transport the defeated Caribs,

to some unfrequented part of the coast of Africa, or to some desert island adjacent thereto, care being taken that they be treated upon the voyage with every degree of humanity their situation will admit of; and that when put on shore, they be supplied with provisions, and whatsoever may be judged necessary to subsist them for a reasonable time, an with such tools and implements as may enable them to provide for their future subsistence.

Although couched with every justification and expressions of concern for the Caribs' welfare, the imperial orders were conveyed in absolute secrecy, considering 'the propriety of avoiding as much as possible, any discovery of our intentions, lest these infatuated savages should become desperate, and commit some fatal acts of hostility before the arrival of the troops'.[11]

In the event, the 'infatuated savages' did successfully resist the imperial troops, obtaining the option of a negotiated peace in 1773 which assigned them the northern third of St Vincent (some 30,000 acres), under terms that duly echoed those agreed with the Jamaican Maroons 34 years earlier – both in the way of apparent concessions and in the canny insertion of clauses bound in due course to favour the colonial regime.[12] This therefore merely postponed the implementation of the colonists' plant to expel the recalcitrant Caribs from St Vincent for a further quarter century. Significantly, moreover, when the great majority of the Black Caribs were transported from St Vincent in 1797, it was not back to Africa, but to the shores of the Central American mainland, where their descendants are to be found today.

The equivocal terms of the 1773 treaty, the tireless expansionism of the British plantocracy, the Caribs' support for the French occupation of St Vincent during the American War, and their subsequent alliance with French Jacobin elements during the 1790s (all considered in rather more detail below) were inherently predictable, and the 1797 expulsion of the Black Caribs also takes on an air of inevitability in the plantocratic and imperialistic accounts. This tradition survived strongly at least until the publication of Lowell J. Ragatz's 1928 study of the planter class between 1763 and 1833, as is borne out by a quotation of the passage concerning the events in St Vincent of 1763-73 in its self-confident entirety:

> The work of surveying was hindered by the Black Caribs who were descendants of shipwrecked Guinea slaves and the indigenous yellow Caribs. These mongrel peoples declared themselves to be independent owners of the soil and disputed the British occupation. They committed numerous depredations on the plantations which had been laid out and matters reached such a point that it became necessary to launch an expeditionary force of North American troops against them in 1772. Their resistance was soon broken. By a treaty the following year, they recognised British control and accepted a block of land in the northern part of the island, set aside for their exclusive use. The affair aroused considerable opposition in England among well-meaning but misinformed individuals who say in it nothing but wanton aggression against an inoffensive local people. It was actually a necessary preliminary step to the development of the colony.[13]

One might take exception to almost every clause in Ragatz's statement not least to his condescending dismissal of those who defended the rights of the Caribs in 1772-73. The majority were no doubt well-meaning, but the motives of all were subtly overlaid by political considerations and concerns at best tangential. Besides, those engaged in the debate were remarkably well-informed by the standards of the day: the official paper which Lord North ordered to be laid before Parliament in December 1772 were as complete and revealing as any up to that time.[14]

The Carib controversy certainly came at a significant juncture in impe-rial affairs, as in the evolution of British ideas about race and empire. At the same time, controversy over Britain's role in India was reaching a climax in the parliamentary and public debates that led to Lord North's Regulating Act in 1773. These concerned the extent of the political powers of the East India Company in India, the status rights of Indians within the realms controlled by the British, the involvement of the Company in British internal politics, and above all, the behaviour of the most fortunate and unscrupulous Company servants, nicknamed 'nabobs', of whom the great-est and most notorious was Robert Clive. Animosity towards *nouveaux riches* nabobs had long been paralleled by dislike for West Indian absentee planters and now expressed itself in distrust for the new wave of would-be planters seeking their fortunes in the Ceded Islands.[15]

A second underlying theme was the criticism of imperial government and the treatment of subject peoples associated with sympathy for the North American colonists and a concern for the most politic way to treat with native Amerindians – divisive issues in British politics particularly since the Stamp Act crisis in 1765-76 and Pontiac's rebellion of 1763. Some of the leading critics of the government in the Carib affair were simply taking a routine opposition line. Chief of these, and the actual proponent of the parliamentary motions of censure in February 1773, was Thomas Town-shend (1733-1800), briefly Secretary at War under Rockingham and Home Secretary under the 'liberal' Lord Shelburne. The appeals of others to larger matters of principle, though were give greater credibility by direct American connections and experience. Prominent among these was Alder-man Barlow Trecothick (1718-75) who, although a London magnate (and successor as Lord Mayor to the Jamaican grandee, William Beckford), had lived 18 years in New England and seven in Jamaica. An ardent opponent of the Stamp Act, he was, however, himself an owner of properties in Jamaica and Grenada, and had been a government contractor. His speech in favour of the Caribs, in which he called them 'a defenseless, innocent and inoffensive people' against whom the colonists were emulating 'the barbarities of the Spaniards against the Mexicans', was his last in Parlia-ment.[16]

A rather less equivocal figure was Colonel Isaac Barré (1726-1802). A professional soldier of Huguenot extraction and radical ideas, he had seconded Beckford's motion against the Stamp Act, spoken strongly against the Declaratory Act, and was briefly Paymaster-General under Shelburne. Barré's service in India had made him the enemy of Robert Clive (and candidate for the governorship of Bengal had Lawrence Sulivan's interest defeated that of Clive in the parliamentary inquiry of 1772-73); and service in North America had made him the ardent friend of the American colonists, while at the same time admiring the martial spirit of the Red Indians. The Caribs, said Barré on December 9, 1772, were 'fighting for liberty, and every English heart must applaud them'.[17]

Such sentiments found a ready response in those members of the public still influenced by the notion of the Noble Savage, whose generalised sentiments about the inherent Rights of Man were to be recruited sequentially (if somewhat ambiguously) on behalf of the rights of the American colonists and the Afro-American slaves. Their most famous spokesman was the all-purpose liberal, Granville Sharp, who strongly supported the Caribs' cause at the same time as he was winning his most famous victory in Lord Mansfield's judgement in the case of the slave James Somerset.[18]

This phase in the history of ideas is best told in Wylie Sypher's almost forgotten *Guinea's Captive Kings: British Anti-Slavery Literature of the XVI-IIth Century* (1942). Sypher shows how the attraction felt by Aphra Behn for her Surinamese Oroonoko (1688) or, less sentimentally, by Daniel Defoe for his fictional Carib Friday (1719) gradually spilled over into the sympathy expressed for the Negro slave in Thomas Chatterton's *African Ecologues* (1770) and Thomas Day's *Dying Negro* (1773), or the deeply ambiguous (and Freudian) homage accorded by Bryan Edwards and William Blake to the *Sable Venus* (1794). As much the same time as anthropologists, Richard and Sally Price have shown, John Gabriel Stedman's relationship with the mulatto slave, Joanna, as portrayed in his 1796 *Narrative*, similarly expressed deep ambivalences. This whole process is brilliantly encapsulated, although, in Sypher's analysis of the gradual transmutation of the legend of Inkle and Yarico.[19]

Originally told in 1657 by Richard Ligon as a simple take of the tragic betrayal of an ingenuous Indian maid by a Barbadian 'redleg' (who during a brief idyll impregnates her, then sells her into slavery, upon which she kills her baby and herself), the story was taken up by Richard Steele in the eleventh issue of the *Spectator* (1712) and transformed into a parable of the conflict between natural innocence and the imperatives of commerce. Over the following century, the legend was retold innumerable times in plays and poems in England and France, with Inkle being the servant or symbol of the greedy West Indian plantocracy, and Yarico symbolising the unfortunate slave, now more often a 'Nubian Dido' than an Amerindian. As Wylie Sypher summarised the transformation that had already occurred when Parliament was debating the fate of the Black Caribs:

> This amalgam of Dido with Yarico was inevitable; the noble Negress, like the noble Negro, became all things to all poets. Anti-slavery found ready for its purposes a symbol, the African who united the traits of the white man, so that he might not be repulsive; the traits of the Indian, so that he might not be base; and the traits of the Negro, so that he might rouse pity. By 1773 [Thomas] Day did not need to invent but simply to adopt this hero, the Negro who is not a Negro, a creature who lives, moves, and has his being in the arcadia of primitivism. Poetry is indeed more marvelous than history – or ethnology.[20]

What better subject for such liberal sentiments than the Black Caribs, who not only combined the genetic and cultural traits of the African and the Amerindian, but could be portrayed as nature's noblemen, eager for the benefits of civilisation (like the intelligent, French-speaking Chatoyer) but instead the tragic victims of crass commercial imperialism!

However, such popular ideology was not yet general or coherent enough to outweigh political realities, or to command a parliamentary majority. The parliamentary opposition itself was ill-focused. As we have seen, even the chief critics of the government were ambivalent in their attitude towards the Vincentian Caribs, finding it difficult to reconcile support for white colonials, Amerindian natives, and for the ordinary white soldiers transferred from garrison duty in North America to active duty in the fever-ridden West Indies – even where they did not have countervailing personal interests. A significant and perhaps crucial absentee from the debate was Edmund Burke, who seems to have abstained less from the ideological confusions involved than from embarrassment at his brothers' speculation in lands in the Ceded Islands.[21]

Similar conflicts seem to have confused the attitudes of those concerned with the military aspects of the controversy. Those who felt that the soldiers transferred at the height of the fever season were as much victims of imperial greed as the Caribs they were called on to fight, were quick to notice that the military commanders tended to behave like Spanish conquisitadores, or Clive in India. General Monckton MP had already been rewarded for his services in America during the Seven Years' War with a large tract of Vincentian sugar land, and the expeditionary commanders Dalrymple and Etherington were more directly rewarded by grants of appropriated Carib lands after the conclusion of hostilities in 1773. Thus while a retired military radical like Barré could speak for the ordinary soldiers and Caribs alike, and hint at collusion between generals and planters, other military spokesmen, while prepared to criticise the Secretary of State and War Office for mismanagement, were at pains to stress that all soldiers would always perform their duty as directed.[22]

Perhaps the most critical issue in the debate, though, was raised by Hans Stanley MP, who claimed (in an argument that might equally have been applied to Red Indians on the North American frontier, to French Canadians, or to the natives of British India) that it was essentially a question of suzerainty and the status of native subjects. Stanley disclaimed any personal interest in the West Indies and strongly, if somewhat rhetorically, deplored the slave trade and the worst aspects of colonialism, including racist discrimination, while asserting more basic imperial principles. 'He should not think of either the stature or complexion of any man,' Stanley was reported by Cobbett as saying,

> whether he was a pygmy or a Patagonian, or whether he was a white, yellow or black; he only looked to the present measure so far as it was founded on natural justice and good faith, and supported by sound policy, and that necessity by which those who are entrusted with the executive part of the government are compelled to act.

The crux of the matter was simply deciding whether the Caribs were 'subjects or sovereigns', and for Stanley and many other parliamentarians there was no doubt. For such a stateless and disjunctive people to claim sovereignty was a nonsense; the Caribs had been accepted as subjects at least since Lord Willoughby's treaty in 1668, and the subject status of those in the Ceded Islands had been clarified and confirmed by the Treaty of Paris in 1763. This status provided the benefits of British protection and British laws (including those that guaranteed their lands and customs and forbade their enslavement) but reciprocally required peaceable acceptance and civilised behaviour. No one seems to have noticed however, that this 'liberal imperialist' stance placed the unfortunate Caribs in a Catch 22 position. If they denied British suzerainty (a stance which seemed to accord with some planters' wishes) they might have justice on their side, but would be proceeded against as foreign enemies; yet if they were subjects, they had no options to submission but to rebel and take the consequences, which would be at least equally severe.[23]

As might have been expected, the government was vindicated in the parliamentary debate. The motion that the expedition against the Black

Caribs was undertaken without sufficient provocation at the instigation of persons interested in the 'total extirpation' of the Caribs was defeated by 206 to 88, and that which asserted that it was undertaken without direct orders from the government, and so mismanaged as to invite disaster as well as to incur dishonour, by 199 to 78. These votes (taken on February 15, 1773) came too late to forestall the signing of a maroon-type treaty with the Black Caribs (published in the *St Vincent Gazette* on February 27, 1773), although they gave the planters encouragement to ignore and undermine it as far as they could.[24]

How the Black Caribs viewed the 1773 treaty is open to speculation based upon their subsequent actions and a more careful analysis of their existing culture. But the plantocratic viewpoint (overlaid with conventional European symbolism at least as old as Columbus) is nicely conveyed in the well-known painting of the treaty negotiation commissioned around 1775 from the itinerant artist, Agostino Brunias, by Sir William Young, former First Commissioner of Lands and now Governor of Dominica. Lithographs of this painting appeared as late as 1810 variously to depict British nego- tiations with Maroons in Jamaica and Dominica as well as St Vincent, but what it depicted in fact was the meeting between General Dalrymple and the Black Carib chieftains led by Chatoyer in February 1773. On the right hand side are the elegantly clad representatives of civilisation guarded by an armed soldier in regimental dress, with an officer reading out the formal terms of the treaty and a seated General Dalrymple holding out a symbolic hand to the Caribs. For their part, the Caribs, standing on the left, are depicted as almost naked savages of African physiognomy and hue, ponder- ing the British terms but clearly submissive – their bows, muskets and knives being laid on the ground at Dalrymple's feet. Chatoyer, whom Brunias also painted in picturesque domesticity with his similarly half-clad wives, is the central figure; an image of the savage on the point of redemption.[25]

Chatoyer was indeed a central figure in the subsequent phase, but in the planters' interpretation the epitome of Carib treachery. The Black Caribs were at first peaceable and a greater number seemed to be adopting European ways (particularly the French language and Catholic religion) and becoming settled small planters. But as the numbers of British settlers increased (including the smallholders brought in by the controversial Governor Valentine Morris) and more plantations were developed even in the northern third of the island, the Black Caribs did not all become assimilated or passively succumb as the whites had planned.[26]

During the American and Maritime War, the Caribs actively encouraged the French takeover of St Vincent in 1779, and its return to Britain at the Treaty of Versailles in 1783 was a disappointment to them and probably the death-blow to any chance of reconciliation. What precipitated actual hostilities, though, were the whites' realistic fears of the encouragement which the 1791 revolt of the Haitian slaves might have on the Black Caribs, the spread of French revolutionary ideas and the actual aid provided by the French once the Anglo-French war began in 1793. As recounted by Charles Shephard, the agents of the Jacobin commissioner, Victor Hugues, invited the Caribs 'in the name of the glorious French republic as friends and citizens to accept of liberty and equality, to rouse themselves from inglorious sloth, and assert the natural prerogatives of men'. With canny rhetoric (which if it did not fully take in Caribs, certainly frightened the British) Hugues proclaimed (in French and English but not in Island Carib):

> Behold your chains forged and imposed by the hand of the tyrannical English! Blush,
> and break those ensigns of disgrace, spurn them with becoming indignation, rise in a

moment, and while we assist you motives of the purest philanthropy and zeal for the happiness of all nations, fall on these despots, extirpate them from the country, and restore yourselves, your wives and children to the inheritance of your fathers, whose spirits from the grave will lead on your ranks, inspire you with fury, and help you to be avenged.[27]

Seemingly well-organised into two divisions and well-armed by the French, the Black Caribs struck at the colonial regime in March 1795 under the command of Chatoyer and Duvallé, just after news reached St Vincent of Fédon's successful rebellion in Grenada. For a time it seemed likely that the Caribs and their allies would take over St Vincent entirely. The first turning point occurred on march 18, 1795, in the desperate battle for the control of Dorsetshire Hill, commanding the colonial capital, when Chatoyer was killed in personal combat with Major Leith of the militia. According to the plantocratic writers, in Chatoyer's pocket was found an inflammatory French proclamation, although he wore round his neck a gorget presented to him by Prince William Henry (later King William IV), and held in his hand a sword given to him by Sir William Young.[28]

British reinforcements steadily built up till more than three regular regiments were engaged. Far from collapsing, the Black Caribs resisted for more than a year, being forced to surrender only after the landing of a huge expeditionary force under General Abercromby, many guerrilla skirmishes, a scorched-earth policy on the part of the British and the threat of starvation. Significantly, the way in which the defeated Black Caribs were rounded up, the shocking conditions under which they were detained on Balliceaux Island, and their deportation to Roatan in March 1797, created little stir in Britain and aroused nothing like the wave of sympathy for the Caribs some 25 years earlier. It is probably true to say that not only were the plantocratic accusations of Carib perfidy underlined by the exigencies of the French Revolutionary War but that the general reaction against popular radicalism which brought about Pitt's notorious domestic repressions was reinforced by a general fear of concerted rebellion by Afro-Caribbean subjects following the Haitian explosion and subsequent events in the Antilles.

In a numerical sense at least, the identification of some 4,200 rebel Caribs for concentration on Balliceaux in October 1796, the sending back to St Vincent of 44 slaves and 102 'Yellow Caribs' (not to mention the less intentional weeding out caused by the death of some 2,400 by 'malignant fever') gave the Black Caribs a more recognisable identity than ever before. From the nucleus of the rather less than 2,000 Black Caribs actually shipped to Roatan, moreover, can be traced the origins of all the present-day Garifuna in Central America and elsewhere. What remains for the historian and ethnographer to decide, however, is whether the events of 1763-97 were significant in the creation of a Black Carib (or Garifuna) nation.[29]

PART TWO

Slave Trade, Slavery and Slave Society

7

The African background
of American Slavery

Introduction: Systematic work on the origins of the slaves destined for British colonies in the Americas, and on the volume and morphology of their flow, really only dates from Philip Curtin's *The Atlantic Slave Trade: A Census* (1969), and it has been even more recently that slavery historians have come to acknowledge (what was well-known to seventeenth and eighteenth century planters as slave owning practitioners) the significance of the variations of the African peoples enslaved and their native lifestyles and cultures upon their behaviour, 'suitability' and usefulness as slaves. This essay attempts to go one step further, to summarise the degree to which the variations among those enslaved were themselves determined by geographical as well as purely historical factors. Originally written for a Dictionary of Afro-American (that is, US) Slavery, the essay has been modified to apply more generally to the origins of slaves carried to all the British American colonies, in the Caribbean as well as mainland North America.

The 2.5 million Africans brought to be slaves in British colonies in the Americas between 1619 and 1807 derived from an area even more extensive and diverse than that to which they were transported. They came from an African coastal belt as wide as 500 miles, stretching 7,000 miles from Mauritania to northern Mozambique. Even though the great majority hailed from a relatively smaller swathe of West Africa, the range of climatic, geographical and ecological areas, and ethnic and cultural types, remained much greater than those from which the non-African migrants to the colonies came.

This great variety, coupled with the part-accidental, part-calculated mixing of different Africans, tended to ensure that African influences were general rather than specific, while the African links were much weaker and less continuous for the comparatively healthy colonies of the North American mainland than for the Caribbean, which needed a far larger and steadier flow of African replacements. As Philip Curtin has demonstrated, a mainland slave population eventually similar in size to that of the British West Indian colonies derived from a flow of imported Africans no more than a fifth as large as that to the British West Indies. Consequently, the African component of the Afro-American culture on the mainland was quickly diffused, and progressively more generic.

Yet it is still vital for mainland as for West Indian colonies to examine and differentiate the African background with as much precision as possible. This will enable us to understand the differences between the Africans transported and the degree to which they shared common and easily transferable features. It will also provide insights into both those cultural elements that could be carried and retained over generations and those which were so intrinsically African that they were left behind for ever.

Despite the steadily increasing involvement of North Americans in the slave trade (with up to 70 per cent of their slaves coming directly from Africa rather than by way of the West Indies), similar preferences on the part of slaveowners and the same exigencies of trading conditions determined that the catchment area for North American slaves was essentially the same as that for the Caribbean. British West Indian and mainland planters alike generally preferred slaves from west of Dahomey to those from further east or south. Angolans, however, were preferred to Congolese or any slaves from the Bights of Benin and Biafra, particularly the latter. Mainland buyers like West Indians were constrained by availability and cheaper prices to take progressively more slaves from trading areas further east and south, and especially from the Bight of Biafra. This important trend, though, was offset by other factors. Mainland traders, using smaller ships and without many shore establishments, increasingly took a higher proportion of captives than traders based in England or the West Indies from the Upper Guinea Coast, from African traders around the mouth of the Congo, and from Portuguese traders established at Luanda and Benguela.

The number and types of slaves available for transshipment at the African coast were determined by local geographical as well as political, social and economic conditions. Population densities were largely determined by the means of subsistence. This in turn was mainly decided by climate, soils and topography. West Africa, broadly, is characterised by latitudinal regions shaped by the amount of rainfall and its seasonal variations. These range from the immense central belt of equatorial rain forest, outward from the equator to north and south through woodland savannas, grassy steppe lands with only seasonal rains, to outright desert with hardly any rain at all. There are, though, significant coastal variations, particularly in the bulge of West Africa north of the equator, affected by elevation, prevailing winds and offshore currents. These include the summer 'monsoonal' belt of Upper Guinea with its interior mountain variants in the Futa Jalon, the fairly dry coastal region of modern Ghana (always relatively healthy for European traders), and the monsoonal-equatorial excess of the Cameroon Mountains, with an annual rainfall as high as 400 inches. The upper slopes of Mount Cameroon may be 30 degrees cooler than the nearby coast, and desert temperatures may fall as much as 50 degrees in the nights, but only at the northern and southern extremes of the coast is there a significant annual variation. Although soils vary (and are not often really good), the critical regime boundaries are formed by the 60-inch and 20-inch isoyets. The former delimit the range of tropical forest; the latter, the limit of agriculture without irrigation. A valuable further indicator might be the lines showing the areas that receive at least 4 inches of rainfall each month, allowing for all types of plant growth throughout the year (and thus several crops), and the considerable area in the savanna and Sahel that receives less than one inch of rain for six or more months each year.

Each region has its distinctive native vegetation and indigenous agriculture, ranging from an almost exclusive reliance on hunting and gathering in the densest equatorial forest, through predominantly root, bean and tree cultivation in the tropical forest belt, various kinds of cereals in the woodland and savanna areas (including rice in the best irrigated areas), to pure nomadic pastoralism in the Sahel. Only the desert, mountaintops and substantial areas of coastal mangrove swamp stand virtually unproductive. One great cultivation boundary was the line between the predominance of the yam and the area where grains provided the chief subsistence. Another was that region, roughly coincident with the forest belt, beyond which the tsetse fly reigned, and raising cattle, save for an inferior dwarf variety, was almost impossible.

As a consequence of these divisions, which were greatly intensified by the introduction, mainly into the coastal and forest belts, of bananas and new forms of yams from Asia, and cassava and maize from North America, there was, north of the equator, one belt of dense and increasing population close to the coast. Another stood some 500 miles inland, in the optimal areas for growing grains and raising domestic animals, with an intermediate area of low population density. South of the equator, the coastal region was less populated except around the major settlements and the mouths of the great rivers. The areas of densest population tended to follow the river valleys, particularly those of the Congo River and its southern tributaries, and the Kwanza River, where they traversed the richly diversified area between tropical forest and savanna. In any region, however, there could be local population variations. These depended on the degree of political stability, the stimulus of mining or trade, and the existence of rivers or lakes to provide irrigation or resources of fish. Other factors – the incidence of tribal conflict, religious war, or the disastrous incursions of slave-catching enemies – had negative demographic implications.

Regional variations in traditional African occupations and skills played almost as significant a role in buyer preference as did the age, health and stereotypical characters of slaves purchased. And such transferable attributes certainly shaped and sustained the Afro-American culture. Farming techniques from the African forest, such as rotational slash-and-burn and swidden agriculture, were of less use in North America than in the American tropics. But the drudgery of hoe cultivation – with its far from simple techniques of breaking, aerating ad irrigating the soil, planting and weeding – became as distinctive a feature of American slave plantations as of much West African farming. Even more direct carryovers were the knowledge of rice cultivation and cattle herding. The former made slaves from parts of Upper Guinea and the 'Inland Delta' of the Niger vital to the development of South Carolina. Expertise with cattle inclined planters to choose Africans from the pastoral cultures of the northern savanna, such as the Malinke, to manage their stock.

Of almost equal utility on the plantations were the wonderful skills in wood-working found throughout West Africa. Important too were the rarer, quasi-magical crafts of working in iron and other metals that gave black blacksmiths, even on plantations, mystery and reputation. Other West African crafts – of a sophistication lost on most whites, and denigrated or ignored by masters because they were not obviously valuable – also influenced the quality of life in the quarters. To different degrees in different places, these included sometimes interrelated skills and styles of carving, pottery, dyeing, weaving and basketry. Much the same held true of the richly varied and subtle traditions of music, drumming, dancing and folklore carried from Africa to the New World.

Afro-American slaves, however, exhibited an ethnic and cultural diversity far beyond variations in traditional technical and creative skills. This

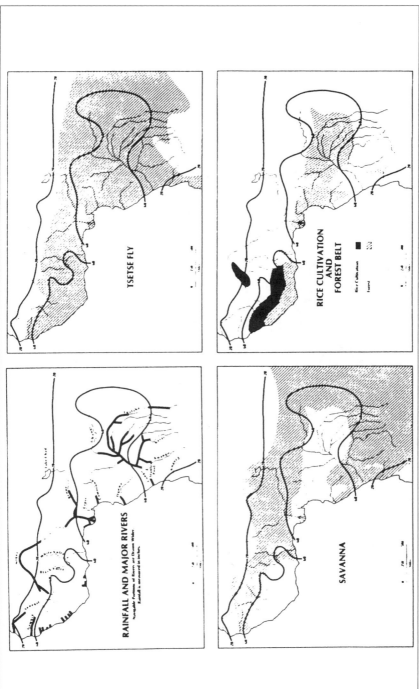

Figure 1: Latitudinal regions of West Africa shaped by amount of rainfall and seasonal variations

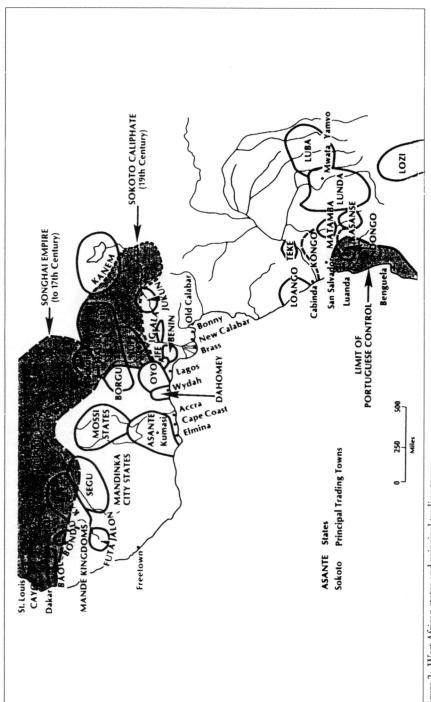

Figure 2: West African states and principal trading towns

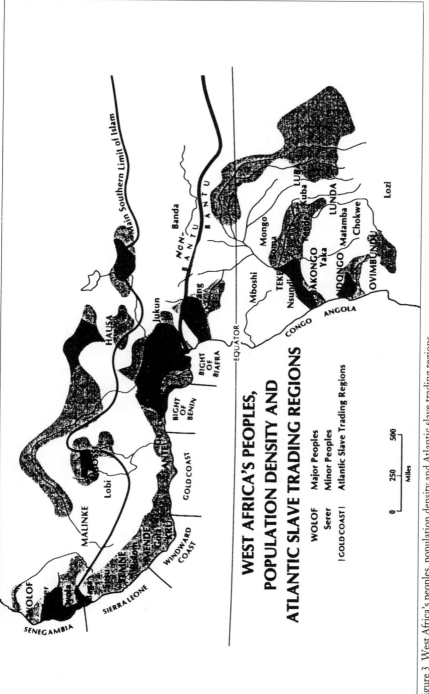

Figure 3 West Africa's peoples, population density and Atlantic slave trading regions

owed far less to planter preferences, or even African ecological variations, than to sociopolitical factors that, among other things, helped to determine which Africans should be delivered to the coast for trade. West African conditions, moreover, went through immense changes during the 400 years of the Atlantic slave trade, many of them resulting directly from the trade itself. It should be remembered, though, that the trade to North America occurred almost entirely within the second half of the process.

Perhaps the most important ethnic boundary in western Africa is the northern extent of Bantu-speaking people. This line coincides roughly with the Congo-Benue-Chad watershed and the Cameroon Mountains. Yet the basic distinction between the several hundred Bantu languages and dialects, and a similar number of non-Bantu languages, meant nothing to American planters. Much more important were the distinctions – owing as much to ecology as to the patterns of trade and warfare – between 'stateless' chieftainly or monarchical, and imperial systems of political organisation. Perhaps the most important boundary in the Atlantic slave trade era was the southern extent of the Islamic religion, with its fundamental sociopolitical and cultural implications.

In Bantu and non-Bantu West Africa alike, even in sovereign states, the basic units of political organisation were the village and the kinship group. Villages were clusters of family households, usually polygynous and patriarchal, but also internally interdependent. Within the household, the roles of women were multiple and vital, involving most of the lighter farming tasks, the tending of stock and marketing, as well as purely domestic chores. The men were engaged in the heavier farming tasks such as clearing new fields, in cattle husbandry, and in hunting and fishing. But men also monopolised the more important crafts and most of the creative arts. At seasonally busy times – such as the harvesting of grains – the whole household was employed together. Children were put to work from an early age in such light but important tasks as weeding, tending stock, or fetching water. These African village and household functions and traditions were easily carried over into North America, particularly where the slave quarters were well-integrated and family life was possible, or even encouraged.

With very close kinship links and internal ranks and canons of honour, reputation and seniority, African villages were in most respects self-sufficient. Broadly speaking, it was a peasant existence. Land was the common property of the folk, and concepts of freehold tenure were as strange to most Africans as was the notion of producing crops for surplus and export. Typically, village land was allocated to household heads, according to need and the ability to farm it. And the village was effectively governed by councils of elders, sometimes in parallel with quasi-religious 'secret societies'. Religion, indeed – contrary to the ignorant assertions of most European travellers – played an essential part in all African lives. It provided a satisfying explanation for natural phenomena, a means of intercession through priests exercising rituals of sorcery and magic, as well as, in most cases, a reinforcement of the social order.

A belief in a universal spirit continuum served as the common denominator in most African religions. This linked persons with the spirits of past kin and folk, as well as with those yet to be born. It also bound the spirits of humankind with all living things, and with numinous objects – rivers, springs, prominent rocks, or certain trees – generally regarded by Europeans as inanimate. Certain objects, locations, or phenomena were sacred, sometimes personified in a pantheon of lesser gods. Such, however, were always subordinate to a supreme spirit-principle, too vast and unimaginable to be easily personified.

The burial sites of kin – often located in the core of the village or even in the household compound – were especially sacred. So too were natural objects vital to the community (such as rivers, springs, or refuge-rocks), or places associated with the origins of the group in folk mythology. Precise structures of belief, pantheons of gods and forms of ritual extended beyond the narrowest groupings towards ethnic boundaries. These included associations of priests and initiates, and often the existence of a central oracle almost defined some larger ethnic units. Such ethnic entities were sometimes political units too, and imperial rule could even subsume different ethnicities. At the basic sociopolitical level, though, the individual villages were linked to contiguous units, more by concentric bands of wider kinship deriving from common lineage than by the need for trade or common defence. Considerable long-distance trade existed everywhere before the years of European contact. And village markets, concerned with local barter as part of larger commercial networks, served much as social meeting places, just as clannish confederacies were often the limit of political concentration. This was particularly true in areas – such as Iboland before the slave trade intensified – isolated by poor communications with no shortage of subsistence land and an absence of external enemies.

Elsewhere, however, more formal states emerged. These existed under dynastic rulers who, despite the often minuscule extent of their sway, were commonly accorded semi-divine, or at least mythically exotic status, buttressed by the authority of a priestly caste. Debate continues as to whether this system of dynastic monarchy developed from intrinsic forces, or as a result of wars of conquest and cumulative diffusion radiating from across Sudan. Certainly, the presence of ruling, leisured, warrior and priestly castes, and subordinate classes, including slaves, was usually associated with earlier migrations and wars of conquest. The size and effectiveness of West African states, moreover, related to the importance of trade. Commerce flowed by river or overland caravan, with important market towns at trade crossing places, large capital cities and in the Niger Delta even what might be termed commercial city-states.

The extent and power of West African states, at least until the Atlantic trade was under way, also tended to increase from the forest belt northwards and westwards towards the Sahara and Sudan, and southward into the savanna. In the north they reached their apogee in the areas of nomadic pastoralism, transhumance, frequent migrations and long-distance trade. It was here that the earliest known Sudanic kingdoms – Takrur, Ghana and Kanem – and their successors developed during the European medieval period. These were centred on Senegambia, the Upper Niger and Lake Chad. Large and sophisticated states – the sixteenth-century Songhai Empire being as extensive as Western Europe – were created by armies of camel or horse cavalry, with powerful dynastic rulers, nobles and priests. They were sustained by networks of trade that tapped gold, kola nuts and slaves from the forest belt partly in exchange for salt. Traders also distributed gold and slaves northwards to the Maghrib and Mediterranean, and eastwards to the Nile. From the tenth century onwards, their power was indissolubly related to the spread of Islam, with its tendency towards holy wars of conquest and the development of literacy and higher education. The Sudanic rulers administered large dispersed states and organised long-distance trades with complex credit machinery. They subsumed and refined, if they did not originate, racial and chattel slavery.

Although there had long been substantial kingdoms in the southern savanna, the coming of the Portuguese, with their Catholic religion, European weapons and growing demand for slaves, ushered in rapid political change. Indeed, north and south of the equator alike, the European opening up of the West African coast shifted the directions of trade. It also accelerated political changes – processes, though, that already were well established before the first slave cargo ever left for North America. Except for the Senegambian gateway to the Guinea goldfields and 'interior delta' of the Upper Niger, and the Congo-Kwango and Kwanza River routes deep into the interior of south-central Africa, the Atlantic slave trade affected mainly the area within 250 miles of the coast. It reinforced those African states that traded most effectively with the Europeans and, less directly, aided in the development of the more aggressive kingdoms through the import of firearms.

The chief of these changes south of the equator were the disruption, eclipse and eventual depopulation of the Bakongo Empire of Kongo. This resulted from pressures from all sides, the absorption of the Ndongo into a Portuguese sphere of influence, and the emergence of the Matamba and Kasenje kingdoms as powerful middlemen between the deep interior and the coast. The Portuguese developed a large-scale slave trade through Luanda, and likewise subverted the Ovimbundu in the service of the port of Benguela. Yet an even more active trade remained in African hands north of the Congo River – particularly that carried on by Loango with the help of Teke middlemen north of Stanley Pool.

North of the equator, similar processes saw limited European establishments along the coast – notably in Senegambia and on the Gold Coast. These led to the expansion or entrenchment of African polities – such as Benin, the city-states of the Niger Delta and numerous small states on the Upper Guinea Coast – that functioned as independent middlemen. The most spectacular changes, though, during the seventeenth and eighteenth centuries were the parallel, and partly conflicting rise of Asante, Dahomey and Oyo. They expanded at the expense of their neighbours both towards the coast and inland.

In almost all cases, this process of political ferment exacerbated the indigenous system of slavery, whether directly to satisfy the rising Atlantic demand for slaves, or as an incidental by-product of state-building wars. True, as Philip D. Curtin and others have suggested, the Atlantic slave trade as a whole may not have resulted in a net decline in the African population. Nevertheless, much local depopulation and demoralisation resulted. Many societies were disrupted by increasing slave raiding from outside. And others, such as the Kingdom of Kongo or the Tio north of Stanley Pool, were dispersed when kings and traders sold their own free peoples to European traders.

Virtually all Africans carried to America were familiar with one form or another of slavery. But very few had experienced the extreme form of hereditary chattel slavery involving intense exploitative labour and social alienation that evolved in the Americas. Exceptions included those mainly Muslim savanna areas where slaves were needed for labour-intensive enterprises such as gold or salt mining, or were shipped as commodities in distant markets themselves, carrying other commodities on their heads. In time there were even some plantations growing crops for export, as in the Sokoto Caliphate of Upper Nigeria, where slaves toiled in the fields in gangs and lived in separate quarters. In an almost exact parallel with plantation America, their masters provided them with one or two days off per week to work their own provision grounds.

Even so, few such Muslim slaves were transported to the Atlantic Coast, and traditional slavery in the areas most tapped was generally of a more 'domestic' kind. Nearly all African slaves belonged to a caste whose separate status reflected earlier conquests and subjugations. Almost by definition, slaves belonged outside the tribal lineage. But they were usually valued and protected members of the community nonetheless. They could even rise to wealth and power by fulfilling roles – military, commercial, priestly or administrative – denied to members of the lineage. African slaves, indeed, were rarely sold after the first generation of enslavement. There was a reluctance as well to sell women of any kind because of their value as brides.

Who then were the Africans sold to the Europeans in the Atlantic trade? The best recent estimates conclude that at least half were war captives. Less than one-third were acquired by 'normal processes' – through 'lawful conviction of crime, indebtedness, dependency and various types of servitude'. The remaining one-sixth were made up of 'kidnap victims, strangers and unfortunates'. The American slave owners' preference for males (which was reflected in slave prices in the Americas) was congruent with the Africans' desire to retain enslaved females (whose value as brides was reflected in their invariably higher prices within Africa itself). As Paul E. Lovejoy has calculated, of all slaves carried to the Americas, 14 per cent were children under 14 years of age, 56 per cent were adult males, and only 30 per cent were adult females. This resulted in an overall predominance of 63 per cent males to 37 per cent females. Put in other terms, Lovejoy computed that of these Africans available for enslavement, 46 per cent of females between the ages of 14 and 30 (who represented 25 per cent of the total) were retained in Africa. But virtually all men in that age range (amounting to another 25 per cent of the total) were exported. of all children under 14 (representing 30 per cent of the total), only 21 per cent were exported. Virtually none of the mature adults (20 per cent of those available) were exported.

Clearly, slave traders favoured the stronger and healthier elements in the African population. And it is significant to note that many of the least fit failed to survive the rigorous journey to the coast by coffle or canoe. The rigour of their transportation suggest an artificial factor that might have given the Africans an advantage over the more chance-chosen European migrants. Yet there were other physical characteristics of the slaves brought to North America that had important implications for the Afro-American slave population. Recent research shows that African slaves were on the average perceptibly shorter not only than Europeans, but also than their own Creole descendants. African slaves aged between 25 and 40 imported into the West Indies in the first decade of the nineteenth century, for example, averaged 5 feet 4¼ inches for males, and 5 feet 0¼ inches for females. This was no less than 3¼ inches and 2¼ inches shorter, respectively, than American slaves (Africans as well as Creoles) in the same age range between 1828 and 1860. This differential may have been even greater in the earlier years of the traffic, before new food crops began to improve the West Indian diet.

The maturation of Africans, moreover, was slower than that of American-born bondsmen. African males apparently reached maximum height around 20 years of age, more than a year later than male Creole slaves. And the age of menarche in African females, at over 18 years, occurred as much as two years later than for Creole blacks, and even more than that for European females at that time. In addition, the low percentage of females carried to America, the effects of dislocation, the carryover of the common African custom of prolonged lactation, and the fact that female slaves in Africa tended towards a very low fertility rate, explain the comparatively low birthrate of African-born slaves in the Americas. At the same time, though, because the climatic regime in North America was healthier than in Africa itself, these deficiencies were less critical in North America than in the Caribbean and Latin America. As fewer slaves died the percentage of Africans needed rapidly grew less, and the proportion of African-born slaves in North America fell below 10 per cent as early as 1750. Two other demographic factors also contributed significantly to the impact of the African heritage of American slaves. First, throughout the slave-trade period slaves from different African ethnicities were inextricably mixed. And, second, even in the plantation colonies and states, the blacks never outnumbered the white free settlers. Altogether, these forces explain why the African background faded and a distinctive Afro-American identity surfaced more quickly in North America than anywhere else in the hemisphere.

BIBLIOGRAPHY

J. F. Ade Ajayi and Michael Crowder (eds), *History of West Africa*, 2nd ed., 1976.

Philip D. Curtin, *The Atlantic Slave Trade: A Census*, 1969.

Philip D. Curtin, *Economic Change in Precolonial Africa: Senegambia in the Era of the Slave Trade*, 1975.

Philip D. Curtin *et al.*, *African History*, 1978.

Richard Gray (ed.), *The Cambridge History of Africa*, Vol. 4; *From c. 1600 to c. 1790*, 1975.

Ronald James Harrison Church *et al.*, *Africa and the Islands*, 3rd ed., 1971.

Jean Hiernaux, *The People of Africa*, 1975.

Ray A. Kea, *Settlements, Trade and Politics in the Seventeenth Century Gold Coast*, 1982.

Igor Kopytoff and Suzanne Miers (eds), *Slavery in Africa: Historical and Anthropological Perspectives*, 1977.

M. Kwamena-Poh *et al.*, *African History in Maps*, 1982.

Robin Law, *The Oyo Empire c. 1600-c. 1836: A West African Imperialism in the Era of the Atlantic Slave Trade*, 1977.

Paul E. Lovejoy, *Transformations in Slavery: A History of Slavery in Africa*, 1983.

David Northrup, *Trade without Rulers: Pre-Colonial Economic Development in South-Eastern Nigeria*, 1978.

Claire C. Robertson and Martin A. Klein (eds), *Women and Slavery in Africa*, 1983.

8

Slavery and Slave Society in the British Caribbean

Introduction: Written for a general encyclopedia of slavery edited by Seymour Drescher and Stanley Engerman to be published in 1998, this essay can be regarded both as an up-to-date introductory overview and as a glossary of the concepts currently regarded as of salient importance by the author. Distinguishing the slavery of the British West Indies from other forms, it stresses the distinctions between true slave colonies and mere slaveowning colonies, between the slave systems of sugar plantation, non-sugar plantation and non-plantation colonies, between types of slaves, and between slaves as economic units and as human beings. Besides defining such key current terms and concepts as slave society, plantocracy, creolisation, proto-peasants and proto-proletarians, the essay introduces such hotly debated issues as slave resistance versus accommodation, the reasons for abolition, amelioration, apprenticeship and emancipation, and even the fact of the ex-slaves once nominally freed. It includes a short selective bibliography up-to-date in 1996.

Africans were enslaved in all the English colonies of the Caribbean region virtually from the beginning, and black slavery became the predominant system of labour from the time it superseded the use of Amerindians and white indentured 'servants' in the mid-seventeenth century, until emancipation was enforced in 1834-38. The slave labour system involved a trade in blacks from West Africa that suddenly surged with the introduction of large-scale sugar cultivation and increased along with the expansion of plantations to reach an annual peak of around 38,000 before the abolition of the trade in 1807. Because of the deadly climate and diseased environment as much as the harsh work regime and overt cruelty, a traffic totalling some 2 million over 180 years left a population of no more than 670,000 slaves in 1834 (compared with a slave population of 3 million in the USA in 1865 from some 400,000 imported), but these still outnumbered resident whites by nearly ten to one, and the intermediate class of non-white free persons in similar proportion.

The English colonies of the Caribbean region were not only scattered but extremely diverse. Largely as a consequence, their slavery systems (as well as differing from those of the other imperial powers) also varied in important ways; broadly according to the type and intensity of the economic system, but more subtly according to the time when, and the circumstances under which, each colony was acquired, its relative stage and pace of development, and the form of its government. The majority were plantation colonies, and sugar (with its by-products, molasses and rum) was much and most important crop, accounting for as much as 80 per cent of exports by value. But geographical factors such as mountains, low rainfall or sparse soils determined a degree of diversification (cotton, coffee, spices, stock animals, provisions), and some of the colonies acquired later, despite their fertility, had not fully developed plantations before the slave trade or slavery ended. Besides this, there were non-plantation or marginal colonies, dedicated to maritime activity (Bermuda, Bahamas), logwood cutting (Belize), salt production (Turks & Caicos) and turtling (Caymans).

Politically, all English Caribbean colonies can be termed 'plantocracies' in that the white slave-owners ruled, although there were subtle variations between colonies that were English from the beginning and those acquired later from the French or Dutch, and the fact that planters made their own laws in most colonies led to subtle legal variations within a broad general pattern. Towards the end of slavery an important distinction also occurred between the original self-legislating colonies and those acquired during the Napoleonic Wars which were directly ruled as Crown Colonies, and thus came more under the influence of an increasingly liberal Colonial Office.

Sociologically, however, just as all were true slave rather than mere 'slave-owning' colonies, all English Caribbean colonies were 'slave societies' in the sense defined by Elsa Goveia; that despite the whites' pretensions to be a socially distinct elite, the entire social fabric was shaped by the slavery system, encompassing whites and free non-whites as well as the slaves themselves. Slave society, though, was by no means static, and the overarching process was that termed creolisation, in both its demographic and cultural aspects. Confusingly, the adjective creole has often been applied narrowly either to local whites or to persons of mixed race; but more conveniently it describes all persons (or even animals) not indigenously native but born and bred in the region, as well as aspects of the creoles' locally shaped and essentially syncretic culture. As a process, the term creolisation is used both for the gradual increase in the proportion of creoles in the population (blacks and whites who were no longer true Africans or Europeans, as well as persons of mixed race), and for the equally gradual evolution of their distinct regional culture. In its limited and covert way, racial miscegenation was the most extreme, but by no means a necessary feature of creolisation. The most general notable aspect of cultural creolisation – which can stand as a paradigm for all other aspects – was the evolution out of the slavetraders' pidgin of a genuine creole language (or rather languages, for every colony had its own); a *lingua franca* in which, as befitted the origins of masters and slaves, the lexicon was predominantly European, while much of the grammar, sentence structure and intonation was generically, and some of the vocabulary specifically, African in derivation.

The slave codes which the plantocrats constructed could derive little except general concepts of property, punishment and the control of labour out of an English legal system from which the ideas of chattel slavery and serfdom had long since faded. Instead, the slave laws of the English colonies (which, unlike those of the other imperial powers, were not codified until the last years of the eighteenth century, when each self-legislating colony passed its own Consolidated Slave Act) reflected the planters' pragmatic needs and prejudices as well as borrowing from Roman Law principles found in the Spanish *siete partidas* and the French *code noir*. The general purposes of these laws were simple: to define slaves as chattel, to restrict their mobility, to control their lives and work, and to punish them for infractions. In many islands, slaves were defined as real estate so that they could be tied to their owners' other goods, chattels and land. Everywhere, manumission was made almost impossible; the uterine law that children inherited their mother's status was generally adopted; and strict pass laws and savage punishments were enacted for running away, as well as for acts of sabotage, insubordination and overt resistance.

Until the late eighteenth century laws remained on the books decreeing or permitting mutilation, and execution by slow burning or starving to death in gibbets for the worst offenses. However, the inequity and impracticality of the laws (punishing runaways with lashes but their harbourers with death, slave insolence with death but white slave-murderers with fines; never quite determining whether a slave as a chattel could actually commit a crime like theft) meant that usage and custom were always more important, and generally more lenient, than enacted slave laws, and that when 'ameliorative' laws were introduced under metropolitan pressure from the 1780s they were mostly dead letters, simply enacted what had long been customary, or endorsed changes – such as the wholesale adoption and adaptation of Christianity by the slaves – that were occurring independently.

In the age of the buccaneers, slaves were acquired from foreign plantations or ships, but as English plantations developed, the West African trade was formalised through a series of chartered monopoly companies of which the Royal African Company (1672-1750) was the most important. In contrast to the continuing protection afforded sugar and other plantation products (thanks to a powerful lobby of merchants and planters), slave-trading was deregulated and thrown open to free trade by 1712 – partly explaining, perhaps, why the slave trade lost its imperial support and was abolished a quarter of a century before the institution of slavery itself.

The lethal process of acclimatisation called seasoning (which carried off nearly half of all new slaves within three years), as well as the steady expansion of plantations throughout the slavery era, ensured the vigorous continuation of the slave trade until 1807 and the consequently continuous cultural links with Mother Africa. Yet the wealth of African retentions and degree of creolisation varied greatly at any given time. Barbados and the marginal colonies, having become economically fully developed or static and demographically self-sustaining, no longer needed African imports, and as many as 90 per cent of their slaves were creoles when the African slave trade ended. On the other hand, 37 per cent of Jamaican slaves were still African-born as late as 1817, and those of Trinidad and Guyana (where the labour demand was exacerbated by a natural decrease in the slave population of around 15 per thousand a year) no more than 45 per cent were colony-born.

The slaves' lives were shaped by the dominant economy and their culture reshaped by the creolisation process, but within the variations of their Caribbean environment and assigned functions, the slaves preserved what they could of their existential identity, and in fact increased their own contribution to the English Caribbean economy and culture as the institution of slavery ran its course.

Domestic and town slaves lived in smaller groups in closer proximity to their white masters, and tended to experience a more intimate intercourse with them, than did the majority of slaves who lived on large plantations. Mariner and woodcutting crews also enjoyed to a degree the essential freemasonry of the sea and interior forests – their relative freedom being a transactional equation based on the comparative ease with which they could abscond or arm themselves. Yet such a large proportion of English Caribbean slaves lived their whole lives within the sizeable community and closely guarded cellular bounds of a single plantation, that the plantation may be taken as the quintessential form of their existence.

At the apex of the plantation hierarchy, the owner, known by the slaves as Massa, was often an absentee (most commonly in Jamaica, least in Barbados) and could therefore exercise aristocratic luxuries, even noblesse oblige. When resident, he occupied a so-called Great House, proprietarily overlooking his land, slaves and factory. The harsher realities, however, were handled by subordinate whites; attorney-managers (generally resident in the colonial capital), overseers and undermanagers called bookkeepers. Those whites set in immediate authority were an isolated and beleaguered minority, non-gentlemen of limited education, dissolute and shiftless for the most part, outnumbered fifty to one by their charges, tied by contract and the requirement to make a profit, with only the parlous rewards of power to offset unpleasant work in a harsh climate, the ever-present threat of lethal or crippling disease, and the perils of insurrection.

As far as the plantation management was concerned, slaves were graded according to their usefulness, which was roughly equivalent to their monetary valuation. The able-bodied labourers were divided into three or more gangs by age and strength with little regard to gender, with only the roughly 10 per cent who were hopelessly diseased, senile or under six years of age regarded as unproductive. Yet even within the managers' own formulation there was a complex implied hierarchy which separated out the domestics and those of mixed race from the labourers, the factory workers and artisans from the field workers, and gave at least some delegated, if reversible, authority to trusted slave headmen. Africans were regarded as inferior to creoles only to the degree that they were less acculturated, with fewer useful skills or amenable attitudes. That field headmen were often Africans rather than creoles, however, suggested that there was an underlying hierarchy among the slaves that owed more to traditional canons of reputation than to the simple economic imperatives of the plantation. In that fraction of the day, week and year that the slaves had to themselves, and within their own quarters and grounds, they fashioned a social, economic and cultural life of which the masters were largely ignorant or dismissive, but which came to have a critical effect on plantation life and culture as a whole before slavery ended.

Much of this influence went unnoticed not just because it was so gradual but because it was syncretic and thus more easily accepted by the whites, or even assimilated by them. Besides strongly influencing the development of creole languages, Africans introduced new foods and methods of cooking, and new music and modes of dancing that employed European as well as African instruments and adapted European measures and rhythms. African festivals and festival forms such as Crop-over and Junkanoo were melded to European celebrations like Harvest Home, Carnival or Christmas mumming. African games, folklore, proverbs and even beliefs also found their way into the creole culture.

Even more significant was the way that the English Caribbean slaves adopted and adapted Christianity. Unlike the slaves of the Catholic imperial powers, the English slaves were not actively proselytised from the beginning, and the established Anglican Church was regarded as mainly for whites, as well, as in England, as having a secular role in local government and society. The Anglican Church had considerable success in attracting slaves in Barbados and Antigua, and there were many nominally Catholic slaves in the colonies acquired from France and Spain after 1763. But when nonconformist missionaries – the first invited by planters in the expectation that they would have a socialising or 'civilising' function – became widely active from the 1780s onwards, the great majority of English Caribbean slaves became baptised Christians. As the more perceptive (mainly Anglican) planters recognised, however, the majority of slaves were attracted to theologies and liturgies that were mostly consonant with African beliefs and practices, as well as to the more participatory churches. Most popular of all were the Baptists of Jamaica and the Bahamas, whose first congregations were formed by evangelical slave preachers who had come from the mainland with their Loyalist owners after 1783, a whole generation before white Baptist missionaries appeared on the scene from England.

Most important of all, however, was the influence that the slaves themselves had on English Caribbean socioeconomic patterns both during and after slavery. Despite the intentional jumbling of Africans by the traders and slave-owners, Afro-Caribbean slaves quickly reconstituted kinship networks, beginning as early as the 'shipmate bond' yet soon reinforced by more or less inevitable endogamy and the sense of belonging to a localised plantation community. Contrary to the arguments of some scholars that slave sales inevitably broke up families and that family dysfunction was increased by sexual relations between slave women and whites that were tantamount to prostitution and rape, English Caribbean slaves had a strong commitment to the immediate family, in which the roles of father and mother owed more to African traditions of domestic economy than to any concern on the masters' part.

Of fundamental importance in this respect were the ways in which slave mothers dominated in the domestic economy in and around the family house, and that slave families were able to control and exploit the provision grounds they were allotted by their owners. Slaves cultivated gardens and raised small stock around their hutments, and on some plantations there were 'shell blow' grounds near the canefields where slaves were set to grow provision crops during the mid-day breaks. But slave family heads were assigned more extensive grounds wherever there was sufficient and sufficiently cultivable land on the margins of the areas most suitable for planting export crops. It was clearly in the owners' interest for the slaves to be as self-supporting in food as possible, but many slaves went much further. Working as families in the evenings and one and a half days at weekends when they were released from plantation labour (and surely working with greater enthusiasm than ever for their owners), they raised small stock, fruits and surplus ground provisions, collected wild produce and made simple craft items. These goods were marketed, particularly by the slave women who carried them for sale to the Sunday markets in town, to informal markets at plantation intersections, or even to their own owners. The money received was used to purchase small semi-luxuries (such as crockery, cutlery, glassware, mirrors and combs), or fancier items of clothing than were issued by their owners, from itinerant peddlers or market stall-holders. So prevalent did the system of informal slave production and marketing become (most notably in Jamaica) that scholars, following the lead of Sidney Mintz, commonly refer to slaves in the late slave period as proto-peasants. One Marxist, Ciro Cardoso, has even referred to 'the peasant breach in the slave mode of production'.

Other scholars, like Mary Turner, Nigel Bolland and Howard Johnson, bearing in mind that the fate (if not the ideal) of ex-slaves was to fill the ranks of that peculiarly Caribbean hybrid class of 'part-peasant, part-proletarian', have stressed the ways in which slaves organised themselves to challenge and mitigate the terms under which they worked and to receive fixed rewards, even cash for work beyond the normal call, to the degree that we may call them proto-proletarians. Considering what slaves did with the money they earned to ease the poverty of their material life – and thus contribute in a small way to the incorporation of the plantation periphery into the industrialising world – one might even go as far as to term them proto-consumers. In all three ways of anticipating later trends slaves probably contributed almost as much to the transition out of slavery as did any external actors or forces, quite apart from what they did to discredit and bring down slavery by manifold more aggressive forms of resistance.

The simplest, earliest and least effective way to work slaves was to form them into gangs and force them to labour under duress as long as was physically possible. The general substitution for pure gang labour of fixed daily tasks –after which slaves would be free, to rest or labour for themselves as they willed – was an early recognition that slaves worked better under some form of incentive. As time went on, slaves showed great enterprise in reducing the size of tasks that could reasonably be expected, and in raising the level of incentives by playing upon their managers' need to maximise their labour. At one extreme, slaves in Bermuda and the Bahamas helped to crew privateers during wartime, but would only fight with a will if they received a seaman's share of the booty. In all colonies, surplus and skilled slaves were often hired out, and were usually able to command a share of their hire in return for performing satisfactorily. Some were even allowed to hire themselves out and simply pay their owner for the privilege. Even on the strictest plantations, the levels of tasks and rewards (including more time to work the grounds) became so customary that managers risked virtual strikes, or even a sacking from the attorney or owner, if they attempted to extract more than was practicable from their charges.

Beyond the transactional calculus of such primitive industrial relations was the fearsome threat of escalating forms of slave resistance: from malingering, recalcitrance and running away, to arson, cattle-maiming and other acts of sabotage; through individual acts of violence against the whites (including poisoning and the casting of African spells), to widening plots, and the ultimate horror of a general slave uprising. Although there was never a completely successful slave revolt in the English Caribbean like that in Haiti (1791-1804), it is clear that English slaves, like those everywhere, perennially resisted their enslavement however they could; that they rose up 'whenever they could or had to' (for example, when the forces of control were weakened or distracted by war, or when the slaves were driven intolerably); and that their resistance, ultimately, drove home the impracticality of slavery as a labour system compared with its alternatives.

Overt slave resistance in the English Caribbean, as elsewhere in plantation America, went through several distinct phases. The earliest manifestations involved mass running away and the forming of obdurate maroon communities in the forested and mountainous interior, sometimes cooperating with Amerindian survivors. Fighting when they had to, maroons forced the planters into making treaties, although these were not permanently honoured by the whites. The fierce Black Caribs of St Vincent and the maroons of Dominica were not finally subdued until the 1790s, while the Bush Negroes and maroons of the Guianese and Belizean riverine hinterlands were able to survive permanently beyond the reach of planter imperialism. The fate of the most famous maroons of the English Caribbean, those of Jamaica, was rather more equivocal. They fought a successful guerrilla war against the colonial regime in the 1730s, but were divided by the subsequent treaties of accommodation. The more troublesome Leeward maroons were expelled to Nova Scotia and Sierra Leone after a second war in the 1790s, but the remaining maroons retained a nominal independence as the planters' allies to the end of slavery and beyond, keeping a distinct if fading cultural identity right up to the present day.

While African-born slaves remained the majority, African-led revolts were the worst threat to plantocratic hegemony, particularly when Akan-speaking 'Coromantine' slaves from the warrior culture of Ghana were involved. The most serious such crisis was the islandwide Coramantine-led rebellion of 1760 in Jamaica, which occurred when British forces were heavily engaged in the Seven Years' War. Subsequent plots and localised uprisings were weakened by divisions in aims and leadership between African and creole slaves, and the worldwide ferment that included the American, French and Haitian revolutions did not lead to a general slave uprising throughout the English Caribbean, both because British naval and military forces were heavily mobilised, and because a majority of English slaves were persuaded to stay neutral or actually to fight for the regime by promises, largely unfulfilled, or ameliorated conditions of manumission.

To the consternation of the English planters, however, the progressive creolisation of their slaves did not lessen the incidence of overt rebellion, but rather the reverse. As the creole slaves became gradually more aware of philanthropic allies in Britain, and of a changing climate of opinion about slavery in the British Parliament, the three most serious slave revolts occurred in the three most important sugar plantation colonies of the British Caribbean: in Barbados in 1816; in Demerara (British Guiana) in 1823; and in Jamaica in 1831-82. These involved tens of thousands of slaves, led by the most creolised and trusted slave headmen, who in the latter two cases included black Christian deacons. What the rebels wanted above all, of course, was freedom from chattel slavery. But there is overwhelming evidence that they did not seek violence, retribution or the destruction of the plantation system. Rather, they wanted the freedom of choice to live either as free townsfolk, or more like free peasants, retaining the option of working for wages how, when and only for as long as it suited them.

All three rebellions were suppressed with bloody savagery. Planters and imperial conservatives alike were convinced that slavery must continue and that less rather than more leniency was called for. Yet in the British parliamentary debates rising to a climax even as the Jamaican insurrection occurred, the philanthropic minority was joined by two types of realists: those economic liberals who believed with Adam Smith that a system of competitive wage labour was superior to the coercion of slavery, and those who were convinced that if freedom of this kind were not granted from above, it would be seized from below, and the very existence of the colonial empire in the Caribbean jeopardised. In these respects, therefore, the slaves of the British Caribbean can be said to have contributed to their own emancipation.

Emancipation for all slaves in the British Caribbean (as well as South Africa, Mauritius and Ceylon) was decreed by the imperial Parliament a year in advance, to come into effect at midnight on July 31, 1834. It was endorsed by the colonial legislatures with a promptitude spurred by the fear of losing the monetary compensation voted for the owners (not, of course, for the slaves), and the right to impose a transitional period of compulsory labour called apprenticeship. Apprenticeship was designed to last six years but in the event was terminated after four. This was partly because it proved unworkable and provoked scandal, but mainly because it was deemed unnecessary. The legislators of Bermuda and Antigua, where there was no spare land and ex-slaves had no option but to work for their former owners, even chose to forgo apprenticeship altogether. As the disciples of Adam Smith predicted, labour relations fell into a natural pattern without regulation or physical coercion, although only in colonies with a surplus of land and a shortage of workers were these conditions even remotely favourable to the ex-slaves.

With their numbers for the first time increasing everywhere, the ex-slaves of the British Caribbean and their descendants were faced with a rapidly declining economy, an increasingly indifferent imperial government, and a local ruling class able to sustain its hegemony through the control of land and commerce, if not also, absolutely, the structure of local politics. Although still proudly struggling to construct a life of their own and intermittently continuing the fight against oppression, in an age driven by *laisser-fair* ideas as well as the racist distortions of Social Darwinism, formal slavery's black legatees were condemned to a century or more of a different, and scarcely preferable, form of involuntary servitude, while the racism that stemmed from the correlation between functional, class and ethnic divisions was an even longer-lived legacy.

BIBLIOGRAPHY

Hilary Beckles, *Natural Rebels: A Social History of Enslaved Black Women in Barbados*, New Brunswick, NJ, 1989; *White Servitude and Black Slavery in Barbados, 1627-1715*, Knoxville, TN, 1989.

Hilary Beckles and Verene Shepherd, *Caribbean Slave Society and Economy: A Student Reader*, Kingston, 1993.

Nigel Bolland, 'Systems of Domination after Slavery: The Control of Land and Labor in the British West Indies after 1838', *Comparative Studies in Society and History*, 23, 4, 1981, 591-619.

Edward K. Brathwaite, *The Development of Creole Society in Jamaica, 1770-1820*, Oxford, 1971.

Barbara Bush, *Slave Women in Caribbean Society, 1650-1838*, Bloomington, IN, 1990.

Ciro F. S. Cardoso, 'The Peasant Breach in the Slave System: New Developments in Brazil', *Luso-Brazilian Review*, 25, 1988, 49-57.

Frederic G. Cassidy, *Jamaica Talk: Three Hundred Years of the English Language in Jamaica*, Kingston, 1961.

Michael Craton, *Sinews of Empire: A Short History of British Slavery*, New York, 1974; *Searching for the Invisible Man: Slaves and Plantation Life in Jamaica*, Cambridge, MA, 1978; *Testing the Chains: Resistance to Slavery in the British West Indies*, Ithaca, 1982; 'Reshuffling the Pack: The Transition from Slavery to Other Forms of Labour in the British Caribbean, c. 1790-1890', *Nieuwe Westindische Gids*, 1995.

Philip D. Curtin, *The Atlantic Slave Trade: A Census*, Madison, 1969.

Richard S. Dunn, *Sugar and Slaves: The Rise of the Planter Class in the English West Indies, 1624-1713*, Chapel Hill, NC, 1972.

Barry Gaspar, *Bondmen and Rebels: A Study of Master-Slave Relations in Antigua*, Baltimore, MD, 1985.

Elsa Goveia, *Slave Society in the British Leeward Islands at the End of the Eighteenth Century*, New Haven CT, 1965.

Douglas Hall, *In Miserable Slavery: Thomas Thistlewood in Jamaica, 1750-86*, Basingstoke, 1989.

Barry W. Higman, *Slave Populations of the British Caribbean, 1807-1834*, Baltimore, MD, 1984.

Howard Johnson, *The Bahamas in Slavery and Freedom*, Kingston, 1991.

Kenneth Kiple, *The Caribbean Slave: A Biological History*, Cambridge, 1984.

Roderick McDonald, *The Economy and Material Culture of Slaves: Goods and Chattels on the Sugar Plantations of Jamaica and Louisiana*, Baton Rouge, 1993.

Sidney Mintz, *Caribbean Transformations*, Chicago, 1974.

Richard Pares, *A West Indian Fortune*, London, 1936.

Orlando H. Patterson, *The Sociology of Slavery: An Analysis of the Origins, Development and Structure of Negro Slave Society in Jamaica*, London, 1967.

Frank W. Pitman, *The Development of the British West Indies, 1700-1763*, New Haven, CT, 1917.

Lowell J. Ragatz, *The Fall of the Planter Class in the British West Indies, 1763-1833*, New York, 1928.

Richard B. Sheridan, *Sugar and Slavery: An Economic History of the British West Indies, 1623-1775*, Baltimore, MD, 1974; *Doctors and Slaves: A Medical and Demographic History of Slavery in the British West Indies, 1680-1834*, New York, 1985.

Mary Turner, *Slaves and Missionaries: The Disintegration of Jamaican Slave Society, 1787-1834*, Urbana, IL, 1982.

John R. Ward, *British West Indian Slavery, 1750-1834: The Process of Amelioration*, Oxford, 1988.

Eric E. Williams, *Capitalism and Slavery*, London, 1944.

9

Jamaican Slavery

Introduction: This fairly early work, a contribution to the landmark slavery conference held at Rochester, New York in 1974, had as its main task to show how Jamaican slavery was as distinct from that of other British West Indian colonies as US slavery was from those of the Caribbean and Brazil. It does indeed provide an accurate and comprehensive a survey of Jamaican slavery as was then available, but is perhaps most interesting now as an enthusiastic compendium of ideas and methods, many of which were new at the time and later proved useful in the analysis of slave systems elsewhere and at large. One paradox proposed is that the asperities of slavery may have been mitigated by the masters' sense of proprietorship over their slaves as well as their land, and by the Creole slaves' growing sense of belonging to the plantation where they lived all their lives. Less controversial, probably the chief of the new methods was the use of comparative and sequential age profiles of slave populations, pioneered in an article in the *Journal of Caribbean History* in 1971. It is hoped that the fact that the 1971 JCH article has been more often praised than any of my others betokens an unfair neglect of my later offerings, rather than an actual decline in their quality!

In the eighteenth century – for ideological purposes and with dubious accuracy – British slavery was carefully differentiated by British writers from that of other European imperialisms, almost invariably to Britain's advantage. At the same time, Jamaica, being the richest British colony of the type regarded as the most valuable during the mercantilist period, tended to be treated as the British colonial norm, in slavery as in other respects.[1] In this century, a similar imperialism of scholarship has tended to generalise from American mainland slavery – particularly that of the cotton plantations in the nineteenth century – for slavery throughout the

British Empire as well, if not for all slavery.[2] This tide has recently been reversed, most notably by Eugene Genovese in *The World the Slaveholders Made*.[3] The model of a pre-industrial (or extra-industrial), pre-bourgeois culture, paternalistically closed, in which profitability was less important than social reciprocation between masters and slaves, was perhaps plausible in the nineteenth-century US context. But it could not be traced equally in the earlier 'slave societies' of the British West Indies, with their practical absence of a recognisable master-culture, their absentee owners and exploitative managers both exceedingly interested in profitability and uninterested in the slaves as human beings, and their indubitably alienated blacks.

The result of this revisionism, however, has been to treat the British Caribbean once more too generically. The time has now arrived to show the ways in which Jamaican slavery was peculiarly different from that of other British West Indies colonies, conditioned by differences of geography, topography, historical morphology and demography. It is also necessary to concentrate on the relatively undocumented Jamaican slavery of the eighteenth century, since the period between the ending of the slave trade in 1807 and the emancipation of the slaves in 1838 about which most is known because records and accounts proliferated, or even the period after 1787 when general amelioration laws were first passed, were not typical of Jamaican slavery but significantly atypical.

Situated about 1,000 miles to leeward of those small islands of the Lesser Antilles which the earliest British colonists found most accessible, defensible and developable as plantations, Jamaica was not acquired until Britain had a firm base in the Caribbean, and could not be exploited properly until the demands of Barbados and the Leewards for capital, labour and shipping had more or less been satisfied. Consequently, in its first settlement and in the development of sugar plantations, Jamaica lagged behind by about 30 years, and even after it became the richest British island always suffered from the anxieties, delays and higher prices for slaves and other imported commodities which followed from its geographical location.[4]

For other reasons Jamaica's development was not only telescoped but never really completed until the sugar industry passed its apogee around 1755. Jamaica was to remain the largest island developed by the British during the mercantilist period, containing half the population of the British West Indies and responsible for a like share of Britain's Caribbean production and profit, and with some of its 1,000 sugar growing estates situated as far as 25 miles inland. Yet although it contained at least 1.5 million cultivable acres, Jamaica was densely forested and riven with mountains and impenetrable tropical *karst* 'cockpit' country.[5] These were all the more difficult to tame by the presence of maroons and their runway recruits, who resisted encroachment until 1739 and final reduction until 1796. Ten times as close to Spanish Cuba and French Saint Domingue as to other British colonies, Jamaica was also very vulnerable to outside attack, particularly until two trans-island carriage roads were completed in the later eighteenth century. In all these senses Jamaica remained a dynamic 'frontier' society even after Barbados and the Leewards were stabilised and stagnant.

Unlike the islets first colonised, Jamaica was large enough almost to swallow the limited number of whites who were willing to settle there and able to survive. Its original settlement was made by the survivors of the 'conquering' army of 1655, who almost immediately established an aristocracy on Harringtonian lines, in which political power, landowning and rank in the militia were closely matched. Capital and labour poor, these shabby oligarchs were land rich, having been able selfishly to pre-empt huge acreages long before development was possible. This retarded progress early, but once the 'takeoff' occurred around 1730 – chiefly through improvements in credit and marketing machinery and the supply of African slaves – the transition to a socioeconomic system dominated by slave sugar plantations was not only rapid but also remarkably uniform. This process was aided by the fact that by that time sugar husbandry and technology, if not slave management as well, had become more or less standardised throughout the Caribbean.[6]

Although, as the largest in size and population, Jamaica after 1750 had more townsmen than any other British West Indian colony, the proportion of its population in rural areas, about 90 per cent, was if anything even higher than elsewhere. Jamaica, however, did not develop quite the degree of sugar monoculture suffered by the smaller islands to the windward. In 1774, Edward Long estimated that besides 680 sugar plantations, there were 600 'polinks and provision places', 500 'breeding pens', 150 coffee, 110 cotton and 30 ginger plantations, 100 pimento walks, and eight indigo works.[7] Nineteen years later, Bryan Edwards claimed that besides 767 sugar plantations there were 607 coffee estates and no less than 1,047 grazing pens, as well as innumerable smallholdings.[8]

These figures, however, are somewhat misleading and a clear picture would emerge only if the size of each unit, its ownership and relationship to others were fully analysed. The majority of provision grounds and a high proportion of the pens listed by Long and Edwards were probably tied directly to the sugar plantations. Moreover, most of the coffee, cotton, ginger, pimento and indigo plantations were small and, like the unspecified smallholdings, many grew sugar as well. In 1793, Edwards estimated that 80 per cent of the Jamaican slaves lived on plantations (the remainder living on smallholdings or in the towns), but only 56 per cent on sugar planta- tions.[9] If the typical Jamaican unit of factory-based sugar plantation with tied grazing and provision land is used, the proportion of the Jamaican slave population involved either directly or indirectly in the production of sugar might be calculated as high as 75 per cent, with the average population of integrated units about 240.[10] Corroborating evidence is provided by the facts that in 1770, sugar, rum and molasses accounted for no less than 89 per cent of Jamaica's exports by value, and that this proportion did not fall below 80 per cent before the end of slavery.[11]

Slave sugar plantations predominated in Jamaica but it was clearly a monoculture with peculiar characteristics. The topography of Jamaica and the nature of its early colonisation determined that the average estate was laid out on more generous lines than in other sugar colonies. This explains the rather high average slave production, but also the degree to which Jamaican estates were relatively self-sustaining, self-contained and socially closed.

As elsewhere, the amount of cane planted was determined by the capacity of mills and factory, the optimal unit varying between 250 and 400 acres according to soil fertility and rainfall. The average West Indian plantation produced about three tons of sugar per year from every four acres in canes, with a work-force equivalent to one slave per acre.[12] Yet in Jamaica, the availability of second – and third-class land decreed that for the acreage in canes there would normally be as much improved pasture-land, and up to four times the area of forest and mountain, in which there would be glades for rough grazing and polinks for the growing of provisions. Because of non-sugar employment there would therefore be a total population on an average Jamaican estate equivalent to three slaves for every two acres of canes, with a complement of steers and mules at least two-thirds as numerous.[13]

The ease with which cattle could be grazed and provisions grown aided the cultivation and fertilisation of Jamaican estates and made them, and Jamaica as a whole, less dependent upon outside supplies. Cattle pens and provision grounds – useful also for 'seasoning' new African slaves – were often separated from the core sugar land of an estate, in the case of inland plantations frequently serving as way stations on journeys to and from the coast.[14] Some Jamaican planters owned several or many estates, but these

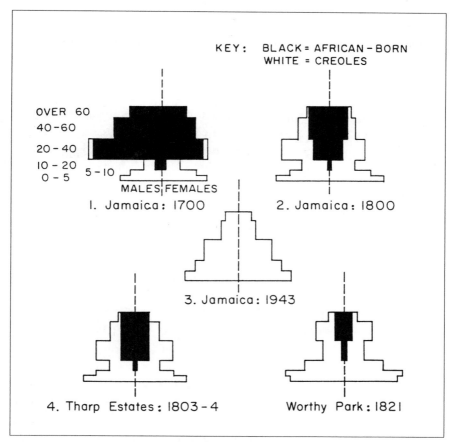

KEY: BLACK = AFRICAN – BORN
WHITE = CREOLES

OVER 60
40 – 60
20 – 40
10 – 20
0 – 5   5 – 10

MALES | FEMALES

1. Jamaica: 1700

2. Jamaica: 1800

3. Jamaica: 1943

4. Tharp Estates: 1803 – 4

Worthy Park: 1821

Jamaican Population Pyramids, 1700 - 1943

aggregations (never more profitable than single fortunate estates) did not really represent economic or social consolidation of the type that reached its peak in late nineteenth century Cuba.[15] The factory-based units were rarely contiguous or even adjacent, and their work-forces remained almost self-contained and therefore relatively stable. Besides, within each unit there was a much wider range of available jobs than estates on islands like Barbados where sugar monoculture was almost absolute (93 per cent in 1770), if not also a relatively larger degree of occupational mobility.[16]

Despite constant attempts to recruit more whites and the fact that Jamaica's white population became the largest in the British West Indies, the Jamaican ratio of blacks to whites became and remained the highest in the British Empire during the slavery period, stabilising around 1780 at 10:1 overall but being up to six times as high on the estates and those farthest inland. These ratios, compared with overall proportions of 4:1 for Barbados, parity for Bermuda, Virginia and Georgia, and a white preponderance of 15:1 for the American Middle Colonies, were among the most important of all social determinants.[17]

Because opportunities outran the available whites, the white indentured labourer almost became an extinct species in Jamaica,[18] and there were no such pockets of poor rural whites as found in Barbados and other plantation colonies. Jamaica's white population of up to 30,000 included about 3,000 troops, 1,000 merchants, shopkeepers, and urban craftsmen, and 4,000 smallholders.[19] Yet as many as 20,000 were tied to the plantation system, although not as proletarians. Far from ever approaching the Negro slave in status as a labourer and thus identity, the poorest Jamaican whites were found in the very senior and most skilled craftsman posts or on the lower rungs of the managerial ladder. They enjoyed not only an absolute social distinction from all blacks, but also considerable upward mobility and real power from their indispensability as managers, voters and militiamen for external and internal defence.[20]

Jamaican towns, in which probably 26,000 or about 10 per cent of the total population lived in 1775,[21] provided a contrast to rural life but acted more as an irritant or stimulus than a determinant or society as a whole. Spanish Town was crowded with planters during the winter legislative season and at other times, and in all other towns the minority of white merchants and shopkeepers dominated. Yet the Deficiency Laws – taxing estates which did not keep a certain proportion of whites – and the owners' preference for Britishers determined that the towns would largely be filled by second-class citizens aspiring to middle-class status and the most mobile and ambitious of the slaves. Freed Negroes – who by mutual consent left the plantations as soon as they were manumitted – probably outnumbered the ruling white townsmen by four or five to one, and competed commercially and socially against an almost equal number of Portuguese Jews. Even the urban slaves, numbering perhaps 15,000 by 1775, differed from the plantation majority in enjoying, or suffering from, the aspirations toward locational, occupational and social mobility which their smaller groupings and the greater variety of town life seemed to offer.

All these factors sharpened the dichotomy between country and town life and between country and town, merchant and planter factions in colonial politics, which in turn tended to reflect the division between colony and metropolis. Yet, just as fear of social discord concentrated power in the hands of the town whites, who tried to keep the garrison tied to the major towns and tended to play Jews against free blacks and both against the slaves, so it was the plantocracy which throughout the eighteenth century was able to impose its will on the towns. For example, in mid-century the planters were able to promote the building of roads at the island's expense directly to serve their estates and to insist on the building of barracks at strategic inland locations to guard against a Maroon resurgence or organised slave rebellion in the backwoods. Plantocratic power was, only occasionally, partially and temporarily curtailed when an unfriendly governor was able to concentrate opposing forces, as Charles Knowles did in 1755.[22]

Generally, the importance of the plantation colonies led the imperial government to connive at the process whereby the metropolitan laws were 'wonderfully altered' to suit the socioeconomic needs of the colonists.[23] The peculiar needs of each colony's dominant class were therefore catered for. In the case of Jamaica, this called for the establishment of security and social control on behalf of the planters. This in turn implied extreme severity at tension points such as towns and isolated estates, or in times of stress such as wars and slave rebellions; but not to the same degree when and where standardisation and stability had been achieved. It is easily arguable that by 1790 or thereabouts, such a form of stability – amounting to a dynamic equilibrium – had been achieved in Jamaica, based upon the entrenchment of a standard system of estates and the relative stabilisation of the population. The best evidence for this lies in the fact that by 1787 it was possible for the slave laws to be moderated considerably and to change their purpose.

As the most valuable colony of all, Jamaica came close to legislative autonomy even though the solidarity of interest among all Jamaican whites meant that there was a greater degree of 'democracy' there than almost anywhere within the imperial system. Such plantocrats as Edward Long were able to discuss the colonial constitution in Lockean terms that were even more ironic and absurd than those employed by Locke's disciples in England or the American colonies since the Jamaican free coloureds as well as the slaves were totally excluded as well as being legislated against.[24]

Indeed, the legislation constricting the right of 'free' Negroes, along with the general harshness of the slavery laws, reflected a classic case of social 'siege mentality', stemming from racial imbalance coupled with strategic insecurity. In two of the four principles discerned in the informal slavery code that had evolved in the West Indian colonies by 1789, Jamaica could be judged normal in defining property in slaves and even comparatively enlightened in its laws protecting slaves. Yet in regulations designed

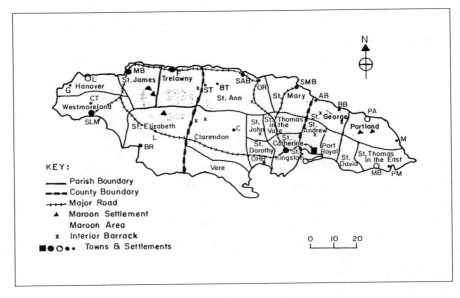

Jamaica around 1790

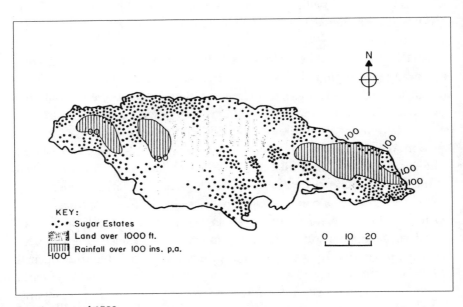

Jamaica around 1790

to preserve the social order and police the blacks, Jamaica was exceptionally severe.[25]

In Jamaica slaves were regarded absolutely as chattel property at least until 1787, save that provisions were made not to separate slaves from the plantations which depended on their labour. In normal circumstances slaves could not be sold or bequeathed apart from the lands on which they lived, though it was not until 1788 that an act was passed to forbid the break-up of slave families, where they existed. Despite the development of contrary custom, Jamaican law maintained as along as it could that slaves, being property, could not themselves own property, appear in normal courts on their own behalf, or be manumitted except on the initiative and under the continuing responsibility of their masters or the legislature.

Manumission was made so difficult that free Negroes never amounted to more than four per cent of the Jamaican population before 1800 — or less than half of the total of whites.[26] Moreover, clear legal distinctions were made, in a subtly ascending order of practical freedom, between Negroes who had been manumitted by private deeds and public acts, between those who had themselves been freed and the sons and daughters of freedmen, and between those who were free on the basis of legal form and those who were free by being 'recognised as white'. The Jamaican custom recognising mustees' children as white was the most generous to persons of colour in the West Indies, but although this was obviously a result of the shortage of whites, it was not really evidence of the slackening of racial and class lines; rather the reverse, since it was based on a redefinition of the quality 'white'.[27]

The most savage of the Jamaican laws were directed against the slaves who resisted the system. Particularly in the early years described by Hans Sloane and in the aftermath of Tacky's 1760 rebellion described by Long and Edwards, the penalties for rebellion and murder by slaves were medieval in their barbarity. But draconian controls were also applied against the threat of violence, the carrying of weapons, riotous or unsupervised assembly, travel without a pass, running away, drumming and the practice of *obeah*.

Elements of social control were evident in such laws as required regular Vestry returns of slaves, including runaways (and later, details of ages, origins, colour and health), the listing of slaves belonging to absentees, widows, minors and lunatics, the inventorising of slaves in wills, the enrolment of deeds involving slave purchases, and the bonding of masters for slaves manumitted. Yet even laws ostensibly aimed at protecting the slaves' interests contained similar elements, as Elsa Goveia has demonstrated for the Leewards. For example, those laws which laid down rules for holidays compelled masters to maintain their sick and superannuated slaves, regularly to issue food and clothing and to detail slaves to grow ground provisions were as much designed to standardise practice and prevent the slaves becoming a burden on or an embarrassment to the government as strictly to ameliorate conditions.[28]

The Jamaican slave plantation was, however, largely a law unto itself as long as it posed no threat to general stability and security. Planters and the managerial staffs were hardly controlled at all in the way they established and maintained control over their slaves. The Jamaican legislature was the most reluctant of all to lay down specific scales of punishment for slaves. Moreover, since blacks could not testify against each other, prosecutions would depend upon the whites themselves, who would naturally be reluctant to crack the facade of social solidarity. Any such legislation was likely to be as much a dead letter as the clause in the 1696 act enjoining the Christianising of slaves.[29]

Yet the fact that Jamaica set up a system of slave courts – even with juries, though of freedmen, not peers – in advance of other colonies, and passed legislation uniquely laying down punishments for whites who violently abused the slaves, did hint that it was recognised that in such a volatile slave colony excessive severity – overstepping the delicate line in slave husbandry between firm management and outright sadism – was as dangerous to social security in general as weaknesses or lack of uniformity.[30]

The actual quality of life on Jamaican slave plantations (being a subject which naturally has always aroused animus on all sides and has thus been obscured by polemic) is difficult absolutely to ascertain. Yet, given the predicates of uniformity, stability and self-containment, much can be inferred, both from general data and accounts and from the particular example of Worthy Park Estate, on which detailed analytical work continues.[31]

Jamaican plantation life in the eighteenth century was conditioned by the insecurity and crudity of the backwoods, the disproportion between whites and blacks, and the tendency of the dominant class to limit locational, occupational and cultural mobility; but also by absenteeism and purely demographic factors such as the proportion of males to females, Africans to creoles (island-born).

In an island not only separated by an eternity of longing from Africa and by months of sailing from the imperial metropolis, but also with plantations which might be a day's hard ride from the sea or the nearest hamlet and three days from the colonial capital and garrison, the sense of insularity, isolation and introspection could have been overwhelming. Paradoxically, this may have been in the long run less damaging for the slaves, who were permanently located and had no choice, than for the masters who hankered for the life of the capital or their motherland, or the managerial whites who became almost peripatetic in their restlessness.

Owners, especially if they were resident, might acquire an affection for the land which brought them profit and power and even, in a paternalistic way, for the slaves who provided 'the very sinews of West Indian property'. The slaves themselves could likewise, in course of time, become attached to the estates as the places of their birth, the burial places of their kin, the only home they knew. Only the salaried whites had no ties with the estate as home or a source of wealth. On an average they probably spent no more than three years on each estate. They therefore tended to be restless, rootless, callous, being to the blacks they ruled an undifferentiated a force as the mass of blacks appeared to them.[32]

Blacks and whites alike escaped the bonds of the plantations as far as they could, but for the whites this was physically easier. Yet for the whites as well as blacks there were ties which bound them to the system and to each other. There was an unacknowledged degree – immediately recognised by some outsiders – to which the whites were occupationally tied, dependent on the blacks and symbiotically related by a subtle admixture of fear, hatred, sex and grudging respect. This relationship shaped plantation society to the point that foreign visitors saw the owner and upper managerial class as philistinely imitative of metropolitan society and their white hirelings as brutalised barbarians little different in language or habits from the slaves themselves. In the age of the Noble Savage there was also a type of black who was regarded by enlightened men as superior to the 'worst sort' of white man, although, like Oroonoko, Friday or Rasselas, they tended to sound like golliwog dummies of *philosophe* ventriloquists.[33]

When owners were resident (and even more so while they were on extended visits), plantation conditions came closest to that idyllic or quasi-feudal model which romantics detect in the pages of M. G. Lewis.[34] Yet by 1790 probably no more than 10 per cent of Jamaican owners lived permanently in the Great Houses on their estates. Both success and failure increased absenteeism and its effects. Most West Indian planters sent their children to be educated in England from the beginning and retired there themselves just as soon as they could afford to live in style upon their profits.

The very success of Jamaica decreed that from 1730 onwards absenteeism became the norm, although many planters reversed the process by sending their eldest sons out to their estates for a period of practical apprenticeship. Even when profits declined few planters returned to Jamaica, preferring to increase their debts by continuing to live in the style to which they had accustomed themselves. Accordingly, more and more Jamaican properties sank under the burden of mortgages, falling in due course into the often reluctant hands of the mortgagors, who rarely felt any compulsion to visit the island.[35]

The normal Jamaican estate was therefore run on behalf of an impersonal or quasi-mythical owner, indirectly by a local attorney who often controlled many estates and was paid a percentage of the gross returns, and directly by an overseer and white underlings (called bookkeepers) forced to seek consolation for their poor salaries in the exercise of petty power and in conspicuous consumption.

The very scarcity of whites led to two particular areas of social tension and ambivalence. In Jamaica, to a greater degree than elsewhere, senior craftsmen's as well as drivers' functions were performed by blacks. This provided not only an area of occupational overlap but a comparatively large slave élite. This unique body of slaves with specialised functions were torn three ways: between the African traditions which provided the means of their leadership, acceptance of the white man's system which provided them with occupational rank, and frustration at the racial lines which remained uncrossable.

Second, because plantation whites (often contracted to remain single) were even more deprived of womenfolk of their own colour than were the imported blacks, miscegenation was general. This exacerbated the sexual and familiar anarchy of Jamaican plantation life, particularly since it was invariably of the artificially one-sided kind of free white men mating with black slave women. The overall effects of miscegenation were limited by the huge preponderance of blacks and the tendency of free coloureds to leave the estates, but the average incidence of coloureds in the population of Jamaican plantations may have been as high as 10 per cent by 1834 or five per cent by 1775.[36] Permanent liaisons were rare and open acknowledgements of love unthinkable, but since white men often freed their coloured bastards and sometimes their mistresses too, miscegenation possessed the attractions for the black women of the easiest route to manumission or even, over the minimum four generations needed to produce a 'Jamaican White', towards full entry into the white man's world.[37]

At the very least, any 'lightening of the skin' offered a better chance of occupational mobility since the élite jobs of domestic servants and crafts-men generally went first to the coloured slaves. Drivers – the third compo-nent of the plantations' slave elites – were generally black rather than coloured, yet they were rarely African-born save in the earliest years. Such important posts were almost invariably reserved for the apparently most faithful and assimilated creoles. In these ways, the equations not only between labourer and slave and slave and black were perpetuated, but also the correlation between the degree of assimilation and responsibility, and even between assimilation, responsibility and degrees of blackness.

Nonetheless, relative to the slaves in other British islands, Jamaican plantation slaves had by 1775 achieved a high degree of locational stability, were likely to be left much to their own devices if quiescent, and had the chance of limited improvement and even responsibility as long as they were creoles.

Although a few percipient masters recognised the excellent skills many Africans possessed as stockmen or in crafts such as woodworking, the vast majority of new African slaves recruited after Jamaica's early years as a British colony or the very first years of a new estate were shuffled off to join the labouring gangs, there to toil out the remainder of their lives. They were treated as nearly as possible as human draft animals, women as well as men. Given names that were mere labels, they were not educated or Christianised, theoretically not allowed to even own the simplest property, not encouraged to form stable sexual relationships or even set up a perma-nent house as home. Provided with none but the most rudimentary skills (some not even allowed to work with tools, being simply carriers), and trained only where necessary to fill the limited number of more sophisti-cated plantation tasks, the gangmen and women did not even acquire the language of the master class save for the fractured degree necessary to understand the words of command transmitted by semi-assimilated and notoriously brutal drivers.

None of these conditions of absolute deprivation and depersonalisation could be continued once the slaves were generations removed from Africa. Yet the very degree to which the Jamaican plantation majority was unas-similated, a separate identity was retained. Beyond the ken or care of the master class, in the separate language, music, folklore and spiritual beliefs of the black labourers, in their cramped cantonments (which sometimes even looked like African villages) or the often-distant provision grounds which the slaves worked with little supervision on Sundays and even

Saturdays out of crop times with almost African methods of slash and burn and hoeing, a vivid culture or individuality lingered. Until 1807 this was constantly refreshed from Africa, but even before the links were severed, it was subtly developed and shaped by the Jamaican environment.[38]

The Jamaican slave culture was in any case syncretic from the beginning. Large trial groupings such as the Coromantines, Ibos, Congos, Papaws, Chambas, Bandas, Mandingos did retain their separate identities to a degree, but the partly calculated, partly accidental mingling of the Middle Passage determined that black culture was only generically African at most. As time went on, moreover, the generic African lifestyle was modified by West Indian foods, European clothing, musical instruments and modes, and such status symbols as household possessions, money, the English Language and finally (and probably the most important) Christianity. This process of insensible acculturation or 'creolisation' reached a point before the ending of slavery that the dominant culture of the white Jamaicans was itself substantially influenced by the 'African', particularly in language, music and religion.

The Anglican Church was to prove most obdurate of all elements in the white colonial society. The planters throughout the slavery period were a godless lot and the Anglican Church, as far as it operated at all, was strictly a function of the Jamaican Establishment. Only towards the end of slavery days was it persuaded to proselytise the slaves, in the hope of cramming them under the wing of the master church and forestalling the missionary activities of Baptist, Wesleyan and Moravian sectaries. This hope proved largely vain and most Anglicans unregenerate – for example, using the church as the aegis of the savage oppression of the Baptists and Methodists which occurred after the 1831 rebellion.

For their part, the sectarian chapels, particularly those with separate congregations and black preachers, provided a chance of an alternative society outside the plantation's orbit, complete with its own status patterns and freedom of expression. This began to occur, however, only after about 1785, once the preachings of the Moravians began to take effect and Jamaican blacks were inspired by the words of the black evangelists George Lisle and Moses Baker.

By this time, the Jamaican slaves had already made great gains in the acquisition of status through possessions and money. Many witnesses stated that in practice Jamaican slaves had tenure in their homes and plots, grew provisions and raised stock to sell on their own behalf, and on special occasions dressed in finery which they bought for themselves. In 1789, testimony before the British House of Commons claimed that nine-tenths of the silver coin in Jamaica was in the hands of slaves and that very many of them had the means to purchase their own manumission *if they wished*.[39] If not contentment, this evidence seems to indicate at least a fair degree of acceptance; a preference for slavery as it normally was to those conditions of severe restraint imposed upon free blacks. Even if hopelessly exaggerated, it does imply conditions of stability, or at least equilibrium, in which custom could outweigh the law.

Yet, from beginning to end, uncertainty bedevilled plantation life, for all segments of plantation society. Economic fortune affected the population from top to bottom either directly or indirectly. The fact that the determining forces – hurricane, flood, drought, disease, war, rising costs and fluctuating produce prices – were beyond human control, tended to load the owners and attorneys with manic depression and contribute to the callousness and fatalism of resident whites and blacks alike.[40] Nothing was more important yet so frustrating as the factors determining health, mortality and fertility, since the causal elements – geography, epidemiology and demographical factors – were not only immutable but little understood.

Towards the end of the eighteenth century the philanthropists believed that the planters' cruelty and the harshness of the work on plantations contributed most to the lamentable health record of the slaves, and that amelioration, by leading to natural increase, would in due course make the slave trade unnecessary. At the same time, some planters favoured a measure of amelioration in the cause of improving slavery's notorious record of inefficiency. In neither respect did amelioration work, and, T. F. Buxton's horrified disclosure in 1830 of continuing natural decrease convince the philanthropists that only emancipation would improve conditions, although even the wisest planters were merely converted to a further phase of amelioration while redoubling their efforts to retain slavery itself.[41]

Edward Long, though biased as a planter, was probably more accurate than the philanthropists in attributing the poor health of the slaves chiefly to geographical location and the type of work engaged in rather than overt cruelty and the intrinsic harshness of the work. From personal experience Long reckoned in 1788 that the annual natural decrease (excess of deaths over births) in Jamaica was two per cent, observing that the least healthy estates were large sugar plantations on the marshy plains (with a natural decrease as high as six per cent), and the most healthy small coffee plantations in the mountains, many of which maintained their demographic equilibrium.[42]

Edward Long also remarked that fresh Africans could be expected to die off at the rate of ten per cent per year during the first three years of 'seasoning' and provided figures which showed that on his own estate in Clarendon a disastrously low birthrate was accompanied by a very low proportion of fertile females, though apparently he had neither the medical knowledge nor the demographic insight to draw the correct etiological conclusions. Philip Curtin, however, has recently pointed out the epidemiological factors which made the Middle Passage a crossroads for the diseases of Europe, Africa and America, and the inevitability that fresh Africans in the plantations, like all people with low resistance and little immunity, would be bound to suffer disastrously from diseases.[43] This would be especially true in crowded conditions, in areas close to the breeding grounds of mosquitoes, or in conditions of extremes of heat, cold and damp, insufficient or ill-balanced diet and crushing toil. Modern medical knowledge has also suggested that unstable sexual conditions (resulting partly from the low ratio of women), by encouraging the 'promiscuity' for which slaves were notorious, contributed to the very low fertility rates among slave women as much as poor diet, hard work, and the general ignorance concerning infantile diseases and child care.

Since Africans suffered from higher mortality and lower fertility rates than creoles, and cargoes of fresh Africans averaged about 60 per cent males and contained very few slaves under 20 years of age, the demographic health of Jamaica as a whole and of individual estates at different times can be determined very largely by projections showing ratios of Africans to creoles and males to females.[44] In Jamaica as a whole around 1670 and on estates in the early years or periods of rapid expansion, when the population would be virtually all African-born, the average age around 25 and the proportion of males as high as sixty per cent, it would be likely that the annual birth rate would be no higher than ten per thousand, and the death rate as high as 100 per thousand, requiring an annual importation of nne per cent simply to keep numbers level.[45]

Once Jamaica as a whole or individual estates had become established, these disastrous rates would have modified, but since the period from 1700 to 1775 was one of general expansion, the average annual inflow of fresh Africans merely declined from about six per cent around 1700 to about four per cent around 1775. By 1778 however, the rate of general expansion had slowed almost to a stop and the Jamaican need for imported slaves was probably close to Edward Long's figure of two2 per cent per year. This implies a death rate for Jamaica as a whole (and thus for the average estate) of about 40 per thousand if the overall birth rate was as high as 20 per thousand per year.

African slave importations ceased, perforce, in 1808 with the ending of the slave trade, at a time when Jamaica (thanks partly to the five per cent longer life expectancy of females) had almost reached a healthy 50:50 ratio of females to males. Natural decrease continued, amounting to about five per thousand as late as 1834, but this was as much due to the 'aging and wasting' effect of the cutoff in slave imports as to the continuation of high mortality and low fertility figures. Slave census returns in the 1830s showed that creole slaves were already increasing naturally, and projections show that Jamaica would have achieved an overall natural increase little later than it actually did (around 1842) had slavery continued. It also seems likely that these demographic effects may have occurred had the amelioration laws never been passed.

A demographically stable and closed society of creoles – in which the ratio between the sexes was close to parity, which did not demonstrate an unhealthy 'bulge' in any age-range, which reproduced itself naturally, and suffered from neither in- nor out-migration – was likely to be socially stable as well, as long as political and economic conditions were not severely disrupted by external events. These criteria were as true, in microcosm, for individual estates as for islands as a whole.

Unlike some islands such as Barbados and the Leewards, Jamaica had not quite reached this degree of demographic stability even by the time slavery ended, and in 1775 males still made up about 57 per cent of the overall slave population and Africans 64 per cent. Yet although profits declined, sugar production continued to expand until 1805, to the degree that sugar plantation work-forces were frequently augmented by gangs of 'jobbing slaves' brought in from failing coffee and cotton plantations. As long as the chances of socioeconomic improvement continued to exist for creole slaves a dynamic social equilibrium was likely. This seems as true for Jamaica as a whole as for the individual estates which continued to flourish most.

Since the social stability of society, however, depends as least as much on the incidence of psychological adjustment as to material well-being and demographic health, it is necessary, in conclusion, to consider the question of assimilation and resistance to the system by the Jamaican slaves and to speculate on the ways these subtly changed.

Resistance – the slaves' escapism – existed in so many forms short of open rebellion that it is possible to maintain that it was general, and provided as important a social determinant as the constraints which slavery imposed or the assimilation which the system encouraged. At the least obvious and measurable level, the low state of state health – mental as well as physical – might be largely attributed to resistance. Masters certainly accused slaves of malingering, self-wounding, culpable carelessness in health matters, of procuring abortions, and even committing suicide in order to frustrate them. More calculable, the abysmal level of Jamaican slaves' productivity – probably no higher than 25 per cent of that of modern wage-earners performing similar tasks – was almost certainly due more to unwillingness to work than to physical incapability.[46] Most masters recognised that overuse of the whip was counter-productive but they were faced with a dilemma. Whatever incentives they tried did not greatly or permanently raise productivity. Freedom from work was the only 'incentive' which the slaves really sought and this was economically unacceptable. Instead, working in no sense for themselves and with no hope of improvement in a system from which all those involved in it tried to escape, slaves rarely produced more than the minimum, not even caring that thereby they gained a reputation for incurable sluggishness, laziness and dishonesty.[47]

The pessimistic stereotyping of 'Negro' traits by frustrated whites can itself be seen as a subtle victory for the blacks in resisting the system. It took percipient outsiders who noticed the energy, thrift and honesty of blacks working their own lands to detect the irony. Plantation whites were also notoriously blind, or forced to turn the blind eye, to the degree to which their slaves were covertly insolent. Even Edward Long recognised that some work-songs satirised the 'obishas' and other 'buckras', though there were innumerable more subtle ways of 'putting on ole Massa' which escaped his notice.[48]

Running away was a far more obvious form of resistance though equally difficult to cure. The overall number of runaways at any one time was probably no more than one per cent of the island's slave population, but the Worthy Park records suggest a rather higher proportion of slaves went absent without leave at some time in their lives, perhaps as many as five per cent. An increasing number of them, however, were the semi-assimilated who 'pulled foot' for the towns, almost inevitably to return or be recaptured. Those few Africans who ran away, and those who escaped into the impenetrable forests and hills, were far more damaging to the system, for by so doing they were totally rejecting slave society, urban as well as rural.

A similar distinction in the nature of rejection can be detected in a study of Jamaican rebellion – the most extreme of all forms of resistance. Compared with the American mainland colonies (and later USA), where Herbert Aptheker was able to detect over the entire slavery period no rebellion involving more than 70 slaves, and only some 250 mutiny-like outbreaks of ten or more slaves, Jamaica suffered several prolonged revolts involving at least 1,000 slaves, resulting in immense property damage and horrific loss of life.[49] Orlando Patterson tends to equate all these outbreaks,[50] but they should perhaps be distinguished into three main types, dating from the periods 1655-1793, 1740-1775 and 1807-1834, with the period 1775-1807 being one of significant transition and comparative, though uneasy, quiescence.

From the earliest period of 1739, the maroons carried on a tradition from the days of the Spaniards that runaway slaves could find a refuge in the hills and defend their freedom against encroachment. This phase, in which a nomadic enclave of almost totally unassimilated Africans with Amerindian allies steadily expanded with fresh recruits such as those who fell after the St John's rebellion of 1690, came to an end with the treaties signed by Cudjoe and Quao at the end of the First Maroon War. By these treaties the maroons nominally agreed to hunt down and return runaways, alive or dead, in return for an acknowledgement of continued independence.

Thereafter, the maroons somehow maintained their separation but gradually lost their dynamism as well as their bond of empathy with the plantation slaves. In due course they suffered much the same fate as the indigenous minorities of the American mainland in the face of the inexorable advance of the Europeans. In 1796, after a second war provoked more by the whites' paranoid fear of a spread of the Haitian Revolution than by maroon provocation, the Windward maroons were extirpated and the remainder shut up firmly in the western cockpits. In this Jamaican equivalent to Wounded Knee, slaves and free blacks assisted the whites in their campaign, many slaves, indeed, being manumitted as a reward for their faithful services.[51]

Tacky's five-month rebellion of 1760, although not the first such outbreak, was a different case entirely; a classic revolt led by the fiercest of the unassimilated Africans, the Coromantines. It was possible only in a comparatively early stage of plantation development. The forces of control were distracted by a mercantilist war, yet far more important were the facts that the population in the areas most affected was overhelmingly African, the tribes comparatively unsplit, and the natural leaders, for the most part, as yet uncorrupted by the attractions of limited power and ease within the system.[52]

Despite the paranoia and military power which enabled the whites to persecute the maroons in the Second Maroon War and deport half of the survivors to Nova Scotia, it was not the strength of the forces of control or even the tightening of the slave code immediately after 1760 which chiefly explain the remarkable lack of Jamaican slave rebellions over the period of the American, French and Haitian Revolutions. A far more plausible explanation is that Jamaican plantations were now relatively stabilised, with creole slaves approaching parity and complete monopoly of subordinate power and status, and the Africans relatively divided and repressed.

Unrest revived after the French wars ended, reaching a dramatic climax in the Christmas Revolt in western Jamaica in 1831. Yet this phase, while no less serious in its manifestations, was of an entirely different kind again. The 1831 rebellion was led not by the most repressed, the African labourers, but (like the Guyanese revolt of 1823) by the creole élite of craftsmen and drivers, particularly those who were active in the Baptist chapels. It was a response to the frustration of the rising expectations of open-ended economic improvement and social mobility consequent upon the last-ditch efforts of the whites to retain their socioeconomic and racial superiorty.[53]

Since the 'Silver Age' of 1783, both the social equilibrium and the relative prosperity of Jamaican sugar plantations had been upset. Creole slaves were now in the majority, but conditions were actually deteriorating for them as well as for their masters. The general decline in the sugar industry which had begun in earnest after 1805 meant greater exploitation and hardship for the slaves. Masters tried to maintain profits by greater production, while having less money to provide services.[54] At the same time the fund of money in general circulation, which the slaves had come to rely on, gradually dried up.

Moreover, outside the plantations tensions mounted as the result of changes which had occurred since 1807 or 1787. Following the great increase in manumissions, the growth of towns and the decay of many of the weaker plantations, the number of dissidents in the non-plantation Negro population increased. The number of free Negroes had risen by 1830 to 45,000, outnumbering the whites by 3:2, and town slaves probably numbered 25,000 exclusive of runaways and the unrecorded masterless.[55] Yet what set the seal on the general unrest was the intransigence of the whites. Their siege mentality was exacerbated both by their actual military weakness since the wars ended in 1815, and by the feeling that their economic plight and the pretensions of the Negroes alike were the products of an inimical and erroneous liberalism emanating from Westminster and the headquarters of the missionary societies. Only by a counterattack by the forces of law, order and the established church, they considered, could they retain what they had.[56]

In many ways the 1831 rebellion was more akin to the 1865 Morant Bay Rebellion of the nominally free than to the true slave rebellions of a century earlier. In 1865 as in 1831, the rebels made appeals to African identity, just as the white dominated régime in 1865 regressed to the form of retributive brutality employed in 1831, 1760 and 1690. But in the rebels' case this was now as much an appeal from the head as from the heart, and in the régime's case as much a calculated policy as an automatic reflex conditioned by two centuries of uneasy mastery. With even less realism than ever before, the Jamaican whites were resisting the fact that they were as much a part of creole society as the free Negroes or the slaves themselves.

In conclusion, then, it can be maintained that the distinctive unit in Jamaican slave society was the relatively stable, almost closed sugar estate, and that this was generally attained by about 1790. Moreover, as the determinants of health and mortality fertility were 'accidents' of geography, epidemeology, and demography, the most important factors in the development of Jamaican society —slave and post slave —were not the imposition of the slave system of such or even the resistance to it. Rather, it was those elements of syncretisation and symbiosis which contributed towards the insensible creation of an integrated society: not European or African (or even plural) but creole.

Yet Jamaican slave society was characterised also by certain dynamic tensions, consequent upon the location, topography and size of Jamaica, racial imbalance and ambivalences, absenteeism, the premature decline of the sugar economy, the ending of the slave trade, and the way in which the amelioration and emancipist policies were enforced from Britain, and polarised the social elements. These factors together determined that while Jamaican society would be neither the unmodernised Africa transplanted of Haiti nor the stagnant little black England of Barbados, it would not be the sick plural society which the USA had inherited from the American South.

Table 1 **The Growth of Jamaica, 1670 - 1830, Compared with the British West Indies, 1630 - 1830**[a]

Period	1. Jamaica: slaves (thousands)[b]	2. Whites	3. Coloured	4. Free negroes (black and coloured)	5. Barbados: slaves	6. Whites	7. Leewards: slaves	8. Whites	9. British West Indies: slaves	10. Whites	11. B.W.I.: annual slave trade	12. Jamaica: annual slave trade	13. B.W.I. annual sugar production (thousand tons)	14. Jamaica: annual sugar production (thousand tons)	15. Jamaica: sugar estates[c]	16. Jamaica: sugar products of total exports, by value	17. Jamaica: sugar profits: per cent of capital
1630	—	—	—	—	—	2	—	1	4	7	—		—		—	—	—
1650	—	—	-	-	15	25	2	3	17	—	1.4	—	2	—			
1670	9	8	-	—	35	25	4	4	49	40	3.0	1.0	10	1	57	75.0	20.0
1690	34	7	-	-	45	17	13	5	93	—	6.5	2.0	18	4	70		
1710	49	7	1	-	42	13	27	7	120	32	7.8	2.5	25	5	150	85.0	17.5
1730	80	8	4	1	46	16	55	11	188	—	9.5	4.5	45	16	300		
1750	122	11	9	2	57	15	73	10	255	43	12.4	6.7	42	20	525	90.0	12.0
1770	185	17	23	6	63	16	86	10	389	—	15.8	8.0	90	40	650		
1790	250	25	32	10	64	16	83	9	483	71	16.1	8.0	100	50	900	75.0	7.5
1810	325	30	55	17	69	14	82	9	670	—			150	75	750		
1830	312	30	60	45	82	15	70	8	702	75	—	—	230	70	600	75.0	2.5

[a] See Michael Craton, *Sinews of Empire: A Short History of British Slavery*, London, 1974, Chapters 2, 3. Population figures in cols. 1-10 largely from Great Britain, Commons, *British Sessional papers*, A/P, 1789, xxvi, 646a, pt iv; 183, xxi, 674; 1838, xviii, 215; 1845, xxi, 426; also F.W. Pitman, *The Development of the British West Indies, 1700-1763*, New Haven, 1917, App. 1, 369-390; Brathwaite; Sheridan, 41. Slave totals and trade figures in cols. 11, 12, largely from Philip D. Curtin, *The Atlantic Slave Trade: A Census*, Madison, West Indies, 1969. Sugar production in cols. 13, 14, from Noel Deerr, *The History of Sugar*, 2 vols, London. 1949-50, I, 176, 193-204. Sugar estates in col. 15 from Edward Long, *History*, 1, 301; Edwards, *History*, 11, 466. Percentage monoculture in col. 16 largely from Long, *Jamaica*; Edwards, *History*; R. M. Martin, *Statistics of the British Empire*, London, 1839, Profitability in col. 17 from Craton, *Sinews of Empire*, Chapter 3.

[b] All figures of persons in cols. 1-12 given in thousands.

[c] These figures, unfortunately, must remain approximate since, as is discussed in the text, authorities obviously differ as to criteria, without explanation given. Where possible the criterion used here has been estates growing a substantial amount of sugar, with their own mills and factory.

Table 2   The Population of a Typical Large Jamaican Sugar Estate around 1793
(Worthy Park, St John's: 1,200 acres, 400 acres canes, 577 slaves)

	Ages	Colour	African or creole	Male or Female	Salary or approx. value (Jamaica currency, £)[a]
A. WHITES (10-11)					
Owner (absent in England			English		
Attorney (in Kingston)[b]			C		2,000-4,000
Overseer	42	White	C		200
Overseer's Wife	40	White	C		—
Head Book-keepers	38	White	C		100
3 Under Book-keepers	20-30	White	3C		50-80
Head Boiler	40	White	C		100-150
Head Distiller	42	White	C		50-100
Doctor	47	White	C		6/8 d.p. slave
Settler & Wife "to save Deficiency"		White	2C		—
B. NEGRO ELITE (21)					
7 Drivers & Driveresses	40-60	Black	5A 2C	5 M 2F	120-150
2 Head Housekeepers[c]	35, 40	Sam./Mul.	2 C	2 F	60-80
Head Cooper	35	Mulatto	C	M	140-300
Head Potter	40	Black	C	M	140-160
Second Boiler	40	Black	C	M	180-200
Head Mason	50	Black	C	M	170-180
Head Sawyer	45	Black	C	M	150
Head Carpenter	65	Black	A	M	140-300
Head Blacksmith	50	Mulatto	C	M	180
Head Cattleman	35	Black	A	M	120
Head Muleman	45	Black	C	M	120
Head Home Wainsman	40	Black	C	M	150-200
Head Road Wainsman	23	Black	C	M	150-200
Head Watchman	50	Mulatto	C	M	80
C. SPECIAL WORKERS or LOWER ELITE (95)					
2 Waiting Boys	15, 16	Mulatto	2 C	2M	60-80
Groom	35	Sambo	C	M	80
2 Seanstresses	15, 20	Black	2 C	2F	50-60
2 Washerwomen	19, 41	Black/Mul.	1 A, 1 C	2F	50-60
Cook	35	Black	C	F	50-60
Midwife	60	Black	A	F	150-200
2 Hothouse Nurses	30, 35	Black	1 A, 1 C	2F	90-120
Black Doctor	49	Black	A	M	140
6 Coopers	25-50	5 B./ 1 Sam	1 A, 5 C	6M	120-200
9 Carpenters	25-50	7 B./2 Mul	3 A, 6 C	9M	140-250
3 Sawyers	20-32	Black	3 A	3M	100-120
2 Masons	22-35	Black	2C	2M	120-200
Under Blacksmith	31	Black	C	M	120-200
9 Boilers	40-50	Black	9C	9M	140-250
4 Distillers	30-45	Black	4C	4M	140-300
2 Potters	40-50	Black	1A, 1C	2M	120-200
2 Sugar Guards	25-30	Black	2C	2M	50-70
6 Home Wainsmen	25-40	Black	2A, 4C	6M	90-120
7 Road Wainsmen	20-40	Black	7C	7M	90-120

Table 2   The Population of a Typical Large Jamaican Sugar Estate around 1793
(Worthy Park, St John's: 1,200 acres, 400 acres canes, 577 slaves) cont'd

	Ages	Colour	African or creole	Male or Female	Salary or approx. value (Jamaica currency, £)[a]
C. SPECIAL WORKERS or LOWER ELITE (95) cont'd					
14 Mulemen	20-35	Black	7A, 7C	14M	90-120
3 Hog Tenders	10-40	2 B./ 1 Mul.	1A, 2C	3M	80
2 Poultry Tenders	55-60	Black	1A, 1C	2F	50-60
3 New Negro Tenders	30-60	Black	3C	1M, 2F	50-80
8 Cattlemen & Boys	15-60	5B/3 Sam	3A, 5C	8M	80-120
2 Ratcatchers	19-21	2 Mulattos	2C	2M	80-100
D. GANGS (364)					
147 Great or First Gang	26-40	Black	70% A	60% F	50-125
67 Second Gang	16-25	Black	75% A	64% F	50-100
68 Third Gang	12-15	Black	51% C	54% F	50-80
21 Grass or Weeding Gang	5-11	Black	66% C	69% F	50-60
13 Vagabond Gang[d]	18-40	Black	66% C	60% F	50-100
48 " Pen Negroes" (at Mickleton & Spring Garden Pens)[e]					
E. MARGINALLY PRODUCTIVE OR UNPRODUCTIVE (97)					
25 Watchmen		Black	20 A, 5 C	25F	30-70
7 Grass Gatherers		Black	5A, 2C	4M, 3F	60
3 Child Watchers		Black	2A. 1C	3F	50
2 Pad menders		Black	2A	1M, 1F	80
3 Women with Six Children		Black	1A, 2C	3F	50-80
18 Hopeless Invalids		16 B/2 Mul.	10A, 8C	9M, 9F	5
2 Superannuated		Black	2A	2F	5-10
37 Infants		33 B/4 Mul.	37C	18M, 19F	10-60

[a] The valuations in the last column are approximate, being estimated from data in the Wedderburn Papers at the Institure of Jamaica. prices of new African slaves ranged £50-70 for males, £50-60 for females. For seasoned slaves, the ranges were £80-125 and £70-110.

[b] The Attorney's high salary was based on the management of 5-6 estates. Some managed 15-20 and may have made £8,000-10,000 a year.

[c] When the owner, or his son, was in residence, the nominal Great House staff of two may have been raised as high as 25.

[d] The Vagabond Gang consisted of persistent runaways and other miscreants.

[e] Mickleton Pen was 12 miles distant, Spring Garden 20. They were used as resting places to and from Kingston and Old Harbour respectively; also for breeding cattle, growing provisions and seasoning new slaves.

10

The Rope and
the Cutlass
Slave Resistance in
Plantation America

Introduction: The aim of this essay, presented at an international congress on slavery at Rio de Janeiro (Niteroi) in June 1988, was to test the validity on a hemispheric scale of the analysis and conclusions of a study of slave resistance within the British West Indies, published six years earlier. This reversing of the normally recommended method of proceeding from the general to the particular is, I believe, justified, with three possible reservations. 'Plantation America' is here defined virtually to exclude the USA, incidentally almost sidetracking the work of one of the most important analysts of slave resistance, Herbert Aptheker. The exceptional nature and unique success of the Haitian Revolution may be understated, along with its integration into what Eugene Genovese and others see as a worldwide Age of Revolutions. Besides, an admittedly wide definition of slave resistance (coming close to including what others have seen as forms of accommodation) may be thought to justify Richard Dunn's assertion that the predominant theme should not be, as here, the heroic resistance of the slaves, but rather the prevailing success of the master class in enforcing slavery as a system.

In making an overdue and perhaps over-ambitious attempt to review slave resistance throughout plantation America, we start with axioms so obvious that they are probably commonplace. As even arch-plantocratic writers like Edward Long and Bryan Edwards recognised, slave resistance was as inevitable as slavery was unnatural. It was a constant feature of slavery; only the forms varied from time-to-time and place to place.[1]

While resistance was endemic, it was only overt in special circumstances. I think it is true to say that slaves in the Americas would always tend to engage in open rebellion 'whenever they could, or *had to*'. But this was not very often; so infrequently in fact that even a liberal writer like Richard S.

Dunn inclined to exaggerate the power of the masters.[2] Yet defining slave resistance merely as plots and acts of rebellion is unduly limiting, giving a misleading impression of the effectiveness of slavery as a socioeconomic system. To discover fully how the slaves themselves shaped slavery, contributed to its evolution, helped to speed its demise, it is necessary also to understand forms of resistance short of actual (or proposed) overt action. These ranged from covert violence, to manifestations of internal rejection and anomie, to forms of apparent (though dissimulated) accommodation and acceptance that were, perhaps, as subversive as other forms.

Resistance then was a constant. If there was a process, it was part of that described for the immediate post-slavery period by Nigel Bolland and Eric Foner; a perennial dialectic between change and continuity.[3] For our purposes, it was a dialectic of adjustments between masters and slaves and in respect of all forms of resistance, open and covert, gradually verged from total rejection towards forms of industrial action and proto-peasant activity as part of the process of creolisation, and in due course spilled over into the post-emancipation period.

In the last analysis, the effectiveness of slave resistance should be judged not in comparison with the Haitian Revolution of 1791-1804 – the only example of a complete and permanent overthrow of the socioeconomic system, if scarcely an unequivocal model of success in all respects – or even by the comparative evidence of forms of open revolt, but by the degree to which the enslaved were able to overcome the constraints of the master system to 'make a life of their own'. In this light, the slaves were at one with all oppressed peoples, before, during and after the phase of formal enslavement – a point of view that aligns with the potent apothegm of Herbert Aptheker that 'History is the story of resistance, not acquiescence.'[4]

Since there was a spectrum of forms of slave resistance, let us consider briefly a descending typology of these forms in general, before allotting most of our space to an examination of the historical continuum.

The prospect of a general slave uprising was the slave-owners' ultimate nightmare. A Haitian planter wrote: 'A colony of slaves is a town menaced by assault; one lives on top of a powder magazine.'[5] The master class therefore deployed all the available instruments of power and expended much psychic energy and money to prevent slave rebellions. Army garrisons were sought and all local whites enrolled in a militia as much against internal as external enemies. The annual military reviews and exercises, particularly the firing of guns, were as much to overawe the slaves as to gratify and reassure the whites.[6] All free persons were given vigilante duties, while the more substantial whites were legislators and judges to pass and execute draconian policing laws. The unauthorised movement of slaves, large slave gatherings, the possession of guns and other weapons, the sounding of horns and the practice of secret rituals were rigorously suppressed, while the punishments for actual or threatened violence against whites were savage. In extreme cases, the legal systems allowed for punishments in any form, however barbarous – a reflection not only of the savagery of rebel behaviour (for instance, the mutual decapitations and display of enemy heads which were a feature of many slave rebellions), but of the masters' paranoid fears.

These fears naturally increased at times of plantocratic weakness; for the occasion of slave rebellions were the inverse of the planters' ability to exercise their power. Slave rebellions were most likely in the years before the instruments of power were fully installed, when they were weakened by distractions or the depletion of garrisons during times of war, or when the planters' powers were depleted by absenteeism, epidemic, economic decline or the loss of whole-hearted support from the imperial authorities. Robert Dirks' recent observation that slave rebellions most commonly occurred around the licensed slave holidays of Christmas, Easter or 'crop-over' or after the weekly Sunday rest-day, points up the danger of temporary imbalances of power – although the planters themselves recognised this and strove to guard against it.[7]

To a degree, the relative infrequency of slave rebellions was an index of the planters' power, although the Barbadian planters, for instance, complacently claimed that their immunity from slave rebellions was due both to their mild and judicious regime and to the pacific nature and general satisfaction of the Barbadian slaves – this on the very eve of the major slave uprising of 1816.[8] Other slave colonies whether the slaves were far more quiescent, such as Bermuda and Antigua, never had a major slave uprising. But the threat of insurrection remained; and plots one stage beyond the perennial slaves' mere dream of freedom, were surely far more common than actual outbreaks of rebellion. This was certainly true of Bermuda and Antigua.

What gave slave plots added force was the secrecy with which they were enshrouded. Picturesque slave rituals, such as the *ikem* dances performed by the Antiguan slaves in 1736, took on an altogether more sinister face when they were found to be associated with a binding to rebel and to oaths of secrecy. Such all-encompassing secrets, of course, could not be kept perfectly or for long, even without the existence of slave informers – persons whose actions the slave-owners defined as fidelity, but who were as likely to be those calculating few who feared the bloody consequences of rebellion. Once teased out, through systematic interrogation, torture and savage exemplary punishments, such plots usually terrified the whites by their extent and aims. Like a guinea worm in the body politic, they called for drastic remedies. In the 1736 Antigua case, the rebel-hunt went on for months, revealing a plot affecting every parish, if not every single estate. Some 88 slaves were put to death – broken on the wheel, starved to death in gibbets or burned alive – and 47 transported from Antigua. Nearly all these were élite slaves chosen to make an example. One has a sense that the plantocracy, having decided that almost all Antiguan slaves were implicated and after making their counter-attack in the most forthright terms, then simply decided to close up the gaping wound, determining thereafter to be ever more strict and vigilant.[9]

Mass running away (*grand marronage*) was almost as much a threat to the planter regime as rebellions and plots, and, indeed, often more associated with them. Would-be rebels were encouraged by the existence of successful Maroon communities (*palenques*) or, having risen up, rebel slaves fled into nearby woods or mountains to escape, concentrate their forces and regroup. Naturally, the largest and longest-lived *palenques* were found on tropical mainlands –the areas most like West Africa –and nothing quite as extensive as the Palmares *quilombos* or the Bush Negro communities of Surinam were found in the Antilles. But all islands had their Maroon communities, especially in the earlier phase of colonisation; with those of Santo Domingo, Haiti, Cuba, Jamaica and Dominica including thousands of Maroons and outlasting slavery itself, and smaller groupings found in tiny Barbados in the 1650s, Antigua up to the 1730s, St Croix in the 1770s and even New Providence in the Bahamas as late as 1823.[10] At the very least, these communities of runaways compromised the plantocratic system.

Yet even more common and insidious was the multiform phenomenon of short-term, short-distance running away by individuals and very small groups (*petit marronage*). Despite the severe penalties, including mutilation, for persistent runaways or harbourers, perhaps two per cent of slaves were absent at any one time, and up to ten per cent were absent at some time in their lives. Some were new Africans, misfits or even what one might truthfully style criminals; but far more were protesting intolerable material conditions or special grievances. Still others were seeking an outlet for grievous psychic repression, seeking an alternative life not necessarily outside the system (as sailors on naval vessels, for example); or they were not, strictly, running away, but rather running *to* a lover, spouse or other family members. In all these respects runaway slaves were merely express-ing variations of forms of protest and resistance that were continuously found among the slaves who remained behind on the plantations.

For a slave to offer physical violence to a white was drastically counter-productive when the slave laws allowed great latitude in what punishments could be arbitrarily administered in the course of 'legitimate correction', and custom decreed even greater licence. But poisoning was a safer, and to the masters a more worrying, alternative. So expert were the slaves thought to be in the use of poisons and spells, and in any case intestinal disorders were so common through over-indulgence, that plantation whites, it seems, went in constant fear of being poisoned by their cooks.

Though not frequently punished for it, slaves were also universally suspected of industrial sabotage. This could include arson, especially in the sugar cane pieces, where fires were not only spectacularly fearsome but also made cane-cutting easier for the easier for the slaves, or the covert killing of cattle, which had the bonus effect of providing meat for the slaves. More direct attacks on the industrial system, such as the breaking of carts, mill machinery or utensils, also served to reduce the tempo of work. Even more subtly, the slaves feigned stupidity to explain industrial accidents or low productivity and became experts at malingering. Gordon Lewis has even suggested that the Caribbean slaves' notorious loquacity was a tactic of procrastination.[11]

The slaves' lack of incentives made slavery generally inefficient, as Adam Smith argued. But what the planters at least intuitively recognised was that even achieving the maximum efficiency possible was dependent on achiev-ing a subtle balance between force and reward, so that the slaves as much as the masters were the determinants of the level of production and profit. In all respects, the role of the black slave driver became critical – an intermediate functionary rewarded with relative power and material bene-fits, but chosen as much for qualities that could command the respect of subordinate slaves, as for mere strength, skills and apparent fidelity.

Planters prided themselves on their skill in dividing the slaves in order to rule them; separating the African ethnicities and Africans from Creoles, sundering coloured domestics from black field slaves, and splitting drivers and craftsmen from ordinary workers. What the whites were less willing to acknowledge was that the slaves were at least as adept in similar skills, performing in real life many of the subterfuges attributed to their chief folk hero, Anansi, the spider-trickster. These stratagems involved exaggerated deference and disguised satire as well as outright cunning, duplicity and mendacity. They also could involve the subtle insertion of divisions between white bookkeepers and overseers, and between overseers and owners. This is somewhat surprisingly conveyed by the planter Edward Long, who is more famous or notorious, for this crude Negrophobia:

> Their principal address is shown in finding out their master's temper, and playing upon it so artfully as to bend it with most convenience to their own purposes. They are not less studious in sifting their master's representative, the overseer; if he is not too cunning for them, which they soon discover after one or two experiments, they will easily find means to overreach him on every occasion, and make his indolence, his weakness, or sottishness, a sure prognostic of some comfortable terms of idleness to them; but if they find him too intelligent, wary and active, they leave no expedient untried, by thwarting his plans, misunderstanding his orders, and reiterating complaints against him, to ferry him out of his post; if this will not succeed, they perplex and worry him, especially if he is of an impatient, fretful turn, till he grows heartily sick of his charge, and voluntarily resigns it. An overseer, therefore, like a prime minister, must always expect to meet with a faction, ready to oppose his administration, right or wrong; unless he will give the reins out of his hands, and suffer the mob to have things their own way; which if he complies with, they will extol him to his face, condemn him in their hearts, and very soon bring his government to disgrace.[12]

Thus the internal politics of the slave plantation! At the individual internalised level, the slaves also resisted the whites' mastery, though at a high psychic cost. More positively, however, the cultural hegemony of the master class was resisted through the creation of a separate culture in the slave quarters and provision grounds.

Acts of internalised rejection included abortion, suicide, violence turned inwards within the slave community, even forms of madness (fittingly termed 'alienation' until modern times). Acting the 'Quashee' persona of craven obedience, childlike behaviour and stupidity, the slaves' true personality was bound to an extent to become deformed.

Yet at the same time, slaves resisted the dislocation of the Middle Passage by the retention of African language, beliefs, folklore, music, customs and crafts. They resisted the depersonalisation and the masters' lack of concern for family ties through a vigorous customary family life and the reconstitution of kinship networks and canons of 'reputation'. They resisted the imposition of such socialising factors as a common European language and European religion by shaping them into distinctly Afro-American Creole forms. Above all, the slaves were able to mock their legal status as non-persons, unable to own property for themselves, by the way that they not only grew much of their own food in family groups with traditional farming methods, but also sold their surpluses in a widespread informal market network. With the slaves indirectly feeding their masters as well as themselves and in some colonies possessing a majority of the coin in circulation, this 'proto-peasant' activity had become an essential component of the local colonial economies long before slavery ended.

Before I go further and stand accused of proposing the obvious absurdity that even accommodation by slaves was a form of resistance, I must turn, as promised, to consider how forms of resistance changed and did not change over time and from place to place.

In crucial respects, Afro-American slave resistance was rooted in the response of the Amerindians to their enslavement by the Spaniards. Besides structural similarities in the modes of resistance, there were actual links in the way that many blacks collaborated, before becoming dominant, in the earliest *palenques.*

Broadly speaking, the Spanish invented a Manichean polarity of Amerindian types: the 'good Indians' who were initially subjugated with ease; and those 'bad Indians' who resisted subjugation from the beginning – and thus were legally enslaveable once overcome because of their 'unnatural' resistance. Not that the initial subjugation of the 'good' Arawaks and others was irreversible, and not soon qualified by those generic types of covert and subtle resistance already mentioned. The Antillean Taino, for example, resisted by non-cooperation, even by dying, but also by running away when they could, and by turning to desperate rebellion, even collaborating with their traditional enemies, the fearsome Caribs.[13] It was these Caribs – the original cannibals who were the prototype obdurate resisters, setting up what Troy S. Floyd has cogently termed a 'Poisoned Arrow Curtain' in the Lesser Antilles and parts of coastal South and Central America – that retarded European colonisation for many years.[14]

The structural link with later slave resistance was forged by the way that black African slaves (imported to replace the 'unsuitable' Amerindians as labourers in plantations and mines) ran away to Amerindian dominated areas and islands and collaborated in some of the earliest *palenques.* Here they were usually allied subjects at first, but soon miscegenated and in due course in most cases became demographically and culturally dominant. Such a process can be traced, for example, in the permanent *palenque* of Bahoruco-Le Maniel in Santo Domingo, in the Windward Maroon communities of Jamaica and among the partially miscegenated Indians termed Seminoles and Miskito on the American mainland.[15] But the classic case was that of the Black Caribs (now usually called Garifuna) originating on the island of St Vincent. These traced their origins to a cargo of African slaves wrecked on the adjacent island of Bequia around 1690 who were harboured by the 'Yellow' or 'Red' Caribs still in control of St Vincent. Within a few decades (and not, it seems, without some internal disruption) these blacks – reinforced by runaway slaves from nearby islands, especially Barbados – had become the dominant element in a miscegenated warrior community, which fearsomely combined African with Amerindian forms of resistance.

The Black Caribs resisted the European colonial incursion as best as they could, fighting two fierce wars against the British planters in the 1770s and 1790s. This phase of resistance came to an end with the deportation of 5,000 of the Black Caribs to Roatan in 1797. Once firmly established in the Bay Islands and on the nearby coast of Honduras, however, being comparatively free from imperialist forces for another century, the Black Caribs flourished and multiplied, proudly retaining their distinctive Afro-Amerindian culture in vigorous enclaves scattered through most of the countries of Central America. In this respect they offer a notable contrast to the sad remnant of Caribs left behind in St Vincent and Dominica.[16]

The African forebears of the Black Caribs were almost certainly 'Coromantees' ('Minas'), drawn from the warlike Akan-speaking tribes of modern Ghana, such as the Ashanti. These proud and obdurate people, who as warriors and slave-owners made captive through the fortunes of war, were naturally less willing to accept their own enslavement than those Africans who were slaves already, at least until it was discovered that slavery in the Americas was altogether different and harsher than the normal African kind. A high proportion of the early slave revolts were led, and the consequent Maroon communities dominated by Akan-speaking slaves, though the fact that the influence of the Akan language and culture was pervasive out of proportion to the numbers of Coromantees involved argues in general for the normative influences of the most resistant African cultures.

African resistance to American enslavement began with the uncounted number of shipboard revolts on the Middle Passage that occurred throughout the 300-year history of the Atlantic Slave Trade. These 'mutinies' were desperate, and the epic of the *Amistad* in 1839 was one of the few that achieved even qualified success once the slave ships were clear of the African coast.[17]

Once in the American slave plantations, the African slaves had a rather better chance to rise up and run away, though little better chance of permanent independence. Revolts of African slaves occurred in many colonies, but especially in the early years of development and in frontier conditions, where there was a dangerous disproportion between the number of whites and slaves, large nearby areas of undeveloped forest, mountain or riverways, and Maroon communities already established in the wilds. These African-dominated slave rebellions were similar in many respects to native African wars – with the rebels demonstrating incredible obduracy and hardihood, expertise of a guerrilla type in the use of terrain, great skill in the use of muskets (developed in West Africa soon after the Atlantic slave trade got underway), the ability to travel at great speed over rough country and to communicate almost instantly over long distances with African drums. The aims of the rebels were essentially separatist (Genovese calls them 'restorationist') to do what damage they could to their white oppressors and to fight them as long as was necessary, but wherever possible to establish their own separate transplanted African regime, even if it required making compromising treaties with the whites.[18]

One example of an heroic doomed cause was the 'Amina' slave uprising in the Danish island of St John in 1733. Here the slaves killed or drove off all the whites and took control of the entire island for half a year – although when faced by starvation and the overwhelming military superiority of colonial troops borrowed from French Martinique, the rebels committed mass suicide.[19]

Far more successful but at a high political cost were the Jamaican maroons who fought a 50-year war with the British before achieving a qualified degree of independence in 1738-40. Almost continuous fighting on the fringes of the expanding plantations began after 1690, when a 'Coromantee' slave called Cudjoe led a revolt on Sutton's Estate and a mass running away. The fighting climaxed under Cudjoe's son and namesake and another Akan-speaking leader called Quao in the 1730s, when the colonial regime was virtually forced to come to terms. Two treaties were signed, providing the maroons with a fair degree of political and juridical autonomy, land, hunting and trading rights. This, however, was in exchange for agreeing to return slave runaways, even to track them down for bounties, to provide military aid for the white regime in times of war and to accept white superintendents in the chief maroon settlements. The Jamaican maroons first paid their new treaty dues at the time of the last great Coromantee uprising of 1760, when they stood more or less neutral while pretending to aid the plantocracy, rather than throwing in their lot with their fellow Africans.[20]

The greatest and most permanent success was achieved by those African runaways who formed the many Bush Negro communities along the tropical forested riverways of inland Surinam from the earliest days of Dutch colonisation. Although some political and economic linkages were retained with the white coastal regime – with tacit agreements not to harbour runaways in return for trading rights –the Bush Negroes were able to retain their independence and predominantly African culture with or without formal treaties, competing almost as much against each other and against rival Amerindians as against the whites, just as they might have done had they remained in West Africa.[21]

However, the classic case of an African slave rebellion in the Americas which almost achieved complete success also occurred in Guyana, in the Dutch colony of Berbice, in 1763. Here a revolt of the 'Delmina' slaves (the fifth since 1733), led by a privileged slave called Cuffee, seized Upper Berbice and threatened to take over the entire colony. Faced by the fidelity to the whites of most of the creole, coloured and company-owned slaves, and by the arrival of Dutch reinforcements, Cuffee modified this demand to a division of the colony into reciprocal halves; Upper Berbice becoming an independent black federation of different African ethnic groups (in diplomatic association with the Surinam Bush Negroes), while Lower Berbice remained a white plantation colony. Cuffee, though, still couched his missive to the Dutch governor in terms befitting an African king or princely diplomat:

> If Your Excellency makes the war, the Negroes are ready too. The Governor Cuffee requests that your Excellency come and speak with me, and Your Excellency must not be afraid, but if Your Excellency does not come, fighting shall last as long as there is a Christian in Berbice. The Governor Cuffee will give Your Excellency half of Berbice and his people will all go upriver, but you must not think that the Negroes will be slaves again.[22]

Cuffee's proud vision was destroyed, not by plantocratic power so much as by divisions among the slaves themselves. Cuffee's chief rival, Atta, preferred absolute Akan hegemony to a diplomatic solution, with all creole slaves and even Angolan Africans placed under subjection. After a civil war and their leader's suicide, Cuffee's two chief lieutenants defeated Atta and restored the entire colony to the Dutch, leaving us with one of history's most fascinating 'might-have-beens'.[23]

In Berbice we see that there was already a fatal division among the slaves between unacculturated Africans and the local-born creoles. Such an inevitable division in outlook and aims, and thus in strategies and tactics of resistance, was a critical transition found in every colony at a certain stage in its development; that is, when the locally born slaves came close to outnumbering those born in Africa. The transition, with its damaging effects upon slave unanimity, can be traced in Barbados as early as the abortive plot of 1683. Divisions between African and Creole leaders hindered the Antiguan plot of 1736, and contributed to the failure of the Hanover plot in Jamaica in 1776. The way that differences between African and creole leaders affected the outcome of the Haitian Revolution of 1791-1804 has yet to be fully explored, but they were clearly significant – although St Domingue, as a late-developing colony, still had a large majority of African-born slaves at the time of the outbreak.

We would define distinctively creole forms of slave resistance as those attempts to achieve freedom that did not necessarily involve the destruction of, or even separation from, the predominant economic system in favour of a reconstituted African lifestyle. The perennial constants, of course, were the will to be free from the bonds of chattel slavery and the wish for more power, and a majority of slaves would doubtless have chosen to reject plantation labour in favour of the life of a creolised peasantry. But many creole slaves had rather less radical and more rational aims: simply to widen the ambit of freedom already won within the plantation system, by becoming resident free wage labourers or, best of all, predominantly peasants with the opportunity to work for fair wages when they wished.

Besides becoming more sophisticated in taking advantage of the temporary and longer-term weaknesses of the plantocratic regime and of political discord between white colonists and imperial authorities, the creolised Afro-American slaves were increasingly adept at profiting from the rising tide of anti-slavery sentiments in the metropole, whether these stemmed from libertarian, philanthropic or religious principles, or from new 'liberal' economic theories. None of these factors, however, fundamentally reshaped the slaves' own aims and ideology.

Not that the external impact of the so-called Age of Revolutions between 1775 and 1825 did not influence and reinforce, as well as complicate, the increasingly creolised slaves' quest for freedom. Literate and especially domestic slaves were naturally taken by the political conversation of creole whites who condemned imperial oppression upon principles of the 'Rights of Man', and talked of seizing freedom through armed rebellion. The slaves borrowed the slogans if not the intrinsic ideology, particularly once both the North Americans and the Latin American whites demonstrated that political independence did not encompass slave emancipation.

Similarly, the great Haitian Revolution of 1791–1804 was more than conditioned by the tremendous upheavals associated with the French and Napoleonic Revolutions; it could not have succeeded without them. The explosion of 1791 was facilitated by the distractions caused by the conflicting visions of the French Revolution held by *grands blancs*, *petits blancs* and *gens de couleur*. French Revolutionary ideology provided slogans for the disparate leaders of the slave revolt and the victory of the Jacobins gave legal freedom to the slaves and legitimacy to their leaders. Despite Napoleon's *volte face* over slavery and an American empire, yellow fever and the international war against Bonapartism ensured that the Haitian Revolution was irreversible.

Yet these causal factors were secondary and accidental. The primary force and essential ideology of the Haitian Revolution, as Fouchard and Manigat argue, were provided by the cumulative and catalytic effect of a form of *grand marronage* heavily infused with *vodun* elements, combined with the volcanic will of the mass of slaves to throw off their bonds, whatever the cost.[24]

The Haitian Revolution had a direct influence in several colonies, provided even more widespread inspiration to the slaves, and served to raise all slave-owners' fears to the level of paranoia. But it had no exact replicas, and its effects were curiously transmuted in non-Francophone colonies. Events in France, particularly the Jacobin emancipation declaration, encouraged the slaves of the French colonies to throw in their lot with the revolutionary cause. Jacobin ideals were also crucial in motivating the Black Caribs of St Vincent in their second war against the British and in persuading the French-speaking slaves of Grenada to take part in Julien Fédon's heroic revolt. According to plantocratic sources, the examples of Haiti and French Revolutionary slogans were instrumental in stirring up the Jamaican Leeward maroons in the Second Maroon War, a swell as slave plots in several other colonies. Yet far more slaves remained quiescent rather than seized the chance of overt rebellion, and tens of thousands volunteered to take up arms on the British side against the French. In so doing, they were surely making an essentially creole response, whether this amounted to resistance or not: choosing quiescence for fear of losing what they had already gained in return for a dubious outcome; volunteering to wear a uniform and carry a gun in preference to toiling with a hoe, in the hope if not promise of the reward of freedom; defending what by now was almost their native homeland against foreign enemies, including blacks.[25]

The outcome of such tactical calculations was almost universally disappointing, and this certainly affected slave behaviour in the last decades of formal slavery in the British colonies. Resistance became more general and increasingly took on the features of industrial action. In every colony, including those in which plantations had decayed or never been established, slaves proved harder to drive and impossible to move from their established houses and grounds more aware of their allies in Britain, their rights and power, and more adept in negotiating the terms of their employment. In the Bahamas, for example, where the slaves were no longer producing plantation profits and spent most of their time working for themselves, they agitated whenever they were threatened by removal or felt their statutory food and clothing allowances were being withheld; while in Antigua, the slaves resisting the abolition of the Sunday markets by rioting and demonstrating in 1831 actually stood on the legalistic point that the plantocracy had no right to remove a general statutory provision in favour of a vague promise of a half-day Saturday market which was voluntary to the masters.[26]

Even more shocking to those imperialists who believed that fully creolised slaves would not resort to armed revolt was the fact that the period also saw the three largest of all British colonial slave rebellions: in Barbados in 1816; in Demerara in 1823; and climactically in Jamaica over the Christmas and New Year of 1831–32, which spread over 750 square miles and involved 60,000 slaves. These rebellions were truly creole manifestations. They were led by the élite of 'confidential' slaves, many of whom were literate and nearly all of whom were Christians. The millenarian aspects of the slaves' own version of Christianity ran counter to the 'civilising' message of the white missionaries, but the slave leaders (who in Demerara and Jamaica included sectarian deacons) were quite capable of manipulating the missionaries whom they rightly saw as the forward edge of a rising tide of anti-slavery sentiment in the metropolis. Cleverest of all the black leaders' tactics, though, was the almost universal dissemination of rumours; that freedom was already decreed by the King and was being illegally withheld by the colonial planters, the slaves' direct aggressors.[27]

The aims and demands of the slaves were far from revolutionary. Chief among them was the removal of slavery's formal bonds; but the form of freedom envisaged generally extended no further than more days in the week to work with their own lands, with wages paid for remaining days of plantation labour. By calculated policy, the rebels wreaked little material damage and tried to abstain from bloodshed.[28]

The plantocracies, however, were savage in their repression and reprisals. In the three rebellions, the 100,000 slaves involved killed less than 20 persons; yet at least 350 of them were slaughtered in the field and 700 judicially murdered, with an equal number flogged, imprisoned or deported. This level of overkill raised a sympathetic storm among British philanthropists, at the same time that the parliamentary debate over slavery was reaching a climax in a general climate of liberal reform. The full revelations about the Jamaican Christmas Rebellion were followed within months by the Emancipation Act of August 1, 1833.[29]

Although the claims of Richard Hart and Eric Williams that the British slaves virtually emancipated themselves by their late rebellions are exaggerated, it is almost certainly true to say that the concurrence of major outbreaks and a general slave malaise finally convinced those legislators inclined to believe that slavery was an uneconomic labour system compared with 'free wage labour', pushing them into the same voting lobby with those who thought emancipation was politically timely and the minority of truly philanthropic emancipators.[30]

Three-quarters of a million British slaves were emancipated on August 1, 1834 and given nominal 'full freedom' four years later. Elsewhere, of course, slavery and the slave trade continued wherever, and as long as economic imperatives and the power of plantocracies dictated, with British capital heavily, if quietly, involved. Although it is a phase needing much more scholarly work, this period also saw continuing and even escalating slave resistance, along lines foreshadowed in the British colonies.

The most remarkable case was that of the Danish Virgin Islands, where Buddoe's carefully planned slave uprising in St Croix on Monday, July 2, 1848 – a general work stoppage followed by a mass descent on the capital Fredericksted and the sacking of the police station and the house of a prominent planter – was followed almost immediately by Governor Van Scholten's declaration of slave emancipation. In this sense, the Danish slaves achieved their own liberation, although considerable violence followed during the months of transition from slave to free wage labour, and Van Scholten's spontaneous declaration was not formally ratified by the Danish Parliament until 1851.[31]

A similar process climaxed rather less dramatically in the French colonies with the freeing of the slaves in the very same year of European liberal revolutions. As in Britain a few years earlier, the metropolitan debate over the justice, economy and political wisdom of slavery was punctuated and speeded by general slave unrest and frequent plots and revolts. The Guadeloupean blacks revolted fiercely against the reinstitution of slavery in 1802, there were serious plots and rebellions in Martinique in 1822, 1824, 1831 and 1833, and in all French colonies the months before the implementation of the emancipation decree were torn with slave unrest. According to a Guadeloupean *beké* quoted by Eric Williams, the condition of slavery in the French plantation colonies in 1848 was one in which '. . . the Negro works as little as possible, five days a week, for his master, who dares not remonstrate with him'.[32] A few years later, the declaration of slave emancipation in the Dutch West Indian colonies was actually delayed by three years while the authorities reinforced the military garrison and instituted a system of Negro education, against the very real threat of unrest on the part of slaves and ex-slaves during the transition period.[33]

In the Spanish colonies, especially Cuba, slave resistance likewise conditioned the transition from slavery to alternative labour systems, including the importation of indentured labourers from Galicia, China and other regions in the Antilles. As Díaz Soler shows, the slaves of Puerto Rico plotted and rebelled on many occasions during the nineteenth century, especially in conjunction with planned or rumoured republican invasions, or in response to harsh government proclamations such as General Prim's notorious *Banda contra la raza africana* of 1848, which itself was a response to the events in St Croix and the French Antilles.[34]

Uniquely, a large proportion of the white creoles of both Cuba and Puerto Rico were in favour of slave emancipation, mainly on economic grounds, against the will of the conservative sugar planters and the imperial authorities; so the struggle of Cuban and Puerto Rican slaves for freedom was associated with the liberal fight for political independence. The slaves were therefore naturally involved in the short-lived uprising in Puerto Rico called the *Grito de Lares* in 1868 and the Ten Years' War in Cuba which followed the liberal revolution in Spain, with its emancipation proclamation of September 17, 1868.[35]

In Puerto Rico where slaves constituted only 14 per cent of the population in a predominantly peasant economy, partial freedom began with the Moret Law of 1870, with full freedom following in 1873. But, as Rebecca Scott has shown, the Cuban case was far more complex. The revolutionary junta declared slave emancipation and a large number of blacks joined in the fighting to achieve their liberty. These *libertos*, whoever, were rarely treated as equals even in the fighting ranks, and when the Treaty of Zanjón was signed in February 1878 it no more guaranteed full emancipation than it made Cuba independent. A general amnesty was proclaimed and slaves within the 'insurrectionary lines' were recognised as free. But outright abolitionists like Maceo as well as the slave majority were disappointed, and the struggle continued.[36]

For a short while, the conservative Cuban planters felt that the system of slavery remained indispensable, although to impose it required the continuous presence of imperial troops. For their part, slaves rioted, ran away in droves and did as little work as they could get away with. The governor-general reported to Madrid in 1879 that many masters had felt compelled to offer their slaves wages and the promise of freedom, while others reported that fires had been set in the canefields by slaves who vowed: *Libertad no viene, cana no hay*; 'If liberty doesn't come, there'll be no cane.' This resistance, as much as the planters' change of heart and alternative labour arrangements, contributed significantly to the passing of the *patro-cinado* law in 1880, and to the final emancipation of the Cuban slaves in 1886.[37]

Then, to round off this brief historical survey, what of the involvement of slave resistance in the ending of slavery in its last American stronghold, Brazil, barely 100 years ago? The earlier historiography, at least as late as C. H. Haring's *Empire in Brazil*, like that of the British Empire down to Reginald Coupland and G. R. Mellor, saw slave emancipation as mainly a product of an external abolitionist movement, mainly philanthropic. Toplin, Conrad and others, however, have surely shown us the vital importance of slave resistance in the process.[38]

Generalisations about such a vast country as Brazil, with its varied economy and wide range of slave and slave-owner types, are especially dangerous. But it does seem certain that the myths of a relatively benign slave system and a relative lack of slave resistance, promoted most notably by Gilberto Freyre and Frank Tannenbaum, must be superseded by a far grimmer and more dynamic picture, with slave resistance rising to a climax in the period between 1882 and 1888.[39]

As illustrated by the excellent collection of essays published by the journal *Estudos Económicas*, the whole spectrum of slave resistance found in the Caribbean basin was also discovered in Brazil along with some distinctive local variants, although the details were often discreetly hidden in the archives and the literature.[40] The scholarly works of Almeida Barbosa, Carneiro, Freitas, Magno Guimaraes, Schwartz and many others have shown how nowhere outside Brazil were runaway slave communities – *quilombos* or *mocambos* –more numerous or widespread, with African slaves being most active in attempts to escape plantation slavery altogether. As far a covert resistance on the plantations was concerned, many other scholars have recently shown how the sugar plantations in particular were constantly racked by the threat or actuality of slave uprisings, not just the well-known disturbances in and around Bahia in 1798, 1806, 1814 and, best-known of all, 1835, but in Pernambuco, Sergipe and elsewhere. Many of the plantation rebellions in the nineteenth century, as Stuart Schwartz demonstrated with the documents from Bahia in 1806 published in the *Hispanic American Historical Review* in 1977, were seemingly well-articulated in aims and ideology, amounting, indeed, to forms of industrial action.[41]

But no Brazilian slave unrest was more coherent and purposeful than that which combined with the climax of abolitionist fervour in the 1880s. This last phase of slave violence was so manifold and widespread (occurring in mining and coffee as well as sugar plantation areas, and spreading into the towns) that even more rational slave-owners joined the abolitionists, converted to the prophecy published by Francisco Antonio Brandao in the year of slave emancipation to the USA and quoted by Robert Brent Toplin: that 'the slave will sign his letter with the blood of his oppressor and, to the disbelief of all, the decayed edifice of our society will fall'.[42] From their different point of view — which we now share, of course — the Afro-Brazilian slaves were doing no more nor less than pursuing by means of their resistance a dream, not merely of freedom but of taking their proper place in the reconstituted society of a great emerging nation.

If the foregoing analysis is convincing, we can indeed generalise about the nature and importance of slave resistance throughout plantation America. But if we agree on the general importance of slave resistance, we must not exaggerate its success. A final postscript, even disclaimer, is called for.

We would suggest that just as slaves in their constant search for freedom — or at least for an ecological 'niche' or 'life of their own' within the confines of slavery — had constantly to respond to changing conditions and to the masters' own adjustments, so the struggle was far from over anywhere once emancipation was decreed. If chattel slavery was formally ended in the half century after 1838, and with it the crude equation between slavery and racism, the class struggle was exacerbated.

At the same time that the new forces of international capitalism were in the process of fixing plantation America in a stranglehold, the former slaveholding class was easily able to reshuffle the cards it held, sustaining and even entrenching its hegemony through the control of wages, land and inter-territorial migration, not to mention, in most cases, the system of government, the franchise, the legal system and the police. Popular unrest and explosions of resistance in the post-emancipation period thus showed many similarities with at least the later forms of slave resistance and rebellion.[43]

11

Hobbesian or Panglossian?

The two extremes of Slave Conditions in the British West Indies, 1783-1834

Introduction: Demographic cliometrics, as here related to causal factors and compared, enable us not only to demonstrate and explain the wide range of conditions under which slaves lived and laboured, but also to estimate the degree of blame that can be assigned to the masters for the relative severity of each regime. This essay, originally delivered at the New York Academy of Sciences symposium on comparative slave studies in 1976, was probably the first to deploy such a range of data and causal factors in a comparative study. Focusing on slave communities that were almost polar opposites by most criteria, its main intention was to shed light on the degree to which the variations in the slaves' demographic perform-ance could be attributed, respectively, to the relative severity of the work extracted, to planters' calculated policies, and to factors beyond the masters' control or understanding, tending to come down most strongly on the last of these explanations.

It has long been recognised that there were considerable variations in slave conditions from colony to colony within the British Empire, and the relationship between material circumstances and the quality of life on slave plantations has long excited debate. However, there has hitherto been a tendency to generalise and to relate slave conditions to simple causes, imprecisely measured. Depending on their point of view and the population of slaves used as an example, some writers have suggested that the charac-teristic life of slaves was 'nasty, brutish and short' and have argued that this stemmed largely from the brutality of the economic system and the callous-ness of the white master class. Others have been able to point to areas where conditions were ostensibly better and draw the conclusion that this was as much owing to benign masters and docile slaves as to a non-intensive labour system.[1]

Such oversimplification and selectivity are giving way at last to rigorous quantification, detailed comparison, and the analysis of causes in an intensive examination of slave conditions. This has placed under close surveillance for the first time the factors influencing demographic success, which were largely beyond the key and control of masters and underexplored by previous historians, but which clearly had an important bearing on the quality of life. In particular, recent research on slavery in the British Caribbean has suggested that the achievement of a healthy demographic balance and the maintenance of families may have been as important as the type and severity of the work required and the healthiness of the plantation location in determining whether a slave population increased naturally or required importations even to keep up its numbers.[2]

Although it is impossible in the present stage of research to order the variables in this multiple hypothesis precisely, the discovery of data on a slave population for which virtually *all* causal elements were favourable permits comparisons with the data from less favourable slave regimes on which demographic research has so far concentrated. Conditions better than elsewhere in every respect seem to have been enjoyed by the population of slaves owned by Lord John Rolle of Stevenstone and established on the island of Great Exuma in the Bahamas, as detailed in the Register of Returns of Slaves for the period 1822–34.[3] Analysis of this slave unit along lines already pursued for Jamaica and Trinidad[4] suggests that the augmentation of Lord Rolle's slaves from 254 to 376 in 12 years by natural increase alone was the result of a fortunate combination of demographic, familial, occupational and locational characteristics. These placed the Rolle slaves at the benign end of a scale of demographic health, on which sugar plantation slaves such as those of Worthy Park, Jamaica, occupied a far lower position.

Great Exuma, straddling the Tropic of Cancer, north of Cuba, was one of the majority of Bahamian islands uninhabited before the American War of Independence. As large an area as Antigua, although less compact, and consisting mainly of flat coral limestone and very thin soil, the island was first settled in 1784 by groups of Loyalists from East Florida, Georgia and New York, and their slaves. Chief among these newcomers was Denys Rolle, who brought about 150 slaves from East Florida and settled them on two tracts at opposite ends of the island, totalling 2,000 acres of the choicest land, patented from the Crown. These two holdings, called to this day Rolleville and Rolle Town, were later increased to 5,000 acres by the purchase of two blocks in the centre of the island.

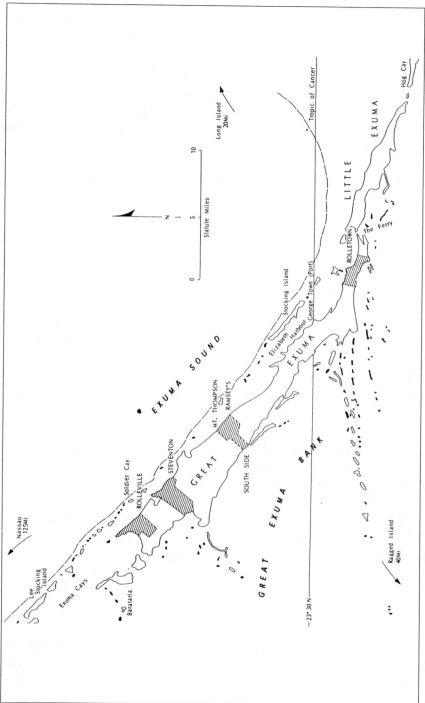

Exuma, Bahama Islands: Showing Rolle family lands, 1784-1838

As in most of the newly settled Bahama Islands, cotton plantations were optimistically begun in Exuma. But they never flourished, falling victim first to the chenille bug and then to soil exhaustion.[6] Denys Rolle himself became an absentee, living in London, while his plantations and slaves were managed by an overseer resident in Exuma and an attorney in Nassau, the Bahamian capital. When Rolle died in 1791, land and slaves were inherited by his only son John, who, as a faithful parliamentary adherent of William Pitt, had been raised to the peerage as Baron Rolle.

Although they may have also acquired the few resident slaves when they purchased their second two tracts of land in Exuma, it seems clear that the Rolles bought no more slaves on the general market after 1784.[8] When the first triennial return of Bahamian slaves was made in January 1822, following the imperial Registration Act of 1815,[9] Lord Rolle's holding had grown to 254. Of these 51 – 19 Africans and 32 Creoles – were over 40-years-old, and thus almost certainly survivors of the immigration of 1784. The remaining 203 were under age 40 in 1822, and therefore almost certainly born in Exuma.

In regard to mortality and fertility, the Rolle slaves contrasted strikingly with those of the long-established sugar plantation of Worthy Park. Before the slave trade ended in 1808, Worthy Park's annual crude mortality seems to have fluctuated between 27 and 25 per thousand, except in the years of large importations of Africans, when it soared to over 60 per thousand, with the death rate of new Africans well over ten per cent. During the registration period (for Jamaica, 1817–32), recorded mortality being 37.7 per thousand per year, with that of the creole majority being 33.7 per thousand. These rates were by no means disastrous in themselves. They were, for example, matched by Italy as a whole between 1760 and 1860, and exceeded by most European cities during the same period.[10] However, when associated with recorded live births that averaged around 20 per thousand per year over the entire period 1783-1834[11], they meant that Worthy Park – like most sugar estates – rarely came close to sustaining its population by natural increase. During the registration period, Worthy Park's crude birth rate averaged 21.7 per thousand per year, falling from 27.7 in 1817-25 to 15.6 in 1820–29.

Among Lord Rolle's slaves during the registration period (for the Bahamas, 1822–34), the crude annual birth rate averaged 42.5 per thousand, actually rising from 41.5 per thousand in 1822–25 to 53.7 per thousand in the final triennium. The crude death rate of Rolle's slaves was even more remarkable, averaging only eight per thousand per year between 1822 and

1834, with the death rate of creoles a mere 5.5 per thousand, one-sixth the rate at Worthy Park (see Tables 1 and 2). In sum, the Rolle slaves in slavery's last years exhibited demographic characteristics that match the most fruitful populations in Latin America today, with a birth rate much like that of Mexico and a death rate as low as Cuba's. Indeed, the only modern country in the Caribbean region with a comparable rate of natural increase is Costa Rica, where between 1955 and 1959 the crude birth rate was 43.5 per thousand per year, the crude death rate 9.1 per thousand, and the natural increase 36.2 per thousand[12]— compared with the Rolle figures of 42.5, 8.0 and 34.5.

To what can the remarkable differences in vital statistics between the Rolle and Worthy Park slaves be attributed? A study of the demographic balance of the Rolle slaves discloses some characteristics very unlike those of Worthy Park and other slave populations in the Caribbean proper. British slave cargoes towards the end of the slave trade contained on the average 62 per cent males.[13] A slave population with a high proportion of Africans therefore tended to have a preponderance of males, especially in the age range of highest female fertility, with corresponding effects on general fertility. Worthy Park's population in 1793, shortly after an influx of new African slaves, was 54.5 per cent male, with 156 men to 90 women in the 20 - 44 age range and a crude birth rate just under 20 per thousand. In the Rolle slave plantation in 1822, however – with only 19 elderly Africans surviving –the sexes had almost exactly evened out, with 119 males to 116 females, or 50.6 per cent males. In the 20 –44 age range there were 25 men and 35 women, all creoles.

After achieving a balance, the sex ratio of the slave populations in the colonies of the Caribbean proper tended to reverse as the proportion of creoles rose, especially after the ending of the slave trade in 1808. The reason was that slave women there lived at least five per cent longer than men on the average. In 1834, only 40.4 per cent of Worthy Park's slave population was male, and for Jamaica as a whole there was a preponderance of females of over five per cent. This feminisation of the population, however, was accompanied by an 'ageing and wasting' effect, with the proportion of fertile women actually declining. Consequently, the crude birth rate at Worthy Park, after having reached a peak of almost 35 per thousand between 1811 and 1817, relapsed in the 1830s to below 20 per thousand.

In the Bahamas (where all the conditions of life appear to have been equally shared), men seem to have lived at least as long as women, and the sex ratio stayed fairly constant until the end of slavery. Indeed, in Exuma

TABLE I

WORTHY PARK SLAVES: MORTALITY AND FERTILITY, 1817 to 1832[13]

	Total Population (actual)	Males	Females	Africans	Creoles	Median Population (3 years)	Males	Females	Africans	Creoles	Total Deaths (3 years)	Males	Females	Africans	Creoles
1817	527	241 45.73%	286	169 32.07%	358	517	232	285	159	358	51*	24	27	15	36
1820	508	223 43.90%	285	149 29.33%	359	501	217	283	139	362	50	29	21	19	31
1823	494	214 43.32%	280	130 26.32%	364	481	204	277	122	359	47*	27	20	16	31
1826	468	195 41.67%	273	115 24.57%	354	449	189	260	102	347	48	13	35	23	25
1829	430	184 42.79%	246	89 20.70%	341	401	170	231	80	321	69	30	39	17	52
1832	372	156 41.94%	216	71 19.09%	301										
1817-1832 Totals and Averages											265	123	142	90	175

Table 1 cont'd

	Crude Mortality (3 years), ‰	Males of All, ‰	Males of Males, ‰	Females of All, ‰	Females of Females, ‰	Africans of Africans, ‰	Creoles of Creoles, ‰	Total Births	Male Births	Female Births	Total Fertile Females (15-44)	% Fertile Females of Females	Crude Birth Rate, ‰	Birth Rate, Fertile Females, ‰	Natural Increase, ‰
1822	7.6	6.3	12.5	1.3	2.5	37.0	5.4	33	15	18	47	35.6	41.5	234.0	34.0
1825	4.6	2.3	4.6	2.3	4.6	19.6	3.6	33	16	17	54	37.0	37.7	203.7	33.1
1828	7.5	4.3	8.6	3.2	6.4	44.4	5.6	36	18	18	57	36.5	38.5	210.5	31.0
1831	11.9	6.0	12.1	6.0	11.8	151.5	7.2	52	26	26	63	37.3	53.7	285.7	41.8
1822-1834 Totals and Averages	8.0	4.7	9.4	3.3	6.6	52.1	5.5	154	75	79	Mean 56	37.1	42.5	229.2	34.5

* Manumitted: 1825-1828, 2 males, 3 females; 1828-1831, 5 males, 6 females; 1831-1834, 5 males, 1 female.

TABLE II
ROLLE SLAVES: MORTALITY AND FERTILITY, 1822 TO 1834[14]

	Total Population (actual)	Males	Females	Africans	Creoles	Median Population (3 years)	Males	Females	Africans	Creoles	Total Deaths (3 years)	Males	Females	Africans	Creoles
1822	254	129 / 50.78%	125	19 / 7.48%	235	265	133	132	18	247	6	5	1	2	4
1825	281	139 / 49.47%	142	17 / 6.05%	265	292	146	146	17	275	4*	2	2	1	3
1822	305	151 / 49.51%	154	16 / 5.25%	289	312	156	156	15	297	7*	4	3	2	5
1831	323	160 / 49.54%	16:	14 / 4.33%	309	335	166	169	11	324	12*	6	6	5	7
1834	357	175 / 49.02%	182	9 / 2.52%	348										
1822–1834 Totals and Averages											29	17	12	10	19

Table 2 cont'd

	Crude Mortality (3 years), ‰	Males of All, ‰	Males of Males, ‰	Females of All, ‰	Females of Females, ‰	Africans of Africans, ‰	Creoles of Creoles, ‰	Total Births	Male Births	Female Births	Total Fertile Females (15-44)	% Fertile Females of Females	Crude Birth Rate, ‰	Birth Rate, Fertile Females, ‰	Natural Increase/Decrease, ‰
1817	32.9	15.5	34.5	17.4	31.6	31.5	33.5	43	15	28	130	45.6	27.7	110.2	−5.2
1820	33.3	19.3	44.6	13.9	25.0	45.6	28.5	39	19	20	124	43.8	25.9	104.8	−7.4
1823	32.6	18.7	44.1	13.9	24.1	43.7	29.0	25	11	14	125	45.1	17.3	66.6	−15.3
1826	35.6	9.6	23.0	26.0	44.9	75.2	24.0	21	9	12	113	43.5	15.6	61.9	−19.3
1829	57.3	24.9	58.9	32.4	56.3	70.9	54.0	24	12	12	105	45.5	20.0	76.2	−37.3
1817-1832 Totals and Averages	39.3	18.2	41.2	21.0	37.7	50.0	35.4	152	66	86	Mean 119	47.4	22.5	85.2	−16.7

* Manumitted: 1817, 2 males; 1824, 3 males, 2 females; 1834, 2 males, 1 female

as a whole, there were 70 male slaves over 45 years of age in 1822, compared with 50 females, and in the far longer-established Out Island of Eleuthera there were 92 males and 66 females over age 45. The Rolle population, with no new Africans bought after 1784, retained an even healthier balance of sexes than Exuma and Eleuthera in general. In 1834 Lord Rolle owned 175 males and 182 females, or 49 per cent males and the population showed none of the ageing and wasting noticed in the colonies further south.

The comparison of age profiles points up many significant contrasts. New Africans were normally purchased in the 12-25 age range, and thus a slave population with a large proportion of Africans demonstrated a dispro-portionate bulge in the middle age ranges. When to this is added the notoriously low birth rate of the African-born (probably no more than half that of creoles)[14] and a high mortality rate, a modular age-cohort diagram for a slave population often appears more like a lopsided Christmas tree than the truer pyramid shape that indicates a normal stable population.

The age profile of Bahamian slaves in 1822 exhibited a very different shape from that for plantation slaves in the Caribbean proper at the height of slavery. Although there was a notable deficiency of elderly slaves, the populations on Eleuthera and Exuma alike displayed a regular pattern far closer to that of the modern West Indies and Central America than to the same areas in slavery days. The Rolle slaves exhibited a pattern close to the Bahamian average but, with no Africans remaining in the fertile-age range, had perhaps the healthiest demographic balance of all.

It seems plausible then, although not directly provable, that a balanced sex ratio and a 'pyramidal' age profile, as exhibited by the Exumian slaves, would be generally conducive to viable fertility as well as mortality levels. Yet, flaws in the correlations suggest that these were by no means the only causal factors involved.

Compare, for example, the fertility of women in the fertile-age range at Worthy Park and on the Rolle estate. During the registration period, the birth rate for females at Worthy Park aged 15-44 averaged only 84.6 per thousand per year, whereas among the Rolle females in the same age range it averaged 229.2 per thousand, nearly three times as high. This was despite the fact that because of natural increase the proportion of total population in the 15-44 age range was smaller in Exuma than at Worthy Park. So large a differential is surely only partly attributable to a far higher proportion of women in the fertile-age range among the Rolle slaves than at Worthy Park, a more healthy distribution between young and old, and a complete absence of fertile-age African females. Moreover, these demographic conditions do

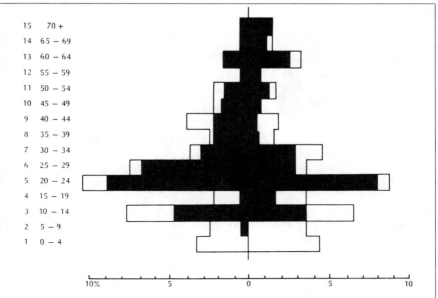

FIGURE 1. Population Pyramid for Worthy Park, 1794

Each Tenure cohort is divided to show the percentage of women in the total population on the left and of men on the right; the proportion of Africans in each group is indicated in black.

Cohort	Ages	African Males	African Females	Creole Males	Creole Females	Total Males	Total Females	Total Males and Females	% African Males of All	% African Females of All	% All Males of All	% All Females of All	% Cohort of All
1	0-4	0	0	15	19	15	19	34	0.00	0.00	3.33	4.21	7.54
2	5-9	1	0	11	16	12	16	28	0.22	0.00	2.66	3.55	6.21
3	10-14	21	17	14	12	35	29	64	4.66	3.77	7.76	6.43	14.19
4	15-19	3	8	7	8	10	16	26	0.67	1.77	2.22	3.55	5.76
5	20-24	40	36	7	8	47	44	91	8.87	7.98	10.42	9.76	20.18
6	25-29	31	13	3	3	34	16	50	6.87	2.88	7.54	3.55	11.09
7	30-34	13	13	4	7	17	20	37	2.88	2.88	3.77	4.43	8.20
8	35-39	10	3	2	4	12	7	19	2.22	0.67	2.66	1.55	4.21
9	40-44	10	2	8	6	18	8	26	2.22	0.44	3.99	1.77	5.76
10	45-49	8	3	2	0	10	3	13	1.77	0.67	2.22	0.67	2.88
11	50-54	7	5	3	2	10	7	17	1.55	1.11	2.22	1.55	3.77
12	55-59	3	3	0	0	3	3	6	0.67	0.67	0.67	0.67	1.33
13	60-64	8	11	0	3	8	14	22	1.77	2.44	1.77	3.10	4.88
14	65-69	3	5	0	1	3	6	9	0.67	1.11	0.67	1.33	2.00
15	70+	3	6	0	0	3	6	9	0.67	1.33	0.67	1.33	2.00
	Totals	161	125	76	89	237	214						
			286		165		451	451	35.70	27.72	52.55	47.45	100.00

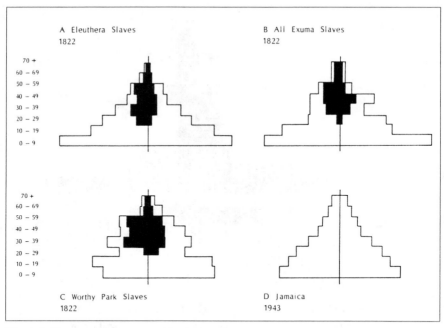

Figure 2: Four population pyramids compared

not explain why towards the end of slavery – when at Worthy Park, the number of Africans declined, the bulge in the middle age ranges ironed itself out, and the proportion of females in the total population in the age range 15-44 actually increased – not only the crude birth rate but even the birth rate of fertile-age females at Worthy Park fell – from 110.2 per thousand per year in 1817-20, to a dismal 61.9 per thousand in 1826-29. Another argument against the primacy of the 'pyramid factor' is that the fertility of the slave population of Eleuthera was lower than that of Exuma, despite the fact that the Eleutheran slaves exhibited an almost perfect demographic pyramid.

Fortunately, the Register of Returns of Slaves for the Bahamas between 1822 and 1834 discloses evidence of family and household patterns for some groups of slaves – including those owned by Lord Rolle in Exuma –which suggests that these were important additional factors. In the Bahamas, as in the West Indian colonies farther south, most returns listed all males before all females, and the old before the young, or employed some scale of economic or socioeconomic evaluation. Such was the case, for example, at Worthy Park. A few slave groups in the Bahamas, however, were listed in a manner which suggested that families and households were the most

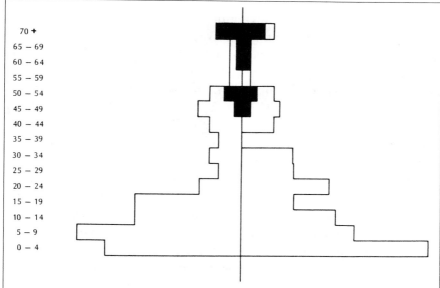

FIGURE 3. Population Pyramid for Rolle Slaves, Exuma, 1822

Cohort	Ages	African Males	African Females	Creole Males	Creole Females	Total Males	Total Females	Total Males and Females	% African Males of All	% African Females of All	% All Males of All	% All Females of All	% Cohort of All
I	0-4	0	0	22	30	22	30	52	0.00	0.00	8.66	11.81	20.47
2	5-9	0	0	26	18	26	18	44	0.00	0.00	10.24	7.08	17.32
3	10-14	0	0	17	15	17	15	32	0.00	0.00	6.69	5.91	12.60
4	15-19	0	0	17	8	17	8	25	0.00	0.00	6.69	3.15	9.84
5	20-24	0	0	7	14	7	14	21	0.00	0.00	2.76	5.51	8.27
6	25-29	0	0	4	8	4	8	12	0.00	0.00	1.57	3.15	4.72
7	30-34	0	0	5	8	5	8	13	0.00	0.00	1.97	3.15	5.12
8	35-39	0	0	4	0	4	0	4	0.00	0.00	1.57	0.00	1.57
9	40-44	0	0	5	5	5	5	10	0.00	0.00	1.97	1.97	3.94
10	45-49	1	1	6	5	7	6	13	0.39	0.39	2.76	2.36	5.12
11	50-54	3	2	2	3	5	5	10	1.18	0.79	1.97	1.97	3.94
12	55-59	0	0	2	1	2	1	3	0.00	0.00	0.79	0.39	1.18
13	60-64	1	1	1	0	2	1	3	0.39	0.39	0.79	0.39	1.18
14	65-69	2	1	0	0	2	1	3	0.79	0.39	0.79	0.39	1.18
15	70+	3	4	0	1	3	5	8	1.18	1.57	1.57	1.97	3.55
	Totals	10	9	119	116	129	125						
		19		235		254		254	3.94	3.54	50.78	49.22	100.00

convenient criteria, with children grouped after some parents where they lived together, and other cohabiting slaves listed together. Perhaps because of the scattered nature of the population (which by the end of slavery was the largest under single ownership in the colony), this was particularly true for Lord Rolle's slaves. Because of the consistency in the listing methods used, it was easy to corroborate the family groupings of the Rolle slaves indicated in 1822 by comparing the original list with the triennial returns for 1825, 1828, 1831 and 1834, in which the names of slaves born later were entered under those of their families listed earlier.

Although absolute certainty is not possible, particularly about household rather than family groupings, some notable patterns are suggested by the Rolle slave data, especially when placed in conjunction with the data from the West Indies culled by Barry Higman and with the data for families in modern rural Jamaica gathered by Edith Clarke.[15]

Easily the most common grouping among Lord Rolle's slaves —accounting for nearly half of the population in 1822 —was the simple nuclear family, with man and woman living together with their children. Although some of Higman's best data deal with 'housefuls' rather than households, and thus may play down somewhat the true proportion of nuclear families, the Rolle data suggest an incidence of the nuclear family at least twice as high as in the populations studied by Higman, and almost as high as in the modern West Indies. The proportion among the Rolle slaves for the years after 1822 would most certainly have been higher than in that year, for few families broke up, some of the couples listed in 1822 were young and had children later, and others listed as children in the first roll later began to live together and have children themselves.

Extended simple families – with grandparents living with parents and their children – were apparently more common than in the Higman examples, though less common than in modern Jamaica. Denuded families, with children living with a single parent, usually the other, were about as common in the 1822 Rolle holding as in the Higman sample for 1813, but less common than in the population of Lord Seaford's Montpelier Estate in Jamaica in 1825 (see Tables 3 and 4). In all cases, however, the proportion of such denuded families is considerably higher in the data from slavery days than in data derived from modern Jamaica, contrary to the importance attached by modern anthropologists such as Edith Clarke to the incidence of children living with their mother alone.[16]

The proportion of Rolle slaves in some form of family grouping was an astounding 86.4 per cent in 1822 and probably over 90 per cent by the end

TABLE III

FAMILY PATTERNS IN THE LAST YEARS OF SLAVERY;
ROLLE SLAVES, EXUMA; TRINIDAD SAMPLE; MONTPELIER, JAMAICA

Exuma Group-Types (1822)	A. Rolle Slaves, 1822					B. Trinidad Sample, 1813					C. Montpelier, 1825				
	Total Slaves	Family Units	Mean Size	% in Type	Sub-total	Total Slaves	Family Units	Mean Size	% in Type	Sub-total	Total Slaves	Family Units	Mean Size	% in Type	Sub-total
1. Man, Woman, Children	110	26	4.23	46.6		248	63	3.9	19.1		204	50	4.1	25.1	
2. Man, Woman (no Children)	14	7	2.00	5.9		110	55	2.0	8.5		76	38	2.0	9.3	
3. Woman, Children	40	12	3.33	16.9		186	62	3.0	14.4		309	66	4.7	38.8	
4. Man, Children	11	2	5.50	4.7		22	7	3.1	1.7		0	0	0.0	0.0	
5. Three-Generation Groups	29	5	5.80	12.3		42	8	5.3	3.2		33	8	4.1	4.1	
6. Men Alone, or Together	11			4.7											
7. Women Alone, or Together	9			3.8											
8. Children Alone (with Nurse)	12			5.1											
Totals	236			100.0		1296					814				
A. Nuclear Family (Types 1, 2, 5)	153	38	4.03	64.8	86.4%	400	126	3.17	30.9	46.9%	313	96	3.26	38.5	76.5%
B. Denuded Family (Types 3, 4)	51	14	3.64	21.6		208	69	3.01	16.1		309	66	4.68	38.0	
C. No Family (Types 6, 7, 8 etc.)	32			13.6		661			51.0		190			23.5	
				100.0					98.0*					100.0	

* 2.0% Unknown

TABLE IV
FAMILY HOUSEHOLD PATTERNS IN MODERN RURAL JAMAICA

		Percentages of Total Population		
Type of Household		'Sugartown'	'Orange Grove'	'Mocca'
I.	Simple Nuclear (Man, Woman, Children)			
	Marriage	12	25	14
	Concubinage	35	8	27
	Total	47	33	41
3-4.	Denuded Simple (Parent, Children)			
	Male	2	3	2
	Female	7	5	6
	Total	9	8	8
5A.	Extended Simple (Grandparent, Parents, Children)			
	Marriage	10	31	12
	Concubinage	8	5	18
	Total	18	36	30
5B.	Denuded Extended (Grandparent, Parent, Children)			
	Male	1	1	1
	Female	9	15	11
	Total	10	16	12
6-7.	Single Persons			
	Male	11	–	3
	Female	4	–	4
	Total	15	–	7
	Siblings	2	2	2
		100	100	100

Source: Edith Clarke, *My Mother Who Fathered Me: A Study of the Family in Three Selected Communities . . . in Jamaica*, 2d ed. (London, 1966 [orig. publ. 1957]), 192.

of slavery. This proportion compares with the figure of well under 80 per cent on the exceptional Jamaican estate of Montpelier in 1825, and under 50 per cent for Trinidad as a whole in 1813, and is well in line with the figures for modern rural Jamaica.

Higman's work on the Montpelier date indicates a positive correlation between nuclear slave families and high fertility,[17] a finding strongly corroborated by the data for the Rolle slaves. Moreover, the discovery that, in populations less well-established and less paternalistically organised than the Montpelier slaves, fertility and the incidence of nuclear families were at lower levels – together with the evidence of a much higher incidence of nuclear families and higher fertility in modern Jamaica – suggests a definite progression towards the nuclear family, as well as higher fertility. This seems to point to a European, rather than African or specifically slave, origin for modern West Indian families – a conclusion that is strengthened by the hint in Higman's work that African-style polygyny was still common in populations where the African influence remained strong, but declined as the incidence of stable monogamous unions and nuclear families increased.[18]

These suggestions about the general morphology of the West Indian family must remain tentative until much more research has been completed. Moreover, even the suggestion that stable families were the main determinants of viable fertility levels requires modification once the data for the Rolle slaves are more fully analysed and compared. Why, for example, was a degree of family nucleation that was similar to, but not greater than, modern Jamaican patterns accompanied by a far higher level of natural increase? What of sexual, physiological and customary, but not necessarily familial, patterns affecting fertility and mortality?

One factor that clearly inhibited normal sexual relations and the establishment of stable families on West Indian plantations was miscegenation between white managers and slave women. At Worthy Park, miscegenation was common: between 1816 and 1838 a rounded yearly average of 27 slaves (7.3 per cent of the total) were listed as coloured (that is, of mixed blood) – 15 'mulatto', five 'quadroon', one 'mestee', six 'sambo'. Among the Rolle slaves, on the other hand, there was apparently no miscegenation whatsoever, since in a system that allowed for the identification of coloured slaves, all were listed as black. Moreover, in the islands of the Bahamas where miscegenation was common the fertility rates were definitely lower than on Exuma. For example, in Eleuthera – for which the natural rate of increase during the registration period was approximately a third less than for the Rolle population[19] – there were 131 'coloured' slaves out of a total of 1,263 in 1822, or 1.04 per cent (98 being listed 'mulatto', 27 'yellow' and six 'sambo').[20] However, the case should not be overstated. Even if real, the effects of miscegenation on overall fertility were indirect, since there is little evidence that black women who engaged in miscegenation had fewer children than other slave women. Besides, it should be pointed out that at Worthy Park a decline in the rate of miscegenation in the last years of slavery was accompanied by a decline, rather than an increase, in general fertility.

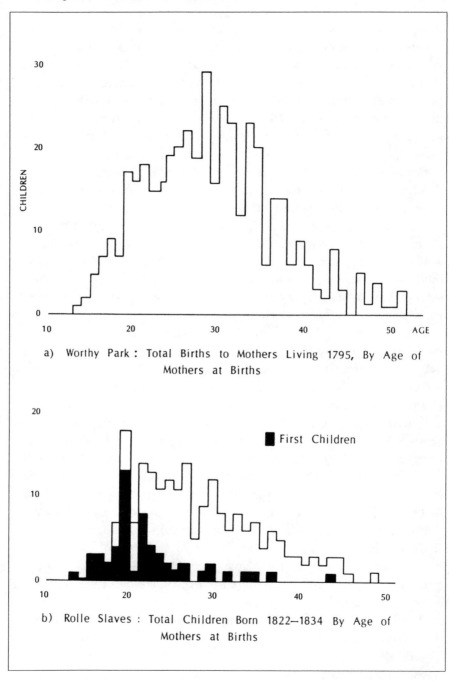

a) Worthy Park : Total Births to Mothers Living 1795, By Age of Mothers at Births

b) Rolle Slaves : Total Children Born 1822–1834 By Age of Mothers at Births

Figure 4: Fertility graphs, Worthy Park and Rolle slave mothers compared

Because mothers are not specifically identified in the Bahamian returns, it is difficult to assess individual fertility with complete accuracy. But it is clear that while female Bahamian slaves who had children may have had only a few more births than Jamaican slave mothers, a far higher proportion of the females in the fertile-age range became mothers, perhaps as many as 95 per cent compared with Worthy Park's 70 per cent – a figure even lower than for some modern populations approaching zero growth. Comparison is also aided by the fortunate existence of a unique census of slave mothers ordered by Rose Price, the son of Worthy Park's owner, in May 1795.[21] The census discloses that of the 240 females then at Worthy Park (of whom approximately 125 would have been in the fertile-age range),[22] 87 or 36.3 per cent (possibly 70 per cent of the fertile-age females) had given birth at some time. The total births was 352, an average of 4.1 births per mother. However, an alarming 77 per cent of these births, or 21.8 per cent, were said to have miscarried[23] Besides, a further 116 of the offspring were already dead by 1795, leaving only 159 or 45.2 per cent still living.

No fewer than 70 of the 87 Worthy Park mothers had lost one or more children by miscarriage or early death. Of the remainder, 13 had borne and raised a single child; three, two children, and a solitary mother, three. Under these circumstances, to give birth to six live children, let alone successfully raise them so as to be excused from manual labour under the law of 1787, was something of a triumph. As many as 17 women at Worthy park in 1795 claimed to have given birth to six or more live children, but only three mothers were excused from work in that year for having six still living, and no more than eight mothers were so excused in any subsequent year.

Among the 62 Rolle females over age 15 in 1822, 50 were listed as having children living with them or in subsequent years. Yet nine of those listed without children were over 52-years-old and may have had children who were no longer living with them. Only three of all females aged 15–51 in 1822 (aged 18, 19, and 21) had no children listed between 1822 and 1834. In all, 55 mothers were identified, with a total of 213 surviving children, an average of 3.9 each. No fewer than 21 mothers had five or more children living simultaneously at some time between 1822 and 1834 – eight mothers with five children each, five with six, three with seven, and five with eight.

Yet the Rolle mothers do not appear to have been unduly precocious. On the average they seem to have given birth for the first time at the age of 21.6 years, far higher than for most populations in the Caribbean region today. The Rolle mothers also seem to have had their children at a healthy average interval of three years –not so frequently that they were soon worn

TABLE V

ROLLE SLAVES, 1822 TO 1834: AVERAGE AGES OF MOTHERS AT BIRTHS, INTERVALS BETWEEN BIRTHS, BY FAMILY TYPES
(COLUMNS SHOW SEPARATE MOTHERS, WITH AGES AT BIRTH OF EACH CHILD)

Number Births	Average Ages	Ages at birth of each child	Child Intervals	Intervals in Years
A. Simple Nuclear Families (Male, Female, Children)				
1	22.07	19 19 23 18 18 19 21 29 15 18 21 24 28 15 19 22 25 16 21 22 33 19 21 21 31 36	1-2	3.46
2	24.63	21 22 25 28 20 21 20 25 30 19 21 23 27 31 25 22 25 34 19 24 26 36 22 25	2-3	2.91
3	27.64	24 24 28 29 22 23 23 28 37 21 23 25 29 34 27 26 29 36 24 26 29 41	3-4	2.72
4	29.83	26 26 32 30 25 26 26 31 40 22 26 28 31 37 29 32 32 38	4-5	2.69
5	31.50	28 29 36 33 28 28 28 33 40 25 32 29 33 39	5-6	2.44
6	33.89	30 32 37 37 30 31 30 35 43	6-7	2.33
7	35.17	32 33 41 38 32 35	7-8	2.50
8	38.50	34 35 43 42		
B. Denuded Simple Families (Mothers, Children)				
1	23.50	19 16 19 19 21 23 19 26 34 24 43	1-2	2.20
2	23.70	21 18 21 21 20 22 24 22 30 38	2-3	2.71
3	23.86	24 19 23 26 22 24 29	3-4	5.50
4	27.20	24 23 30 34 25	4-5	7.00
5	31.00	31	5-6	2.00
6	33.00	33	6-7	3.00
7	35.00	35	7-8	3.00
8	38.00	38		
C. Three-Generation Families (All Types)				
1	22.27	22 17 19 22 17 26 21 29 16 36 20	1-2	4.10
2	28.40	27 19 22 20 34 24 32 18 39 29	2-3	2.50
3	28.50	27 20 24 36 26 37 19 39	3-4	4.00
4	34.33	30 27 41 41 23 44	4-5	3.40
5	38.20	35 44 42 25 45	5-6	1.50
6	35.00	44 26	6-7	4.00
7	48.00	48		
D. Other Mothers				
1	17.25	19 13 18 19	1-2	1.00
2	20.00	20		

out, but possibly more frequently than among African mothers accustomed to greatly extended periods of lactation.[24] The average age of all identified Rolle's mothers at the birth of their children was 26.9, and the median, 25.4, giving a fertility peak something like five years earlier than for the slave mothers at Worthy Park.

Stable families, the absence of miscegenation, a healthy spacing between births and a comparatively early peak of fertility (though not necessarily an earlier onset of menarche) all appear to have contributed to the high levels of fertility among Lord Rolle's slaves. But it is also obvious that the general health factors that led to a high general mortality, extremely high infant mortality, and a catastrophic level of miscarriages of various kinds were among the chief reasons why it was so difficult for populations of sugar plantations such as Worthy Park, to increase naturally.

Overt cruelty on the part of masters would clearly have inhibited fertility, as well as adversely affecting the general quality of slave life; but perhaps this factor has been overstressed by anti-slavery writers. True, the Exuma slaves benefited from the virtual absence of white supervisors. But in Jamaica and other Caribbean colonies dominated by plantations, it was the system itself and conditions in general, even more than harsh overseers, that served the slaves cruelly. The beneficial effects of the planters' policy of encouraging childbirth during the period when – in response to metropolitan pressure as well as for their own advantage – the local legislators passed 'amelioration' laws (1783-1832), have also probably been exaggerated by later writers, as they were by the planters themselves.[25]

The relative availability of food adequate in quality and quantity was obviously important, although a firm answer as to how vital it was must await more study of native African as well as slave diets. Recent research has suggested that changes in diet have contributed to modern fertility patterns, particularly the early onset of menarche, and that serious diet deficiencies can adversely affect fertility.[26] Worthy Park slaves were by no means badly fed, although their diet was starch-rich and protein-poor (like that of native Africans). In contrast, Exumian slaves could enjoy fresh seafood, including that incomparable mollusk, the conch, to which modern Bahamians ascribe fabulous properties, including aphrodisiac.

Besides, the Bahamian slaves lived under extremely favourable climatic conditions. With definite seasons but none of the extremes, for example, of Virginia, Exuma was (and is) healthfully dry and without the almost seasonless, unwavering high temperatures and high humidity of the true tropics, where the environment is conducive to debilitating and fatal

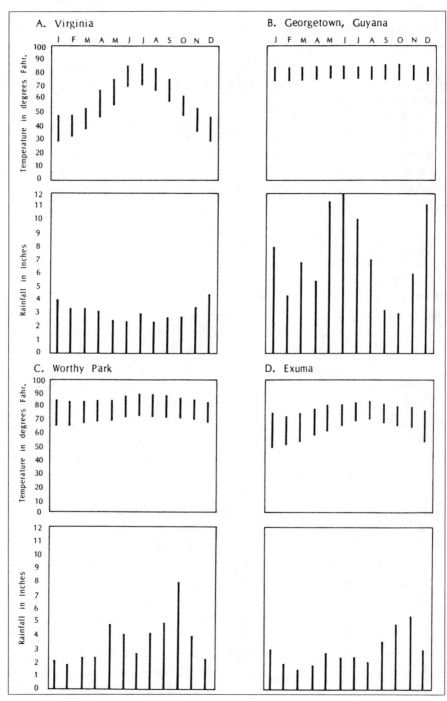

Figure 5: Climate graphs for four areas compared

diseases. The effects of such differences in disease environments – not just the macro-environments of areas and whole colonies, but the micro environments of single plantations and other settlements – require further study, as do the phenomena of epidemiology first noticed by Philip Curtin.[27]

Curtin's work also points to an additional feature distinguishing the Rolle slaves from the majority of West Indian slaves: they were descended from mainland American slaves – that parcel of about 150 brought from East Florida by Denys Rolle in 1874. Only a handful of the original migrants remained by the time of the initial registration in 1822, but the American connection may well have had subtle influences on both the health and cultural patterns exhibited by the Exumian population.

Yet when all the foregoing causal factors have been fully considered, what remains is perhaps the most important of all – the type and intensity of the work required of the slaves. In 1834, when the question of differential compensation for slaveholders was being aired, the Bahamian slaves were identified for the first time according to employment, as well as sex, age and continent of birth.[28] The categories into which Lord Rolle's slaves were placed show superficial similarities with those listed at Worthy Park over a far longer period, but they also reveal significant differences. The percentages of those regarded as unproductive were remarkably similar. For the three-quarters of each population regarded as usefully employed, there was also a fair similarity between those in preferential and prestigious jobs, and between those in labour categories in each population.

Yet among Lord Rolle's slaves there were conspicuously fewer headmen than at Worthy Park. The proportion of domestics was similar, but in 1834 all but the three who looked after the overseer's house at Rolleville were off in distant Nassau. The number of craftsmen in Exuma was also far smaller than at Worthy Park, and virtually none of Rolle's were employed in what might be regarded as functions indispensable to a dominant economic system. All in all, the proportion of what could be called élite slaves was far smaller in Exuma than in the Jamaican sugar economy, indicating a comparatively low level of socioeconomic stratification.

The proportion of stock workers listed among Lord Rolle's slaves was similar to that of Worthy Park, yet the proportion of pure field workers were far higher. Almost all of Worthy Park's labourers were listed in the four field gangs normal in Jamaican sugar plantation practice, but perhaps a third of these were usually employed in the factory rather than in the fields. No less than 60 per cent of the Rolle slaves were true agricultural workers. In addition, there were 14 male 'Mariners' – employed in the

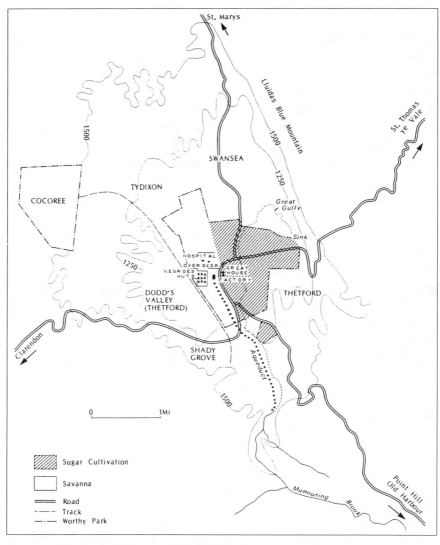

Figure 6: Worthy Park Estate and Lluidas Vale, Jamaica 1783-1838

healthiest and, in practical terms, the most free occupation open to slaves anywhere. Some were 'droguers', engaged in the coastal communication between the Rolle settlements or perhaps in the Nassau trade, but most were fishermen, who provided Exumian slaves with the fresh protein so sadly lacking on Jamaican slave plantations.

These essential differences between the two populations clearly lay in the nature of the economic system in which each was employed. Worthy

Park's system was the 'factory-in-a-field' of sugar production, while Exuma's was an almost decayed open plantation system with a negligible 'industrial' component.

Today, Worthy Park Estate, with its 1,000 workers, extends to 12,000 acres, or 19 square miles, and includes nearly the whole of Lluidas Vale. Yet in slavery days the estate was only one of five sugar plantations in the valley. The slave population of up to 550 was crammed into a central block of land less than 2 miles square, producing up to 525 tons of sugar from some 500 acres of cane, in a factory season that extended from January to July. In those last decades of slavery, moreover, Jamaican sugar workers such as those of Worthy Park were driven harder than ever before, as masters attempted to maintain gross profit levels in the face of declining sugar prices and a steady reduction in the effective labour force resulting from natural decrease, ageing and wasting, since the slave trade ended.

The working conditions on Exuma always contrasted sharply with those in Jamaica, and toward the end of slavery they actually grew easier. Cotton production, even before the introduction of the gin, was far less labour-intensive than sugar. An anonymous writer, describing the earliest Loyalist cotton operations in the Bahamas, stated in 1788: 'The number of acres which one Person can attend cannot yet be exactly ascertained, the lowest computation is 5 acres exclusive of Provisions for each hand and almost all Ages and Sexes can be employed'.[29] At the time, however, Denys Rolle had only 150 acres in cotton on Exuma, a sixth of the total for the island. Production was reckoned to average 140 pounds of 'clean cotton' per acre. At the current price of 14 pence per pound this implied a total income of some £1,225 from Rolle's cotton, or about £8 3s. 5d. per working slave. This fell far short of the average income of about £50 (at least £20 of it profit) which each of the 500 Worthy Park slaves generated between 1785 and 1800, and was less even than the average annual profit of £10 per slave which Bryan Edwards, in 1793, reckoned was achieved in Jamaican sugar production.[30]

At the average of five acres of cotton for each working slave estimated in 1788, the Rolle plantations were clearly open to expansion. With a field work-force that rose as high as 225, the Rolles might have developed 1,125 acres of cotton, producing 157,500 pounds of cotton wool a year, worth £9,188 at 1788 prices or £25 7s. 7d. for each of the total population of slaves. This may explain why Denys Rolle's original holdings at Rolleville and Rolle Town were augmented by the purchase of Steventon, Mount Thompson, Ramsey's and South Side, at the same time that the population

TABLE VI
CATEGORIES OF EMPLOYMENT COMPARED:
WORTHY PARK, 1783 TO 1834, ROLLE SLAVES, 1834

	Worthy Park		Rolle Slaves	
	%	No.	No.	%
Slave Elite (Drivers, Headmen)	3.23	16	6	1.66
Lower Elite: Domestics	4.08	20	14	3.87
Hospital	1.12	6	6	1.66
Craftsmen, Factory	2.37	12	–	–
Other Craftsmen	3.44	17	8	2.21
Laborers: Factory	1.45	7	–	–
Stock Workers	2.40	12	9	2.49
Field Workers	53.68	268	217	59.93
Others	1.00	5	14	3.87
Unproductive:	24.73	124	88	24.31
Unspecified:	2.50	13	–	–
	100.00	500	362	100.00

Notes: Worthy Park Unproductive include watchmen, aged, young, sick, women with six
children, runaways, manumitted. Rolle Slave Craftsmen were three "Platters," two
"Jobbing Carpenters," one mason, one basketmaker, one "Learning Shipwright."
Other Labourers were 14 "Mariners," either listed as "Fishing" or "in Droguing
Vessel." The Unproductive included those under six years of age, and those listed
"Nil," "Attending Infants," "Attending Light Work." One slave called Joe, aged 56,
was listed as "employed on own account, formerly as Mariner."

of slaves was gradually doubling by natural increase. Eventually, Rolle's 300
slaves in Exuma seemed scattered in six separate settlements – five of them
on hilltops – on the four blocks of land, at an average density of one person
per 17 acres, or 36 per square mile, compared with one to each four acres,
or 160 per square mile at Worthy Park.

Yet the expansion of landholdings, the natural increase of the slaves, and
even the introduction of a local variant of the cotton gin around 1800, did
not lead to any intensification of the plantation system in Exuma. It is
unlikely that the Rolles ever cultivated more than 500 acres in cotton at any
one time, and the total annual production, after reaching a peak of perhaps
60,000 pounds in 1791,[31] gradually fell with the working out of the thin
soils and periodic depredations by insects and drought. The steady decline
in prices as American cotton production expanded was an additional burden. Consequently, the Rolles, like the other Loyalist planters, were forced
into progressive diversification. Corn and peas, always easily grown between the cotton rows and cropped at a different time, were produced for
export; salt was raked from at least two salinas; and cattle, sheep and goats
were increasingly raised on the marginal lands.

This form of enforced diversification was decreasingly profitable.[32] Loyalist slaveholders, evading the laws against slave trading, shipped their slaves to the expanding sugar colonies of Trinidad and Guiana.[33] Lord Rolle himself conceived a plan to send his slaves to Trinidad, claiming that only by doing so could he staunch an outflow of capital he could ill-afford. Uniquely, he suggested that once they had earned their purchase price, the transferred slaves should be freed and allowed to work for wages. This proposal was turned down by the Colonial Office, either because it was felt that such a radical departure would upset the socioeconomic system in Trinidad or because of scepticism over Rolle's good faith.[34] Instead, Rolle merely relocated 61 of his slaves elsewhere in the Bahamas in the last five years of slavery – 37 in New Providence, 20 in Grand Bahama and four in the Berry Islands.[35]

Those slaves who remained on the Rolle lands in Exuma were increasingly left to their own devices, with a single overseer at Rolleville and only one field headman at each of the six settlements. No longer bringing in any profit, they were expected to be self-sufficient as to food production and as self-sufficient as possible in other ways. Conditions, in fact, were quite in line with those noted for the Bahamas as a whole by the abolitionist James Stephen in *Slavery Delineated* in 1824:

> The planters, unable for the most part to find any article of exportable produce, were obliged to employ their slaves in raising provisions and stock. What were the results? To the proprietors, distress enough I admit, and to many of them ruin; to the slaves, the effects have been ease, plenty, health, and the preservation and increase of their numbers by native means, all in a degree quite beyond example in any other part of the West Indies.[36]

By 1830, Lord Rolle's slaves were already sufficiently entrenched in their mode of life and independent enough to threaten revolt when they heard rumours of plans to shift them to islands more suitable for plantation agriculture. When word reached them of impending transfers (although nearby Cat Island and not distant Trinidad was thought to be the intended destination), a dozen slaves under one Pompey seized Rolle's salt boat and took flight to Nassau to plead their cause. Thrown into the workhouse and severely whipped, they nevertheless returned to Exuma reassured that they and their fellows would not be removed against their wishes.[37]

Though a true-blue Tory in British politics, and despite the dubious motivation of his philanthropic gestures, Lord Rolle has earned an almost legendary reputation in the Bahamas as a liberal master. This may have

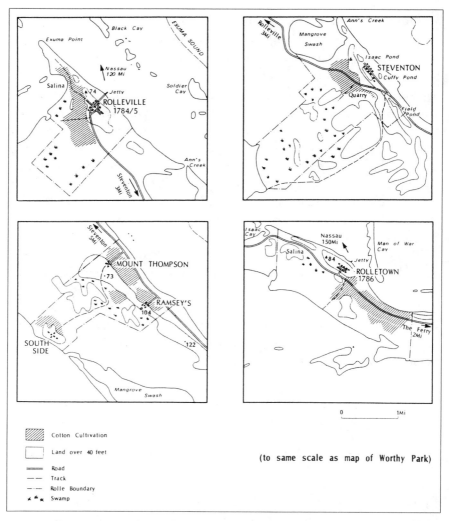

Figure 7: Great Exuma, Bahamas: The Rolle Lands 1784-1838

been as much for an exception policy of *laissez faire* before emancipation as for his plan to allow his slaves to work their freedom in Trinidad and for the fact that in 1838 he, alone of all Bahamian ex-masters, deeded his lands in Exuma to his slaves in perpetual commonage.[38] Even today, any one of the 2,000 Exumians surnamed Rolle, or their kin, may claim land to work or a plot for a house, rent free. But it is highly likely that even before they were freed in 1838, the Rolle slaves had come to regard the land they worked for food, and the tenements they lived in, as virtually their own. In

1830, at the time of the Pompey affair, a police magistrate noted that nearly all Rolle's slaves had their own provision grounds, that they ran flocks of goats and sheep of their own, and that the men were often away from the settlements for a week at a time, either fishing or working distant lands.[39] In other words, the transition from 'proto-peasant' to true peasant, of which Sidney W. Mintz writes,[40] was probably further advanced in Exuma and similar Bahamian islands than anywhere else in the British colonies, even if development after the end of slavery was to be less pronounced.

In conclusion, this brief study of populations at opposite ends of a demographic scale indicates that the causal explanation of living conditions among slaves in the British colonies was far more complex than previously thought. A multiplicity of values is suggested, but a great deal of work on other types of slave populations, in different locations, at different times, is needed before something like regression analysis is attempted and the many variables are satisfactorily placed in order. It is already clear, however, that many factors enter the analysis which have not been hitherto recognised, including some that are not directly related to the slave status of the populations as such.

Where slave lives were 'Hobbesian' in the sense of 'nasty, brutish and short', this could largely be attributed to the evils of a system that sanctioned slavery wherever the most profitable type of agriculture was extremely labour-intensive and situated in unhealthy areas. Where slave conditions – though nowhere quite 'Panglossian' – were relatively benign, this could largely be attributed to the fact that slavery, once it had been instituted for the most intensely cultivated and profitable areas, spilled over into those colonies that probably could not have justified the Atlantic slave trade on their own behalf alone. The relative cruelty or kindness of individual masters was not directly relevant, any more than the relative resistance or docility exhibited by slaves. Slave masters argued endlessly about their labour problems and possible solutions, but many factors were beyond their knowledge or control. Some unfortunate demographic characteristics were, indeed, simply transitional features of an enforced migration – lasting for different periods in different colonies, and in the British West Indies as a whole suddenly curtailed in 1808 – that were in the gradual process of ironing themselves out, whether or not slavery remained in existence.

Incomplete as it is, this essay offers possible causes for many demographic phenomena that have hitherto been unexplained. Among these are the reasons why the slaves of the Grenadines were far healthier than those of Grenada and St Vincent at either end of the same island chain; why the slave population of Barbados, though intensively engaged in sugar production, was already increasing naturally before slavery ended; why the black population of Jamaica (which never increased naturally under slavery) so quickly achieved natural increase after emancipation in 1838; and why there was such a superfluity of slaves in the decaying tobacco plantations of Virginia in the 1850s, and so large a trade in surplus slaves to the expanding cotton plantations of the south-west, that some misguided commentators have written of 'slave breeding farms'.[41]

However, one final caution is necessary in the turbulent wake of Robert Williams Fogel and Stanley L. Engerman's *Time on the Cross: The Economics of American Negro Slavery*.[42] It must be humbly admitted that even to quantify all slave plantations, and to comprehend all the components of the demographic equation for slave populations, will not be to understand fully all the ingredients of slave existence, or to explain how slaves themselves assessed the quality of their lives. To move from an understanding of the quantifiable variables to a deeper comprehension may never prove possible in the absence of direct slave testimonies. Nonetheless, the material here, and a sense of common humanity, do suggest at least a working hypothesis: that slaves were contented in reverse correlation to the intensity of the labour system, and in positive correlation to the degree to which, even as slaves, they were able to make a life for themselves.

12

Changing Patterns of Slave Family in the British West Indies

Introduction: This essay, dating from 1978, if not being quite the first to discover the existence of slave families in the British West Indies, shares with the work of Barry Higman, the credit of extending to the Caribbean the work on slave families in the USA initiated by Herbert Gutman. It goes beyond the previous essay in this collection in singling out the formation of slave families from other factors in the complex equation determining the nature and quality of slave life, taking into account demographic realities and the variations in work, climate and disease regimes at opposite ends of the Caribbean and over time. Although it is subject to the familiar problems of patchy documentation and of certainly distinguishing true families from mere households, the clinching argument for the importance of family is thought to rest on the essay's so far unique comparison of the experience of a single set of families transferred from one colony to another. At the very least it challenges received interpretations of the roles of Africans, white masters and the system of slavery in the formation of slave families. It might also lead future scholars to face the problem of explaining why, if slavery was not so inimical to formal close-knit families as previously suggested, the structure and cohesion of Caribbean families became progressively weaker rather than stronger after slavery ended.

> any Attempt to restrain this Licentious Intercourse between the Sexes amongst the Slaves in this Island in the present State of their Notions of Right and Wrong, by introducing the Marriage Ceremony amongst them, would be utterly impracticable, and perhaps of dangerous Consequence, as these People are universally known to claim a Right of Disposing themselves in this Respect, according to their own Will and Pleasure without any Controul from their Masters.[1]

Writers on the West Indies have echoed the negative statements of Alexis de Tocqueville and E. Franklin Frazier on slave and modern black families in the USA.[2] In this vein, Simey, Henriques and Goode exaggerated the

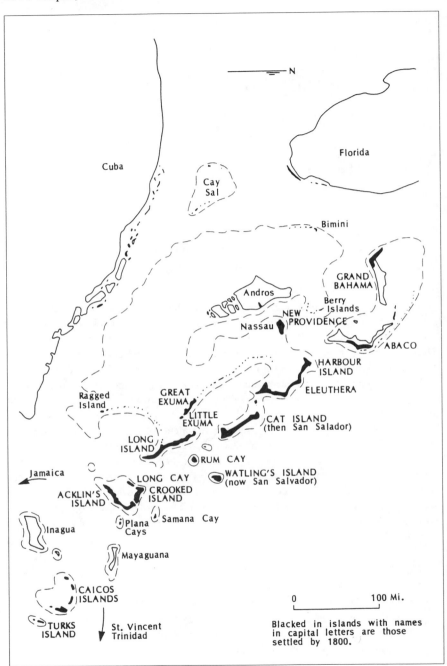

Bahama Islands, 1783-1838

matrifocality and instability of modern Caribbean families as 'deviant' results of an alleged absence of family life in slavery, while Smith and Patterson confidently backed up their analyses of modern family with assertions that 'the women normally acted as the sole permanent element in the slave family, whether or not the male partner was polygynous', and that 'the nuclear family could hardly exist within the context of slavery'.[3]

In work published since 1973, Higman has proved these assertions to be wrong and thus has reopened the whole study of the West Indian family and its roots. Although concentrating on sugar plantation colonies and the period of slave amelioration and registration (1807-34), he has shown that family life – even in patterns recognisable to Europeans – was then the norm for British West Indian slaves. Although polygyny and other African practices persisted, the nuclear, two-headed household was extremely common among the African-born as well as creole slaves. More remarkably, single-headed maternal households were in a minority in every area studied by Higman, save for the towns. The frequency of matrifocal families and the general disruption of slave families had become exaggerated, he suggested, because of the practices of those slaves with whom whites were most familiar: domestics and urban slaves.[4]

The purpose of this present paper is fourfold. It adds to Higman's evidence by using material chiefly from the Bahamas, a non-sugar, largely non-plantation colony. It also summarises the evidence hitherto gathered, sketches the varieties of slave family from place to place and time to time, and, finally, discusses developmental models. Despite great variations according to location, employment and ownership (not to mention the difficulties presented by fragmentary and uneven evidence) a consistent pattern does emerge. This suggests both the place that the rediscovered West Indian slave family of the late slave period occupies in the continuum between West African roots and the modern West Indian black family, and some of the ways in which the dynamics of West Indian black family have differed from those of the USA and Latin America.

As Stephen noted as early as 1824, slave conditions in the Bahama Islands were at the benign end of a scale on which the sugar colonies further south – particularly the newly acquired colonies of Trinidad and Guyana – represented the opposite extreme. An influx of Loyalist planters after 1783 had changed the tone and pace of the archipelagic colony, doubling the white population and trebling the number of slaves; but the population density remained a twentieth of that of Jamaica and a fiftieth of that of Barbados, while the ratio of black slaves to white freemen and the average

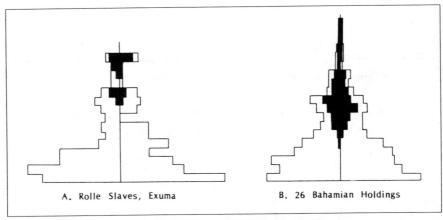

Figure 1: Population pyramids, Rolle slaves and 26 Bahamian holdings

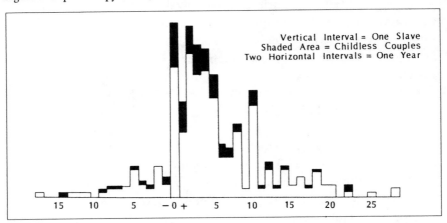

Figure 2: Bahamas, 26 holdings, 1822; Age differences between males and their mates

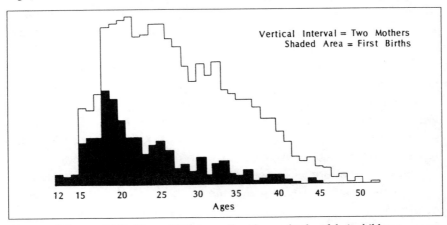

Figure 3: Bahamas, 26 Holdings, 1822; Ages of mothers at births of their children

size of slave holdings remained among the lowest in the British West Indies.[5]

Most of the Loyalist emigrés settled their slaves on Bahamian 'Out Islands' until then unpopulated, attempting to replicate the plantation conditions they had left behind in the Carolinas, Georgia and Florida. They found the climate ideal for growing sea island cotton, but the exhaustion of the thin soil and the depredations of the chenille bug left them unable to compete with American cotton once Whitney's gin became effective after 1800. Although a local planter, Joseph Eve, invented a wind-powered variant of the gin, Bahamian cotton production had almost faded away by 1820. Plantations were turned over to stock or the growing of grains and other provisions, and many of the slaves had to fend for themselves.

Those planters who could, sold up and migrated once more. Many of them attempted to transfer their slaves to the old colony of Jamaica or the new sugar plantations in Trinidad and St Vincent, where fresh slaves were at a premium after the African supply had been cut off by the abolition of the Atlantic slave trade in 1808. Although slaves were registered in the Crown Colony of Trinidad as early as 1813, this opportunistic trade was not revealed until the first returns under the Bahamian Slave Registration Act of 1821 reached London, after which it was effectively scotched by the abolitionists under Stephen Lushington in 1823. By then, perhaps 2,000 Bahamian slaves (a fifth) had already been transferred.[6]

The meticulous triennial returns of British West Indian slaves produced by the registration laws were of great value to the emancipationists, who were able to prove the persistence of 'natural decrease' as well as to end the intercolonial trade. Modern demographers, however, can put them to much wider use, reconstituting and comparing whole colony populations by age, sex, African or creole birth, mortality, fertility and life expectancy. In at least two colonies, Trinidad and the Bahamas, it is also possible to discover and compare patterns of slave family. Unlike the Trinidadian instructions, the Bahamian law did not require the listing of slaves' families or households-by-name. But approximately a quarter of Bahamian slaves were voluntarily listed by their owners in such a way as to indicate family relationships, though with limits on the range of family types identifiable. Comparison between the original lists of 1821 and 1822 and those of 1825, 1828, 1831 and 1834, moreover, allows both for corroboration of relationships and the testing of their permanence.

In all, it has proved possible to analyse 26 slave holdings in the first Bahamian census of 182-22 in which owners listed slaves in family groups,

Table 1 Household Patterns, Rolle Slaves, and 26 Bahamian Holdings, 1822

FAMILY TYPE	ROLLE SLAVES, EXUMA				26 BAHAMIAN HOLDINGS			
	TOTAL SLAVES	NUMBER OF UNITS	MEAN SIZE OF UNITS	PERCENT OF TOTAL IN TYPE	TOTAL SLAVES	NUMBER OF UNITS	MEAN SIZE OF UNITS	PERCENT OF TOTAL IN TYPE
1. Man, Woman, Children	110	26	4.23	46.6	1,629	308	5.29	54.1
2. Man, Woman	14	7	2.00	5.9	178	89	2.00	5.9
3. Woman, Children	40	12	3.33	16.9	377	95	3.97	12.5
4. Man, Children	11	2	5.50	4.7	16	3	5.33	0.5
5. Three-Generation Groups	29	5	5.80	12.3	358	46	7.78	11.9
6. Men Alone, or Together	11	—	—	4.7	264	—	—	8.8
7. Women Alone, or Together	9	—	—	3.8	173	—	—	5.8
8. Children Separately	12	—	—	5.1	16	—	—	0.5
Totals	236	—	—	100.0	3,011	—	—	100.0
A. Nuclear Family (1,2,5)	153	38	4.03	64.8	2,165	443	4.89	71.9
B. Denuded Family (3,4)	51	14	3.64	21.6	393	98	4.01	13.0
C. No Family (6,7,8)	32	—	—	13.6	453	—	—	15.1

rather than by alphabetical order, age, sex or any other method. This sample comprised 3,011 out of a Bahamas grand total of about 12,000, an average of 116 slaves per holding, but with a range between 20 and 840, drawn from 11 different islands. The findings not only illustrate the contrasts between the Bahamian slave population and those in sugar plantation colonies farther south, but also point up the typicality of the only Bahamian slave group previously studied, that of the slaves owned by Lord John Rolle on the island of Exuma.[8]

Ten times the size of the Rolle holding, this widespread fourth of the Bahamian slave population exhibited almost as balanced, 'modern', and 'unslavelike' a demographic pattern, with a broad base of youngsters and a fair number of elderly slaves. The sexes in the fertile age ranges were almost as equally balanced as Rolle's slaves, and the only features reminiscent of slave populations farther south were a slight 'bulge' in the age range from 40-54, representing in this case survivors from the migration of Loyalists' slaves in the 1780s, and a substantial remnant of Africans, 18.8 per cent of the total. Unlike the Rolle holding, there also was evidence of considerable miscegenation, 6.9 per cent of the 3,011 slaves being listed as 'mulatto' or 'yellow'.[9]

These slight differences and the less optimal work and living conditions accounted for a rather lower average net population increase than with Lord Rolle's slaves, but the incidence of family in the sample of 26 holdings was very similar. As Table 1 shows, 85.0 per cent were found in some type of family, with no less than 54.1 per cent of the 3,011 slaves over 20-years-old, 854, or 63.1 per cent, were listed in couples. The normal pattern was for males to be a few years older than their mates. On the average, males were some four-and-one-half years older, but this figure was skewed by some much older males and by the few older females. Of 397 couples who were the parents in nuclear families or were childless, in 303 cases the males were from zero to ten years older, with an average of three years and ten-and-one-half months. Although the presence of elderly mothers whose first children had left the household or had died makes it difficult to count exactly, the average age of mothers at the birth of their first children appears to have been under 20 years. As Table 2 shows, the spacing between children was regular and healthy, with the overall average almost exactly three years. Of all women in the age range 15-49, a high proportion, 65.8 per cent, were indicated as mothers, having had on the average almost exactly three children.[10]

Table 2   Bahamas, 26 Slave Holdings, 1822—Average Ages of Mothers at Births and Child Spacing

WHICH CHILD	NUMBER OF MOTHERS	PERCENT TOTAL MOTHERS IN EACH GROUP	AVERAGE AGES AT BIRTHS	AVERAGE SPACING (YEARS)
1st	479	100.0	22.37	
				3.36
2nd	356	74.3	26.53	
				2.93
3rd	244	50.9	30.00	
				2.93
4th	170	35.5	32.60	
				2.42
5th	105	21.9	33.38	
				2.81
6th	59	12.3	35.22	
				2.95
7th	31	6.5	40.10	
				2.67
8th	8	1.7	43.46	
				1.87
9th	2	0.4	38.75	
				1.00
10th	1	0.2	38.00	
Averages			34.84	3.02

Besides these basic statistical findings, a study of the Bahamian returns allows for some general observations and analysis along lines followed by Gutman and other scholars of slavery in the USA. First, important implications concerning the incidence of endogamy and exogamy — or at least of in-group and out-group mating — arose from the tendency of slave families to appear most clearly in the records of the larger and more isolated holdings, which were mainly in islands distant from Nassau, the colonial capital.[11] In contrast, on New Providence (Nassau's island) and the nearer, long-established settlements of Harbour Island and Eleuthera, conjugal patterns seem to have been more disrupted. Many of the holdings were too small to include whole families and this clearly contributed to the custom of choosing mates from other holdings. But there were other factors. Among a heavily creolised population (with some slaves six generations removed from Africa), in small units, marital mobility was not only possible but probably seen as desirable to avoid too close a consanguinity. Miscegenation was also rather more common in New Providence and Eleuthera than farther afield, those slaves listed as mulatto or yellow constituting eight per cent of the few holdings analysed, and probably more than ten per cent overall.[12]

In general, it seems that these conditions led not to familial cohesion but the reverse, with many male mates absent or even temporary. Female-headed families were most common in the listings for New Providence (where almost a quarter of all Bahamian slaves lived), not only in the several holdings that consisted solely of slave mothers and their children, but also in such groups as the 37 slaves of Elizabeth Mary Anderson, where nine men aged from 22 to 60 were listed together but separately from five female-headed families averaging five children each. Only in the exceptional holding of William Wylly at the isolated western end of New Providence, were families distinct and clearly permanent.

In the distant, more recently established settlements, populations were on the average larger, more isolated and, perhaps of necessity, more cohesive. The choice of mates was limited, and thus relationships were likely to be not only well-known but also more permanent. In relatively large populations, consisting in most cases primarily of first and second generation creoles, such enforced in-group mating would not yet come into conflict with any customary ban on cousin-mating that may have existed (whether derived from Africa or Europe). In all, it is possible that conditions in the Out Islands, which Nassauvians, both white and black, might consider primitive, were more conducive to stable family formation than those closer to the colonial centre. Certainly, in modern times, Otterbein has documented a greater awareness of the value of stable families in 'primitive' Andros Island than that to be inferred in the less affluent sections of modernised Nassau, which include large groups of displaced Out Islanders. Yet these conditions seem to have also obtained in slavery days, a conclusion that runs counter to Gutman's contention that the dislocating effects of urbanisation postdated emancipation, at least in the USA.[13]

The listings of families headed by single females may disguise the existence of serially shifting, or even polygynous, relationships. But in the series of five censuses spread over 12 years (1822-34) there is very little positive evidence of serial monogamy, and only rare and equivocal evidence of polygyny.[14] Naming practices were little help in tracing family patterns. Bahamian slaves did not universally adopt surnames before emancipation, and then it is by no means certain that surnames were patronymics in the modern style.[15] The practice of taking the surname of the former owner tends to exaggerate consanguinity as well as to confuse relationships – the most extreme case being Lord Rolle's 372 slaves, all of whom took the surname Rolle in order to share common rights in their former master's land. The discernment of immediate relationships was aided, however, by the frequent practice of naming a male child after his father or grandfather, and the occasional custom of naming a female after her grandmother.[16]

Such three-generation links sometimes allowed for the identification of extended family units, but the positive evidence of wider kinship links was disappointingly meagre, and the direct evidence from the records of related families living close together in clusters of huts or 'yards' was non-existent, although such groupings are known to have been a feature of Out Island life in later times. However, the frequent listing of a young girl with her first child in the household of her parents, or mother, does permit some inferences about sexual customs. Few girls under 20 cohabited with their mates; few mothers over 20 lived with their parents, and most, as we have seen, lived with mates. Nearly all girls who bore their first children in their mothers' households began separate cohabitation at, or shortly before, the birth of their second children. It therefore seems likely that premarital sex was not uncommon, and even that virginity at marriage was not excessively prized; but that separate cohabitation in a nuclear household was the accepted norm for couples over the age of 20.[17]

The evidence proves the vigorous existence of families among Bahamian slaves during the registration period and, indeed, points to the existence of types of families classified as 'modern' by Europeans among the least modernised groups of slaves. It remains to be decided, though, whether this was a social pattern chosen by the slaves themselves – and thus likely to have existed before the recorded period – or one determined, or at least encouraged, by the Eurocentric, pro-natalist, or publicity-conscious masters.

Strong evidence for the latter conclusion is found in the case of the slaves of William Wylly, Attorney-General of the Bahamas. An ardent Methodist who arranged for a minister to preach regularly to his slaves, he came to be regarded as a crypto-emancipationist by his fellow planters because of a legal decision made in 1816, and was at the centre of a bitter wrangle between the plantocratic Assembly and three successive governors, lasting until 1820. Close examination of the evidence, however, shows that Wylly was a strict paternalist, and suggests that if he wished to turn his slaves loose it was because they were no longer profitable.[18]

By 1818, Wylly's three estates in western New Providence had ceased to grow cotton, Tusculum and Waterloo being turned over to stock raising and Clifton, the largest, being devoted to growing provisions for the slaves and the Nassau market. The Attorney-General's many enemies accused him both of allowing his slaves more time to work for themselves than laid down by Bahamian law, and of supplying them with less than the provisions specified. In response, Wylly produced convincing proof of the degree to which his slaves were self-supporting, and stated: 'My principal object has been, to accustom them to *habits of Industry and Oeconomy* – which I am convinced, never will be found to exist among any Slaves, in this part of the World, who are victualled by their Masters.'[19]

At the same time, Wylly forwarded a revealing set of regulations for his slaves which he had caused to be printed and published in Nassau in 1815. Apart from his concern for religious instruction and regular prayers, and details of clothing, feeding, work and punishment regulations, these clearly illustrated his views on slave marriage, sexual continence and motherhood. 'Every man, upon taking his first wife,' read Article VII of the regulations, 'is entitled to a well built stone house, consisting of two apartments, and is to receive a sow pig, and a pair of dunghill fowls, as a donation from the proprietor.'[20]

'In cases of Adultery,' read Article XI, 'the man forfeits his hogs, poultry, and other moveable effects; which are to be sold, and the proceeds paid over to the injured husband. Both offenders are moreover to be whipt; their heads to be shaved, and they are to wear *Sack cloth* (viz. gowns and caps made of Cotton bagging) for the next half year; during which time they are not to go beyond the limits of the plantation, under the penalty of being whipt.'

With far less Mosaic severity, Article XIX enjoined that, 'On working days, the children are to be carried, early every morning, by their mothers, to the Nursery, where proper care will betaken of them during the day; and their mothers are to call for them when they return from their work in the afternoon. Women who have children at the breast, are never to be sent to any distance from the homestead.'

Predictably, Wylly's slave lists in the registration returns disclose a neat pattern of families and a healthy natural increase. Since his regulations were published and his views on slave management became well-known, it is possible that they became normative. The very decision to list slaves according to families and households may indicate owners who shared Wylly's concerns. Certainly, the other two Bahamian owners known to have engaged in correspondence on the management of their slaves, Lord Rolle of Exuma and Burton Williams of Watling's Island, demonstrated an awareness of the value of stable families in producing healthy, fertile and contented slaves.[21]

It is likely, though, that such planters as Wylly, Rolle and Williams were self-deluding if not self-serving. The widespread incidence and consistent form of slave families suggest customary choice on the part of the slaves rather than the dictates of the masters. Few plantations were owner-managed, especially in the Out Islands, and it seems strange that orderly patterns of slave family should be more common the further from Nassau (where slaves were commonly under the daily scrutiny of their owners), unless this was the slaves' own choice. Nor can the growing influence of Christianity be given unequivocal credit. The established Anglican Church, which held a monopoly on formal weddings until 1827, did not proselytise the slaves, and the few sectarian missionaries concentrated on Nassau and the nearer islands. The underground 'Native Baptist', who were active among the Loyalists' slaves in Nassau as early as in Jamaica, may have had more widespread influence. But they were known to be tolerant about informal marital ties, being regarded by whites as hardly Christians at all. Indeed, the common impression held by the whites of the mass of the slaves was that those who were not heathen practisers of *obeah* were infidel 'followers of Mahomet'.[22]

This at least suggests strong African cultural retentions, particularly in the Out Islands. Numerically the Africans were few by the registration period but, as elderly survivors, seem to have been highly respected members of the slave community. Indeed, it became clear on further analysis of the 26 holdings that the African slaves had influence out of all proportion to their numbers, and even that they were dominant in shaping family life in the Bahamas. Although most of the African-born slaves were grouped together towards the end of the rolls, in more than a third of the slave holdings analysed an African couple was at the head of the list. Thus usually indicated that the owner had chosen the most prestigious married African as head driver.[23]

As in all slave communities the role of such leaders was ambivalent. They were chosen for what was termed 'confidentiality' – fidelity, reliability and respectability. But they were known to be effective because they commanded respect and 'reputation', among creoles as well as African blacks. For example, Wylly's African head driver and under-driver, Boatswain and Jack, practically ran his estates. Strong family men, they were expected to lead prayers at Sunday services and conduct funerals. Boatswain at least was literate, and was paid for each slave taught to read; both were rewarded with 12 guineas a year, the right to own and ride a horse, and the power to inflict punishment on their own initiative up to 12 stripes. But did their authority, ultimately, stem from their paternalistic master, or from their position as family heads and from African roots? And what did the family pattern at Clifton, Tusculum and Waterloo owe, respectively, to memories of Africa, the examples of Boatswain and Jack, and the encouragement of Wylly?

Strong clues emerged from the discovery that, when African-headed families – those in which both parents, either parent, or the only parent were African-born – were separated from purely creole families, it became obvious that Africans were considerably more inclined towards family formation than creole slaves. Of the Africans, 65.3 per cent lived in couples, compared with less than 60 per cent of the creoles over the age of 20. Of all African-headed families, 61.0 per cent were of the simple nuclear type, with an additional 9.4 per cent indicated as extended family households. This compared with 48.4 per cent in nuclear units and 14.4 per cent in extended households among creole families. Only 11.9 per cent of Africans lived alone, compared with 16.7 per cent of adult creoles.

By a Bahamian law of 1824, owners were forbidden to separate slave husbands from wives by sale, gift, or bequest, or to take their children away from them before they were 14-years-old. Although the act did not expressly forbid the splitting of families by shifting slaves from island to island, or the separation of children from single parents, it would seem to have provided owners with a motive for discouraging rather than encouraging slave families. Yet the evidence strongly suggests that masters were not only forced to acknowledge slave marital arrangements and to sell or transfer slaves only in families, even before 1824, but also to consider carefully the social consequences before they shifted slaves from their customary houses, plots and kin at all.[24]

Wylly, although an alleged emancipationist, only manumitted three of his slaves after 1822 and did not scruple to scatter them by sale and tranfer between 1821 and his death in 1828. Families, however, were carefully kept together. In another case, Rolle proposed an ingenious scheme in 1826 to shift all of his slaves to Trinidad, where they were to work to earn their freedom in the Spanish style. Fortunately for the slaves, the project was vetoed by the Colonial Office. But the word must have filtered down to Exuma, for in 1828 when Rolle's agent set about transferring some slaves to Grand Bahama, all of the slaves, fearing a move to Trinidad, became so mutinous that troops had to be sent down to keep order. Two years later, when they heard that the agent planned to ship them from Exuma to Cat Island, 44 slaves (five men, eight women, and their families) actually rebelled. Under the leadership of a slave called Pompey they first fled to the bush, then seized Rolle's salt boat and sailed to Nassau to put their case to Governor Smyth, who was widely thought to be a friend of the slaves. The fugitives were thrown into the workhouse and the leaders flogged (including the eight women). But Smyth was angry when he heard about it

Table 3   Bahamas, 26 Slave Holdings, 1822 Comparison between African-Headed and Creole Families

FAMILY TYPE	A. AFRICAN HEADED FAMILIES[a]				B. CREOLE FAMILIES			
	TOTAL SLAVES	NUMBER OF UNITS	MEAN SIZE OF UNITS	PERCENT OF TOTAL IN TYPE	TOTAL SLAVES	NUMBER OF UNITS	MEAN SIZE OF UNITS	PERCENT OF TOTAL IN TYPE
1. Man, Woman, Children	830[a]	154	5.39	61.0	799	154	5.19	48.4
2. Man, Woman	138[a]	69	2.00	10.2	40	20	2.00	2.4
3. Woman, Children	91	21	4.33	6.7	278	72	3.86	16.8
4. Man, Children	11	2	5.50	0.8	5	1	5.00	0.3
5. Three-Generation Groups	128[a]	19	6.73	9.4	238	29	8.21	14.4
6. Men Alone, or Together	114	—	—	8.4	150	—	—	9.1
7. Women Alone, or Together	48	—	—	3.5	125	—	—	7.6
8. Children Separately	—	—	—	—	16	2	8.00	1.0
Totals	1,360	—	—	100.0	1,651	—	—	100.0
A. Nuclear Family (1,2,5)	1,096	242	4.53	80.6	1,077	203	5.31	65.2
B. Denuded Family (3,4)	102	23	4.43	7.5	283	73	3.88	17.1
C. No Family (6,7,8)	162	—	—	11.9	291	—	—	17.7

a   African-Headed Families were taken to be those in which both parents, either parent, or the single parent were of African birth. Thus in categories 1, 2, and 5 in Section A mixed couples were included.

and none of the slaves in the end were sent to Cat Island; so it can be said that Pompey and his fellows won the principle that Bahamian slaves could not with impunity be shifted against their will.[25]

The largest single transfer of slaves had been the shipment in 1823 of most of the 840 slaves of James Moss from Acklin's Island and Crooked Island to Jamaica, where their fate remains obscure. Yet the most interesting of all Bahamian transfers was that to Trinidad between 1821 and 1823 of the majority of the slaves of Burton Williams of Watling's Island and his family, since it allows for comparisons between the fortunes of those transferred and other slaves in Trinidad, and between all those and the slaves left behind in the Bahamas.

Early in 1825, after he had been in Trinidad three-and-half years, Williams gave evidence to the Trinidad Council about his slaves. He claimed that in '30 odd' years of Bahamian residence he had seen the group of seven slaves inherited and 'about 100' bought augmented by 224 through natural increase. This remarkable growth (as rapid as that indicated for Rolle's slaves, and sustained over a longer period) was attributed by Williams to his own residence among the slaves, to firm management, and to the encouragement of marriage 'by giving a feast to the Gang when they come together and a sharp punishment when they part'.[26]

Certainly, the 450 Williams slaves found in the Bahamian in 1821 exhibited an even healthier demographic balance and a higher incidence of family formation than the Bahamian average, as is shown in Figure 4 and Table 4. The proportion of young children was higher, there were only two-thirds as many Africans, and yet a fair number were very elderly slaves. The proportion of slaves in nuclear families, 55.8 per cent, was some two per cent higher than the average for the 26 holdings analysed earlier, and the total in some kind of family more than five per cent higher, at 90.2 per cent. Yet by Williams' account, the situation in the Bahamas had become economically and demographically critical by 1821, so that he could neither clothe nor feed his slaves adequately, although he owned 13,000 acres of land. Taking advantage of the inducements offered by Trinidad, he therefore transferred 324 of his slaves in five cargoes between 1821 and 1823.[27]

Although one or two couples were split and an unknown number of extended family members separated, Williams clearly attempted to transfer his slaves predominantly in family units. Comparison of the slaves settled at Williamsville, his new estate in Naparima, in the Trinidadian returns of 1825 with those left behind listed in the Bahamas returns of the same year, indicates also that the majority of the elderly and Africans were left behind,

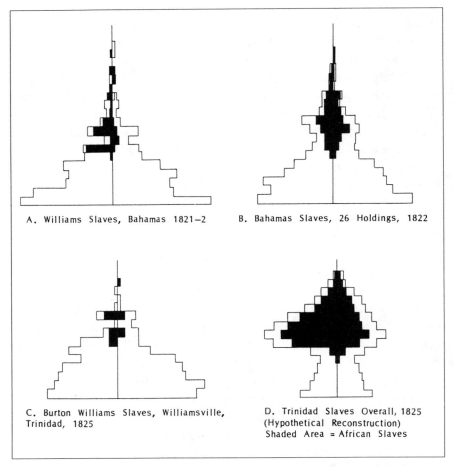

A. Williams Slaves, Bahamas 1821–2

B. Bahamas Slaves, 26 Holdings, 1822

C. Burton Williams Slaves, Williamsville, Trinidad, 1825

D. Trinidad Slaves Overall, 1825
(Hypothetical Reconstruction)
Shaded Area = African Slaves

Figure 4: The Burton Williams slaves, 1822 and 1825, compared with Bahamas and Trinidad slaves, 1825; Population Pyramids

and that rather more young females were carried than young males. The transferred population therefore exhibited many characteristics sharply different from those of the generality of Trinidad slaves. Only 5.3 per cent of the Williamsville slaves were African-born, compared with the Trinidadian average of over 40 per cent, and females outnumbered males by 7.8 per cent, more than reversing the general Trinidadian pattern. Whether using the categories used elsewhere in this paper or those employed by Higman, the contrast in family formation is even more noticeable. Because of the greater detail given in the Trinidadian registration returns, more types could be differentiated, but the total of Williamsville slaves in some type of family was as high as in the Bahamas sample, and almost twice as

Table 4 Bahamas, Family Formation, Williams Slaves 1822 and 1825 compared with 26 Holdings, 1822

FAMILY TYPE	A. WILLIAMS SLAVES, 1822				B. WILLIAMS SLAVES, BAHAMAS, 1825				C. 26 BAHAMIAN HOLDINGS, 1822			
	TOTAL SLAVES	NUMBER OF UNITS	MEAN SIZE OF UNITS	PERCENT OF TOTAL IN TYPE	TOTAL SLAVES	NUMBER OF UNITS	MEAN SIZE OF UNITS	PERCENT OF TOTAL IN TYPE	TOTAL SLAVES	NUMBER OF UNITS	MEAN SIZE OF UNITS	PERCENT OF TOTAL IN TYPE
1. Man, Woman, Children	251	47	5.34	55.8	103	20	5.15	46.0	1,629	308	5.29	54.1
2. Man, Woman	28	14	2.00	6.2	10	5	2.00	4.5	178	89	2.00	5.9
3. Woman, Children	45	10	4.50	10.0	38	14	2.71	17.0	377	95	3.97	12.5
4. Man, Children	2	1	2.00	0.5	0	0	—	—	16	3	5.33	0.5
5. Three-Generation	80	9	8.88	17.8	25	4	6.25	11.2	358	46	7.78	11.9
6. Single Men	15	—	—	3.3	22	—	—	9.8	264	—	—	8.8
7. Single Women	14	—	—	3.1	8	—	—	3.5	173	—	—	5.8
8. Separate Children	15	—	—	3.3	18	5	3.60	8.0	16	—	—	0.5
Totals	450	—	—	100.0	224	—	—	100.0	3,011	—	—	100.0
A. Nuclear Family (1,2,5)	359	70	5.13	79.8	138	29	4.75	61.6	2,165	443	4.89	71.9
B. Denuded Family (3,4)	47	11	4.27	10.4	38	14	2.71	17.0	393	98	4.01	13.0
C. No Family (6,7,8)	44	—	—	9.8	48	—	—	21.4	453	—	—	15.1

high as the Trinidadian average indicated by Higman. The percentage in simple nuclear households, 57.3 per cent, was slightly higher than in the Bahamas, and three times as high as the Trinidadian average. Mothers living alone with their children accounted for only six per cent of the Williamsville slaves, half of the Bahamas figure, and little more than a quarter of that for Trinidad as a whole.

As a consequence of the division of the Williams slaves, those left behind in the Bahamas were less well-balanced in composition than the Bahamian average and therefore increased in number rather less rapidly after 1823. Yet those transferred were less healthy than those left behind and increased even more slowly. However, they did increase, in contrast to Trinidadian slaves in general, who suffered an alarming depletion throughout the registration period. By the end of 1826, 33 of Williams' Trinidadian slaves had died, while 57 were born (49 having been sold and two manumitted), an annual rate of natural increase of roughly 16 per thousand. This was half the Bahamian rate, and compared with an annual net decrease at least as high for Trinidadian slaves on the average.[28]

Although his 1825 evidence was twisted to justify the transfer, Williams had to admit that the health and morale of his slaves had suffered in the first three years – the seasoning period. 'Fevers and Agues and bowel Complaints', as well as unfamiliar 'Sores', although not great killers, were common among the transferred slaves. These ills Williams attributed to his having arrived in the middle of the wet season, settling in a wooded and marshy area, and being forced to feed his slaves on plantains and saltfish rather than their customary guinea corn (millet or sorghum). He deplored the laxity of Trinidadian morals and the effects on family life of the disparity in the sex ratio. He also pleaded that the demoralising effects of Colonial Office regulations would encourage the idleness of slaves and limit the powers of correction of their masters. Against the evidence, he denied that the work required of slaves was harder than in the Bahamas, and claimed that slaves had more opportunity in Trinidad to dispose of the surplus food that they grew on their own allotments. However, he admitted that most of the slaves would have returned to the Bahamas if they had been given the choice.[29]

The research undertaken so far not only indicates a far wider existence of family in slave society than hitherto expected, but has also clarified the varieties of family within the range of West Indian slave communities in the late slave period. At one end of the scale were the virtual peasants of the Bahamas, Barbuda, and, perhaps, the Grenadines, with locational

Table 5 Family Structure, Williams Trinidadian Slaves, 1825 compared with Trinidadian Total, 1813 (Higman, 1978)[a]

FAMILY TYPE	A. WILLIAMS SLAVES, 1825				B. TRINIDADIAN SLAVES TOTAL, 1813			
	TOTAL	UNITS	MEAN SIZE	PERCENT IN TYPE	TOTAL	UNITS	MEAN SIZE	PERCENT IN TYPE
Man, Woman, Children	142	24	5.9	57.4	4,675	1,162	4.0	18.3
Man, Woman	6	3	2.0	2.4	1,036	518	2.0	4.0
Woman, Children	15	3	5.0	6.0	5,690	2,066	2.8	22.2
Man, Children	0	0	—	—	357	138	2.6	1.4
Polygynists	0	0	—	—	31	7	4.4	0.1
Three-Generation and Extended[b]	47	8	5.9	18.9	445	97	4.6	1.7
Siblings	14	4	3.5	5.7	547	197	2.8	2.1
Siblings, Children	9	2	4.5	3.6				
Man, Woman, Cousins	5	2	2.5	2.0	0	0	—	—
No Family[c]	10	—	—	4.0	12,892	—	—	50.2
Totals	248	—	—	100.0	25,673	—	—	100.0

a Data from Public Record Office, London, T. 71/513 (1825); T. 71/501–503; Higman, "Family Patterns in Trinidad," 32.

b In the Williams Population: Man, Woman, Children, their Children (8); Man, Woman, Children, Man's Sister, her Children (7); Man, Woman, Children, Woman's Brother, his Spouse (6); Man, Woman, Child, Man's Brother, his Spouse (5); Man, Woman, Man's Sister, her Child (4); Man, Woman, Children, Spouses (5). In the Higman Total: Woman, her Children, her Grandchildren (227); "Extended" (218).

c In the Williams Population, Men and Women living alone, unrelated separated Children.

stability, a small proportion of African slaves, natural increase, and a relatively high incidence of nuclear and stable families. At the opposite pole were the overworked slaves of new plantations such as those of Trinidad, Guyana and St Vincent, with a high rate of natural decrease, a majority of slaves living alone or in 'barrack' conditions, and a high proportion of 'denuded', female-headed families. In between came the mass of West Indian slaves, all but ten per cent living on plantations of one sort or another, with a wide range of demographic patterns but a generally declining rate of natural decrease and a rapidly dwindling African population, and varying degrees of practical exogamy, miscegenation with whites, and family formation.[30]

Unfortunately, statistical information on West Indian slave families is practically limited to the registration period, 1813-34, after the slave trade with Africa had ended, when all plantations were starting to decline, amelioration measures were being applied, and missionaries were beginning to make their influence felt. It remains to be seen whether a morphology of slave family during the entire period of slavery can be inferred, or projected, from this material alone; what additional light is shed by the white-produced literary sources from an earlier period; and, finally, what other arguments can be adduced, including the incorporation of West African material.

Earlier speculation led the present writer and Higman to postulate, and then to refine to the point of dismissal, two successive models. First, if one took the nuclear two-headed family as the quintessentially modern family form, it was beguilingly easy to propose its different incidence during the registration period as relating to the degree of maturation, creolisation, or modernisation of each slave unit, and thus to suggest a historical progression from some aboriginal African form of family. Such a progression initially seemed borne out by the closer parallels among the modern Jamaican rural communities analysed by Edith Clarke and the Exumian slaves of Rolle, as compared with Jamaican slave plantation examples, and by the highly developed family patterns traced by Colin Clarke and Lowenthal among the completely creolised peasants of Barbuda in 1851.[31]

However, the discovery by Higman, amply corroborated by the Bahamian material examined here, that Africans were at least as likely as creoles to form nuclear families, modified the original mode. This revision, coupled with the likelihood that the registration records largely concealed the existence of extended families, and the apparent paradox that creole men were more likely to be polygynous than Africans, led Higman to a second developmental model, based on the seemingly progressive differences between Trinidad, Jamaica and Barbados.[32] By this formulation, the establishment of 'elementary nuclear families' was the primary response of the displaced Africans in the first slave generation. This was the stage of fictive kin such as the 'shipmate' relationship described by Edwards. Owing to high mortality, the further shifting of slaves and a high male ratio, families were able to practice polygyny. A second slave generation began to establish extended families based on the formation of virilocal 'yards' within single plantations; but, because mortality remained high and fresh Africans were continually arriving, the elementary family continued to be the dominant norm. At this stage polygyny may actually have increased, as an index of status and property. In subsequent generations, kinship networks expanded as slaves increasingly practised exogamy. This occurred earliest and most rapidly where holdings were small and contiguous and the proportion of creoles high. The process tended towards matrifocality rather than the nuclear family, especially where lack of slave-controlled provision grounds, money and property deprived slaves of the chance of 'marriage strategies'.[33]

It was clearly right to de-emphasise the normative role of the slave-owners and to stress that slaves largely determined their own family arrangements. Higman's schematic formulation also properly recognised that a wide variety of family types coexisted in all periods, since different islands and sectors developed at different rates and in different ways. A closer study of the Bahamian materials, however, suggested that it was the Bahamas rather than Barbados which represented the forward extreme of slave family development. Higman's most recent analysis of the 1813 registration returns also suggested that Trinidad was a more special case than previously thought: an area directly supervised and rapidly expanding on the eve of emancipation and changing technology, rather than a frontier area exactly analogous to Barbados in 1650 or Jamaica in 1720. In particular, his scrutiny pointed up three conclusions apparent or latent in the Bahamian material considered here: the critical importance of slave family development of plantation size; the effects of urbanisation; and the difficulty of tracing simple cultural transfers from Africa. Even more critically, Higman's earlier model underestimated the formative changes that occurred over the century and a half before the slave trade ended. These included great changes in the intensity of the plantation system and the gradual evolution of systems of slave management aimed at greater efficiency in general, and thus at increasing slave fertility as well. Perhaps most important of all was the filtering down into the West Indies of evolving concepts of the 'modern'

Table 6   West Indian Family from Slavery to the Present; A Comparison of Trinidad, Jamaica, and the Bahamas in Slavery Days with Barbuda immediately after Slavery, and with Modern Rural Jamaica, 1813–1955

FAMILY[a] TYPE	A. TRINIDAD, 1813				B. MONTPELIER, JAMAICA, 1825			
	TOTAL SLAVES	NUMBER OF UNITS	MEAN SIZE OF UNITS	PERCENT OF TOTAL IN TYPE	TOTAL SLAVES	NUMBER OF UNITS	MEAN SIZE OF UNITS	PERCENT OF TOTAL IN TYPE
1	4,675	1,162	4.0	18.3	204	50	4.1	25.1
2	1,036	518	2.0	4.0	76	38	2.0	9.3
3	5,690	2,066	2.8	22.2	328	70	4.7	40.3
4	357	138	2.6	1.4	0	0	—	—
5	445	97	4.6	1.7	24	6	4.0	2.9
6								
7	12,892	—	—	50.2	182	—	—	22.4
8								
Others	578	204	2.8	2.2				
	25,673	—	—	100.0	814	—	—	100.0
A	6,156	1,777	3.5	24.0	304	94	3.2	37.3
B	6,625	2,408	2.8	25.8	328	70	4.7	40.3
C	12,892	—	—	50.2	182	—	—	22.6

a 1 = Man, Woman, Children; 2 = Man, Women; 3 = Woman, Children; 4 = Man, Children; 5 = Three-Generation Groups; 6 = Men Alone, or Together; 7 = Women Alone, or Together; 8 = Children Separately;

family, which gradually gained hold in the practice of creolised slaves, as well as in the minds of white masters.

It is notable that the two most important early writers on British West Indian slavery gave sympathetic accounts of the slaves' society and customs. Ligon (1657) and Sloane (1707) described the early slaves as having a great sense of decorum. Unlike Europeans, they were not ashamed of nakedness and, although with a healthy sex drive, fastidiously avoided public displays of 'wantonness'. They married when they could, and had a rigorous distaste for adultery. Sloane wrote:

> They have every one his Wife and are very much concern'd if they prove adulterous, but in some measure satisfied if their Masters punish the Man who does them the supposed injury, in any of his Hogs, or other small wealth. The care of the Masters and Overseers about their Wives, is what keeps their Plantations chiefly in good order, whence they even buy Wives in proportion to their Men, lest the Men should wander to neighbouring Plantations and neglect to serve them.

The males appeared to be dominant and the practice of polygyny by no means uncommon, being enjoyed, 'by certain brave fellows . . . of extraor-

	C. BAHAMAS, 26 HOLDINGS, 1822			D. BARBUDA, 1851				E. RURAL JAMAICA, 1955b 1. "SUGARTOWN" 2. "MOCCA"	
)TAL AVES	NUMBER OF UNITS	MEAN SIZE OF UNITS	PERCENT OF TOTAL IN TYPE	TOTAL POPULATION	NUMBER OF UNITS	MEAN SIZE OF UNITS	PERCENT OF TOTAL IN TYPE	PERCENT OF TOTAL POPULATION IN TYPE	PERCENT OF TOTAL POPULATION IN TYPE
,629	308	5.3	54.1	425	76	5.6	67.7	} 46	41
178	89	2.0	5.9	28	14	2.0	4.5		
377	95	4.0	12.5	50	12	4.2	8.0	16	17
16	3	5.3	0.5	6	1	6.0	0.7	3	3
358	46	7.8	11.9	90	18	5.0	14.3	18	30
264	—	—	8.8	7	7	1.0	1.1	}	
173	—	—	5.8	10	10	1.0	1.6	17	9
16	—	—	0.5	13	6	2.2	2.1	}	
,011	—	—	100.0	629	144	4.7	100.0	100	100
165	443	4.9	71.9	543	108	5.0	86.3	65	71
393	98	4.0	13.0	56	13	4.3	8.6	19	20
453	—	—	15.1	30	23	1.3	3.1	17	9

= Nuclear Family (1,2,5); B = Denuded Family (3,4); C = No Family (6,7,8).
Edith Clarke, *My Mother Who Fathered Me* (London, 1957), 191–194.

dinary qualities', from the earliest days. In contrast to later reports there was a strong bond of affection between parents and children, particularly between mothers and infants, who, in African fashion, were carried to work in the fields and not weaned for two years or even longer. Great respect and care were shown for the aged, whether or not they were actual kin.[34]

Ligon and Sloane wrote with exceptional objectivity before the plantation system was intensified, and also in a period when extended families were more important than nuclear families in Europe itself, and modern ideas of childhood and parental affection were still relatively strange. Besides, during Ligon's period in Barbados and Sloane's in Jamaica, miscegenation had not yet become institutionalised because there was still a sizeable proportion of whites of both sexes in the labouring population, and the majority of blacks were unacculturated Africans.

Echoes of Ligon and Sloane could still be heard in later writings, but most gave a far less sympathetic account of the slaves. As Barbados, followed by the Leeward Islands and Jamaica, became dominated by sugar plantations, the planters became more callous and indifferent to slaves' social arrangements. Spurred by the plantations' demands, the slave trade also intensified, and now men imported outnumbered women by three to two. Meanwhile, bourgeois social values increasingly added insult to injury. As far as they were concerned at all, planters disparaged, as natural faults, characteristics in their slaves for which the whites themselves were chiefly to blame, and often similarly guilty. Thus, although marriage and family life were practically discouraged and forcible miscegenation was rife, planters condemned the slaves' 'promiscuity', 'polygamy' and apparent indifference to their children, or even to having children at all.

Behind the planters' ignorance and exaggeration, however, lay the undoubted truth that the quality of slave life had nearly everywhere deteriorated seriously. In this phase, West Indian families were probably at a low point of integration – before extended new kinships had been built up and laws passed forbidding the separation of husbands and wives, and mothers and children. Except for the polygynous favours enjoyed by privileged slaves like drivers – the slaves' 'worst domestic tyrants' – conjugal unions were rare and impermanent, and the majority of infants lived with single mothers or grandmothers – up to ten per cent of whom were, or had been, the casual mates of plantation whites.

In the last phase of slavery, as the profits of plantations dwindled, the price of slaves rose, and in 1808 the supply of fresh Africans was cut off and the West Indian slave-owners came under economic constraints at the same time as they were coming under pressure from metropolitan philanthropists. Writers on slave society attacked or defended plantation customs, or proposed methods of raising the dismal level of slave fertility. The encouragement of Christianity and family life were seen by some as methods for making slaves contented, peaceable and fertile. Some measure of local reform would, moreover, vitiate the arguments of the emancipationists and undermine the sectarian missionaries, who shared none of the establishment's reluctance to proselytise the slaves and promote respectable marriage. Accordingly, in the 1820s, plantocratic Assemblies passed acts ostensibly encouraging slave marriage and actually authorising fees to Anglican ministers for slave baptisms.

Few writers, though, acknowledged the slaves' own motives. Since all slaves yearned chiefly to be free, if adherence to the Church and its formulas were conditions of freedom, a growing number of slaves would aspire to baptism and formal marriage, with their official registrations, as potent indicators of improving social status. Most writers also ignored the degree to which slaves actually possessed property and virtual tenure of houses and plots, which they were able, in custom if not in law, to bequeath to whomever they wished. Long before emancipation, a fair proportion of West Indian slaves had ample reasons, on the grounds of respectability and conformability to the laws of inheritance, to adopt the familial norms of the master class.

But nearly every commentator, from Ligon and Sloane to 'Monk' Lewis and Mrs A. C. Carmichael, did share two absolute certainties: that as to marriage, whatever the masters did, the slaves always had and always would (in the words of the Jamaican, John Quier) 'claim a Right of disposing of themselves in this Respect, according to their Own Will and Pleasure without any Controul from their Masters'; and that within certain obvious constraints these voluntary arrangements were African rather than European. 'We restrain their Actions sufficiently, to our conveniences,' wrote Lindsay, Rector of St Catherine's, Jamaica, 'tho' we inslave not the Inclinations of the Heart, against their Natural Habits and Native Customs, which may well be injoy'd separately from their Obedience to us.'[35]

Few Africans carried their children with them in slavery, and fewer still accompanied marital partners from West Africa into West Indian plantations, let alone the members of the extended family and kinship groups which were of prime importance in West Indian society. The ethnic mixing which was standard plantation policy meant additionally that the legacies of Africa were transmitted in a haphazard or generalised way. Yet the impress of Africa was indelible, and African patterns were replicated where possible, and reconstituted as soon as possible where not, surviving slavery itself in modified forms.

On large plantations there were sometimes subcultural groups – such as 'Ibo' or 'Congo' – and some forceful cultural traditions, particularly the Akan (or 'Coromantee'), seem to have been normative. Yet the very variety of West African roots allowed for creative syncretism, or the choice of alternative customs – for example, concerning the role of women, and the acceptability of cousin-mating and premarital intercourse – as the slaves made the necessary adjustments to the new environment, the dictates of the plantation system and the shifting demographic conditions.[36]

Some features of the plantation system, such as the expectation that women would work in the fields, that men would monopolise the skilled and privileged roles, and that slave drivers and other élite slaves such as head craftsmen would be likely to practise polygyny, actually facilitated the continuation of West African customs. Other continuities were of necessity more covert, having to exist in the narrow scope of private life left to the

slaves by the master class: rites of passage, courtship and premarital negotiations, marriage ceremonies and celebrations, and the role of elderly slaves
as 'councils of elders' to determine custom and settle domestic disputes.
While the slave trade lasted, direct links with Africa were never cut, native
Africans being brought in groups to expand plantations or, more commonly, arriving in ones and twos to make up the shortfall in slave fertility.
As Edwards testified, these Africans were welcomed into family units,
especially those of their own tribe and language.[37]

From the simple pairings which were all that the planters provided for,
the slaves built up extended family relationships beyond the masters' ken
or concern and, in the course of generations, whole new kinship networks
based on the cohesive 'village' of a single plantation holding but gradually
extending beyond the plantation's bounds into nearby groups. In Barbados,
a small island covered with small contiguous plantations, the process of
social diffusion had gone on longest; but even there, as in Africa, the primary
allegiance remained the village, the birthplace, the home and burial-place
of closest family, kin and ancestors.

In 1808 the direct connection with Mother Africa was cut, but by that
time the area of social autonomy had significantly expanded for most slaves.
Slaves owned their own property (in some colonies even in law), bequeathed
and inherited houses and land, and in some islands virtually controlled the
internal market system. On declining plantations they were encouraged to
be as nearly self-sufficient as possible, and on decayed plantations were left
almost entirely to their own devices. Yet, contrary to the masters' pessi-
mism, the young and the aged were better cared for than under more
rigorous slave regimes, and the unfavourable ratio between deaths and
births began to reverse. In the phrase of Sidney Mintz, the most fortunate
British West Indian slaves were proto-peasants long before slavery ended,
and made an easy transition into 'full freedom' in 1838.[38]

Four influences militated against the continued development of peasant
lifestyles and family systems: the breakup of the old slave quarters and the
consequent 'marginalisation' of many ex-slaves; the persistence of plantations in a more impersonal form; an accelerated urbanisation; and the
spread of the canons of respectability. The closing down of the slave
cantonments after emancipation, as plantations decayed or turned to less
intensive forms of agriculture (particularly, grazing 'pens'), or as ex-slaves
who refused to work on the planters' terms were evicted from houses and
plots, was as traumatic a change as the cutting of the African link or the
ending of formal slavery itself. The more fortunate ex-slaves were able to

form their own villages and develop a healthy peasant society; but many others without land of their own were forced into a marginal existence, depending on the increasingly mechanised plantations for wages, but competing with each other, and with newly imported indentured labourers, in a cruelly seasonal economy. Far fewer women worked as plantation labourers, and most of the men became transients, living in barracks or strange villages during crop-time and being unable to form permanent or stable attachments, while women provided the only permanence and stability for children. A similar continuation of the worst features of the slave period occurred among the poor of the towns, which burgeoned after emancipation. The new towns had a high proportion of migrants from the countryside, a disproportionately high ratio of women, and thus a majority of impermanent, fractured and matrifocal families.

As we have noticed, many slaves in the last phase of slavery were attracted by the apparent advantages of respectable, European-type families. After emancipation these became the norm among the small emergent middle class, many of the members of which were the coloured descendants of domestic slaves who had engaged in miscegenous relationships. Under the growing influence of the churches, a far wider spectrum of the ex-slaves continued to subscribe outwardly to the canons of respectability, especially in islands like Barbados where the Anglican Church was deeply entrenched and conditions were unfavourable for true peasant development. Yet, as Wilson has plausibly argued, the subscription to respectability is superficial among the majority of British West Indian blacks. Far more deeply engrained are the tenets of 'reputation': those elements of custom which place greater stress on community, kinship and extended family, and place greater value on social worth, than on introspective family forms, bourgeois manners and material wealth. In this analysis, reputation provides a continuous thread of tradition passing back through slavery to Africa itself.[39]

Therefore, in assessing the nature of slave family and its place in the continuum, we emphasise not the ways that slavery destroyed or distorted family, but the ways in which the slaves' own forms of family triumphed over adversity. In this light, we evaluate slavery not by the manner in which it controlled and shaped slaves' destinies, but by the degree to which it allowed slaves to make family lives of their own.

PART THREE

Transformations
and
Continuities

13

Slave Culture, Resistance and Emancipation in the British West Indies

Introduction: This essay serves as a bridge between the second and third sections of this collection in showing how essential features of British West Indian slave culture, particularly the Christianisation that occurred late in the slavery period, contributed both to slave resistance and to the emancipationist process in the metropole. Derived largely from a paper in the Shaffer lecture series at Northwestern University in 1977 on the general theme 'Christianity and Africa', the essay's main task is an attempt to resolve two apparent puzzles or paradoxes. If the elements of African culture were strong as they apparently were, how was it that Afro-American slaves, and colonised Africans too, so ardently adopted – if after a marked delay – the religion of their enslavers and colonisers? Secondly, if the function of Christianity as practised by the masters was largely to socialise the underclasses, how was it that Afro-Caribbean Christians became the most active resisters of the slavery system? Briefly, the resolution proposed is that the Afro-Caribbean slaves (like colonised Africans) made of Christianity what they wished, incorporating many elements of traditional African religion, and adopting the radical and millenarian implications of the Evangelical Revival to their own theology of redemption and liberation.

> The negroes . . . believed that Massa King George had said they were all to be free –
> a term very differently understood by the negroes and by their advocates on this side
> of the water. By free, a Briton means that the negro is no longer to be the property of
> his master, but situated as labourers are in England; that is, he is to work for his own
> and his family's support, or starve. But the word *free* means quite another thing in the
> negro sense; for they tell me that it means 'there is to be no masters at all, and Massa
> King George is to buy all the estates and give them to we to live upon.'
>
> (Mrs A. C. Carmichael, 1834).[1]

Like most of her white contemporaries, Emma Carmichael, a planter's wife who resided in Trinidad and St Vincent between 1821 and 1826, thought

263

very little of the intrinsic qualities of native Africans. But she set great store by the process of 'creolisation' whereby Africans and their descendants adapted to the New World, and the 'civilising' effects of what she regarded as the sounder forms of Christianity. She was therefore puzzled and disappointed as anyone that a crescendo of slave unrest occurred during the period between the ending of the Napoleonic wars and 1832, while the proportion of creole (or island-born) slaves rose above 80 per cent and perhaps a quarter of all slaves became at least nominally Christian. This included the three largest and widest-ranging of all British West Indian slave rebellions: in Barbados in 1816, Demerara in 1823 and climactically, Jamaica in 1831 - 32. Yet even in other colonies where the plantation system had decayed or never been firmly established, slaves proved more confident and assertive of their rights the more their conditions seemed to have improved.

Familiar explanations for slave unrest had gradually lost their force. The notion that rebellion was a peculiarly African response was vitiated by the slaves' palpable creolisation. The well-attested fact that slaves seized on the disruptions caused by wars between the European powers did not apply now that peace was re-established. The planters' fears that slaves would be 'infected' by the ideologies of the American, French and Haitian Revolutions had been found to be greatly exaggerated, and faded almost completely once the revolutionary wars were over. Apart from this, the widespread ameliorative legislation passed since 1783 could be produced as evidence against the accusation that rebellion occurred because of excessive cruelty on the part of the slave-owning class.

Predisposed to ignore their own internal divisions and mismanagement, and unable to give credit to the slaves, the West Indian planters were bound to look to outside forces to account for the actual increase in slave resistance in the period after 1815. At a time when a wave of new philosophical, political and economic ideas was sweeping the imperial metropole, and Britain was also in the throes of a religious revivalism almost equally foreign to the plantocratic style, slave-owners placed the blame firmly on those whom they regarded as ignorant metropolitan liberals and the misguided missionaries who acted as their agents. For the most part they concluded that education and Christianisation were dangerously unsuitable for West Indian slaves.

Though it distorted the truth, there was considerable plausibility in the West Indian lobby's case. As the anti-slavery forces in Britain grew in number and power, infiltrating the Colonial Office and influencing Parliament, publishing hundreds of books and pamphlets and sending out dozens of missionaries to the West Indies, they provided increasing, if rarely direct, encouragement to slaves resisting the system. Borne up by the intellectual and moral certitude that were features of the secular Enlightenment and Protestant revivalism, they were able to paint the planters' denial of education and Christianity to slaves as morally evil as well as a mere socio-political stratagem, loftily ignoring the possibility that the slaves themselves might not want the types of education and religion they would thrust upon them.

Imperial politicians, philanthropists and missionaries alike were eager to claim credit for British slavery's downfall after the event, although their innate conservatism and pusillanimity led them to play down both the effectiveness of slave rebellion in speeding change and their own roles in promoting unrest. This interpretation has been followed – swallowed – by many historians. The sheer volume of the paper debate over slavery, and the fact that it was carried on by white protagonists not slaves, have tended to an attribution of more influences to metropolitan polemics and polemicists than either warrant. If the effect of the rebellions in speeding the process is acknowledged at all, planter contempt for the intellectual capabilities of black slaves, philanthropic conceit and an exaggerated view of the role of pure ideas in shaping history have concurred to maintain that it was metropolitan ideas which mainly stirred up the British West Indian slaves in the late rebellions. On the contrary, we would not only ascribe more influence to rebellion, and its threat, in promoting change, but much more weight to the slaves' own motives and aims. To turn the usual proposition around, slave unrest just as much influenced metropolitan ideas and actions as vice versa.

To assert that slaves actually achieved their own emancipation by resistance would be to overstate the case. The freeing of the British slaves in 1838, in common with the ending of the British trade in slaves years earlier, could only be achieved by parliamentary decree. Parliament did not act until a majority of its members had been convinced that slavery was, at the same time, morally evil, economically inefficient and politically unwise. Yet the outcome would certainly have been delayed and different had the planters been able to convince Parliament that the slaves they owned were all humanely managed, contented and efficient. Instead, though the evidence of day-to-day resistance and the major risings of 1816, 1823 and 1831-32, it became gradually apparent that the British West Indian slaves could never be ruled without intolerable repression and would never be contented or make efficient workers while slavery lasted.

The British anti-slavery forces certainly worked the slaves' purposes. Yet they were incapable of recognising the ways in which their ideas and actions were cleverly used by the slaves, not depended upon. While Wilberforce became a synonym for reform, he was no more than a distant symbol to the slaves, an ally of convenience. Even more telling was the slaves' attitude to the king. Though in fact very far from being an anti-slavery advocate, he was flatteringly conflated with the Deity as Big Massa – a kind of *deux ex machina* who, along with the anti-slavery lobby, could be pictured as having the slaves' own interest at heart. In this the slaves may have learned from their white masters, who had cloaked their rebelliousness at the time of the American War of Independence in Loyal Addresses.

Similarly, missionaries led and guided the slaves far less than they imagined. They congratulated themselves on the way in which the slaves joyfully accepted Christianity in slavery's last phase, but failed to notice how the new religion was shaped by the slaves to their own needs and ends, making it an instrument of political as well as spiritual change. As ever, the ruling class apprehended only the mimetic idiom of slave behaviour and the surface of slave resistance, ignoring their deeper structures. The mainsprings of slave resistance in the last years of plantation slavery, and its most positive achievements, owed little or nothing to metropolitan inspiration or aid and, indeed, ran counter to even the revised interests of the imperial economy.

From the time of the first anti-slavery publications of Granville Sharp, Anthony Benezet and John Wesley between 1769 and 1774, those with an interest in plantation slavery and the slave trade knew that there was a rising tide of opposition in Britain. But it was not until the 1780s, with the formation of the first abolitionist organisations and the publications by John Ady, James Ramsay, John Newton, Thomas Clarkson and William Wilberforce, that the debate spilled over into the West Indies and began to be heard by the slaves. James Ramsay's *Essay on the Treatment and Conversion of African Slaves in the British Sugar Colonies* (1784) was particularly influential. For the author was a clergyman of the established church with 20 years' experience in the West Indies, who argued not only for the abolition of the slave trade, but also the advisability of switching from slavery to free wage labour and the need to improve the moral climate of the plantation colonies.

The debates in Parliament and the pioneer parliamentary inquiries into the slave trade and conditions in the plantation colonies were accompanied by a flood of polemical writings which reached its high point between 1788 and 1792. While the French wars lasted the number of new books and the vigour of the slavery debate drastically declined, although so steadily did the arguments of the first generation of abolitionists enter the general consciousness that when the debate revived after 1815 the new wave of anti-slavery works began where its forerunners had broken off. Thomas Clarkson remained one of the most forceful anti-slavery advocates, but was equalled or surpassed by Henry Brougham, Zachary Macaulay, Thomas Cooper, James Stephen and James Cropper. Of the second and greater flood of polemic the influential equivalent of Ramsay's *Essay* was probably James Stephen's magisterial two-volume *Slavery Delineated* (1824, 1830) since, like Ramsay, the author had many years' first-hand experience in the Leeward Islands, and added a crushing weight of legal and statistical evidence to evangelical fervour. He was also a brother-in-law of William Wilberforce and became official legal adviser to the Colonial Office – which made him doubly distrusted by the West India interest.[2]

By the time slavery ended no more than one or two slaves in a hundred were literate enough to read books. Besides, masters kept anti-slavery works from their slaves as being more dangerous than guns. Of far wider circulation were the colonial newspapers, which multiplied after 1783. Many of these were no more than gazettes, publishing government notices and proclamations, shipping intelligence and news randomly brought in by visiting captains, planters' letters, current prices and advertisements. But the better newspapers in the more sophisticated colonies sometimes reviewed anti-slavery books and reported anti-slavery speeches if only to condemn them, gave at least a partial and delayed account of transactions at Westminster, and provided full, even verbatim, reports of debates in local legislatures and vestry meetings.[3] Such papers were eagerly acquired by literate slaves, and read aloud or retailed to their illiterate fellows. But, as perceptive whites realised, the most common way in which political news and views were spread among the slaves was by domestics overhearing and passing on their masters' incautious table talk. In these ways, an ever-widening group of slaves became aware not only that they had friends and allies in the imperial metropolis, but that the masters felt increasingly embittered, besieged and desperate.

Change was clearly impending, posing a threat to the masters and hope for the slaves. But *rumours* of change played an even more important role in slave unrest than actual changes, becoming part of a common pattern. After every plot or revolt, from at least 1790 onwards, the planters provided evidence that rumours of impending changes had been circulating among the slaves, usually in the form that actual decrees had been made by the king, the imperial Parliament or the Colonial Office, and withheld by the local regime. By stressing the effect of rumours of change the planters hoped to forestall actual changes. They also hoped that by attributing slave unrest to actual or imagined changes imposed from outside they might draw attention away from local causes, and deflect blame from themselves.

But if they overemphasised the rumours, the planters did not invent them. The rumour syndrome in the late slave rebellions was of far deeper significance than a mere plantocratic ploy. That the rumours could only be transmitted by the élite of literate and 'confidential' slaves and yet were spread widely and uniformly through the mass of slaves implied not only an efficient network of communication but also a degree of concurrence between the élite and ordinary slaves that was deeply disturbing to the master class. Equally disconcerting to them was the consistent form of the rumours and the ways in which their very inaccuracy was of use to the cause of slave resistance. Even the most literate and best-informed of élite slaves were unlikely to be informed with complete accuracy, and the manner of dissemination, with many slaves receiving information at fourth and fifth hand, was bound to lead to exaggeration and distortion. But the facts that the rumours were not only consonant with the wishes of ordinary slaves but of remarkable consistency in the circumstances, suggest that they were intentionally shaped by those who stood to gain most – the potential leaders of a slave revolt. Rumours such that an act of emancipation had been signed by the king in London could neither have been invented by the most ignorant nor believed in by the most literate and informed of slaves. The rumours fulfilled the classic canons of successful propaganda – use of half-truths falling midway between fact and wish.

For the would-be leaders of the slaves the rumours were doubly useful – encouraging the mass of their followers that change was inevitable, with outside help available in the fulfilment of their wishes, and driving the masters deeper into their siege mentality. That they no longer enjoyed the sympathy of the British public and could not any more call upon the unquestioning support of the imperial government was bad enough for the planters. But what wounded them most was the loss of a dream of aristo-cratic mastery such as was to sustain the planters of the US South through a bloody civil war. It became gradually clear that none of the slaves would ever be contented with their assigned socioeconomic roles. The most privileged were the least contented. Dissatisfied slaves of all types, far from looking to their temporal masters for justice, bounty and mercy, now looked to 'Big Massa' and to metropolitan leaders hated and distrusted by the planters for support in their resistance. Such was the subversive propaganda message conveyed in the slave ditty recorded by Matthew 'Monk' Lewis in western Jamaica in 1816:

> Oh me good friend, Mr Wilberforce, make we free!
> God Almighty thank ye! God Almighty thank ye!
> God Almighty, make we free!
> Buckra in this country no make we free!
> What negro for to do? What negro for to do?
> Take force with force? Take force with force?

The rapid Christianisation of British West Indian slaves after 1783 clearly had a vital effect on their general consciousness, and an important bearing on slave resistance. But it is far less certain that the missionaries themselves were ever quite the 'Enemies of Caesar' claimed by Dr Thomas Coke, the chief Wesleyan evangelist in the West Indies.[5] Until 1754 the Anglican Church had a monopoly of Christianity in the British West Indies, steadfastly upholding the regime as was the proper function of an established church, and solving any doubt as to the compatibility of Christianity and servitude by neglecting to proselytise the slaves at all. The Catholic Church, entrenched in the colonies acquired after 1763, had a more integrating approach, but for that reason was treated with extreme distrust by the British planters. Contrary to Protestant legend, however, Catholic planters did seem to enjoy closer and more fruitful relations with their baptised slaves than those enjoyed by Protestant planters with pagans. Consequently, a minority of optimistic British planters – most of them nonconformist converts themselves – came to speculate on the practical as well as spiritual value of allowing missionaries to work with their slaves. Some were completely cynical in their motivation. 'I must in candour own that I am not influenced by religious principles myself in this matter but simply by self-interest', a prominent Jamaican planter told Rev. H. M. Waddell in 1830:

> I have a bad set of people: they steal enormously, run away, get drunk, fight and neglect their duty in every way; while the women take no care of their children, and there is no increase on the property. Now, if you can bring them under fear of a God, or a judgement to come, or something of that sort, you may be doing both them and me a service.[6]

A steadily growing number of nonconformist sectaries proved willing to enter the field but they were tolerated, if at all, to the degree they supported the *status quo*. The Moravians were first – in Jamaica and Antigua from 1754

– and most adaptable of all, having no doubts that slavery was God-or-dained. They actually owned plantations and slaves, and two of their earliest missionaries even tried, in vain, to become slaves themselves.[7] The first Methodist missionary went to Antigua in 1778 at the invitation of a prominent white convert, and Methodism greatly expanded under the direction of the judicious Thomas Coke from 1786 onwards.[8] Methodist missionaries suffered more opposition than Moravians, partly because they were not formally structured and controlled by a missionary organisation until 1812, but mainly because of the uncompromising abolitionist state-ments in John Wesley's *Thoughts on* Slavery (1774). However, as in Britain, Methodism turned out to be almost a force of conservatism. The quest for respectability led to racial segregation within chapels, or even between them. Much the same was true of the small number of Presbyterian missions, which ministered almost as much to expatriate Scots as to the slaves, and became virtually a second established church in the Bahamas and British Guiana.[9] Such compromises did not occur to anything like the same extent in the chapels founded by the London Missionary Society, an interdenominational body dominated by Congregationalists which began work in 1808, or by the Baptist Missionary Society, which sent out its first pastors to Jamaica in 1814. Their ministers had fewer social aspirations and their congregations were, and remained, almost exclusively black.[10]

Without exception, though, the missionary societies carefully instructed their ministers not to engage in politics or to upset the social order. Count Zinzendorf wrote to a Moravian missionary that he was,

> not to work against the police, or regard the government with suspicion . . . Do not interfere between employer and employed; do not play any part in party politics, but teach the heathen by your example, to fear God and honour the King . . . The right way with savages is this: you must set them such a dazzling example that they cannot help asking who made these delightful characters . . . You must labour with your hands until you have won the love of the people.[11]

The LMS instructed the Rev. John Smith on his way to Demerara in 1816 that 'not a word must escape you in public or private which might render the slaves displeased with their masters or dissatisfied with their station. You are not sent to relieve them from their servile condition, but to afford them the consolations of religion'.[12] And another LMS missionary wrote to his superiors from Tobago in 1808:

> I am persuaded that it is neither my business nor in my power to deliver them [the slaves' from the bondage of men. I have always conceived it my duty to endeavour

thro' divine assistance to direct the poor negroes, how they may be delivered from the bondage of sin and Satan, and to teach them the pure principles of Christianity, which will not only lead to sobriety, industry and fidelity; but will make them loyal subjects, obedient servants and children . . . I not only endeavour to avoid any expression which might be misunderstood in this respect but always endeavour to endear them to each other, and particularly their employers, in fact all who have authority over them.[13]

In practice, of course, such instructions and intentions proved impossible to follow to the letter and, wittingly or not, Nonconformist missionaries became slaves' allies in resistance. As the planters quickly realised, many of the missionaries came from a class closer to the labourer than to the landowner. By living godly lives missionaries pointed up a glaring contrast to the lifestyle of the average planter. Not inured to the system by profit or long acquaintance, and living close to the slaves, missionaries found it impossible totally to ignore slavery's manifest inhumanity. 'I felt exceed-ingly distressed and was scarcely able to rest though the night', wrote one missionary from Jamaica in 1829. 'I though I would rather, if I could have my choice, be lying in jail as I was last year, than hear as I do now, from day to day, of the sufferings of the poor defenceless negroes.' Similarly, throughout the most poignant and telling of all missionary records, the private journal of John Smith of Demerara, the crack of the punishment whip sounds like an unbidden yet unstillable conscience.[14]

Although, as Madeline Grant has written, 'most missionaries were political innocents with an unconscious bias towards conservatism',[15] some were less ingenious and all, in time, came to be regarded as dangerous by the planters. William Knibb, the Baptist gadfly, when giving evidence before the parliamentary inquiry in 1832, made a careful distinction: 'I did not say our doctrines led to implicit obedience; I said we taught it.'[16] And in its own heavily biased report, the Jamaican Assembly declared that:

The preaching and teaching of the sects called Baptist, Wesleyan Methodist, and Moravians (but more especially the sect called Baptist) had the effect of producing in the minds of the slaves, a belief that they could not serve both a temporal and a spiritual master, thereby occasioning them to resist the lawful authority of their temporal, under the delusion of rendering themselves more acceptable to a spiritual master.[17]

By this time though, the tide of missionary activity and slave conversion was irreversible. By 1834 there were 63 Moravian missionaries in the British West Indies, 58 Methodists, 17 Baptists and perhaps a dozen other Non-conformist missionaries; a total of 150. In the Nonconformist chapels there were about 47,000 communicating slave members and a claimed total of some 86,000 'hearers or inquirers', about 11 per cent of the total slave population of 776,000.[18] To this should be added perhaps twice as many nominal adherents of the Anglican Church, which had long since been goaded into proselytising the slaves on inoculative principles. As early as 1788 the Rev. John Lindsay, Rector of St Catharine's Jamaica, had argued in response to James Ramsay's *Essay* that the slaves should be

> stamp'd with the Seal of Religion. From this Quarter (in times to come) it is we, or at least many of us, shall be served with Honest, Attentive, Sober, Obliging House Servants . . . And the Saltwater, Stupid, Selfish, Thieving, Vexatious Pack we are commonly served with will be driven where they ought to be – to the Hoe and Bill.
> . . . Negroes are ill adapted to receive Instruction, from a Natural sulkiness, stupidity and prejudice – a want of Natural feelings – of Capacity – and an Unusual carelessness about everything which does not forcibly strike their conceptions. But if there be a possibility to bring Negroes, by a Religious knowledge to be Orderly – Neat in their Persons – Sober and Sensible in their Carriage – Diligent – Faithful – and Industrious . . . Why may not the British Cathechist [i.e., the Anglican] gain them to this, as well as the Moravian or Methodist?[19]

Spurred on not by the words of the egregious Dr Lindsay (whose outburst did not find a publisher) but by the Saints of the Clapham Sect, Anglicans founded the Church Missionary Society in 1799. In 1824 bishoprics were established for Jamaica and Barbados, and by 1834 the number of Anglican ministers in the British West Indies had trebled to about 100. Under metropolitan urging, new colonial laws were passed with encouraged slave baptism, church marriages, Christian instruction and sabbatarianism. The Rev. George Bridges, for example, claimed in 1823 to have baptised 10,000 slaves within two years in Manchester parish, Jamaica, though he neglected to mention the fee of 2/6d a slave decreed by the Jamaican legislature.[20]

The Rev. George Bridges, who was later the founder of the Colonial Church Union which physically attacked nonconformists and burned their chapels, quite candidly saw the role of the Church of England as to counter the sectaries and defend the social order. But after slavery ended even those missionaries who claimed to have opposed slavery from the beginning disclaimed any part in the rebellions of 1816–32, and all tended to stress the function of Christianity (especially their own particular brand) in 'civilising' the slaves and smoothing over the social transition from slavery to free wage labour. Yet almost universally the white ministers in the West Indies exaggerated their own role in the conversion of 250,000 slaves to Christianity within a quarter century, and distorted the slaves' motivation in making the voluntary transition.[21] The part played by Christianity in creolisation and slave resistance can only be truly assessed by examining more closely what Christianity meant to the slaves themselves.

Because of the natural blending of religious elements in Africa itself, and the nature of the African slave trade to the New World, one would expect African religion to have taken on Christian elements during the creolisation process even without active proselytisation. The extent of religious blending in the New World was determined partly by the degree to which the African components were mixed and the extent to which they faded and became generalised, and partly by the degree to which Christianity – or rather, its variants – proved culturally adaptable, assimilable and attractive to slaves.

There was much in Christianity that was strange to native Africans, if not objectively ridiculous.[22] Two missionaries wrote home from Grenada in 1820 that many slaves were too ignorant to be admitted to chapel membership, being unable to understand the content of the teaching. Yet in the same letter the missionaries listed the following as the subjects on which they had preached to the slaves: 'the Fall of Man, Redemption by Jesus Christ, the blessings of Redemption such as Justification, Regeneration, Sanctification and eternal glory, the Resurrection of the Dead and eternal judgement'.[23]

Nonetheless, there were many more common or transferable elements in European and African religion that is usually recognised, especially by Eurocentric Christian writers reluctant to acknowledge that Africans had any proper religion at all. As had been especially apparent in Haiti, Cuba and Brazil, with their syncretic religions of *vodun*, *santeria* and *candombe*, many rituals, iconographies and beliefs were more easily blended than separated out. Africans and European Christians alike believed in a supreme creator and a pantheon of saints or personified spirits who proved easily interchangeable. And what is being done at the baptism of a baby, or of an adult by total immersion, or when flowers are carried to a graveside – even to the bedside of the sick – which a native African would not instantly recognise?

From the first crusading period of contact, European Christians, with their sacred relics and pilgrimage sites, their mystery-guarding, miracle-working priests and their holy liquids, were far closer to what was disparagingly termed animistic African religion (or 'superstition') than they were prepared to own. Even Protestants, who dismissed Catholic practices along with African as idolatrous or superstitious, retained easily transferable symbols and imagery: the cross, communion wine as blood and sacrifice, the almost talismanic reverence for the Holy Book, the 'Rock of Ages, cleft for me'. Even the solemn oath sanctioned and enforced by religion, which was so vital both to subversive organisation and to its uncovering, was a feature common to Europe and Africa.

Apart from becoming increasingly accessible, Christianity offered real attractions to the increasingly creolised slaves of the British West Indies – social, political and psychological. Conversion was in its nature a sudden hopeful change, though the way in which this change was visualised, and the motivation of slave converts, was distinctly two-fold. At the level most willingly recognised by the master class, conversion was a token of at least partial acceptance, in a quest for social respectability. At a deeper level, conversion could signify resistance, even revolution – the most positive manifestation of that reidentification which Peter J. Wilson has called the quest for reputation.[24]

At first –and in some colonies such as Bermuda and Barbados, for a very long time – the established Anglican Church had a monopoly of respectability. Only Anglican persons were authorised to baptise, marry or give Christian burial to slaves. At the very end of slavery these privileges began to be extended to sectarian ministers, as long as they were properly ordained and licensed. Far from weakening the hold of respectability this reinforced it by spreading it more widely. Chapels, especially those presided over by white missionaries or what commonly came to be called 'black Englishmen', became almost as property, conventional and respectable as Anglican churches. This was particularly true of Presbyterians, Moravians and Wesleyans, but even the Baptist church divided into relatively respectable and 'primitive' or 'native' wings in which the ministers remained unlicensed and unordained.[25]

Even in adhering to respectable religious slaves, in the words of E. D. Genovese, were developing a 'most powerful defense against the dehumanization implicit in slavery . . . drawing on a religion that was supposed to ensure their compliance and docility [they] rejected the essence of slavery by projecting their own rights and values as human beings'.[26] Yet the Native Baptists and their equivalents were at least as important in West Indian history and society as the more respectable churchgoers, and far more important in their history of resistance. The strictly relative sense of social worthiness acquired by joining a respectable church became almost a personality change under the influence of the more fundamentalist Christian teaching and practice in the popular churches, combining personal

validation with spiritual regeneration. In a memorable passage, the Guyanese historical Robert Moore has analysed the description of slaves'
testimonies given in the Demerara journal of the Rev. John Smith. The
slaves' sense of sin, wrote Moore,

> was rather a sense of social worthlessness or inferiority than the concept of personal
> depravity in which the missionaries believed. Services in slave chapels usually followed
> the pattern of people weeping for their sins, people crying out loudly for their guilt,
> and then coming away refreshed by a new confidence ... no longer feeling the peculiar
> mixture of guilt and unworthiness which characterised the typical Creole slave. Even
> if the experience of a conversion was not followed by baptism or a particularly close
> adherence to the church the effect seems to have been to change the Creole slave not
> necessarily into an outwardly less obedient slave but inwardly into a less accepting
> one.[27]

Quite apart from this, Nonconformist chapels with all-black congregations,
such as Shrewsbury's in Barbados, Smith's in Demerara and Burchell and
Knibb's in Jamaica, provided an alternative society and refuge from the
plantation ethos. They were places in which slaves from different plantations could meet regularly, which offered opportunities for self-expression
and spiritual release. They also created their own hierarchies independent
of plantation society – although for obvious reasons those who became the
leaders in chapel were often those who had already emerged as the plantations' slave élite.

In such chapels the black deacons usually had a closer rapport with the
lowlier members of the congregation than did the white ministers – a source
of later tension. In a profound sense (in a phrase quoted by Genovese in
the US context) 'The whites preached to the niggers and the niggers
preached to theyselves.'[28] This was most apparent in the most popular black
churches of all, those founded 25 years or more before the first white
missionaries appeared on the scene by black 'Loyalist' slaves: the Wesleyan
Joseph Paul and the Baptists Frank Spence, Prince Williams and Sharper
Morris in the Bahamas, and the Baptists George Lisle, Moses Baker,
Andrew Bryan, Prince Hoare and George Gibb in Jamaica. These all had
to fight a running battle not only with the colonial regimes and the
established church, but also with the official missionaries sent out from
Britain. For example, the bigoted Anglican Rev. D. W. Rose (as quoted by
the historian of the SPG) ridiculed the Native Baptists of Long Island,
Bahamas, in 1799 as having been,

> 'misled by strange doctrines'. They called themselves 'Baptists', the 'followers of
> St John' and were 'not so happy and contented' as in other parts of the West Indies,

though 'every indulgence and humanity were exercised towards them by their Masters'. Their preachers, black men, were 'artful and designing, making a merchandize
of Religion'. One of them was 'so ingenious' as to proclaim that he had 'had a familiar
conversation with the Almighty, and to point out the place where he had seen Him'.
At certain times of the year the black preachers used to 'drive numbers of negroes into
the sea and dip them by way of baptism', for which they extorted a dollar, or stolen
goods. Previously to Mr Rose's arrival an attempt 'to check their proceedings'
occasioned some of the slaves to 'abscond and conceal themselves in the woods.'[29]

Even more telling evidence can be found between the lines of the Rev. John
Clarke's *Memorials of Baptist Missionaries in Jamaica* (1869), which over-
praised such white missionaries as Knibb and Burchell but was far more
guarded about Lisle, Baker and their numerous following. Besides the
inevitable references to the blacks' affection for fervent hymn singing and
call-and-response in chapel services, there are clear references to more
obviously African practices: to drumming and dance, spirit possession and
speaking in tongues. 'Some of them', wrote Clarke,

> thought the old men were to dream dreams, and the young men were to see visions
> . . . There was certainly much superstition mingled with their religious exercises; many
> had wonderful dreams to tell, which they considered as prophetic visions; some excited
> themselves by fanatical notions, and fell into wild extravagances which they called '*the
> convince*' in which they had full faith, as much as in Divine Revelation . . . and from
> others we had learned that they had gone out at night to what they called *the
> wilderness*.[30]

Another pioneer black preacher, George Gibb, who went to Jamaica from
the USA in 1784, practised baptism by triune immersion, at night, in secret,
in unfrequented places.[31]

It should not then be surprising that the members of such recessive,
apocalyptic churches should predominate in the late slave rebellions of 1823
in Demerara and 1831–32 in Jamaica; that they should be led by élite slaves
and chapel deacons such as Quamina, John Smith's chief deacon at Le
Resouvenir, and Samuel Sharpe, Baptist head deacon in Burchell's chapel
in Montego Bay; or even that several modern commentators should char-
acterise the outbreaks as classic millenarian phenomena. The voluminous
evidence from the rebellions stressed the rebel chapel-goers' emphasis on
membership and leadership, their fervent, secret meetings, their use of
dream, trance and oaths, their almost cabalistic reverence for the Holy
Bible, their choice of biblical texts stressing atonement, redemption, regeneration, apocalypse. Then one is easily reminded of the famous five-point
formulation of Norman Cohn: like classical millenarian outbreaks these

slave rebellions can be seen to have been collective, to be engaged in by all the faithful. They were immanent, to be realised on earth not in heaven, and imminent, coming soon and suddenly. They were perhaps, to be total, utterly transforming, bringing not only improvement but perfection. Finally, they would be seen as miraculous, invoking God's direct intervention.[32]

Such an analysis is beguiling but too formulistic, and too Eurocentric. Christianity had a vital role where Christian slaves predominated or where the forces of evangelical revivalism were particularly strong, but it was not a *necessary* condition. It seems to have played no part, for example, in the Barbados rebellion of 1816 or the disturbances that upset the Bahamian Out Island of Exuma in 1828–30. What then, in general, did motivate British West Indian slaves, and what did they seek? If we rely on the evidence of the Jamaican slave ditty of 1816 (which, incidentally, Monk Lewis claimed originated from a person whom he described as 'a brown priest'), the overwhelming wish for all slaves was, simply, for freedom. Slavery was a condition so absolute and intolerable that it must be ended, however much it had been mitigated by familiarity, custom and law. Its very mitigation, indeed, made slavery's ending easier, the result, in part, of friendly forces in the metropolis, and resulting in a more sophisticated generation of creole slaves.

How slaves visualised freedom and the means by which it should be achieved is far less straightforward. Leadership was of crucial importance and the motives and aims of leaders were likely to differ substantially from those of ordinary slaves. The rebel leaders, paradoxically, emerged from those who had gained most from the system of slavery. As in the independence movements of the twentieth century, they knew the ways of the master class, but the superiority which they had gained over the mass of their follows made them more rather than less frustrated. There is nothing more energising for a rebel leader than, while feeling to be superior to his fellows, to be treated as a second-class person by the master class, especially when close association and privileged information provide a sense that the power of the masters is crumbling. For the members of the slave élite who became the rebel leaders (and in certain cases for free coloureds too) rebellion offered the open-ended extension of what they had already gained. At one extreme this might have meant a complete takeover from the master class: the retention of the factories, great house and government buildings, and the substitution of black (or brown) for white overseers, owners and plantocratic legislators. At the other extreme, in which rebellion led to a total destruction of the socioeconomic machinery of the planto-cratic system, the rebel leaders might have entrenched their leadership by a return to an autocratic African style. In the context of the Haitian Revolution these were, broadly, the divergent approaches of Henri Chris-tophe and Jacques Dessalines respectively. Neither was easily applicable in pure form to the British West Indies, the first being unrealistic, the second outdated. A far more realisable scenario lay somewhere in between, with the rebel leaders simply reinforcing the leadership gained in plantation and chapel in a reorganised system, with slavery abolished, the power of the planters curtailed and the black majority free to work for planters or themselves as and when they wished.

These comparatively moderate ambitions had the supreme advantage of consonance with what seem to have been the wishes of the mass of slaves. Leadership was vital but rebellion depended upon a mass following. To win over the ordinary slaves, the rebel leaders used their established authority as leaders on the estates, in the slave quarters and in the chapels, playing on the slaves' dissatisfactions and aspirations. They also relied cleverly on millenarian tactics, employing the Bible, preaching and oaths upon a susceptible people, and used convenient rumours that they themselves knew to have been untrue, unlikely, or half truths. In sum, the rebellions occurred because the leaders were able to mobilise the slaves, harnessing their seething discontent and potential for retaliatory violence, and offering fulfillment for their deepest aspirations.

The chief of these aspirations was, naturally, to be free. Yet the form of that freedom seems to have become visualised as that of an independent peasantry, about which the slaves had quite clear notions and of which, in most cases, they already had considerable experience. As has been notably argued by Sidney Mintz and Douglas Hall, many West Indian blacks were already what might be called 'proto-peasants' well before the end of formal slavery.[33] Besides the ways in which they worked their provision grounds, with their own methods and with minimal supervision, this was demon-strated by the way in which they had developed an internal marketing system quite independently, and managed to enter the cash economy on their own terms. More deeply, the slaves retained and developed concepts of family and kin quite beyond the comprehension and control of the master class, and a concept of land tenure that was in contradiction to that of the dominant European culture. In brief, for ordinary slaves freedom meant being free to be small farmers, working for the plantations, if at all, only for wages and on their own terms. They wanted to live in family units, to have ready access to land of their own, and to be free to develop their own culture, particularly their own syncretised religion. These were the basic aspirations, amounting to an ideology, though varying according to the different conditions in each of the colonies.

In some cases slaves were ready to seize a peasant lifestyle before their masters were ready to grant it; in others they became rebellious because their masters sought to erode what had already been achieved. Only in the very last period was the slaves' drive toward Christianity involved, and even then not in all colonies affected. Probably the earliest example occurred in Dominica in 1791, when the slaves on the windward side downed tools and refused to work unless they were granted half the week to cultivate their own provision grounds. This claim, reported the island merchants and planters, 'occurred in pursuit of what they term their "rights", which in their interpretation extend to an exemption from labour during four days out of seven'.[34] A similar instance happened in Tobago in 1807, when a type of 'industrial action' on the part of the slaves was narrowly quelled short of actual rebellion.[35] But such early cases were mere straws in a wind that rose to a gale and then a hurricane in Barbados, Demerara and Jamaica between 1816 and 1832.

All slave aims and aspirations were most neatly demonstrated, perhaps, in the Demerara rebellion in August 1823 – though our account and interpretation has to be filtered through the words of white officials. On the first day of the outbreak the Governor, John Murray, went forward to speak with a small group of armed slaves, asking them what they wanted. The more vocal called out: 'Our right'. Murray expostulated with them for half an hour, explaining the limits of the recent Bathurst reforms, but was unable to satisfy them. 'These things they said were no comfort to them,' he reported. 'God had made them of the same flesh and blood as the whites, that they were tired of being Slaves to them, that their good King had sent Orders that they should be free and they would not work any more'.[36]

Two days later some 2,000 slaves confronted the 300 colonial militia and imperial troops as they marched through the plantations. The military commander, Colonel Leahy, spoke with the rebels under flag of truce. 'Some of the insurgents called out that they wanted lands and three days in the week for themselves, besides Sunday, and they would not give up their arms until they were satisfied,' wrote one eyewitness.[37] 'At first there was more demand for freedom and three days than anything else, went Leahy's own account, given at the trial of Parson Smith, 'but latterly when I came out again they were all for freedom, and all of them dwelt considerably on going to Chapel on Sunday.'[38] Refusing to disperse, the rebels were mown down with musketry, with 100–150 killed for the loss of one white wounded. Thereafter, Leahy and the troops proceeded up and down the coast, shooting rebel leaders after drumhead courts martial and hanging their bodies in gibbets as an example '*in terrorem*'. The rebellion collapsed with almost pathetic suddenness. But while such barbarity was still necessary to suppress it – and still possible – yet could no longer be concealed from disinterested or antagonistic persons of influence in the motherland, the days of British plantation slavery were surely numbered.

In 1816 the Barbados slave rebellion had been comparatively little impact on Britain at large. In parliament it reinforced the decision not to impose the Registry Bill on the self-legislating colonies, and it resulted in a successful parliamentary petition to the Prince Regent to declare that slave emancipation was not an immediate object of British policy.[39] The impact of the Demerara uprising and the subsequent destruction of Shrewsbury's chapel in Barbados was far greater. The news, relayed chiefly through the publication by the LMS of the details of John Smith's trial and articles in the *Edinburgh Review*,[40] provoked an uproar among British emancipationists, who seemingly regarded the ordeals of Smith and Shrewsbury as far outweighing the deaths of 250 slaves. Two hundred petitions were delivered to Parliament in April and May 1824, led by one from the LMS, and in June an acrimonious debate occurred on a motion of censure, during which Lord Brougham delivered two of his marathon speeches against the colonial regime.[41] However, the motion was lost by 193 to 146, the majority agreeing with John Gladstone (father of William Ewart, and owner of the estate on which the revolt had centred) that philantrophy was misplaced and Christianity dangerous when dealing with slaves whose only ambition was 'the freedom to live in indolence'.[42] At one level, then, the concurrence of the Demerara rebellion with the policy of amelioration pursued by Lord Bathurst set back rather than speeded the emancipation cause.

The news from Jamaica in 1832, though, overwhelmed the remaining opposition to emancipation. It came at a time when the political atmosphere was already electric with the debates over and passage of the Great Reform Bill, and was relayed more completely and quickly than ever before. The details of the suppression of the rebellion and of the scale and scope of the rebel trials provoked official inquiry and public censure, but this was nothing to the storm that arose over the retaliatory prosecution of the nonconformist missionaries and their black congregations by the Jamaican regime. Most of those in the British government and many middle-class philanthropists were ambivalent about the exercise of law and order in suppressing rebellion. But quite another and unambiguous matter was the lawless behaviour of ostensibly Christian whites as described in Governor Belmore's despatches, in Henry Whiteley's lurid *Three Months in Jamaica*, or by refugee missionaries like William Knibb and Thomas Burchell in person, before the parliamentary inquiry during the summer of 1832 and on the speaking and preaching circuit in England and Scotland throughout 1832 and 1833.[43]

Once again the missionaries bid fair to steal the martyr's crown, but no longer could they fully disguise who were the true victims and heroes in the conflict. In all, some 200 Jamaican slaves were killed in the fighting and no fewer than 540 put to death after military or civil trials. Their paramount leader, Samuel Sharpe, was one of the last to die, hanged at Montego Bay on May 23, 1832. By a fitting coincidence, just one week later the House of Commons in London appointed a Select Committee with the significantly worded mandate, 'to consider and report upon the Measures which it may be expedient to adopt for the purpose of effecting the Extinction of Slavery throughout the British Dominions, at the earliest period compatible with the safety of all Classes in the Colonies'.[44] The committee heard evidence during June and July 1832 which provided a background for the General Election for the first reformed Parliament, when, it was reported, all successful candidates were bound to give pledges of support for emancipation. The evidence in the report, ordered to be printed in August 1832, provoked a deluge of petitions that eventually included 1,500,000 names, and when Parliament reconvened at the beginning of 1833, the emancipation debate was its first priority.[45]

Soon debate centred on the questions of compensation for owners of property in slaves, and ways in which the labour of ex-slaves could be guaranteed in order to sustain the British West Indian sugar plantation. But emancipation itself had become inevitable. Samuel Sharpe's dying affirmation in May 1832, 'I would rather die on yonder gallows than live in slavery',[46] can therefore stand as the noble if poignant epitaph for all those thousands of mostly anonymous slaves who, fighting and dying with little hope for the right to make a life of their own, in the fullness of time helped bring slavery down.

14

Proto-Peasant Revolts?

The late Slave Rebellions in
the British West Indies,
1816-1632

Introduction: This essay should be read in counterpoint with the previous one, since it stresses the more important secular rather than the spiritual motivations of the late slave rebellions in the British West Indies. Forerunner of *Testing the Chains* (1982) and published in *Past and Present* in November 1979, it was probably a pioneering work in two respects. It may have been the first by any scholar to make a systematic comparison between the three late slave revolts which were among the most serious ever to occur within the British West Indies, and it was certainly the first to examine the contention that these outbreaks were inspired by the aspirations of slaves to be free peasants. Somewhat anticipated in this collection by the essay 'The Rope and the Cutlass' in Part II, its conclusions are further developed, and somewhat modified, in essays 15, 16, 17, and 19 (including the suggestion that slaves were also in key senses proto-proletarians). This essay can be contrasted, however, not only with the preceding one in this collection, but also with an article entitled 'The Passion to Exist: Slave Rebellions in the British West Indies, 1650-1832', published in the *Journal of Caribbean History* in 1980.

> So varied are the reports from the different parts of the island relative to the disaffection of our peasantry, that we can scarcely rely with certainty on any of them.[1]

Three major slave revolts occurred in the British West Indies in the last two decades of formal history: Barbados in 1816, Demerara (Guyana) in 1823 and Jamaica in 1831–32. It was remarkable enough that the revolts erupted in three very different colonies on the very eve of freedom after a period thought to have been one of legislated amelioration. But they also followed a phase of comparative slave quiescence (despite the French Revolution and the revolution of the French slaves in Santo Domingo) and were led by an élite of assimilated, 'confidential' slaves, many of them Christians. The late revolts, moreover, constituted a crescendo of resistance, each one more extensive, disruptive and influential than the one before.

At one level it is not surprising that slaves should always rebel if they had the chance, as long as slavery lasted. 'resistance is the core of history, not acquiescence', asserted Herbert Aptheker, the pioneer historian of American slave rebellions, in 1976.[2] 'They are always ready to revolt', wrote Père Labat of the Martinique slaves as long ago as 1693, 'to risk everything and commit the most horrible crimes to obtain their liberty . . . It is a truism that the desire for liberty and for vengeance is the same among all men, and makes them capable of risking all to satisfy it'.[3] Yet although slave rebellions were seemingly inevitable, even a casual examination discloses that there were significant differences in their nature and causes, and several recent writers have classified them into types.[4] In my own attempt at a general survey in 1974 I proposed four situations conducive to slave rebellions. These were: 'conditions of extreme repression; the presence of unassimilable elements; the weakening of the forces of control; and the frustration of slave expectations'. At the same time a sequential model was suggested, with slave revolts divided into those of the maroon type, those led by unassimilated Africans, and the late slave rebellions led by the creole, or colony-born, slave élite.[5]

Since 1974, however, decided flaws have come to light in this model, at least in its sequentially. It is now clear that the maroons continued to provide an admired example for rebellious slaves even after most maroon groups had come to terms with the slave-holding class, and that the pull of 'Mother Africa' remained strong even the umbilical cord was cut by the ending of African slave imports in 1808. Besides, it is now known that creole and élite slaves were prominent in slave unrest far earlier than previously thought. For example, they were dominant in the serious slave plot in Hanover parish, Jamaica, in 1776.[6] Indeed, as early as the 1660s a governor of Barbados said, in effect: we can control the Africans by jumbling up the tribes, but what will happen when all our slaves are creoles?[7]

Typologies of slave rebellion, chiefly through concentrating on one colony, one period, or even one revolt, have tended hitherto either to generalise too much from the particular, or to over-differentiate. The late slave revolts in particular seem to require a fresh analysis; comparing and contrasting them both with earlier outbreaks and with each other, assessing their contexts and the causes attributed to them by planters, philanthropists and previous scholars, before attempting a new synthesis. What follows are successive descriptions, necessarily succinct although the result of detailed research, and objectively presented. Only thereafter are new conclusions tentatively ventured.

Barbados is a small island, comparatively flat, and evenly fertile. In 1816 it was the longest established of the British slave colonies, densely populated, a sugar monoculture dependent upon imported provisions, with small, contiguous estates mainly owned by resident planters. These owners, allied to a sizeable population of poor whites, constituted an immensely strong, self-legislating plantocracy. Because of political conservatism and a comparatively low level of miscegenation, the 'free coloureds' remained a small, oppressed minority. Slaves outnumbered the free by five to one, were demographically self-sustaining, and 93 per cent creole. There had not been a slave upheaval since 1702, and this undoubtedly bred complacency among the whites.[8]

In the year before the Barbados revolt there were short-term hardships and political ferment. The end of the Napoleonic Wars in 1815 led to a slump in the sugar market, and provisions were dear because trade with the USA was still curtailed. The Barbadian assembly had vigorously debated these matters and pleaded with the imperial government for relief, while bitterly complaining about the imperial bill of 1815 calling for the registration of colonial slaves. 'Even in the newspapers of Barbados', it was reported, 'formal Resolutions of the Assembly were published only three or four months before the insurrection broke out, denouncing the Registry Bill as a plan for the emancipation of the slaves'.[9]

The rebellion broke out with shocking suddenness on Easter Sunday night, April 14, 1816, at a time when the slaves were free from work and had ample opportunities for organisation under cover of the permitted festivities. Cane-fields and cane-trash houses were fired as beacons in the south-eastern parishes, particularly St Philip, one of the driest areas, with the highest ratio of slaves to whites.[10] Up to 70 estates were affected, the resident whites fleeing to Oistins Fort or Bridgetown in considerable panic. Martial law was promptly declared and the military commander, Colonel Codd, acted vigorously, only to discover that the rebels unsportingly faded away like guerillas.[11] Although the rebels initiated no massacre, and damage to property was initially limited to burned canes and plunder, the method of suppression were draconian, especially on the part of the local militia.[12] Only two whites were killed in the fighting but probably about 100 slaves, with a further 144 executed, 170 deported, and innumerable floggings.

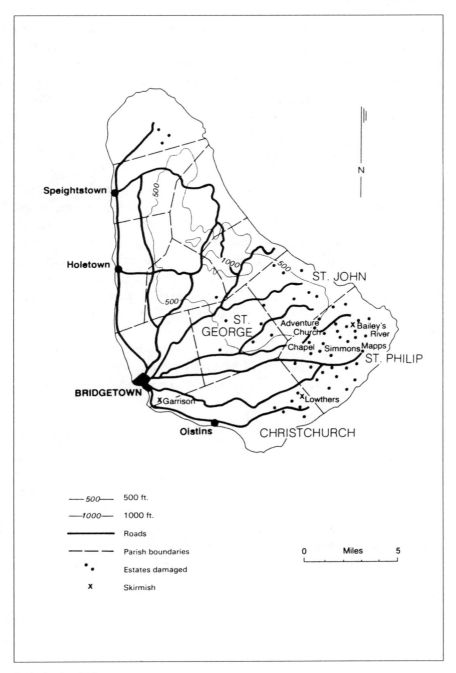

Barbados in 1816

Roaming slaves were shot on sight and Negro houses burned, especially where, as at Mapp's, Bailey's, Three Houses or The Thicket estates, they virtually formed separate villages or were set amid slave provision grounds.[13] Captives were commonly tortured to extract confessions or to incriminate others. Convicted rebels were publicly executed in different parts of the island and their bodies – sometimes just their heads – in many cases exposed on their home estates.[14]

Perhaps because it began prematurely, the rebellion did not spread over the whole island and was effectively over within a week, although the last implicated slaves were not transported to Honduras until January 1817. Long before that the army and naval commanders and the governor had reported the details and their own view of the causes. The Assembly's version, after much heart-searching, was not published until 1818,[15] although it did not differ substantially from the immediate accounts. The revolt came to be known as Bussa's Rebellion by ordinary Barbadians after a slave from Bailey's estate, St Philip, but it was said by the whites to have been hatched by disaffected free coloured men, especially one Joseph Pitt Washington Franklin, 'a person of loose morals and abandoned habits, but superior to those with whom he intimately associated'. These associates, most of the rebel leaders, and a very high proportion of those executed, were élite slaves: drivers, 'rangers' and craftsmen, some of them literate. Very few indeed were Africans.[16]

'The general opinion which has persuaded the minds of these misguided people', claimed Colonel Codd to the governor on April 25, 'since the proposed Introduction of the Registry Bill [is] that their Emancipation was decreed by the British Parliament. And the idea seems to have been conveyed by mischievous persons, and the indiscreet conversation of Individuals'.[17] Whites asserted that slaves never gave bad treatment as a cause of revolt, and masters were eager to demonstrate, against their metropolitan critics, that Barbadian slaves were well-fed, clothed and housed, were not cruelly punished, received good medical treatment, and had opportunities to grow their own provisions and raise livestock, even to sell their surpluses.[18]

'They maintained to me', wrote Colonel Codd of the slaves he interrogated, echoing an ancient theme,

> that the island belonged to them, and not to white Men, whom they proposed to destroy, reserving the Females, whose lot in case of success, it is easy to conceive . . . Among the Flags used by these Insurgents, a rude drawing reserved to influence the Passions, by representing the Union of a Black Man with a white Female.[19]

Besides the emancipation rumour and the idea that William Wilberforce was their saviour, the slaves were said to have believed that the black troops of the 1st West India (Bourbon) Regiment would not fight against their own kind, and that aid would come from Santo Domingo (independent as Haiti since 1804).[20] Indeed the slave revolution in Santo Domingo was claimed to have inspired the slaves, although few seemed to have the haziest facts of the case, or to know the correct name of the island, calling it 'Mingo'.

The suppression of the rebellion seems to have doused neither the slaves' unrest nor the masters' brutally reawakened fears. 'The disposition of the Slaves in general is very bad', wrote a Barbadian to London in June 1816:

> They are sullen and sulky and seem to cherish feelings of deep revenge. We hold the West Indies by a very precarious Tenure, that of military strength only and if they do not change at home their system of reduction I would not give a year's purchase for any Island we have.[21]

These proprietary sentiments were expressed even more crudely by Speaker Beckles of the Barbadian assembly two weeks later. 'The Insurrection has been quelled', he said in a speech,

> but the spirit is not subdued, nor will it ever be subdued whilst these dangerous doctrines which have been spread abroad continue to be propagated among the Slaves. It behoves us to be upon guard – to keep watch that we may not again be caught so shamefully unprepared. The comfort and happiness of our families require it – the safety and tranquillity of the Island call for it. We must all determine to sacrifice our private interests for the public good. It is a duty which we owe to our Constituents – it is a duty which we owe to our country.[22]

Demerara in 1823 was one of the three contiguous British colonies in South America acquired from the Dutch in the last French war only 20 years before. All three had a huge tropical interior laced with rivers, but development had been limited to a coastal strip, much of it reclaimed from the sea. Since the British takeover there had been an intensification of the plantation system towards sugar monoculture. Although there were comparatively few resident plants and the Guyana colonies were intended to have less autonomy than those with ancient assemblies, the local whites effectively formed a plantocracy based on Georgetown. This was despite an overwhelming majority of slaves who outnumbered the whites 20 to one. The slaves, perhaps half of whom in 1823 were African-born, were demographically unhealthy, suffering a serious annual net decrease in numbers. The number of free coloured inhabitants was negligible, and the few

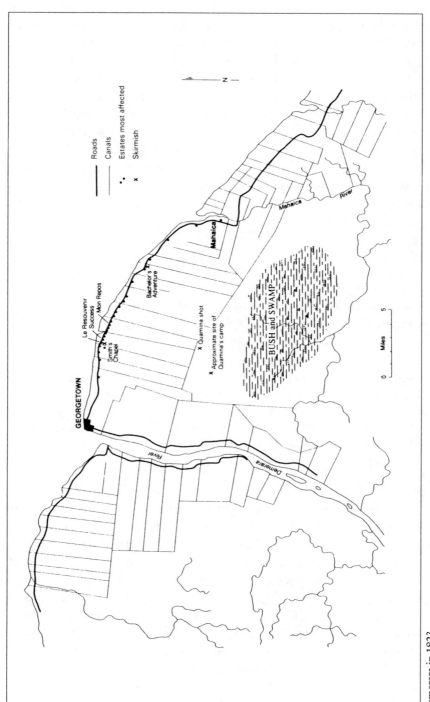

Demerara in 1823

Maroons (called Bush Negroes) and Amerindians were far inland, almost outside the ambit of the colonial polity.[23]

The plantocracy of Demerara, divided over the activities of missionaries but united in opposition to metropolitan 'interference', angrily debated the circular of instructions for ameliorating slave conditions sent out to Crown Colonies by the Colonial Secretary, Lord Bathurst, in mid-1823, and dragged their feet over its implementation.[24] The quasi-legislature (Court of Policy) was to promulgate the reforms at the end of August but the rising began, with stunning suddenness, on Monday, August 18, 1823, immediately after the slaves' official rest-day when, as was well-known, there was considerable movement between estates, either clandestine or, with passes, ostensibly to attend chapel services. The outbreak centred on Le Resouvenir estate, the site of the chapel of the London Missionary Society's pastor, John Smith, and the adjacent Success estate (owned by the father of William Ewart Gladstone), and spread to over 50 estates in the 25 miles between Georgetown and Mahaica. The most prominent leaders were Quamina, Smith's chief deacon, and Quamina's son, Jack of Success, but perhaps 30,000 slaves were affected in all.

In remarkable contrast to the brutality of the regime on many estates, no violence was initiated by the rebels.[25] Whites who did not flee to town were placed in the slaves' punishment stocks. However, martial law was declared, and after the governor and military commander failed in parleys the army and militia acted decisively to save the bridges and rescue the whites. Armed parties of rebels were dispersed with great bloodshed and many Negro houses were fired. Over 100 slaves were killed and dozens summarily executed, though only two whites were killed in all. Implicated slaves not executed were sentenced to up to 1,000 lashes, with hard labour in chains for life. Quamina, who like many rebels had fled to a secret provision ground in the bush, was tracked own with Indians and dogs, shot on September 20, and gibbeted at the roadside in front of Success Estate. Jack appears to have been deported after turning King's evidence.[26]

The planters' version of details and causes established with suspicious rapidity, and sustained with great consistency by Governor Murray, himself a planter, in his first dispatch, by the chief naval officer on station, Captain Thomas Cochrane, and by the London Committee of Guianese Planters.[27] For example, Captain Cochrane wrote that 'they were told by a Missionary whose Church most of the leaders attended, that they were Free; that the King had given them their Freedom of which their Masters still determined to deprive them'. According to Cochrane a plan was made to murder the white men and keep the white women as slaves. 'The Missionary was to be Emperor', he claimed, "the black man 'Quamina' to be King and his son 'Jack' now on his trial, & next to his father the deepest in the plot, some other great personage". Forces were to have been collected eastward of Georgetown; these would then march on the capital, the flames of which would serve as a signal for the slaves of Essequibo, the neigbouring colony. The rebels were said to have believed that the regular soldiers, white as well as black, would not fight against them, being under the command of London, not Georgetown.

Although real resistance was over in two weeks, martial law was continued until the end of January 1824, five months after the outbreak. This was mainly to round up the last bands of runaway rebels deep in the bush; but another purpose was to try the Reverend John Smith, for complicity, under military law. The trial dragged on from October 13 to November 24, when Smith was found guilty and condemned to death (with a recommendation for mercy). He died in prison, of galloping consumption on February 6, 1824.[28]

The response of the British Parliament to the Barbados rebellion had been to withdraw the imperial Registry Bill and to vote addresses to the Prince Regent deploring the outbreak and disavowing slave emancipation. The death of Smith, the 'Demerara Martyr', aroused a public furore in Britain. However, the general response in Parliament was shock at the rebellion of the Demerara slaves, which seemed to come in response to amelioration measures and to occur on what were regarded as the most benevolently ruled estates. The overall effect was to slow the pace of emancipationism.[29]

Parliamentary deceleration was not to be the result of the Jamaican 'Christmas Rebellion' of 1831–32, which was by far the largest, longest and most serious of the three revolts. Although Jamaica had never become a complete monoculture and by 1831 sugar produced by traditional methods was facing a catastrophic decline, the island was still among the most important British colonies, producing a third of the total of British colonial sugar and containing half the total population of the British West Indies. Jamaica had much undeveloped, undevelopable mountain land, and there were many non-sugar plantations and other 'settlements', especially in the highlands. Some sugar estates had already collapsed, with their slaves consequently underworked, while other estates and slaves were being worked harder in the search for economies of scale in the face of declining sugar prices. Jamaican salves were now 75 per cent creoles, but their numbers continued to suffer an annual net decrease of about five pr thousand for the whole island, and much more on many sugar estates. Yet the resident whites, despite being outnumbered 12 to one by slaves and even now, by the free coloureds, constituted an intransigent, self-legislating plantocracy.[30]

The Jamaican legislature had long resisted change dictated by the imperial government. There had been crises over non-compliance in the 1820s (when several slave plots were uncovered), which had been somewhat eased by the passing of ameliorative local acts in 1830. However, the emancipation debates begun at Westminster in April 1831 refuelled the planters' paranoia, which was not mollified by a royal proclamation author-ised in June 1831 that slave freedom had not immediately anticipated.[31]

Signs of slave unrest were general in Jamaica, especially in the western parishes where, it transpired later, where there was a widespread rumour that that slaves would refuse to return to work after the Christmas holiday. A significant incident of insubordination occurred at Silver Spring near Montego Bay in mid-December involving the hot-headed and unpopular Colonel Grignon (nicknamed 'Little Breeches' by the slaves). Christmas Day, moreover, came on a Saturday, giving the slaves two consecutive days officially free from work and, as in Barbados and Demerara, opportunities to move around between estates and meet under cover of the traditional holiday celebrations or religious services. All the same, the concerted outbreak of Monday, December 27, 1831, astounded by its suddenness, its extensiveness, and the clear evidence of careful preparation.

The insurrection was concentrated on St James and the adjacent parts of the neighbouring five parishes, but involved in all some 300 estates containing perhaps 60,000 slaves. The outbreak was signalled by beacons made of the cane-trash houses; there was little other damage at first. The whites not already in towns for Christmas fled to Montego Bay, Falmouth, Lucea, Savanna-la-Mar and Black River, and the only militia unit in the interior (commanded by Colonel Grignon) beat a strategic retreat to Montego Bay after a skirmish at Old Montpelier on December 28.[32]

Governor Lord Belmore proclaimed martial law, and the military com-mander, Sir Willoughby Cotton, acted promptly and efficiently with a five-pointed pincer campaign against the rebel fastnesses on the upper Great River. But the suppression took fully two months because of the slaves' maroon-like guerrilla tactics, for which the country was extremely well-suited. On the margins of nearly all estates there were tropical woods and mountainous cockpits, many of them already developed as slave provi-

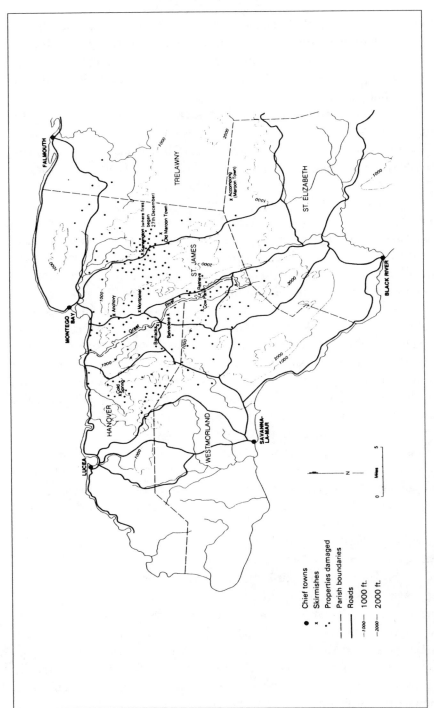

Western Jamaica in 1831-1832

sion grounds, into which the slaves fled at the approach of the military, firing on their red-coated pursuers from the shelter of tangled trees and rocks. A particular target of military operations was Old Maroon Town high above Montego Bay, empty since the end of the Second Maroon War in 1796, but feared as a rebel refuge and rallying point.[33]

The maroons of other settlements, though, stayed loyal to the regime, and the authorities, especially the local militia, acted with exemplary savagery. Many slaves, including women and children, were shot on sight, slave huts and provision grounds were systematically burned, and there were numerous judicial murders by summary courts martial.[34] After the revolt, damages were assessed by the planters at well over £1 million, but this total included damage caused by the military themselves and by the slaves simply in retaliation, and also the estimated value of the slaves killed.[35] Only 14 free men died in the rebellion but over 200 slaves were killed in the fighting, with 312 executed and 300 others flogged, imprisoned for life or transported. An amazingly high proportion of these victims were élite slaves, particularly drivers and craftsmen, and so many of them were Baptist converts, including deacons, that the rebellion was popularly called 'The Baptist War'.[36] Despite the attempts by the plantocracy to implicate them, neither non-Baptist-Nonconformist converts (Moravians, Wesleyans, Presbyterians) nor free coloureds were generally involved in the revolt.[37] Some of the rebel leaders were killed in the fighting; others were captured or surrendered. Samuel Sharpe, a Baptist deacon widely known as 'Daddy Ruler Sharpe' and commonly held to be the chief leader, was almost the last to be executed, being hanged at Montego Bay on May 23, 1832. Just before his execution Sharpe told the Reverend Henry Bleby: 'I would rather die upon yonder gallows than live in slavery!' Bleby also reported that Sharpe,

> expressed deep regret that such an extensive destruction of property and life had resulted from the conspiracy which he had promoted; but declared this formed no part of his plan. He did not wish to destroy the estates, nor did he desire that any person should be injured: his only object was to obtain freedom.[38]

The Jamaican Assembly rapidly appointed a self-serving commission of enquiry, protesting the kindliness with which the slaves had been treated, insisting on the bloody and destructive intentions of the slaves' leaders, and placing the chief blame on an alleged conspiracy in Britain, including Westminster itself, in which the missionaries were said to be the chief local agents. Much play was made of the dissemination of false rumours, particularly concerning a 'free paper' emancipating the slaves, said either to have been granted by the king and withheld by the local whites, or to be arriving in the hands of the Baptist missionary, Burchell. The climate of opinion in Britain, however, had significantly changed since 1823. The long intransigence of the Jamaican plantocracy, the full evidence of the rebellion and the savage suppressive measures – not least the persecution of Nonconformist missionaries by the Anglican vigilantes of the Colonial Church Union – convinced not only the vast majority of British but Parliament as well that only by emancipation could the situation be remedied. The following year the first Emancipation Act was passed.[39]

What, then, is to be made of these late slave rebellions: their causes, nature and ends? Were they sufficiently similar to each other and different from earlier revolts to amount to a separate phenomenon? Were they manifestations of changing conditions, or productive of important changes in themselves?

First, the testimony of the planters should be treated with caution since much of it consisted of automatic assumptions based on outdated experiences and ancient prejudice, buttressed by selective evidence often obtained from slaves under torture. Yet the planters' plea between 1816 and 1832 that events in Britain and emancipationist pressure helped to cause the outbreaks is not implausible in the light of the coincidental rumours that freedom was impending, or actually granted and withheld. The Registry Bill of 1815, the Bathurst circular of 1823 and the Westminster debates of 1831 all had an exaggerated impact upon the slaves, although it was not clear to contemporaries whether the rumours were planted on purpose, or grew naturally through a combination of indiscreet discussion and secretiveness on the part of the plantocracy.

Similarly the planters' complaints about missionaries were not entirely unfounded, at least in Demerara and Jamaica. Although missionaries were carefully instructed by their societies to preach obedience, and all protested their innocence of inflammatory intent (many, indeed, believing that what they called 'Civilisation' should come before freedom), there is little doubt that their message and activities were inimical to slavery. However, although some claimed credit after emancipation was achieved, these almost certainly overstated and misunderstood their real role. John Smith's journal, for example, provides plentiful hints that what missionaries preached was not necessarily what the slaves heard and saw as the benefits of the Word or membership in the church. It should also be remembered that in 1816 missionary activity had not yet properly begun in Barbados.[40]

In confronting and putting the blame on the colonial plantocrats, the missionaries and metropolitan philanthropists were much nearer the mark. The attitudes and behaviour of the local whites exacerbated conditions, if they did not alone provoke the outbreaks. Before each rebellion the whites showed little solidarity. Nearly all selfishly pursued their own concerns and they were dangerously divided. A few planters genuinely believed that concessions and Christianity had pacified the slaves, but this attitude merely reinforced the siege mentality of the majority, who held that with Negro slaves, severity and constant vigilance were the price of socioeconomic security. Once rebellion occurred, the whites closed ranks and reverted to traditional behaviour. Initial panic was followed by over-reactive suppression and, in the post-mortem period, by exculpatory special pleading and the use of racist arguments to defend what was essentially a socioeconomic interest.

The masters had not changed much since the days of the earliest slave rebellions; and they were incapable of seeing what had changed. Their reactions, moreover, emerged from deep in the collective plantocratic psyche. Sustained, as Bryan Edwards, the greatest of their writers, acknowledged, by naked power,[41] the planters were conditioned to ascribe nothing but anarchy and blind destructiveness to their slave opponents. Their emphasis on damage and pillage reflected fears for their property; their emphasis on rape, a deep sexual insecurity. In a profound and double sense the issues were visualised by them in black and white. As an aside, it is worth remarking that the notorious modern phrase 'Law and Order' takes on a special, classic, connotation in a system where not only is the work-force enslaved and of a different race, but both the magistracy and the militia are exclusively of the master class and race.

Although modern commentators have no direct interest either in condoning or combating slave rebellions, they are presented with a wide and often contradictory, choice of causal elements to add to the contemporary analysis. Economists and economic determinists would stress the politically disruptive effects of capitalistic intensification in the transition phase between old and modern plantations, between the mercantilist and industrial phases of capitalism, though most would also insist that the change from formal slavery to what was generally called 'free wage labour' was a change in form not substance.[42]

Non-Marxist historians might tend instead to favour the causal structure attributed to revolutions in general by Crane Brinton and others, arguing that in all the late slave rebellions were to be found an oppressive socioeconomic and political system, leadership by a relatively privileged élite on the spot supported by intellectuals standing outside the conflict, with generally rising expectations on the part of the underdog class and yet, at the critical moment, short-term grievances.[43]

Historians of ideas might well-prefer to see the late slave rebellions as consonant with – even manifestations of – the abstract spirit of the age. The most eloquent of modern writers on slavery, David Brion Davis, points out that this was an era of general reform and a change in general sensibility amounting to a revolution, though in his latest work he himself veers towards the formulation of the neo-Marxist, Antonio Gramsci: that this was one of those periods in which the ruling class, with its focus now more firmly on the imperial metropolis, was shifting its ground in order to sustain its ideological hegemony in a changing world.[44]

More strictly idealist historians might be even more ingenious. Looking at the remarkable success of Nonconformist sects in the last days of slavery (which presented a contrast to Christianity's meagre initial impact on Africa), and considering the religious overtones of the Jamaica and Demerara rebellions, they might well be intrigued by the possibility that the outbreaks exhibited classic symptoms of millenarianism. This is particularly plausible if one studies the role of sectarian deacons in the underground 'native Baptist' churches in Jamaica or the small independent classes on individual estates in Demerara, with their emphasis on membership and leadership, their fervent, secret meetings, their use of dream and trance, their almost cabalistic reverence for the Holy Bible. Then one is easily reminded of the famous five-point formulation of Norman Cohn. Like classical millenarian outbursts these slave rebellions can be seen to have been collective, to be enjoyed by all the faithful. They were immanent, to be realised on earth, not in heaven; imminent, coming soon and suddenly. They were, perhaps, to be total, utterly transforming, bringing not only improvement but perfection. Finally, the rebellions could be seen as invoking the miraculous, calling for God's direct intervention.[45]

The concept of millenarianism is intellectually beguiling, but it does not fit perfectly and is not all-inclusive. Moreover, it is descriptive rather than causal. Indeed, all the foregoing explanations, singly or in combination, are flawed and incomplete. Almost exclusively they hinge on the views of contemporary whites and later outside commentators, and they stress the play of abstractions. Worse, they deny the same degree of will to the rebels as to the master class – a tendency that itself smacks of racism. To redress the balance one should look more at the slaves' side – their aims, aspirations, leadership – seen, where possible, through their own words and actions.

Clearly the role of the rebel leadership has hitherto been understated. This perpetuates the contemporary response of the whites who, with their low estimation of the capabilities of blacks, were perennially amazed at, and incredulous of, the evidence of careful, concerted planning and coherent aims. Nearly all previous accounts have played down the intelligence and awareness of the rebel leaders. This may be the result of a tendency to lump all slaves together, not only denying their individuality but ignoring the fact that the leaders were almost a separate class in what had already become a three-caste 'slave society': masters, slave élite and ordinary slaves.

The importance of a new type of slave leadership, with aims and tactics shaped to the new context, is clear for those with eyes to see. Earlier leaders had tended to be desperate warriors, sometimes transported African chieftains, using traditional African means of communication and warfare, and prepared to die if they could not overthrow and supplant their plantocratic enemies. Now the leaders were far more versatile: a relatively privileged élite, often Christian and sometimes literate. Aware of previous rebellions and the value of African traditions, they had additional means of communication, a wider range of tactics, and new, and infinitely more practical, aims.

Only a form of transferred prejudice can prevent us viewing the new slave leadership as being at least sophisticated as the leadership of contemporary proletarian movements in Europe.

Consider the following examples drawn from each of the late slave rebellions. At the time of the trial of Samuel Sharpe in Jamaica in April 1832, Robert Rose, one of the slave witnesses, testified that in a house on Retrieve estate before Christmas:

> Saml. Sharpe put the Book on the Table & asked me to take the oath. I said Yes. The oath was if we would agree to sit down. I said Yes & so did everybody in the house say Yes. [We] Must not trouble anybody or raise any rebellion – [we] sat down all Wednesday & Thursday [December 29-30, 1831].[46]

Likewise, at the trial of Inglis, one of the lesser Demerara rebels, in August 1823, the defendant testified that:

> On Sunday [the day before the outbreak] Daniel [one of the deacons] called a meeting of the Negroes and then ordered the women to leave them. After remaining an hour Joseph [another deacon] came having a Bible in his hand which he gave to Daniel who ordered us to kiss the Bible, for the King had sent us a good thing, but the Planters said it was too good for us, & that all the Negroes were to join from Town upwards and to be joined by 1,000 Bush Negroes.[47]

After the Barbados rebellion a slave called Robert, of Simmon's Estate, made an even more telling confession. He said that Nanny Grigg, 'a negro woman at Simmon's who said she could read', had put around a rumour late in 1815 that all the slaves were to be freed on New Year's Day, and that,

> she said she had read it in the Newspapers, and that her Master was very uneasy at it: that she was always talking about it to the negroes, and told them that they were all damn fools to work, for that she would not, as freedom they were sure to get. That about a fortnight after New-year's Day, she said the negroes were to be freed on Easter Monday, and the only way to get it was to fight for it, otherwise they would not get it; and the way they were to do, was to set fire, as that was the way they did in Santo Domingo.

Robert went on to say:

> Jackey, the driver at *Simmon's*, said he would send to the other Drivers and Rangers, and to the head Carters about, and to Bussoe (at *Bayley's*), to turn out on Easter Monday to give the Country a light, and let every body know what it was for; and that John (at *Simmon's*) was the person who carried the summons from Jackey: that Jackey was one of the head men of the Insurrection, and that he had heard him say he was going to point out a good great house to live in, but he did not say which: that Jackey sent also to a free man in *The Thicket* (who could read and write), to let the Negroes at *The Thicket* know, that they might give their assistance . . . That Toby, of *The Chapel*, came with a gun in his hand, and gave orders to shoot, every one that did not join them, and marched about the yard with a gun on his shoulder. That Little Sambo, belonging to *The Adventure*, came with a gang to *Simmon's*, armed with a sword, and began to lick down the old mill door, in which they kept the provisions. That Jack belonging to Mr Doughty, had a sword and a long knife in his hands, and came up to him [Robert] and said, 'I will chop you down if you do not join us.'[48]

Leaders such as Bussa, Jacky, Sambo and Nanny Grigg in Barbados, Quamina, Jack, Telemachus and Daniel in Demerara, and Sharpe, Johnson, Gardner, Dove and Dehany in Jamaica, were intelligent persons who had risen to positions of authority, responsibility and confidentiality through their own abilities. Their privileged positions provided opportunities to move between the estates and meet their fellows, under the cloak of their work, Bible-reading, chapel meetings or, in the case of Barbados, the Sunday evening dances. Some of the few literate slaves were among their number, conversant through the newspapers and the idle talk of the plantation whites not only with colonial but also imperial affairs. The leaders were surely quite aware of precisely what was going on in Britain, and quite capable of calculating the chances that the slaves by concerted action could serve their own cause well, by showing up the immorality and inefficiency of the system and the intransigence of the whites.

It appears that despite the whites' imaginings, none of the rebel leaders wanted bloody revolution unless there was no alternatives. It is unlikely that any of them visualised a complete overthrow of the economic system. The best interpretation of their strategy is to see it as a kind of strike action: leading the slaves in a refusal to work, immobilising the whites by driving them to town and taking their arms, but resorting to fighting only where necessary, destroying houses only in retaliation, and mills and factories as a last resort, in desperation. In all cases, though, along lines developed by the maroons in their heroic resistance to the imperialist tide. Living off the land and taking advantage of familiarity with the terrain and the support of their fellow slaves, they would confront the soldiers trained in European methods with ambushes and skirmishing, moving quickly in small bands, refusing pitched battles and fading away when threatened with frontal assault.[49]

Leadership was vital but rebellion depended upon a mass following. To win over the ordinary slaves, the rebel leaders used their established authority as leaders on the estates, in the slave quarters and in the chapels, playing on the slaves' dissatisfactions and aspirations. They also, it seems, relied cleverly upon millenarian tactics, employing the Bible, preaching and oaths upon a susceptible people, and used convenient rumours that they themselves must have known to have been untrue, unlikely or half-truths.

At their trials many rank-and-file rebels complained bitterly that they had been misled. Yet strong evidence remains, in contemporary accounts and the fading oral tradition, that attitudes of resistance, even revolutionary potential, were deeply ingrained in ordinary slaves. As early as 1816 Matthew Gregory Lewis, a visiting absentee planter, had recorded with alarm, a subversive ditty (already quoted in the previous essay) which invoked the aid of God and William Wilberforce alike, and enjoined the use of force if the planters remained obdurate.

A clear derivative of the song was remembered in 1973 by aged informants in Lluidas Vale, central Jamaica, as variants of the 'Tenke Massa Song':

King give mi mi freedom;
Tenke Massa . . .

Driber 'tan mi side, but let mi talk to mi 'busha;
Whan 'busha gan, is mi an' yu de yah . . .
If yu kick mi, mi kick yu back;

Tenk yu Massa.
If yu buck me, mi buck yu back;
Tenk yu Massa.
If yu lick mi, mi lick yu back;
Tenk yu Massa.'[51]

In sum, the rebellions occurred because the leaders were able to mobilise the slaves, harnessing their seething discontent and potential for retaliatory violence, and offering fulfilment for their deepest aspirations. The chief of these aspirations was, naturally, to be free. Yet the form of that freedom – and here we arrive at the crux of the argument – seems to have been that of an independent peasantry, about which the slaves had quite clear notions and of which, in most cases, they already had considerable experience. Because the slaves were virtually mute and the literature was dominated by white writers, the evidence is meagre. But it does exist 'between the lines' of plantocratic and missionary accounts (as was convincingly demonstrated by Sidney Mintz and Douglas Hall in 1960 in their article on the origins of the Jamaican internal marketing system),[52] and in the unpublished accounts of the rebels' trials.

Although by the time of the late rebellions a high proportion of the slaves were already creoles, their African peasant roots clearly predisposed all slaves to regard plantation agriculture as being unnatural as the institution which sustained it. From the earliest days, runaway slaves settled around provision grounds (called 'polinks' in the British colonies, 'palenques' in the Spanish),[53] worked in a manner owing something to African farming, something to the *conuco* agriculture of the Amerindians. From the earliest days too, masters were constrained to give slaves their own garden plots, and provision grounds wherever space was available, when time-off from plantation labour to work them – Sundays and holidays and, in some areas, alternate Saturdays too.[54] By the last phase of slavery the custom had become institutionalised. As Bryan Edwards testified in 1793, slaves in Jamaica had some come to regard the provision grounds as their own that they bequeathed them at their death, and even expected compensation from their masters if the lands were required by the plantation for other purposes.[55]

In other words, and in the term coined by Sidney Mintz, many of the slaves were already 'proto-peasants' well before the end of formal slavery. Besides the ways in which they worked their provision grounds, with their own methods and with minimal supervision, this was demonstrated by the way they had developed an internal marketing system quite independently, and managed to enter the cash economy on their own terms. More deeply, the slaves retained and developed concepts of family and kin quite beyond the comprehension and control of the master class, and a concept of land tenure that was in contradiction to that of the dominant European culture.[56] In brief, for ordinary slaves freedom meant being free to be small farmers, working for the plantations, if at all, only for wages and on their own terms. They wanted to live in family units, to have ready access to land of their own, and be free to develop their own culture, particularly their own, syncretised religion. These were the basic aspirations, which varied according to the different conditions in each of the colonies affected.

Jamaica by 1831 was particularly primed for this type of revolt. The island's economy and society were both approaching crisis, the plantocracy locked in combat with the imperial government. Conditions were ideally suited for the slaves to seize the initiative and switch from bondage to the life of peasants, or at least the status of quasi-peasants – working their own land much of the year, and for the estates for wages when they wished. Because of the crescendo of metropolitan interest in conditions and the growing concern of the planters to defend themselves, the Jamaican evidence is plentiful. All plantocratic writers made much of the slaves' enjoyment of grounds of their own, although most saw this as an argument for continuing slavery not a fundamentally weakening aspect of the system.[57] More perceptively, a Jamaican overseer, William Taylor, like other witnesses before the British parliamentary inquiry into the Christmas Rebellion, gave his opinion in June 1832 that because of their peasant proclivities no ex-slave would continue working on sugar plantations a moment after slavery ended, given viable alternatives.[58] And to return to Samuel Sharpe's trial just two months earlier, Edward Barrett, a second slave witness, testified: 'Sharp[e] said we must sit down. We are free. We must not work again unless . . . [we] got half pay. He took a Bible from out of his pocket, made me swear that I would not work again until we got half pay.'[59] 'Half pay' here plainly meant the right to be paid for plantation labour, but also to work only for that period which could be spared from peasant cultivation. The inference is clear that the slave rebels wanted to control the terms of the arrangement, an ideal that continued – though all too rarely realised – from emancipation to the present day.

Demerara in 1823 was at least as volatile as Jamaica in 1831 – quite ready for a peasant-type revolt, although for slightly different reasons. The slaves were driven to revolt as much by the harshness of the socioeconomic and political regime as by finding conditions especially conducive to seizing the initiative. Yet at the same time they too felt that they were strong enough to dictate the terms of their involvement in the system – free from bondage, with land of their own, and working for wages if and when it suited them. The evidence from the Demerara revolt, although scantier than for Jamaica, is still good. For example, Lieutenant-Colonel Thomas Leahy of the 21st Regiment described at the trial of the Reverend John Smith in November 1823 how on the first day of the Demerara revolt he advanced with his men to meet the rebels. Coming to Bachelor's Adventure Estate he found thousands massed, some with guns and some with cutlasses, but still went forward alone, twice, to parley. Leahy spoke with Jack, Telemachus, and other leaders, listened to their complaints (even writing them down, though he later destroyed the paper 'as useless'), saying that he would carry the complaints to the governor only if the slaves would lay down their arms and disperse. He gave the leaders half-an-hour to convince their followers. 'At first', he reported to the court, 'there was more demand for freedom and three days than anything else [that is, three days' private labour, four days for wages], but latterly when I came out again they were all for freedom, and all of them dwelt considerably on going to Chapel on Sunday'. Jack and the other leaders did not come forward when Leahy returned, and when the slaves refused to disarm or disperse the colonel ordered his troops to advance with shot and bayonet.[60]

Only in Barbados was the revolt truly desperate. With a plantation system so long established, white supremacy so firmly entrenched, and with so little spare or waste land to move to and work for themselves, the slaves could not easily visualise a compromise with the dominant order. To escape the yoke, the white regiment and the plantations might both have to be destroyed. Uniquely too in Barbados, the free coloured minority – or at least some of them – saw their only chance of advancement in throwing in their lot with the rebel slaves. In so doing they doubtless hoped to take over the leadership role of the whites, if not their absolute dominance. In the unlikely event that the rebels had achieved a takeover, the self-emancipated slaves would have aimed to have established themselves as peasants, while their leaders (coloured as well as black) might have tried to revive or continue the sugar plantations.

The Barbadian evidence, predictably, is weakest of all. But it can be inferred, for instance, from the planters' own testimony when they were at pains to describe how well they treated their slaves, and how free in practice many of the slaves were by 1816. Thomas Stoute, manager of Mapp's Estate, for one, testified to the Barbados assembly that:

The condition of the slaves was comfortable and they were (generally speaking) healthy. They had warm and comfortable houses, always as much food as they could consume, and frequently had such a superfluity as to enable them to dispose of a part – which consisted of corn and other grain, of roots of different sorts, such as the Country produces.[61]

Edward Thomas, manager of Bailey's estate, testified that no labour was ever required of the slaves there on Sundays,

or any of the Festivals or great Fast-Days, and that these days were exclusively theirs. Each negro cultivates a garden of his own, in which he raises, with great facility, corn, ocros, yams, &c . . . a great part of the ginger exported from this Island is raised by the negroes in their gardens; and he has known individual negroes to make from £10 to £20 per annum from the sale of their ginger. They also raise great quantities of hogs, goats, and poultry, and he thinks that the market is chiefly supplied with these articles by the negroes.

Thomas also reckoned that there had 'been an obvious change in the negro character within the last few years, and that they were fully sensible of their importance'.[62] Many other commentators remarked that by 1816 slaves of the island were already calling themselves 'Barbadians', though it was probably only the actual rebels who believed, in the words of Colonel Codd, 'that the Island belonged to them, and not to white Men'.[63]

In conclusion, although one must agree with Aptheker that the late slave rebellions in the British West Indies illustrated the fundamental tendency of all slaves to resist their enslavement and rebel whenever possible, they shared characteristics peculiar to the last phase of formal slavery. Although occurring in three distinctly different colonies, they can all be portrayed as responses to the accelerating pace of emancipationism and the declining importance of old-style sugar plantations and their owners. More subtly, they could all be partly attributed to a dangerous imbalance between overworked and undeworked slaves on states in different stages of economic flux, and to tensions created by the contradiction between official policies of amelioration and the tightening of control on the part of some owners over-compensating for their loss of power. Most important of all, the late slave rebellions unequivocally demonstrated the growth of a sense of identity and power among the enslaved blacks, particularly creoles, and the emergence of a new leader class.

However, one should not perpetuate the tendency simply to assess the causes of the revolts and to underestimate the results. In striking for freedom in advance of imperial legislation all three of the slave communities studied were, in different ways and to an increasing degree, far more effective than the dominant whites acknowledged or later writers have generally recognised. In the long view, none of the slave rebellions was a failure, and the Jamaican rebellion at least was a notable success.

In Barbados the planters and their chosen historian, Sir Robert Schomburgk, did their utmost to bury the events of 1816 along with the killed and executed slaves. Yet the rebellion undoubtedly shattered plantocratic complacency beyond repair, while providing a cause for secret pride among the blacks. From this standpoint it is quite plausible to argue that the 1816 rebellion did as much as to crystallise the social matrix in Barbados as the ending of slavery itself, 22 years later. Socioeconomic freedom did not come for the Barbadian majority with emancipation in 1838, and the sugar plantations and their owners showed remarkable resilience for at least another century. But today it is the name of Bussa, not those of Governor Leith, Colonel Codd, or even Joseph Franklin, which is remembered by ordinary Barbadians.

The Demerara rebels, by proclaiming their refusal to take part in the socioeconomic system on the masters terms, likewise made a contribution of huge significance to the development of Guyanese society. True, the 1823 rebellion did not speed, indeed rather retarded, the official ending of slavery; nor did it immediately overthrow the master class. Yet when emancipation came 15 years later the sugar system was only maintained by the initiation of an alternative form of imported servile labour, the use of Asian 'coolies'. This consigned Guyana, even more than Barbados, to the fate of a plural society. Yet it must be noted that it is the heirs of the rebel slaves who are the dominant class in modern, independent Guyana, and that the heroic resistance of Quamina, Jack and their fellows is an inspiration to modern Guyanese, of Asian as well as African stock.

It was the Jamaican rebellion, however, which had the most important, immediate and lasting effects. The Barbadian whites judiciously suppressed the true nature of the 1816 rebellion and the feelings of the rebels. The evidence from Demerara in 1823 only leaked out in partial and edited forms. But thanks to the missionaries on the spot and the metropolitan philanthropists (who had by now infiltrated the imperial government itself) the intrepid actions of the Jamaican blacks at last aroused the conscience of the imperialists. Even more significant in the long run, the Christmas Rebellion signalled the birth of a Jamaican national consciousness. As early as 1833 a British commentator prophetically wrote:

I little doubt that the day will come when the names of *the rebels* Sharp[e], and Gardner, and Dove, will be dwelt upon in the proud recollections of another black republic, with the same satisfaction with which we look back to the first authors of British freedom.[64]

Slavery distorts the personality and all human relationships, so that only in resistance can the self be realised and dignity restored. This can be said of all slave rebellions. Yet the late slave revolts in the British West Indies went further. In the phrase of John Fowles in another context, they celebrated on the part of the rebels 'more than the fact of being; the passion to exist'.[65]

15

What and Who, to
Whom and What

The Significance of Slave Resistance
in *Capitalism and Slavery*

Introduction: Probably the most influential of all books written on British West Indian history, Eric Williams' *Capitalism and Slavery* was for a generation the unshakable orthodoxy among young West Indians. As *Sinews of Empire* attests, the present author was himself almost an unqualified Williamsite in 1974. Time has wrought its usual modifications. Yet, given the animus provoked by his increasingly conservative political career and the intellectual arrogance which declined to debate his historical work with other historians, Williams still emerged strongly, if not unscathed, from the counterattacks of the traditionalists and the quibblings of the numbers crunchers at a memorable retrospective held at the Rockefeller Centre, Bellagio, five years after his death. The present essay was typical of those delivered at Bellagio, in criticising aspects of Williams's work while not denying its general validity and significance. Specifically, it criticises Williams for not convincingly integrating the factor of slave resistance into the general explanation for British slave emancipation given in *Capitalism and Slavery*, while at the same time giving him credit for being, with C. L. R. James, one of the first to recognise the slaves' own contribution to the achievement of their freedom.

The essence of *Capitalism and Slavery* for most of its readers – what is commonly termed 'the Williams thesis' – is the book's concern with the degree to which the origins, the nature, and most of all, the ending of formal slavery were determined by global economics. The twelfth and last chapter in *Capitalism and Slavery*, however, does not fit comfotably into this restricted view of Williams's ideas, and therefore tends to be ignored.

Unlike the rest of *Capitalism and Slavery*, Chapter 12 deals almost exclusively with the colonies rather than the metropolis, to show the ways in which 'the colonists themselves were in a ferment which indicated, reflected, and reacted upon the great events in Britain'.[1] In broad terms, it concentrates on questions of political power and expediency rather than on economics and abstract humanitarianism. In Chapter 12 Eric Williams argues that, quite apart from economic or moral considerations, metropolitan legislators became concerned with the way that both slave unrest and plantocratic recalcitrance jeopardised the very fabric of British imperialism in the West Indies. As the slavery debate intensified in the metropolis, it exacerbated the existing tension between masters and slaves within the colonies. Planters tightened their repressive system and openly threatened secession if slavery were decreed abolished, while the slaves responded by an escalating series of plots and open rebellions, climaxing in the Jamaican Christmas Rebellion of 1831 – 32. 'In 1833, therefore, the alternatives were clear', concludes Williams: 'emancipation from above, or emancipation from below. But EMANCIPATION.'[2]

The purpose of the present essay is twofold. Its longer part will test the validity and strength of Williams' arguments in Chapter 12 of *Capitalism and Slavery* against the historical evidence. Then, having decided that Williams's arguments are at least plausible, it will more briefly and tentatively address the more difficult task: deciding whether questions of power politics, particularly the active role of the slaves themselves, are, or even can be, reconciled with the familiar understanding of the Williams thesis.

With remarkable brevity and brilliant illumination through selective quotation, Eric Williams shows in Chapter 12 how rapidly change came to the British West Indies after the French Revolution and the Napoleonic Wars. The West Indian planters responded first to the Registry Bill of 1815 and then to the proposed amelioration measures from 1823 to 1832 with a panicky rearguard action. Even more serious to them than the threat of losing their fortunes was the prospect of losing power over their slaves and all non-whites, a system of control that they feared would be undermined if legislation were ever imposed upon the colonies by a metropolitan government fallen under the sway of meddling ideologies.[3]

For its part, the growing community of free coloureds was for the first time threatening to exercise an influence proportionate to its size. Feeling superior to the enslaved blacks, the free coloureds sought civil rights hitherto denied them by a plantocracy that they already outnumbered. More respectable than either slaves or the white élite, however, they threatened neither rebellion nor secession. Unlike the mulattos of Saint-Domingue, they were not fired up by a partial interpretation of the ideals of the French Enlightenment. Their interest, indeed, was to keep the slaves to heel, while professing extreme loyalty to a Crown that might yet use them as counterweights to an overweening plantocracy. From the historian's privileged perspective they were thus the men of the future. But for the present, they were too preoccupied with short-term gains and personal security to pose a radical threat.[4]

For Eric Williams it was the mass of the black slaves who constituted the most dynamic force for change in the British West Indian colonies. 'Not nearly as stupid as his master thought him,' he writes with residual condescension, 'the slave was alert to his surroundings and keenly interested in discussions about his fate'. Williams slights the effect upon the British slaves' group consciousness of the events in Saint-Domingue between 1791 and 1804, making far more of the effect of the subsequent 'economic dislocation and the vast agitations which shook millions in Britain', as relayed to the slaves through the distorting lenses of their masters' unguarded conversations. 'The consensus of opinion among the slaves whenever each discussion arose or each new policy was announced' (or each new governor was sent out), writes Williams confidently, 'was that emancipation had been passed in England but was withheld by their masters ... No state of the Negro mind was so dangerous as one of undefined and vague expectation'.[5]

Whether or not one agrees with Williams that such invariable rumours and exaggerations could have been unintentionally circulated, rumour certainly did play a significant role in the sequence of slave revolts in British slavery's last decades, indicating a causal connection between metropolitan debates and colonial revolts. Williams argues a direct abolition in 1807 and an alleged revolt in British Guiana in 1808 (which in fact never occurred), between the Registration dispute and the Barbadian revolt of 1816, between the first Bathurst Amelioration Circular and the Demerara revolt of 1823, and between the news of wide-ranging political reform in Britain between 1829 and 1831 and the Jamaican Christmas Rebellion of 1831–32.[6]

With his less than ideal view of the slaves' intelligence and his failure to identify any coherent leadership among the rebellious slaves, Williams could not see the late slave revolts as being anything but spontaneous reactions to ill-founded rumours, bound to fail in their immediate objects. Yet, in the long run and indirectly, he claims, they did succeed. On the strength of the rumour syndrome, the planters were able to attach blame to false philanthropists, pernicious bureaucrats and misguided missionaries working on the minds of ignorant blacks – and thus justify their tactics of propaganda, obstructionism, threats of secession, and the extension of repression from slave to Nonconformist missionaries. On their side, the legislators at Westminster gradually came to believe, with Lord Brougham, that the colonial whites were a self-interested rabble, indifferent alike to Christian principles and the larger imperial issues, whose behaviour in provoking the slaves and threatening secession was jeopardizing the very integrity of the British Empire.[7] Thus, argues Williams, by 1833 a majority came to believe that only by freeing the slaves could the West Indian colonies be made safe within the Empire – a sixth and clinching argument for emancipation.[8]

William's chief concern in Chapter 12 is to assess the influence of purely colonial events and forces upon imperial decisions. Just as he had earlier dealt with the crescendo of debate in Britain, now he describes a parallel tide of colonial unrest. His argument is that the relationship was reciprocal. Yet, whereas he makes much of the effect that the various phases of the anti-slavery campaign had upon colonial masters and their slaves, he does not integrate successive colonial events into the metropolitan debates with sufficient precision to prove the countervailing influence convincingly.

Williams almost ignores the ways in which the question of slave rebellion conditioned the metropolitan debate almost from the beginning, and this leads him to underplay the way that changes in the nature of slave resistance crucially shaped the course of debate. Also, by understanding the horror felt by most imperial legislators for any form of popular rebellion, he fails to convey the way in which most West Indian slave rebellions were counterproductive to the anti-slavery cause. There was a fundamental difference – in effect as in form – between the earlier 'African' and later 'Creole' forms of slave resistance. While slave revolt could be termed the product of 'African savagery', the anti-slavery lobby could argue that the process of 'civilisation' – including abolition, amelioration and even eman-cipation, as well as the insensible process of creolisation – could lessen the chances of colonial insurrection and disturbance. Thus, the evidence that it was the élite, most creolised, even most Christianised, of slaves who were instrumental in the later slave rebellions, was to be a serious blow to the emancipatinists of Wilberforce's generation, calling for new attitudes and tactics.

Long before Bryan Edwards, the greatest of British plantocratic writers, made his famous admission that slaves would always rebel when they could because their enslavement was unnatural, depending as it did upon 'that absolute coercive necessity which. Leaving no choice of actin, supersedes all questions of right',[9] it was taken for granted by abolitionists such as Wilberforce that uncivilised Africans were particularly prone to rebel, since law and order – and their acceptance – were concomitants to civilisation. This belief could even be used as an argument against the African trade, particularly once the abolitionist debate came under the show of the French Revolution and the terrific slave revolt in Saint-Domingue, which began in 1791.

In a great speech on April 2, 1972, William Wilberforce tried to meld his fellow legislators' beliefs and fears to abolitionist ends. Citing Edward Long, a plantocratic writer altogether cruder than Bryan Edwards, he pointed out that after the 1760 slave rebellion, the Jamaican planters had attempted to place a prohibitive duty on the importation of Coromantine (that is, Gold Coast, Akan-speaking) slaves. 'Surely', he declared,

> when gentlemen talk so vehemently of the safety of the islands and charge us with being so indifferent to it; when they speak of the calamities of St Domingo, and of similar dangers impending over their own heads at the present hour, it ill becomes them to be the persons who are crying out of further importations. It ill becomes them to charge upon us the crime of stirring up insurrections – upon us who are only adopting the very principles which Mr Long – which in part even the legislature of Jamaica itself – laid down in the time of danger, with an avowed view to the prevention of any such calamity.[10]

Wilberforce disavowed any intention of damaging the plantation economy. On the contrary, abolition should aid the plantations by obviating insurrections. 'Why should you any longer import into those countries that which is the very seed of insurrection and rebellion?' he asked.

> Why should you persist in introducing those latent principles of conflagration, which, if they should once burst forth, may annihilate in a single day the industry of a hundred years? Why will you subject yourselves to the imminent risk of a calamity which may throw you back a whole century in your profits, in your cultivation, in your progress to the emancipation of your slaves?'[11]

Whatever short-term penalties the planters might incur, claimed Wilberforce, would be as nothing to the grander, long-term socioeconomic, political and moral advantages. 'It amounts but to this, he argued,

> the colonies on the one hand would have to struggle with some few difficulties and disadvantages at the first for the sake of obtaining on the other hand immediate security to their leading interests; of ensuring, Sir, even their own immediately commencing that system of progressive improvement in the conditions of the slaves which is necessary to raise them from the state of brutes to that of rational beings, but which can never begin until the introduction of these new disaffected and dangerous Africans into these same gangs shall have been stopped.'[12]

These arguments were reiterated and refined in the debate that finally led to the ending of the British slave trade, 15 years later and three years after the black republic of Haiti came into existence. 'The abolition of the trade is the only way of avoiding, in your islands, the horrors which have affected St Domingo,' Lord Grenville told his fellow peers in February 1807:

> I look forward to the period when the negroes in the West Indian islands, becoming labourers rather than slaves, will feel an interest in the welfare and prosperity of the country to whom they are indebted for protection, and of the islands where they experience real comforts, and when they may be called upon to share largely in the defence of those islands with a sure confidence in their loyalty and attachment.[13]

To this, Lord Howick added a rider in the subsequent Commons debate, in response to a suggestion that the cutting of the African link might incite the remaining slaves. 'The prohibition to import fresh negroes could not be fairly adduced as a motive why the old ones should revolt,' he claimed. 'It was proved by experience and fact that in those islands where there was no regular supply of fresh negroes no insurrection ever took place.'[14] This confident assertion, however, was very soon proved false.

Once the Napoleonic War was over, Wilberforce and his allies returned to the attack, stressing the civilisation of the slaves as a necessary corollary to the preservation of the prosperity and tranquillity of Britain's West Indian colonies. In June 1815, during the debate on the Registry Bill, Wilberforce spoke of 'the duty of parliament to provide for the moral and religious instruction of the negroes'. 'Above all other circumstances,' the was reported as saying,

> he had looked to the encouragement of marriage among the slaves as a necessary and most beneficial consequence of the abolition of the trade . . . How desirable would it be to convert the slaves into a free and happy peasantry, capable of defending the islands which they inhabited, instead of endangering them by their presence.[15]

Besides the inadvertent but telling use of the verb 'convert', it should be noticed that by implication, Wilberforce had come round to the belief that it was not just African but all socialised slaves who were likely to rebel. In this respect he was almost prophetic, for in May 1816 came news of a stunning slave rebellion in Barbados, where well over 90 per cent of the slaves were island-born.

Involving some 20,000 slaves from more than 75 estates, the Barbados rebellion occurred a whole generation after the Haitian Revolution, in a colony where not even a plot had ruffled the planters' complacency for 115 years. Although the planters also implicated a handful of disaffected free coloureds, the revolt in fact was led by a vanguard of slave drivers, rangers and craftsmen, some of whom were literate, though very few formally Christian, and only two African-born. The mass of the rebels almost immediately took over the south-eastern third of Barbados, chasing the whites to town but committing no immediate bloodshed and remarkably little property damage. Setting up defensive positions, they fully expected the regime to negotiate, but were soon disillusioned, being savagely suppressed by regular troops and militia. Some 120 slaves were slaughtered in the field at the cost of one white and one black soldier killed, with 144 slaves executed later and 132 deported to Honduras.[16]

Once the Barbados revolt was suppressed, the plantocracy was at pains to exculpate itself. They argued that since the slaves were not badly treated, and in any case were incapable of organisation or even rational thought, the revolt must have been generated by outside forces, namely the British emancipationists and those at Westminster whom they were encouraging to impose an imperial slave registration act upon proudly self-legislating British West Indian colonies. 'The general opinion which has persuaded the minds of these misguided people [the slaves] since the proposed Introduction of the Registry Bill,' summed up the official report of the Barbados House of Assembly in 1818, '[is] that their Emancipation was decreed by the British Parliament. And the idea seems to have been conveyed by mischievous persons, and the indiscreet conversation of individuals'.[17]

For his part, William Wilberforce – who in 1815 had supported the Corn Law ostensibly in return for government support of the Registry Bill, and had his windows broken by the mob in consequence[18] – was desperate to disavow blame for the rebellion, or any intention of undermining the Barbadian plantocracy. He vehemently denied that he had ever advocated immediate emancipation – rather, simply, abolition of the slave trade followed by amelioration, with emancipation as an eventual natural consequence. He further disclaimed any intention to abrogate the local planters' legislative rights; rather, he argued, the Barbadian plantocracy was undermining itself. 'The insurrection, which all lamented,' he was quoted as saying in the Commons on June 19, 1816, 'had proceeded from the intemperance of the colonists themselves, and was to be attributed to the imprudence of their language and conduct. Whatever had happened had no reference to himself or his friends; he had no share in creating the explosion that had been felt; he washed his hands clean of the blood that was spilt'.[19]

Unfortunately for Wilberforce, the very next speaker was the pro-slavery MP C. N. Pallmer, who referred obliquely to the news recently brought to Britain by 'Monk' Lewis that rebel slaves in Jamaica were invoking Wilberforce's name, along with God's, in their struggle for freedom against their masters. 'Persons had been found', asserted Pallmer,

assuming the sacred office of religious instructors, making their way into the interior of the islands, instilling into the minds of the negroes doctrines subversive of the public tranquillity, mixing with the truths of Christianity the dreadful principles of insubordination and insurrection . . . It had appeared the nightly assemblies had been held at which a sort of religious ceremony was performed, and a hymn was sung, the purport of which was to return thanks to Providence, that their good friend, naming the hon. gentleman, had made them free, but that their masters would not allow them to be so.[20]

This quite clearly referred to the subversive slave ditty recorded by Lewis on March 22, 1816, though not published until 1834, which, while neatly encapsulating the creole slaves' new ideology of resistance, challenged two of Wilberforce's most dearly held tenets: that Christianised slaves would not rebel, and that he himself was at least as concerned as the West Indian planters to maintain the social order.[21]

Not surprisingly, this was the juncture at which Wilberforce decided that the emancipationists had better 'rest on their oars' awhile, going so far as to risk a breach with his brother-in-law James Stephen for his pusillanimity.[22] Wilberforce never forsook his belief that slavery was incompatible with civilisation, but the idea of popular insurrection was anathema to him, in Britain, even more so than in the West Indies. In the period 1817-19, indeed, he spent almost as much effort in supporting the government's repressive measures at home as he did on the West Indian cause, and he was never more than a figurehead of the anti-slavery campaign thereafter.[23]

The second generation of emancipationists, led and epitomised by Thomas Fowell Buxton, were clearly men of a different, more pragmatic stamp, living in a subtly different age. In contrast to the anti-revolutionary panic triggered by the Jacobin Terror in France, and the counter-revolutionary overreaction that followed the downfall of Napoleon, British politics entered a new phase of inoculative liberal reform – the era ushered in by Canning in the Commons and Huskisson at the Board of Trade. In the dozen years after the suicide of Castlereagh in 1822 – which saw the achievement of Catholic Emancipation and the troubled passage of the Great Reform Bill – a turning point occurred in the perennial political dialectic between expediency and principle, in which the former (though never previously absent) firmly took over from the latter.

In due course, in response to what was essentially a new constituency, Buxton and his colleagues were not only able to turn the blame for slave rebellions from godless slaves to their ungodly masters, but to suggest that slavery threatened both Britain's reputation and her imperial mastery. This position was already close to the Victorian liberal precept that if Empire were to prevail (as prevail it must) it should be just.[24]

The transition, however, was far from sudden. The next major episode in the West Indian process, in 1823-24, almost replicated the events of 1815-16, although with significant advances on both colonial and metropolitan sides. Moderate liberal reforms, promulgated in response to wide-ning emancipationist activity, triggered a stunningly coordinated slave revolt, which in turn led to overreaction from the colonial regime and, successively, dismay, caution and a reshuffled policy on the part of the anti-slavery lobby.

In January 1823, buoyed up by the growing moral and political fervor in the country, the new Anti-Slavery Society was founded and T. F. Buxton took over leadership from the ailing William Wilberforce. In response to Buxton's demand for gradual emancipation, Canning and Bathurst cannily substituted an ameliorationist policy clearly designed to promote Wilberforce's idea of a civilised, Christianised labouring class. A six-point programme, including the promotion of religious instruction, the banning of Sunday markets, the encouragement of marriage and families and the setting up of savings banks, as well as some easing of the restrictions on manumission and the banning of the flogging of female slaves, was to be experimentally imposed on the Crown Colonies, and only strongly recommended to the self-legislating colonies.[25] But even such a programme was too radical for the Guianese planters who, powerless to reject it, dragged their feet over implementation. This provoked the Guianese slaves, 30,000 of whom, from over 60 estates on a 30-mile stretch of eastern Demerara, rose up on Monday, August 18, 1823.[26]

As in Barbados in 1816, the rebels committed little property damage, contenting themselves, for the most part, with placing captured whites in the slave punishment stocks. When on the first morning, Governor Murray met a spearhead of rebels and asked them what they wanted, they replied simply, 'Our rights'. However, when Murray tried to satisfy them with details of the forthcoming Bathurst reforms, they became more specific. 'These things were no comfort to them', Murray reported them as saying. 'God has made them of the same flesh and blood as the whites, that they were tired of being Slaves to them, that their good King had sent Orders that they should be free and they would not work any more.'[27]

Such strike action elicited as savage a response from the plantocratic regime as in 1816, with some 120 slaves butchered in the fighting – compared with three whites killed and a handful wounded – with another 60 shot out of hand and an equal number more ceremonially executed after military trials. Outweighing these 250 black victims in the minds of the British public, however, was the fate of the Congregationalist missionary, John Smith, whose chapel had been the focus of the slaves' discussion and planning. Smith was tried for complicity, found guilty and condemned to death (with a recommendation for mercy). He died in prison in February 1824.[28]

The news of the Demerara revolt, which reached Britain early in October, 1823, disappointed the anti-slavery lobby and gave strength to its opponents. The fact that, unlike Barbados in 1816, missionaries had been active in Demerara and a majority of rebel leaders had not only been élite slaves but also Christian converts, was particularly embarrassing to the metropolitan 'Saints'. Even they regretted the timing, if not the contents, of the Bathurst instructions, Zachary Macaulay going so far in his attempt to reassure Buxton and Wilberforce as to claim that the revolt was 'the work of Canning, Bathurst and Co and not of your firm'.[29]

No one dared, at least in public to defend the actions of the Demerara slaves. Yet an alternative line of attack presented itself to the anti-slavery forces over the next few months, as the disgraceful details of Smith's trial reached Britain, along with news of the concurrent wrecking of Shrewbury's Methodist chapel in Barbados, and the Jamaican planters' overreaction to a threatened revolt in Hanover parish. Clearly, the blame could be laid on the West Indian planters even more directly than in 1816. Not only had they agitated the slaves by repression, resistance to reform, and loose threats of secession, but they had also demonstrated a lawless godlessness in attacking the Christian Church and its adherents. This was the core of Lord Brougham's marathon attack on the colonial plantocracies on June 1, 1824; a speech that Charles Buxton claimed 'changed the current of public opinion'.[30] Two weeks later, in his last ever Parliamentary speech, William Wilberforce argued that such an ungodly body as the Guaina planters would never voluntarily reform, and helped win the minor concession that the Bathurst measures would be imposed on British Guiana and the other Crown Colonies despite the Demerara revolt.[31] In a parallel move, moreover, the Canning government in 1824 instituted the first two Anglican bishoprics in the West Indies, in Jamaica and Barbados, with the express intention of pushing forward the ideal of amelioration under the safe aegis of the established church.[32]

The period between 1824 and 1833, as Eric Williams suggests, saw events accelerate toward an ultimate crisis and resolution. The gulf between the metropolis – Colonial Office, public and even Parliament – and the colonial plantocracies rapidly widened. As their support throughout Britain increased, the emancipationists made the critical transition from gradualism to immediatism in May 1830.[33] At the same time, unrest increased in the West Indies as the slaves became increasingly adept at taking advantage of developing conditions. All colonies were affected. But, not surprisingly, it was in the richest, most populous, most plantocratic colony, Jamaica, that the climactic slave revolt erupted around Christmas 1831, spreading over an area of 750 square miles and involving perhaps 60,000 slaves from over 200 estates.[34]

Besides having one of the harshest regimes and the most turbulent history of slave resistance, Jamaica was by 1831 the colony in which Christianity had most firmly taken root. This was a development over which the planters were perilously ambivalent. Some had encouraged the resolutely regime-supporting sects, such as the Moravians, Presbyterians, or even Methodists, in the belief that they might fully socialise the slaves, and in recent years there had even been cautious proselytising by the established Anglican Church. Yet what slave converts made of Christianity was rarely what planters intended or missionaries recognised. By far the most popular Nonconformist Church was the Baptist, which owed its vitality as much to its foundation by 'native' black preachers who had come to Jamaica and their Loyalist masters over 25 years before the first white missionaries arrived from Britain, as to its encouragement of popular participation.[35]

The Jamaican rebellion of 1831 occurred in the centre of 'native Baptist' activity, and so many black deacons and their congregations were involved that the uprising was popularly known as the Baptist War. Without doubt there were politically explosive – even millenarian – elements in the rebels' preferred type of Christianity. Yet Christianity was by no means essential to the slaves' resistance. As in Demerara, the chapels and the slaves's more or less authorised Sunday activities provided cover for the organisation and planning, chapel services contributed to rebel rhetoric, and contact with missionaries even provided a sense that the slaves were linked with sympathetic allies overseas. As the reported speeches of Sam Sharpe, the Baptist deacon who was the slaves' chief leader, indicate, the revolutionary message in 1831 was only marginally religious. One condemned rebel described how Sharpe, referred to the manifold evils and injustices of slavery: asserted the natural equality of man with regard to freedom ... that because the King had made them free, or resolved upon it, the whites ... were holding secret meetings with the doors shut close ... and had determined ... to kill all the black men, and save all the women and children and keep them in slavery; and if the black men did not stand up for themselves, and take their freedom, the whites would put them at the muzzles of their guns and shoot them like pigeons.

The slaves, counselled Sharpe, should therefore be prepared to fight, but merely to use the threat of force as the backing for what was essentially strike action, binding 'themselves by oath not to work after Christmas as slaves, but to assert their claim to freedom, and to be faithful to each other'.[36]

Once again, these tactics of strike action, with force only used to counter force, proved ineffectual in the face of an implacable and overwhelmingly well-armed local regime. Some 200 slaves were killed in the fighting and 'pacification' process (for less than a dozen killed by them), while no less than 340 were executed, including more than 100 after civil trials once martial law was lifted in February 1832. Beyond this, the local whites, largely under the cover of an Anglican organisation called the Colonial Church Union, carried out a veritable pogrom against the Nonconformist missionaries and their congregations, burning down virtually every chapel in the rebel parishes.[37]

The response of the Jamaican plantocracy was traditional, but this time it was undoubtedly a case of overkill, tending to speed the ending of the very institution it was desperate to preserve. The news of the Jamaican rebellion reached Britain in mid-February 1832, at a time when the complex struggle for the reform of Parliament itself was approaching its climax. This phase found the Lords fighting a desperate rearguard action, as mobs stoned the houses of unpopular Tories, radical workingmen's associations armed and drilled, and the petty bourgeois were being encouraged, in the slogan recorded by Francis Place, 'To stop the Duke, go for gold.'[38]

The pro-slavery forces responded to the news from Jamaica with a campaign designed to outmatch that of the anti-slavery Agency Committee, with their public meetings still able to attract up to 6,000 people. Many converts to anti-slavery wavered, with those most terrified of insurrection at home and abroad deserting the camp, and many others, convinced of the involvement of converted slaves in the rebellion, retreating to a gradualist position.[39] Yet, after much agonising, T. F. Buxton and his staunchest allies chose a bolder and, in any event, more strategic line, propagating the notion that only by immediate and complete emancipation could a disastrous conflagration be averted. 'If the question respecting the West Indies was not speedily settled,' Buxton warned the Commons as early as March 7, 1832, 'it would settle itself in an alarming way, and the only way it could be settled was by the extinction of slavery'.[40] Two weeks later, strengthened by reports from Jamaica about the whites' attacks upon missionaries and slave Christians, and planters' threats of revolt and secession from the Empire, Buxton was able to place the blame for slave unrest and rebellion firmly on the regime.[41]

Between April and May 1832, Buxton's resolve was transferred to the anti-slavery movement at large. Governor Belmore's revelations about the destruction of sectarian chapels were underlined by the arrival in Britain of refugee missionaries. The Anti-Slavery Society held its annual meeting on May 12, in the middle of what William Cobbett called 'The Days of May' – the tumult occasioned by the obstructionism of the Lords, the king's refusal to create reformist peers and the consequent resignation of the Whig Prime Minister, Earl Grey. The Anti-Slavery Society members were spurred on by the elder James Stephen, one of the earliest advocates of immediate emancipation, who, through his son and namesake, was ideally placed both to understand the obduracy of West Indian planters and to influence imperial policy. But the keynote speaker was Buxton himself, who stated that it was now 'unquestionable that only by the interposition of parliament [that] any hope can be entertained of peacefully terminating [slavery's] unnumbered evils, or any security afforded against the recurrence of those bloody and calamitous scenes that have recently affected Jamaica'. As a result, the Anti-Slavery Society almost unanimously voted that parliament be pressed to fulfil without delay the promise to end slavery made, in the vaguest possible terms by Canning in 1823.[42]

The ultra-conservative Wellington failed in his attempt to form a government, and Grey's Whigs returned to power on May 19 with a commitment to reform. Taking advantage of the change, Buxton made a crucial speech in the Commons less than a week later, calling for the appointment of a select committee 'to consider and report on the measures which it may be expedient to adopt for the purpose of affecting the extinction of slavery throughout the British Dominions, at the earliest period compatible with the safety of all Classes in the Colonies'.[43] Buxton's motion, which was aimed to supplant the Lords' mere committee of inquiry, was outvoted 136 to 90. But a Commons committee was appointed nonetheless, if with an ostensibly milder mandate, and the anti-slavery momentum was maintained. The evidence heard by the committee over the following months, coupled with the cresting wave of anti-slavery campaigning throughout the country and the growing number of members in the newly constituted House of Commons pledged to reform, made the passage of an Emancipation Act by the Whig government within 18 months seem – at least in retrospect – almost inevitable.

The refugee missionaries were key figures in this final phase of the emancipation campaign, particularly the Baptist William Knibb, whose evidence before the Parliamentary committee covered 40 pages, and whose highly coloured lectures drew hisses and boos for the Jamaican planters up and down the country. Perhaps significantly, the British public, as in 1823, was far more easily moved by the maltreatment of white missionaries than by the wholesale slaughter of black rebels. True Christians, it was felt, were bound to be innocent of insurrection, and even Knibb was at pains to argue that neither he nor his parishioners were involved in actual rebellion, conveniently ignoring the fact that he would scarcely have had a case were it not for the rebel slaves' initiative.

The attitude of parliament itself was far more pragmatic. Neither slaughtered rebels nor martyred Christians were as effective at Westminster as the real threat perceived to the empire at large by the catastrophic breakdown in relations between West Indian masters and their slaves. For a majority of Parliament, the question was essentially political, not moral. It was a matter of morality only in the limited sense that in liberal ideology empire can only be sustained if its morality was justified. Thus, the crux of the debate was probably Buxton's speech of May 24, 1832, in which he brilliantly argued the coincidence of slavery's corrupting immorality with its political unwisdom. 'Was it certain', he asked,

> that the colonies would remain to the country if we were resolved to retain slavery? . . . How was the government prepared to act in case of a general insurrection of the negroes? . . . a war against a people struggling for their rights would be the falsest position in which it was possible for England to be placed. And did the noble Lords think that the people out of doors would be content to see their resources exhausted for the purpose of crushing the inalienable rights of mankind?[44]

That Buxton's words were no mere parliamentary rhetoric or debating point is borne out by his private correspondence at that time. Immediate emancipation was vital, he argued in response to a radical critic a few months later, 'for I know *our* power of emancipating in one way or another is fast drawing to a close. I mean they [the slaves] will take the work into their own hands'.[45] Whether or not Buxton's speech of May 24, 1832, was instrumental in swaying Parliament, the decisive watershed certainly occurred during the next six months. In November 1832, the government privately invited Buxton to present a specific plan for freeing the slaves, and so confident did the emancipationist leader feel of the outcome that he counselled a less militant campaign for fear of alarming conservatives, especially in the Lords. In the event, such expediency proved, once more, wise. In effect, only the timing and details of emancipation remained to be debated and resolved, although since the agenda included the mechanics of imposing a transitional phase of compulsory labour and the amount by which the owners should be compensated for their forfeited slave property, as well as the means of ensuring 'the safety of all classes in the colonies', it was to be more than a year before the first Emancipation Act became law, and fully six years before, on August 1, 1838, the 750,000 British West Indian slaves became 'fully free'.[46]

In sum, Eric Williams' subordinate thesis in Chapter 12 of *Capitalism and Slavery* is broadly consonant with the historical record. Slave revolts and plantocratic unrest in the last decades of British slavery were interrelated, and the degenerating sociopolitical climate of the colonies did contribute to slave emancipation in 1834-38. Most of the elements in Williams' analysis at which criticism can be levelled are simply the result of the type of compression inevitable in such a work. As in much of the rest of the book, further detail does little more than flesh out and refine the revisionary groundwork originally laid some 40 years ago.

As we have indicated, more detail of the effect of the Haitian revolution on slaves, their masters and the imperial government, would simply have shown that the threat of slave rebellion conditioned the anti-slavery debate almost from the beginning. More information than Williams provided on the terror felt by emancipationists such as William Wilberforce for any form of popular unrest, would merely have strengthened the theme that emancipation was the culmination of a civilising and socialising process aimed at preventing such manifestations. Similarly, the discovery that imperialist concern for the injudicious, even barbaric, behaviour of the colonial planters came much earlier than previously thought, actually reinforces the theme that contradictions between imperial policy and plantocratic behaviour were as dangerous as actual slave rebellions.

Rather more damaging to a balanced evaluation is the way in which Williams's 12-page treatment ignores the process by which the emancipationists' attitudes and tactics changed, as it was progressively realised that not only the mass of ignorant Africans, but also élite creole and finally, Christian slaves were likely to make a bid for freedom through rebellion. Williams' assumption was that slavery was so obnoxious that all slaves were likely to rebel, but the fact that this truth only gradually dawned upon the imperial master class greatly refines our understanding of the emancipation process – the way in which a naive civilising mission, promoted by an idealistic minority, gradually shifted to a more sophisticated, even cynical, pragmatism, eventually endorsed by a parliamentary majority.

Even more remarkable in the work of one at pains to argue the slaves' contribution to their own emancipation through resistance and rebellion, is Eric Williams' almost complete silence about the precise ideology, aims and tactics of the slaves, and of the ways these subtly changed in the shift from 'African' to 'Creole' forms of resistance. Unfriendly critics might blame this upon an ignorance stemming from an indifference to, even contempt for, mere human aspirations and endeavours in the face of larger, mechanistic forces. Rather, we would see it as an oversimplifying general-isation. The objective reality that slaves consistently sought their freedom and repeatedly rebelled, and that the colonial slave resistance rose to a climax in intimate conjunction with the emancipation process, were suffi-cient facts for Williams's revisionist purposes in *Capitalism and Slavery*.

Finally, then, how does Eric Williams's twelfth chapter fit into the rest of *Capitalism and Slavery*? However convincingly he shows that metropoli-tan decisions over the ending of slavery were accompanied and influenced by slave revolt and planter reaction in the colonies, how well can such political dynamics be integrated into an analysis that is primarily concerned with the articulation of West Indian plantation slavery into the world economy?

Despite the author's late deviations as a practical politician, and despite whether or not as C. L. R. James has alleged, Eric Williams simply adopted whatever imperfect ideology the book contained from sitting at his former schoolmaster's feet in London in the late 1930s, *Capitalism and Slavery* must be regarded –and itself analysed –as essentially a work of Marxian analysis. Besides a resolute economic determinism, Williams explicitly adopts in *Capitalism and Slavery* at least the structural centre of the Marxist historical framework: the shift from feudal to mercantile and then to industrial capital phases and modes of production and social relations. Reinforcing this Marxist structure are Williams' peculiar contributions to the analysis of the process; his emphasis upon the opening of the West African coast as a vital influence in the switch from the Middle Ages to the age of mercantilism, and his stress on the contribution of the profits of the Triangular Trade to the next great transition in the development of capital, the British Industrial Revolution.

Slavery and plantations, indeed, loom larger in Williams' work than in Marx's, where the crucial difficulty lay in deciding the degree to which they constituted a feudal mode.[47] By implication, Williams saw slave plantations as comprising those elements of feudal ownership and socioeconomic relations that conveniently spanned the expansive phase of European merchant capital. These feudal elements, in Williams' view, became outmoded once industrial capital demanded a different mode and scale of production and a changed set of relations of production – that is, demanded a wage-earning proletariat rather than a servile, dependent labouring class.

This analysis underpins and illuminates the relationships described in Chapter 12 of *Capitalism and Slavery*. The continuance of empire depended upon a new phase of industrial capital that made both slavery and the quasi-feudal attitudes of the West Indian planter class dangerously *demodé*. While the achievement of British West Indian slave emancipation in 1834 – 38 was only the first stage in a 50-year process of legislated emancipation in the Americas as a whole, it was speeded by Britain's primacy in the industrialising process, the unique concurrence in Britain of practical secular and idealistic liberal ideas, and by the peculiar nature of British slave resistance.

Complex circumstances decreed that the Haitian slaves achieved a revolutionary overthrow of the industrialising process between 1791 and 1804, while, at the other extreme, in Cuba, Brazil and the USA, a catastrophic confrontation was long delayed and, in due course, easily defused. The case of the British West Indies was intermediate. Slave resistance was endemic and rebellions frequent, reaching, indeed a climax in the period 1816-32. Imperial and colonial forces, however, remained sufficient and sufficiently coordinated to suppress even the most widespread of the slave revolts. Moreover, when these occurred they were no longer truly revolutionary.[48] Led by creolised, and eventually Christianised slaves, they no longer aimed at the annihilation of the whites or the total destruction of the economic system. Rather, the British West Indian slaves in slavery's last phase demanded a form of freedom that might rationally include free wage labour on the plantations as well as peasant farming. This, of course, was the 'part peasant–part proletarian' lifestyle that was, in fact, substituted for slavery in most of the British West Indian colonies after 1838, although the terms of relationships remained resolutely in favour of the land-owner/employer master class.[49]

Thus, while Eric Williams's analysis in *Capitalism and Slavery* and his subsequent works concurred with the neo-Marxism of C. L. R. James and Herbert Aptheker in respect of slave resistance – seeing it as part of a perennial undercurrent of resistance by the underclass – it is also, at least by implication, attuned to the hegemonic interpretations of the greatest of all neo-Marxists, Antonio Gramsci.[50] Although the Italian theorist did not specifically address the case of the British West Indian slaves and their allegedly free descendants, undoubtedly he would have used the evidence adduced by Williams – in the twelfth chapter of *Capitalism and Slavery*, in the post-emancipation chapters of *From Columbus to Castro*, and in the brilliant short analysis of neocolonialism included in *Inward Hunger* – a perfect illustration of the hegemonic principle: the subtle way in which a ruling class can maintain its domination by apparently adopting liberal changes, thereby recruiting a willing underclass into a new, and initially unrecognised, form of subordination.[51]

A Gramscian analysis, moreover, would perfectly integrate the matter treated in Chapter 12 with the rest of *Capitalism and Slavery*. At different levels, imperial and plantocratic hegemony in the seventeenth and eight-eenth centuries stemmed from the control of the Triangular Trade and the system of social controls that defined Negro slaves as chattel. In the later eighteenth and early nineteenth centuries, conflict threatened between an industrialising metropolis and a less progressive planter class, as well as between planters and their slaves, as theorists and humanitarians edged the imperial government towards liberal policies of free trade and free wage labour. Yet at both levels, disastrous conflicts were avoided and hegemony maintained. At the imperial-colonial level, this was achieved by engineering a peaceful transition from slavery to wage labour through the apprentice-ship system, by generous compensation to ex-slave-owners, and by the introduction of new measures of social control aimed at sustaining hege-mony in a liberal guise. At the purely colonial level, it could be argued, hegemony was facilitated more subtly still, and over a longer period, through the very process of creolisation and Christianisation which, as Wilberforce dreamed, came close to creating a respectable, hard-working, thrifty, long-suffering – and only nominally free – black wage-labouring class.

16

Continuity not Change

Late Slavery and Post-Emancipation Resistance in the British West Indies

Introduction: The discovery that Barbados, Demerara and Jamaica, where the three largest late slave rebellions in the British West Indies occurred, were also the locations of what were probably the most serious outbreaks of civil unrest in the half century after emancipation, naturally invited a comparative analysis. Just as the examination of the late slave rebellions given earlier showed that they shared essential features in respect of the slaves' rejection of the dominant socioeconomic system, a delving beneath the obvious but superficial differences between what happened in Demerara in 1856, Jamaica in 1865 and Barbados in 1876, revealed crucial similarities both between each other and with the pre-emancipation manifestations. Readers will have to decide for themselves whether or not the evidence adduced is overly selective and the arguments convincing. But the exercise does prove to at least the writer's satisfaction that the continuities illustrate an application of Antonio Gramsci's hegemonic principle: that since ruling classes always attempt to sustain their dominance by changes more apparent than actual, so there is a continuum in the resistance to them by the underclass.

The observation that ruling classes tend to sustain their hegemony by shifts that are merely superficial, and the contention that oppressed classes will always resist their oppression, are ideally tested by focusing attention on the plight and political behaviour of the ex-slaves of the British West Indian colonies in the period after slave emancipation, particularly between 1838 and 1876.[1]

At the imperial level, the adoption of 'liberal' social and economic policies gave British slaves their nominal freedom while allowing freer trade with areas outside the formal empire where profits were greater and chattel slavery continued for a further 50 years. At the colonial level, plantocracies continued to dominate. No colony with its own Assembly lost its power of self-legislation before 1866, and in all colonies – including Crown Colonies directly ruled from London – the ex-slaves were cleverly kept in their place. Education was minimal, the franchise restricted, and law and order maintained by a scarcely reformed and even more impersonal magistracy and police force, and by the translation from Britain to the colonies of allegedly liberal but in fact class-regulating masters and servants, vagrancy, police and poor laws.

Most ex-slaves aimed to be peasant proprietors, yet they were denied cheap land by the application of Wakefieldian principles, and kept from squatting by the increased efficiency of government surveyors and lawyers insisting on proper title. In colonies with little spare land they were forced to compete with each other for the limited wage employment available, but elsewhere the planters' 'labour problem' was solved by the importation of cheap and reliable 'coolie' labourers from India. As a result, British West Indian ex-slaves were less a free peasantry than a wage-slave proletariat, employed only when needed on their former owners' terms, and competing with each other and with new immigrants of different ethnicities.

A closer look than has previously been given shows that the ex-slaves were far more restless and resistant than has been suggested by imperialistic writers or those who considered that emancipation was an end in itself. Unrest in the earliest years of nominal freedom stemmed from problems of adjustment, from official opposition to a return to traditional ways, especially in religion, from tensions occasioned by questions of rents, wages and the availability of land, and from conflict with new immigrants, government surveyors and the police. These incidents multiplied and spread in times of economic slump such as the late 1840s, early 1860s and mid-1870s, or in times of natural disaster, such as drought, flood or cholera epidemic.

In Jamaica, for example, recent research has shown that there were dozens of riots hitherto unpublicised between 1838 and 1865; localised for the most part, but approaching island-wide revolts in 1848 and 1859.[2] This essay, though, concentrates on the three most serious outbreaks in the British West Indies as a whole; the 'Angel Gabriel' Riots in Guyana in 1856, the Morant Bay Rebellion in Jamaica in 1865, and the Federation Riots in Barbados in 1876. It argues that the fact that these happened in the same colonies in which the chief of the late slave rebellions occurred (Barbados in 1816, Guyana in 1823, and Jamaica in 1831-32) was not coincidental, pointing up the telling parallels between slave and ex-slave grievances, the tactics, aims and expectations of rebels and rioters, and the savage responses of the white colonial plantocrats.[3]

In Guyana by 1856 the slave revolt of 1823 was a long closed entry in official ledgers but still a potent folk memory, for attitudes, issues and conditions had not changed fundamentally. In August 1823, the slaves on the East Coast of Demerara had come out in their thousands to demand freedom, or at least far better conditions of labour and more time to work their own provision grounds, from which they supplemented their meagre diet and made some money at informal local markets. For the most part, they were convinced that they had already been granted concessions by the imperial government which were being withheld by the oligarchy of planters and Georgetown merchants. Many of them recently Christianised, the slaves did not willfully damage the estates and offered little violence to the whites, calculating that the imperial troops (some of them black) would not be used against them except in retribution. In fact, the rebels were dragooned by the regular troops, white militia and Amerindian auxiliaries at the behest of a governor who was himself a soldier-planter, and as many as 250 slaves lost their lives.[4]

With emancipation in 1838 the ex-slaves had moved to achieve their aspirations, but with very limited success. As many as could left the estates, some to settle in the colonial capital, Georgetown, but more to find land for themselves and form 'free villages'. Yet these ex-slave villages were free only in the senses of being unregulated and neglected by the plantocratic regime, emancipation having chiefly freed the planters from their previous legal and moral responsibilities. In a country where the only fertile land was near the coast and rivers, and extensive drainage works were necessary, suitable land was scarce and expensive. Although they often cooperated to buy land, the ex-slaves were unable to grow export staples and were restricted even in marketing local produce. Increasing cash needs (exacerbated by a growing population) could only be met by continuing to work for wages on plantations on terms compatible with peasant proprietorship, at a time when increased mechanisation and economies of scale meant that the ordinary labour was ever more cruelly seasonal. Planters, however, complained that Negro labour was spasmodic, unreliable and insufficient – arguments used to justify the importation of Madeiran, Chinese and Indian labourers from 1835 onwards.[5]

The cultural gap between whites and blacks remained as wide as the socioeconomic. In Georgetown, considerable numbers of both races lived close together, with resulting tensions. Yet over the rest of the colony, only two small categories of whites lived in permanent contact with the Afro-Guyanese, both of them acting in an intermediate role between ruling whites and peasant-proletarian blacks. The few Nonconformist missionaries willingly accepted the function of bringing 'under a more efficient moral culture'[6] a people whom Governor Wodehouse referred to as being 'a good measure beyond the reach of the law, and who lead a life little less savage than that of the beasts of the fields'.[7] Such missionaries admired the religious fervour of the black congregations, but no more understood what Christianity meant to them in terms of solace and inspiration than had Rev. John Smith, 'The Demerara Martyr' in 1823.[8] The Madeiran Portuguese were in an even more uncomfortable position, being not only foreign and Catholic, but having been encouraged by the white merchants and planters to move from mere labouring into the local retail trade, at a time when credit was almost entirely denied to those of black complexion. 'The negro was envious', wrote a negrophobic local historian, James Rodway, in 1894, 'but not ashamed of his own laziness or want of thrift. Instead therefore of blaming himself for his poverty he ascribed it to cheating and overreaching on the part of his competitor, and unfortunately the Madeiran gave some slight cause for this'.[9] In a situation where blacks were very easily indebted to the retailers and the truck system was not unknown, some would place much less equivocal blame on the Portuguese, but a fairer assessment might see them as the unfortunate catspaws of, and scapegoats for, an extremely exploitative ruling class.

Guyana was ignited in February 1856 by an apocalyptic coloured preacher called John Sayers Orr, who had recently returned from a stormy itinerary of 'sixteen of the United States, the Canadas, Nova Scotia, New Brunswick, . . . Scotland, England and the Protestant part of Ireland'. A sort of proto-Paisley, who announced his meetings with a blast on a trumpet and was nicknamed 'The Angel Gabriel', he purveyed an inflammable mixture of Protestant zeal, populist radicalism, racism and appeals to patriotism, along the lines of the doggerel on one of his American posters:

Scorn be on those who rob us of our rights
Purgatory for Popery and the Pope
Freedom to man be he black or white
Rule Britannia![10]

In his native Georgetown, Orr was at first received kindly by the governor, but 'immediately after he commenced walking about the Town and its vicinity, carrying a flag, wearing a badge, and blowing a horn occasionally at the corners of the Streets, followed by small groups of the rabble of the place'.[11] His preachings at the market place on Sundays attracted huge crowds of town and country blacks, in Wodehouse's words, 'blending together skillfully and amazingly . . . political and religious subjects in a manner calculated to arose the passions of the Black and Coloured Population against the Portuguese immigrants'.[12] Rioting began on Saturday and Sunday, February 16-17, 1856, after Orr was summoned for unlawful assembly, and spread like wildfire throughout the colony once he was committed to prison on Monday, February 18. 'In the afternoon the town may be said to have been in open insurrection, and the true character of the disturbances was at once revealed', wrote Wodehouse.

> The Pope, the Bishop, the Nuns were clean forgotten – Nothing remained in the minds of the actors but the long subsisting hatred and jealousy of the Portuguese Immigrants from Madeira and the love of plunder, aggravated by the gross and brutal character of the female population, who have throughout the Colony taken a most active part in the Riots, and who are of course the most difficult to punish.[13]

Long before the forces of law and order could be fully mobilised, the riots had spread throughout Demerara and into the nearer parts of Essequibo and Berbice, and within four days virtually every Portuguese shop had been ransacked and plundered, with the few local policemen who tried to intervene being pelted with broken bottles and brickbats. It was reported that 'men, women and children all joined in, and in some parts of the country every creole of the lower orders seems to have been one of the mob'.[14] So unexpected, sudden and general were the disturbances that the governor at first presumed a deep conspiracy. The most likely conspirators, he suggested, were the members of a black mutual aid society wishing to invest their funds in a trading association, who, disappointed by the way in which previous efforts had failed because 'either the Members were defrauded by their own leaders, or the shops from mismanagement gradually dwindled away', had used the coming of Orr to fement a plot to destroy the opposition and promote 'the establishment of creole Shops upon its ruins'. In this imaginative scenario the agents of the black syndicate went rapidly through the country districts, not waiting for the actual riots but sowing the seeds by showing fictitious orders from the government not to kill the Portuguese but to seize all their property and give it to the people.[15] Certainly such wish-fulfiling rumours of benevolent actions by the imperial government did circulate in 1856, as they had in 1823 and all the late slave rebellions, although their origins were never ascertained and none of the members of the mutual aid society were actually implicated in the riots.

Wodehouse himself found it incredible that anyone would be so ignorant as to believe that the government supported the plunder of the Portuguese, though he could not 'quite assert that they altogether disbelieved a statement which harmonized so agreeably with their own inclinations'.[16] The more plausible alternative that the riots stemmed from a universal socio-economic malaise only gradually dawned on the governor, and he never publicly drew the most obvious conclusion from the fact that it was mostly food which the mobs plundered from the Portuguese shops.[17]

Governor Wodehouse, whom even the Colonial Office called 'an energetic officer with no disinclination to the old planter system, and with many of his advisors no doubt attached to it',[18] quickly disabused the rioters of the notion that the government was on the people's side and acted as forthrightly as had Governor Murray, his predecessor in 1823. Martial law was not declared, probably because the garrison consisted almost entirely of the black troop of the Second West India Regiment. But the troops were rapidly deployed, reinforcements called for from Barbados and offers of assistance from warships stationed in the neighbouring Dutch and French colonies gratefully accepted. Hundreds of whites and 'respectable' coloureds were sworn in as special constables and the old militia regulations, in abeyance since 1839, reintroduced.[19]

Loss of life was minimal, but so many rioters were arrested that the jails overflowed and a special penal settlement was set up. At the trials, more than 100 'ringleaders' were sentenced by the plantocratic judges to terms of one to three years at hard labour, in addition to fines or floggings. John Sayers Orr, despite being the only prisoner defended by counsel, was sentenced to three years at hard labour, with sureties of £600 to keep the peace on his release.[20] Another 600 prisoners were treated in what Wodehouse regarded as an ingenious and magnanimous way but which nonetheless betrayed his plantocratic bias; they were given a conditional pardon, dependent on the satisfactory conclusion of contract labour on designated estates, at a rate of six months' work for each month's sentence. Such an unprecedented measure Wodehouse defended by declaring 'that a Negro requires to be under a necessity to do right. As long as that necessity exists, he not only obeys but appears to have no wish to avoid. Remove the necessity, and the spirit of licence comes into operation at once.' He went on to state his belief,

> that the people of England are no longer under the delusion that these people can be controlled by precisely the same forms of laws as prove sufficient in highly civilized communities; and that they no longer wish freedom from slavery to mean anything

less than freedom from all legal control . . . The late events have shown beyond the possibility of doubt that the mass of the population are in no degree able to govern themselves than they were at the time of the Emancipation – some will even say less so.[21]

Subsequent actions by the Guyanese regime reflected Wodehouse's dire assessment, and were endorsed by the Colonial Office because they were cleverly consonant with contemporary trends towards sociopolitical efficiency and *laissez-faire* principles, particularly the belief that colonies should be as self-supporting financially as was possible. A flurry of ordinances passed by the Court of Policy reformed and extended the police force and system of local courts and tightened the code against petty offenders (including, incidentally, a ban on the use of 'horn or other instrument to call people together'). An ordinance against vagrancy virtually defined as 'idle and disorderly persons', 'rogues and vagabonds' or 'incorrigible rogues' any persons who chose not to work for the estates and were far from their settlements without visible means of support, at the same time as masters and servants legislation put all the onus of observing labour contracts on the labourers.[22]

The most controversial legislation, though, involved the payment of compensation to the Portuguese. Claims for damages amounted to some £59,000, of which no less than £53,000, or 91 per cent was allowed by a local tribunal – not so much because of representations made by the Portuguese government to the Foreign Secretary Lord Wodehouse (a relative of the governor), as through the determination of the Guyanese regime to rescue and restore the retail system, and its superstructure of Georgetown merchants. The compensation, more than the entire annual budget for the colony, was to be paid over five years and financed ostensibly out of the general revenue, but in fact through a novel poll tax. A special registration ordinance was promulgated on the pretext of facilitating the payment of compensation claims in this and possible future cases, but with two other quite different purposes; to arrive at an accurate census of population and property for taxation purposes and to facilitate the control of the free villages.[23] These purposes were transparent to the persons upon whom the new taxation pressed most heavily, at a time of special economic hardship. It was opposed in Britain by the Anti-Slavery Society, which made a deputation to the Colonial Secretary, and condemned in a petition from the ordinary people of the colony carrying 18,000 signatures.[24] When Governor Wodehouse left Georgetown on vacation in August 1857, he was pelted with stones, cane stalks and offal at the dock and when he finally left the colony in May 1861 without ceremony and at the dead of night, it was suggested that it was 'to avoid a salute of dead cats and dogs'.[25]

In Jamaica, the great slave rebellion at Christmas 1831 and the Morant Bay Rebellion in October 1865 occurred at opposite sides of the island, but in both cases they were merely the conflagration of island-wide tinder. Besides, the combustible material remained unchanged in many respects between 1831 and 1865, despite emancipation in 1838.

By 1831 the creolised slaves of Jamaica had become intolerably frustrated, while at the same time seeing a glimmer of hope that by concerted action they might enforce improved conditions or even speed their own emancipation. Over the previous 50 years, slaves had come to regard the working of provision grounds as a customary right and had established an effective informal market network; yet the more recent decline of the plantation economy and the ending of the slave trade in 1808 had led many masters to extract more work, while expecting the slaves to be more self-supporting. Likewise, the spread of Christianity – originally through the agency of black preachers from America and only later through white missionaries from Britain – had given slaves opportunities for organisation and self-expression, as well as a message with apocalyptic overtones; yet the slaves' sense of self-justification through religion was frustrated, or at least challenged, by plantocratic opposition, to the point of martyrdom. Meanwhile, liberal reform – economic, political and social – was gathering momentum in the metropolis, and the planters' reactions to the threats of free trade, political interference and enforced emancipation occurred in dangerous conjunction with the slaves' growing realisation that they had allies, of a sort, in Britain.[26]

Certainly, the slaves' most implacable enemies were the local whites, but rumours circulated by the élite slaves among their humbler brethren exaggerated the case for external support, claiming, for example, that emancipation had already been granted by the king and withheld by the Assembly, and that governor, military and missionaries alike would support them if they rose to assert their freedom. In fact, all whites, including missionaries, had a horror of social unrest, particularly when it involved 'uncivilised' blacks. They ignored the clear evidence that a majority of dissidents simply planned a stoppage of work without harming any persons or even damaging the estates, and concentrated their paranoid fears on the minority of realist slaves who knew that the regime would never surrender without a fight and consequently drilled black guerrilla 'regiments'.

The revolt centred on the Great River Valley in western Jamaica, far from the centre of government and the colonial armed forces, in ideal peasant farming (and guerrilla) country – a traditional area of Maroon resistance. It was also the part of Jamaica where the Native Baptists had made their most, and most fervent, converts; indeed, so many of the participants in the rebellion were Baptist church members and so many of their leaders Baptist deacons, that it became popularly known as 'The Baptist War'. Over 200 estates were involved, on which lived some 60,000 slaves. For a week the rebels controlled a fifth of the island, and it was six weeks – after thousands of troops, militia and maroons were deployed, using terror tactics – before the last embers were extinguished. Though no more than a dozen whites were killed in all, about 200 slaves perished during the campaign and no less than 340 were executed after court martial or civil trial.

The Jamaican Assembly assessed damages as well over £1 million and the planters received compensation from the imperial government despite the fact that the largest item was the value of 540 slaves 'lost' in the rebellion. In the wake of the suppression, white Anglican vigilantes torched nearly all the Nonconformist chapels in western Jamaica, and it was this and the maltreatment of white missionaries, rather than the death of the 540 slaves, which convinced waverers in Britain of the need to enforce emancipation upon West Indian slaveholders. The parliamentary select committee to consider the means to effect emancipation 'at the earliest period compatible with the safety of all Classes in the Colonies', was convened just one week after the execution of Sam Sharpe, the noble chief of the Jamaican rebels.[27] Pretty soon the debate centred entirely on the question of how much compensation the slaveholders should receive for their emancipated property and the means by which the ex-slaves could be compelled to work for their former owners as 'free' wage labourers.

It was, indeed, the attempted enforcement of local adjustments by the plantocracy that provoked much of the tension of the first phase after emancipation. Even in the initial period of optimism, when land seemed plentiful and the prices of peasant produce remained satisfactory, localised disturbances occurred between the employers and employed over the trimming of wages and attempts to tie the labourers by charging rents for houses and provision grounds, and between planters and missionaries over the establishment of church-related free villages. With the economic collapse of the later 1840s and in subsequent slumps brought by drought, hurricane, epidemic or worldwide depression, tension heightened. By 1865 Jamaica enjoyed only a fraction of its former prosperity, but the decline of the richest of all British plantation colonies did not mean that the ex-slaves were left to enjoy the life of free, if impoverished, peasants; rather the reverse. Sporadic conflict occurred over the more efficient application of the laws governing labour contracts, vagrancy and petty offences, through a magistracy that remained essentially plantocratic and a more officious police force, following a policy of stationing officers in parishes other than their own. Conflicts also broke out with more obvious strangers; the new Africans, Indians and few poor whites cynically introduced by the legislature to provide a more reliable plantation work-force while driving down wages through labour competition.[28]

Meanwhile, land for peasant farming grew scarcer; not so much because of a rapid growth of population as the tightening of rules about formal title and the payment of a 'sufficient price' for Crown lands. The situation was particularly anomalous in the light of the steady decline of sugar plantations – so many of the decayed estates being brought up for conversion into inefficient cattle 'pens' by middle-class Jamaicans (coloured as well as white) that one writer has referred to as the creation of a 'penocracy' to reinforce the traditional plantocracy.[29] Fights flared between government surveyors and peasant farmers and over the eviction of squatters, and the police were kept constantly busy over cases of praedial larceny, fence breaking, and the rustling and maiming of stock.

The Jamaican countrymen remained a deeply religious people, and the normally high level of observance was periodically raised by waves of frenzied revivalism, particularly during the 1850s and early 1860s. Yet even the people's preoccupation with revivalist religion heightened rather than lowered tensions. Missionaries deplored the way in which the revivalists reverted to spontaneous and unsupervised worship (much of it akin to traditional African 'myal'), and the local whites, as usual, treated what they could neither understand nor control with a mixture of contempt and fear, complaining at the same time that episodes of religious fanaticism kept labourers from the estates and even led to a shortage of peasant-grown ground provisions.[30]

Localised disturbances became general during the depressed mid-1860s, and erupted into a major revolt in St Thomas-in-the-East in October 1865. A few months before, a Baptist missionary, Edward Underhill, had written a forceful letter to the Colonial Office calling attention to the desperate plight of the Jamaican blacks, particularly now that provisions were scarce because of drought and prices of imports high because of the American Civil War. At the same time, some peasants of St Ann's parish sent a petition for relief to Queen Victoria herself. The Underhill letter was debated throughout Jamaica, but the only official response was the so-called Queen's Advice to the St Ann's petitioners callously enjoining hard work and thrift as the only solutions to the hardships.[31]

The Queen's Advice was inspired by the recently-appointed governor, an obstinate mediocrity and ardent Anglican named Edward Eyre who, on the basis of experience with Australian natives and Indian 'coolies' in Trinidad and St Vincent, believed that West Indian blacks should be ruled with an iron rod.[32] Eyre's most formidable opponent in the Jamaican Assembly was George William Gordon, an upwardly mobile coloured planter, businessman and independent Baptist church leader, who made himself the people's champion in a personal quest for political status. The real rebel leader in 1865, though, was the equally remarkable Paul Bogle, one of Gordon's black deacons, a peasant smallholder of Stony Gut in St Thomas, a parish backed by the traditional maroon fastness of the Blue Mountains, with many decayed estates owned by absentees and thousands of land-hungry former slaves and recently freed indentured African labourers.

Events accelerated after Gordon was sacked as a St Thomas Vestryman and JP for criticising the operation of justice and a lack of social services in the parish, blaming by implication the Anglican Rector and the Custos (who, rather absurdly, was a German baron, Von Ketelhodt). In August 1865, Gordon allegedly told an audience of St Thomas blacks 'You have been ground down too long already . . . Prepare for your duty. Remember the destitution in the midst of your families, and your forlorn condition', and went to say of the Queen's Advice, 'it is a lie; it does not come from the Queen'.[33] Shortly afterwards, Governor Eyre refused even to see the petitioners, including Bogle, who had walked the 45 miles from St Thomas into Spanish Town. Unknown to Gordon, oaths were taken and drilling began in Stony Gut, based on Deacon Bogle's chapel.[34]

On Saturday, October 7, a market day, a band of Bogle's men rescued a black whom the police was trying to arrest for a breach of the peace at Morant Bay Courthouse, a commotion that immediately preceded a case involving eviction for non-payment of rent (in which the plea was 'on the ground that the land was free, and the estate belonged to the Queen').[35] Three days later, police sent from Morant Bay to arrest Bogle were driven back the seven miles from Stony Gut. Von Ketelhodt called out the Volunteers and sent to Spanish Town for troops, while at the same time Bogle and 19 others signed a letter to the governor asking the 'due protection' which, if refused, would compel them 'to put our shoulders to the wheel, as we have been imposed upon for a period of 27 years with due observance to the laws of our Queen and country'.[36]

Before any response could come from Governor Eyre, on Wednesday, October 11, hundreds of crudely armed men marched, to the sound of drum, cow horn and conch sell, upon Morant Bay, where the hated Vestry was in session. Fired on by the Volunteers, who killed seven in their only volley, Bogle's forces burned down the courthouse, released 50 prisoners, looted the town and estate provision grounds, and in all killed 20 whites, including Custos Ketelhodt and several unpopular estate managers. Back at Stony Gut, Bogle held a prayer meeting, allegedly declaring, 'It is now time for us to help ourselves. War is at us; black-skin war is at hand.' Within three days, insurrection had spread from Monkland in the west to Elmwood in the north-east, a distance of 75 miles.[37]

Retribution, though, was swift and terrible. Martial law was immediately declared in the County of Surrey, the eastern third of the island. Two naval vessels were sent from Port Royal to Morant Bay and the troops at Kingston and Newcastle were force-marched through the mountains. The Moore Town maroons crossed the Blue Mountain ridge and fell on the rebels, and even the Hayfield maroons, whom Bogle thought were behind him, sided with the government. More than 430 men and women were shot down or put to death after trial —scarcely fewer than 1832 —with 600 publicly flogged and more than 1,000 houses burned. Paul Bogle, caught by maroons in a canepiece, was hanged from the burned-out Courthouse. George William Gordon, carried by ship from Kingston to Morant Bay so that he could be tried by court martial, was hanged within three days, on October 23.

In keeping with better established methods of parliamentary inquiry, a more realistic effort was made by the imperial government to arrive at the causes of the revolt and the details of its suppression than in 1832. Over a three-month period, a three-man commission took evidence from 730 witnesses in 60 separate sittings, including some in the actual locations of the revolt. Yet some of the difficulties and prejudices of the commissioners can be gauged from remarks at he beginning of their 1,200-page report:

> As regards the negroes, it is enough to recall the fact that they are for the most part uneducated peasants, speaking in accents strange to the ear, often in a phraseology of their own, with vague conceptions of number and time, unaccustomed to definiteness or accuracy of speech, and, in many cases, still smarting under a sense of the injuries sustained.[39]

In their conclusions, the commissioners found that the revolt was at least partly fuelled by racial animosity and constituted 'planned resistance to lawful authority'. Governor Eyre was praised for his 'skill, promptitude and vigour', and it was stated that though there was no evidence directly implicating Gordon, had there been in fact a long-plotted conspiracy he must have known of it. Yet the commissioners also ascertained that the rebels were 'for the most part what are called free settlers, occupying and cultivating small patches of land', whose "great desire was to obtain, free from the payment of rent, what are called the 'back lands' ", and added that 'disputes between employers and labourers, and questions relating to the occupation of land, which are decided in the first instance at Petty Sessions, are adjudicated upon by those whose interests and feelings are supposed to be hostile to the labourer and the occupier'. Particularly in St Thomas-in-the-East the existing bench of magistrates was unfit to dispense justice in the cases that most commonly came before it, and Jamaica as a whole was in sore need of a 'good Master and Servant Act', arrived at and administered by an independent and impartial tribunal. In their most damning passage of all, the commissioners concluded that in the suppression of the revolt martial law had been kept on far longer than was necessary, that punishments by death were 'unnecessarily frequent', that the floggings were 'reckless' and sometimes 'barbarous', and that the burning of 1,000 houses was 'wanton and cruel'.[40]

These findings provoked scandal among conservative imperialists and, as Bernard Semmel and Gertrude Himmelfarb have shown, the controversy that raged in Britain in the later 1860s over the conduct of Governor Eyre polarised attitudes and helped to crystallise imperial policy.[41] Yet even the 'liberal' position in the debate went no further than the principle 'that if British rule was to prevail (as prevail it should), it should be just'.[42] For the ordinary black Jamaicans the only obvious change was the self-dissolution of the Jamaican Assembly and the substitution of Crown Colony government in 1866, but this was far from a benefit to them. The voluntary change was motivated by a fear, inspired by the career of George William Gordon, that popular radical elements might in due course take charge of an elective Assembly, and by the thought that the plantocracy might more easily sustain itself through Councils nominated by 'right-thinking' governors. Events after 1866 proved the Jamaican ruling class largely correct. Although an extremely limited franchise was gradually reinstated after 1884, land policy, laws and magistracy were not substantially changed in the nineteenth century, and what V. S. Reid called Jamaica's 'New Day' – democratic self-government – did not dawn until 1957, 119 years after slave emancipation.[43]

An even more repressive scenario characterised Barbados, where the widespread revolts of 1816, 1876 and 1937 punctuated, at remarkably even intervals, a largely unchanging tale of plantocratic dominance. The revolt of 1816 that was to take its popular name from its chief slave leader, Bussa, came as an immense shock to the Barbadian whites, whose slaves had not even been detected in a plot for over 100 years. With the threat of invasion removed by the ending of the French wars, the whites were preoccupied by the effects of reduced economic protection on sugar prices, and almost upin arms about plans by the imperial government to impose a slave registration bill with or without the consent of the Barbadian Assembly, loosely talking in terms of revolution and secession much like the Americas in 1775. Over 95 per cent of the Barbadian slaves were island-born, regarding themselves as much Barbadian as the whites. They grew much of their own food on their tiny plots and even made money selling surpluses, including ginger for export.[44]

Yet the Barbadian slaves were far from content, particularly in the south-east of the island, the area with the highest density of slaves, the driest soils, the harshest working conditions and a tradition of resistance that went back to marronage in the early seventeenth century. Groups of élite slaves in St Philip parish, in conjunction with a few disgruntled free coloureds who had more slave than free kin, plotted at weekend dances. They believed, on the evidence of newspaper reports and loose talk overheard, that the imperial government was in favour of slave emancipation, and calculated that if they closed down the mills and drove the whites into Bridgetown, the plantocracy would be forced to come to terms. The majority convinced themselves that if they refrained from violence the governor and imperial troops would be on their side; only a few believed that their only option was to follow the lead of the 'Mingo' slaves (that is, the Haitian rebels of 1791-1804).[45]

The revolt erupted on Easter Sunday, April 14, 1816, with the firing of trash houses as beacons. Within hours the rebels controlled a third of the island, over 100 estates. Bussa's followers seized the armoury of the St Philip's militia and marched toward the town under the captured standard, as if they were now the effective parochial militia.[46] Not a single white was killed at this stage and very few injured, though hundreds were at the slaves' mercy.

The regime, however, showed no mercy at all. Martial law was declared, and the army commander confidently sent forward the black regular troops with orders to shoot when necessary and unleashed the undisciplined white militia, who shot on sight and wantonly burned slave huts and grounds. Two whites died in all, but 50 slaves were shot in the fighting and another 70 summarily executed in the field. Later, a further 144 were executed (including three of the four free coloureds charged) and 132 deported. The bodies of dead rebels – sometimes just their heads – were displayed on their home estates, and security measures were tightened up in all respects. Yet an official local report published in 1818 insisted that the Barbadian slaves had no grounds for discontent, putting blame firmly on meddling by the imperial government.[47]

Unequivocally, 1816 was a lasting victory for the Barbadian white oligarchy of planters and Bridgetown merchants. Alone of the older sugar colonies, Barbados was able actually to increase production after slavery ended through the planter's complete monopoly of fertile land and control of the former slaves, who had virtually no chance of owning farmland and no alternatives to labour on the estates on the planters' terms.[48] The increase in production tapered off in the 1870s with declining world prices, and many planters and even merchants were threatened with bankruptcy. But their socioeconomic dominance was not seriously eroded. The few middle-class coloureds and blacks with money were denied the chance of competing as sugar producers by a united front of white planters and their merchant bankers, and the minority of blacks who owned parcels of freehold land were denied the capital and favourable legislation necessary to cooperate and become more efficient producers even of non-sugar crops.[49]

The lot of the black majority, crowded into Bridgetown or tied to agricultural labour, was bleakest of all. Though the population increased by more than 50 per cent between 1838 and 1876 despite serious cholera epidemics, emigration was positively discouraged,[50] at least until 1870. In a community which the whites – like those of the American South – claimed was uniquely civilised, eight out of ten blacks were technically illegitimate, a majority of the children of school age received no schooling whatever, there was no free medicine and no medical facilities at all outside Bridge- town, the poor law system brought practical relief only to poor whites, and the Bridgetown jail and workhouse were accurately described as dungeons. In 1876 the only efficient institutions were the assembly, the Anglican Church, the police force and the magistracy.[51]

The linchpin of the planters' dominance was the oppressive Masters and Servants Act of 1840.[52] By this, every agricultural labourer was required to be located on a plantation, his tenancy of a minute house and plot requiring him to work when called, five days of nine hours' work per week. If he failed to turn out, he was liable to the forfeit of a month's wages and/or 14 days in jail, with or without hard labour. If no work were offered, the labourer, theoretically, could go to court to sue for five days' wages, but was then liable to eviction at one month's notice. In fact labourers never went to court for wages due, and worked on the average far less than 45 hours a week while at the same time having to pay rent for houses and plots which, by another law, was deducted by owner/employer before wages were paid. Many planters also trimmed wage-bills by selling ground provisions to their labourers which the labourers could not grow for themselves.

The consequences were inexorable. At the best times wages were close to subsistence, and in times of depression or drought destitution was common and starvation not unknown. For example, in 1870 an inquest was held at Clifden in St Philip on a labourer named Samuel Dottin, aged 55, who was found dead in his hut while his wife was away at The Crane scavenging sea urchins for food. It was testified that Dottin had been receiving 10 pence a day as a contract labourer, but that most weeks he worked only three days and some weeks not at all. Even the estate manager admitted that Dottin 'tottered as he walked' and the coroner decided that he had suffered 'from no disease but starvation'.[53]

Yet the Barbadian proletariat was not so long-suffering and compliant or the whites so calm and confident, as the plantocracy pretended. At the day-to-day level, by far the most common cases that came before the local magistrates involved canefield arson and other forms of malicious damage, trespass and, especially in times of hardship, stealing of food. For example, in the month before the 1876 riots, no fewer than 152 persons were charged with food stealing, compared with a total of 75 charged with all other offences.[54] As to more serious and general manifestations of resistance, there had been riots in St Philip in 1863 which Governor Walker confidentially attributed to insufficient wages,

> although the planters are very angry with me when I say so. They aver that there has been little or no reduction of wages, but whatever it may have arisen from, whether from the inability of the planters to give the same quantity of work, or from the difficulty with which the labourer can, on account of the hardness of the soil, accomplish his ordinary task, or from the task of having been increased, the labourer is undoubtedly not earning the same amount of money which he has been accustomed to do.[55]

A few years later, a disillusioned Anglican curate leaving for Britain wrote:

> One predominating characteristic of the white people of Barbados is their abject fear of the negroes. Whether, on the principle that 'conscience doth make cowards of us all', this feeling be only the natural offspring of past tyranny and present scant or unwillingly rendered justice, or has any more solid foundation, I am unable to say.[56]

Governor Pope Hennessy, who quoted the anonymous curate in 1876, added that even in comparatively good years when food was cheap and the people apparently worked cheerfully, 'panics sometimes spring up among the white people that are quite inexplicable', quoting Colonel Clements, the Inspector General of Police, as saying that he hardly knew an Easter over the previous 18 years (that is, the anniversary of Bussa's Revolt) 'to pass without some leading white people talking of an insurrection amongst the labourers'.[57]

Conditions were desperate by 1876, but what triggered an explosion, as in 1816, was not the whites' fears of the blacks so much as of imperial interference, coupled with the blacks' reaction to white paranoia and their own miserable servitude. In this case, the immediate issue was the imperial government's campaign to create a Windward Islands Federation including Barbados.[58] The Barbadian blacks saw no practical advantage in a federation, but instinctively felt that if the planters and merchants were so adamantly against it, it must be good, especially since it was strongly espoused by a governor, John Pope Hennessy, who was clearly on the side of the ordinary blacks.[59] From his arrival in Barbados in late 1875, Hennessy went on personal missions of inquiry into local conditions, being accused by the planters of holding court for disgruntled blacks at his country retreat, what is now called Sam Lord's Castle, in St Philip.[60] In speeches before the Council and Assembly the governor not only promoted federation but condemned the level of wages, the burden of taxation on ordinary people, the lack of social services and the appalling state of the Bridgetown jail. On one occasion his carriage was dragged by exultant black townsfolk from the legislative building back to Government House.[61]

As so often in the past, exaggerated rumours spread through the rural areas, to gain additional force when relayed to the master class. For example, the fervently plantocratic *Agricultural Reporter* claimed on April 4, 1876, that pro-federation agents,

> have been going about the country with Federation petitions for people to sign, have invariably employed as their great argument, a promise to the labourers, not only of higher wages, but of 20 acres of land in some neighbouring el dorado, where they would become gentlefolks, and be elevated from the position of labourers to that of landed proprietors in their own right . . . [and] have not scrupled to impose upon their

illiterate dupes the lying impression that the land of estates in Barbados is to be freely apportioned to them, that they are to drive in their carriages, and indulge in other luxuries. The consequences is that the labourers are already heard selecting the spots of land for which they have a preference, and otherwise manifesting the results of the evil influences which are thus brought to bear upon their impressionable and excitable natures.[62]

An even more authoritative statement was made in a document signed by all the Anglican clergy from the Bishop downwards, sent to the governor on May 26 after the riots subsided:

There was a general impression made upon the minds of the labourers that the ground provisions of the planters and their live stock were given to the labourers by the consent of the governor . . . The belief is still very general that the land and other property of the white, coloured, and respectable black owners, is wrongly held back from the blacks, to whom at the governor's insistence it had been awarded by the Queen.[63]

However, it was anti- not pro-Federation agents who provoked the first bloodshed. On March 28, 1876, a group of white members of the Barbados Defence Association attempting to hold a meeting at Mount Prospect, St Peter's, was stoned by the audience and in the resulting fracas a black labourer, Moses Boyce, was shot.[64] Far worse was to follow as the true issues came to the fore, beginning, significantly on Byde Mill Estate, at the junction of St Philip's, St John's and St George's, on Easter Tuesday, April 18, 1876 – almost exactly the sixtieth anniversary of Bussa's Revolt.[65]

Labour conditions at Byde Mill, under a hated manager called Reece, were notorious even by general Barbadian standards. In 1870 there had been a case of labourer's child dying of starvation, and earlier in 1876 a female labourer, Emily Howell, had been served with notice of eviction after ten years' residence for complaining of wages of sixpence for a full week's work. On Easter Sunday, most of the labourers received from two to eight and-a-half pence for the week, the estate's attorney later telling the governor, 'he supposed the wind had been slack and there had not been full work for them all', while calmly adding as justification that these were net wages, Reece having duly deducted all rents due.[66]

On Easter Tuesday, the labourers went to Reece's house, told him they were starving and asked for potatoes. When he refused, a mob of several hundred ransacked the estate's provision grounds. They were led by two brothers called Dottin, said to be relatives of the man starved to death at Clifden in 1870, the one blowing a conch shell, the other carrying a red flag.[67] From Byde Mill, semi-organised bands of labourers fanned out in all directions, to plunder provision grounds on 50 estates. Local constables and armed and mounted whites were defied with sticks and stones, but no lives were threatened and very few buildings damaged. At Welch's for instance:

> The cellars, pantrys, potato store, pigsties, rabbit hutches, etc. had been completely rifled, and in some cases pulled down, but the mob seemed to have been under control of some leaders with a system of their own, for no glass had been damaged in the dwelling house proper, nor had it been entered, although there were marks of bill hooks on the doors and other woodwork.[68]

In this manner, it seems, the labourers intended mainly to bring attention to their miserable condition, making the points that they intended no destruction of the plantation system, wanting merely a living wage, along, perhaps, with more land of their own from which to feed themselves and their families.

Neither white nor black Barbadians expected that Governor Pope Hennessy would act forthrightly, but he surprised all by the degree to which he emulated earlier governors. He resisted demands by panicked whites who fled into Bridgetown that he declare martial law, issue guns to the police and permit public flogging of prisoners, but he immediately mobilised the troops, formed a column of irregulars from the ships at anchor and authorised the JPs to swear in hundreds of special constables. These last, needless to say, were exclusively whites and avowed anti-federationists, and pursued the rioters with traditional venom. There were skirmishes at Halton, Applethwaite's and elsewhere, but within a week the riots had been suppressed, with eight blacks killed, at least 36 wounded, and 450 taken prisoner.[69]

When they were eventually brought to trial in October 1876, before a judge specially imported from Natal, the prisoners were treated with comparative magnanimity – only 47 being given further terms in jail.[70] But the Barbadian regime successfully used the Federation Riots as a pretext to retain and reinforce its socioeconomic system, finally to defeat the Windward Islands Federation proposal and to pursue the vendetta against Governor Pope Hennessy. Alone with Bermuda and the Bahamas – the other two colonies in the region with sizeable minorities – Barbados never lost its right to self-legislation, although in the 1870s the franchise was exercised by only 1,300 out of 162,000, and no more than one in 20 adults ever voted before 1945. The Colonial Secretary, Lord Carnarvon, made only a token effort to support Pope Hennessy's actions, the Federation project was quietly shelved and the governor himself transferred to Hong Kong before the end of 1876.[71] In one of their last petitions calling for Pope Hennessy's removal, the arrogant whites of the Barbados Defence Association had almost the last word, consigning the black majority of Barbadians back into the apolitical limbo from which they were not to emerge for another 70 years:

> Our society [that is, the B. D. A.] consists of persons belonging to every class, colour, and condition in life, representing the owners of property in contra-distinction to those not possessed of any property . . . This class of people being possessed of no real property whatever, never had shown the slightest disposition to take any interest in political questions, politics having all along been confined to people possessed of property without regard to colour or class.[72]

Elsewhere, I have tried to show how all three of the chief late slave rebellions in the British West Indies not only followed traditional patterns of slave resistance but also foreshadowed the will of the slaves to become free peasants.[73] This essay attempts to show the degree to which the major outbreaks in the same colonies in the 40 years after emancipation not only demonstrated the frustration of would-be free peasants forced to continue to toil for former owners, but also harked back to the mass outbursts of slave resistance, on the part of rebels and masters alike. Of course, there were differences between the colonies affected and changes over time, but these, it is felt, were outweighed by fundamental similarities and continuities. Over an even longer period, if there were any important changes at all they were regressive.

There were substantial differences between the colonies in respect of racial composition, population density and the intensity of plantation agriculture, yet these resulted in socioeconomic differences that were quantitative rather than qualitative. Jamaica had proportionally less land suitable for efficient sugar production than either Barbados or the settled parts of British Guiana or Jamaica — as well as having a proportion of white inhabitants some five times as high as either. Yet these differences were reflected, if at all, in the form and intensity of the plantation system rather than in the relative strength and weakness of the planter and peasant class.

Jamaica, it is true, steadily declined as a sugar producer, falling behind Barbados around 1860, while British Guiana went ahead of Barbados around 1850, and by 1875 produced twice as much as Barbados and three times as much as Jamaica. By then, British Guiana obtained its 100,000 tons of sugar a year from only 70,000 acres of canes, processed through a mere 70 factories — nearly all steam powered — but needed 90,000 sugar workers.

This system was almost as labour intensive as Jamaica's, which required 40,000 workers to produce 33,000 tons from 30,000 acres, with over 150 factories. Barbados' 50,000 tons a year, on the other hand, were produced by only 42,000 workers, but most inefficiently, from about 75,000 acres of canes through no fewer than 440 factories, only a fifth of them powered by steam.[74] Had labourers been willing or able to migrate from one British West Indian sugar colony to another they could have found few differences, and certainly no improvements in respect of the balance of wages received, work required and social conditions.

Each of the colonies had a different constitution, and from time-to-time there were imperial moves for simplification and consolidation. Yet with an imperial government dedicated to the principles that colonies be efficiently self-sufficient and left as much as possible to their own devices, constitutional issues remained largely academic. British Guiana was a Crown Colony from the beginning and Jamaica became one in 1866, but both were almost as free of Colonial Office control and as plantocratic as Barbados, which remained self-legislating from beginning to end. Paradoxically, the meek endorsement of Governor Wodehouse's spate of 'liberal' ordinances by British Guiana's Court of Policy in 1856-57 and the Jamaican Assembly's 'surrender' of 1866, had much the same plantocratic purpose as the fervent opposition by the Barbados Defence Association to dictation from Westminster over the question of the Windward Islands Federation.

This pragmatic uniformity applied to the local administration of laws as well. Stipendiary Magistrates, intended to be impartial, were introduced into all colonies from the time of Apprenticeship (1834-38), but they were never numerous or independent enough and, as in Britain, unpaid JPs drawn from the propertied classes remained the backbone of the system of petty justice.[75] Backing this plantocratic magistracy were police forces which, in line with metropolitan reforms, were intended to be an impartial and efficient alternative to the traditional militias and military garrisons. Yet to the very degree that they impartially administered the law, the police were seen as the agents of a hated system. Moreover, financial stringencies continually hampered the ideal. Trained professional policemen were augmented in the country districts by untrained local constables who were not only unreliable in times of stress but actually heightened tensions by insensitive officiousness.[76] In times of widespread riot, police forces had to be augmented; by special constables drawn from the 'respectable' classes who were realistically seen by blacks as little different from the old racialist militias and, in extreme case, by the regular armed forces, kept in reserve throughout the age of the Pax Britannica as in slavery days, as much against internal as external foes.

In each colony throughout the period the will of the planters effectively determined local policy and planters controlled the magistracy and forces of order, while the black majority of former slaves were kept tied to the plantation economy, depoliticised, denied education and other social services, yet disproportionately taxed. Although metropolitan interest in the British West Indies declined along with plantation profits, no-one, it seems, could conceive of an alternative to the plantation system, let alone encourage West Indian blacks to determine their own socioeconomic fate. Whatever help was given – such as the delay in the removal of protection, the passing of the Encumbered Estates Act or the authorisation of 'coolie' immigration – was designed to shore up the plantation system, not to improve the lot of the black majority.

As we have seen, there were special features of each of the three outbreaks of 1856-76 – especially from the metropolitan point of view. But each of these differences cloaked fundamental realities. In British Guiana the riots concentrated on the Portuguese shopkeepers, in Jamaica the disturbances were overshadowed by Governor Eyre's actions and the fate of George William Gordon, and in Barbados the ostensible issue was whether or not the island should become part of the Windward Islands Federation. But the real local issues were common; the way in which the blacks were denied land and forced to work on their masters' terms, competing with immigrants and each other within a local economy over which they had no control, subject to actual starvation when times were bad, and with no means of being heard save through violence or its threat.

Over the longer duration, significant major changes did occur, but like the switch from formal slavery to competitive wage labour, they were more apparent than real, or represented simply a deterioration of general conditions. The world economic order shifted so that old-style sugar plantations within formal colonies became less profitable, but for the British West Indian labourer this simply meant working more for less in a system that became yearly more impersonally exploitative in the quest for economies of scale. The black population also grew steadily, pressing on the limited land available, increasing the competitive squeeze on wages, and crowding poor people into towns woefully unprepared to receive them.[77]

The planters themselves became ever more subject to outside economic forces, and merchants and bankers proportionately grew in power. Many whites, defeated, retreated to the metropolis, but at the island level, merchants and planters acted in unison in order to preserve the socioeconomic system – refusing in Barbados, for example, to break up even bankrupt estates before the twentieth century.[78] Likewise, as the proportion of whites declined, the middle class was gradually reinforced by coloured or even black recruits, even in Barbados. Yet all this represented in a structural way an extremely gradual shift away from the complex dialectic of race and class in slave society, to that simpler class structure in which Paul Bogle would spare even policemen who would join his cause but to encourage the beating to death of the black man, Price because 'he has a black skin but a white heart'.[79]

Some white commentators have argued for the occurrence of a gradual change in imperial sensibilities, humanising relations between races and classes as a continuation of the noble cause that created the Anti-Slavery Society and sent out missionaries to the benighted blacks.[80] From slavery days too blacks themselves were predisposed to imagine a sharp disjunction between their immediate oppressors and benevolent 'others'. Slaves expected help from distant authorities – an owner who was an absentee, the governor in the colonial capital, 'Saint Wilberforce', or 'Big Massa', the English king – while, with remarkable unanimity, slave rebels and later black rioters alike believed in rumours that granted concessions were being withheld by the local regime, and that they would receive at least a tacit assistance from imperial authorities if they acted positively in their own interests.

These were the cruellest delusions in all. In the event, governors invariably aligned themselves with plantocracies in the cause of law and order, and the imperial authorities automatically endorsed the activities of local regimes in suppressing disorder. Even the most ardent philanthropists, seeing riots as evidence of setbacks in the 'civilising' process to which they were dedicated, found it far easier to condemn barbarities committed in the maintenance of law and order than actually to condone civil unrest. Bloodshed may have been rather less in 1865 and 1876 than it might have been 50 years earlier, but the suppression of the Morant Bay Rebellion was quite as savage and cynical as that of the late slave rebellions, and missionaries were just as much concerned to dissociate themselves from the unrest in 1856-76 as in 1816-32.

Theoretically, control by the Colonial Office over the colonies was facilitated by improved communications, particularly the extension of the submarine cable to the West Indies in the 1870s. Formal Royal Commissions certainly became more frequent, efficient and voluminous after 1847, and the volume of printed materials on colonial affairs available for circulation also increased hugely with the introduction of the Command Paper system in the 1860s.[81] Yet faster mailboats and the telegraph made it easier to control and frustrate governors than to curb colonial regimes – as Governor Pope Hennessy found in contrast to Governors Eyre and Wodehouse – while the outpouring of Command Papers was more an index of the vastly increased efficiency of British printing than of greater metropolitan interest, and the reports of the Royal Commissions remained little more than 'maps of oblivion'. In each of the major inquiries into the British West Indies, at least one commissioner noted with amazement, if not shame, that nothing had changed since the last report.[82]

Yet, from the present perspective, the most remarkable of all continuities was the steadfast behaviour of the black majority; to endure when they had to, to resist however and whenever they could. In the period 1856-76, as in slavery days, the plantocratic regimes, with at least the tacit support of the imperial government, were everywhere able to localise and stamp out unrest. It was not until 100 years after emancipation that concurrent unrest occurred throughout the British West Indies and major changes became inevitable. Even then similarities prevailed. For example, the scrupulous historian of the Federation Riots, writing in 1959 (in a book actually published by the Colonial Office), noted with surprise the remarkable parallels between 1876 and 1937 Barbados riots he had witnessed for himself, in respect of the aims and methods of the rioters and the forces of law and order alike.[83] Moreover, although the wave of unrest throughout the British West Indies between 1935 and 1938 shook the imperial fabric in a way that the outbursts of 1856, 1865 and 1876 had not, an increasing number of commentators now feel that even the sweeping changes that occurred after the catalytic delay of the Second World War were by no means as revolutionary as they were once thought to have been.[84]

17

Changing Sugar Technology
and the Labour Nexus
The Search for a Unified Field Theory

Introduction: This brief essay was delivered as the summary commentary at the final session of a panel at the 1988 Americanists Conference in Amsterdam. Written between 2 and 4 o'clock on the final morning of the meeting, it was published exactly as delivered, and is essentially unchanged here. This is not to show off or to establish some kind of a record (other essays in the collection took six months to write and underwent editorial changes), or even because it is believed that the piece presents an absolutely convincing conclusion. Rather, it is felt that it did draw together quite successfully all the factors involved in a complex equation, the resolution of which would provoke much further work and endless debate. Most of the factors mentioned had been discussed in the panel sessions, with a wealth of sophisticated cliometrics, in papers also later published in the *Nieuwe Westindische Gids*. But the commentary did relate them much more to each other within the larger context, over space and time. It also added at least two less quantifiable factors: the role of extraneous and unpredictable contingencies and the effect of decisions made by the planters based on human rather than purely economic considerations. Thus the essay, despite its seemingly confident ending, did serve the dual purposes of discouraging facile explanations and encouraging further work – some of the fruits of which are to be found in the two essays following.

The conference sessions I had been asked to comment on were dedicated to the discussion of the interrelationship of changing labour systems and technologies in Caribbean sugar plantations between 1750 and 1900. What made the exercise frustrating and incomplete as well as challenging and important was that it clearly involved many more variables besides those of labour and technology. However widely labour and technology are defined, at least five other related and intertwined factors have to be considered: the availability and suitability of land; the supply of capital; the access to markets and market prices; management strategies, attitudes and personnel; and finally, changing economic policies – specifically those designed to speed the transition from narrow mercantilist units to a worldwide 'free trade' system.

In seeking a causal explanation for the complex process of change in Caribbean sugar plantations over 150 years, we are all surely seeking the simplest possible key; what might be called – if the pun be pardoned – a kind of unified field theory. But besides making sure that we leave out of consideration none of the obtruding factors mentioned above, we must surely not look at one place or area in one time period, but at the whole region over the whole period of global changes.

As for special comparisons and interrelationships, we have gone some way, but probably not far enough. It is not enough to seek similar processes in different places over different time scales; we should seek to show how developments in one area led to, or related to, developments elsewhere, and how all related to global developments. This may seem a crass commonplace; but nonetheless ignoring it does seem to be the root of some of the confusions, for instance, in the 'Williams-Drescher' debate, as well as in some of our own labour/technology discussions.

For example, what was true about the relative importance of economic and humanitarian arguments in the 1780s was surely very different from arguments under the same heads after the British slave trade was abolished in 1807. And what might be felt about the relative efficiency of slave versus free wage labour and the value of technological innovation before slaves were emancipated anywhere and industrialisation had not anywhere gone far, was surely very different from labour-technology considerations once the slave trade had ended and technological changes were ever more widely available.

There are also the questions of reason versus chance or contingency in the quest for optimisation. We have to decide in a given case whether planters did what they knew or thought was best, or what was the best alternative actually open to them; or whether they did what they thought was best and were proved to be wrong; or whether they optimised rationally under certain conditions and were overtaken by events and developments that were unforseen.

We could carry on this line of relativistic and hypothetical argument ad infinitum. But let us turn instead to a more relevant issue. How well have we answered some of the questions posed, or reaffirmed or refuted some of the claims made, in the initial position paper written by Peter Boomgaard and Gert Oostindie (1989)?

First, was slavery inefficient (as well as unjust) as the abolitionists argued? In other words, were slaves under any circumstances more productive than other forms of labour? Were slave plantations ever more profitable than the same plantations might have been with 'freer' forms of labour, given that such were freely available? Second, was slavery incompatible with technological change, sustaining a conservative class of owners and retarding progress, as Marxists aver?

Broadly, I take it, Boomgaard and Oostindie's answers to both questions were 'No'. But what of areas where slavery did continue because the quest for profits seems to have called for it to do so, at least for a time, as in Puerto Rico and Cuba, as well as in Brazil and the USA? Were these forms of slavery really the same as those that had expired? Or were the alternative labour systems loosely called free – indentured 'coolies', part-time peasant labourers, migrant workers bound by debt peonage or other forms of constraint – really no more than slaves, as Michiel Baud (1988) seems to argue? And were the levels of technological change or innovation under formal slavery itself of which several authors, notably Richard Sheridan (1989), have written, really as substantial as those that came after slavery ended – whether or not emancipation was the only reason or not?

Other less central questions put forward by Boomgaard and Oostindie have surely been aired, though not finally solved. These include, third, the question of the relative abundance of available labour; fourth, the importance of the periodicity of labour demand during slavery and after; fifth, the role of slaves' and other workers' resistance to plantation labour, or, in particular, of all workers to cutting cane; and sixth, the significance of tariff barriers, or their lack, in the establishment and maintenance of sugar prices, and thus of the levels of profitability.

We have all surely come away with fresh or reinforced ideas about these, and perhaps many other questions. Other differential factors which have occurred to me since include the significance of the great variations in the growing cycle of sugar cane and thus the length of the cane cutting season, between areas with very marked winter and summer seasons and those like Guyana where cane could be planted almost any time of year and harvested almost continuously; of the difference between mixed cane farming systems based on the Brazilian counterpoint between share-cropping *lavradores* or *colonos* and true plantation slaves, and the more intensive monolithic slave labour systems preferred by the Dutch, British and French; or of the special 'cultural' conditions that allowed a colony like Barbados to expand its sugar production to a peak after slavery ended without the availability of virgin land, without notable economies of scale or even substantial technological change.

My own chief feeling, though, is that the best place to look for firmer answers to the questions posed is in the words and writings of the planters themselves – those with greater personal experience, and with more personal interest, than we as contemporary historians can ever have. The article I would have liked to offer at this time had I the time to write it, would have been called 'Worthy Park Revisited' – being a re-examination and re-evaluation of some of the material concerning a single Jamaican sugar estate which James Walvin and I studied and wrote about between 1968 and 1978 (Craton & Walvin 1970, Craton 1978).

In particular, I thought to look again at the three persons with very different characters and significantly different roles who gave evidence on behalf of Worthy Park in the 1848 Parliamentary Inquiry into the crisis facing the British Caribbean sugar industry. The hope was that each would provide a different facet of the problem of plantation management under changing conditions. First of these featured actors was George Price, fifth of six sons of the former owner, who had gone out to manage and revive the struggling family estate in 1843 at the age of 31 with an infusion of fresh capital provided by his father-in-law, Lord Dunsany. George Price made valiant but vain attempts to mechanise Worthy Park and reorganise its work-force, mainly by offering competitive wages. He remained in Jamaica for more than 20 years despite the estate's economic collapse, an important figure in local politics and a resolute opponent of Governor Eyre. Second was Thomas Price, George's youngest brother (later, Lieutenant-Governor of Dominica and British Honduras), who had already been to Worthy Park in 1841 and returned in despair. As an absentee increasingly gifted with hindsight, he was a severe critic of what he regarded as his brother's 'visionary' expenditure and mismanagement, unfairly blaming him for cutting off the family's Jamaican income. Third was Viscount Ingestre, Worthy Park trustee and mortgage-holder since 1835 by virtue of the last will of his brother-in-law, the father of George and Thomas Price. He now regretted the family connection which had led to such disastrous investment, bewailed the way in which his money was locked up, and would dearly have liked to deploy it elsewhere (British Sessional Papers 1848: 4963-5170).

The planned paper was not written, largely because the counterposed roles of the three *dramatis personae* did not come clearly enough through the written record. On a re-reading, most of the evidence given before the

1848 Commission was found to have been given by Thomas Price, who had far less direct involvement in the running of Worthy Park than had his brother George, and whose financial interest was less direct than Viscount Ingestre's. Yet the dozen pages of evidence presented to the 1848 Commission did touch on almost all the critical factors mentioned at the beginning of this essay and discussed in the conference sessions.

First, the evidence showed that at Worthy Park during the 1840s, the availability of suitable *land* was not an immediate problem. Although the original estate had optimised its own cane lands since the 1790s, adjacent decayed or abandoned estates could be, and were, bought up for a song. Had the Prices been otherwise able to create a very large central sugar operation at Worthy Park, they would have been constrained in time by the surrounding mountains; in fact their enterprise failed altogether before suitable land ran out.

Second, *capital* was available to a degree, but what it could achieve was severely limited by labour and technical constraints. Third, *technological modifications* were tried, but they failed for reasons unrelated to whether they could, or did, increase productivity. Fourth, *labour* was a problem, but chiefly on account of the need to reorganise it efficiently into a two-tier system of a small corps of permanent workers and a larger seasonal cane-cutting gang, its availability *when needed*, and its *cost*. Fifth, *imperial policy* was an extremely contentious issue, Thomas Price arguing that the economic situation might be remedied, if narrowly, if the imperial government maintained the sugar price at ten shillings a hundredweight by subsidies, and if it subsidised the immigration of foreign labourers to allow the reduction of the daily rate of wages from one shilling and sixpence to twopence or fourpence.

But the bottom line, sixth, was surely the *world sugar price*. This had reached a catastrophic low in 1846-7, so that even with optimisation and maximum production, Worthy Park's total income from sugar and rum was well below the cost of production. In existing circumstances the total income was actually less than the *wage bill* – quite ignoring all the other costs, including that of servicing the standing debt. Under such circumstances, it was inevitable that capital would migrate elsewhere, and even relatively fortunate Jamaican estates like Worthy Park would be forced to close.

What happened in the face of these and similar problems and crises? It depended, of course, on who you were and what were the options, if any, available to you. First, the workers (whose role and behaviour have hardly been considered at this meeting) did what they could to find alternative work or ways of subsisting, or to obtain the best type of work and the best wages, and to shape and optimise and determine conditions as best they could by forms of industrial action or resistance.

Second, the planters and their managers did what they could to adjust and juggle and make new equations. These included changing field and factory practice as best they could, to get new capital if they could, to make technological changes as far as their knowledge and means allowed, to diversify (and here the comments about the moves towards coffee, cotton and, later, bananas are very apposite) and, in the last resort, to shut up operations altogether.

For those, third, who provided the capital – absentee family members or associates like Thomas Price or Lord Ingestre, or faceless bankers – the options and strategies were different again. They might be satisfied with local attempts to adjust and reform the labour and technical systems, or to diversify, to cut back production temporarily, or to practise economies of scale as far as possible. But they were far readier than resident owners or managers to close down operations and switch elsewhere. In many cases they were only frustrated by the inertial provisions of the existing laws of inheritance, entail and bankruptcy, which made it practically impossible to dispose of 'encumbered' estates until 1854 (Craton & Walvin 1970: 208-233).

These are the three main levels of human behaviour and practices. But we ought also to distinguish three, or even four, other more determinant levels on the material plane: those of individual plantations, of the larger island or colony units, and of the Caribbean region as a whole – placed, of course, within the total world economy.

For itself, Worthy Park staggered on somehow as a sugar producer, until the years of stunning success following the Second World War – although under several different owners. This story is written in *A Jamaican Plantation* and *Searching for the Invisible Man* (Craton & Walvin 1970; Craton 1978). The island colony of Jamaica as a whole, however, almost ceased to be a sugar producer by 1900, becoming a rather more diversified but still desperately poor backwater, notable mainly as an exporter of migrant labourers at a time when capital migrated to sugar production in Cuba and banana plantations in Central America. Within the island, as Verene Shepherd has pointed out in a recent dissertation, cattle pens largely took over the best former sugar land, and the cattle pen owners turned themselves into, or became part of, what Douglas Hall and Verene Shepherd have termed a 'penocracy' (Hall 1959, 1979; Shepherd 1988).

In the context of the wider Caribbean this points up a curious but significant development very relevant to our current discussions. Whereas Jamaica was one of the greatest sugar producers during the heyday of slavery, islands like Spanish Puerto Rico and Cuba, and other Spanish mainland colonies, were largely cattle ranches and small-scale producers of minor crops. Once Cuba and, to a certain extent, Puerto Rico became great sugar producers, though, the positions were almost reversed, with Jamaica reverting to a largely ranching and peasant subsistence economy. Viewing this transition in the widest perspective, it was clearly a local function of an age that saw great developments in the internationalisation of capital, the spread of free trade and *laissez-faire* principles, the worldwide organisation of transportation, processing and marketing, and, not least, the much more efficient organisation of migratory labour on a global scale (Moreno Fraginals 1978; Scott 1985; Zanetti & Garcia 1988).

Out of a reading of the articles and our discussions of them, I make the following preliminary, tentative and personal conclusions. If we look for the *single* overriding principle in the labour: technology equation or the sugar plantation debate at large, we cannot do better than accept the truism that sugar plantations are 'ultimately in the business of making profits'. But beyond that, an only slightly less simple formula gives me slightly more satisfaction, at least for the time being: 'Change (including technological change) was ultimately driven by the quest for profit in the face of the world sugar price. Change, however, was limited not so much by the availability of capital or labour as by the availability of plentiful, cheap, fertile and politically unencumbered *land* — since both capital and labour would readily migrate or become available to such areas, and *only* to such areas'.

REFERENCES

Alan H. Adamson, *Sugar Without Slaves: The Political Economy of British Guiana, 1838-1904*, New Haven, Yale University Press, 1972.

Michiel Baud, *Sugar and Unfree Labour: Reflections on Labour Recruiting in the Dominican Republic, 1870-1940*, Paper ICA Amsterdam, 1988.

Peter Boomgaard and Gert J. Oostindie, *Nieuwe Westindische Gids*, Spring 1990, 1-12.

British Sessional Papers, Accounts & Papers XXIII, *Select Committee on Sugar and Coffee Planting*, London, 4,963-5,170.

Michael Craton, *Searching for the Invisible Man: Slaves and Plantation life in Jamaica*, Cambridge, MA, Harvard University Press, 1978.

Michael Craton and James Walvin, *A Jamaican Plantation: The History of Worthy Park, 1670-1970*, London, W. H. Allen and Toronto, Toronto University Press, 1970.

Seymour Drescher, *Econocide: British Slavery in the Era of Abolition*, Pittsburgh, Pittsburgh University Press, 1977.

_____The decline thesis of British slavery since *Econocide. Slavery and Abolition*, vii, 3-24.

Douglas G. Hall, *Free Jamaica 1838-1865: An Economic History*, New Haven, Yale University Press, 1959.

_____'The flight from the estates reconsidered: the British West Indies', 1838-1842, *Journal of Caribbean History*, x-xi, 7-24.

Francisco Moreno Fraginals, *El ingenio; complejo economico social cubano del azúcar*, 3 vols, Havana, Ediciones Ciencias Sociales, 1978.

Walter Rodney, *A History of the Guyanese Working People, 1881-1905*, Baltimore, Johns Hopkins University Press, 1981.

Stuart B. Schwartz, *Sugar Plantations and the Formation of Brazilian Society, 1550-1835*, New York, Cambridge University Press, 1985.

Rebecca J. Scott, 'Explaining Abolition: contradiction, adaptation and challenge in Cuban slave society, 1860-1886', *Comparative Studies in Society and History*, xxvi, 83-111.

_____*Slave emancipation in Cuba: the transition to free labor, 1860-1899*, Princeton, Princeton University Press, 1985.

Verene Shepherd, 'Pens and pen-keepers in a plantation-society: aspects of Jamaican social and economic history, 1740-1845', unpublished PhD dissertation, University of Cambridge, 1988.

Richard B. Sheridan, *Nieuwe Westindische Gids*, Spring, 1990.

Eric E. Williams, *Capitalism and Slavery*, Chapel Hill, North Carolina University Press, 1944.

Oscar Zanetti and Alejandro Garcia, *Caminos para el azúcar*, Havana, Ediciones Ciencias Sociales, 1987.

18

Reshuffling the Pack

The Transition from Slavery to
other forms of Labour in the
British Caribbean, 1780-1890

Introduction: Written for a conference comparing adjustments to the ending of slavery, held in Rio de Janeiro in 1992, this essay followed on from the more general and bibliographic study of the same theme written earlier but actually printed next in the present collection. Its presumed purpose was twofold: to summarise and add to work currently under way in what seems to be the most vital area of British Caribbean scholarship, and to inform non-Caribbean scholars, working in parallel but largely in isolation, of the existence of this trend. As its title indicates, the general conclusion of the essay is that the transition from slavery to other forms of labour and labour relations exemplifies the principle of Antonio Gramsci that ruling classes are adept at adapting to inevitable changes, even adopting them, if that is the only means of sustaining their hegemony. This was well-received at the Rio conference and after publication (with an excellent translation by Carlos Hasenbalg) in *Estudos Afro-Asiaticus*. The publication in English in *Nieuwe Westindische Gids*, however, did touch at least one conservative nerve. In a subsequent exchange in the same journal, Pieter Emmer wilfully ignored the tide of scholarship of which the author represents but a wavelet, while virtually accusing him of arguing that the condition of slavery was preferable to what followed in the subsequent century.

The separate and rival imperialism of the mercantilist era gave the First British Empire a distinctive functional identity, and the British system passed through successive stages of commercial and industrial capitalism in advance of others. Yet there is an artificiality in separating the transition out of a slave labour system within the British colonies from later processes elsewhere, and this is made all the more unacceptable by the general decay of mercantilism, the progressive spread of free trade and *laissez-faire* principles, and the concurrent substitution of a worldwide and intensifying capitalist system. The British slave trade from Africa was ended in 1808 and

British slaves were formally freed in 1838, whereas both the trade and the institution of slavery lingered on in other imperial systems. Slavery survived in the USA until 1865 and in Cuba and Brazil into the later 1880s. But this should no longer invite sequential comparisons, or even an analysis that features simply a cumulative widening of principles initiated in Britain. Instead, the transition should be viewed in its entirety. Even if there is a concentration on the British West Indies, we must conscientiously relate what happened in that restricted ambit to the larger hemispheric, Atlantic and worldwide process. What happened in the British sphere initiated and to a degree set up the model for developments lasting almost a century. But it was itself but a part of the larger, longer process, with what happened outside the British colonial sphere flowing back and fundamentally affecting the pattern within.[1]

EVOLUTIONARY RATHER THAN REVOLUTION CHANGE: PREMATURE FORMATIONS

The socioeconomic transformation of the British West Indies, if more complete, was much more gradual and subtle than the violent change which occurred in Haiti between 1791 and 1804. There, a bloody servile revolution seizing the opportunities provided by the French Revolution as much as inspired by its ideals, quite suddenly transformed the most intensively developed slave plantation colony in the world into an independent black republic based on peasant cultivators. This proud new country and its economy were instantly marginalised, by the Haitians' own independent spirit and by the calculated indifference, or active antagonism based on racist paranoia, of the major powers, including the USA. Haiti, though exploited by the imperialists whenever they could, was thereby largely spared the trammels of developing world capitalism, at least until the twentieth century.

In the British West Indies there were also serious slave rebellions after the last French wars: in Barbados in 1816, British Guiana in 1823 and Jamaica in 1831-32. All seem to have had similar socioeconomic agendas, and the example of Haiti was a widespread inspiration. But they all failed, partly because of political confusion among the rebels, but mainly because the colonial regimes, alerted and fearful of the Haitian precedent, and no longer distracted by war, were easily strong enough to suppress them. The British West Indian slave colonies (like those of the other European powers including the French) were therefore preserved for the luxury of more leisurely change, upon principles ostensibly liberal. The result was a more orderly dismantling of the slavery system, the substitution of different forms of planter and other local oligarchies in different guises, and the gradual incorporation of the island economies into a more generic world system.

Whether or not it arose from the often-alleged British national tendency towards evolutionary rather than revolutionary change and a concomitant facility for pragmatic adaptation, the process within the British West Indies demonstrated aspects of a continuum, with anticipations and survivals on each side of the formal emancipation of the slaves, rather than sharply marked phases and abrupt changes. According to recent analysts, long before the British slaves were freed they exhibited features of both proto-peasant and proto-proletarian behaviour; while it has long been a commonplace that many aspects of labour relations after 1838 were no better than a modified form of slavery, with the chances of a pure peasant lifestyle little greater than in the last decades before emancipation. Put in other terms (and perhaps mixing Marxian and Braudellian concepts), the evolution of the dialectic between the classes of capitalists and their workers was of long duration, transcending the mere punctuation of events such as the statutory outlawing of the African slave trade in 1808 and the proclamation of Full Freedom in 1838.

Slaves as proto-peasants

It has taken modern analysts of the slavery system in the West Indies a long time to acknowledge what were probably empirical commonplaces for practical planters, recognised by at least some contemporary writers on plantation management: that it was self-interest for planters to provide incentives as well as punishments for slaves; that allowing slaves opportunities for producing their own foodstuffs (even selling the surplus) cut down the cost of their upkeep and made them less unhappy; and that gang labour under the white man's lash was counterproductive and less effective than customary task allotments mediated by drivers drawn from the slaves' own natural leaders. It can even be argued that the terms of employment for slaves were as much the product of a species of transactional negotiation as they were of the exercise of the relations of naked power.[2]

From the earliest days of the sugar revision in the British West Indies, slaves were put to grow provisions on land and at times that could be spared from export staple production. On islands suitable for absolute monoculture, like Barbados, where there was almost no marginal land and each acre of fertile land could make profits from sugar that could pay for imported produce it would take five acres to grow locally. Thus such slave provision grounds were a luxury, and slave provision production was more or less limited to the small plots on which the slave cabins stood. Two consequences were subsistence crises at times when importations were curtailed, such as in wartime, and the problem of controlling slaves who wandered from plantation to plantation or dissipated themselves in traditional dances once they were given Sundays to themselves.[3]

On some islands, and areas within islands, without much space and accessible fertile land a small proportion of estate land was allocated for food crops, which were then rationed out to the slaves – a system that became more common under metropolitan monitoring and with the intensification of staple crop production towards the end of slavery (Turner 1991:93). On most islands, and most notably in Jamaica, however, there was much land unsuitable for plantation production, and the most effective plantations had large areas of wooded hillside and mountain glade, either adjacent or within walking distance, that could be designated slave provision grounds. As Barry Higman's (1988:262) painstaking analysis of the huge trove of estate plans preserved in the Institute of Jamaica has illustrated, by 1780 'only where almost all of the land within an estate was suited to the cultivation of sugar and backlands were not accessible did planters choose to purchase food or produce provision crops by supervised gang labour'.

On many plantations, indeed, slaves had access to three tiers of grounds to grow their own crops: 'kitchen gardens' immediately adjacent to their houses (which included fruit trees and pens for small stocks as well as vegetable plots), allocated areas called 'shellblow grounds' close enough to the canefields that they could be worked during the two-hour midday break, and more distant provision grounds, worked at the weekends under minimal supervision (Higman 1988:261-67).

Despite the planters' habitual indifference to slave family arrangements and their attempted discouragement of all things African, all three types of land facilitated the preservation or reconstitution of African patterns of peasant family production. Hut plots and shellblow lands were allocated at the will of the planter to male household heads (as were issues of provisions, supplies and clothing), and were subject to permanent oversight, sometimes mapped out, and scrupulously reclaimed once the slaves were freed. Yet even these nearer allotments often took on a customary African appearance

– huts and plots seemingly laid out haphazardly and differing in size according to need, with female household heads dominant around the domestic hearth and the surrounding kitchen gardens.

Slaves in their quarters had a more independent existence than was once acknowledged; but it was in the more distant provision grounds that they were most able to shape a life of their own, albeit in that fraction of the week – a day and a half at most in the true plantation colonies – when they were left more or less to their own devices. Each family cleared and worked what land they could manage in what one exasperated surveyor called 'a straggling way, here and there where they find the best soil . . . so that it is impossible to form a judgement of the extent of it in the aggregate'.[4]

Enterprising families not only grew most of the food they ate and provided extra food tribute to their owners, but were able to produce surpluses, as well as pigs and fowls raised in their kitchen yards, which the women sold in the informal Sunday markets that sprang up at crossroads or plantation intersections – bartering or purchasing with the money received such items which they were not issued by their owners or could not make for themselves. By the last half century of slavery, not only were the slaves providing most of their own subsistence but had so far upset the theory that as chattel property they could hardly own property or money themselves as to participate substantially in the cash economy. Of Jamaica it was said by Edward Long (1774,I:537) as early as 1774 that a fifth of the coin in circulation was in the hands of the slaves, much of it made by actually selling their produce to their owners.

As Sidney Mintz and Douglas Hall (1960) first suggested such a customary system was a prototypical form of peasant production – or more accurately, a foreshadowing of the common post-emancipation mode in the British West Indies whereby the largest section of the black population spent what time they could in peasant production, what time they had to in wage labour on the plantations; in Richard Frucht's (1967) formulation, as part-peasants, part-proletarians. The Brazilian Marxist analyst, Ciro Cardoso (1987), identifying similar examples throughout plantation America, has fittingly termed this phenomenon 'o brecha camponesa no modo de produco escravista', [the peasant breach in the slave mode of production].[5]

Though proto-peasant activity among the slaves was common before the end of slavery – being concurrent with, and facilitated by, the demographic normalisation and accompanying creolisation of the slave population – it was most evident in areas and colonies where there were decayed plantations, or where plantations had failed altogether, leaving a population of slaves surplus to formal labour requirements. Such slave populations also tended to grow by natural increase because of the lightening of the workload. In a situation where the power of the slave-owners was absolute, this would simply have led to the redeployment of slaves from such 'breeding areas' to areas of high labour demand. In the USA, this was to account for the steady transfer of slaves from the declining tobacco plantations and demographically favourable environment of Virginia to the burgeoning and chronically labour-short cotton plantations of the south-west.[6]

In some parts of the British West Indies too, the owners of slaves surplus to former labour requirements ingeniously explored alternative ways of making a return on their human property; employing them in tasks previously thought uneconomic compared with plantation labour; hiring them out in gangs of 'jobbing' labourers or, if skilled craftsmen, as individuals, and in extreme cases, shipping them off to other colonies where there was a labour shortage. The economic weakness of slave-owners in decaying or decayed plantation areas, however, was further and progressively exacerbated by pressures from two directions: on the one side, by the rising concern for the condition of the slaves emanating from the metropole (which the slave-owners, of course, termed ignorant meddling), and on the other by the slaves' own growing awareness of their increased bargaining power, their sense that they now had allies and even rights, and their consequently heightened resistance.[7]

The abolition of the British trade in slaves from Africa between 1805 and 1808 highlighted the continuing shortage of slave labourers which was general in the sugar plantation colonies, with the single exception of Barbados. The need was greatest in those underdeveloped but promising colonies acquired in the last French wars: St Lucia, Trinidad and the Guianas. Slave-owners unable to find alternative gainful employment for their slaves therefore tended to ship them off to other colonies where there was a marked labour shortage, until this practice, like the African trade itself, was outlawed by the British Parliament in 1824. One island within the Caribbean to which such conditions applied was Tortola once sugar production there was no longer economic. But the most notable case was the Bahamas, where the failure of cotton plantations begun by the Loyalists led to the underemployment of a slave population which, largely for the same reason, was increasing at a phenomenal rate. Some owners managed to redeploy their slaves at the salt-pans of the central and southern islands of the archipelago, while those who could fulfil the requirement that they were simply transferring their slaves to their own estates elsewhere, transported them to new sugar plantations, mainly in Trinidad. In this way, over 2,000 Bahamian slaves, a fifth of the total, were moved before 1824, although the depletion was made up within a decade by natural increase (Eltis 1972; Higman 1984:79-85; Craton & Saunders 1922:291-96).

Where slaves were too numerous for profitable employment, and the imposition of statutory requirements over issues of food and clothing further increased the owners' maintenance costs, a majority of the slaves were left to their own devices as virtual peasant subsistence farmers. They combined their own will to support themselves by farming and fishing rather than engage in estate labour with their owners' reluctance further to erode already exiguous profits by the cost of issues of imported food. The practical bargaining power which such slaves held over their owners was reinforced by the slaves' growing sense that they had allies in Britain and that the new statutory requirements were tantamount to their rights; so that they refused to be moved, in the case of the Bahamas, first out of the colony and then from one island to another within it. They even began to claim that the land was their own.

The behaviour of the troublesome slaves of Lord Rolle in Exuma was an extreme example of incipient bargaining powers held by a proto-peasantry. In the 1820s the Rolle slaves claimed that they had been promised the land on which they lived by Lord Rolle's father (who had brought them to the Bahamas from Florida in the 1780s) and resolutely refused to agree to be transferred to Trinidad. In 1830 some of them actually rebelled when a proposal was made to transfer them from Exuma to Cat Island within the Bahamas as a jobbing gang, seizing Lord Rolle's salt boat and sailing to Nassau to put their case to Governor Carmichael Smyth, who was thought to be sympathetic to the slaves. Although punished with whipping, they were not moved from Exuma, and thereafter performed ever less work for Lord Rolle, Governor Smyth's successor reported that the Rolle slaves only worked for the estate when there were soldiers present, and even then had completed their assigned tasks around midday – although at the same time he admitted that the slaves' claims that they were undersupplied by their owner according to the law was not unjustified (Craton & Saunders 1992:381-91; Craton 1979, 1983).

After Lord Rolle's proposal to manumit his costly slaves early had been turned down by the Colonial Office, they continued to work only under military supervision, and during the transitional apprenticeship period

(1834-88) performed only nominal tasks. Lord Rolle was glad to be relieved of his turbulent charges in return for by far the largest Bahamian slave compensation payments, tacitly allowing the ex-slaves to assert commonage rights over the virtually unsaleable Rolle lands in Exuma. In the final twist in a complex transactional relationship extending over more than a half century, the Rolle ex-slaves expanded the alleged promise by Lord Rolle's father to claim that their commonage rights were based on a donation (seemingly just as mythical) in Lord Rolle's will. Wittily encapsulating the ambivalencies of all such 'paternalistic' relationships, the Rolle ex-slaves all took their former owner's name; possession of the Rolle surname remaining to this day sufficient authority for a share of the use of the Rolle common-ages in Exuma (Craton & Saunders 1991).

Variations on the same theme, with the interdependence of slaves and owner being yet more obvious, and the outcome being labour tenancies and sharecropping rather than commonage-working peasantry, are apparent in the case of the Farquharson estate on San Salvador island, one of the few remaining Bahamian estates with a resident owner at the end of slavery, as well as the only one of which a day-by-day record survives (for 1831-32). Charles Farquharson, the aged owner, had scarcely more options than his slaves. His over-mortgaged land not only made absentee ownership impos-sible but produced no more than was necessary to keep him and his family at the planter's level of subsistence. And even this depended on the labour of the slaves over whom, in his isolation, he had limited practical power. Since buying imported provisions for a steadily growing population was out of the question, at least a half of the estate's limited fertile land, and a similar proportion of the slaves' labour, was given over to the production of corn and other food crops for feeding the slaves. In an island without any alternative demands for labour and seemingly without informal slave mar-kets – indeed, almost out of range of the cash economy – the slaves fed themselves from their master's land but were completely dependent on him for the issues of clothing and other items not produced on the estate.

Consequently, proximity, familiarity and interdependence bred a deli-cate reciprocity, a customary balance, between owner and slaves. Although it was in the owner's self-interest to get what returns he could from his land and labour resources, and in the slaves' self-interest to perform the mini-mum work for the necessary benefits, it was the enlightened self-interest of the former not to exact too much, and of the latter not totally to upset the boat in which all sailed together. Even on the one occasion when excessive work at the height of the corn harvest and unusual punishment led to a strike and riot, one of the more obdurate slaves actually intervened to prevent the driver from committing murder, and, although the arraignment of the ring-leaders in the Nassau slave court was regarded as inevitable, all the other slaves returned to work without enforcement the following day, to gather the remains of the corn upon which their subsistence depended.

When slavery ended, Charles Farquharson's heirs, like many Out Island owners, gratefully took the parliamentary compensation for their slave property but did not (probably could not) sell their land. Instead, they sought to capitalise on this residual resource and on the habits of dependency engrained in ex-slaves unwilling or unable to find either wage labour or suitable land on which to squat without legal tenure. This was achieved by making either sharecropping contracts or labour tenancies – sometimes both. By such arrangements, the ex-slaves and their descendants retained the occupation and use of their familiar houses and grounds, and received issues of seed, fertiliser and tools, even handouts if not cash advances in times of special hardship, at the price of a third or a half of their crops and/or the obligation to work from time-to-time on their former owner's demesne. As with the black Rolles, this special relationship was often signalised by the assumption and retention of their former owner's surname, which also sometimes remained the name of the settlement in which they lived (Craton & Saunders 1992).

Slaves as proto-proletarians

In respect of the tacit negotiations and customary arrangements made with their owners, Rolle, Farquharson and similar slaves were already almost as much proto-proletarians as proto-peasants. But elements of similar relationships were to be found throughout the British West Indian slave system, climaxing in the period between abolition and emancipation (1805-34), but with roots traceable almost to the earliest years of the slave plantation system.

Despite the attempts of the plantocratic system to treat slaves simply as parts of an animate machine, slave labour clearly was a commodity with a negotiable cash value from the beginning, and this reality soon became manifest. Manuals of slave management continued to stress the importance of ganging the slaves according to their labour effectiveness, and assigning work to them as a gang unit under the impetus of the drivers' whips (Ligon 1657:43; Beckford 1790, II:47-48; Stephen 1824, I:54). It was regarded as the index of a planter's efficiency, moreover, how well he balanced his work-force against the needs of his plantation throughout the year. John Pinney of Nevis (1740-1818), for example, took pride that he never had to hire extra slaves and was actually able to capitalise on his surplus labour by hiring out his slaves from time-to-time (Pares 1950:103-40). Nonetheless, the very fact that slaves were commonly hired out, either as jobbing gangs or as individuals with special skills, brought home the measurability of their value, not just to the owners but to the slaves themselves. Estate record books that list the slaves in their gangs and include alongside each slave his or her assessed market value are therefore not merely an indication of an owner's assessment of his capital assets, but an indicator of the slaves' actual value, potential bargaining power, and consequent status (Craton 1978:135-87).

Jobbing gangs were naturally assigned specific tasks for costing purposes, and perceptive owners soon noted that preassessed daily tasks that made it possible for energetic slaves to finish early were more efficient than unlimited drudgery through the hours of daylight. All that then had to be determined from the point of view of labour efficiency was what was the optimum level of work that could be extracted under this method; what was the maximum amount of work that could still provide an incentive to the worker. This was a differential equation; as many commentators noted, the amount of work that could be expected or extracted from slaves varied according to the relative power of masters and slaves, and steadily decreased over time. The Barbadian, William Dickson (1814:121, Morgan 1988), the most perceptive of all planter commentators, for example, remarked that pure gang work was 'a vulgar system which perhaps was the only one that was practicable 150 years ago, with an untamed set of savages'. Even those experts on plantation slave management who continued to believe that ganging was essential as a means of control, advocated what Philip Morgan (1988) has called 'collective tasking'. By the end of slavery, it is likely that the seemingly rigid allocation of slaves into separate gangs in plantation record books was more a system of classification by age and strength than a reflection of reality in the allocation of work.

Similarly, the need for owners to provide an incentive for individual slaves to go off to work for others, to work efficiently, and, most important, to return when they were instructed to do so, inevitably led to the slaves first to expect a share, and then to negotiate an increasing proportion of their hiring charge. The practices of allowing slaves to retain a share of their hire and of assigning slave gangs fixed daily tasks began first and developed most quickly in marginal plantation or non-plantation areas, but became widespread and almost general in slavery's last decades. The fact that the amount of work that could be expected – as measured by the size of tasks assigned and the number of hours worked – steadily declined towards the end of slavery attests at least as much to the growing negotiating power of the slave proto-proletariat relative to their owner-employers, as to the increasing vigilance of the imperial authorities as to what the owners extracted out of their slaves.

The eagerness of slaves to become at least partial wage-earners – as of slaves in general to become involved in the cash economy by whatever means – was also determined by the chances of obtaining manumission by purchase, which steadily increased towards the end of slavery (speeded, among other things, by the increasing willingness of owners in a declining economy to capitalise on their chief remaining asset, their property in slaves). Moreover, the way that slaves were able progressively to negotiate smaller tasks and a larger share of their hiring wage underlines the fact that the switch from slavery to wage labour was not only inevitable but also a steady transition rather than a sudden change. Mary Turner (1991:102) even characterises this phase as a 'cash labour breach in the coerced labour system'.

Premature transformations under slavery: Antigua, Jamaica, Belize, Bahamas

The processes described above could be illustrated in any colony in the British West Indies. Certainly they are consistent with all that has so far been analysed in scholarly detail; by Hilary Beckles and Andrew Downes (1987) for the 'old' sugar monoculture of Barbados, Barry Gaspar (1985) for the declining monocultural system of Antigua, Barry Higman (1990)and Mary Turner (1988, 1991) for the incomplete monoculture of Jamaica, and Nigel Bolland (1981, 1991, 1993), Howard Johnson (1991), Gail Saunders and the present writer (1992, 1997) for the marginal colonies of Belize and the Bahamas. From this recent work and these significantly different territories alone a convincing composite picture has already emerged.

As the work of Elsa Goveia (1965) and Barry Gaspar (1985:160-62) shows, the socioeconomic system of Antigua had initially developed in a more relaxed and less efficient manner than that of Barbados. The unravelling of the slave plots of the 1730s revealed that not only were some Antiguan planters (notably Christopher Codrington) ingenuously lax in not controlling their Akan slaves or punishing runaways, and in willing to manumit slaves no longer capable of useful work, but African and creole slaves alike were allowed a dangerous latitude in self-employment. The Act of 1757 to limit manumission and tighten controls in general, declared that 'a Custom hath prevailed . . . for permitting slaves to go about the Towns and Country to hire themselves and take their own liberty and pay their Masters and Mistresses for their Time, by which many Negroes who were actually Runaways, under Pretence of working out, or being at Liberty to hire themselves, have been employed in the Towns or Country unknown to their Masters and Mistresses, and often Robberies are committed by such slaves'.[8]

Fines were enacted for delinquent owners and the manumission require-ments tightened, but the continued need for re-enactments argues for the ineffectiveness of the laws and the strength of custom rather than the reverse – as does, perhaps, the curious fact that Antigua never suffered from a major slave uprising, or even a repetition of the island-wide slave plot of 1736. A large proportion of Antiguan slaves – probably around 40 per cent – were employed in non-plantation labour (as domestics, craftsmen, mari-ners, or hired labourers at the port and naval base) and as the profitability of Antiguan plantations declined, leading to the collapse of sugar estates, increased absenteeism, and general emigration of whites, the practical control of the Antiguan plantocracy over their slaves reached a point where it appeared that the slaves controlled the terms of labour.

In Antigua, as throughout the Leeward Islands, managers wrote to their absentee owners of the ineradicable laziness of their slaves and their tendency to larceny. This can be decoded to mean that managers obtained progressively less production on a daily basis and in a similar way were unable to prevent the slaves from engaging in the informal market economy of the island. One reason why the Antiguan planters were the first in the British West Indies to allow Christian missionaries – first Moravians and then Methodists – into the colony to proselytise the slaves may well have been a calculated effort to socialise them as dutiful and hardworking servants. If so, the attempt was a failure. The missionaries had such success in religious conversion that by the 1820s virtually all Antiguan slaves could be categorised as adherents of the Moravian, Methodist, or Anglican churches.[9] But this simply attested to the slaves' degree of creolisation and to the benefits they themselves perceived from Christianisation. Far from leading to greater productivity and malleability, it seems to have produced a greater sense of self-worth or even political power, backed up by an awareness of sympathetic allies in Britain and of the declining economic and political clout in the metropole of the planter lobby.

Certainly, the creolisation process was accompanied by a growing assertion of the slaves' customary rights. As Gaspar (1988) has shown, the climax occurred in 1831, fittingly over the banning of the slaves' long-established Sunday markets. Under the influence of the sabbatarian evangelicals of the Clapham Sect, the Bathurst Circular of 1830 had suggested this measure — and the granting of a half-holiday on Saturdays instead — under the impression that it was genuinely 'amelioration'. Not only would it give the slaves a better chance to attend divine worship on Sundays, but it would cut down on the disorder and dissipation that were often associated with Sunday activities, and leave the slaves in better condition for labour on Monday mornings. That the slaves saw the matter differently was revealed by the fact that the first weekend the ordinance came into effect thousands of them marched to Government House in St John's and demonstrated noisily against it.

Although their behaviour bordered on the riotous, the Antiguan slaves' political position was quite sophisticated and their combined action might also be taken as evidence of a nascent proletarian consciousness. It was not just that Sunday markets were both customary and convenient; they had actually been enacted by the laws of Antigua and were therefore a right, taken away in favour of an alternative which depended not on law, but the will of individual masters. Although the crowds were dispersed and their informal petition for the continuation of Sunday markets formally rejected, the protests were in fact successful in two respects. Not only did the governor decree that all masters would henceforth grant a Saturday half holiday without a choice, but the government forces found themselves unable to prevent the Antiguan slaves carrying on much as before, including the holding of informal markets on Sundays.

Although a careful re-reading of planters' writings — such as the absentee 'Monk' Lewis's (1834) account of master-slave relations on and around his two Jamaican estates (1815-17), or even of the journal of the brutal and insecure eighteenth-century plantation manager Thomas Thistlewood (Hall 1989) — reveals how the relations of power were less unbalanced than usually described, the actual process of labour bargaining within the slave system has only been unravelled through Mary Turner's brilliant micro-historical studies (1988 and 1991) of the two related estates of Grange Hill and Blue Mountain in eastern Jamaica between 1770 and 1830.

Of the two estates, Grange Hill was the more marginal as a sugar producer and had a longer-entrenched slave population, and these features gave its slave work-force a bargaining power in advance of that of Blue Mountain. The estates shared a proprietor absent in Britain and an attorney in distant Kingston. Moreover, they had, like most Jamaican estates, neighbouring maroon and free coloured smallholders who illustrated the possibility of an alternative lifestyle, and were adjacent to the small port and market town of Manchioneal, which gave ample evidence of the value of labour and the opportunities it provided for skilled wage labourers, and for the exchange of the surplus produce of the slaves' more or less voluntary labour in their provision grounds for cash.

Even by 1770, the Grange Hill slaves had been granted Thursdays as well as Sundays to work their provision grounds and attend the market in town. There was a marked hierarchy of slaves, with privileges proportional to their value to the estate, and some of the most skilled craftsmen were hired out and probably kept at least some of their wages. When the black slave carpenter Joe (who lived three months a year at attorney Malcolm Laing's house in Kingston) complained of a dispute with the Grange Hill overseer to the attorney, the overseer was dismissed. The slaves then refused to work for the overseer's militaristic replacement, David Munroe, ran to the woods and sent delegates 60 miles to Laing in Kingston. The slaves returned to work when Laing promised to investigate and, in the event, Munroe too was sacked (Turner 1988:15-18).

In 1825, to counteract the steady decline in profits, the estates' owners appointed an 'improving' overseer, Charles Lewsey, from Barbados, an island widely believed to have established firm but effective relationships between masters and slaves. Lewsey found the situation at Grange Hill almost hopeless. Under a defiant and powerful black head driver, John Reay, the slaves spent more effort in producing provisions than sugar. Most of the heaviest labour, such as digging cane-holes and making sugar, had to be performed by jobbing gangs at up to two shillings and sixpence a day per slave or £7.10s per acre, the Grange Hill slaves were accustomed to carrying their own produce as much as 30 miles to Morant Bay, using either their own mules (worth up to £8 apiece) or those belonging to the estate. The provision grounds became the customary refuges of 'skulking runaways' – that is, slaves individually protesting working conditions. Threats to sell all the slaves if any more runaways were found in the provision grounds or to send Reay to the workhouse had no effect. The threat to rent out the provision grounds to strangers and issue the slaves with corn instead, which prompted the slaves to be more industrious, effected only a temporary improvement. Surrounded, as he claimed, by 'A set of subjects which meet me on every Quarter with Low Cunning and Vile Cant', Lewsey decided to give up the struggle to produce sugar at Grange Hill and turned it to pasture and livestock. This 'complemented the slaves' provision ground production and rationalised the economic transformation which they had effected' (Turner 1988:26; see also Craton 1978:1-49; Higman 1976:9-44).

The situation at Blue Mountain Charles Lewsey found almost equally problematic. There the concentration on sugar had been achieved by Malcolm Laing and his successor as attorney through importations of Africans before the slave trade was ended. This may initially have divided the slaves in a manner beneficial to the owners. But since the new Africans found it difficult to obtain provision grounds of their own, the move entrenched an increasingly troublesome slave élite who even employed some of the 'poorer sort' of slaves to work their grounds for wages (eventually at up to one shilling and eightpence a day). As early as the 1790s, when the Haitian Revolution and the French and maroon wars exacerbated the threat of slave unrest, the Blue Mountain slaves had been able to effect the dismissal of two of their overseers. But after the slave trade was ended and the continued mortality among Africans led to a decline in the Blue Mountain slaves from a peak of 350 to 1765, the overseer was faced by an ever more unified 'village interest bloc', cemented by adherence to a black Baptist preacher, and led by a powerful black slave driver called Becky.

In order to sustain sugar production at Blue Mountain, Charles Lewsey was forced to make considerable changes in the estate's management, which amounted to concessions in the labour bargaining process: a reduction in the level of work expected, occasional rewards such as a steer for cropover, and a closer attention to the slaves' notion of justice in the matter of punishments. This was in response to threats of work stoppages, go-slows and running away, to near riots, or more subtle tactics such as the complaints against Lewsey's white Barbadian under-manager of misdemeanours and inefficiency. While Lewsey's decision to rationalise estate production by cutting down the cane acreage and the hours of factory operation could be justified to the owner by a genuine local labour shortage, his reduction of the slaves' individual workload and the granting of other concessions could only be rationalised on grounds similar to those put forward by Adam Smith under the principle of Enlightened Self-Interest:

that inhumanity and coercive attempts to raise the tempo of work were counterproductive.

As Lewsey testified to the Parliamentary Inquiry of 1831-32, before he made concessions concerning the hours of sleep allowed the slaves during the cane harvest (thus cutting down the number of tasks to be completed) his head field driver had found it impossible to wake up his gang in the morning or to keep them at work without the whip. Always a half dozen labourers had gone absent, either hiding in the cane pieces to sleep or running farther away. As the driver expressed it, 'those that had *Heart* to take the Flogging would come up and receive it and go to work and those that none would *Run*'. In this, Charles Lewsey was more or less echoing Robert Scott, a planter-attorney of Trelawny parish at the other end of Jamaica, who commented of the slaves at the same Inquiry: 'They are excessively impatient of control, if you exact more from them than you ought to do, they will not submit to it, but they know very well what duty they have to do on a plantation, and if no more is exacted they are very easily managed and require no harsh treatment whatever.'[10]

Similar processes can also be detected in the marginal colonies of Belize and the Bahamas. Despite significant differences in their economies – between logwood and mahogany cutting in the former and a mainly maritime economy punctuated by an era of attempted plantations in the latter, with only the economy punctuated by an era of attempted plantations in the latter, with only the economy centred around the small colonial capitals more or less similar – the proto-proletarianisation of the Bahamian slaves showed remarkable parallels with those of Belize as analysed by Nigel Bolland (1991:600-11).[11] In 1784, before the Loyalist influx, a German visitor said of the slaves of the 'Old Inhabitants' that they were able to earn money for themselves in their free time, being left 'undisturbed in the enjoyment of what they gain from other work' on the payment of 'a small weekly sum' to their owners. Bahamian slaves, he added, had 'never experienced the inhuman and cruel treatment which draws so many sighs from their brethren in the neighbouring sugar-islands or the rice-planta-tions of the main-land' (Schoepf 1911; see also Craton & Saunders 1992:171-74).

Several thousand of the latter slaves involuntarily migrated with their Loyalist owners in the 1790s after the American War of Independence and were put to the onerous work of clearing the bush for cotton production or toiling at the salt-pans. The owners' preference was for gang-work, but the difficulties of control and Bahamian traditions, as much as the failure of the cotton plantations made inevitable by poor soils and insect pests, determined that task-work soon became the general norm. By 1823, Bahamian slave-owners reported that task-work had been universal throughout the islands 'within the memory of the oldest of us' for all slaves except domestics, tradespeople, or sailors.[12]

For the two latter categories, and for an ever-widening spectrum of Bahamian slaves, moreover, partial self-employment became ever more firmly entrenched. Governor Carmichael Smyth reported in 1832 that it had 'long been a custom in this Colony to permit the more intelligent of the Slaves, & more particularly Artificers, to find employment for themselves & to pay to their owners either the whole or such a proportion of what they may gain as may be agreed upon between the Parties'.[13] Two years earlier the governor had similarly reported (with some exaggeration): 'The greater part of the slave population here are seafaring people. The crews in the wrecking vessels are in great measure composed of slaves – these people are paid in shares, & they almost all invariably work out their freedom.'[14]

Although modest, the rate of manumission in the Bahamas towards the end of slavery was still the highest in the West Indies, rising from 3.1 per 1,000 slaves in 1808, to 4.5 per 1,000 in 1820, and 11.4 per 1,000 in 1834. The usual method was for owners to allow the slaves to pay their agreed value in return for manumission (plus the owner's bond until that was abolished) either in a lump sum or instalments – even allowing the slaves to build up a credit balance by retaining their share of hiring wages. By the system of self-hire with manumission as a goal, the will of the slaves to achieve full wage-earning independence could be said to have reciprocated neatly with their owners' determination to capitalise on a declining resource; first by gaining a share of the slaves' wages by hiring them out (having no profitable employment at home), and then receiving recompense for their slave property through manumission (at a time of generally low and further declining slave prices) (Higman 1984:380-81; Craton & Saunders 1992:8-10, 258-96).

On the other hand, it might be argued that even in the Bahamas the rate of slave-bought manumissions was surprisingly low (barely reaching one per cent) and that countervailing forces were at work. The majority of slaves actually wanted the best of both systems – virtual self-employment while retaining those handouts that their owners were obliged by law to provide –whereas the masters did their utmost to retain all their slaves' labour value, raising the price of manumission as high as possible, and at the very end of slavery holding on to their property in the hope of generous compensation from the imperial government.

Certainly, as Howard Johnson (1991) and the present author with Gail Saunders (Craton & Saunders 1992:358-80) and Godwin Friday (1984) have shown, the prevalence of 'working out on wages' in the Bahamas and the problems which resulted are attested to by the governors' correspondence, the often frenzied manoeuvrings of the Bahamian legislators, and by the numerous advertisements concerning hiring and running away in the local newspapers. In 1808 a local act was passed with the expressed purpose of controlling the practice of hiring out. It was no longer lawful for slave-owners on New Providence (Nassau's island) to allow their slaves 'to hire themselves out to work, either on board of vessels or on the shore, as porters or labourers, without first registering the names of such slaves in the police office, and obtaining therefrom a copper badge, with the number of such slave marked thereon; which badge is to be work on the jacket or frock of the slave, in a conspicuous manner'.[15]

This act (which in any case only applied to labouring slaves) seems to have been ineffectual, and slave-owners resorted to more subtle forms of controlling or appropriating the slaves' labour value. As Governor Carmichael Smyth went on to report in 1832:

Almost every Slave is anxious to enjoy this species of Liberty [self-hiring] & will readily promise & undertake to pay more than, at times, he may be able to acquire. Many of them have a sort of account current with their owners; & in hopes of better times get deeper into debt each month. There are of course some dishonest and dissolute Slaves who will spend whatever they may gain & state to their owners that they have not been able to get work. The day of reckoning is however sure to arrive at last & I have had occasion to observe, in the weekly returns, Slaves repeatedly confined in the Work-House & punished for not paying wages.[16]

A rising proportion of the 500 or so slave runaway advertisements in the local newspaper related to disputes over wages and hiring conditions. One remarkable early absconder was the African-born ship carpenter Dick, who broke out of jail in 1799 after being put there for 'not paying his wages regularly'. Returned to his owner, the master ship carpenter Timothy Cox, who had offered a $20 reward, Dick was absent again within a month. 'Run away on Monday last, immediately after having received his Wages for four Days Hire from Mr. Ritchie,' advertised Timothy Cox, 'a Negro Man called Dick belonging to the Subscriber, a Ship Carpenter and well known about Town. He frequently saunters around the Western Suburbs, and there is Reason to suspect he is occasionally employed there'.[17]

Runaway advertisements frequently mentioned or suggested disputes over wages. They often referred to slaves who had stayed away after their job was supposed to have finished, and almost always referred to persons, whites and free coloureds as well as slaves, who "harboured" them – these persons being sometimes threatened with direr punishments than the runaways themselves. Some runaways were clearly seeking a better job or a more congenial or complaisant employer, while others ran away for fear of being transported away from their familiar location, family, or customary employment – such as Nassau tradesmen or domestics threatened with fieldwork in the Out Islands or agricultural labourers consigned to work on the dreaded salt-pans. In nearly all such cases, slaves were making a statement of wishes and placing pressure upon their owners. On their side, owners ran the whole gamut of threats and inducements in order to get their workers back, or at least to regain control over their labour value. From the beginning, however, the advertisements disclose that the nego-tiating power was not entirely one-sided. A surprising number of advertisers promised that they would not punish slaves who 'returned to their duty'. And at least one (as early as 1784) made the remarkable offer to permit the slaves to choose another owner – presumably if such a person would be willing to buy them (Craton & Saunders 1992:379). Such a symbolic mutual rejection of power or even paternalistic relationships was surely the closest one could ever get to a true dialectic between a proletariat and a bourgeois employing class within a system of chattel slavery.

METROPOLITAN LIBERAL IDEOLOGY AND THE
TRANSITIONAL PERIOD, 1808-38

The will of the British West Indian slaves to work their own grounds whenever they could, and to work for wages when they had (or wanted) to, was quite congruent with what metropolitan philanthropists and their missionary agents considered civilised alternatives to slavery, and what imperial policy-makers, under the influence of liberal economists, were coming to regard as a more generally efficient, as well as more polite system. Few planters, however, were won over by arguments that free wage labour would be preferable to slavery and, standing on their property rights in the slaves and their labour; stood out for compensation and a transitional period of compulsory labour where necessary (called apprenticeship). They also, of course, argued vehemently for the continuance of their plantocratic privileges – asserting that direct imperial rule in the new Crown Colonies was contrary both to the historical right to self-legislation enjoyed by the older colonies and to the liberal ideal of *laissez-faire* itself.

The ending of the British slave trade by 1808 had already greatly affected labour conditions in the West Indies and changed attitudes towards slavery and its alternatives on all sides. Denied fresh recruits and faced by a declining and strongly resistant slave population in those colonies with the greatest labour need, planters dug in their heels, while philanthropists and policy-makers, appalled at the evidence of population decline revealed in the slave registration returns after 1815, moved with increasing resolution towards what colonial official James Stephen (1824) among others, argued was the healthier, as well as more efficient, alternative of a free wage labour system.[18] A staged emancipation with slave-owners' compensation was imposed on the Crown Colonies and negotiated for those that were self-legislating in 1834. But the four-year apprenticeship phase and following few years was a period of even more vigorous adjustment on both sides, in which gains for the more fortunate ex-slaves in the form of workable lands, saleable produce and liveable wages were predictably countered by planter complaints that their former slaves would only continue to work on the plantations when it suited them, for wages were so high that they threatened the economy's ruin.

It was not mainly the wage labour system that threatened the plantation economy, however, but the larger adjustments to a free worldwide market economy, the first-fruit of which was the catastrophic collapse of the prices of export produce at the end of the 1840s. The former slave-owners and their legatees showed a tireless ingenuity in retaining political power, adjusting to new economic realities (becoming to some extent an agrocommercial bourgeoisie), and even adapting allegedly liberal reforms to their own advantage. They were helped by a metropole that while ostensibly dedicated to *laissez-faire* principles directed what aid it gave to the West Indies to the plantation sector rather than aiding peasant production. Ironically, for most of the former slaves the status of part-peasant, part-proletarian which had seemed so preferable to slavery was now an unavoidable choice, with the cards stacked in favour of those who continued to control the political system, the allocation of land and at least the local aspects of the economy. So, as was instinctively felt by many ex-slaves at the time, and has been more clearly discerned by most recent historians, the British West Indian plantocracies and other local oligarchies, imperial policy-makers, and even missionaries, in the longer term conspired to fix the peasant and labouring classes in a Gramscian hegemonic grip.[19]

Missionaries, education and the liberated Africans

The role of white missionaries was most equivocal of all. In the early days of plantation slavery, British planters had been ambivalent about Christianising their slaves, for just as Roman Law continued to subsume slavery as an institution after English law (at least in the metropole) had given it up, so established Protestantism lacked the confidence long enjoyed by Roman Catholicism that religion could help to make good slaves (as well as godly masters). While occasional lip service to Christianising the slaves was made in the British colonial codes, sectarian missionaries specifically targeting the 'godless' slaves – first Moravians (1754) and Methodists (1787), with LMS (London Missionary Society) Congregationalists, Baptists and Presbyterians following between 1808 and 1820 – were only tolerated as long as they upheld slavery, and to the degree that they aimed to make their converts good Christian workers (Grant 1976; Turner 1982).

Many planters remained bitterly opposed to sectarian missionaries, especially when LMS slave converts were prominent in the 1823 Demerara rebellion and so many Baptists were involved in the 1831-32 Jamaican uprising that it was popularly known as the Baptist War. But the tide of conversion was irreversible, and efforts were being by regime and missionaries alike to ensure through preaching and teaching that the Christian message was not subversive. Even the established Anglican church made belated efforts – including mass baptisms – to ensure that they would not entirely 'lose' the slaves.[21]

Although the attractions of Christianity to the slaves were more spiritual than social, the established church and missionary societies alike were as concerned to teach 'civilized behaviour' as to preach correct theology. All churches played a vital role in providing education for West Indian blacks in the transition out of slavery, beginning with Sunday schools in the last decades of slavery and providing the majority of full-time schools after emancipation, with some help from the Negro Education Grant voted by the imperial government between 1834 and 1846.[22]

Once emancipation removed the ambivalencies of the churches' role, what the white clerics preached and taught was unequivocally conservative and intended to sustain the socioeconomic order. Some sectarian missionaries – largely to ensure close-knit communities of client adherents – sponsored peasant-style villages, and were thus accused by the planters of encouraging the ex-slaves' 'flight from the estates'. Missionaries in general also seem to have had more success with peasant and urban blacks than with wage-earning proletarians, catering, indeed, more effectively to those who were most free to make their own choices. But all missionaries accepted the desirability and inevitability of the ex-slaves' shift into the cash and wage economy, and the qualities they aimed to inculcate were the 'civilised' and 'respectable' virtues of hard work, reliability, fidelity, thrift and the stable, monogamous, nuclear family. More fundamentally, church inspired schools (virtually all West Indian schools for blacks) taught only those subjects that would be useful for 'useful citizens' of the 'lower orders': no skills that would help them to a different or better employment, bare literacy in reading and writing, minimal arithmetic, plentiful doses of the Christian scriptures and homiletic anecdotes masquerading as history (Gordon 1963:19-42).

Such values were perfectly attuned to what the policy-makers at the Colonial Office – headed by the ardently evangelical Anglican James Stephen – believed were the essence of liberal principles. The marriage of official policy with the missionary impulse, and the role of both in guiding the British West Indian blacks through the transition out of slavery, is best exemplified by the confident statement by Colonial Secretary Lord John Russell in 1841 that explained the reduction and removal of the Negro Education Grant by 1846: that the purposes for which it had been instituted had now been effected (Gordon 1963:38).

The Negro Education Grant of 1834-46, however, was only one of the means by which liberal policy-makers induced or facilitated the translation of a predominantly slave into a predominantly wage-earning work-force in the British West Indies, without permanently upsetting the established local white regimes. The process had been latent since the British slave trade itself had been abolished, in the provisions for the 'apprenticing' of slaves liberated from illegal British or foreign slave-trading vessels. As early as March 1808, an Order-in-Council decreed that such recaptured slaves as could not be repatriated or voluntarily recruited into the British Army or Navy (the war still being on) were to be placed in charge of the Collector of Customs in the nearest British colony. The Collector would then bind them as apprentices (usually for seven but sometimes for 14 years) to 'humane masters or mistresses to learn such Trade and Handicrafts or Employments as they seem from their bodily and other Qualities most likely to be fit for and to gain their livelihood most comfortably after their terms of Apprenticeship or Servitude shall expire' (Asiegbu 1969:27).

The largest total of liberated Africans – some 33,000 – were resettled in the recent colony of Sierra Leone. But from the first slave cargoes seized and adjudicated in 1811, through the treaties imposed on Portugal and Spain in the 1820s, down to the effective ending of the slave trade to Cuba and Brazil in the 1860s, many thousands of liberated Africans were resettled in the British West Indies; not just in colonies like the Bahamas and Belize with more space than obvious labour needs, but in the newly acquired Crown Colonies of Trinidad, Guyana and St Lucia where there were genuine labour shortages. In Jamaica, the planters claimed a labour shortage after the legitimate slave trade ended, and after emancipation they were eager for any labourers who might be more easily coerced than the local ex-slaves. In all colonies, officials were instructed to supervise the welfare of the liberated Africans, and such provisions may have been relatively effective in the Crown Colonies. But as Monica Schuler (1980) has shown, the liberated Africans in Jamaica were treated little different from – and suffered even worse than – slaves, having only their inevitably slow acclimatisation, their lack of usable skills, and their native ingenuity, to protect them from complete exploitation.[23]

As Howard Johnson (1991:55-68) has recently suggested, though, it is the way that the liberated Africans were regarded and treated in the Bahamas that tells us most about the transition from slavery to an allegedly free labour system (see also Dalleo 1984; Saunders 1985:193-204). At first the Africans were kept in camps at government expense, but females and those males not willing to sign up for the navy or the local battalion of the West India Regiment were offered as domestic or labouring apprentices. Local employers, openly complaining of the Africans' lack of sophistication, treated them as far as they could as an underclass. At first, these newcomers could be more easily exploited than slaves, and after slavery ended they constituted a competitive reservoir of cheap labour. An African Board was appointed to prevent liberated Africans being given short rations or extended working hours, tricked into an extension of their apprenticeship terms, or illegally shipped off to the Out Islands in labouring gangs, particularly to work the salt-pans. But officials lacked the power, money and probably the will to remedy all abuses. They measured their success by the number of liberated Africans for whom they found employers, regretting the alternative, which was to settle them on tracts of Crown land, where it was feared they would be an expensive embarrassment to the government.

Such a case was the scandalous deployment in 1832 of some 400 'Angolans' on barren Highborne Cay in the Exumas, where many perished from hunger and thirst. In fact, the majority of liberated Africans once freed from their indentures and left on their own succeeded quite well. But the official attitude towards them can be gauged from the correspondence of the allegedly liberal Governor Smyth and his appointed supervisors concerning the government settlements, such as Carmichael, named after Smyth himself. The first superintendent appointed complained of the Africans' godlessness and inveterate promiscuity, their failure to work to order, their tendency to squat on unappropriated land, and to wander away from the settlement. The governor professed a strict paternalism, sponsoring an Anglican chapel, regular visits by a clergyman and doctor, a schoolhouse for adults as well as children, a 'female school of industry', and a resident policeman. Moreover, there was no shortage of high-minded volunteers, mostly single ladies, eager to bring 'civilisation' to the unfortunate Africans. Of the 20 children under the tutelage of a Miss Scott in the Adelaide School in 1835 it was said by the slightly less reactionary of the two local newspapers:

> Some of them have learned the Alphabet and are spelling words of three letters, are spending part of the day in reading and attending to the various lessons that are taught, and part in learning to sew. When it is remembered that these children of African parents were growing up in ignorance of all that is useful and good, and to whom the English language was almost unknown . . . [we] cannot but regard the establishment of a School among them as one of the most valuable favours that they have received from the British nation.[24]

Certainly, those outside the protective orbit of government often fared worse, in New Providence competing, as the master class intended, in the local produce and labour markets, and in the Out Islands sometimes almost becoming debt peons under a prototypical 'truck system' of payment in kind rather than cash, and credit advances. In 1827, for example, Governor Smyth's predecessor described liberated Africans working in the fields, at the salt-pans, in cutting ships' timbers and quarrying stones in the Turks Islands for a white family called Lightbourne, 'The Holder Lightbourne would be earning two Dollars and a half for each pr. week,' he wrote, 'and the Africans would be receiving from him each 8 Quarts of Corn pr. week and two suits of Osnaburgs pr. ann; which together would not cost the Holder one days earnings of the Africans – a quarter Dollar pr. week which was given also, I believe, to the African might make the weekly cost to the Owner about one days earnings.'

Governor Smyth's successor reported to Lord John Russell in 1840 of other liberated African apprentices toiling at the salt pans: 'In some instances they work on Shares [that is, some salt for themselves, most for the master], in others they receive from their employers, Eight Quarts of Indian

Corn – 2 lb of Salt Fish or Meat, 2 Hs of Molasses or Sugar Weekly – Two Dollars a Month as Wages and three Suits of clothes annually with Medical attendance when sick.'[25]

The ex-slave apprenticeship system

In all respects, the method of apprenticing the liberated Africans provided a trial run for the more general system of apprenticeship by which the West Indian white oligarchies effected the transition out of slavery between 1834 and 1838, if not also suggesting means by which some of the methods of exploitation from the slavery era could be perpetuated.

Although the general form of apprenticeship emanated from the Colonial Office, there were local options and variations in its operation. Two colonies, indeed, opted out of the apprenticeship phase altogether and went straight from slavery to the free wage labour: Bermuda and Antigua. In Bermuda, the mainly maritime and domestic slaves had long been involved in the cash and wage economy, and in any case had virtually no alternative but to continue working for their former owners. In Antigua, the planters in 1826 had somewhat whimsically offered to sell the whole island and its slaves to the Colonial Office for large-scale experimentation in the operation of a free wage system (Ward 1978:203). Many plantations were struggling but continued to monopolise the land, so that ex-slaves had no chance of setting up as independent peasants, and were immediately forced to compete for the limited and declining wage-earning opportunities. Antigua can even be accorded the dubious distinction of instituting, by a local act of 1834, a system of labour contracts enforced by the local courts which as 'the Antigua system' served as a useful model for other colonies once apprenticeship was terminated (Hall 1971:28; Bolland 1981:595).

It is perhaps surprising that the two colonies where conditions were most similar to Bermuda and Antigua, respectively the Bahamas and Barbados, actually opted for apprenticeship; in the former case probably because of the surplus of underdeveloped land, and in the latter perhaps because of the planters' fear of organised unrest and of the ex-slaves upsetting the social equilibrium by roaming the island in search of the best employers.

In all colonies where apprenticeship was imposed or adopted, there were great local variations in the amounts of work exacted for the 45 hours per week of compulsory labour for former owners, and in the wages paid for work in the remainder of the working days. As far as was possible, the standards were laid down by committees of planters and other employers at the parochial level. But the very variation in what constituted a daily or hourly task in every branch of labouring activity – indeed the very assumption that tasks rather than simple hours of work would be the measure – showed that what had been customarily negotiated in slavery was at least as deciding as the variations in soils, topography, climate and season of the year. Even more significantly, the variation in hourly and daily wages paid reflected great practical differences in the cash value of labour and the relative power of labourers and employers, even before a fully competitive free wage labour system came into operation.

The tendency of the former owners to assess their slave property at the highest possible level for compensation purposes, and their willingness to negotiate self-manumission even up to the last months of the apprentice-ship period, gave the apprentices a sense of both their relative and absolute labour value, as well as valuable transactional experience. Apprenticeship, though, was scarcely anywhere successful from either the planters' or the ex-slaves' viewpoint. The planters set the task-rate as high and wages as low as they thought possible, while the apprentices naturally went even further than to resist both tendencies – to show unwillingness to work at all without wages when a free wage labour system was already scheduled so soon ahead. It was because of the effects of the coercion which had to be employed to get the apprentices to work as much as the feeling that apprenticeship was neither necessary or workable that brought the system to a premature conclusion in 1838.[26]

The ending of apprenticeship, however, merely accelerated the process of adjustment by masters and employees already well under way. Suggesting the fulfilment of prophecies made since the 1820s, planters complained of a wholesale flight of the labourers from the estates and a consequent shortage of labour, especially at the busiest times in the agricultural cycle – for planters and peasants alike – when labourers were most needed on the estates but expected wages which the planters regarded as uneconomic. Undoubtedly ex-slaves did transfer into preferred lifestyles – peasant agri-culture on their own lands or life in towns – and this caused problems in many colonies, especially in British Guiana, Trinidad and Jamaica. But studies by Douglas Hall (1978) and the present author (1978:275-315) have suggested that the alleged 'flight' has been exaggerated and that the process was much more complex than the planters claimed (Chace 1988; Higman 1990; Trouillot 1989).

IMMEDIATE POST-SLAVERY ADJUSTMENTS

A detailed look at most sugar estates still active during the first decade after 1838 discloses that most of the adjustments made on both sides were entirely consonant simply with the ending of a system whereby all slaves were tied to their masters and for whom the masters had legal responsibility, irrespective of the precise labour demands of the estate. Responsibility for the ineffective members of the community – infants, elderly and the incurably sick – immediately shifted from owners to the ex-slaves' families. A more resolute shift into subsistence farming was therefore a necessity. A more rational management of the plantations, moreover, demanded a much greater periodicity in the employment of labourers, so that efficient plantations maintained a comparatively small nucleus of permanent workers; predominantly factory operatives, craftsmen and other types of relatively élite workers, virtually all males. At the times of peak demand, especially the cane-cutting season, a large temporary work-force was employed. This also naturally tended towards the partial peasantisation of the labouring force. A third major way in which the simple change out of a slavery system subtly transformed plantation society was the tendency, in which the choice of planters and ex-slaves concurred, to make the field work-force as predominantly male as that of the factories had always been, cutting down as far as possible the 60 per cent female component of the field work-force.

All these trends are detectable in the few early plantation wage employment records that have survived. When the planters complained (as to the British Parliamentary Inquiry of 1848) of the flight of the ex-slaves from wage employment and of their inability to get enough workers (especially males) except at ruinous wages, what they really meant was that they were unable to persuade enough ex-slaves to fit their ideal; that is, to keep a minimal nucleus of faithful retainers throughout the year and for sufficient male labourers to be available when they were wanted, for the lowest possible wages. The quest for this ideal, in the face of the ex-slaves own preference for peasant framing, the incompatibility of the annual cycles of peasant and plantation production, and the ex-slaves' sheer ingenuity in negotiating the best possible terms, explains both the tension between planters and ex-slaves and the forms of employer-employee transaction.

In Jamaica, planters more or less unsuccessfully tried to reduce their wage bills by charging ex-slaves rent for their cottages and customary grounds. In practice, there was generally enough adjacent undeveloped land to enable the ex-slaves to desert their former quarters for new villages and to squat on farmable hillsides and glades. In many cases, the planters did not even discourage squatting on lands they technically owned, especially if those lands were surveyed and the squatters identified, regarding the squatters as a convenient, and theoretically evictable, reservoir of seasonal labour. In Jamaica and Barbados alike, permanent workers became tied cottagers, while in nearly all colonies forms of labour tenancy were negotiated. The terms of employment, wages offered and conditions under which tenants could be evicted, varied according to the relative availability of labour, the demand for it and the harshness of the local laws.[27]

Only in colonies like Trinidad and Guiana with a genuine labour shortage and much fertile spare land was the balance weighted towards the ex-slave labourer, and even there only relatively, and not for long. In marginal or decaying colonies, such as Belize, the Bahamas and, perhaps, the Virgin Islands, some ex-slaves were left in a kind of benign neglect, at least for a time. At the other extreme, though, was Barbados, where labour was plentiful, spare land virtually non-existent and wages a quarter of those in Trinidad. At the same time, plantocratic laws and courts applied the harshest conditions concerning the tenure of tied 'chattel houses' and condoned eviction for failure to work on the employers' terms, yet placed great difficulties in the way of those labourers wishing to migrate to more favourable areas (Beckles 1990:102-47).

Stipendiary magistrates, law and order

The interests of first the apprentices and liberated Africans, and then the ex-slaves and all other ordinary blacks, were supposed to be protected by Stipendiary Magistrates (SMs), appointed by the imperial government from 1834 onwards to counteract the locally appointed white Justices of the Peace (JPs). With certain honourable exceptions, however, the SMs were reluctant to challenge and incapable of effectively countering the interests of the local whites. The SMs (retired military officers and impoverished gentry for the most part, including many Anglo-Irishmen) were, moreover, indelibly predisposed by class and temperament to favour an ordered over a more open society, and employers and landowners over employees and the landless. They were also exponents of a corpus of law that while ostensibly liberal was similar slanted, and in the final analysis were the salaried servants of an imperial authority that in the face of tightening economic conditions gave what help it afforded to the plantations, planters and other colonial oligarchs, rather than to mere peasants and proletarians (Burn 1937; Green 1976; Marshall 1977a; Cox 1990; McDonald 1990).

A study of the writings left by the SMs, particularly their correspondence through colonial governors to the Colonial Office, discloses that their primary concern was to establish peaceful, orderly and effective relations between ex-slaves and their former masters, now landlords and employers. Many SMs prided themselves on the promotion of written contracts – dealing with share-cropping arrangements and labour tenancies as well as labour contracts strictly defined. These contracts were assumed to be of reciprocal advantage, and undoubtedly gave ex-slaves a legal status as negotiating parties for the first time. But they were still subject to the general operation of laws slanted towards the landlord and employer and against the tenant and employee. Despite the steady liberalisation of metropolitan law throughout the nineteenth century, land law still greatly favoured the holders of registered freehold title over those with leasehold or squatter tenures. Vagrancy, police and poor laws virtually made it a crime not to have 'visible means of support' and made the workhouses for the unemployed and unemployable as unattractive and arduous as possible. In addition, masters and servants and combination laws actually made criminal the failure by workers to fulfil implied contracts by leaving employment in mid-week or mid-task, or any attempt by labourers to organise themselves. And as in the metropole, the liberalisation of the law was accompanied by the creation of new police forces, which, although doubtlessly better regulated and less corrupt than formerly, were at the same time more effective in enforcing the law (Beckles 1990:102-47).

To describe the process in just one colony, the first SMs in the Bahamas in the 1830s and 1840s zealously toured the Out Islands, tried disputes and negotiated contracts between former slaves and former owners, praised those ex-slaves who industriously and peacefully worked for themselves and for what wages were available, and actually chastised those landowners who tried to exact excessive shares, evicted unwilling workers, or insisted on payment in kind instead of fair cash wages. But at the same time the SMs and the governors to whom they reported had a predilection for those Out Islanders who were hard-working, law-abiding, thrifty, regular church-go-ers with a respectable family life and eager to provide education for their children. In supervising the communities of ex-slaves, the ideal of SMs and governors seems to have been an integrated and nucleated village based on the old slave units, dominated by church, school and government building that could serve as court, police station and lock-up.

For it was not an ideal that was expected to be achieved simply by the magic of *laissez-faire*. In the colonial capital, Nassau, the focus of all social, political and economic activity, a small but efficient, professional and eventually even paramilitary, police force was gradually created between 1835 and 1888, at first locally recruited but, following imperial practice, increasingly drawn from outside the colony particularly from Barbados (Johnson 1991:110-24; Craton & Saunders, 1997). This force, however, was of limited effectiveness throughout such a scattered archipelago. From the time of emancipation, governors and SMs were also involved in setting up a local constabulary – necessarily on the cheap – drawn from those members of the community who already enjoyed a good reputation and respect, and were often in fact former slave headmen. As Governor Cole-brooke wrote when originating the system in 1835, such unpaid Special Constables ought to be appointed in a ratio of one to each ten families 'according to local circumstances'. They would have no power to act unless called on by a magistrate 'to assist in the suppression of tumults and disorder', although they would be at all times 'competent to advise the Apprentices to preserve order' and could always advise the magistrates of trouble before it got out of hand. Ideally, wrote Colebrooke, they would therefore be drawn from the 'Heads of families who are thought well of by their employers, and who are possessed of some influence with the Apprentices'.[28]

Imperial government and colonial oligarchies

Imperial administrators naturally assumed that colonial social legislation would echo 'liberal' trends in the metropole but certainly wold not exceed them. Given the incomplete 'civilisation' of the Afro-Caribbean majority, indeed, they would rather expect to lag behind. Imperial inertia, moreover, decreed that, despite *laissez-faire* ideology, what aid continued to be given to the colonies would accrue to the planation system, the plantocracies, and other local ruling classes, rather than to peasant production, the emergent peasantries, or other ex-slaves and liberated Africans.

At the most general level, such inertial thinking (rather than the principle of not meddling unnecessarily in colonial affairs) explains the reluctance to extend the principle of direct Crown Colony rule beyond those colonies acquired in the late French wars: British Guiana, Trinidad and St Lucia. It spread nowhere else before the scandal of the suppression of the Morant Bay Rebellion of 1865 led to the dissolution of the Jamaican Assembly in the following year. It was applied very slowly elsewhere, and never imposed on Barbados, Bermuda and the Bahamas. These colonies were regarded both as sufficiently untroubled to be left alone, and, not coincidentally, to have sufficiently large white minorities to manage efficiently and peacefully their own affairs through self-legislation (Ayearst 1960; Lewis 1968:95-288; Dookhan 1975:112-28).

The colonial office vetoed blatant attempts to deny the franchise to Africans and all ex-slaves, and the most extreme cases of local legislatures using the taxation system to deprive poor non-whites of the fruits of their labour (or to force them in effect to work for wages against their will). But this did not lead to a democratic or predominantly non-white electorate, or to more than an ineffectual handful of non-white members of the legislatures, in any colony. The bulk of colonial revenues, moreover, continued to be paid by the under-represented non-white majority in all the self-legislating colonies. Even in the colonies ostensibly ruled directly by the Colonial Office the white planters retained disproportionate influence or even power; in British Guiana by monopolising the Court of Policy left over from the Dutch system of local government and in all colonies by continuing to be chosen for the Governors' Councils.

At least four policy decisions by the imperial authorities were more directly aimed at aiding the beleaguered planters – in the Crown Colonies at least as much as in the self-legislating. The decision to postpone the final removal of the protective sugar duties from 1848 to 1854 in response to desperate pleas from the planters was no more than a temporary palliative. The Encumbered Estates Act of 1854 (designed by the formerly slave- and plantation-owning but now Liberal Chancellor of the Exchequer and future Prime Minister, William Ewart Gladstone) changed the laws of bankruptcy to enable the sale of estates hopelessly encumbered with debt and was also intended merely as a relief for distressed planters, but seems to have had more fundamental effects. Far from unlocking the prime plantation lands for peasant farmers, in the fertile Crown Colonies of Guiana and Trinidad it facilitated the consolidation of plantation holdings which, with the help of improved technology, made possible the necessary economies of scale that led to the nearest British equivalents to the Cuban *centrales*. In Barbados and Jamaica too it permitted some consolidation, but in the former more notably enabled the resilient local plantocrats sufficiently to redeploy and refinance their holdings that they were able to maintain a united front against any desperate renegades who wished to break up their estates for sale to non-white smallholders or independent villagers. Even in Jamaica, where the sugar industry was almost beyond saving and a considerable number of decayed estates were in fact broken up into small-holdings, a more obvious effect on the Encumbered Estates Act was the purchase of former sugar plantations by enterprising capitalists for knock-down prices (although still out of the reach of smallholding peasants) and their conversion into virtual cattle ranches called pens (Beachey 1957:1-39; Shepherd 1990).

East Indian indentureship

Much more wide-reaching was the decision of the Colonial Office to, permit if not always encourage, what Hugh Tinker (1974) has termed 'a new system of slavery', in the form of indentured labour, imported over-whelmingly from the Indian subcontinent. From the end of formal slavery up to its termination during the First World War, this system brought some 420,000 East Indians to the British West Indies, only a quarter of whom ever returned home. Of the total number of migrants, some 240,000 went to British Guiana, 144,000 to Trinidad, 36,000 to Jamaica, and about 10,000 divided between St Lucia, St Vincent and Grenada – an average flow at least half that of the African slave trade at its peak and having an even greater sustained impact in the two areas of greatest concentration.[29]

East Indian migration stemmed from the ability of the Indian subcontinent to fulfil the absolute need for labour in the new plantation colonies, a need which was exacerbated by the comparative ease with which the 'Creole'-ex-slaves were able to obtain lands and set up 'free villages' of their own and were consequently unwilling to toil on the plantations save when they wished to do so, for adequate wages. After 1834, Guianese and Trinidadian planters sought voluntary labour recruits wherever they could: from Portuguese Madeira, China and Africa. John Gladstone, the future prime minister's father, tapped a new source of migrants in the south-east-ern and central regions of British India. Gladstone found that 'hill coolies' could be persuaded to agree to work under indentures for five years, for nine to ten hours a day compared with the apprentices' 7.5 hours, for monthly wages that in effect (along with free housing and some issues of food and clothing) were equivalent to the going rate for two daily tasks (Adamson 1972:42; Checkland 1971).

The mortality and general conditions for the first migrants were so horrific that the Colonial Office was led to impose the 'Stephen regulations' in September 1838, limiting written contracts to one year and verbal contracts to one month (as in most other colonies), which virtually amounted to a free wage labour system. For a time the planters tried to live with this system by relying on the flow of recruits, but the economic crisis of the late 1840s and the appointment of a series of planter or pro-planter governors enabled the local planters to persuade a vacillating Colonial Office to let them change the rules. The planters now funded immigration largely on the colonial revenues, constructed cunning systems of bounties for reindentures (coupled with monetary penalties for non-fulfilment of labour contracts), and cruelly tightened the terms of indenture and their enforcement. In this they were only intermittently and ineffectually challenged by the British Indian Government (Adamson 1972:42-47).

Even before the supposedly liberal Earl Grey left the Colonial Office in 1852, the Guianese planters had been able to obtain local ordinances that while theoretically establishing a one year minimum, made the normal indenture last three years, required a minimum five years' 'industrial residence' before the immigrant qualified for a return passage, and included provisions intended to ensure that immigrants reindentured themselves for a second five years. Immigrants not under contract were obliged to pay what amounted to a monthly fine equal to two daily tasks. For each monthly sum unpaid, the immigrant could be sentenced to 14 days at hard labour. Immigrants under contract could be apprehended without a warrant if found more than two miles from their estate without a ticket of leave. For every day away from work the immigrant not only forfeited his wages but was also required to pay his employer 24 cents. Six dollars per annum for lodging and three dollars for medical expenses were deducted from his wages.[30]

In the years between 1855 and 1870, when East Indian immigration was actually rising rapidly to its peak, conditions governing work tasks, wages and punishments were also at their tightest. The daily tasks, set at the time of apprenticeship, were so unrealistic that scarcely half the work-force was able to complete the weekly requirement of five daily tasks (worth a shilling each), and the average number of tasks completed per year was scarcely half the required annual total of 260. Yet since the minima were established by statute, the employer could obtain a judgement in the local courts against their employees 'every week or any week in the year'. As Alan Adamson (1972:111-12) states, the employer 'could also get a conviction for badly done or unfinished work, for neglecting or refusing to perform work, for drunkenness at work, abusive language, carelessness of employer's property, inciting to strike, or desertion'. Desertion itself was so loosely defined in the employer's favour – with the muster rolls used in evidence without question – that 'by this means a technical offence was every day laid up in store for every immigrant who behaved badly or could not be convicted on other grounds'.[31]

Although exceptional liberals such as Chief Justice Beaumont (dismissed by Governor Hincks in 1868) and ex-SM George Des Voeux spoke up for the East Indians against the Guianese plantocracy, magistrates, including the SMs, almost invariably took the planters' side. As Edward Jenkins memorably quoted an East Indian immigrant (speaking for so many British Indian labourers at that time) in *The Coolie: His Rights and Wrongs* (1871:103-4): 'O massa, no good go mahitee [magistrate] – Mahitee know manahee [manager] – go manahee's house – eat um breakfus – come court – no good Coolie go court – mahitee friend manahee: always for manahee, no for Coolie.' 'Not coincidentally, British Guiana was, in Adamson's words, 'the most heavily policed in the British West Indies', with its constabulary 'organized along military lines' (Adamson 1972:263; see also Ramsarran 1985).[32]

Working conditions in British Guiana reached a nadir in 1869 when there were serious strikes and riots centred on plantation Leonora. A Parliamentary Inquiry was held in the following year, but this did not in itself remedy conditions. So well-established was the system of indentured labour – and so many East Indians were still willing to migrate and stay in the West Indies – that in 1877, the year that British Guiana harvested the largest sugar crop in its history, the local plantocracy felt strong enough to abolish the system of reindentures. What this meant was simply that the real problem of a 'labour shortage' had now been solved. There was now a sufficient supply of indentured immigrants to provide the necessary permanent force on the plantations, while there were also enough freed East Indians competing with black creoles for seasonal labour that the employers were guaranteed workers when they needed them at wages they considered affordable. Thus the employers enjoyed the luxury of a competitive labour pool, with the additional bonus (for them) of a competition increasingly tinged with ethnic discord.

Much the same process explains the apparent anomaly that Jamaica (and to an extent the colonies of St Lucia, St Vincent and Grenada), a declining plantation economy without a labour shortage strictly defined, nonetheless engaged in the business of importing East Indians. These provided a reliable, tied and ethnically distinct work-force that would both guarantee a small permanent (and generally faithful) labour pool, while forcing the unwilling seasonal labourers to come in to work when needed for minimal wages, through competition. Being such a minority component in the colony's work-force, moreover, they were denied even the limited chances of coordinating and operating as an ethnic subclass enjoyed by the East Indian workers of British Guiana and Trinidad (Sohal 1979).

The immigration of East Indians had its most obvious effects in propping up, and in the cases of Trinidad and British Guiana even extending, a sugar industry threatened with decline. Also, in providing a new work-force of bound labourers and enlarging the competitive labour pool, it both rein-forced the sociopolitical power of the planters and militated against any attempt by the wage-earning ex-slaves and liberated Africans (as well as the formerly indentured East Indians themselves) to become an effective proletariat. The interests of those whose ambitions were to be peasants (or at least peasant-proletarians) were compromised even more by the fourth feature of imperial policy designed to aid the old plantocratic regime: the way that the doctrine of dear land (or Crown Land sold only at a 'sufficient price') was applied to the British West Indies, despite the fact that in its original formulation by Edward Gibbon Wakefield (1849) it was intended solely for colonies of new white settlers, such as Australia, New Zealand and Canada (Marx 1867; Bloomfield 1961).

Land, peasantisation and the Morant Bay Crisis

The privileged access to freehold land had always been one of the chief defining characteristics of British West Indian plantocracies,[33] and the British imperial government's attitude to Crown Land after emancipation entrenched rather than challenged this traditional dominance. Private land that was not protected from would-be peasant owners by high competitive prices as well as the united determination of planters not to split large estates into affordable small parcels, often reverted to the Crown for the non-payment of nominal quit rents. But this, despite the huge number of new freedmen eager for land, merely led to a steady increase in the amount of Crown Land rather than its redistribution to smallholders. The Colonial Office did authorise the sale of Crown Lands for as little as £1 an acre in the later 1830s, but local provisions (as in the Bahamas) first decreed that the land be auctioned with an 'upset' (and thus minimum) price of £1, and then laid such a high lower limit on the size of parcels sold as to place it out of the reach of ordinary blacks – even when the price was nominally reduced as low as 12 shillings an acre. This trend had the effect of encouraging planters or penkeepers, who had sufficient capital to buy large tracts at low prices per acre while effectively excluding impecunious freedmen (Craton 1987:88-114).

Freehold possession for would-be peasants was further restricted by the laws relating to squatters, by the attitudes of the authorities and planters towards the squatters, and by the tendency among Afro-Caribbean people to develop informal systems of customary tenure called family or generational land. The British tradition that uninterrupted possession for 21 years gave squatters the right to claim freehold tenure was adopted in the British West Indies, but the provision was extended to require 60 years' uninterrupted possession in the case of Crown Land. Needless to say, the requisite court procedures dealing with providing title and eviction were complex, protracted and expensive, and thus heavily slanted against the poor and often illiterate squatters. Obtaining land by squatters' rights over private land was therefore extremely difficult, and in the case of Crown Land virtually impossible.

As already mentioned, those planters with secure title (unable to obtain rents for houses and lands, formal labour tenancies, or free part-time labour in lieu of rents) were often quite content to allow ex-slaves to squat on their lands on the tacit assumption that they would offer their labour for wages when it was needed, only making sure that the squatters' possession was technically 'interrupted' from time-to-time, and that the threat of eviction was always held over the squatters' heads. Some canny planters, as in Jamaica, even went so far as to go through a form of sale of land to those squatting on their lands, ensuring that the sale and title were not formally registered, and having the additional assurance that custom would decree that the land would soon devolve to such a swathe of family members that it would be impossible to prove formal tenure in the courts, even by squatters' rights (Otterbein 1964; Clarke 1966; Besson 1987:13-45; Craton 1987).

That it was imperial policy as much as planter obstructionism which kept the would-be peasants from freehold ownership is borne out by the example of what happened in Jamaica after the plantocratic Assembly was disbanded and Crown Colony rule came into effect in 1866. The planters' virtual mortmain over the land had been one of the primary causes of the peasants' revolt around Morant Bay in 1865. Two years previously a recommendation by the Baptist missionary, Edward Underhill, and petitions from poor framers in St Anne's parish to provide relief in the form of cheap lands in small parcels had met with a cynical response called the Queen's Advice, enjoining hard work and thrift instead; that is, in effect, a proletarian rather than peasant means of subsistence.[34]

The most obvious and immediate effect of the Morant Bay Rebellion was the assumption of direct rule by the Colonial Office, but, as Veront Satchell (1991) has recently demonstrated, this was soon followed by a systematic tightening of the controls over Crown as well as privately owned lands that contributed to the progressive proletarianisation of the Jamaican rural population. Satchell singles out the District Courts Law and Quit Rent Forfeiture Laws of 1867 and the Registration of Titles Law of 1888 (all of which could be paralleled in most other British West Indian colonies) as ostensibly liberal reforms that had quite opposite effects. The first represented a general demand – backed up by extremely active Surveyor General's and Registrar General's department – that all lands be surveyed and all holdings registered. The second, although initially aimed at those holdings on which quit rents were in arrears, represented a more forceful policy of evictions for non-existent or dubious tenure. The final law, in due course, facilitated the redeployment of lands to those who, it was thought, could most efficiently develop them – which meant not smallholding peasants but new wage-paying plantation investors, particularly banana exporters.

As Satchell shows, between 1869 and 1900, 1,381 Jamaican squatters were evicted by the government from 33,208 acres of land (86 per cent of them between 1869 and 1879), the overwhelming majority of whom claimed less than 10 acres apiece. Evictions by private owners – sometimes without recourse to the courts or the aid of the police – at least doubled these figures. Besides this, the Jamaican government between 1887 and 1902 alone repossessed no less than 240,368 acres of land for the non-payment of quit rents. Contrary to the argument of Gisela Eisner (1961) that this process was paralleled by a willingness of the government to distribute lands to the peasants in leaseholds, Satchell points out that the seemingly impressive total of 63,500 acres leased by the government between 1869 and 1900 went to a mere 195 lessees, an average of 325 acres per person – scarcely peasant-sized holdings. Over the same period, the Jamaican government sold 53,400 acres in 817 lots, but to a mere 81 persons – an average of 659 acres per purchaser. As Satchell (1990: 7-8, 125-27) states, the majority of lessees and purchasers were 'merchants, professionals and business companies, who were actively acquiring land to help them take advantage of the lucrative banana, fruit and cinchona trades'. Only in the late 1890s did the Jamaican government make a calculated effort to sell

Crown Lands to small settlers, and then only on a small scale with limited success, while at the same time making extravagant concessions to private companies, such as the 76,800 acres granted to the West Indian Improvement Company alone.[35]

Thus far from speeding the process of peasantisation, during the period when the Jamaican population rose from 450,000 to 750,000, Crown Colony government policy, endorsing the will of the ruling class, ensured that the land formally owned by peasant farmers actually decreased, and that those denied formal tenure would be more than ever before constrained to offer themselves as wage labourers to more fortunate landowners or employers, either at home or abroad (Bryan 1991:266-77).

THE BRITISH WEST INDIES AND THE GLOBAL ECONOMY, 1865-1938

Jamaica and its people were the most obvious victims of the regional and global changes following the triumph of free trade and *laissez-faire* principles and capitalistic intensification. The number of Jamaican sugar plantations fell from 646 at emancipation to 162 in 1890 (to fall further to 74 by 1910), while Cuban sugar production over the same period multiplied ten times and eventually represented three-quarters of the world's cane sugar total – with the largest *centrales* each producing as much sugar as the whole of Jamaica. With only slight exaggeration it can be said that while in the 1790s Jamaica was the world's foremost sugar producer and Cuba was predominantly a ranching economy, by the 1890s the positions had been almost reversed – with Jamaica desperately searching for an alternative plantation export crop and its people forced by declining wage opportunities at home into seasonal or short-term migration elsewhere in the region (Moreno Fraginals 1978, 1985; Stubbs 1985; Zanetti & García 1987).

However, the transformation of world markets and the patterns of finance, transportation, refining and distribution (analysed most cogently, perhaps, by the Cuban scholar Francisco Moreno Fraginals) had parallel effects throughout the British West Indies, differing substantially according to local economic variations and varying more subtly through differences in the local class structure, but having the depression and exploitation of the work-force in common, and sharing, if unequally, its gradual transformation into an international class of migrant workers.

Hitherto, scholarship has concentrated on the most obvious areas: the new sugar colonies of British Guiana and Trinidad which remained competitive longest, and the oldest British sugar colony of all, Barbados, which retained its sugar monoculture, and even reached an all-time peak of production after Jamaica had entered its period of most rapid decline. There has also been some solid analytical study of the fast-fading sugar colonies and more diversified (and slightly more flexible) small plantation and peasant economies of the Leeward and Windward Islands (Lewis 1936; Hall 1971; Chace 1988; Marshall 1965, 1975; Phillips Lewis 1990). More recently, though, studies of even more marginal colonies, of the timber colony of Belize and of the maritime-based failed plantation colony of the Bahamas, have enabled Nigel Bolland and Howard Johnson to shed oblique new light on the British West Indies as a whole, particularly on the ways in which the local black peasants and proletarians became subject not just to global trends and forces, but, more directly, to the ways in which the local oligarchies transformed themselves into agro-commercial bourgeoisies (Bolland 1981, 1988, 1990; Johnson 1991).

Belize and the Bahamas

In Belize the ratio between land and available labour had always been high, so that the 'timber barons' had always been able to cut more or less where they wished and slaves in 1834 were valued higher there on the average than anywhere else in the British West Indies. Long before the end of slavery, the log-cutting work-force was virtually an undifferentiated proletariat in a competitive wage labour market, with slaves working alongside liberated Africans, non-white freedmen, and a few indigenous Mayas and Garifuna (Black Caribs, originally transported from St Vincent). After slavery ended, however, the Belize City timber magnates, with the connivance of the imperial government, were able to perpetuate their power through the control of the laws relating to land and labour, and by playing off the Belizean labourers against Mayan migrant workers from the Mexican Yucatan.

The control by the creole élite over the work-force became so strong that when mahogany prices fell in the late nineteenth century (mainly because of competition from other sources) the creole master class continued to prosper without being forced to resort to substantial mechanisation. In other words, the chief victims of the global intensification of timber extraction (which provided cheap elegance quite far down the social scale in the metropolitan countries) were the log-cutting labourers on the periphery – in Burma, Indonesia, South America and new African colonies, as well as in the original logwood cutting areas of Central America, including Belize.

In Belize, the timber barons held a near monopoly over the freehold lands close to the capital and other coastal towns, and alone were able to obtain leaseholds over the forest lands in the interior held by the Crown. The only lands offered to ex-slaves were either infertile or too high-priced, and virtually no Crown Lands were sold before 1868. Except for some squatters on river banks and Maya and Garifuna subsistence farmers in the north and south, a peasantry was almost non-existent in Belize, the majority of the population remaining landless and dependent for wage labour on the merchant and landowning elite. This class (almost unique in the British West Indies in being far from 'pure' white) was able to control the terms of wage labour legally by contracts enforced under masters and servants laws through compliant local courts. For example, in 1869 the magistrate at Corazal tried 286 cases under the labour laws, all at the instance of employers and virtually all decided in their favour, 245 for labourers being absent without leave, 30 for 'insolence and disobedience', six for assaults on masters and bookkeepers, and five for entering into second contracts before the expiry of former engagements. In the same period, of 156 cases tried in the police court at Belize City, 146 were brought by employers against employees, of which only one was dismissed; of the ten cases brought by employees against their employers, only one resulted in conviction and a fine of two dollars. The normal punishment for a convicted employee was three months' imprisonment at hard labour (Bolland 1981, 607-610).

The chief means of ensuring the enthralment of the labouring class, however, was the system of payment in advance, less in cash than in 'truck' goods, and as far as possible on credit. Hiring for the seasonal work at the timber camps in the interior usually occurred around Christmas, when the log-cutters were in town with their families. Advances were given ostensibly for stocking up for the interior but were usually dissipated, so that the labourers purchased most of their provisions on credit, paying high prices for substandard goods either in town or, even more extortionately, in the employers' own commissaries in the forests. In the words of Nigel Bolland:

> Sometimes labourers never saw any wages, as the company bookkeeper would simply reduce their debts by the amount of their earnings. Often, the balance of the wages a worker received in the forest was insufficient to meet his expenses, he ended the season in debt to his employer, and had to work off the debt in the following season. The

effect of the combination of the advance and truck systems, therefore, was to bind the labourer to his employer by keeping him eternally in debt (Bolland, 1981, 608).

As Howard Johnson has pointed out, the credit and truck systems were found throughout the British West Indies from the 1860s onwards, including the plantation colonies of Jamaica, British Guiana, Trinidad and Tobago (Johnson 1991, 103-105). But the credit and truck systems probably reached their fullest development in the Bahamas, a colony with neither plantations nor a continuous staple export and where the growing black population had since slavery days pressed on the available subsistence resources, yet where the white oligarchy of failed planters showed wonderful ingenuity in manipulating the laws and adapting the economy in order to maintain and even extend their local hegemony.

We have already seen how the Bahamian ex-planters retained their hold over the land, sought to capitalise on it through labour tenancies and sharecropping arrangements, and used the liberated Africans to experiment in systems of payment in advances, credit and truck, even before slavery ended. These methods were refined and intensified after emancipation until they characterised all economic activities involving subordinate capital relations as well as wage labour. In the first category came the practice of advances on seeds, fertilisers and future crops by which landowners reinforced their involvement in the systems of labour tenancy and sharecropping, and the way in which Nassau merchants, by making necessary advances to Out Island boatbuilders on a share of the product, gradually came to dominate boat ownership as well as the boatbuilding industry. Consequent, the merchants' commanded an ever larger share of all the maritime activities of a colony more than any other dependent on the sea (except, perhaps, Bermuda), as well as a dominance in the export of produce outside the archipelago. At least until steamships came to supersede sailing vessels as the normal mode of transportation in such a poor and scattered colony in the twentieth century, the very need for larger vessels than those suitable for inter-insular traffic militated in favour of the merchants who had the necessary capital or control of credit to finance their building (Johnson 1991, 100).

Even when ordinary Bahamian wreckers, woodcutters, turtlers, fishermen and spongers (poor whites as well as blacks) retained a share in the ownership of their boats, they found themselves economically dependent on the merchants of Nassau's Bay Street for the disposal of their produce as well as for advances. When they were simply wage-earning mariners, their lot was far more dire, reaching its nadir in the sponging industry, as memorably described in *Land of the Pink Pearl* by L. D. Powles in 1888. At its peak, the sponging industry engaged a full third of the Bahamian male labour force, almost 600 sailing vessels and nearly 3,000 open boats, effectively competing with each other. Employed on shares, rather than formal wages, the ordinary sponger had to sign seaman's articles, which made him even more subject to prosecution than the wage-earner under the Masters and Servants laws. Without wages, the seaman was completely dependent on advances mainly paid not in cash but in inferior truck items from the shipowner-merchant's store. After eight weeks or more of broiling, backbreaking labour, the sponges had to rely on a share of a product sold by the shipowner-merchants in the Nassau Sponge Exchange for as little as one-fiftieth of its final retail cost in metropolitan shops. As the local market became dominated by aggressive Greek middlemen and worldwide competition developed, cheap spongers in London, Paris and New York were paid for by housing and health conditions in the black Out Islander spongers' settlements worse than those in slavery days (Powles 1888; Craton 1986, 238-241; Craton and Saunders 1994, IV, c .8 Johnson 1991, 96-100).

The full process of labour degradation, though, was demonstrated in the development of the Bahamian pineapple industry. Discovering viable metropolitan markets shortly after slavery ended, pineapples could initially be grown profitably by small farmers, but these depended on the resources commanded by Bay Street merchants for their efficient collection and distribution. Mercantile interests moved into agricultural production first through sharecropping and providing advances for independent small farmers (including those on the Eleutheran commonages) and then, in the interests of economies of scale in the face of competition, into plantation-style production on their own account, using the local blacks as wage labourers. In the final stage of mini-capitalist development, to optimise profits and obviate the difficulties of transporting such a perishable and short-seasoned crop to market, certain white Nassau merchants set up canning factories in Eleuthera and Abaco in the 1870s, supplied from their own fields, from sharecroppers on land they owned, and from small independent pineapple farmers. Before the Bahamian pineapple industry was more or less destroyed by American protection and the far more efficient production in Hawaii, the Philippines and elsewhere, it was reported that the factory at Governor's Harbour, Eleuthera, was paying all its labourers and suppliers solely in tokens redeemable at its company store.

For years this was the only money to be found in local circulation, although the company forbade any other store to take the tokens and refused to redeem them save against their own high-priced retail goods (Johnson 1991, 94-96).

In the face of the exploitation and other difficulties faced by would-be peasant farmers, mariners and other wage labourers, by the end of the nineteenth century the ordinary black Bahamian had no recourse but to migrate in hope of better conditions. An expanding trickle of seasonal and short-term labourers found their way to Cuba, Central America and Florida, but the largest numbers offered themselves from the 1870s onwards as contract stevedores on the American and German steamers that symbolically stopped in the southern Bahamas on their way to and from Cuba and other more profitable territories only to pick them up and drop them off. Ironically, even these subjects of the new informal capitalist empire of the Caribbean were not free of the Bahamian truck and credit systems.

Most of the stevedores were based on Inagua, which already had a flourishing small local mercantile community and pervasive credit and truck system because of the expansion of the Inaguan salt industry by Bay Street capitalists after 1847. Stevedores were freely given advances on their wages which were paid in rum for immediate consumption and provision for the families they left behind. The families too were encouraged to run up debts on credit. When the stevedores returned they often had difficulties in obtaining their wages from merchants who were also commission agents, and were again offered payments only in kind. When the contract system at Inagua was later expanded to engage labourers on one-year contracts in Mexico, Panama and South America, it was said that labourers and their families were allowed to run up debts of £40, a sum that could rarely be earned by a year's hard labour abroad (Johnson 1991, 91-93, 101-102).

The migration of Bahamian labourers was, of course, only a minor stream of a complex flow. New forms of industrial capital entered the region: the industrialised Cuban sugar *centrales*, the railways and new railway and steamship-served plantations of Mexico and other parts of Central America, and, most attractive of all, the extravagant but premature attempt of a French company to build a Panama Canal. In this process, international capital tapped into the growing reservoir of workers, distressed by the shortage of subsistence land and the insufficiency of local wages as well as the oppression of their colonial masters. It drew mostly from destitute colonies like the Bahamas, decaying but overpopulated colonies like Jamaica or Grenada, or the ambitious, relatively well-educated and restless black populace of Barbados; and least from those colonies like British Guiana and Trinidad where wage opportunities still existed, however limited. It was an expanding flow (involving migration within as well as outside the British West Indies), the full story of which, from first trickle in the 1840s to flood in the 1920s, traumatic cutback in the 1930s, and renewal in and after the Second World War, still awaits its definitive historian.[36]

Doubtless the British West Indian labour migrants of the last third of the nineteenth century were victims of blind and indifferent supernational forces (the first awareness of which, along with the germs of a matching proletarian consciousness, were to emerge only with the First World War and the Great Depression), but they were voluntarily taking up options that in prospect and initially at least were preferable to conditions in their home islands. Emigration in most cases was a sociopolitical safety valve, and the money brought back or sent back by settled migrants was an important contribution to the economies of impoverished homelands. As Bonham Richardson (1985), Woodville Marshall (1987) and Cecilia Karch (1980, 1982, 1983) have shown in the case of remittances of 'Panama money' to Barbados, these financed the first substantial wave of smallholding and house lot purchases by Barbadian blacks, and helped to keep afloat and even expand the regional mini-capitalism of the white Barbadian agrocommercial bourgeoisie. The latter operated through banks and insurance companies and the control of the local wholesale trade as well as the ownership of virtually all agricultural land (Chamberlain 1991).

Elsewhere too the meagre flow of outside wages may have helped to loosen somewhat the strangehold of local capitalism by providing an injection of cash into the popular and folk systems of saving and banking. Even in the Bahamas, there seem to have been the first gains by the blacks in the perennial struggle with the government and the Bay Street legislators over the control of the people's friendly and savings societies. For the first time blacks also gained a precarious toehold on the lower end of the capitalist economy; through craftsmen's shops, retail stores, specialist services (such as livery stables, boat carriage and undertaking), renting houses, subdividing land-lots and managing technically illicit forms of saving and gambling.

These token advances (or subdivision of the underclass), the anodyne of a marginally increased cash flow, and the often illusory prospects of gains from migrant labour, as much as the increased efficiency of the forces of law and order and the other features of liberal hegemonic legerdemain already discussed, account for the success of the British West Indian ruling class, as measured by the general decline in the incidence of popular unrest towards the end of the nineteenth century. The British Caribbean was certainly not as quiescent after slavery as the emancipationists wished to believe, and recent scholarship has rightly emphasised the popular explosions that punctuated each colony's history. But these uprisings were most numerous in the earlier years, more or less climaxed in the Morant Bay Rebellion of 1865, and can be broadly classified as the British West Indian equivalents of peasants' revolts – bearing, indeed, more similarities in common with the 'proto-peasant' late slave rebellions of 1816, 1823 and 1831-32 than true proletarian upheavals (Craton 1988).

The earliest of such localised uprisings was probably the 'Guerre Nègre' of 1844 in Dominica, recently analysed by Russell Chace (1988). This seems to have exhibited most of the characteristics of later turmoils, such as in St Lucia in 1849 (which still await their historian), and of the 'Vox Populi' riots in St Vincent of 1862, studied by Woodville Marshall (1983), and the much better known and well-studied Jamaican Rebellion of 1865.[37] All of these upheavals were triggered by short-term hardships and antipathy towards unpopular government measures, particularly taxation, and brutal behaviour by the colonial police. In all there was some element of anti-white racialism. In the Jamaican case at least there was the additional complication of religious revivalism. But all manifestations were basically fuelled by deep-seated grievances predictable among a predominantly peasant population. In all cases, there was animosity over the shortage of land and its retention or monopolisation by an unfriendly government and absentee landlords, over the terms imposed upon sharecropping métayers and labour tenants, and by the difficulties experienced among peasant farmers to obtain either a fair return for their produce or equitable treatment in the local courts.

Although even the Dominican, St Lucian, Vincentian and Jamaican outbreaks included grievances over wage labour conditions, it was the Angel Gabriel Riots in Demerara in 1856 and the Barbadian Federation Riots of 1876 which first exhibited (for those who wish to find them) some of the necessary elements of proletarian rather than peasant uprisings. Although they were set off by seemingly irrelevant occurrences or issues (which have tended to distract most subsequent commentators), both outbreaks occurred in colonies in which plantations and plantocracies remained dominant, and they spread with almost spontaneous combustion among plantation populations suffering cruel hardships and oppression by the master class. They also (like all slave revolts and most nineteenth- century popular uprisings) were suppressed with exemplary rigour by the united forces of government and the local white militias.

In the Demerara case, John Sayers Orr, a revivalist radical preacher returning from abroad – nicknamed the Angel Gabriel for his habit of announcing a sermon at street corners by blowing on a trumpet – retailed a heady mixture of populist rhetoric and anti-Catholic millenarianism. But he could scarcely have had an inkling of the way his demagoguery was to ignite the smouldering grievances of poor urban wage-earners, plantation labourers and part-peasant seasonal workers alike. The ensuing riots focused on the retail shops owned by Catholic Portuguese immigrants, who had themselves graduated from plantation labour but were now, as petty bourgeois middlemen, surrogate targets for the white wholesale merchants. Thus, it might be argued, the nascent Guianese proletariat was striking out at both elements of its oppressive ruling class: the planation landowners and the commercial bourgeoisie (Craton 1988:146-50).

The Barbadian explosion of 1876 was even more obviously the spontaneous collective action of a subject work-force against its oppressive employers. As the subsequent official inquiry disclosed (without formally acknowledging it) the lack of land and alternative employment and the system of labour tenantries were so absolute that with declining profits in the sugar monoculture, wages were everywhere below the subsistence level, and deaths from starvation not uncommon. Coupled with this were an inequitable justice system, a harsh police regime, disgraceful conditions in prisons and workhouses, and almost no social services save a rudimentary education system, not to mention a complete lack of political representation for the working class in a colony that prided itself on having the second oldest self-legislating system in the British Empire. The ostensible or original cause of the uprising was the opposition by the plantocrats to an imperial scheme to include Barbados within a federation of the Windward Islands. Rather optimistically placing confidence in the wishy-washy liberal Governor Pope Hennessy sent by London to promote the federation scheme, the Bridgetown blacks initiated riots in favour of federation and other reforms that quickly led to a conflagration throughout the island.

No doubt most black Barbadians took up the federation issue on the simple principle that if it was opposed by the white plantocracy and supported by a liberal-sounding governor, it must be good. The real issues, of course, went far deeper. Nonetheless, there were at least two aspects of the federation proposal which were basically attractive to Barbadian blacks (and equally unattractive to their masters): almost certainly it would lead to a general dilution of the power of the white plantocracy and more specifically, it would facilitate emigration of Barbadians to greener pastures which hitherto had been resolutely denied them by their legislative masters (Craton 1988:155-61; Hamilton 1956; Levy 1980; Belle 1984).

Yet this is almost special pleading. Over the entire area and period, only in those colonies or areas where plantations continued to be dominant and relatively successful and in the small craftsmen and wharfinger sections of the few port towns can we look for true proto-proletarian activism, the necessary leadership and the first faint emergence of a proletarian consciousness, in the form of strikes, formal combinations and the first tentative ventures into polemic writing and speaking. Before his assassination, Walter Rodney made what he could of the evidence for such activity in his brilliant study of workers in British Guiana from the 1880s to 1905. But only if he had been spared to carry his story forward at least another three decades might he have been able to entitle his book 'The Making of the Guyanese Working Class', rather than simply *A History of the Guyanese Working People, 1881-1905* (1981).[38]

Sugar workers were rarely quiescent and always resisted the employers' attempts to lower wages and raise workloads. In British Guiana they often struck and were even more often disorderly, and on sugar plantations everywhere similar manifestations sometimes occurred. But the sugar workers were nearly always divided and disorganised. The system, as in slavery days, cleverly divided the élite from the ordinary workers, the factory workers from the field labourers. Now the divisions were exacerbated by differences between permanent and seasonal workers, between the indentured contract workers and wage labourers, and between East Indians and creole blacks. Beyond this, plantation workers almost never found common cause with peasant farmers or townsfolk even of their own ethnicity. Consequently, what industrial action occurred was almost bound to be defeated, even without the overwhelming control by the masters of the law, the courts and the police.

There were no truly successful strikes anywhere in the British West Indies in the nineteenth century, and it was only in the 1890s that the first faltering steps were made towards forming trade unions, beginning with the carpenter E. A. Trotz's Guianese Patriotic Club and Mechanics Union of 1890, the Trinidad Working Men's Association of 1894 and the Jamaican Carpenters, Bricklayers & Painters Union of 1898 (Lewis 1939; Hart 1973). Thus it is possible to argue that even in the nearest equivalents to a true proletarian sector in the British West Indies, resistance was always inchoate throughout the nineteenth century; while among the remainder of the people, except for occasional spontaneous small-scale eruptions equivalent to peasant revolts for the first few decades after slavery ended, quiescence and acceptance rather than organised resistance was the rule.

As the Norman Commission was to notice in 1897, it was certainly not any advance in economic, health and educational conditions (which were almost uniformly disgraceful) that accounted for the placidity of the ordinary British West Indian – although the commissioners opted for the torpor of hopelessness rather than any more subtle cause. That there were more likely reasons – the division between peasant and proletarian elements, competition and division within the work-force itself, an inability to organise, and above all the lack of a class consciousness – remained masked. This accounted for the fact that the Commission was able once more to concentrate on only one section of the people, recommending improvements in the peasant rather than wage sector (and trifling improvements at that), while almost ignoring the faults of the system of wage-employment and the continued dominance of the landowning class, and resolutely refusing to recommend any political changes at all. Those who are not purblind admirers of Sydney Olivier, allegedly the most progressive member of the Norman Commission, might even argue that his advocacy of the West Indian peasantry was merely one more hegemonic tactic; dividing in order to continue to rule, or even stave off revolution, by favouring the least against the most dangerous elements in the populace.[39]

More radical and fundamental change was to await the Caribbean-wide ferment of the 1930s, and the catalysts of the Second World War and the United Kingdom's related decline in the will and ability to sustain a formal empire. Whether this, however, really represented the final emergence of a dialectic between classes, let alone a triumph of the underclass over the capitalist bourgeoisie, remains, to say the least, open to debate.

REFERENCES

Roger Abrahams and John F. Szwed (eds), *After Africa: Extracts from British Travel Accounts and Journals of the Seventeenth, Eighteenth and Nineteenth Centuries Concerning the Slaves, Their Manners, and Customs in the British West Indies*, New Haven, Yale University Press, 1983.

Alan H. Adamson, *Sugar without Slaves: The Political Economy of British Guiana, 1838-1904*, New Haven, Yale University Press, 1972.

Johnson U. J. Asiegbu, *Slavery and the Politics of Liberation, 1787-1861: A Study of Liberated African Emigration and British Anti-Slavery Policy*, New York, Africana, 1969.

Morley Ayearst, *The British West Indies: The Search for Self Government*, London, Allen and Unwin, 1960.

Alexander Barclay, *A Practical View of the Present State of Slavery in the West Indies*, London, Smith, Elder, 1826.

Raymond W. Beachey, *The British West Indian Sugar Industry in the Late Nineteenth Century*, Oxford, Basil Blackwell, 1957.

William Beckford, *A Descriptive Account of the Island of Jamaica*, 2 vols, London, T. & J. Egerton, 1790.

Hilary Beckles, 'Slaves and the Internal Marketing System of Barbados', *Historia y Sociedad*, 2, 1989a, 9-32.

_____ *White Servitude and Black Slavery in Barbados, 1627-1715*, Knoxville, Tennessee University Press, 1989b.

_____ *A History of Barbados: From Amerindian Society to Nation State*, Cambridge, Cambridge University Press, 1990.

Hilary Beckles and Andrew Downes, 'The Economics of Transition to the Black Labour System in Barbados, 1630-1680', *Journal of Interdisciplinary History*, 18, 2, 1987, 225-247.

Hilary Beckles and Karl Watson, 'Social Protest and Labour Bargaining: The Changing Nature of Slaves' Responses to Plantation Life in 18th Century Barbados', *Slavery and Abolition*, 8, 3, 1987, 272-293.

William Belgrove, *A Treatise upon Husbandry and Planting*, Boston, D. Fowle, 1755.

George Belle, 'The Abortive Revolution of 1876 in Barbados', *Journal of Caribbean History*, 18, 1984, 1-35.

Jean Besson, 'A Paradox in Caribbean Attitudes to Land', in Jean Besson and Janet Momsen (eds), *Land and Development in the Caribbean*, London, Macmillan Caribbean, 1987, 13-45.

Robin Blackburn, *The Overthrow of Colonial Slavery, 1776-1848*, London, Verso, 1988.

Paul Bloomfield, *Edward Gibon Wakefield: Builder of the British Commonwealth*, London, Longman, 1961.

O. Nigel Bolland, 'Systems of Domination after Slavery: The Control of Land and Labor in the British West Indies after 1838', *Comparative Studies in Society and History*, 23, 1981, 591-619.

_____ 'The Extraction of Timber in the Slave Society of Belize', unpublished paper, 1989.

_____ 'The Institutionalisation of Planter Hegemony in the Colonial Polity of the British West Indies after 1838', unpublished paper, 22th Annual ACH Conference, Trinidad, 1990.

_____ 'Proto-Proletarians? Slaves Wages in the Americas: Between Slave Labour and Wage Labour', unpublished paper, Conference 'From Chattel to Wage Slavery', London, 1991.

_____ 'The Politics of Freedom in the British Caribbean', in Seymour Drescher and Frank McGlyn (eds), *The Meaning of Freedom: Economics, Politics, and Culture after Slavery*, Pittsburgh, University of Pittsburgh Press, 1993, 113-146.

Peter Boomgaard and Gert J. Oostindie, 'Changing Sugar Technology and the Labour Nexus: The Caribbean, 1750-1900', *Nieuwe West-Indische Gids*, 1989, 63/3-22.

Bridget Brereton, 'Post-Emancipation Protest in the Caribbean: The 'Belmana Riots' in Tobago, 1876, *Caribbean Quarterly*, 1984, 30/110-123.

Patrick Bryan, *The Jamaican People, 1880-1902: Race, Class, and Social Control*, London, Macmillan Caribbean, 1991.

W. L. Burn, *Emancipation and Apprenticeship in the British West Indies*, London, Cape, 1937.

Mavis C. Campbell, *The Dynamics of Change in a Slave Society: A Sociopolitical History of the Free Coloreds of Jamaica, 1800-1865*, Rutherford, Fairleigh Dickinson University Press, 1976.

Ciro Flamarion Cardoso, *Escravo ou campones? O protocampesinato negro nas Americas*, Sao Paulo, Editora Brasiliense, 1987.

Selwyn Carrington, 'The State of the Debate on the Role of Capitalism in the Ending of the Slave System', *Journal of Caribbean History*, 1988, 22/20-41.

Russell E. Chace, 'Religion, Taxes, and Popular Protest in Tortola: The Road Town Riots of 1853', unpublished paper, South-South Conference, Montreal, 1984.

_____ 'The Emergence and Development of an Estate-Based Peasantry in Dominica', unpublished paper, 1988.

_____ 'Protest in Post-Emancipation Dominica: The Guerre Nègre of 1844', *Journal of Caribbean History*, 1989, 23/118-141.

Mary Chamberlain, 'Renters and Farmers: The Barbadian Tenantry System, 1917-1937', unpublished paper, 23rd Annual ACH Conference, Santo Domingo, 1991.

S. G. Checkland, *The Gladstones: A Family Biography, 1764-1851*, Cambridge, Cambridge University Press, 1971.

Edith Clarke, *My Mother Who fathered Me: A Study of the Family in Three Selected Communities in Jamaica*, London, Allen and Unwin (orig. 1957), 1966.

Edward L. Cox, 'Ralph B. Cleghorn of St. Kitts in the 1830s', unpublished paper, 12th Annual ACH Conference, Trinidad, 1990.

Michael Craton, *Sinews of Empire: A Short History of British Slavery*, New York, Doubleday/London, Temple Smith, 1974.

_____ *Searching for the Invisible Man: Slaves and Plantation Life in Jamaica*, Cambridge MA, Harvard University Press, 1978.

_____ 'Proto-Peasant Revolts? The Late Slave Rebellions in the British West Indies, 1816-1832, Past and Present*, 1979, 85/99-125.

_____ 'Testing the Chains: Resistance to Slavery in the British West Indies*, Ithaca, Cornell University Press, 1982.

_____ 'We Shall not be Moved: Pompey's Proto-Peasant Slave Revolt in Exuma Island, Bahamas, 1829-1830', *Nieuwe Westindische Gids*, 1983, 57/19-35.

_____ 'White Law and Black Custom: The Evolution of Bahamian Land Tenures', *in* Janet Momsen and Jean Besson (eds), *Land and Development in the Caribbean*, London, Macmillan Caribbean, 1987, 88-114.

_____ 'Continuity Not Change: The Incidence of Unrest Among Ex-Slaves in the British West Indies, 1838-1876', *Slavery and Abolition* 9/2, 1988, 144-170.

_____ 'A transicao da escravido para o trabalho livre no caribe (1780-1890): um estudo com particular referencia à recente produco academica', *Estudos Afro-Así-ticos, 1992a, 22/5-32.

_____ 'The Transition from Slavery to Free Wage Labour in the Caribbean 1780-1890: A Survey with Particular Reference to Recent Scholarship', *Slavery and Abolition*, 13/2, 1992b, 37-67.

Michael Craton and D. Gail Saunders, 'Seeking a Life of their Own: Aspects of Slave Resistance in the Bahamas', *Journal of Caribbean History*, 24, 1991, 1-27.

_____*Islanders in the Stream: A History of the Bahamian People, Volume One. From Aboriginal Times to the End of Slavery*, Athens, University of Georgia Press, 1992.

_____*Islanders in the Stream: A History of the Bahamian People, Volume Two. From the End of Slavery to the Twenty-First Century*, Athens, University of Georgia Press, 1997

Michael Craton and James Walvin, *A Jamaican Plantation: The History of Worthy Park, 1670-1970*, London, W. H. Allen, 1970.

G. O. Cumper, 'Employment in Barbados', *Social and Economic Studies*, 8, 1959, 105-146.

Peter B. Dalleo, 'Africans in the Caribbean: A Preliminary Assessment of Recaptives in the Bahamas, 1811-1860', *Journal of the Bahamas Historical Society*, 6, 1984, 15-24.

David Brion Davis, *Slavery and Human Progress*, New York, Oxford University Press, 1984.

William Dickson, *Letters on Slavery*, London, J. Phillips, 1789.

_____ *Mitigation of Slavery*, London, J. Phillips, 1814.

Isaac Dookhan, *The Post-Emancipation History of the West Indies*, London, Collins, 1975.

Seymour Drescher, *Econocide: British Slavery in the Era of Abolition*, Pittsburgh, University of Pittsburgh Press, 1977.

_____ *Capitalism and Antislavery: British Mobilization in Comparative Perspective*, New York, Oxford University Press, 1987.

Geoffrey Dutton, *The Hero as Murderer: The Life of Edward John Eyre*, London, Collins, 1967.

Bryan Edwards, *The History, Civil and Commercial of the British Colonies in the West Indies*, 2 vols, London, J. Stockdale, 1793.

Gisela Eisner, *Jamaica, 1830-1930: A Study in Economic Growth*, Manchester, Manchester University Press, 1961.

David Eltis, 'The Traffic in Slaves between the British West Indian Colonies, 1807-1833', *Economic History Review*, 25, 1972, 55-64.

Godwin L. Friday, 'Fifty Years of Freedom: Runaway Slaves in the Bahamas, 1784-1834', MA thesis, University of Waterloo, 1984.

Richard Frucht, 'A Caribbean Social Type: Neither Peasant Nor Proletarian', *Social and Economic Studies*, 16, 1967, 295-300.

David Barry Gaspar, *Bondmen & Rebels: A Study of Master-Slave Relations in Antigua; With Implications for Colonial British America*, Baltimore, Johns Hopkins University Press, 1985.

_____ 'Amelioration or Oppression?: The Abolition of the Slaves' Sunday Markets in Antigua (1831)', unpublished paper, 20th Annual ACH Conference, St Thomas, 1988.

Bentley Gibbs, 'The Establishment of a Tenantry System in Barbados', in Woodville K. Marshall (ed.), *Emancipation II. Aspects of the Post-Slavery Experience in Barbados*, Bridgetown, Department of History, University of the West Indies, 1987, 1-23.

Shirley C. Gordon, *A Century of West Indian Education: A Source Book*, London, Longman, 1963.

Elsa V. Goveia, *Slave Society in the British Leeward Islands at the End of the Eighteenth Century*, New Haven, Yale University Press, 1965.

Madeleine Grant, 'Enemies to Caesar? Sectarian Missionaries in British West Indian Slave Society, 1754-1834', MA thesis, University of Waterloo, 1976.

William A. Green, 'The Apprenticeship in British Guiana, 1834-1838', *Caribbean Studies*, 9, 1969, 44-66.

_____ *British Slave Emancipation: The Sugar Colonies and the Great Experiment, 1830-1865*, London, Oxford University Press, 1976.

_____ 'The Perils of Comparative History: Belize and the British Sugar Colonies after Slavery', *Comparative Studies in Society and History*, 26, 1984, 112-125.

Douglas G. Hall, 'The Apprenticeship Period in Jamaica, 1834-1838', *Caribbean Quarterly*, 3, 1953, 142-166.

_____ *Free Jamaica, 1838-1865: An Economic History*, New Haven, Yale University Press, 1959.

_____ *Five of the Leewards, 1834-1870. The Major Problems of the Post-Emancipation Period in Antigua, Barbuda, Montserrat, Nevis and St. Kitts*, St Laurence, Barbados, Caribbean Universities Press, 1971.

_____ 'The Flight from the Estates Reconsidered: The British West Indies, 1838-42', *Journal of Caribbean History*, 10/11, 1978, 7-24.

_____ *In Miserable Slavery: Thomas Thistlewood in Jamaica, 1750-86*, London, Macmillan Caribbean, 1989.

Bruce Hamilton, *Barbados and the Confederation Question: 1871-1885*, London, Crown Agents, 1956.

Kusha Haraksingh, 'Control and Resistance among Overseas Indian Workers: A Study of Labour on the Sugar Plantations of Trinidad, 1875-1917', *Journal of Caribbean History*, 14, 1981, 1-17.

Richard Hart, 'The Formation of a Caribbean Working Class', *The Black Liberator*, 2, 1973, 131-148.

_____ 'The Working Class in the English-speaking Caribbean area 1897-1937', in Malcolm Cross & Gad Heuman (eds), *Labour in The Caribbean: From Emancipation to Independence*, London, Macmillan Caribbean, 1988, 43-79.

Gad Heuman, *Between Black and White: Race, Politics and the Free Coloreds in Jamaica, 1792-1865*, Westport, Greenwood Press, 1981.

Barry W. Higman, *Slave Population and Economy in Jamaica, 1807-1834*, Cambridge, Cambridge University Press, 1976.

_____*Slave Populations of the British Caribbean, 1807-1834*, Baltimore, Johns Hopkins University Press, 1984.

_____*Jamaica Surveyed: Plantation Maps and Plans of the Eighteenth and Nineteenth Centuries*, Kingston, Institute of Jamaica, 1988.

_____ 'To Begin the World Again: Responses to Emancipation at Friendship and Greenwich Estate, Jamaica', unpublished paper, 22th ACH Conference, Trinidad, 1990.

History Task Force (Puerto Rico), *Labor Migration under Capitalism: The Puerto Rican Experience*, New York, Monthly Review Press, 1979.

Thomas C. Holt, *The Problem of Freedom: Race, Labor and Politics in Jamaica and Britain, 1832-1938*, Baltimore, Johns Hopkins University Press, 1992.

Edward Jenkins, *The Coolie: His Rights and Wrongs*, London, Strahan, 1871.

Howard Johnson, *The Bahamas in Slavery and Freedom*, Kingston, Ian Randle and London, James Currey, 1991.

Cecilia A. Karch, 'The Role of the Barbados Mutual Life Assurance Society during the International Sugar Crisis of the Late Nineteenth Century', unpublished paper, 12th Annual ACH Conference, Trinidad, 1980.

_____ 'The Growth of the Corporate Economy in Barbados: Class/Race Factors, 1890-1977', in Susan Craig (ed.), *The Contemporary Caribbean: A Sociological Reader*, I, Port-of-Spain, Susan Craig, 1982, 213-241.

_____ 'The Transport and Communications Revolution in the West Indies: Imperial Policy and Barbadian Response, 1870-1917', *Journal of Caribbean History*, 18, 1983, 22-42.

Sir John Lefroy, *Memorials of the Bermudas*, 2 vols, London, Longman, 1877-79.

Charles Leslie, *A New History of Jamaica*, London, J. Hodges, 1740.

Claude Levy, *Emancipation, Sugar and Federalism: Barbados and the West Indies, 1838-1876*, Gainesville, University of Florida Press, 1980.

W. Arthur Lewis, *The Evolution of the Peasantry in the British West Indies*, London, Colonial Office, 1936.

_____ *Labour in the West Indies*, London, Gollancz, 1939.

Gordon K. Lewis, *The Growth of the Modern West Indies*, London, MacGibbon & Kee, 1968.

Kathleen Phillips Lewis, 'The Poor and the Powerful: The Working of the Cocoa Contract System in Trinidad at the End of the Nineteenth Century', unpublished paper, 12th Annual ACH Conference, Trinidad, 1990.

Matthew Gregory Lewis, *Journal of a West India Proprietor, Kept during a Residence in the Island of Jamaica*, London, John Murray, 1834.

Richard Ligon, *A True and Exact History of the Island of Barbados*, London, H. Moseley, 1657.

Richard S. Lobdell, 'British Officials and West Indian Peasants, 1842-1938', in Malcolm Cross and Gad Heuman (eds), *Labour in the Caribbean: From Emancipation to Independence*, London, Macmillan Caribbean, 1988, 195-207.

Edward Long, *History of Jamaica*, 3 vols, London, T. Lowndes, 1774.

David Lowenthal and Colin G. Clarke, 'Slave-Breeding in Barbuda: The Past of a Negro Myth', in Vera Rubin and Arthur Tuden (eds), *Comparative Perspectives on Slavery in New World Plantation Societies*, New York, New York Academy of Sciences, 1977, 510-535.

John Luffman, *A Brief Account of the Island of Antigua*, London, T. Cadell, 1788.

Jay Mandle, *The Plantation Economy: Population and Economic Change in Guyana, 1830-1960*, Philadelphia, Temple University Press, 1973.

Woodville K. Marshall, 'Métayage in the Sugar Industry of the British Windward Islands, 1838-1865', *Jamaican Historical Review*, 5, 1965, 28-55.

_____ 'The Termination of Apprenticeship in Barbados and the Windward Islands', *Journal of Caribbean History*, 2, 1971, 1-45.

_____ *The Colthurst Journal: Journal of a Special Magistrate in the Islands of Barbados and St Vincent, July 1835-September 1838*, Millwood, KTO Press, 1977.

_____ 'Vox Populi: The St Vincent Riots and Disturbances of 1862', in Barry Higman (ed.), *Trade, Government and Society in Caribbean History: Essays Presented to Douglas Hall*, Kingston, Caribbean Universities Press, 1983, 85-115.

_____ 'Apprenticeship and Labour Relations in Four Windward Islands', in David Richardson (ed.), *Abolition and its Aftermath: The Historical Context, 1790-1916*, London, Cass, 1985, 203-244.

_____ '19th Century Crisis in the Barbadian Sugar Industry', in Woodville Marshall (ed.), *Emancipation II: Aspects of the Post-Slavery Experience in Barbados*, Cave Hill, Barbados, Department of History, University of the West Indies, 1987, 85-102.

Woodville K. Marshall, Trevor Marshall and Bentley Gibbs, 'The Establishment of a Peasantry in Barbados', in *Social Groups and Institutions in the History of the Caribbean*, Papers Presented at the 6th Annual Conference of Caribbean Historians, Puerto Rico, April 1-9, 1974, 1975, 55-104.

Samuel Martin, *An Essay on Plantership*, Antigua, S. Jones, 1756.

Karl Marx, *Capital*, I, Hamburg, O. Meissner, 1867.

Roderick A. McDonald, 'The Journal of John Anderson, St Vincent Special Magistrate, 1836-1839', unpublished paper, 12th Annual ACH Conference, Trinidad, 1990.

Sidney W. Mintz, 'Slavery and the Rise of Peasantries', in Michael Craton (ed.), *Roots and Branches: Current Directions in Slave Studies*, Oxford, Pergamon Press, 1979, 213-242.

Sidney W. Mintz and Douglas G. Hall, 'The Origins of the Jamaican Internal Marketing System', in Sidney W. Mintz (ed.), *Papers in Caribbean Anthropology*, New Haven, Yale University Press, 1960, 3-26.

Benjamin M'Mahon, *Jamaica Plantership*, London, E. Wilson, 1839.

Brian L. Moore, *Race, Power, and Social Segmentation in Colonial Society: Guyana after Slavery, 1838-1891*, New York, Gordon & Breach, 1987.

Francisco Moreno Fraginals, *El ingenio: complejo económico social cubano del azúcar*, 3 vols, Havana, Editorial de Ciencas Sociales, 1978.

_____ 'Plantations in the Caribbean: Cuba, Puerto Rico, and the Dominican Republic in the Late Nineteenth Century', in Francisco Moreno Fraginals, Frank Moya Pons and Stanley Engerman (eds), *Between Slavery and Free Labor: The Spanish Speaking Caribbean in the Nineteenth Century*, Baltimore, Johns Hopkins University Press, 1985, 3-21.

J. B. Moreton, *The History, Civil and Commercial, of the British Colonies in the West Indies*, 3 vols, London, W. Richardson, 1790.

Philip D. Morgan, 'Task and Gang Systems: The Organization of Labor on New World Plantations', in Stephen Innes (ed.), *Work and Labor in Early America*, Chapel Hill, University of North Carolina Press, 1988, 189-220.

_____ 'Encounters with Africans and African-Americans, circa 1600-1780', in Bernard Bailyn and Philip D. Morgan (eds), *Strangers within the Realm: Cultural Margins of the Fist British Empire*, Chapel Hill, University of North Carolina Press, 1991, 157-219.

Velma Newton, 'British West Indian Emigration to the isthmus of Panama, 1850-1914', MA thesis, University of the West Indies, Kingston, 1973.

_____ 'Aspects of British West Indian Emigration to the Isthmus of Panama, 1850-1914', unpublished paper, 9th Annual ACH Conference, Barbados, 1977.

_____ *The Silver Men: West Indian Labour Migration to Panama, 1850-1914*, Mona, Institute of Social and Economic Research, 1984.

_____ 'The Panama Question: Barbadian Emigration to Panama, 1880-1914', in Woodville K. Marshall (ed.), *Emancipation II: Aspects of the Post-Slavery Experience in Barbados*, Bridgetown, Department of History, University of the West Indies, 1987, 102-130.

Sydney Olivier, *The Myth of Governor Eyre*, London, L & V. Woolf, 1933.

Keith Otterbein, 'A Comparison of the Land Tenure Systems of the Bahamas, Jamaica and Barbados: The Implications It Has for the Study of Systems Shifting from Bilateral to Ambilineal Descent', *International Archives of Ethnography*, 50/1, 1964, 31-42.

Richard Pares, *A West India Fortune*, London, Longman, Green, 1950.

Elizabeth McLean Petras, *Jamaican Labor Migration: White Capital and Black Labor, 1850-1930*, Boulder, Westview Press, 1988.

George Pinckard, *Notes on the West Indies*, 3 vols, London, Baldwin, Cradock & Joy, 1806.

Latchman Ramsarran, 'Governor Francis Hincks of British Guiana (1862-1869)', PhD Dissertation, University of Waterloo, 1985.

Paul Rich, 'Sydney Olivier, Jamaica and the Debate on British Colonial Policy in the West Indies', in Malcolm Cross and Gad Heuman (eds), *Labour in the Caribbean: From Emancipation to Independence*, London, Macmillan Caribbean, 1988, 208-233.

Bonham C. Richardson, *Caribbean Migrants: Environment and Human Survival in St Kitts and Nevis*, Knoxville, University of Tennessee Press, 1983.

_____ *Panama Money in Barbados, 1900-1920*, Knoxville, University of Tennessee Press, 1985.

_____ 'Caribbean Migrations, 1838-1985', in Franklin W. Knight and Colin A. Palmer (eds), *The Modern Caribbean*, Chapel Hill, University of North Carolina Press, 1989, 203-228.

Emanuel W. Riviere, 'Labour Shortage in the British West Indies after Emancipation', *Journal of Caribbean History*, 4, 1972, 1-30.

Walter Rodney, *A History of the Guyanese Working People, 1881-1905*, London, Heinemann, 1981.

Thomas Roughley, *The Jamaica Planters' Guide*, London, Longman, 1823.

Veront Satchell, *From Plots to Plantations: Land Transactions in Jamaica, 1866-1900*, Mona, Institute of Social and Economic Research, 1990.

_____ 'From Peasants to Proletarians: The Case of the Jamaican Peasants during the Late Nineteenth Century', unpublished paper, 13th Annual ACH Conference, Santo Domingo, 1991.

Gail Saunders, *Slavery in the Bahamas, 1647-1838*, Nassau, s.n., 1985.

Johann David Schoepf, *Travels in the Confederation, 1783-1784*, Philadelphia, Campbell, 1911.

Monica Schuler, *'Alas, Alas, Kongo': A Social History of Indentured African Immigration into Jamaica, 1841-1865*, Baltimore, Johns Hopkins University Press, 1980.

_____ 'The Recruitment of African Indentured Labourers for European Colonies in the Nineteenth Century', in Pieter C. Emmer (ed.), *Migration: Indentured Labour before and after Slavery*, Dordrecht, Nijhoff, 1986, 125-161.

Bernard Semmel, *Jamaican Blood and Victorian Conscience: The Governor Eyre Controversy*, Cambridge MA, Houghton Mifflin, 1962.

Verene Shepherd, 'Livestock Farmers and Marginality in Jamaica's Sugar Plantation Society: A Tentative Analysis', unpublished paper, 12th Annual ACH Conference, Trinidad, 1990.

Richard B. Sheridan, 'Changing Sugar Technology and the Labour Nexus in the British Caribbean, 1750-1900, with Special Reference to Barbados and Jamaica', *Nieuwe West Indische Gids*, 63, 1989, 59-93.

Lorna E. Simmonds, 'Riots and Disturbances in Jamaica, 1838-1865', MA thesis, University of Waterloo, 1982.

Adam Smith, *An Inquiry into the Nature and Causes of the Wealth of Nations*, 2 vols, London, W. Strahan & T. Cadell, 1776.

Harinder Singh Sohal, 'The East Indian Indentureship System in Jamaica, 1845-1917', PhD Dissertation, University of Waterloo, 1979.

James Stephen, *The Slavery of the British West India Colonies Delineated*, 2 vols, London, J. Butterworth, 1824, 1839.

Jean Stubbs, *Tobacco on the Periphery: A Case Study in Cuban Labour History, 1860-1958*, Cambridge, Cambridge University Press, 1985.

Richard Sutch, 'The Breeding of Slaves for Sale and the Westward Expansion of Slavery, 1850-1860', in Stanley Engerman and Eugene Genovese (eds), *Race and Slavery in the Western Hemisphere: Quantitative Studies*, Princeton, Princeton University Press, 1975, 173-210.

Hugh Tinker, *A New System of Slavery: The Export of Indian Labour Overseas, 1830-1930*, Oxford, Oxford University Press, 1974.

Michel-Rolph Trouillot, 'Discourses of Rule and the Acknowledgement of the Peasantry in Dominica, W.I., 1838-1928, *American Ethnologist*, 16, 1989, 704-718.

Mary Turner, *Slaves and Missionaries: The Disintegration of Jamaica Slave Society, 1787-1834*, Urbana, University of Illinois Press, 1982.

_____ 'Chattel Slaves into Wage Slaves: A Jamaican Case Study', in Malcolm Cross & Gad Heuman (eds), *Labour in the Caribbean: From Emancipation to Independence*, London, Macmillan, 1988, 14-31.

_____ 'Slave Workers, Subsistence and Labour Bargaining: Amity Hall, Jamaica, 1805-1832', in Ira Berlin and Philip Morgan (eds), *The Slaves' Economy: Independent Production by Slaves in the Americas*, London, Cass, 1991, 92-106.

Edward Bean Underhill, *A Letter Addressed to the Rt. Hon E. Cardwell, with Illustrative Documents on the Condition of Jamaica and an Explanatory Statement*, London, A. Miall, 1866.

Edward Gibbon Wakefield, *A View of the Art of Colonisation*, London, J.W. Parker, 1849.

John R. Ward, 'The Profitability of Sugar Planting in the British West Indies, 1650-1834', *Economic History Review*, 2nd series, 31, 1978, 197-213.

_____ *British West Indian Slavery, 1750-1834: The Process of Amelioration*, Oxford, Clarendon Press, 1988.

Judith Weller, *The East Indian Indenture in Trinidad*, Rio Piedras, Institute of Caribbean Studies, University of Puerto Rico, 1968.

Eric Williams, *Capitalism and Slavery*, Chapel Hill, University of North Carolina Press, 1944.

Swithin Wilmot, 'Strikes for Freedom: The Ex-Slaves and the Introduction of the Apprenticeship System in the British West Indies', *Jamaica Historical Society Bulletin*, 8, 1984a, 333-338.

_____ 'Not Full-Free: The Ex-Slaves and Apprenticeship System in Jamaica, 1834-1838, *Jamaica Journal*, 17, 1984b, 2-10.

Donald Wood, 'Kru Migration to the West Indies', *Journal of Caribbean Studies*, 2, 1981, 266-282.

Oscar Zanetti and Alejandro García, *Caminos para el azúcar: historia de los ferrocarriles en Cuba*, Havana, Editiones Ciencas Sociales, 1987.

19

Transition to Free Wage Labour in the Caribbean, 1780-1890

Introduction: This essay was originally presented a year before the preceding one, at the Latin American Studies Association Congress held in Washington, DC, in April 1991, in a session including appears by Ciro Cardoso and Nancy Naro on Brazil and by Ira Berlin on the USA. It cannot lay claim to great originality, being mainly an attempt to provide a useful survey of current work being undertaken in the Caribbean in parallel with (but too disparately from) that in the other two major areas of slavery and post-slavery studies in the Americas. It does, though, point out a commonplace, the significance of which is too often forgotten: that slavery ended at widely separated dates, not just in the British colonies, the USA and Brazil, but within the many different political units of the Caribbean. Accordingly, any simple emulative model of the transition from slavery to 'free' wage labour has to be modified both in relation to similar changes that had already occurred elsewhere, and in accord with general changes across the globe.

The study of the transition from slavery to wage labour and related transformations throughout the Caribbean sphere is greatly more complicated but potentially more rewarding than examining the single (if not simple) process at either end of the spectrum of plantation America in the USA and Brazil. More than 100 years separates the first concentrated onslaught of the secular and religious opponents of British slavery in the Caribbean in the early 1780s from the freeing of the last slaves in Cuba in 1886. Apart from including the immediate and indirect effects of the slave revolution in Haiti between 1791 and 1804, such a study should look at the sequential termination of slave trading between 1805 and 1860, and the subsequent revision and ending of slavery itself between 1834 and 1886 in five different imperial systems: the British, French, Danish, Dutch and

Spanish. Moreover, it should not restrict itself, as many studies have done, to the slavery of large plantations (especially sugar plantations) where black slaves hugely outnumbered free coloureds and whites, but should also include non-plantation slavery, the areas where slavery co-existed with other forms of production and labour and slaves did not necessarily out-number the free, and the many marginal areas where slavery legally existed but was not the primary mode.

Yet this very complexity and prolongation allows us to consider what was unique and what common in each phase and area, what constituted a standard pattern, what was the result of cumulative internal developments, and what of changing external forces. Covering such a broad spectrum in the central arena of the plantation system also provides the best of oppor-tunities to distinguish all the distinct and often counterposed ideologies that were involved: those of the planters, the imperialists, the philanthro-pists, the slaves and ex-slaves, and by no means least, the many historians who have described and analysed the process.

Above all, the micro-study of slavery and its aftermath in each subre-gional area should provide a clearer macro-historical view of those trans-formations which reshaped the Atlantic world between 1780 and 1890; changes in the pattern of European imperialism, imperialist theories and policies, and structural changes in the world capitalist system, which included massive if gradual changes in the systems of financing, production, processing, transportation and distribution, with their concomitant changes in patterns of labour management and migration, and in the relations between labourers, landowners and employers. Put another way, a comprehensive and accurate survey of the myriad but generally narrowly focused monographic works on slavery, its abolition and its aftermath throughout the Caribbean should help us to test those almost equally numerous works which make global generalisations about the nature of slavery and its transformation into a system of wage labour as part of the modernisation process. This ambitious (and possibly impossible) agenda would, of course, if successful, also help to illuminate what has happening beyond the northern and southern bounds of the Caribbean, and place it within a global schema.[1]

The most fitting way to begin is to examine the historiography still swirling about the most dramatic and traumatic episode during the entire process, the bloody 13-year war in which the Haitian slaves freed them-selves and created the first black republic in the modern world. Considering the causes, nature and effects of the Haitian events 1791 to 1804 (or rather, interpretations of them) leads naturally to a discussion of the resistance of slaves to their enslavement in general, and of the ideologies involved on every side. In the broadest terms, the debate counterposes those who see the Haitian Revolution and related instances of slave resistance as part of a western worldwide movement and ideology, and those prepared to grant a separate ideology of resistance to the slaves.

Of the former, the most extreme, despite his subtle qualifications, is Eugene Genovese. In *From Rebellion to Revolution* (1979) he equals James and Aptheker in stressing the importance of the Haitian Revolution in the history of slave resistance, but exceeds them both in ascribing the centrality of the French Revolution to the events in Haiti, to the extent that he characterises the Haitian slaves as participants in a general 'bourgeois-democratic' enterprise. Prior to 1791, Genovese argues, slave revolts were mere rebellions. Slaves aimed to escape from plantation slavery and colonial slave society, but not necessarily to destroy them. Their main intention was to restore traditional African ways, which might even include the enslave-ment of their enemies. After 1789, though, says Genovese, 'the conquest of state power by the bourgeoisie in France', coupled with bourgeois radical rhetoric, inspired the slaves to destroy slavery as a system and to replace it with bourgeois property relations. 'The traditional-restorationist ideolo-gies of the early slave revolts gave way before a new bourgeois-democratic ideology, which imparted to subsequent slave revolts new quality and power.' Almost all subsequent slave revolts 'increasingly aimed not at succession from the dominant society but at joining it on equal terms'. The fact that the plantation system was actually destroyed in Haiti and declined elsewhere along with slavery, and that the mass of Haitian and many other ex-slaves became conservative peasants, is simply called by Genovese the result of a 'grimly ironical counter-revolution'.[2]

The most thorough and persuasive scholar of the Haitian Revolution, David Geggus, points out many of the salient flaws in Genovese's argu-ment. Both in Haiti and the wider Caribbean sphere, the French and Haitian Revolutions had more impact on free coloureds and blacks than on slaves. The influence of the French Revolution, he claims, 'was political rather than ideological; it promoted resistance less through the propagation of libertarian ideas, than through affecting the distribution of power'. Thirdly, and perhaps most important, the Anglo-French anti-slavery movement was at least as important (and significantly antedated) the French and Haitian revolutions in generating new forms of slave resis-tance.[3]

Quite apart from the fact that it was a free coloureds' rebellion led by Vincent Ogé that initiated the turmoil in Haiti and provided the conditions that facilitated the slave uprising of 1791, the leaders of the Haitian and later slave rebellions who most employed Jacobin rhetoric and ideas were either an upwardly mobile slave élite or actually freedmen, black or mulatto. Toussaint himself was already a free black in 1791, and Pétion – in many ways the most radical of Haitian reformers – was a mulatto. Similar leaders included Fédon in Grenada (1795), the prime movers in the Coro and Maracaibo rebellions in Venezuela (1795, 1799), and in the Cuban Aponte conspiracy (1811). Although the mass of slave rebels were easily persuaded to wear tricouleur cockades and sing revolutionary songs, it is far more difficult to ascribe consistent Jacobin ideology to them. As ever, they were far more likely to seize opportunities and seek allies when and where they could, rising up when their masters were distracted or weakened, and actually fought in large numbers against the French revolutionary forces when it seemed pragmatically advantageous.[4]

Robin Blackburn, author of the most impressively wide-ranging survey of anti-slavery to date, *The Overthrow of Colonial Slavery, 1776-1848*, concurs with Geggus in asserting that 'slavery was not overthrown for economic reasons but where it became politically untenable', while at the same time impressively widening and deepening the concept of the ideology involved. Instead of Genovese's simple 'bourgeois-democratic' formulation, Blackburn postulates a convergence of secular and religious humanitarian impulses, old and new, a growing distaste for the selfish intransigence of colonial planters and slave-trading merchants coupled with a heightened awareness of the initiatives of slaves and free coloureds in the colonies, and above all, a novel (and scarcely likely to be long-lived) concurrence of interests among all those classes in the metropole not involved in slavery's profits. 'Abolitionism, with its roots in a centuries-old anti-slavery reflex,' he concludes,

> also appeared to offer guarantees for the future – basically a guarantee that the enlarged circuit of capital accumulation would not simply reinforce and extend personal bondage. Anti-slavery as a doctrine had a special appeal to those who were caught in the middle or were seeking to construct a cross-class bloc . . . Emancipationism was certainly compatible with ideal projections of wage labour and thus congruent with capitalist industrialisation. But the idea of 'free labour' or 'independent labour' which abolitionism claimed to protect had popular appeal because it could also be taken to refer to the small producer, the artisan or the professional, each of whom were free to work on their own account rather than for a capitalist. Women, normally excluded

from political life, played a significant part in anti-slavery; while abolitionism idealised the family it directly inspired the first campaigns for civic equality for women.[5]

This powerful argument gains extra strength from Seymour Drescher's recent work on the popular support for abolitionism, and it comes close to the magisterial conclusion of David Brion Davis and David Eltis [in the words of Robert Paquette] 'that British capitalism had given birth to a radical new ideology. It would radiate outward, across the Atlantic, attracting adherents and decisively conditioning the specific political struggles that brought about emancipation . . . abolitionism was related to the need to legitimate an emerging system based upon free (i.e. wage) labor . . . [and] the self-sustained growth associated with the social relations of industrial capitalism and the attendant development of mass consumerism.' Blackburn's analysis certainly helps to explain the apparent heterogeneity of a movement that included the disciples of Adam Smith and the French *philosophies*, Quaker and other Non-conformist evangelicals, industrialists opposed to colonial preferences and trading monopolies, artisans who looked back nostalgically to medieval guilds and talked about the Norman Yoke, workingmen who believed that Britons never would again be slaves, militant bluestockings, genuine romantic radicals like Shelley or the new Coleridge, or wishy-washy radicals like the Wordsworth who wrote the thrilling, if ideologically muddy, 'Ode to Toussaint l'Ouverture' (1802):

> . . . Thou hast left behind
> Powers that will work for thee; air, earth, and skies;
> There's not a breathing of the common wind
> That will forget thee; thou hast great allies;
> Thy friends are exultations, agonies,
> And love, and man's unconquerable mind.[6]

However, as Gordon Lewis caustically emphasises in *Main Currents in Caribbean Thought*, all these anti-slavery proponents and propositions exhibit a metropolitan and idealist bias out of touch with plantation realities and the slaves' own ideology. Few contemporary or later commentators seem to have made much of the sentiments of the maverick Tory Samuel Johnson in the 1770s, with his sarcastic remark that the loudest yelps for liberty seemed to come from the owners of slaves, and his even more outrageous toast to the next successful slave rebellion in the West Indies.[7]

Indeed, the almost universal 'problem of slavery' for contemporary whites in the metropolis (and featuring largest in the majority of modern commentaries too), was how to reform the plantation labour system without destroying the plantations or the supply of labour altogether. Moreover, the promotion of violence was anathema to the most dedicated abolitionists. What the slaves really wanted and how they planned to achieve it has only recently become the focus of scholarship.

In the masterly fourth chapter of his book, Gordon Lewis gives by far the best general account of the West Indian slaves' own ideology, although he is less persuasive over the aims of those later rebels whom Richard Hart has called 'slaves who abolished slavery'. Since the ideology was essentially subtle, private and secret (and also feared by the whites), it has been denigrated, ignored or missed altogether by earlier writers. But a sensitive reading of the evidence makes it clear that slaves developed wonderful skills of accommodation – or apparent accommodation – in order to survive or subsume the rigours of slavery, preserved and developed a vigorous alternative lifestyle, and were ready to pursue any means, up to and including overt revolt, in order to end the slavery system when they could. They were especially adept at finding temporary allies where they could, and at playing one white person, or one European nation, off against another. Their favourite folklore figure was Anansi, the West African and Afro-American spider-trickster.

Once in open rebellion, argues Lewis, the signs became clearer: a fusion of African forms with revolutionary activity (as in *vodun* or *santeria*); black self-confidence, including the purging of white values and white-induced self-denigration to the point of seeing themselves as the whites' avenging nemesis (as with Cuffy in Berbice in 1763); assertive black national consciousness (as with the Haitian maroons throughout the colonial period); a united front not just among all Africans, but all coloured and all oppressed peoples; a tendency to charismatic leadership – though this may take many forms, from the miracle-working of Mackandal to the Robin Hood behaviour of Three Fingered Jack, the biblical Moses persona of Samuel Sharpe, or the militaristic apocalypticism of Daaga. In addition, claims Lewis, maroons throughout the region exhibited two lasting features of Afro-Caribbean ideology: an ardent sense of moral superiority not just over whites but towards those who remain in subjection to them, and a tendency towards political pluralism.[8]

With Lewis's analysis as a gloss, it is possible to deconstruct the famous rebel slave ditty almost inadvertently recorded by his namesake, the Jamaican absentee planter, Matthew Gregory Lewis, in 1816 (although, significantly, not published until after British slavery ended). Freedom is the aim above all, towards which end the slaves will seek whatever allies they can find against their real oppressors. God should properly aid them against the Jamaican planters, through the mediation of the godly leader of the British abolitionists. But if even these forces are insufficient against the implacable slave-owning whites, the blacks must rise to assert their collective ethnic power.[9]

As to what the slaves wanted in freedom, there was clearly some divergence, which has been seized on by those who, reading forwards and backwards from their own ideological standpoint, are predisposed to suggest either a peasant or a proletarian status. Until very lately, the weight of recent scholarship has leaned towards the former. From James's simplistic characterisation of the Haitian rebels as 'revolutionary peasants', through studies of maroon societies which emphasise their African peasant roots, from the study of 'the peasant breach in the slave mode of production' that was initiated by the famous article by Sidney Mintz and Douglas Hall on the origins of the Jamaican internal marketing system (1960), and from the subsequent re-readings of the aims of most of the late slave rebels in the British colonies, have come conclusions that, as far as was possible to them in their own time, and beyond the ken or control of their masters, West Indian slaves engaged in a proto-peasant lifestyle that echoed African and foreshadowed post-emancipation Caribbean modes.[10]

Even more recently, though, several students of British West Indian slavery, taking a lead perhaps from an article written by Richard Hart in 1973, have shown the ways in which towards the end of slavery in several different areas, slaves were engaged in forms of quasi-industrial action and were virtually (in Nigel Bolland's phrase) proto-proletarians. Barry Gaspar, for example, has illustrated how the Antiguan slaves marched on Government House in 1831 to demand the restoration of what had become their traditional (and legal) rights to Sunday markets, while Mary Turner has described in detail how slaves in eastern Jamaica were able to insist on their customary manner and levels of work. In marginal or decayed plantation colonies such as Belize and the Bahamas, where slaves had long been accustomed to being hired out or working on their own for wages not all of which were surrendered to their owners, the process was even more marked, and it became almost a general rule later in colonies where the slavery system survived late into the nineteenth century.[11]

Taken to an extreme, it could be argued that the inevitable dialectic of negotiation that had always occurred between what the slave owners wanted from their slaves and what the slaves were prepared to give in the way of work had always been a form of industrial relations, with the black slave drivers as intermediaries. Philip Morgan for one has suggested that the choice of task over gang work was a product of such an informal dialectic. From the master's point of view, all was in the cause of output optimisation, and it might be argued that the success of the slaves in informal negotiation was both a factor in persuading percipient owners to favour free wage labour, and a precursor of later employer-employee relations. Certainly it seems obvious that the level of work determined by local committees of planters as reasonable for apprentices during the crucial transition from slavery to free wage labour in the British colonies both represented what level in each district the slaves had achieved as the customary expectation, and the basic pattern that was to obtain after slavery ended.[12]

Looking at the way that the Haitian Revolution and later manifestations of slave resistance affected the emancipation process, first in the British and then successively in the French, Danish, Dutch and Spanish colonial systems, the degree to which in each bloc ex-slaves achieved their goals and, conversely, the extent to which the former slave-owners were able to sustain their political and socioeconomic hegemony, helps us to understand the relative power and success of the counterposed ideologies.

In the twelfth chapter of *Capitalism and Slavery*, appended rather awkwardly to his main economic arguments, Eric Williams suggested that the threat of an extension of the Haitian Revolution – as occurred in Barbados in 1816, Demerara in 1823 and Jamaica in 1831 – was a strong additional argument for the expedience of emancipation to British politicians. Emancipation granted from above could save the essentials of the plantation system, whereas the alternative, emancipation from below, would be devastating. Developing Williams' suggestion more broadly, it has been proposed that all forms of resistance by slaves were increasingly seen to be counterproductive, and that the emergent philosophy of enlightened self-interest proposed that by freeing the slaves and providing them with the incentives of wages not only would a civilised concord prevail, but at the same time productivity would be increased and the plantocratic system retained. Rephrased in Gramscian terms, this posited a technique whereby the ruling class would sustain its hegemony through winning over the labouring classes to an apparently liberal change which they approved. The essential fraudulence of the procedure ensured that the labouring class would soon return to forms of resistance not so different from those of the preceding slavery era.[13]

How far were these forces and tactics illustrated throughout the Caribbean throughout the nineteenth century? In the British colonies, although the Haitian Revolution and even the 1816 and 1823 rebellions were followed by tightened controls, the huge Jamaican rebellion of 1831-32 certainly had an important effect on the final stages of the emancipation debate. Yet if either the imperial legislators or any planters believed that the freed slaves, after the transitional four-year stage of apprenticeship in most colonies, would become a contented work-force, they were soon disabused. Except in the few areas where they were able to command satisfactory wages and conditions, the ex-slaves fled the plantations for the life of full-time peasants if they could. The plantocracies, especially in colonies where there was much accessible land for would-be peasants, almost immediately resorted to a strategy of coercion, restricting access to land, charging rents for customary houses and garden plots and tying them to plantation labour, and passing strict coercive laws (already well-established in the metropole), concerning master-servant relations, vagrancy and policing. In addition, in those colonies with large areas of fertile land undeveloped before slavery was ended – particularly Guiana, Trinidad and St Lucia – the plantocracies, with the connivance of the imperial government and the British government in India, began the steady importation of an alternative work-force of East Indians under terms of indentureship that were little better than 'a new system of slavery'.[14]

Although some ex-slaves became true peasants or townsfolk, and a very few proletarian wage-labourers, the most notable creation in the British West Indies was the type which Richard Frucht labelled 'part-peasant, part-proletarian'. All elements exhibited forms of protest and resistance towards oppression, that can be variously characterised as peasant rebellions, urban unrest, or industrial action, complicated by increasing elements of ethnic as well as racial and class discord. In the first category can be placed the 'Guerre Nègre' in Dominica (1844), the 'Vox Populi' riots in St Vincent (1862), the Morant Bay Rebellion in Jamaica (1865) and the 'Belmana' riots in Tobago (1876), more in the second, the Christmas riots in Kingston Jamaica in 1840 and 1841, the 'Angel Gabriel' riots in British Guiana (1857) and the Federation Riots in Barbados (1876). Elements of the third category can be traced in all surviving plantation areas but were most common in the Guianas, where the frequency of strikes, the beginnings of labour organisation, and the first glimmerings of class solidarity between Afro-Guianese and East Indians led Walter Rodney to write, as his posthumous legacy, a book that might almost have been titled 'The Making of the Guyanese Working Class'.[15]

In the French plantation colonies, there was a general climate of non-cooperation climaxing in overt rebellion in 1848 that was an important contributory cause to the emancipation of French slaves by the metropolitan revolutionaries, with a spill-over effect in the nearby Danish Virgin Islands. In 1848 French colonial slaves eagerly picked up the symbols and rhetoric deriving from the earlier and greater French Revolution as well as the Haitian Revolution, and their unrest inspired sentiments in the French Assembly from the bourgeois liberal poet-politician Lamartine that might have been spoken earlier by English anti-slavery advocates:

> We must not forget that each inflammable word pronounced here touches not simply on the conscience of our colleagues or the anxiety of the *colons*, but also reaches the ears of three hundred thousand slaves; that which we discuss calmly and without danger from this tribune, concerns the property, the fortune and the life of our compatriots in the colonies.[16]

So great was slave unrest in the French colonies in response to revolutionary events in the metropolis (coupled with the fear of a planter counter-revolution), that the municipal councils of Martinique and Guadeloupe, on the advice of the governors, independently announced slave emancipation several days before the arrival of the definitive decree from Paris. In Danish St Croix a few weeks later the slaves were even more instrumental in their own emancipation, when a mass uprising led by Martin King and Buddoe persuaded Governor Scholten to declare slave emancipation without any authority from Copenhagen.

The freeing of the French slaves was a climatic triumph for Victor Schoelcher, the 'French Wilberforce', but it is worth noting that he was what one might term a bourgeois type of socialist. The son of an Alsatian factory owner, he was in favour of the industrial modernisation of the Caribbean sugar industry for the way that it would facilitate the association of wage-earning workers, and he resolutely opposed the type of peasant proprietorship which was the ideal of most Caribbean slaves. In the Virgin Islands too, the celebrations of the freed slaves quickly turned to further unrest when it was realised that they would be turned out of their houses and grounds if they did not continue to work on their former owners' estates, and would be forced into harsh labour contracts if they wished to keep them. Van Scholten himself requested troops from Puerto Rico to put down disturbances, and Buddoe was deported.[17]

Although slave emancipation in Dutch Surinam was not decreed until 1863, there was continuous covert resistance and open unrest at the times of British and French emancipation and when the Dutch government dragged its heels in the 1850s. Commissioners' reports concluded that given the slaves' obvious preference for the life of an independent peasantry, some form of coercive labour would be necessary for the continuation of the plantations. Tensions heightened as four successive emancipation bills were defeated between 1856 and 1862, while the government and missionary societies made last-minute attempts to educate the slaves in their forthcoming responsibilities. The final Emancipation Act of July 1, 1863, was received with qualified enthusiasm by the freed people since it called for a ten-year period of enforced labour contracts under state supervision. Significantly, it was noted that many of the ex-slaves celebrated their new status with Afro-Caribbean dances previously banned and that there were riots against the labour contract provisions within a week. In the longer run, the Dutch planters despaired of compelling their ex-slaves to continue plantation labour, and all Christian pastors noted a decided decline in Christian observance after 1863. The wholesale importation of indentured labourers into Surinam from India after 1873 (as into British Guiana and Trinidad since the 1830s) and Indonesia after 1891, was as much an indication of the ex-slaves' resistance to plantation labour and preference for either town life or an Afro-Caribbean peasant lifestyle, as of the planters' failure to create an effective wage work-force from their ex-slaves.[18]

Although slave emancipation was a more protracted, gradual and complex process in the Spanish colonies, slave resistance still had important effects, both in convincing government and planters of the expediency and efficiency of switching to alternative labour systems, and in more direct ways. In their resistance, indeed, the slaves often found allies among liberals and independentists, who — although they might proclaim libertarian principles — needed black support more than they needed slaves, actually favoured free wage labour over slavery on grounds of expedience, or had no direct involvement in the slave plantation system.

In Puerto Rico, as Díaz Soler has shown, slave revolts punctuated the first three-quarters of the nineteenth century. These were mainly of the familiar localised plantation type in the sugar-growing areas, but they also occurred in conjunction with planned or rumoured republican invasions, or in response to harsh government decrees such as General Prim's notorious *banda contra la raza africana* of 1848, which was itself a response to the events in St Croix and the French Antilles. Liberal elements in Spain were in favour of both colonial independence and slave emancipation, and in the debates in the short-lived liberal parliament of 1868, the white creole delegates from the Caribbean, using arguments that were practical as well as idealistic, were instrumental in promoting slave emancipation along with independence. The ideal of independence was buried in the defeat of the liberals in Spain, and general emancipation in Cuba postponed. But Puerto Rican emancipationism survived for lack of a powerful enough counter-advocacy either in the colony or metropole. Even a fair number of the Puerto Rican sugar planters were confident that they could replace their inefficient resistant slaves with an alternative work-force made up of local free blacks and imported workers in competition with each other – citing the example of the Dominican Republic, where sugar plantations had developed despite the final freeing of the Dominican slaves by Jean Pierre Boyer in 1822. Consequently, the Moret Law of 1870 which freed all the new-born children of Spanish slaves was followed three years later by the formal emancipation of all Puerto Rican slaves.[19]

Slave resistance on a small and localised scale, especially involving *marronage*, can be traced throughout the history of Cuba; but it dramatically increased in the nineteenth century in conjunction with the spread of sugar plantations, under the influence of the Haitian and Latin American revolutions, and the early phases of Cuban independence that climaxed in the Ten Years' War of 1868-78. Most of this slave resistance remained localised and opportunistic on traditional grounds, and the slaves naturally identified with any sector that favoured their emancipation, or they seized whatever opportunities arose to better their conditions as the result of civil strife. The case of collaborative plotting with free coloureds in the Aponte conspiracy of 1811 has already been mentioned, and in his brilliant recent book on the complex conspiracy of La Escalera in the 1840s, Robert Paquette quotes the plausible analysis of the chief martyr of the episode, the mulatto poet Placido:

> From what has been said once can deduce that six [in fact, five] plans existed, namely, the abolitionist, which is more of a religious sect than a hostile party; the independents; the *pardos* [free coloureds] deceived by them; the free blacks who have formed themselves from information gathered without any other support than their strong desire to destroy everyone; and the slaves who want to be free.[20]

The activities of Cuban slaves in the Ten Years' War were even more critical. The metropolitan Spanish emancipation decree of 1868 (shortlived in any case) had no general effect in Cuba. But the Cuban revolutionary junta declared slave emancipation, and a large number of blacks joined in the fighting to achieve their liberty,. These *libertos*, however, were rarely treated as equals even in the fighting ranks, and when the Treaty of Zanjón was signed in February 1878 it no more guaranteed full emancipation than it made Cuba independent. A general amnesty was proclaimed and slaves 'within the insurrectionary lines' were recognised as free. But for the remaining slaves the limits of imperial emancipationism were fixed by the gradualist Moret Law of 1870. Outright emancipationists such as the mulatto revolutionary, General Maceo, were as disappointed as the slave majority, and the slaves' struggle continued and actually intensified.

For a short time, the conservative Cuban planters felt that the system of slavery remained indispensable, although to impose it required the continuous presence of imperial troops. For their part, the slaves rioted, ran away in droves and did as little work as they could get away with. The governor-general reported to Madrid in 1879 that many masters had felt compelled to offer their slaves wages and promises of freedom, while others complained that fires had been set in the canefields by slaves who used the slogan *libertad no viene, cana no ha*; 'If Liberty does not come, there will be no cane.'

The last wave of overt slave resistance, as much as the planters' change of heart and alternative labour arrangements, contributed significantly to the passing of the transitional *patronato* law in 1880 which anticipated final emancipation in 1888. During this ultimate phase, the resistance of the Cuban slaves took the forms not only of doing as little work as possible but of purchasing their freedom out of the *patronato* system. So successful were they in this that when full freedom came in October 1886 – two years before it was originally scheduled – there were only 25,000 *patronicados* left to be freed, a quarter of the original total of 1880 and one-fifteenth of the number of Cuban slaves at the outbreak of the Ten Years' War in 1868.[21]

Turning back from a concentration of the role played by the slaves in the transition from slavery to free wage labour to more general motive forces and motivation, mainly external, a second broad way towards understanding suggests itself: a consideration of the current state of the 'Williams Debate' over the centrality of economics in the process.

In trying to explain the rise and fall of Atlantic slavery as a labour system, the best of modern scholarship has tried to reconcile the economic, political and philanthropic factors, and has been at pains to show how multi-casual explanations have always been inherent. This is the drift of William Darity's recent analysis of Eric Williams' forerunners. Even Williams himself in his Oxford doctoral dissertation, as Howard Temperley has bravely pointed out, was merely trying to reassess the economic component in the process against those who unduly asserted the primacy of philanthropic-philosophical and political features. What Temperley terms the reductionist economic determinism of *Capitalism and Slavery* was the result, he suggests, in an ascending order, of an ambitious young scholar's determination to turn his thesis into a publishable book, of the discrimination Williams felt he had suffered as a black colonial, and of the changing political conditions that in due course (after its reissue in 1964) were to make it the 'little red book' of an ardent Caribbean black nationalist.[22]

Yet even though the polarisation of *Capitalism and Slavery* faded along with Williams' personal charisma, an understanding of the economic issues involved remains essential to participation in all facets of the grand debate – involving class and ethnic effects as well as the merely structural changes in the labour system. As Stanley Engerman and Barbara Solow explain the cogent introduction to the papers of the first conference devoted entirely to *Capitalism and Slavery*, held at Bellagio in 1984, these focus on four interconnected sub-disputes, of which the third seems to generate most heat and least final illumination. Put at their simplest, these are the questions of whether slavery was the product of racism or vice versa, the degree to which slavery made the Industrial Revolution possible and thus made the ending of slavery advantageous, the question of when, or even whether, a decline occurred in the profitability of the slave trade and slave plantation nexus, and finally, the precise concatenation between economic concerns and the necessary legislation to end the trade and free the slaves.[23]

The debate concerning whether Africans were enslaved because there was an existing racial prejudice against them, regarding them as inferiors and natural slaves; or because economic necessity required an extreme form of coerced labour and Africans were available – with racism becoming the traders' and planters' *post hoc* justification – has most ardently been played out in US scholarship.[24] Williams' argument that slavery had nothing initially to do with race and that racism was a product of economic realities in the plantation colonies, carrying over to entrench and complicate class relations in the post-slavery period, has had some proponents in Caribbean scholarship. Most notably, Hilary Beckles has striven to show how there was nothing structurally to distinguish white indentured servants from black slaves in the earliest years, and that there was even some form of class solidarity between them in the first instances of servile unrest in Barbados. The purpose and consequences of subsequent racist differentiation, in slavery and after emancipation alike, is therefore manifest: to cloak and muffle the emergence of a genuine proletarian consciousness. The objection that this purpose would have been nullified once there was an absolute coincidence between black ethnicity and slave status can be countered by the argument that in fact the capitalist class ensured and continued its hegemony both by allowing the emergence of black intermediaries – élite privileged slaves, treaty maroons, free coloureds and blacks – and, after slavery, by importing labourers who were non-African.[25]

The view that Africans were especially suited to slavery has recently received some unexpected ammunition from the arguments of Kenneth Kiple in *The Caribbean Slave: A Biological History* about Africans' immunities to certain diseases and their long biological adaptation to low protein diets. Although Kiple clearly intends this to be something of a compliment to Africans and Afro-Americans, the thesis has predictably been called overt racism, and rejected by most Caribbean scholars in favour of the Williams explanation that Afro-American slavery was simply 'a supply of labor, with certain productivity and costs, whose adoption was determined by considerations of profit-maximisation'.[26]

The debate over the contribution of profits from the slave trade and West Indian plantations to European capital accumulation and the Industrial Revolution, which has engaged many fine economic historians (mostly in the anti-Williams camp),[27] is of little direct relevance to the present case, save in the way that the manifest success of the British economy (including its agricultural as well as growing industrial sectors) on the basis of wage-earners rather than a directly coerced work-force argued against the continuation of slave labour in a plantation system that demanded equally efficiency. But what was extremely relevant – engaging even more scholars on both sides of a debate that, it must be admitted, sometimes approaches the tedious – are the still smouldering questions of whether a decline in profitability led successively to the abolition of the slave trade and the ending of slavery or, conversely, whether if a decline occurred it came as a result rather than as a cause of abolition and emancipation.

Eric Williams took up the assumption made by the American, Lowell J. Ragatz that the loss of the Thirteen Colonies was followed by a continuous and irreversible decline in the profitability of the West Indian slave plantation nexus, and assert a casual connection to the subsequent changes in imperial theory and policy which saw, successively, the abolition of the British slave trade, the ending of formal slavery, and the abrogation of colonial protectionism. Brilliantly suggestive, Williams' thesis was vitiated (apart from some manifest errors) by a general fuzziness over statistics, by not distinguishing adequately between the separate components of the slave trade, plantation production and trading nexus, and a complete failure to prove a direct connection between a recognition of falling profits and a decision to switch from slavery to free wage labour. Notoriously reluctant to discuss his own *obiter dicta* in academia, Williams left the debate to lesser mortals, who continue to squabble without satisfactory resolution nearly a decade after his death.[28]

The first thrust against the Williams Decline Thesis came out of the pro-altruist school with the work of G. R. Mellor and Roger Anstey. But its most unrelenting critic has been Seymour Drescher, who argued in *Econocide* (1977) and subsequent work that although there may have been short-term declines in profitability, the general trend was upward until well after the slave trade was ended in 1807. Drescher added that the undeniable subsequent decline, accelerating in the 1820s, 1830s and 1840s, was therefore a consequence, not a cause, of abolition, emancipation and the gradual shift to free trade. Palmerston's continuing persistence against the non-British slave trade was likewise evidence of a policy indefensible on selfish economic grounds. Drescher's case has been strongly supported on the plantation side by John Ward, who stresses the increasing number of technical improvements and the continuance of investments from 1750 to 1834 as evidence that British slave plantations were basically profitable, until slavery ended, and on the slave trading side by David Eltis, with the somewhat counter-factual argument that the profits that might have been made in supplying slave labour to the undeveloped new colonies of Trinidad, British Guiana and St Lucia were so great that stopping the trade and freeing the slaves were indeed economic suicide. Eltis expands his analysis to test the effects of Britain's long campaign against the foreign slave trade, emphatically to argue that it was economically disadvantageous.[29]

Against such an array of econometric talent, the valiant counterattacks of Selwyn Carrington often appear a desperate enterprise.[30] The precise components, dimensions and dating of the decline and imperial policy. Yet the search for a precision over contemporary actualities (unknown, indeed, at the time) may be obscuring more important general points. For whether the actual decline came first or later, it is clear that there was from at least 1783 both a sense of economic decline and a decline in support for a slave-based system, while economic as well as moral arguments were being put forward for changes and alternatives. Moreover, the preservation of what was worth keeping called for changing policies, and any losses in one sector might well be made up in another, along with a general gain in moral credit. Such thinking, rather than precise statistics, or even an exact knowledge of actual conditions, was what determined what happened in the way of legislation.

Thus the ending of the British slave trade was actively favoured by the older sugar colonies scared of competition and overproduction from the new, just as the British colonies later supported the denial of slave trading to their foreign competitors. Amelioration of slave conditions after abolition was aimed at improving the demographic performance, and thus the cheapness and efficiency, of the slave work-force; yet one amelioration was shown to be a disastrous failure in these respects by the revelations of the slave registration returns, publicised by Buxton and Stephen, emancipation became the inevitable option, approved by philanthropists and economic optimisers alike.[31] Emancipation could be painted as a philanthropic gesture, but was only achieved by compensating the slave-owners for their sacred property and guaranteeing the continuation of coerced labour, at least for a time. Even when these measures failed to arrest the decline of planter fortunes or compel the ex-slaves to become plantation wage workers, the imperial government still supported the plantations and plantocracies to an extent, despite free trade and *laissez-faire*, by endorsing policies of dear land and other methods of labour compulsion, and by encouraging alternative supplies of cheap labour. Neither side won a simple or quick victory in the transition from a policy of protection and slavery to one of free trade and free labour, any more than there is a simple solution, or a simple polarisation, in what might now be called the Williams-Drescher Debate.

My own conclusion in 1992 would remain close to the multi-casual formula proposed in *Sinews of Empire* in 1974 (which, in part, inadvertently expanded the conclusion of William Cunningham as early as 1907, quoted by both Darity and Carrington). The 1974 formulation anticipated most of the elements in the 'overarching imperial ideology' described by Davis and Eltis, if somewhat optimistically seeing Adam Smith's notion of Enlightened Self Interest as a universal key:

> Although Adam Smith and his followers believed that the proper operation of enlightened self-interest and the removal of narrow protectionism would result in moral as well as material improvement, their attack on slavery was concentrated on its uneconomic aspects . . . Enlightened self-interest could only work to the public good if it were to the advantage of employers and employed alike that the workers advance in intelligence, usefulness, and the ownership of property. This could only be achieved by emancipation and the consequent decline of plantations based on slavery. Yet by condemning the old plantation system, emancipation might destroy the justification for mercantilist protection and release such energies that all sections in due course would be bound to benefit.

. . . Apparently, philanthropy, *laissez-faire* and enlightened self-interest were neatly blended, at every level.[32]

Although some might feel that the scope and sophistication of Davis and Eltis have relegated the cliometric conflict between Drescher and Carrington to the status of a marginal skirmish, enough problems, however, remain to fuel the 'Williams Debate' for at least the rest of this century. First, there is the question of incalculability. Whatever the proponents of abolition and emancipation argued and believed would be the outcome was a quite different causal factor from arguments generated from the actual results of initial changes. Contingencies in history are invariably so complex as to deny rational expectations. Second, there was the uncomfortable fact that even within the same empire there were at the same time some colonies in which neither slave trade nor slavery were any longer necessary, and others in which both trade and institution were thought to be absolutely vital for economic well-being or expansion. This touches on the question of precisely who was in favour of slavery, and who anti-slavery, at any given time; and finally, on the dating question which bedevils much of the debate. Were not the factors involved in a decision to end the trade necessarily different – not even similar – from those involved in the ending of slavery itself, and those concerned with the initiation of both processes by the British not bound to be very different from those affecting the French, Danish, Dutch and Spanish governments subsequently?

A residual overconcentration on abolitionism – moreover British abolitionism – remains a flaw even of Eltis' impressive work (quite apart from his ill-defined notions of both ideology and economic progress, and his historical tendency towards counter-factual arguments). Only by reconnecting abolitionism and emancipationism and widening our perspective to see what actually happened throughout the region up to 1886, and why it happened, can we hope to arrive at a clearer final notion of what the prevailing or dominant ideology was. One unexpected, and unlooked-for, result might be the vindication of Eric Williams on an even grander scale than that least modest of all historians imagined: by showing that in the long run and over the widest compass, slavery continued wherever it was needed by the dominant class, and finally came to an end only when economic conditions making slavery preferable to that class had irrevocably changed.

Far more than in the quarter-century between the abolition of the British slave trade and the emancipation of British slaves, the half-century between the first freeing of slaves by the British and of the liberation from formal bonds of the last Spanish slaves, saw immense social and economic changes in the Caribbean plantation sphere. By the end of the century, not only had slavery ended, with the ex-slaves and their descendants constituting a new cash and wage-oriented class of consumers engaged in a combination of peasant and proletarian functions, but the whole nature and location of economic activity had changed and shifted. Most obviously, in their battle to retain plantation production the old sugar colonies had almost suffered complete defeat at the hands of Cuba, with its huge modern central factories, producing some 40 per cent of the whole world's supply of cane sugar. A third large cohort of scholars, particularly in the hispanic Caribbean, has in recent years been avidly engaged in describing and explaining the nature of these changes, particularly in the whirling debate (literally so, for many of the arguments become circular) as to which change drove which.

Some of the factors involved, such as the steady increase in Caribbean populations after about 1840, the first worldwide economic slump; at the end of the 1840s and the facilitation of labour migration, were quite clearly new; others were recurrent or continuous survivals, such as the revival of revolutionary and reformist ideals in 1848 and during the last independence wars and the persistent activities of idealist abolitionists; while most of the remaining factors were at least incipient in the initiation of the process of abolition and emancipation by the British. Of these last, however, the most critical – the eternal quest for profit maximisation, optimisation and the need for economies of scale through managerial, organisational, technical and mechanical improvements in the face of increasing competition, freer international trade and a developing capitalist system – became hugely more important and reinforced each other during the period from 1850 to 1900.

The doyen of studies of the development of the Cuban sugar industry and its labour systems is the Cuban writer Francisco Moreno Fraginals, whose magnificent three-volume work *El Ingenio* (1964, 1978) was supplemented by his brilliant overview article for the collection of papers from the conference 'Problems of Transition from Slavery to Free Labour in the Caribbean' held in Santo Domingo in 1981.[33] Moreno argues that however much slavery might have been a necessary feature of the early phases of the Cuban sugar industry, it became progressively less relevant under the accelerating changes that occurred after 1860. These changes were not just technical but also commercial. He produces definitive evidence that it was not just a case of the introduction of steam power allowing for the extension of the orbit of existing factories, but of the creation of whole new *centrales*, with a consequent consolidation that reduced the number of mills by 80 per cent in 35 years, despite the doubling of the total Cuban crop to a million tons a year. This was accompanied by what he calls a new latifundisation that gradually took the new *centrales* out of the hands of the old Cuban sugar-growing families into those of *nouveaux riches*, or corporations, increasingly foreign-owned.

Because field methods increasingly lagged behind factory technology (indeed, remained almost static), a widening gap opened between factory operatives and field labourers, while at the same time shortened cane-cropping seasons magnified the natural tendency of modern factories towards a greater periodicity of labour demand that had obtained in the old slave plantations. Slaves, argues Moreno, were not wanted in the mill, nor was their labour needed throughout the year in the field. Alternative types of labour were sought – indentured short-term workers, seasonal day-labourers, even convicts – or the *centrales* sought their cane from sharecroppers or small cane-farmers, becoming exploitative landowners as well as employers. The process of exploitation went even further as the owner of *centrales* diversified into other forms of industry, commerce and landlordism. They came to own passenger-carrying railways, electricity power-plants, foundries, and all the shops their employees and others could need (including brothels and gaming houses). Not only would employees pay rent for their housing, deducted from pay, they would be given seemingly generous advances, only a small percentage of which would be in cash, the rest in tokens redeemable only in company stores. Thus was gradually created a thoroughly modernised exploited consumer-proletariat.

The Ten Years' War (1868-78) actually aided the process of modernisation, with more aggressive factories buying up the smaller, weaker or war-damaged, consolidating and expanding, at a time when prices remained high because of war conditions. Foreign investment steadily increased, and although American direct investment remained comparatively small before 1900, the US market took an increasingly large share of the product, helped by the oligopolistic structure of production and refining, and the increasing importance of brokerage and speculation in shipping, storage and distribution. Competition from subsidised beet sugar actively favoured the more efficient producers, as did the demand for a single high-quality product, packed in easily stowed bags rather than the unwieldy muscovado hogsheads of the past. Improvements in shipping (which saw the tonnage carried on steamships exceed that carried by sailing ships in 1870) not only brought markets closer, but facilitated the migration of Chinese indentured labour and of poor Spanish *gallegos*. All these factors, concludes Moreno, conspired not only to place the Cuban sugar industry more firmly under the control of foreign capital and subject to world market forces but, by enforcing efficiency, to make a slave labour system progressively outdated.

The conclusions of Moreno Fraginals about the progressive subjugation of the Caribbean economy to world capitalist forces and the consequent embattlement of the Caribbean working class, are underlined by the fascinating study of the interaction of sugar production and the development of Cuban railroads (and of the related growth of a proletarian section within the railway system) by Zanetti and Garcia. The theme of the progressive retardation of indigenous Cuban capitalism in the plantation and plantation-based industrial sectors, with its implications for Cuban labour, is reinforced by Jean Stubb's 1985 book on Cuban tobacco. Moreno's generalisations are also nearly all borne out by the parallel studies of the development of the sugar, coffee and tobacco industries and labour systems in Puerto Rico and the Dominican Republic by Francisco Scarano, Tony Ramos Mattei, Benjamin Nistal-Moret, Frank Moya Pons, Laird Bergad, Michiel Baud and others, as are his generalisations about the growing importance of labour migration by the important study *Labour Migration under Capitalism: The Puerto Rican Experience*, published by the History Task Force of the Centro de Estudios Puertorriquenos in 1982. But Moreno's sweeping assertion that slavery as a labour system was doomed simply because it was incompatible with plantation modernisation has not gone without challenge, notably by Rebecca Scott and, mainly for the non-hispanic Caribbean in an earlier phase, by most of the contributors to the symposium 'Changing Sugar Technology and the Labour Nexus' held at the Americanists' Congress in Amsterdam in July 1988, at which the outstanding problems were posed by the Dutch scholars, Peter Boomgaard and Gert Oostindie, and a concluding summary attempted by the present author.[34]

Against Moreno, Scott points out the fact that far from a reluctance to use slaves in Cuba, slaves were used and even preferred in the technical operations of the modernised Cuban *centrales* (perhaps because they were the most permanent workers), and she posits a far more complex and multi-causal explanation for the phasing out of slavery in Cuba.[35] It is worth noting too that the conditions governing the choice for or against a black slave work-force were bound to be very different in territories (like Puerto

Rico and the Dominican Republic as well as Cuba) in which blacks never made up as much as half of the population, than in those in which blacks were the overwhelming majority. At Amsterdam, preferred explanations were too multi-causal, and the notion that slavery and technological improvement were necessarily incompatible was rejected out of hand. John Ward, for example, pointed out that the failure of the plough, and of many other attempted technical improvements, was due to factors other than the competence of the black slaves. Several contributors pointed out that slaves were never so cheap that there were disincentives on this account to make improvements; nor did their prices ever rise so steeply that for this reason alone the owners were driven to seek technical improvements, or to seek out alternative sources of labour. What were more potent practical arguments for technological improvements and a change from slave labour alike were those conditions of declining market prices (due to increased competition through overproduction or a decline of protection) that made old-style plantations no longer viable, and a seasonal wage work-force preferable to a permanent dependent population (including infants, superannuated and sick), however effectively they were coerced, or even encouraged.[36]

The author's somewhat deflating conclusion was that even the economic equation that explained the transition from slavery to free wage labour,

> clearly involved many more variables besides those of labour and technology. However widely labour and technology are defined, at least five other related and intertwined factors have to be considered: the availability and suitability of land; the supply of capital; the access to markets and market prices; management strategies, attitudes and personnel; and finally, changing economic policies – specifically those designed to speed the transition from narrow mercantilist units to a world-wide 'free trade' system.

Taking his arguments from the case of Worthy Park, Jamaica, which almost totally failed as a sugar estate after 1846 despite strenuous efforts by its intelligent owner-manager, the author pointed out that although land for optimal expansion was not an immediate problem in this case, and that capital was available to a surprising degree,

> what it could achieve was severely limited by labour and technical constraints. Thirdly, technological modifications were tried but they failed for reasons unrelated to whether they could, or did, increase productivity. Fourthly, labour was a problem, but chiefly on account of the need to reorganise it efficiently into a two-tier system of a small corps of permanent workers and a larger seasonal cane-cutting gang, its availability when needed, and its cost.

Imperial policy was seen to be a problem since the owners at that time could not visualise a profit without a subsidised market price of 10 shillings per hundredweight and the subsidised importation of East Indian labourers, who would drive down the going rate of wages from one shilling and sixpence to twopence or fourpence a day. For the bottom line was clearly the world sugar price, which by that time had fallen so low that Worthy Park's total income from sugar (not its level of profit) had fallen below the estate's total wage bill for labour.

The author pointed out the apparent anomaly that while Jamaica, which under slavery had been the richest sugar island, by the end of the nineteenth century had reverted to a largely ranching and peasant subsistence economy (with its male population available to migrate for wage labour), the case in Cuba and Puerto Rico had been almost exactly reversed. 'Viewing this transition in the widest perspective,' the author concluded, coming closer to Moreno's formulation,

> it was clearly a local function of an age that saw great developments in the internationalization of capital, the spread of free trade and *laissez-faire* principles, the world-wide organization of transportation, processing and marketing, and, not the least, the more efficient organization of migratory labour on a global scale.[37]

This oversimple causal formula skates too easily over the vital questions of the ways in which capital migrated and the migration of labour was facilitated. In the former case, much more needs to be known, for example, about when, why and how British capital migrated from old colonies to new, and from formal colonies into informal spheres of investment, such as Cuba and Brazil. In the latter case, much more needs to be said about the ways in which the new imperialism of the free trade era led not only to labour migration within the region but, from an even earlier period, to large-scale migration of labourers into the region from British India, Dutch Indonesia, and from a not formally colonised China.[38] The Amsterdam formula is also — like most of the present essay — concerned too much with causes and not enough with results. In transformations in the planter-capitalist, peasant and proletarian classes, and in the dynamics of interaction between them.

Again in the broadest terms, the process of change over the entire region and period can be separated into four main components, of which the last two, probably rightly, have attracted most attention in the recent secondary literature. First, the protracted and stepped transition out of a slave labour system, representing and itself intensifying the widening and tightening world market and capitalist forces, can be seen in terms of the creation of a cash-oriented consumer society increasingly dependent on wages over which it has little control, with workers being forced to migrate under the dictates of economic necessity.

Second, the constraints and drives which made industries on the colonial periphery more efficiency-oriented and exploitative also made them more impersonal and the workers consequently more depersonalised. Thus ex-slaves and their descendants who were regarded as totally non-productive, were totally ignored – a form of neglect that can rarely be labelled benign. Those in the peasant sector were steadily degraded into part-time labourers, having neither the means for year-round peasant subsistence nor sufficient wages to opt for a proletarian alternative. The remaining pure proletarians had no options at all, but had to migrate where they could for what work there was, competing against each other for what wages were offered, and certain to be paid off when no longer needed or preferred. The dependence of the economy on external and worldwide forces, and the trends of industries towards economies of scale and to corporate and absentee ownership, increased their impersonality and the depersonalisation of the workers.

Third, the capitalist intensification of the post-slavery phase extended beyond the plantation and extractive industries (such as timber and salt) for which slavery had been instituted, to affect virtually all ex-slaves and their descendants. New forms of exploitation and dependency, even new industries, were devised to capitalise upon the labour of the landless; for example, by the systems of truck, credit and binding advances in many forms of urban employment, in the fishing, turtling and sponging industries, and in the increasing varieties of migrant contract labour and stevedoring. For those would-be peasants without the means or will to work for plantations or other wage-payers –and for the womenfolk and families of migrant labourers – there were the many varieties of sharecropping (or *métayage*), none of them, of course, fully advantageous to the sharecroppers/*métayers*.

Fourth, to the ex-slaves and their descendants who continued to work on the plantations, on whom scholarship has so far concentrated (especially as regards sugar plantations), the structural and organisational changes were similarly disadvantageous. Immediately slavery ended, optimising managers were able to trim and shape their work-forces to suit the needs of crop and factory. This had two salient effects besides the general one of making the new wage-earners, not the former owners, responsible for the maintenance of the non-productive members of their families. The first was the bifurcation of the work-force into a small nucleus of permanent workers and a much larger force of seasonal wage labourers. The former were skilled, indispensable, relatively privileged, rooted to the locality, trusty and almost exclusively male – much like the 'confidential élite' slaves of the former era. The latter (whose proportion of the total increased with technological change up to five, even ten, to one) were unskilled, dispensable, of necessity migrant, with their reliability only guaranteed on the shaky grounds of dependence and competition among themselves. The second salient effect of the shift from slavery to wage labour on the plantations was the trimming of the work-force towards the employers' desideratum of making it entirely male. For obvious and well-studied reasons, the field work-force of a slave plantation was at least 60 per cent female; yet optimising managers after slavery ended (such as at Worthy Park, Jamaica) made it as far as possible 100 per cent male. The degree to which they succeeded, and the reasons why they never were completely successful, along with the implications as to gender roles in post-slavery family, village and economic life, remain open for much more study.

To such direct and indirect 'fruits of merchant capital' I would now add only a much greater awareness, derived mainly from the work of Nigel Bolland, of the ways in which capitalistic intensification and the transition from slavery to free wage labour were inevitably associated with a general galvanisation of the dialectic between capital and labour. In the quasi-feudal relations of slavery days, slave-owners, even in marginal plantation colonies such as the Bahamas or non-plantation colonies like Belize, so rejoiced in their paternalistic power that they bitterly resisted emancipation despite all evidence that slavery was uneconomic. Now in a different dispensation, the former owners, continuing as plantocrats or translated into a creole mercantile oligarchy, sustained and even extended the earlier patterns of domination without any pretence of paternalistic responsibility or *noblesse oblige*, be it over plantation wage-labourers, peasant sharecroppers, fishermen or woodsmen paid in truck, or wage-earning urban artisans. For their part, the former slaves, former proto-peasants or proto-proletarians and their descendants continued to resist their exploitation, and moved, if so slowly, towards a true class consciousness and solidarity. This, for some analysts at least, remains the fundamental transformation.[39]

20

A Recipe for the
Perfect Calalu
Island and Regional Identity
in the West Indies

Introduction: The immediate response to this Elsa Goveia Lecture given in Barbados in 1990 was disappointing. Most of the questions and comments concerned the correct way to cook, or even to spell Calalu. It is included here, however, both because it seems to round off the present collection neatly, and is also one of the most personal and heartfelt of the author's pieces. Calalu is, of course, a metaphor, and what this essay attempts to do is to use historical examples to illustrate what, beyond differences of class and ethnicity, and despite the cultural variations between and even within the islands, constitute the essential ingredients of a sense of Caribbean identity. The author feels that as a historian and an outsider he has a perspective and objectivity beyond those of ordinary West Indians, but this belief enshrines an inner poignancy. Much as he loves the area and people to which and whom he has dedicated his working life, age (and the writing and delivery of the present essay) convince him of the truism that we are essentially and ultimately the natives only of the place where we were born and bred.

For a moment I want to invite you to share with me an indulgence normally denied to all self-respecting professional historians; that is, to be completely subjective. Please search your private minds and ask yourselves the following questions. First, what is the place that you call home, and what is it that makes it so? Second, do any of you (as I did recently when my memory was triggered by a reminiscence of Peter Gzowski) recall from your schooldays writing your full address on the cover of some book in something like the following definitive order: house name and number, street, village, parish, county, country, continent, planet, Solar System, Milky Way, The Universe? And if you did, what did this exercise signify?[2]

The answers to these questions, I believe, relate to the essential elements in one's sense of identity, and I've lately pondered about them and compared notes with some of my West Indian friends, as well as reading such evocative works as Kamau Brathwaite's Barbadian *Mother Poem* and Derek Walcott's Caribbean-transcending *Omeros*.[3] Let us then, first consider home and belonging. The following, in descending order, seem to be the crucial elements of a sense of affective identify towards a place to which you belong, and which therefore essentially belongs to you:

1. Where you were born – and bred, up to a certain critical age.
2. Where your family is – and, to a variable extent, where your more extended family, that is, your antecedents, came from.
3. Where your investment is – materially, where you have bought or acquired land and built, and more abstractly, where you have made a psychic investment.
4. (Some way down the scale.) What your passport reads – or rather, what it means in the world at large.

I believe that we are likely to agree about these simple basic elements, but probably differ considerably about their relative weight and order. At the recent ACH conference in Santo Domingo I had a discussion about them with a colleague, a black Grenadian scholar living in the USA. Edward Cox (for it was he) felt, like me, that living in another country and advancing in age naturally sharpens one's concerns for such questions, and he broadly agreed with my components of identity. But as an Afro-Caribbean, he stressed more than I the importance of possessing family land, the maternal bond, and the significance of distant antecedents – in his case, African.

We talked too about the critical age at which one becomes aware of relating to a particular place and people – which we agreed was a common biological function of growing up –and of differences in aesthetic responses to landscape and to other people living within it. Ed Cox concurred with me that an appreciation of the abstract beauty of the larger landscape – rather than of the usefulness of the smaller family holding, which betokens a narrower rootedness –stems from the European sensibility (or *mentalité*), the sense of a larger possessiveness. For the European, one does not merely want enough; one wants it all. One might make similar conclusions from the way in which in standard English, the words 'lack', 'want' and 'need' are almost interchangeable – or, more precisely, how to want something can mean both to lack it and to desire it, and how to be needy is both to be without and to be deficient. What does this apparent verbal cloudiness tell us about the British cultural psyche? Surely, not so much that the differences are obscured, but that they are occluded: it is almost taken as given that to be without something is to desire it; an unnatural deficiency one expects to be remedied.[4]

When discussing the onset of individual awareness, Ed Cox and I may also have uncovered another aspect of the fundamental differences between European and Africans (and perhaps most other non-Europeans). I cited the extreme solipsis noted in myself when young and in so many autobiographical accounts; that which is beautifully encapsulated in the poem called 'The Island' in *When We Were Very Young* by A. A. Milne:

If I had a ship,
I'd sail my ship,
I'd sail my ship
Through Eastern seas;
Down to the beach where the slow waves thunder –
The green curls over and the white falls under –
Boom! Boom! Boom!
On the sun-bright sand.
Then I'd leave my ship and I'd land . . .
And there would I rest, and lie,
My chin in my hands, and gaze
At the dazzle of sand below,
And the green waves curling slow,
And the grey-blue distant haze
Where the sea goes up to the sky . . .
And I'd say to myself as I looked so lazily down at the sea:
'There's nobody else in the world, and the world was made for me.'[5]

It occurred to us, however, that all the examples I could think of this type of solipsistic self-absorption emanated from white Caucasians. Would it not be fair to say that for most non-Caucasians mentally coming of age, the process of coming to know themselves – for example, the nine-year-old George Lamming of *In the Castle of my Skin* or the young Wole Soyinka in *Aké: the Years of Childhood*[6] – is a very different one? Is it not far more the coming to terms with one's own place in the world; in the community of things, people and spirits?

Maybe we can even go further and suggest that through millennia, Europeans have acquired an overdeveloped ego; while the majority of humankind living outside Europe have what European psychologists have condescendingly termed a 'weak ego structure'. What this really means is a predisposition to believe that people belong to the land (with all its attendant spirits) rather than it belongs to them. Therefore, although a seeming paradox, it is not in fact a contradiction that Europeans (and European laws) become obsessive about freehold title (the quintessential manifestation of possessive individualism), while Africans and Afro-Americans are traditionally content with less formal land tenures, simply guaranteeing the *use* of the land, through families over generations.[7]

It surely also relates to a subtle difference in usage between standard English and English-based West Indian creole. Significantly, it used to annoy me when my West Indian wife used the phrase 'it have' instead of 'there are'. It seemed simply 'bad English'. But reading the following in Derek Walcott's recent epic called *Omeros*, I realised that the usage denotes a significant and fundamental difference; even a different concept of the spiritual essence of things. In *Omeros*, Ma Kilman, the St Lucia shopkeeper-sorceress thinks of something that will cure Phíloctete's festering physical and psychic wound:

> It have a flower somewhere, a medicine, and ways
> my grandmother would boil it . . .[8]

So we differ, subtly but fundamentally, in feelings of belonging and ownership. But it is not, of course, a simple polarity, but as befits the most fragmented, mixed and complex (as well as richest and most dynamically creative) region in the world, a mixture and confusion of sentiments. The strength of identification is affected by time; by the degree of creolisation. Rootedness needs firm, long-lived and healthy roots; when family and land are denied or withheld, where race and class pressures continue oppressive, alienation supervenes. And what about where the contributory cultures fail to mix, remain like oil and water; and miscegenation leads not to syncretic creolisation but to a lingering cultural bifurcation? If one is pessimistic about integration and identification (as, most morbidly perhaps, is V. S. Naipaul) one is bound to observe that a prevailing characteristic of West Indian peoples is the will to get away, chasing the rainbows of an idyllic original homeland, or a promised better future land, like Canada.

But travel, or migration, more positively, is surely the key to understanding more clearly where one has come from, where one truly belongs. To return to our remembered youngster, writing his or her address on a schoolbook cover; what this exercise signifies is surely the truth that the *structure* of our identity is a set of concentric circles or nest of Russian boxes. The heart, kernel, or core may be the individual ego; for me it is, although for others with a different ethno-psycho-cultural inheritance it may go deeper yet, into another dimension of radiating circles, connecting a living soul with the ancestors and the spirits of locations far away. Wherever the true heartland lies, however, at each level of separation from it there is a reassessment, an adjustment to a new environment while re-evaluating the place from which one has come. Thus the schoolchild discovers him or herself, the growing youth leaves the family home, the villager comes to town, the small islander alights on a larger or different island, the islander settles on the main. Our present purpose is simply to decide at what stages within this process and continuum does a person truly come to regard themselves as, say, an unhyphenated Barbadian (that is, neither white nor black, rich nor poor, educated nor unlettered, male nor female, young nor old); and under what circumstances does the same person become a West Indian – albeit, perhaps, only of the hyphenated 'Commonwealth Caribbean' subspecies?

What I have mentioned so far has been musingly (perhaps bemusingly) abstract. Let me briefly try to dignify and justify my clumsy musings with some specific examples, drawn from different historical phases, using a whole range of differing sources.

Stretching the historiographical evidence to its elastic limits, we can, perhaps, trace our themes of narrower and larger, present and former identify right back to the aboriginal inhabitants of the Caribbean. Early European writers and modern iconographers alike have asserted that the Taino who inhabited the Greater Antilles and the Bahamas when Columbus came, retained nostalgic ties with the Lesser Antillean islands and the South American mainland from which their ancestors had migrated. Peter Martyr reported that the Spanish plans to relocate the Taino were facilitated by the Tainan priests' encouragement of the belief that the souls of their dead 'after expiating their sins must leave the cold lands of the north for the south', and that a remigration of the living would enable them to 'reach the country where they would find their dead parents, their children, relatives and friends, and where they would enjoy every delight in the embraces of their loved ones'. This spiritual connection with the former heartland was sustained by the numinous value given to heirloom artefacts, particularly the alloyed metal *guanin*, more valued than gold because it derived from South America; and it is further indicated, claims Fred Olsen, by the cult of Jocahu with its triangular icons, reminiscent of the life-giving fire of the volcanic mountains of the Lesser Antilles.[9]

Yet if the ancestral paradise lay to the south, the terrestrial home, through generations of adaptation and family building, lay to the north and west, even in the flat infertile islands of the ultimate archipelago – the

Bahamas. Peter Martyr himself recorded the pathetic response of the Lucayans when they realised that they had been forced (or duped) by the Spaniards away from their beloved Bahamian islands to the mines of Hispanola. Some, wrote Peter Martyr, escaped into the northern mountains, 'where they might breathe the air wafted from their native county; with extended arms and open mouths they seemed to drink in their native air, and when misery reduced them to exhaustion, they dropped dead upon the ground'. Three heroic Lucayans even fashioned their dugout canoe and set out for their native islands, only to be recaptured 200 miles out to sea.[10]

Let us move on a couple of hundred years or more, and consider the conflicts of identity and their partial resolution among the white European settlers of the British West Indies and their involuntary migrant African slaves – especially considering, perhaps, the white, black and brown inhabitants of this island, Barbados – to try to understand what its being called 'Little England' truly means.

From Seeley to Pitman to Patterson, scholars found it difficult to imagine European whites becoming rooted in the Antilles, and regarded absenteeism as inevitable, taking its effects as given. 'Their founders carried no Gods with them,' memorably wrote Seeley in 1883. 'On the contrary they go out into the wilderness of mere materialism, into territories where as yet there is nothing consecrated, nothing ideal. Where can their Gods be but at home?'[11] yet these writers forgot the whole generation of conquest, taming and settlement that preceded the establishment of slave sugar plantations, with their crass commercialism and brutality, in each of the sugar islands; and they ignored the fact that Barbados, the first and model island sugar colony, had a substantial and demographically balanced white planter class, and was not characterised by excessive absenteeism.

Recent scholars with Elsa Goveia and Kamau Brathwaite in the forefront, have, on the contrary, stressed not only that the normative social element in each island was a 'slave society' including masters, freedmen and slaves, but that the prevailing force was the process of creolisation, whereby all permanent inhabitants, whether drawn from Europe, Africa or elsewhere, were socially syncretised in the new environment.[12]

Most recently of all, we have traced this best in the careful analysis of the wonderfully vigorous, coarse and truthful private journal of the white Jamaican overseer-planter, Thomas Thistlewood (1750-86).[13] What we have here is the ingenuous autobiography of a young man from rural Lincolnshire finding his livelihood, his life and eventually his only home, in Westmoreland parish, western Jamaica. Out of the wilderness of mere materialism he carves his own competence, not a sugar estate, true, but a small plantation, remarkably growing among other things, fruit trees and garden flowers. Even more surprisingly, as the English connection fade, out of the brutalised and disordered community of slaves in his care he finds a lifelong mate, the African born Phibbah, mother of his only son.

This was not a sentimental process, on either side, but real enough. Between the lines of the journal we can see something akin happening to Thistlewood's transplanted African slaves. Their African tribal marks were ineradicable and in their early years they retained their native languages and some customs. But Africa had become a generalised nostalgic myth, no longer commanding that desperate wish-fulfilment described by Hans Sloane in the 1690s whereby some Jamaican slaves were so consumed by the belief that their souls would return to Africa when they died that they committed suicide.[14] For Thistlewood's slaves, it seems, it was the shipmate bond –the melding process of the Middle Passage –that was now the closest link with Africa. They had already acquired the creole language that was Jamaica's lingua franca, made family arrangements and reconstructed kinship patterns as best they could, and learned the game of 'playing ol' massa' against their black drivers, white boss and his employer, their owner. Despite the often disgusting realities of power relations on Egypt estate, familiarity bred, if not content, a pragmatic, qualified and conditional form of acceptance.

When almost the whole of Jamaica flared in rebellion in 1760, the Egypt slaves chose not to rebel. Yet most telling of all, when Thistlewood had been transferred into the neighbouring parish in 1757, he was immediately lonely and even homesick for Egypt, was visited nearly each weekend by Phibbah with gifts, and soon returned. Somewhat later he recorded proudly that his slaves actually respected him as harsh but just –the devil they knew. Is not this story more plausible, more likely to be generally true, than most traditional accounts of slave society?

For Barbados, these creolisation processes began sooner and became more deeply imbedded, paradoxically helped, I would argue, by the island's development as a 'Little England' overseas. The early white settlers saw themselves as transplanting English institutions, of which the dearest within the first generation became the right to self-legislation. Lord Willoughby's famous declaration of 1651, entrenched by the accommodation of Barbados to the constitutionalised monarch of the later Stuarts, indissolubly tied the Englishness of Barbados to its independence. However much the Barbadian plantocracy became creolised, however tenuous its direct family and cultural connections with England became, its continuance was guaranteed by the degree to which it cleaved to the English system of government and law – although in due course, changes in the metropolitan system itself as regards democracy would have their ramifications in the extension of rights to the descendants of poor whites and even slaves.

Such a promise, as much as the fading African links, helps to explain how Barbadian blacks too have gained their reputation as Black English.[15] Materially, there was surely benefit in being true to the stereotype that black Barbadians were more Anglican, more educated, more loyal than other British West Indians – ideal imperial soldiers and policemen, reliable migrants – however much this might garner a reputation for arrogant self-confidence or self-serving subservience in other islands. But it was surely more than this. Time brought an identification with Barbados as homeland, pride and a sense of self-worth, that in early rebellions made blacks claim that the island belonged as much to them as to the whites, in the Napoleonic wars willing to don uniforms and bear arms against the foreign French, and in the 1816 uprising to march into hopeless battle under the purloined banner of the St Philip regiment of militia. Later in the century, blacks could claim that their very loyalism made them more authentically Barbadian than their white rulers who, for example, threatened to cut ties with Britain and join either the USA or the Canadian confederation once it suited their socioeconomic purposes.[16]

Also, consider the development of Barbadian cricket in the twentieth century. The Barbadian whites adopted and minimally adapted the game from the English gentry; the blacks emulated their white masters a generation or two later. Cricket was quintessentially English, an elegant and gentlemanly pursuit ordered by rules, but providing an arena where skill gradually transcended class divisions. Likewise in Barbados, cricket was a game in which browns and blacks could aspire to emulate, then excel, and finally exclude, their social superiors; but only if they played correctly by the rules. As I have written elsewhere, far from this process illustrating a 'lackey mentality' on the part of the blacks, it would be fairer to conclude 'that in the distinctive Creole society of Barbados, with its long tradition of sophisticated race relations and its long colonial history, the ethnic stance of most black Barbadians represents a decision that while black remains beautiful and Africa a proud parallel inheritance, to be even more English than the whites is to be a more authentic Barbadian'.[17]

I am pretty sure that this contention does not sit well with Hilary Beckles and his followers; and I am not sure that it is absolutely consonant with the conclusions of that other eminent Barbadian historian and distinguished poet, Edward Kamau Brathwaite. Brathwaite, of course, is the most notable proponent (from the case of Jamaica) of the concept of a creolisation involving the whole spectrum of ethnicities, but he is also the chief anglophone poet of Caribbean negritude, and I have never felt that his argument for the creolisation of the whites is half as convincing, or for that matter as committed, as that for the blacks and browns. Although poetry is naturally a far more subjective medium than history, a similar comment might be made upon Brathwaite's 1977 *Mother Poem*. Here, the mother, wonderfully evoked in human and geographical terms, is Barbados, not Africa directly; but it is as much an Afro-Barbados as it is the young Lamming's:

an she is dream of tears of stone
of dark meroé water lapping at the centre of the world
but then is cries an hungry faces: children
who can hardly shit: tin bones of ancient skeletones

the planter's robber's waggon wheels and whips
and she trapped in within her rusting canepiece plot . . .

an not saying a word to a soul what she see what she dream what
she own[18]

A much more serious charge that can be levelled at Brathwaite's concept of creolisation when applied to the British Caribbean as a whole is that it is concerned mostly with the blacks, only nominally with the whites, and with the East Indians not at all. Indeed, as far as I know, no one, black, white, Indian or other, has yet attempted to argue that creolisation encompasses all equally, or the East Indian even at all. Extremists, Hindu and Muslim cultural missionaries, unfortunately, preach an impossible return to a mythical India as unreal as Garvey's Ethiopia; but V. S. Naipaul speaks for the middle ground, the agonising 'middle passage' of inevitable, unassuagable alienation.[19]

Even the greatest of anglophone Caribbean writers, Derek Walcott, often twists in a torment of conflicting identities. It is a conflict exacerbated (I would prefer 'enriched') by genetic miscegenation: that of a St Lucia with European and African grandparents, bred between the cultures of peasant countryside, fisherman's seashore and small capital port, French Creole, Anglo-Creole, and standard English, Catholic and Protestant, and wandering throughout his adult life between his own small island, the somewhat larger island of Trinidad, the UK and the USA. Consider, for example, the magnificent poem from *The Gulf and Other Poems* (1969) called 'Homecoming: Anse La Raye', which seems to me to prefigure much of Walcott's later poetry, not least the most recent, *Omeros*, written 20 years later:

> Whatever else we learned
> at school, like solemn Afro-Greeks eager for grades,
> of Helen and the shades
> of borrowed ancestors,
> there are no rites
> for those who have returned . . .
>
> . . . because your clothes,
> your posture
> seem a tourist's.
> They [that is, the 'spindly, sugar-headed children' racing towards
>   the visitor] swarm like flies
> round your heart's sore.
>
> Suffer them to come,
> entering your needle's eye,
> knowing whether they live or die,
> what others make of life will pass them by
> like that silvery freighter
> threading the horizon like a toy;
> for once, like them,
> you wanted no career
> but this sheer light, this clear,
> infinite, boring, paradisal sea,
> but hoped that it would mean something to declare
> today, I am your poet, yours,
> all this you knew,
> but never guessed you'd come
> to know there are homecomings without home.[20]

At the risk of being thought what I am not, a reconstructed deconstructionist, maybe I can be allowed here to follow Derek Walcott's own lead and stress the deep (and intentional) significance of the very title of his climactic epic *Omeros*. Omeros is, of course, the Greek form of Homer, the author of *The Odyssey*, that archetypical poem of man's quest to 'find himself' on life's voyage 'from womb to tomb'. But the poem's eponym has deeper resonances. The initial letter, O, is a circle, representing man's circular quest: 'In my end is my beginning'. O is also an egg – at the beginning of the word – as 'os', which means bone', comes at the end. The first syllable of 'omeros' is home (or 'ome') itself – the place where one begins and ends;

if you like, the — *omb* which is the common element of 'womb' and 'tomb'. And in the middle of 'omeros' is *mer*, which is the Creole French mother from whom we spring and to whom we always return. But it is also, in the same French *la mer*, the sea, the encompassing element for all West Indians — the medium of arrival, departure and return.[21]

It is doubtful that Walcott has ever completely found himself, whether at home or abroad (long may his personal odyssey continue!), and his is a quest for identity shared by all his less articulate fellows. Many of them too are restless — if not all such fortunate — travellers, and it is surely their travelling *away* from the native island rather than staying at home that brings more sharply into focus where exactly they belong; or, more specifically, brings a realisation of what part of their being belongs in a particular place, and in what ways they are generically British (or Commonwealth) West Indians.

Speaking at a time when an avidly supported representative West Indian cricket team is currently touring the old imperial metropolis, on the campus of a federal university representing virtually the entire region, I am aware of neglecting two potent crucibles of the divided identity which we are exploring. Perhaps I can wriggle out of the charge by pointing out that the cricket team and the University of the West Indies — invaluable as they are — are voluntary relics (almost the only remains) of a former phase when the only forms of unity sprang from the fact of British imperialism. In any case, the examples I want to use suggest ways in which identities are explored and exhibited in communities of British West Indians abroad, specifically in Canada and the USA.

Just two small examples. A few weeks prior to this event, I was invited to give a talk to the flourishing if small association of Bahamians in Canada, which turned into a long and animated discussion as to what it is to be a Bahamian. First and foremost, it occurred to all of us that we were a very heterogenous mixture — persons of all ages and both sexes, of all colours, classes and personal histories, moreover, from a dozen or more distinct islands in the archipelago —comfortably sharing an experience, an intimacy, that would be rare if not impossible today and unthinkable in former times in the Bahamas itself. Yet this way, perhaps only this way, in detachment, could we consider the essence of Bahamianism.

What Bahamianism is, is not relevant here; but one crucial issue that did emerge was the question of whether, or the degree to which, Bahamians can be regarded as true West Indians. Here the central concern was the nature of Bahamian participation in the annual Canadian Caribbean carnival called Caribana. At one level Caribana is a splendid opportunity for all Bahamians to get together to advertise themselves and strut their stuff: junkanoo, rake 'n' scrape, conch salad and guava duff. But it was also essentially a Commonwealth West Indian occasion, an important opportunity to show Canadians the distinctiveness in diversity of the British Caribbean. Quite what it was that bound the participants in Caribana together was not resolved; but beside the will to inform and show off, it was clearly something to do with a deep-seated need for the different elements to get together in song and dance at least once in the year, to share and cross over where possible, and to diffuse if not cure those sociocultural conflicts which come out of an anguished past.

For whatever reasons, such annual extravaganzas as Caribana are becoming more widespread and important – as they are, indeed, in the islands themselves. Think, for example, of the Notting Hill Carnival in London (and the annual conflict in the media between those who condemn it as riot, praise it as celebration, or intellectualise it as 'bread and circuses' – legitimate catharsis); or the West India Week parade in Brooklyn on Labor Day, which, of course, includes a majority of West Indians who hail from the non-anglophone islands – providing admirable opportunities for the demonstration of a wider Caribbean identity.

On a more permanent and sober basis, similar motives and opportunities occur in the organisation of Caribbean students groups on the university campuses of destination countries. In Santo Domingo, Gwendolyn Midlo Hall, from her experience at Rutgers University, suggested to me the dynamics of such organisations as a rich subject for sociocultural and political analysis. What do we learn, for example, from the fact that at Rutgers the very active West Indian Students' Organisation (WISO) is dominated by Jamaicans, with Trinidadians second? The effect of numbers mainly. Until recently, the Haitians were involved and prominent in WISO, but recently have been numerous enough to form a separate organisation. Yet what are we to make of the fact that Hispanics (mainly Dominicans and Cubans but some Central and South Americans) join the Puerto Rican organisation, Unión de Estudiantes Puertoriquenos (UEP) – which in fact is in danger of being taken over by Cubans? An easy assumption might be that the binding link is both linguistic and racial, since most of the members of UEP are mulatto or mestizo rather than black; except for the fact that there are far closer links between the UEP and the American black student organisation on campus than with the British West Indian dominated WISO!

Apparently there are too few true African students at Rutgers to make conclusions about associational affinities; but I do remember my own speculations on the matter in relation to the Caribbean Students Association (CSA) at Waterloo some years ago. The Africans, nearly all males, were once sufficiently numerous to have their own organisation, but when numbers fell they joined in with the CSA. However, the amalgamation did not last and the West Indian majority voted the Africans out again. Many of the original members of the CSA, particularly the considerable number of non-Afro and East Indian West Indians, claimed that the Africans were not sensitive to the way that the CSA reflected the multiculturalism of the Caribbean. But perhaps the most potent reason was the disgruntlement of the West Indians, of all types, with the somewhat abrupt and unequivocal way in which the Africans approached and attempted to appropriate (with what success I know not) the West Indian women.

Clearly, what West Indians need to do is to find out exactly what or who they are, what makes them distinctive, and what therefore are the reformulations such an identity needs. They will retain, one devoutly hopes, this federal university, their splendid representative cricket team, while forging new associations and institutions – beyond the Caribbean Free Trade Association (CARIFTA), the Caribbean Community (CARICOM) and the Organisation of Eastern Caribbean States (OECS) into such fields as are currently being explored by Sonny Ramphal and William Demas' Independent West Indian Commission. I hope that it is not overly subjective and self-interested to claim that in doing so they should particularly look for guidance to their history, and their historians.

Time is running away, and I am falling short of my hope to provide some practical suggestions. Perhaps, penultimately, I can tentatively and briefly suggest four ways in which what I have said so far points to areas currently in need of more historiographical attention. These are, alliteratively, studies in British West Indian microhistory, macrohistory, migration and *mentalités*.

First, although the current tide runs against microhistory, there is surely still such a large number of gaps in the local history of the British West Indies that the whole is no more than a partial mosaic, incompletely delineated, with the overall picture even distorted. Although all of us hope to find in microstudies some magic new key or prism that will unlock the whole or cast it in fresh light, the more realistic purpose of microhistory is simply to fill in and refine the total picture. But so often we do find significant variations and anomalies, and what differs from the norm is always more interesting than what conforms. And what if such exceptions, cumulatively, show that far from proving the general rule, they *are* the rule?

Mainly but not entirely because of the uneven availability of sources and resources, the larger territories have so far dominated the scholarship – not just in its more traditional forms but, even more, in studies imbued with the new populism and cross-disciplinary methods of social history. Jamaica and Trinidad, and, on the mainland, Guyana and Belize, are relatively well-served; and Barbados, once curiously lagging behind, now has an excellent short modern history thanks to Dr Beckles. But how much we still need good histories of the smaller islands! I hope I am not ignorantly treading on worthy toes when I ask where are the adequate histories of Tobago, St Vincent, Dominica, St Kitts, Nevis, Montserrat, Antigua, Anguilla, the Caymans, the Turks, Bermuda.

These perhaps are more daunting projects than they would seem at first from the islands' small size and historical insignificance in the larger picture; Gail Saunders and I have been working on our social history of the Bahamas since 1983, and it is likely to run to two volumes of 600 pages apiece – as one assessor commented, 'probably an entry for the Guinness Book of Records: largest book on the smallest country'.[22] But there is a wealth of necessary microhistory for this and the next generation of British West Indian historians: not just whole-island histories, but parochial studies (especially in Jamaica and Barbados), studies of individual towns, villages, and estates; and of what someone in a recent conference on microhistory called 'large subjects in small places' termed 'the smallest place of all' – the biographies of individuals, not necessarily, and preferably not, politically prominent. For our present purpose, how better than by such microcosmic studies of places and individuals, of the essential quiddity of different places and the special viewpoint of those who live there, can we expect to understand West Indian identification at its basic core?

At the other end of the spectrum, in the outer rings or Russian boxes which signify what it is to be generically West Indian, there is surely also a need, secondly, for more macrohistorical studies. Macrohistory is only valid where it is consonant with the totality of microstudies; but it is always vital to expand our horizons, to see just how individuals, islands, archipelagos, fit in the larger world, the cosmological whole. In practical terms this means not so much more studies of what British West Indians have and have done in common – for as I have already suggested this is not only pretty well-worked ground but also an imperial legacy – but of what British West

Indians have, and do not have, in common with the other inhabitants of the Caribbean sphere.

Here too we continue to be bound by the linguistic and cultural chains which are the legacies of a half-dozen different imperialisms. Although it was designed to cut down the number of students he would have to supervise, there was a profound truth hidden in Professor Samuel Eliot Morison's requirement that any graduates who wanted to study Caribbean History under him would have to command Spanish, French and Dutch as well as English, and probably Portuguese, German and Latin too. We would today have to add ideally, knowledge of a dozen creoles and at least as many Amerindian languages. But in the real world, we can take heart from the cross-cultural ideals and achievements of the ACH and from the ongoing UNESCO project for a general Caribbean History – the first volume of which should be out within a year or two. Nor should we stop at that but, if warily, continue to engage in comparative studies, such as those that place Caribbean slavery and its aftermath in the context of Plantation America. Inevitably, and hopefully with even more self-aware-ness, we will doubtless also continue the perennial quest for some all-en-compassing world contextual principle, be it neo-Marxist, non-Marxist, post-modern, or totally new and currently unforeseeable.

In recommending the history of migration as the third subject needing further study I need to make several qualifications. I am not referring to the immigration of peoples (along with animals, plants and disease patho-gens) from Europe, Africa and Asia which created the West Indies of the colonial period. This has, of course, been central to traditional West Indian scholarship. Nor am I referring especially to the study of that even greater pan-migration: the exodus out of the Caribbean since the Second World War, on which so much has already been written, mainly by social scientists. Between them, these two large topics dominate the *Bibliography of Caribbean Migration* edited by Rosemary Brana Shute which already in 1983 contained more than 2,500 items.[23]

Rather, what I am advocating is more attention by historians to the internal and external migrations of the later nineteenth and early twentieth centuries which accompanied and helped to shape the transformation from the old colonial system to the modern era, and also helped small islanders conceive of themselves as belonging to a larger cultural if not political and economic regional community. This requires a concentration on, and differentiation between, the details and effects of migration within the region, temporary migrations, the migration of individuals rather than of whole families, and the social, economic, cultural and political effects of emigration and re-migration.

Such modern migration studies are well under way, and Caribbean scholarship has shared in the benefit of the existence since 1980 of the specialist journal *Immigrants and Minorities*. For the British West Indies there are suggestive general outlines by Dawn Marshall, Elizabeth Thomas-Hope and Peter Fraser; and a few excellent monographs, for example, the studies by Olive Senior, Velma Newton, Lancelot Lewis and Bonham Richardson of the migration of labourers from the British islands, including Barbados, to the Panama isthmus.[24] But such studies still need to be injected into the historical mainstream and there is need for much more work, at the detailed micro and more general and integrative macro levels – with at least three large purposes in mind.

A more complete survey needs to be made of the ways in which ordinary West Indians became more mobile after the end of slavery, at first within and between colonies, then between colonies and nominally independent republics, and finally between independent states. This needs to be tied in with studies of population growth and improvements in communications, with global economic changes in the areas of technology, processing, marketing and capitalisation, and with critical changes in the philosophies and policies of the major powers, to decide which factors were causes, which results, and what were the crucial motivating forces. The migrating groups themselves also need much more specific and general study, not only to see how their migration affected the economies, societies and polities of the contributory and destination areas, but also what effects moving to and fro had upon the cultures and minds of those involved.

My own feeling is that more migration studies will not only prove that the facilitation of migration was a vital function of the intensification of capitalism on a worldwide scale, but also that it has led to an important stage in the resolution of the dialectic between capital and labour. Such a quasi-Marxist conclusion may not sit well with all, but at least one can assert that only by more studies of the type advocated can such hypotheses be properly tested.

A fourth and final area needing both more study and tidying up is that which is all too loosely tied together under the borrowed label of *mentalités*. As Gordon K. Lewis complains in his boldly pioneering (although far from completely successful) 1983 book *Main Currents in Caribbean Thought*,[25] imperialism and materialism have led to an almost total neglect of the indigenous intellectual history of the Caribbean. Certainly, a great deal needs to be done to recognise and formulise creole ideas and ideologies, and in particular to look for evidence from the great majority for whom books were unimportant or meaningless. In this, the concept of *mentalités* has very real value, since it comprehends far more aspects of a people's minds and lives than the formulation and expression of formal ideas. It includes (among, I am sure, many other things) the study of languages, folklore, proverbs, poetry, novels, plays and play-acting, music, dance, religion and religious observance, social custom, style of dress and deportment, cooking and medicine, material culture and crafts, architecture (formal and vernacular) furniture, utensils, ornamentation and the purely decorative arts.

One of the delights of studying the West Indies is the richness and diversity of its culture. We are also very fortunate that the region has already attracted a wealth of scholarship from disciplines outside history. Some of the best Caribbean historians, indeed, are by nominal affiliation anthropologists, although the majority of these remain born, bred and based outsiders. I do not know of any region where young historians have better opportunities both to indigenise the scholarship and to follow the ideal of the new Social History to enrich it from almost every other discipline; all this, of course, with the ultimate aim of determining quite what it is to be, at the ascending levels of identity, a true West Indian.

Well, we have come back to our main theme, that which I meant to encapsulate in the title: the search for the perfect calalu. I do hope that it is more or less clear what I mean by the calalu analogy or metaphor. It is perhaps not so far as you thought from history to cookery – and I am not proposing some arcane principle derived from Lévi-Strauss. You have noticed, I am sure, that West Indian bookshops catering for tourists have at least as many recipe books as potted histories; they seem to sell best of all. In fact my distributor in the Bahamas, Henry Lee (whom I once taught history at the Government High School but has gone on to more lucrative pursuits) even came up with what he thought would be a bestseller – which I freely bequeath to any aspiring authors among you if you want it – a Columbus Quincentennial Cookbook!

Cooking may not be quite as significant a cultural indicator as are, say, Caribbean music, dances and festivals, be they in the tradition of carnival, crop-over or junkanoo. But a food savant, a Caribbean Brillat-Savarin might well expiate on the philosophical or historiographical *essence* of local foods. Calalu, as it is lovingly described to me by British West Indians, is the quintessential Caribbean dish, an ambrosial stew of eclectic ingredients, each with its distinct texture and taste. A recipe for the perfect calalu would therefore integrate the ideal mixture, just as the perfectly satisfying analysis of Caribbean identities would decide precisely what it is that defines each island's culture as well as that of the West Indies in its entirety.

The main trouble with making such an analysis, though, also lies in the analogy. For not only do the preferred ingredients of calalu differ from island to island, and even from place to place within each island, but the very word calalu is applied both to the main ingredient and to the whole *mélange*. The common element is the green vegetable called calalu – that in different places even this is either a distinctive spinach-like green, or the green top of the dasheen plant. Thus, the search for the perfect calalu recipe, like the search for the Holy Grail of historical certainty, is never ending. But, I believe, it is well-worth making nonetheless.

Notes

Chapter 1

1. Karl Marx, *Capital: A Critical Analysis of Capital Production*, 3 vols, Moscow, 1961, III. Eric Williams, *Capitalism and Slavery*, Chapel Hill, 1994. For perceptive qualifications of classic Marxism, however, see Elizabeth Fox-Genovese and Eugene Genovese, *Fruits of Merchant Capital: Slavery and Bourgeois Property in the Rise and Expansion of Capitalism*, New York, Oxford, University Press, 1983.

2. Charles Verlinden, *Les origines de la civilisation atlantique*, Neuchatel, Baconnière, 1966; *The Beginnings of Modern Colonization: Eleven Essays with an Introduction*, Ithaca, Cornell University Press, 1970. Also invaluable in preparing this essay were Noel Deerr, *The History of Sugar*, 2 vols, London, Chapman and Hall, 1949-50; J.H. Galloway, 'The Mediterranean Sugar Industry', *Geographical Review*, II, 67, 1977, 176-194; Sidney M. Greenfield, 'Plantations, Sugar Cane and Slavery', in Michael Craton (ed.), *Roots and Branches: Current Directions in Slave Studies*, Toronto and London, Pergamon, 1979, 85-119; David Brion Davis, *Slavery and Human Progress*, New York, Oxford University Press, 1984. See also two important works that appeared after this essay was completed: Barbara Solow, 'Capitalism and Slavery in the Exceedingly Long Run', in Barbara Solow and Stanley Engerman (eds), *Caribbean Slavery and British Capitalism: The Legacy of Eric Williams*, Cambridge University Press, 1987; J. H. Galloway, *The Sugar Cane Industry: An Historical Geography from its Origins to 1914*, Cambridge University Press, 1990.

3. For the parallel and contrapuntal, but as yet largely unwritten, history of cotton plantations, see the hints and suggestions in Eliyahu Ashtor, *Levant Trade in the Later Middle Ages*, Princeton, Princeton University Press, 1983, *passim*.

4. The chief scholars in the New World Group are Lloyd Best, George Beckford, Norman Girvan and Clive Thomas, and perhaps the most influential paper, Lloyd Best, 'The Mechanism of Plantation Type Economies: Outline of a Model of Pure Plantation Economy', *Social and Economic Studies*, 17, 1968, 283-326.
   A useful recent survey of the school is Hilary Beckles, 'Eric Williams' Capitalism and Slavery and the Growth of West Indian Political Economy', in Solow and Engerman *Caribbean Slavery and British Capitalism*.

5. *Encyclopedia Britannica*, 15th edition, Chicago, 1979, Micropedia, IV, 116.

6. 'Adam Smith emphasizes how in his time (and this applies also to the plantations in tropical and subtropical countries in our own day), rent and profit were not yet divorced from one another, for the landlord was simultaneously a capitalist, just as Cato, for instance, was on his estates. But this separation is precisely the prerequisite for the capitalist mode of production, to whose conception the basis of slavery, moreover, stands in direct contradiction.' Karl Marx, *Capital: A Critical Analysis of Capital Production*, 768, quoted and analysed in Elizabeth Fox-Genovese and Eugene Genovese, *Fruits of Merchant Capital*, 19-22.

7. Gerald A. J. Hodgett, *A Social and Economic History of Medieval Europe*, London, Methuen, 1972, 250-28; M. Rostovtzeff, *Social and Economic History of the Roman Empire*, 2 vols, London, Oxford, 2nd edn, 1957.

8. Hodgett, *Medieval Europe*, 113-122; C. Ostrogorski, *History of the Byzantine State*, trans. J. M. Hussey, Oxford, Blackwell, 2nd edn, 1969; J. M. Hussey (ed.), *Cambridge Medieval History*, 9 vols, Cambridge, 1966-80, IV.

9. Deerr, *History of Sugar*, I, 73-99. For the concurrence of agricultural transformation and Islamic conquests, see Andrew M. Wat-

son, 'The Arab Agricultural Revolution and its Diffusion, 700-1100', *Journal of Economic History*, 34, 1974, 8-35.

10. Davis, *Slavery and Human Progress*, 3-6. For the concept of the absentee planters of Basra being proto-capitalists, see Alexandre Popovic, *La Révolte des esclaves en Iraq au IIIe/IXe siècle*, Paris, 1979.

11. Deerr, *History of Sugar*, II, 534-540.

12. Paul Berthier, *Les Anciennes Sucreries du Maroc et leurs Réseaux Hydrauliques*, Rabat, 1966, reviewed by Jean-Marie Salmi-Bianchi, 'Les anciennes Sucreries du Maroc', *Annales*, 24, 1969, 1176-1180. Berthier traced at least 14 water-mills, and presumed the employment of black slaves mainly from place names.

13. Deerr, *History of Sugar*, I, 87-93; S. Lane-Poole, *History of Egypt in the Middle Ages*, London, Methuen, 2nd ed., 1925; M. Lombard, *The Golden Age of Islam*, New York, 1975. The emergence of a quasi-planter class in Egypt was facilitated during the Mameluke era (1250-1517 AD). The Sultan divided the land into estates called *iqta*, which were allocated hereditarily to Mameluke officers according to rank. These acted as absentee proprietors, leaving the *iqta* to be managed by agents and worked mainly by sharecropping peasants – although a corvée was commonly levied for sugar-cane lands. A. N. Poliak, 'La Féodalité Islamique', *Revue des Études Islamiques*, 10, 1936, 247-265; Hassanein Rabie, *The Financial System of Egypt*, AH 564-741/AD 1169-1341, London, Oxford, 1972, 126-172. Eliyahu Ashtor, 'Levantine sugar industry in the later Middle Ages – an example of technological decline', *Israeli Oriental Studies*, VII, 1977, 226-276; *Levant Trade*, 207-209.

14. Davis, *Slavery and Human Progress*, 85.

15. *Ibid*, 85-90; Fernand Braudel, *The Mediterranean and the Mediterranean World in the Age of Philip II*, 2 vols, London, Collins, 1973, II, 815-816.

16. Davis, *Slavery and Human Progress*, 89-97.

17. Steven Runciman, *A History of the Crusades*, 3 vols, London, 1952-54; Joshua Prawer, *The Latin Kingdom of Jerusalem: European Colonialism in the Middle Ages*, London, Weidenfield and Nicolson, 1972.

18. Quoted in Charles Verlinden *Les origines de la civilisation atlantique*, Paris, Albin Michel, 1966, 168.

19. Prawer, *Latin Kingdom*, 46-93; Meron Benvenisti, *The Crusaders in the Holy Land*, New York, McMillan, 1970, 17-21.

20. Prawer, *Latin Kingdom*, 46-59, 355-381; Benvenisti, *Crusaders*, 17-21; Jonathan Riley-Smith, *The Knights of St. John in Jerusalem and Cyprus*, 1050-1310, London, Macmillan, 1967, 18-35.

21. Prawer, *Latin Kingdom*, 382-391.

22. *Ibid*, 355-381.

23. St Bernard of Clairvaux, quoted ibid, 172.

24. *Ibid*, 252-279; Riley-Smith, *Knights of St. John, passim*.

25. In fact, in Templar documents the term *outremer* came to refer not to the Holy Land but to Europe itself; Prawer, *Latin Kingdom*, 277.

26. Riley-Smith, *Knights of St. John*, 426; Benvenisti, *Crusaders*, 247-252.

27. Gino Luzatto, *An Economic History of Italy from the Fall of the Roman Empire to the Beginning of the Sixteenth Century*, London, Routledge, 1961; Wilhelm von Heyd, *Histoire de Commerce du Levant à Moyen-Age*, 2 vols, Amsterdam, Hakkert, 1959, especially 680-692; R. S. Lopez, *Storia delle colonie genovesi nel Mediterraneo*, Bologna, 1938; Prawer, *Latin Kingdom*, 482-503.

28. Verlinden, *Origines*, 162.

29. *Ibid*, 163. Among other Genoese consular families prominent in the Holy Land were the da Voltas. Venetian families included the Michiel, Falier, Contarini, Dandolo and Morosini; Prawer, *Latin Kingdom*, 90.

30. *Ibid*.

31. *Ibid*, 363-381; Benvenisti, *Crusaders*, 247-256.

32. R. S. Lopez and I. W. Raymond (eds), *Medieval Trade with the Mediterranean World*, New York, Columbia, 1955; Fernand Braudel, *Civilization and Capitalism, 15th-18th Century, Vol. II, The Wheels of Commerce*, London, 1982, 556-559. Braudel in particular cites the borrowing of the techniques of bills of exchange, the *commenda*, forward selling techniques, and such words as *douane, fondouk, magazine*. The word for sugar (as for coffee and cotton) was also borrowed from the Arabs, and the Arabic word for mill, *ma'asera*, survives in the English verb, to macerate.

33. R. S. Lopez, *The Dawn of Modern Banking*, New Haven, Yale, 1979, 14-19; Davis, *Slavery and Human Progress*, 46.

34. Benvenisti, *Crusaders*, 213-270.

35. *Ibid*, 254-256.

36. Prawer, *Latin Kingdom*, 496.

37. *Ibid*, 24-33.

38. The work, entitled *Liber secretorum fidelium super Terrae Sanctae recuperatione*, was the result of five journeys through the Levant, and contained four maps. Deerr, *History of Sugar*, I, 83. Sanuto also pointed out that the decline in the demand for wheat to supply the European colonists (coupled with a decline in the indigenous labour force) had also contributed to a great expansion of Syrian cotton production. Since cotton, unlike sugar, could not be grown on the Mediterranean islands as effectively as in the Levant, the expanding Italian (and later German) fustian industries remained dependent upon Syria and Egypt until long after alternative sugar plantations had been developed, and a really substantial European industry awaited the development of cotton plantations in the Americas. Ashtor, *Levant Trade*, 24ff., 93, 184ff.

39. *Ibid*, 93. F. Balducci Pegolotti, *La Practica della Mercatuira* (ed. A. Evans), Cambridge, MA, Harvard, 1936.

40. Verlinden, *Origines*, 164.

41. Brian Blouet, *The Story of Malta*, London, Faber, 1967.

42. There is scarcely any scholarly literature on Byzantine sugar production. The sugar of the Morea, though, was a byword in Venice for the coarsest quality. Deerr, *History of Sugar*, I, 79, 83.

43. Riley-Smith, *Knights of St. John*, 470 sqq.

44. Deerr, *History of Sugar*, I, 83-86.

45. J. M. J. L. de Mas Latrie, *Histoire de l'Ile de Chypre*, 3 vols, Paris, 1852-61; George F. Hill, *History of Cyprus*, 4 vols, London, 1946-52.

46. Mario Abrate, 'Creta, colonia veneziana nei secoli XIII-XIV', *Economia e Storia*, IV, 1957, 251-277; Charles Verlinden, 'La Crète debouché et plaque tournante de la traite des esclaves aux XIVe et XVe siècles', in *Studi di onore de A. Fanfani*, Milan, 1962, III, 593-669; *Origines*, 162; Deerr, *History of Sugar*, I, 83.

47. Ernst Kantorowicz, *Frederick the Second, 1194-1250*, London, Constable, 1931.

48. Charles Verlinden, 'L'esclavage en Sicile au bas moyen-age', *Bulletin de l'institut historique belge de Rome*, XXXV, 1963, 13-113.

49. Denis Mack Smith, *History of Sicily: Medieval Sicily, 800-1713*, London, Chatto and Windus, 185; Deerr, *History of Sugar*, I, 78.

50. In 1410, there were 30 sugar refineries in Palermo alone; Mack Smith, *Medieval Sicily*, 185; Galloway, 'Mediterranean Sugar Industry', 182-183.

51. The Attribution of the invention to Pietro Speciale by Von Lippman (1929) and Deerr (1949) was challenged by Pereira (1955). Mauro (1960) and others claim that the three-roller mill was invented in Peru and introduced into Brazil between 1608 and 1611; ibid, 186-187.

52. Deerr, *History of Sugar*, I, 78-79, citing the German traveller Sebastian Munster, c. 1565.

53. Jacques Heers, 'Le Royaume de Grenade et la politique marchande de Genes en Occident (XVe Siècle)', *Le Moyen-Age*, 63, 1957, 87-121.

54. The Portuguese crown supported this cultivation, and encouraged the involvement of Genoese merchants; H. Gomes de Amorin Parreira, *História do Açúcar em Portugal*, Lisbon, 1962.

55. C. E. Dufourcq, *L'Espagne catalane et le Maghrib au XIIIe et XIVe Siècles*, Paris, 1966.

56. Deerr, *History of Sugar*, I, 80-82, citing Balaguer y Primo (1877).

57. Robert I. Burns, *Islam under the Crusades: Colonial Survival under the Thirteenth Century Kingdom of Valencia*, Princeton, 1973, especially 109-110.

58. Charles Verlinden, 'Italian Influences in Iberian Colonization', *Hispanic American Historical Review*, 1953; *Précédents médiévaux de la colonie en Amerique*, Mexico, 1954.

59. Deerr, *History of Sugar*, I, 82-83.

60. Mas Latrie, *Histoire de Chypre*; Hill, *History of Cyprus*; Riley-Smith, *Knights of St. John*, 470.

61. Davis, *Slavery and Human Progress*, 50-52.

62. Charles Verlinden, *L'esclavage dans l'Europe médiévale*, 2 vols, Bruges, 1965, II, 282, 348-358, cited in Davis, *Slavery and Human Progress*, 87.

63. Verlinden, *l'esclavage*, II, 360-384, 460-461, 566-616, cited ibid, 51.

64. *Ibid*, 47, citing the mid-fifteenth century Venetian explorer Cadamosto. The ubiquitous Genoese had in fact reached Safi on the Moroccan Atlantic coast as early as 1253; ibid, 46.

65. Verlinden, *l'esclavage*, 353-354.

66. But compare Sidney Greenfield, who argues for the crucial importance of virtually new institutions in the Atlantic islands: 'Madeira and the Beginnings of New World Sugar Cultivation and Plantation Slavery; A Study in Institution Building', in

Vera Rubin and Arthur Tuden (eds), *Comparative Perspectives on Slavery in New World Plantation Societies*, New York, NYAS, No. 292, 1977, 536-552; 'Plantations, Sugar Cane and Slavery', 96-116.

67. Virginia Rau, *Sesmarias Medievais Portuguesas*, Lisbon, 1946, cited ibid, 99. One of the three captains appointed by Prince Henry, Bartholemeu Perestrelo, was actually an Italian, born in Piacenza. It was his daughter, Filipa, who was to marry Christopher Columbus in 1479.

68. Jorge Dias and Fernando Galhano, *Aparelhos de Elevar a Aqua de Rega*, Oporto, 1963; F.A. da Silva, 'Levadas', in F.A. da Silva and C.A. de Mennezes (eds), *Elucidaro Madeirense*, Funchal, 1965, cited in Greenfield, 'Plantations, Sugar Cane and Slavery', 100.

69. Deerr, *History of Sugar*, I, 100-101; Greenfield, 'Plantations, Sugar Cane and Slavery', 98-103; Barbara Solow, 'Capitalism and Slavery', 14-17.

70. Felipe Fernandes-Armesto, *The Canary Islands After the Conquest: The Making of a Colonial Society in the Early Sixteenth Century*, Oxford, 1982; Barbara Solow, 'Capitalism and Slavery', 17-19.

71. Deerr, *History of Sugar*, I, 115-116; Michael Craton, *Sinews of Empire: A Short History of British Slavery*, New York, Doubleday, 1974, 1, 29-38.

72. Bentley-Duncan, *Atlantic Islands: Madeira, the Azores and the Cape Verdes in Seventeenth Century Commerce and Navigation*, Chicago, 1972, 11-12; Greenfield, 'Plantations, Sugar Cane and Slavery', 108-110.

73. *Ibid*,111-114,citing Magalhaes Godinho,'A Economia das Canárias nos Séculos XIVe XV', *Revista da Historia*, 10.

74. *Ibid*.

75. Robert Greenfield, 'A History of Sao Tomé Island, 1470-1655', PhD dissertation, Northwestern University, 1971; Greenfield, 'Plantations, Sugar Cane and Slavery', 114-116.

76. *Ibid*.

77. Deerr, *History of Sugar*, I, 101-102.

78. After the opening up of Brazil, Sao Tomé was for a time the most important Portuguese entrepot for African slaves bound for America. Its decline was due not just to the rise of Luanda, but to the depredations of French and Dutch corsairs from the 1540s onwards, and to serious slave revolts in

1536, 1574 and 1595. Barbara Solow, 'Capitalism and Slavery', 24.

79. C.R. Boxer, *The Portuguese Seaborne Empire, 1415-1825*, London, Hutchinson, 1969, 84-105.

80. Eric Williams, *Documents of West Indian History*, Vol. I, 1492-1655, Port-of-Spain, PNM, 1963.

81. Deerr, *History of Sugar*, I, 116.

82. In fact, 20 *ingenios* and four *trapiches* (mills) besides; G.F. de Oviedo y Valdes, *Historia General de las Indias* (1535), quoted in Williams, *Documents*, 26.

83. *Ibid*,142.

84. Eric Williams estimated that there were 50 mills in Hispanola, 40 in Cuba, 30 in Jamaica, 10 in Puerto Rico, and 20 in Mexico and the Spanish Main combined; *From Columbus to Castro; The History of the Caribbean, 1492-1969*, London, Andre Deutsch, 1970, 26-29. For slave totals, see Philip D. Curtin, *The Atlantic Salve Trade: A Census*, Wisconsin, 1969, 25. For Brazil, Frederic Mauro, *Le Portugal et l'Atlantique au XVIIe Siècle, 1570-1670*, Paris, 1960; Boxer, *Portuguese Empire*, 104-105.

85. Williams, *Documents*, 27-30; Craton, *Sinews of Empire*, 6-12.

86. Boxer, *Portuguese Empire*, 84-105; Deerr, *History of Sugar*, I, 102-112; James Lockhart and Stuart B. Schwartz, *Early Latin America: A History of Colonial Spanish America and Brazil*, Cambridge, 1983, 249.

87. Curtin, *Atlantic Slave Trade*, 25-30.

88. Deerr, *History of Sugar*, I, 106.

89. *Ibid*,108. For an excellent analysis of the socio-economic spectrum, see Lockhart and Schwartz, *Early Latin America*, 204-221. For the *lavradores*, see Stuart B. Schwartz, 'Free Farmers in a Slave Economy: The *Lavradores de Cana* in Colonial Bahia' in Dauril Alden (ed.), *The Colonial Roots of Modern Brazil*, Berkeley, California, 1973, 147-198.

90. *Ibid*, 106; C.R. Boxer, *The Dutch Seaborne Empire, 1600-1800*, London, Hutchinson, 1965-105.

91. *Ibid*,105-110. Lockhart and Schwartz provide useful data to underline the effects of the Dutch phase in Brazilian sugar production. The 275-305 *engenhos* in the period 1620-30 produced an annual average of no more than 52 tons of sugar for export. Yet while the total number of *engenhos* first declined slightly and only rose to about 350 between 1630 and 1650, average produc-

tion for export rose to about 90 tons. By 1670 there were already 500 *engenhos*, but the average export production was no more than 60 tons. *Early Latin America*, 249.

92. Deerr, *History of Sugar*, I, 111.

93. Boxer, *Dutch Empire*, 110-113.

94. Craton, *Sinews of Empire*, 13-14, 43-45; R. S. Dunn, *Sugar and Slaves: The Role of the Planter Class in the English West Indies, 1624-1713*, Chapel Hill, NC, 1972.

95. Michael Craton, *Searching for the Invisible Man: Slaves and Plantation Life in Jamaica*, Cambridge, MA, Harvard, 1978, 1-33; Williams, *Columbus to Castro*; Francisco Moreno Fraginals, *The Sugar Mill*, New York, 1977.

96. T. W. Moody, F. X. Martin and F. J. Byrne (eds), *A New History of Ireland, Vol. III, Early Modern Ireland, 1534-1691*, Oxford, Clarendon Press, 1976, 95-98, 113, 174, 196-205, 219-222.

97. Immanuel Wallerstein, *The Modern World-System; Capitalist Agriculture and the Origins of the European World-Economy in the Sixteenth Century*, New York, Academic Press, 1974. Despite his concern for the role of agriculture, Wallerstein gives almost no attention to the development of plantations in the Mediterranean during the European Middle Ages. There is scarcely more than a sentence and a footnote, during a discussion of the origins of African slavery which is almost as scanty. *Op. cit.*, 88-89.

98. Despite his anti-imperialist credentials, this holds as true for Eric Williams as for Immanuel Wallerstein and Marx himself. *Capitalism and Slavery*, indeed, with its concentration on the British slave trade, colonies and industrial revolution, being Britain-centred within its eurocentricity; a bias within a bias.

Chapter 3

1. 'The Voyage of Sir Henrye Colt Knight to the Ilands of the Antilles', in V. T. Harlow (ed.), *Colonising Expeditions to the West Indies and Guiana, 1623-1667*, London, Hakluyt Society, 2nd series, LVI, London, 1925, 54-102.

2. Frank Kermode (ed.), *The Tempest*, by William Shakespeare, the Arden Shakespeare, London, 1954, ixxx.

3. Arthur Percival Newton, *The Colonising Activities of the English Puritans: The Last Phase of the Elizabethan Struggle with Spain*, New Haven, CT, 1914; Kenneth R. Andrews, *The Spanish Caribbean: Trade and Plunder, 1530-1630*, New Haven, CT, 1978; Ernest A. Cruikshank, *The Life of Sir Henry Morgan: With an Account of the English Settlement of the Island of Jamaica (1655-1688)*, Toronto, 1935.

4. Marcus Rediker, *Between the Devil and the Deep Blue Sea: Merchant Seamen, Pirates, and the Anglo-American Maritime World, 1700-1750*, New York, 1986.

5. Edward Long, The *History of Jamaica*, 3 vols, London 1774, II, chapter 13, 319.

6. John Smith, *The True Travels, Adventures, and Observations of Captaine John Smith . . .* (1630), in Philip L. Barbour (ed.), *The Complete Works of Captain John Smith (1580-1631)*, Chapel Hill, NC, 1986, III, 228-233; Egerton MSS 2395, 503-507, British Library, quoted in James A. Williamson, *The Caribee Islands under the Proprietary Patents*, London, 1926, 23.

7. Aucher Warner, *Sir Thomas Warner, Pioneer of the West Indies*, London, 1933; Vere Langford Oliver, *History of the Island of Antigua: One of the Leeward Caribbees*, 3 vols, London, 1894-99.

8. N. Darnell Davis, *The Cavaliers and Roundheads of Barbados, 1650-1652*, Georgetown, British Guiana, 1887; Vincent T. Harlow, *A History of Barbados, 1625-1685*, Oxford, 1926; Vincent T. Harlow, *Christopher Codrington, 1668-1710*, Oxford, 1928; Archibald P. Newton, *The European Nations in the West Indies, 1493-1688*, London, 1933; S. A. G. Taylor, *The Western Design: An Account of Cromwell's Expedition to the Caribbean*, Kingston, Jamaica, 1965.

9. James Harrington, *Oceana*, S. B. Liljergren (ed.), Heidelberg, 1924, 16, quoted in Michael Craton and James Walvin, *A Jamaican Plantation: The History of Worthy Park, 1670-1970*, London, 1970, 18.

10. Craton and Walvin, *A Jamaican Plantation*, 26-94.

11. Stephen Saunders Webb, *The Governors-General: The English Army and the Definition of the Empire, 1569-1681*, Chapel Hill, NC, 1979. But see also Webb's debate with Richard R. Johnson, Notes and Documents, *William and Mary Quarterly*, 3rd series, 43, 1986, 408-459; and Ian Steele,

'Governors or Generals: A Note on Martial Law and the Revolution of 1689 in English America', WMQ, 3rd series, 46, 1989, 304-314.

12. Richard Ligon, *A True and Exact History of the Island of Barbados*, 2nd edn, London, 1673; reprinted 1970, 46.

13. Long, *History of Jamaica*, I, chapter 10, 123-155; Roger Norman Buckley, *Slaves in Red Coats: The British West India Regiments, 1795-1815*, New Haven, CT, 1979; Richard S. Dunn, *Sugar and Slaves: The Rise of the Planter Class in the English West Indies, 1642-1713*, Chapel Hill, N. C., 1972, 140-148; Webb, *Governors-General*, 123-124.

14. 'Q.: How many Parishes, Precincts, or Divisions are within your Corporation? Ans: Each Tribe is a distinct parish.' Answers to queries from Council of Trade and Plantations, July 15, 1679, in J. H. Lefroy, *Memorials of the Discovery and Early Settlement of the Bermudas or Somers Islands, 1511-1687*, II, London, 1879; reprinted 1981, 430.

15. Henry C. Wilkinson, *The Adventurers of Bermuda: A History of the Island from Its Discovery*, 2nd edn, London, 1958, 123; For the early history of Bermuda, see also Lefroy, *Memorials*; Vernon A. Ives (ed.), *The Rich Papers: Letters from Bermuda, 1615-1646*, Toronto, 1984.

16. Williamson, *The Caribbee Islands*.

17. Harlow, *Codrington*; J. Harry Bennett, Jr, *Bondsmen and Bishops: Slavery and Apprenticeship on the Codrington Plantations of Barbados, 1710-1838*, Berkeley, CA, 1958.

18. Codrington to Board of Trade and Plantations, December 30, 1701, CO 152/4, or Great Britain, Public Record Office, *Calendar of State Papers*, Colonial Series, *America and West Indies*, London, 1864, XIV/XIX, 1701, 1132.

19. Carl Bridenbaugh and Robert Bridenbaugh, *No Peace Beyond the Line: The English in the Caribbean*, New York, 1972, 36, 54-59, 78; Dunn, *Sugar and Slaves*, 62-67; Stuart B. Schwartz, *Sugar Plantations and the Formation of Brazilian Society, 1550-1835*, New York, 1985. Barbados adopted what is sometimes called the Pernambuco System after the way the Dutch developed self-contained factory-plantation units in north-eastern Brazil during their conquest. This differed from that system developed around Bahia, farther to the south, whereby the factory owners (*senhors de engenho*) grew only a proportion of the cane that their factory could process, obtaining the rest from the surrounding *lavrador* sharecroppers. The *lavradores* thus provided an intermediate class of dependent poor whites almost unknown in the British West Indies, serving both to augment the white militias and to provide some production elasticity when sugar prices were low and factory output was reduced.

20. Bridenbaugh and Bridenbaugh, *No Peace beyond the Line*, 137-139, 158-159.

21. Ligon, *Barbadoes*, 38-39.

22. Bridenbaugh and Bridenbaugh, *No Peace beyond the Line*, 137-139, 158-159.

23. R. B. Sheridan, 'The Rise of a Colonial Gentry: A Case Study of Antigua, 1730-1775', *Economic History Review*, 2nd series, 13, 1960-61, 342-357.

24. Craton and Walvin, *A Jamaican Plantation*, 26-45.

25. *Ibid*, 71-94; Long, *History of Jamaica*, I, 438; Frank Wesley Pitman, *The Development of the British West Indies*, 1700-1783, New Haven, 1917, 34; George Metcalf, *Royal Government and Political Conflict in Jamaica, 1729-1783*, London, 1965, 186-198; T. R. Clayton, 'Sophistry, Security, and Socio-Political Structures in the American Revolution; or, Why Jamaica Did Not Rebel', *Historical Journal*, 29, 1986, 319-344.

26. Long, *History of Jamaica*, II, chapter 7, 76-78, quoted in Craton and Walvin, *A Jamaican Plantation*, 85.

27. Long, *History of Jamaica*, I, chapter 5, 468, quoted in Michael Craton, *Sinews of Empire: A Short History of British Slavery*, London, 1974, 222-223. An even more remarkably self-centred (and familial) act of *noblesse oblige* was Governor and Lady Nugent's practice of giving their domestic slaves presents on their (the Nugents') wedding anniversary. Entry for Nov. 15, 1801, in Philip Wright (ed.), *Lady Nugent's Journal of Her Residence in Jamaica from 1801 to 1805*, Kingston, Jamaica, 1966, 39.

28. Craton and Walvin, *A Jamaican Plantation*, 79, 91. In general, a study of planter memorials in British West Indies churches illustrates the extent, and the limitations, of plantocratic pretensions and style. Traditionally attracting the interest (as in Europe) mainly of antiquarians and genealogists, the memorials would also repay

the attentions of sensitive demographers, semioticians and iconographers. Often flamboyant in form, and inscribed in terms of poignant, now incongruous, grandiloquence, they differ from similar memorials in British parish churches mainly in showing a much higher incidence of infant mortality and widowhood, and a more complex and fractured pattern of dynasty building. Except for some of the earliest and most ingenuous examples, they are also conspicuously imported artifacts, either carved from Italian marble by transient artists or, in the grandest cases, ordered and shipped out from London studios. See, for example, Lesley Lewis, 'English Commemorative Sculpture in Jamaica', *Jamaican Historical Review*, 9, 1972, 1-24.

29. Peter Laslett, *The World We Have Lost*, London, 1965, 23-54. For the application of Laslett's ideas to the Barbados case, I am largely indebted to Gary A. Puckrein, *Little England: Plantation Society and Anglo-Barbadian Politics, 1627-1700*, New York, 1984.

30. William Belgrove, *A Treatise upon Husbandry or Planting*, Boston, 1755, 51; Puckrein, *Little England*, 79-80.

31. Henry Drax, 'instructions I would have observed by Mr. Richard Harwood in the management of my plantation', Rawlinson MSS, A 348, fol. 7, Bodleian Library, Oxford University, in Puckrein, *Little England*, 78-79.

32. *Ibid*, 80-81.

33. One of the most cogent official statements about the relationship between Christianity and slavery was made by Sir John Heydon, governor of Bermuda, in a proclamation dated Nov. 13, 1669: 'Masters and Servants are hereby advised, and in the kings name required to live in peace, mutuall love and respect to each other, Servants submitting to the condition wherein God hath placed them. And such Negroes as formerlie, or lately have bin baptized by several Ministers, should not thereby think themselves free from their Masters and Owners, but rather, by the meanes of their Christian profession, obliged to a more strict bond of fidelity and service. And if all persons professing Christianity would be careful in the discharge of their duties, living in the feare of God, and in due obedience to his Majestys Laws, complaints of this nature would be prevented, true religion, and civil

conversation would be encouraged, the service of God would be esteemed the greatest freedome.' Lefroy, *Memorials*, II, 293-294.

Chapter 4

1. Charles M. Andrews, *The Colonial Period of American History*, 4 vols, New Haven, CT, Yale University Press, 1934-38, 1, 86-87; Theodore F. T. Plucknett, *A Concise History of the Common Law*, Boston, MA, Little, Brown, 1956 [1929]; 5th edn, 516-574; Frederick G. Kempin, Jr. *Legal History: Law and Social Change*, Englewood Cliffs, NJ, Prentice-Hall, 1959, 55-70; Alan Harding, *A Social History of English Law*, Harmondsworth, Middlesex, Penguin, 1966.

2. Andrews, *Colonial Period*, 1, 86, note 1; 11, 199-240, 282-285; Plucknett, *Common Law*, 521-574.

3. Andrews, *Colonial Period*, 11, 199-240; Samuel Lucas, *Charters of the Old English Colonies in America*, London, Parker, 1850.

4. Andrews, *Colonial Period*, 11, 202, note 3, 274-324.

5. James A. Williamson, *The Caribbee Islands under the Proprietary Patents*, London, Oxford University Press, 1926; Vincent T. Harlow, *A History of Barbados, 1625-1685*, New York, Negro Universities Press, 1969 (1926).

6. Crawford B. Macpherson, *The Political Theory of Possessive Individualism: Hobbes to Locke*, Oxford, Clarendon Press, 1964; John G. A. Pocock, 'British history: a plea for a new subject', *Journal of Modern History*, 47, 1975, 601-628; Immanuel Wallerstein, *The Modern World System, 11 Mercantilism and the Consolidation of the European World Economy, 1600-1750*, 11, New York, Academic Press, 1980.

7. Angus Calder, *Revolutionary Empire: The Rise of the English-Speaking Empires from the Fifteenth Century to the 1780s*, London, Jonathan Cape, 1981; Kenneth R. Andrews, *Trade, Plunder, and Settlement: Maritime Enterprise and the Genesis of the British Empire, 1480-1630*, Cambridge and New York, Cambridge University Press, 1984.

8. John H. Lefroy, *Memorials of the Discovery and Early Settlement of the Bermudas or Somers Islands, 1515-1685*, 2 vols, Toronto, Toronto University Press, 1981 [1879]; 3rd edn; Vernon A. Ives (ed.), *The Rich Papers:*

Letters from Bermuda, 1615-1646, Toronto and Buffalo, Toronto University Press for the Bermuda National Trust, 1984; Henry C. Wilkinson, *The Adventurers of Bermuda: A History of the Island from its Discovery until the Dissolution of the Somers Island Company in 1684*, 2nd edn, Oxford, Oxford University Press, 1958 (1933); Andrews *Colonial Period*, 11, 214-248; Wesley Frank Craven, 'An introduction to the history of Bermuda', *William and Mary Quarterly*, 17, 1937, 176-215, 317-362, 437-465, and 18, 1938.

9. Wilkinson, *Adventurers of Bermuda*, 68 note, 108-110, 241-245. For West Indian surveying in general, see Barry W. Higman, *Jamaica Surveyed: Plantation Maps and Plans of the Eighteenth and Nineteenth Centuries*, Kingston, Institute of Jamaica, 1988, 19-79.

10. Wilkinson, *Adventurers of Bermuda*, 77-95.

11. Answers to queries from Council of Trade and Plantations, July 16, 1679, Lefroy, *Memorials of the Bermudas*, 11, 430.

12. Wilkinson, *Adventurers of Bermuda*, 77-95. Wilkinson cites Beverly W. Bond, Jr *The Quit-Rent System in the American Colonies*, New Haven, CT, Yale University Press, 1919, 15, 109, 131, and Andrews, *Colonial Period*, 1, 867-87.

13. Wilkinson, *Adventurers of Bermuda*, 96-99. the first blacks in Bermuda were apparently a family of 'Spanish Negroes' brought in around 1617 to instruct the settlers in growing cassava, maize and tobacco. Initially free, they may have been later enslaved. The first slaves were captives from the Spaniards and Portuguese around 1620, and were used to work company lands. They were augmented by many others similarly acquired and by the natural increase which the healthy climate encouraged. As a majority of the white inhabitants became engaged in maritime activities and spurned manual labour, the slaves fulfilled agricultural needs in Bermuda, as well as being employed at the salt pans in the Turks and Caicos Islands and in the most menial maritime tasks. The slave population of Bermuda rose from a quarter to a third of the total between 1650 and 1680, not reaching a half until the mid-eighteenth century. Packwood, *Chained on the Rock*, 1-116.

14. Wilkinson, *Adventurers of Bermuda*, 138-141. Brand and petty juries were also estab-lished very early on. Once formed, the Bermudian legal structure was almost frozen in its original Indian colonies because of the colony's small size and population. In 1827, the Bermudian courts consisted of a Chancery court composed of the governor and council, who also sat as a Court of Error to hear appeals from all the island courts. There was a common law court of General Assize, with a chief justice and two associates, which sat twice yearly, and a court of Quarter Sessions to deal with lesser cases. There was, inevitably, an active Vice-Admiralty Court, and officially also courts of Exchequer and Ordinary, although they rarely sat. John Henry Howard, *The Laws of the British Colonies in the West Indies and other Parts of America concerning Real and Personal Property . . . with a View of the Constitution of Each Colony*, 2 vols, London, 1827; reprinted Westport, CT, Negro Universities Press, 1970, 363-364.

15 Wilkinson, *Adventurers of Bermuda*, 246-280.

16 *Ibid.*, 281-384; Henry C. Wilkinson, *Bermuda in the Old Empire, 1684-1784*, London and New York, Oxford University Press, 1950.

17 For the early history of Barbados, see Jerome S. Handler, *A Guide to Source Materials for the Study of Barbados History, 1627-1834*, Carbondale, IL, Southern Illinois University Press, 1971; David Watts, *The West Indies: Patterns of Development, Culture and Economic Change since 1492*, Cambridge and New York, Cambridge University Press, 1987; Robert Schomburgk, *The History of Barbados*, London, 1848; Williamson, *Caribbee Islands*; Harlow, *Barbados, 1625-1685*; Andrews, *Colonial Period*, 11, 241-273; Archibald P. Thornton, *West-India Policy under the Restoration*, Oxford, Clarendon Press, 1956; Richard S. Dunn, *Sugar and Slaves: The Rise of the Plantation Class in the English West Indies, 1624-1713*, New York, Norton, 1972; Gary Puckrein, *Little England: Plantation Society and Anglo-Barbadian Politics, 1627-1700*, New York, New York University Press, 1984; Hilary McD. Beckles, *White Servitude and Black Slavery in Barbados, 1627-1715*, Knoxville, TN, University of Tennessee Press, 1989.

18. For example, N. Darnell Davis, *Cavaliers and Roundheads of Barbados, 1650-1652*,

Georgetown, British Guiana, 1887; Schomburgk, *Barbados*, Harlow, *Barbados, 1625-1685.*

19. Schomburgk, *Barbados*, 261; Fitzroy Augier, Shirley Gordon, Douglas Hall and Mary Reckord, *The Making of the West Indies*, London, Longman Caribbean, 1960, 41.

20. John Poyer, *The History of Barbados*, London, 1808, 30-31; Williamson, *Caribbee Islands*, 23-87; Harlow, *Barbados, 1625-1686*, 1-25. the precise form of the earliest grants of lands in Barbados remains obscure compared with Jamaica after 1660. A useful compilation of the total annual grants allocated between 1628 and 1638, though, was given in *Memoirs of the First Settlement of the Island of Barbados*, London, 1743; reprinted Barbados, 1891. This shows that the average size of grant, excluding the original 10,000 acres granted in 1628 to certain London merchants, was 96½ acres, and that by 1638, 132 square miles, or 80 per cent of Barbados, had been distributed. Some of the land, if not all, was allocated by headright, at the rate of ten acres per dependent white servant – the so-called 'ten-acre men' needed for militia purposes.

Table 1 Average size of land grants in Barbados, 1628-37

Year	Grant	Acreage	Average	Cumulative total
1628 Merchants +	64	16,400	100	16,400
1629	140	15,871	113	32,272
1630	45	14,235	316	46,507
1631	31	2,749	89	49,256
1632	63	4,138	66	53,394
1633	20	905	45	54,299
1634	64	3,511	55	57,810
1635	106	9,055	85	66,865
1636	98	9,810	100	76,675
1637	139	7,604	55	84,279

The figures above are quoted in Richard Pares, *Merchants and Planters*, Cambridge, UK, Cambridge University Press, and the *Economic History Review*, 1960, 57.

21. Harlow, *Barbados*, 17; Schomburgk, *Barbados*, 267.

22. Pares, *Merchants and Planters*, 26-48; Dunn, *Sugar and Slaves*, 46-83.

23. Quoted in J. Harry Bennett, 'The English Caribbees, 1642-1646', *William and Mary Quarterly*, 3rd series, 24, 1967, 367-373.

24. Richard Ligon, *A true and Exact History of the Island of Barbados*, London, 1657, 100-101. In due course, Barbados had the most complete system of courts, closely modelled on England, but with extra courts for special local conditions. As J. H. Howard reported in 1827, 'The courts for the administration of civil justice in Barbados, are the court of Chancery [consisting of the governor and council], the court of Exchequer, five courts of Common Pleas, the court of Ordinary, the court of Admiralty, the court of Error, and the court of Escheat. Besides these general courts, there is, by a local act, a power vested in the governor to appoint a special court of Merchants and Mariners; as also a court to take cognizance of cases of persons about to quit the island in debt. For the administration of criminal justice, the courts are the court of Grand Session, the court of Quarter Sessions, a court for the trial of slaves, and the Admiralty Sessions'. Howard, *Laws of the British Colonies*, 95-101.

25. It is quoted in full in Schomburgk, *Barbados*, 706-708.

26. The terms of the surrender are given in [John Jennings] *Acts and Statutes of the Island of Barbados Made and Enacted since the Reducement of the Same, unto the Authority of the Commonwealth of England . . .*, London, William Bentley, 1654, 1-4.

27. *Ibid.*

28. *Ibid.*, Acts numbered 29, 35, 59, 73, 99; 48, 50, 62; 5-12, 30, 39, 72, 81, 86.

29. *Ibid.*, Acts numbered 28, 41-6. Parallel acts concerned penalties for allowing animals to stray across property lines, and against human vagrants who threatened social order and discipline in a more general sense.

30. Thornton, *West-India Policy*, 36-37; Williamson, *Caribbee Islands*, 180-214; F.G. Spurdle, *Early West Indian Government*, Palmerston, NZ, N. D., 12-20.

31. [William Rawlin] *The Laws of Barbados, Collected in One Volume by William Rawlin, of the Middle Temple, London, Esquire, and now Clerk of the assembly of the Said Island*, London, 1699.

32. Dunn, *Sugar and Slaves*, 46-116; Watts, *West Indies since 1492*, Table 7.5, 311.

33. Dunn, *Sugar and Slaves*, 111-116.

34. For the early history of English Jamaica, see S. A. G. Taylor, *The Western Design: An Account of Cromwell's Expedition in the Carib-*

bean, Kingston, Institute of Jamaica, 1965; Agnes M. Whitson, *The Constitutional History of Jamaica, 1664-1729*, Manchester, Manchester University Press, 1929; Andrews, *Colonial Period*, 111, 1-34; Thornton, *West-India Policy*, 22-123; Michael Craton and James Walvin, *A Jamaican Plantation: The History of Worthy Park, 1670-1970*, Toronto, Toronto University Press, 1970, 12-70; Dunn, *Sugar and Slaves*, 149-187.

35. Thornton, *West-India Policy*, 42.

36. Lord Windsor's Instructions, March 21, 1662, Public Record Office, London, CO 324/1, 37-56; Thornton, *West-India Policy*, 52; Craton and Walvin, *Jamaican Plantation*, 20.

37. Thornton, *West-India Policy*, 53.

38. Analysis of index to Jamaican land patents, 1661-1826, Jamaican Archives, Spanish Town, file 1 B/11, in Dunn, *Sugar and Slaves*, 154. *Calendar of State Papers, Colonial, America and West Indies*, 1674, V11, No. 1236. Governor Thomas Lynch, besides being almost as generous to himself with land grants as Modyford had been, was an even greater speculator in land. As Richard Dunn computed, Lynch 'took out 10 patents for 6,040 acres, but in addition he bought 26,744 acres from other landholders and sold 11,346 acres, so that he ended with 21,438 acres, acquired in 59 separate transactions between 1662 and 1684'. Dunn, *Sugar and Slaves*, 167.

39. C. R. Williams, 'Thomas Modyford, planter-governor of Barbados and Jamaica, 1620-1679', PhD thesis, University of Kentucky, 1979; E. A. Cruikshank, *Sir Henry Morgan: His Life and Times*, Toronto, Macmillan, 1935.

40. See, for example, the early history of the Price family in Craton and Walvin, *Jamaican Plantation*; and of the Helyars in J. Harry Bennett, 'Cary Helyar', *William and Mary Quarterly*, 3rd series, 21, 1964, 53-76; and Dunn, *Sugar and Slaves*, 212-222, 321-323.

41. Dunn, *Sugar and Slaves*, 155; Watts, *West Indies since 1492*, 311.

42. By the mid-eighteenth century, principal courts in Jamaica were the Supreme Court, three courts of assize for what became the counties of Surrey, Middlesex and Cornwall (1756), and 'divers inferior courts of Common Pleas', one for each parish. Besides this, there were island courts for Chancery, Error, Vice-Admiralty and Ordinary. Howard, *Laws of the British Colonies*, 27-33.

43. [Charles Harper] *The Laws of Jamaica Passed by the Assembly and Confirmed by his Majesty's Council, April 17, 1684*, London, 1684. Modyford, in fact, had such a good rapport with the Jamaican planters – who in any case dominated the council – that he found it unnecessary to call the assembly regularly.

44. For the constitutional struggle, see Whitson, *Constitutional History, 1664-1729*; Thornton, *West-India Policy*; Spurdle, *Early West Indian Government*. For the Jamaican maroons, H. Orlando Patterson, 'Slavery and slave revolts: a socio-historical analysis of the First Maroon War, Jamaica, 1755-1740', in Richard Price (ed.), *Maroon Societies: Rebel Slave Communities in the Americas*, New York, Doubleday, 1973; Michael Craton, *Testing the Chains: Resistance to Slavery in the British West Indies*, Ithaca, NY, Cornell University Press, 1982, 61-96.

45. Howard, *Laws of the British Colonies*, 19-26.

46 Richard B. Morris, *Studies in the History of American Law: With Special Reference to the Seventeenth and Eighteenth Centuries*, New York, Columbia University Press, 1930, 83-84, citing 2 Salk., 411 (1694).

47. As J. H. Howard said of the Jamaican Chancery Court in 1827, it 'is composed of the governor or president of the council, with four or more members of the council, and the opinion of the majority is the decision. The court derives its authority from the king's commission, and the judges are supposed to have all the authority of the chancellor of England, except in cases wholly inapplicable to the colony . . . The practice of this court professes to conform to that of the court of Chancery in England, except where it may be altered by local laws, or special rules of their own. There are above a hundred of these rules prescribed by the court itself, written in a book kept by the registrar, often not at all known to persons practising in the profession . . . Many of the early orders are rude and uncouth, some very obscure, and others ludicrous; the latter ones, as far as they go, are generally wise and useful'. Howard, *Laws of the British Colonies*, 96-97.

48. The actual act was 1 Geo. 11, c. 1, 'An Act for granting a Revenue to His Majesty, his Heirs and Successors, for the Support of

the Government of this Island; and for reviving and perpetuating the Acts and Laws thereof'. *Ibid.*, 46. As Spurdle wrote, "Onwards from 1728 each new Jamaican law simply followed the normal course of having to take the chance of confirmation or otherwise in England. Thus, though the details might differ, the result was practically the same: the cream of Jamaican laws gained permanent confirmation; a great many others, being indifferently regarded in England, were allowed simply to 'lie by' and a few, being seriously objected to, were disallowed." *Early West Indian Government*, 31-32.

49. Craton, *Testing the Chains*, 81-87.

50. Watts, *West Indies since 1492*, 311; Michael Craton, *Searching for the Invisible Man: Slaves and Plantation Life in Jamaica*, Cambridge, MA, Harvard University press, 1978, 34.

Table 2   Frequency distribution of landholdings in Jamaica, 1670 and 1754

Acres	1670	%	1754	%
0-99	384	53.0	263	16.0
100-499	234	33.0	566	35.0
500-999	55	8.0	303	19.0
1000-1999	34	5.0	253	16.0
2000-4999	11	2.0	153	10.0
5000-9999	2	0.8	52	3.0
10,000-22,999	0	-	9	0.5
Total	720			

Richard B. Sheridan, *Sugar and Slavery*, Baltimore, MD, Johns Hopkins University Press, 1974, 219; *Calendar of State Papers, Colonial, America and West Indies, 1669-1674*, 99-103. Note that in 1670, the 42.5 per cent of the land in units of more than 1,000 acres was held in only 47 units, or eight per cent of the total, whereas in 1754, 77.8 per cent of the land was held in 467 such parcels – 29.5 per cent of the total. Whereas the number of landholdings of less than 100 acres had actually fallen from 384 to 263, those over 500 acres (which included virtually all the sugar plantations) had risen from 103 to 770. Multiple holdings, of course, determined that the actual number of substantial planters was considerably less than the 1,336 landholdings over 100 acres in 1754.

51. Jamaican Archives, Spanish Town, Patents, 1741, Craton, *Testing the Chains*, 94. The same principle probably explains why Leeward Island planters (most notably Sir William Young, Governor of St Vincent) were at pains to stress the African rather than the Amerindian antecedents of the so-called Black Caribs of St Vincent.

52. W. Jethro Brown, *The Austinian Theory of Law*, London, John Murray, 1912; George L. Haskins, 'Law and colonial society', in David H. Flaherty (ed.), *Essays in the History of Early American Law*, Chapel Hill, NC, University of North Carolina Press, 1969 [1957], 41-52; Mark de Wolfe Howe (ed.), *Holmes-Laski Letters: The Correspondence of Justice Holmes and Harold Laski*, 2 vols, Cambridge, MA, Harvard University Press, 1953.

53. David Brion Davis, *The Problem of Slavery in Western Culture*, Ithaca, NY, Cornell University Press, 1966.

54. Quoted in Andrews, *Colonial Period*, 1, 57, note 1.

55. Morris, *Studies in American Law*, 9-17, 69-125; Zechariah Chafee, Jr, 'Colonial courts and the common law', 1952, Julius Goebel, Jr, 'King's law and local custom in seventeenth-century New England', 1931, Richard B. Morris, 'Massachusetts and the common law: the declaration of 1646', 1925, and George L. Haskins, 'The beginnings of partible inheritance in the American colonies', 1941, all in David H. Flaherty, *Essays in Early American Law*, Chapel Hill, NC, University of North Carolina Press, 1969, 53-82, 83-120, 135-146, 204-244.

56. Peter Laslett, *The World We Have Lost*, London, Methuen, 1965.

57. See the later history of the Prices, including the almost certainly spurious early genealogy contributed to *Burke's Peerage*, in Craton and Walvin, *A Jamaican Plantation*. Also, for example, Jeanette Marks, *The Family of the Barretts: A Colonial Romance*, New York, Macmillan, 1938. For partible inheritance, primogeniture and women's rights in early America, see Morris, *Studies in American Law*, 126-200.

58. For the acts setting up the court system in Barbados, see Act No. 29 of 1652 in Jennings, *Acts of Barbados*, re-enacted after the Restoration as 1 Car. 11, August 29, 1661, Howard, *Laws of the British Colonies*, 105-107. The Jamaican Permanent Revenue Act of 1 Geo. 11, c. 1, dated April 10, 1799, ibid., 341-344. This last act includes

the telling preamble: 'Whereas the common law of England is the best birthright of Englishmen, and of their descendants, but, nevertheless, is not in all respects applicable to the circumstances and condition of new and distant colonies . . . be it therefore declared, That the common law of England, in all cases where the same hath not been altered by any of the acts or statutes hereinafter enumerated, or by any act or acts of assembly of these islands, except so much thereof as hath relation to the ancient feudal tenures, to outlawries in civil suits, to the wager of law or of batail, appeals of felony, writs of attaint, and ecclesiastical matters, is, and of right ought to be, in full force within these islands, as the same now is in that part of Great Britain called England'.

59. Such early acts can be seen in Lefroy, *Memorials*, Bermuda, 1620-1684, Jennings, *Acts and Statutes*, Barbados, 1652-1654, and Harper, *Laws*, Jamaica, 1683-1684.

60. Barbados Acts of 2 Car. 11, September 27, 1661, 9 Car. 11, May 24, 1669, and 11 Car. 11, August 11, 1670 – which last refers to a local act as early as September 11, 1649; Howard, *Laws of the British Colonies*, 107-109, 112-116.

61. For a series of later quit-rent acts, see Jamaican Acts of 2 Anne, c. 7, November 2, 1703, 6 Geo. 11 c. 7 (1733), and 9 Geo. 111 c. 9, December 31, 1768; ibid., 42-43, 50, 60-62.

62. For perhaps the standard ten per cent act, see Barbados Act 8 Car. 11, April 29, 1668; Howard, *Laws of British Colonies*, 111-112. Montserrat in 1735 passed legislation reducing the permissible interest from ten to eight per cent, and Antigua in 1838 even more ambitiously (although at a time of generally falling interest rates, from ten to six per cent). Ibid., 450, 414.

63. [Charles Harper] *Laws of Jamaica, 1684*, xii; *Laws of Jamaica, 1683*, Preface. To the first statement, Harper added the interesting note about Jamaican tenures by crown patent: 'The Tenant holds as in Common Socage, pays a half-penny per Acre, is to serve in Arms, & c.'.

64. See, for example, for the activities of the grandee Sir Charles Price (1708-1772), Craton and Walvin, *A Jamaican Plantation*, 71-94.

65. See the Barbados Acts of 8 Car. 11, April 29, 1668, and 12 Car. 11, January 29, 1672,

and the apparently countervailing 39 Geo. 111 of July 30, 1799; Howard, *Laws of the British Colonies*, 112, 116-117, 139-140. Also see the Nevis Acts 'for ascertaining Lands, as also affixing Slaves, Coppers, & c. to the Freehold', 32 Car. 11, February 8, 1681, and 'for making the Negroes, Coppers, Mills and Stills of Intestates' Estates, Chattels', 10 Wm. & Mary, October 22, 1700, and the Grenada Act 'to make Slaves, Cattle, Horses, Mules, Asses, Coppers, Stills and Plantation Utensils real Estate of Inheritance, and declaring Widows dowable of them, as of Lands and Tenements', 7 Geo. 111, April 29, 1767; ibid., 498-500, 161-163.

66. Elsa Goveia, *The West Indian Slave Laws of the Eighteenth Century*, Barbados, Caribbean University Press, 1970. The Act No. 12 of the second session of the Bermudian Assembly (1622) 'to restrayne the insolencies of the Negroes', is claimed to be 'the first law anywhere in English specifically dealing with Blacks'. Packwood, *Chained on the Rock*, 7; Lefroy, *Memorials of the Bermudas*, 1, 308-311; Craven, 'Introduction', 1937, 362. The first Barbadian Slave Act almost certainly dates from the first Assembly called by the Bermudian Philip Bell in 1639, but details have long disappeared, so that the earliest extant law is that signed by Searle in 1652. An order of the Barbadian governor in council as early as 1636, however, decreed that 'Negroes and Indians that came here to be sold, should serve for Life, unless a Contract was before made to the contrary'. Dunn, *Sugar and Slaves*, 224-229; Acts Nos 48, 50, 62, Jennings, *Acts and Statutes of Barbados*, 1654.

67. Most recently in 'The concept of white slavery in the English Caribbean during the early seventeenth century'. Also, Hilary McD. Beckles, "The English parliamentary debate on 'white slavery' in Barbados, 1659". *Barbados Museum and Historical Society* 36, 4, 1985, 344-352; Hilary McD. Beckles, *White Servitude and Black Slavery*, Knoxville, TN, University of Tennessee Press, 1989.

68. Dunn, *Sugar and Slaves*, 224-228.

69. Preamble to 'An Act for the Security of the Subject to prevent the forfeiture of Life and Estate on Killing a Negro or other Slave', 1730, in Michael Craton, James Walvin and David Wright (eds), *Slavery*,

Abolition and Emancipation: Black Slaves and the British Empire, A Thematic Documentary, London, Longman, 1976, 68.

70. Goveia, *Slave Laws*; 'A Statement of the Laws that at present subsist in the West India Islands respecting Negro Slaves, Prepared by John Reeves, Clerk to the Committee', *British Sessional Papers, Commons, Accounts and Papers*, 1789, XXVI, 646a, quoted in Craton, Walvin and Wright, *Slavery, Abolition and Emancipation*, 181-190; Howard, *Laws of the British Colonies*, passim.

71. Lowell J. Ragatz, *The Fall of the Planter Class in the British Caribbean, 1763-1833*, Washington, DC, American Historical Association, 1928; John R. Ward, *British West Indian Slavery, 1750-1834: The Process of Amelioration*, Oxford, Clarendon Press, 1988.

72 Vincent T. Harlow, *Christopher Codrington*, Oxford, Clarendon Press, 1928; Williams, 'Modyford'; J. R. V. Johnstone, 'The Stapleton Sugar plantations in the Leeward Islands', *Bulletin of the John Rylands Library*, 48, 1965-1961, 175-206; Aucher Warner, *Sir Thomas Warner, Pioneer of the West Indies*, London, West India Committee, 1933.

73 Pares, *Merchants and Planters*; David W. Galenson, *Traders, Planters and Slaves: Market Behaviour in Early English America*, Cambridge and New York, Cambridge University Press, 1986; N. Zahedieh, 'Trade, plunder, and economic development in early English Jamaica 1655-1689', *Economic History Review*, 2nd series, 39, 1986, 205-222; Alexander Boyd, *England's Wealthiest Son: A Study of William Beckford*, London, Centaur, 1962.

74 Richard Pares, *A West Indian Fortune*, London and New York, Longman Green, 1950; Craton and Walvin, *A Jamaican Plantation*; J. Harry Bennett, 'William Whaley, Planter of seventeenth-century Jamaica', *Agricultural History*, 40, 1966, 113-123; Dunn, *Sugar and Slaves*, 212-223; Richard B. Sheridan, 'The rise of a colonial gentry: a case study of Antigua, 1730-1775', *Economic History Review*, 13, 3, 1961, 342-357.

75. Elsa Goveia, *Slave Society in the British Leeward Islands at the End of the Eighteenth Century*, New Haven, CT, Yale University Press, 1965; Edward K. Brathwaite, *The Development of Creole Society in Jamaica, 1770-1820*, Oxford, Clarendon Press, 1971; Douglas G. Hall, *In Miserable Slavery Thomas Thistlewood in Jamaica, 1750-1786*, London, Macmillan, 1989.

76. Thomas Modyford (1620-1679), son of the Lord Mayor of Exeter, enjoyed excellent family, mercantile and political connections. Related both to the wealthy Colletons of his native Devon (a county noted for its conservative gentry) and to George Monck (made Lord Albemarle for engineering the Restoration), he was able to put up £7,000 to purchase and develop half a 500-acre estate on his arrival in Barbados in 1647. Ever the planter first, he was a political opportunist. Colonel of the militia, he was largely responsible for the surrender of Barbados to Ayscue in 1652, and was made Searle's successor as governor by the Council of State early in 1660. Briefly imprisoned by the ultra-Royalists at the Restoration, he was soon back as Speaker of the Assembly under Willoughby, was one of the 13 Barbadians made baronets by Charles 11, and was appointed Governor of Jamaica over several noble contenders in 1664. The largest slave-owner as well as landholder in Jamaica, and great encourager of the slave trade, Modyford was sacked for supporting the buccaneers against the Spaniards and, with Henry Morgan, sent to England in ostensible disgrace in 1671. Both were soon back in Jamaica, although, Morgan being Lieutenant Governor and Vice-Admiralty judge, Modyford (despite no special training) Chief Justice and commission agent for the Royal African Company. When he died at the age of 59, his fellow planters had inscribed on his tombstone in Spanish Town churchyard the apparently sincere encomium:

MISTAKE NOT READER, FOR HERE LYES NOT ONELY THE DECEASED BODY OF THE HONORABLE SIR THOMAS MODYFORD BARONETT, BUT EVEN THE SOULE AND LIFE OF ALL JAMAICA, WHO FIRST MADE IT WHAT IT NOW IS. HERE LYES THE BEST AND LONGEST GOVERNOUR, THE MOST CONSIDERABLE PLANTER, THE ABLEST AND MOST UPRIGHT JUDGE THIS ISLAND EVER INJOYED.

See Williams, 'Modyford'; Williamson, *Caribbee Islands*; Dunn, *Sugar and Slaves*, 68-69, 159.

77. Henry Drax, 'Instructions I would have observed by mr. Richard Harwood in the management of my plantation', British Museum, Rawlinson MSS A 348, fol. 7, quoted also in William Belgrove, *A Treatise upon Husbandry or Planting*, Boston, MA, 1755; Puckrein, *Little England*, 78-80; Richard B. Sheridan, 'Samuel Martin, innovating sugar planter of Antigua, 1750-1776', *Agricultural History*, 34, 1960, 129-139.

78. Pares, *A West India Fortune, Passim.*

79. Frank W. Pitman, *The Development of the British West Indies, 1700-1763*, New Haven, CT, Yale University Press, 1917; Douglas G. Hall, 'Absentee proprietorship in the British West Indies to about 1850', *Jamaican Historical Review*, 4, 1964, 15-35; Clare Taylor, 'The journal of the absentee proprietor, Nathaniel Phillips of Slebech', *Journal of Caribbean History*, 18, 1984, 67-82; Ward, *British West Indian Slavery*.

80. Karl Watson, *The Civilized Island, Barbados: A Social History, 1750-1816*, Barbados, K. Watson, 1979.

81 *Dictionary of National Biography*, L. Stephen and S. Lee, (eds), Oxford, Oxford University Press, 1917, XII, 100-101.

82. Charles Leslie, *A New and Exact Account of Jamaica*, London, 1740; Edward Long, *The History of Jamaica*, 3 vols, London, 1774.

83. 'Somerset *v.* Stewart, June 1772' in Craton, Walvin and Wright, *Slavery, Abolition and Emancipation*, 169-170; James Walvin, *Black and White: The Negro and English Society, 1555-1945*, Harmondsworth, Mx, Penguin, 1973, 117-131; F. O. Shyllon, *Black People in Britain, 1555-1833*, London and New York, Oxford University Press, for the Institute of Race Relations, 1977, 10-38.

84. Goveia, *Slave Laws*; Goveia, *Slave Society in the Leewards*.

85. For the development of this idea, see an essay which is in some ways parallel to the present one, Michael Craton, 'Reluctant Creoles: the planters' world in the British West Indies', in Bernard Bailyn and Philip D. Morgan (eds), *Strangers Within the Realm: Cultural Margins of the First British Empire*, Chapel Hill, NC, University of North Carolina Press, for the Institute of Early American History and Culture, Williamsburg, VA, 1991.

86. David Brion Davis, *The Problem of Slavery in the Age of Revolution, 1770-1833*, Ithaca, NY, Cornell University Press, 1975, 164-212.

Chapter 5

1. Carl Ubbelohde, *Vice-Admiralty Courts and the American Revolution*, Chapel Hill, North Carolina, 1960, for the Institute of Early American History.

2. Charles McLean Andrews, The Colonial Period of American History, 4 Vols., New Haven, 1935-38, IV, 236.

3. Between 1763 and 1815 the Jamaican Vice Admiralty Court handled approximately 3,700 cases, of which some 3,400 were Prize cases. Since the only available overall figures, for nine Courts between 1793-95 and 1803-15, indicate that 1,251 of 3,773 cases, almost exactly one-third, were adjudicated in Jamaica, it seems possible that Caribbean Vice Admiralty Courts dealt with as many as 11,000 cases between 1763 and 1815. Archives of Jamaica, Vice Admiralty Court records; Public Record Office (P. R. O.), London, H. C. A. 49/99, Prize Returns, 1793-1815.

4. Thomas C. Barrow, 'The American Revolution as a Colonial War for Independence', William and Mary Quarterly, 3rd series, 25, 3, July 1968, 452-464, does not go far enough, since it merely shows why the American War of Independence was not a revolution in the classic sense.

5 The first Standing Commissions for piracy trials in special courts of oyer and terminer were sent out to the colonies as early as 1675; C. S. P., Col. A.W.I., 1675-76. Separate Commissions for Prize Courts date from the outbreak of the French wars in 1689, although disputes over jurisdiction were never entirely stilled. Prosecution of Navigation Act cases in colonial Vice Admiralty Courts Date from the Navigation Act of 1673, although the system was not formalised until 1697 and disputes, especially over the definition of a 'Court of Record' and the distinction between Navigation Act and Revenue cases, continued until at least 1775.

6. Decreed by Judge Hedges in 1711; P.R.O., Adm. 1/3668, 49.

7. For the growth of Vice Admiralty jurisdiction up to the beginning of the eighteenth century, Helen J. Crump, *Colonial Admiralty Jurisdiction in the Seventeenth Century*, London, Longman, for the Royal Empire Society, 1931, is useful, despite Miss Crump's tendency to believe that Vice

Admiralty Courts were implanted by conscious policy, her preoccupation with piracy as a formative factor, and her failure clearly to distinguish between the four distinct functions of Admiralty jurisdiction. Some fresh insights and additions to Crump are to be found in A. P. Thornton, *West India Policy under the Restoration*, Oxford, Oxford University Press, 1956. For the period between 1700 and 1763 the best guides to Caribbean Vice Admiralty jurisdiction are Richard Pares, *War and Trade in the West Indies, 1739-1763*, Oxford, Oxford University Press, 1936; and *Colonial Blockade and Neutral Rights, 1739-1763*, Oxford, Oxford University press, 1938, despite the fact that Pares relied almost entirely on metropolitan materials from the H. C. A. series in the P. R. O., London. For the period after 1763 there is, as yet, no published study.

8. When Judge Hinchliffe published his *Rules of Practice for the Vice Admiralty Court of Jamaica* in 1813, he affirmed that the practice of the High Court of Admiralty presided over by Lord Stowell, as delineated in Robinson's reports and Marriott's formulary, were his invariable model. Yet in 1794 when drawing up a summary of procedures for all Admiralty Courts with Sir John Nicholl the Advocate General, Sir William Scott, then Solicitor General, had cited as his own invariable model the rules laid down by Sir George Lee, Judge of the high Court in 1753. Scott and Nicholl to Lord Grenville, September 10, 1794, in Jay-Grenville papers at Columbia.

9. 'In time of peace it is a court of no profit, and of very little if any business', Edward Long, *History of Jamaica*, 1, London, 1774, viii, 78. Judges profits in peacetime scarcely rose above £100 a year, although in wartime they might be at least 20 times that sum.

10. As late as 1789, William Wylly, a Loyalist who became Advocate of the Bahamas Vice Admiralty Court, wrote that 'the present Judge is a most ignorant *Quack Doctor*, and was formerly *Master of a Guinea Ship*'. Wylly went on to recommend that a lawyer be appointed, 'as the Judge of this Court is generally ignorant of any Law at all, and master of no principles, by which to direct his interpretation of the ambiguous clauses of seemingly jarring statutes . . . it is easy to conceive how frequently he must be lost in the Mazes of the Law and left to grope without a thread to guide him – his safest course then is that which chance may point – the *cast of a Dye*, or of a *Halfpenny*', William Wylly, *A Short Account of the Bahamas Islands; Their Climate, Productions, &c. To which are added Some Strictures upon their relative and Political Situation, the Defects of their present Government, &c.*, London, 1789.

11. In Jamaica alone some 120 privateer vessels were commissioned between 1777 and 1783, which between them libelled some 292 prizes in the Jamaican Prize Court. This, however, was only 30.7 per cent of all vessels libelled, the Royal Navy accounting for 659. The scale of business was even greater in the subsequent wars. Archives of Jamaica, J. V. A. series.

12. At Jamaica, for example, the rate of prosecutions for Navigation and Revenue Act offenses more than trebled, from a yearly average of 2.4 cases before 1783, to 7.9 per year from 1784 to 1792. The peak year was 1786, with 24 cases. The average for 1783 to 1802 was 8.4 per year. There were Jamaican prosecutions for the smuggling of coffee, tobacco, tea, porter, brandy, rum and gin. In the Leewards and Windwards, where those prosecuted were largely American or engaged in trade with Americans, most cases involved false registry.

13. A. L. Burt, *The United States, Great Britain and British North America from the Revolution to the Establishment of Peace after the War of 1812*, Yale University Press, 1940. Notable exceptions to the rule that officers of the Royal Navy were less than zealous in upholding the Laws of Trade were the young captain of the *Boreas*, Horatio Nelson, and his lifelong friends the Collingwood brothers. Their stormy dedication to Duty between 1784 and 1787 can best be traced in Thomas Irving, 'Report . . . upon a Correspondence refer'd to him, between the offices of the Navy and the Civil Officers of the West Indies', P. R. O., B. T. 6/75, 743-61 (7747), and B. M. Add. Mss. 38345, ff. 208-13 (210; and in Sir Nicholas H. Nicholas, *The Dispatches and Letters of Vice-Admiral Lord Viscount Nelson*, 7 vols, London, Colburn, I.

14. Original is in Jamaica, *Journal of the House of Assembly*, December 18, 1789; printed copies in Jamaica Archives and P.R.O.

C.O. 137/88. The Jamaican plantocrats felt that the post-1783 imperial regulations were almost exclusively for the benefit (as Irving had written in 1786) of 'the Manufactures, the Commerce, the Revenues and he Naval Power' of Great Britain, and no longer for the protection of the sugar industry nor the benefit of the faithful West Indian colonies.

15 The fate of the Jamaican petition of 1789 is perhaps instructive. It was sent to London on December 22, 1789, Stephen Fuller, the Jamaican Agent, being instructed to press it home. In his usual industrious way, Fuller bombarded William Pitt with requests for an interview to discuss it; but after failing to receive replies to letters dated February 2, May 1 and May 15, 1790, Fuller directed a powerful five-page broadside to Lord Grenville on August 1, backing it up with a letter to Evan Nepean begging for a reply to be sent by the next packet. At long last, on August 18, a reply was sent, although it must have been disappointing to the framers of the petition. Grenville firmly, if somewhat disingenuously disowned the power to make the changes advocated by the Jamaican Assembly. Only the British Parliament, he pointed out, had the authority to repeal or amend any of its own enactments. Fuller to Grenville and Fuller to Nepean, August 1, 1790; Grenville to Fuller, August 18, 1790 P. R. O., C .O. 137/88.

16 In all, 14 Prize Courts were commissioned during the French Revolutionary War: Barbados, Bahamas, Dominica, St Vincent, Grenada, Leewards and Jamaica at the outbreak; Tobago, Bermuda, St Kitt's, Tortola, Montserrat, St Nicholas Mole (Hispaniola) and Martinique later: P. R. O. Adm. 2/1063-64; H. C.A. 49/99; Adm. 5.42.

17 Study of 213 Jamaican Prize cases for 1779 and 1798 shows an average of seven weeks and three days from seizure to decree; and of 56 Jamaican Instance cases, 1784-92, 11 weeks from prosecution to sentence. Appealed cases, however, commonly took years to decide.

18 Out of a total of 943 Jamaican cases before 1783 of which we have record, a mere 19, or less than two per cent were appealed. Of 1,629 cases between 1793 and 1802, no less than 271 were appealed, or about 16 per cent. For 1793-94, only 39 of 299 were ap-

pealed, the peak years being 1798-1800, with 173 out of 913.

19 Sir F. Pigott and G.W.T. Omond, *Documentary History of the Armed Neutrality 1780-1800*, London, 1919; J.B. Scott (ed.), *The Armed Neutralities of 1780 and 1800*, Washington, 1918. For neutral rights in general, see R. Pares, *Colonial Blockade*; or for a particular example of the deterioration of relations towards war, trace the interchange over the Rule of 1756 between Governors Rodier of Curaçao and Dalling of Jamaica in P.R.O., C.O. 137/78, 100 *sqq.*, 1780.

20 Samuel F. Bemis, *Jay's Treaty: A Study in Commerce and Diplomacy*, New Haven, Yale University Press, 1923.

21 Law Officers to Portland, August 9, 1794, P.R.O. 30/8, 351: Grenville to Portland, November 9, 1794, Dropmore MSS 111, 533; Grenville to Jay, March 20, 1795. Ibid., 37; Jay to Grenville, March 21, 1795, Ibid., 533; Grenville to Jay, May 11, 1795. Ibid., 69.

22 Act of 41 Geo. III, c. 96, passed July 2, 1801, created courts only at Jamaica and the captured island of Martinique. Bermuda and the Bahamas were added by 43 Geo III, c. 160, by which all courts were ordered to send regular returns to London. About the same time, Barbados was acknowledged to be a Prize Court and Antigua took over the role of Martinique. Tortola was added in 1804. Further reforms, chiefly in appeals procedures and questions relating to prize agency, were effected by 45 Geo. III, c. 72, xxxviii-ix.

23 As early as 1760, William Pitt the elder had stated the principle that 'the Lords of the Admiralty can very well give directions *consistent with law* to the judges of the courts of Admiralty, founded on the King's pleasure, signified by the Secretary of State', although it was his son who brought the principle into final practice. Yet even the autocratic younger Pitt did not advance without preparing the ground carefully. For example, recent research has shown that James Stephens's famous broadside, *War in Disguise; Or the Frauds of the Neutral Flags* (1805) was sponsored by Pitt on the advice of Sir William Scott. William Pitt to Lords Commissioner of the Admiralty, August 1, 1760, Adm. 1/4124; Scott to Pitt, August 28, 1805, P. R. O. 30/8, 176, 185; Stephen to Pitt, January 6, 1806, P. R.O. 30/8, 180, 185.

24. Trinidad and Curaçao were commissioned in 1801, Berbice, St Croix and Martinique in 1809, and Demerara and Essequibo in 1811. Disputed Courts were set up in Surinam and St Lucia in 1807, and at Guadeloupe in 1811; P. R.O., Am. 5/45-55; Adm. 1/3898; B. T. 3/9, 125 and 5/17; H. C. A. 49/57.

25. The Caribbean Vice Admiralty Court proved remarkably resistant to the institution of a standard scale of fees. From the earliest days, fees were supposed to be based on those of the High Court of Admiralty and to be publically exhibited, but in fact there was great diversity, evasion and actual extortion. The Act of 1801 authorised the government to decree fee scales, but this proved almost equally inapplicable. A fee commission was appointed in 1811 which reported in June 1813 but the suggested scales had not come into effect before the war ended in 1815.

26. This process, detectable in all wars, amounted almost to a 'Law of Caribbean Escalation'. It seems that the predominant naval power tended to force the trade of its enemies into neutral channels; then, applying pressure to the neutrals through its cruisers and courts, it provoked them successively, into war.

27. Frances Armytage, *The Free Port System in the British West Indies; A Study in Commercial Policy, 1766-1822*, London, Longman, 1953. Unfortunately, this author does not even mention the Vice Admiralty Courts.

28. For example, Charles Clark, *A Summary of Colonial Law . . .*, London, Sweet and Maxwell, 1834.

29. A clue may reside in the usage of the very term 'plantation'. It would be instructive to know when the New England and Middle Colonies ceased to be referred to as plantations by the imperial government.

30. The best summaries of recent historiography are Jack P. Greene, 'The Flight from Determinism . . .', *South Atlantic Quarterly*, 61, 1962, 235-259; 'The Plunge of Lemmings. A Consideration of Recent Writings in British Politics and the American Revolution.'

31. Ubbelohde, *American Revolution*.

32. Eric Williams, *Capitalism and Slavery*, London, Andre Deutsch, 1964.

33. Vincent T. Harlow, *The Founding of the Second British Empire, 1763-1793*, 2 vols, Oxford, Oxford University Press, 1952-65.

34. Jack Greene's recent article in the *American Historical Review*, in showing the persistence of the prerogative versus liberty theme from Stuart times until the reign of Queen Victoria, seems extremely persuasive here, Jack P. Greene, 'Political Mimesis: A Consideration of the Historical and Cultural Roots of Legislative Behavior in the British Colonies in the Eighteenth Century', *American Historical Review*, 75, 2 December 1969.

35. Lord Sheffield, *Observations on the Commerce of the United Sates*, London, 1783.

36. R. Robinson, J. Gallagher and A. Denny, *Africa and the Victorians*, London, Macmillan, 1961; D.K. Fieldhouse, 'The Imperialism of Free Trade', *Economic History Review*, 2nd series, August 1953, 1-15.

Chapter 6

1. Michael Craton, 'Caribs to Black Caribs', in Gary Okihiro (ed.), *In Resistance: Studies in African, Caribbean and Afro-American History*, Amherst, University of Massachusetts Press, 1986, 98-99, quoting journal entries of Columbus's first voyage for November 4, December 16, 25, 26, 1492.

2. Proclamation of October 30, 1503, quoted in Eric Williams (ed.), *Documents of West Indian History, 1492-1655*, Port-of-Spain, PNM Publishing Company, 1963, 62-63.

3. Neil L. Whitehead, *Lords of the Tiger Spirit: A History of the Caribs in Colonial Venezuela and Guyana, 1498-1820*, Dordrecht, Foris Publications, 1988, 151-171; Craton, 'Caribs to Black Caribs', 106-113.

4. Sir William Young, *An Account of the Black Charaibs in the Island of St Vincent's, with the Charaib Treaty of 1773, and other original Documents: Compiled from the papers of the late Sir William Young, Bart.*, London, J. Sewall, 1795; Charles Shephard, *Historical Account of St Vincent*, London, W. Nicol. 1831; Lowell J. Ragatz, *The Fall of the Planter Class in the British Caribbean, 1763-1833: A Study in Social and Economic History*, Washington, American Historical Association, 1928; Sir Alan C. Burns, *History of the British West Indies*, London, Allen & Unwin, 1954.

5. Memorials of Sir William Young, First Commissioner for the Sale of Lands in the Ceded Islands to the Lords of the Treas-

ury, April 11, 1767, in William Cobbett *et al.* (eds), *Parliamentary History of England . . . to 1803*, 36 vols, London, Hansard, 1813, 17, 1771-74, 575-582. The papers ordered to be laid before Parliament by Lord North in December 1772 were also published separately as *Authentic Papers relative to the Expedition against the Caribs and the sale of Lands in the Island of St Vincent*, London, Almond, 1773.

6. *Ibid.*

7. 'Draft of Instructions to the Commissioners for the Sale of lands to Survey and dispose of lands on the Windward side of St Vincent', January 1768, Cobbett, *Parliamentary History*, 17, 582-587.

8. Report of Commissioners for Sale of Lands, October 16, 1771, Cobbett, *Parliamentary History*, 17, 605-608; C. O. 106/12.

9. Report of Richard Maitland and others to Lord Hillsborough, n.d. [1771], Cobbett, *Parliamentary History*, 17, 608-614.

10. *Ibid.*, 611; J. Steven Watson, *The Reign of George III, 1760-1815*, Oxford, Clarendon Press, 1960, 154-155.

11. Report of Richard Maitland *et al.*, 613-614.

12. Lord Hillsborough to Governor, April 18, 1772, marked 'Separate and Secret', *Parliamentary History*, 17, 633-635.

13. Michael Craton, *Testing the Chains: Resistance to Slavery in the British West Indies*, Ithaca, Cornell University Press, 1982, 87-92, 151-153.

14. On the events in St Vincent of 1763-73, Ragatz says (116-117): 'The work of surveying was hindered by the Black Caribs who were descendants of shipwrecked Guinea slaves and the indigenous yellow Caribs. These mongrel peoples declared themselves to be independent owners of the soil and disputed the British occupation. They committed numerous depredations on the plantations which had been laid out and matters reached such a point that it became necessary to launch an expeditionary force of North American troops against them in 1772. Their resistance was soon broken. By a treaty the following year, they recognised British control and accepted a block of land in the northern part of the island, set aside for their exclusive use. The affair aroused considerable opposition in England among well-meaning but misinformed individuals who saw in it nothing but wanton aggression against an inoffensive local people. It was actually a necessary preliminary step to the development of the colony.'

15. The Carib debate began on December 9 and 11, 1772; Lord North ordered the papers on December 23, 1772; the debate continued and was concluded February 10 and 15, 1773. For the controversy in the country at large, see *The Scots Magazine* for November 1772 and February, April and May 1773, and *The Gentleman's Magazine* for April 1773 cited in Ragatz, *Fall of the Planter Class*, 177, and for the newspaper and other references in J. Paul Thomas, 'The Caribs of St Vincent: A Study in Imperial Maladministration 1763-1773', *Journal of Caribbean History*, 18, 1983, 71-73. Two parliamentary committees examined the Indian situation throughout the winter of 1772 and spring of 1773; Robert, Lord Clive was examined and received his qualified exoneration in November 1772; Lord North's Regulating Act was passed in March 1773.

16. Lucy S. Sutherland, *The East India Company in Eighteenth Century Politics*, Oxford, Clarendon Press, 1952; J. M. Holzmann, *The Nabobs in England: A Study of the Returned Anglo-Indian, 1760-85*, New York, University Microfilms, 1926.

17. Lewis B. Namier and John Brooke, *The History of Parliament The House of Commons, 1754-1790*, 3 vols, London, HMSO, 1964, 3, 554-556; Cobbett, *Parliamentary History*, 17, 568-570.

18. Lewis B. Namier, *England in the Age of the American Revolution*, 2nd edn, London, Macmillan, 1960, 260-264; Cobbett, *Parliamentary History*, 17, 570-572.

19. Granville Sharp at different times campaigned for the conversion of the Jews, the abolition of press gangs, annual parliaments, the appointment of American bishops, the rights of the American colonists and the improvement of conditions for the British poor, as well as for the Black Caribs and, most famously, the slaves. On this point, see Angus Calder, *Revolutionary Empire: The Rise of the English-Speaking Empire from the Fifteenth Century to the 1780s*, London, Jonathan Cape, 1981, 685. For the Somerset Case (and Strong Case, 1765), see James Walvin, *Black and White: The Negro and English Society, 1555-1945*, London, Allen Lane, 1973, 117-131.

20. Wylie Sypher, *Guinea's Captive Kings: British Anti-Slavery Literature of the XVIIIth*

Century, Chapel Hill, University of North Carolina Press, 1942; Richard Price and Sally Price, *Stedman's Surinam: Life in an Eighteenth-Century Slave Society. An Abridged, Modernized Edition of Narrative of a Five years Expedition against the Revolted Negroes of Surinam John Gabriel Stedman*, Baltimore, The Johns Hopkins University Press, 1992. As the Prices show, Stedman's blunt and revealing original manuscript was drastically edited to catch current tastes for the first edition of 1796, which, like Bryan Edwards' *History*, was illustrated by William Blake.

21. Sypher, *Guinea's Captive Kings*, 122-137.

22. Both Richard and William Burke were involved in land deals in Grenada and St Vincent after 1762, the latter also in speculations in East India Company stock (as was Lord Shelburne); Sutherland, *East India Company*, 206-212; Dixon Wecter, *Edmund Burke and His Kinsmen*, Boulder, University of Colorado, 1939. Edmund Burke himself was hardly disinterested, being at one time Colonial Agent for New York.

23. General Robert Monckton, MP for Pontefract 1751-54 and 1774, had been Governor of New York, 1761-63. For the Monckton, Dalrymple and Etherington grants in St Vincent, 1765-76, see Craton, *Testing the Chains*, 147-153; Ragatz, *Fall of the Planter Class*, 116-119.

24. Cobbett, *Parliamentary History*, 17, 722-741.

25. The pro-planter writer Charles Shephard misrepresented the facts and sequence of events, either through ignorance or, more likely, to justify the planters' actions by putting the blame on Parliament for imposing the treaty on the planters in the first place. 'An enquiry was set on foot by the opponents of Lord North's administration, respecting the justice and propriety of the motives, which give rise to his expedition', wrote Shephard in 1831, 'and after a tedious investigation, it was finally resolved, that the measure was founded in injustice, and reflected dishonour on the National Character, a violation of the natural rights of mankind, and totally subversive of that liberty it gloried to defend. This conclusion was productive of immediate orders to suspend hostilities against the Caribs, and to negotiate a treaty with them on reasonable terms. In obedience to these instructions, General Dalrymple made overtures of peace, which were joyfully embraced by the enemy.' Charles Shephard, *Historical Account of St Vincent*, 30. The treaty itself, signed on the one side of Dalrymple alone, and on the other by 28 Carib chiefs, was reprinted in Young, *Black Charaibs*, 89-97, and Shephard, *Historical Account of St Vincent*, 30-35. It is discussed in Craton, *Testing the Chains*, 151-152.

26. The lithographed version, used by Bryan Edwards in 1794 to illustrate the Jamaican Maroon treaty of 1739, is copied in Craton, *Testing the Chains*, 146 (unfortunately with a somewhat misleading caption). The more famous illustration of Colonel Guthrie's negotiation with the Jamaican maroon Cudjoe in 1739 used by R. C. Dallas in his *The History of the Maroons* (1803) makes for an interesting comparison. In this painting, an unarmed Guthrie likewise holds out a hand but seemingly only for a symbolic exchange of hats with Cudjoe, who is caricatured as a dwarfish hunchback but is fully clothed, armed with musket and knife, and guarded by an armed maroon companion. Craton, *Testing the Chains*, 87-91. See also Diane Kerns, *Black Carib Kinship and Ritual*, Urbana, University of Illinois, 1983, 35-36, 39.

An irresistible parallel may be drawn between the Brunias picture and the pioneer confrontation between Columbus and the Guanahani Lucayans. As Fernandez-Armesto recently described so well, 'Two things in particular impressed Columbus when he disembarked to examine the island in the morning light. It struck him as of pleasant aspect, well watered and wooded with an abundance of fruit: he was beholding it, of course, with a promoter's eye. But before noticing anything but the land . . . Columbus recorded Europeans' first sight of the natives, whom he called 'naked people'. This was not just a description, but a classification. A late fifteenth-century reader would have understood that Columbus was confronting 'natural men', not the citizens of a civil society possessed of legitimate political institutions of their own. The registering of this perception thus prepared the way for the next step, the ritual appropriation of sovereignty to the Castilian monarchs, with a royal banner streaming and a scribe to record the act of possession. Clothes were the standard by which a people's level of civilisation was judged in medieval Latin Christendom . . . At a further level, in terms of the two great traditions of thought to which Columbus and his contemporaries were heirs – those of classical antiquity and medieval Christianity – social nakedness might signify either of two conclusions: it could evoke the sort of sylvan simplicity of which classical poets sang and which humanists associated with the 'age of gold', or it might suggest the state of dependence on God which are starkly symbolised by St Francis of Assisi when he tore off his clothes in the public square . . . [the Amerindians] presented, because of their innocence, a unique opportunity for spreading the gospel; because of their primitivism, an unequalled chance to confer on them the presumable benefits of Latin civilisation; and because of their defenselessness, an irresistible object of exploitation.' See Felipe Fernandez-Armesto, *Columbus*, New York, Oxford University Press, 1991, 82.

27. Chatoyer himself personally owned a considerable amount of land and several slaves, having on one occasion been recompensed by the courts to the tune of £40 for a trespass by white neighbours; Young, *Black Charaibs*, 111. Ragatz, *Fall of the Planter Class*, 117-119; Ivor Waters, *The Unfortunate Valentine Morris*, Chepstow, Wales, Chepstow Society, 1964.

28. Shephard, *Historical Account of St Vincent*, 54-55.

29. *Ibid.*, 74; Young, *Black Charaibs*, 107-125. Chatoyer's sword had formerly belonged to Sir William Young's brother Henry, who had been killed at Saratoga in 1777. Young gave it to the Carib chief 'on the faith of his employing it in loyal service to the King, and (as he promised), in particular defence of the family and its interests'. *Ibid.*, 107-108. For the Second Carib War, 1795-97, Shephard, *Historical Account of St Vincent*, 45-177; Craton, *Testing the Chains*, 190-194, 203-206.

30. Craton, *Testing the Chains*, Gonzalez, *Sojourners of the Caribbean: Ethnogenesis and Ethnohistory of the Garifuna*, Urbana, University of Illinois Press, 1988, 21-22, 33-34.

Chapter 9

1. This stemmed chiefly from Bryan Edwards's 'best-seller' which, although called a general history of the British West Indies, was dominated by Jamaica. First published in 1793, it went through three large editions before 1801. Bryan Edwards, *The History, Civil and Commercial of the West Indies* , 2 vols, London, 1793.

2. A trend which originated, paradoxically, from the very first foray by a modern American scholar into the slavery of the British Caribbean; Ulrich B. Phillips, 'A Jamaican Slave Plantation', *American Historical Review*, 14, April 1914. Probably the best short bibliography of American slavery is in Eric Foner (ed.) *America's Black Past: A Reader in Afro-American History*, New York, 1970, 555 - 577.

3. New York, 1969.

4. See particularly, R. B. Sheridan, *The Development of the Plantations to 1750; An Era of West Indian Prosperity, 1750-1775*, Barbados, 1970.

5. Edward Brathwaite (*The Development of Creole Society in Jamaica, 1770 -1820*, Oxford, 1971), says that Jamaica contains 4 million acres of which 3.75 million are cultivable, citing Edwards, *History*, I, 247-248. Yet Jamaica's total area is only 4,400 square miles, or about 2,800,000 acres of which probably no more than half is actually cultivable in the sense of tillable. In 1752, Governor Trelawny, while estimating that Jamaica's total acreage was 3,840,000 considered 1,706,664 (or 44 per cent) was 'mountainous, inaccessible, rocky or barren land'. and only 2,133,336 acres (or 56 per cent) was 'good plantable land', Trelawny to Board of Trade, August 15, 1752, Public Record Office (P. R. O.), C.O. 137/25, x, 101.

6. For Jamaica's early years, Richard S. Dunn, *Sugar and Slaves: The rise of the Planter Class in the English West Indies, 1624-1713*, Chapel Hill, NC, 1972; and Michael Craton and James Walvin, *A Jamaican Plantation: The History of Worthy Park, 1670 - 1970*, London and Toronto, 12-94. For the remarkable standardisation, as well as the almost completely static technology, of sugar production, see Ward Barrett, 'Caribbean Sugar Production Standards in the Seventeenth and Eighteenth Centu-

ries', in J. Parker (ed.), *Merchants and Scholars*, Minneapolis, MN, 1967, 147-170.

7. Edward Long, *History of Jamaica*, London, 1774, 1, 495 - 496.

8. Edwards, *History*, 1, ii, 311-315.

9. That is, 140,000 out of 250,000 on sugar plantations, 21,000 on coffee plantations, 31,000 on pens, and 58,000 on smallholdings or in towns.

10. That is, as many as a further 60 in addition to 182, or a total of 184,000 out of 250,000.

11. Sheridan, *The Development of the Plantations*, 47. See Table 1.

12. W. Barrett, 'Caribbean Sugar Production Standards 153.

13. That is, about 240 slaves for 160 acres of canes and about 160 animals. In 1739 there were said to be 84,000 livestock to 100,000 slaves in Jamaica, and in 1768, 136,000 against 167,000 but proportionately fewer livestock than slaves were located on sugar plantations, Sheridan, 41.

14. Craton and Walvin, 59-62.

15. The Tharp Estates in Trelawney, developed after 1765, in which half-a-dozen contiguous holdings centred around one of the most elaborate factories in Jamaica at Good Hope on the Martha Brae, may have been something of an exception, although its success was either not conspicuous enough or came too late to invite emulation. Aggregation of holdings could, of course, be profitable in other ways, such as speculative sales of superfluous land, the 'bleeding' of the least profitable areas for labour, or their diversification into pens or coffee farms.

16. Sheridan, 29, 47.

17. Michael Craton, *Sinews of Empire*, London, 1974, Chapter 2; Edward Brathwaite, 'Controlling the Slaves in Jamaica', unpublished paper, Slavery conference, University of Guyana, 1971, 6.

18. The Pinnock estate in St Andrew in 1753 cited by F. W. Pitman, 'The Settlement and Financing of British West India Plantations in the Eighteenth Century', in *Essays in Colonial History Presented to Charles McLean Andrews by his Students*, New Haven, 1931, 261-270, with its 16 white servants to 280 slaves (on 2,872 acres, of which 242 were in canes) was probably one of the last such examples; Sheridan, 45.

19. Brathwaite, *Development*, 135-136.

20. ' . . . The poorest White person seems to consider himself nearly on a level with the richest, and, emboldened by this idea, approaches his employer with extended hand, and a freedom, which, in the countries of Europe, is seldom displayed by men in the lower orders of life towards their superiors. It is not difficult to trace the origin of this principle. It arises, without doubt, from the preeminence and distinction which are necessarily attached even to the complexion of a White Man, in a country where the complexion, generally speaking, distinguishes freedom from slavery . . .' Edwards, *History*, II, iv, 7-8.

21. Barry Higman, 'Some Demographic Characteristics of Slavery in Jamaica, circa 1823', University of the West Indies Postgraduate Seminar Paper, March 1969, 5, 22; Brathwaite, *Development*, Chapters 10, 11.

22. Craton and Walvin, 71-78; George Metcalf, *Royal Government and Political Conflict in Jamaica, 1729-1783*, London, 1965, 58-190. The reorganisation of 1756 which created Jamaica's three counties, however, may have been something of a defeat for the planters, or at least for parochialism.

23. Bermudian law of 1730, quoted in Craton, *Sinews of Empire*, Chapter 4.

24. Long, *Jamaica*, I, x, Appendix, 156-220.

25. 'A General View of the Principles on Which This System of Laws Appears to Have Been Generally Founded', Great Britain, Commons, *British Sessional Papers*, A/P, 1789, 646a, pt. III.

26. It was said to be 3/7 per cent in 1787, when it was 3 per cent in Antigua and 2.6 per cent in Barbados; H. A. Wyndham; *The Atlantic and Slavery*, Oxford, UK, 1935, 284.

27. Brathwaite, *Development*, 167-175.

28. Elsa Goveia, *The West Indian Slave Laws of the Eighteenth Century*, Barbados, 1970.

29. *British Sessional Papers*, A/P, 1789, xxci, 646a.

30. *Ibid.*

31. U. B. Phillips, 1914; Craton and Walvin, *A Jamaican Plantation*, 125-154; Michael Craton, 'Jamaican Slave Mortality: Fresh Light from Worthy Park, Longville and the Tharp Estates', *Journal of Caribbean History*, November 3, 1971, 1-27. Computer analysis of the entire slave population of Worthy Park between 1783 and 1838, to trace mortality, fertility, health, job mobility, male:female ratios, African-creole ratios and individual biographies continued, with the aim of producing a book, entitled

tentatively, *Discovering the Invisible Man* and was incorporated into *Searching for the Invisible Man: Slaves and Plantation Life in Jamaica*, published by Harvard University Press in 1978.

32. For example, between 1783 and 1796 no fewer than 85 white men lived and worked on Worthy Park Estate, yet there were never more than a dozen in residence at any one time. Craton and Walvin, *A Jamaican Plantation*, 144-145.

33. Sir Charles Prices' famous Coromantine 'friend' was one such idealised 'Uncle Tom', *British Sessional Papers*, A/P 1798, xxvi, 646a; Long, *Jamaica*, II, vii, 77. Such exemplary blacks as Francis Williams could be easily ridiculed in London for the incompleteness of their attempted assimilation. Apparently no one thought to measure them against contemporary colonial whites. Francis Williams, though hardly polished, was probably the best Jamaican Latinist of his day, white or black.

34. *Journal of a West India Proprietor, Kept During Residence in the Island of Jamaica*, London, 1834.

35. Edwards reckoned that in 1791, 451 or 59 per cent of Jamaican sugar estates were in the hands of their owners but did not estimate how many of these owners were absentees, held several estates, or lived normally in Spanish Town; *History*, I, ii, 311-315.

36. At Worthy Park, those listed as coloured did not rise about ten per cent before 1800, yet those listed as 'black' may not have been serologically pure. For the debate on the number of 'coloureds' in the Jamaican population, see Brathwaite, *Development*, 168-171.

37. The following partial table of the identification of 393 manumitted in five Jamaican parishes between 1829 and 1835 is telling:

	Negro	Sambo	Mulatto	Quadroon	Mustee	African	Creole	Total
Westmoreland	16	8	29	12	3	1	64	71
Hanover	15	14	16	9	3	2	54	59
St James	24	7	30	23	2	3	83	86
Trelawny	13	13	22	27	3	5	73	78
St Elizabeth	50	23	23	3	-	15	83	99
Total	118	65	120	74	11	26	357	393

Source: Higman, 'Demographic Characteristics', Table 22, Appendix 4.

38. For Jamaican slave society, see U. B. Phillips, 1914; F. W. Pitman, 1917, 1926; H.O. Patterson, *The Sociology of Slavery*, London, 1967; Craton and Walvin, *A Jamaican Plantation*; Brathwaite, *Development* and R. B. Sheridan, *Sugar and Slavery*, Barbados, 1973.

39. *British Sessional Papers*, A/P, 1789, xxvi, 646a.

40. The whites perhaps echoing the brutal fatalism of Captain Phillips (1649); '. . . what the smallpox spar'd the flux swept off to our great regret, after all our pains and care to give their messes in due order and season, keeping their lodgings as clean and sweet as possible, and enduring so much misery and stench so long among a parcel of creatures nastier than swine; and after all our expectations to be defeated by their mortality . . .' . Elizabeth Donnan, *Documents Illustrative of the History of the Slave Trade to America*, 4 vols, Washington DC, 1930-35; I, 410.

41. Charles Buxton (ed.), *Memoirs of Sir Thomas Fowell Buxton, Bart* . . . new ed., London, 1877, 122-126.

42. Edward Long to William Pitt, March 7, 1788; Great Britain P.R.O., *Chatham Papers*, 30/8, 153, 40; *British Sessional Papers*, A/P, 1789, xxvi, 646a.

43. Philip D. Curtin, 'Epidemiology and the Slave Trade', *Political Science Quarterly*, 83, June 1968, 190-216.

44. The average for 121 vessels carrying 41,625 slaves to Jamaica between 1764 to 1786 was 62.2 per cent males, *British Sessional Papers*, A/P, 2789, xxvi, pt. VI.

45. This projection however, probably requires some modification for, as Richard Sheridan has recently argued, slave mortality was almost certainly lower in periods of low agricultural intensity, and sugar plantations did not predominate in Jamaica until at least 1700. The same effect can be traced in Barbados' early years. See Sheridan, *Sugar and Slavery*. If Sheridan's arguments are true, the extrapolated natural decrease figures for 1682-1701 may require some adjustment, although the Jamaican demographic statistics for the earliest period on which Sheridan worked are particularly unreliable – inferior even to those of Barbados.

46. It may have been even less. Between 1776 and 1796 the cane-cutters at Worthy Park (who included a majority of women) probably cut no more than ⅔ ton of cane each

per day on the average, compared with 3.42 tons of cane per man performing essentially the same tasks in 1968; Craton and Walvin, *A Jamaican Plantation*, 103-104.

47. It produced, however, the damaging phenomenon of the 'Quashee' or 'Sambo' mentality. See, for example, Patterson, 174-181; Stanley Elkins, *Slavery*, Chicago, 1959, 82, 130-133, 227-229.

48. Long, *Jamaica*, II, 423.

49. American Negro Slave Revolts, New York, 1943.

50. *Op. cit.*, 260-282.

51. A lively but mythopeic account of the maroons is Carey Robinson, *The Fighting Maroons of Jamaica*, London, 1970.

52. The 1760 rebellion awaits a comprehensive scholarly treatment (as indeed do all Jamaican rebellions).

53. Mary Reckord, 'The Christmas Rebellion, 1832', *Jamaica Journal*, 1970; 'Missions in Jamaica before Emancipation', *Caribbean Studies*, 1968. The most perceptive study of the relationship of religious revivalism to the post-1807 revolts seems to me to be Robert Moore, 'Slave Rebellions in Guyana', unpublished paper, Slavery Conference, University of Guyana, 1971.

54. The same effect has been noted in the French Antilles in the years just prior to the French and Haitian Revolutions by the *doyen* Gabriel Debien in, for example, *Plantations et Esclaves à Saint-Domingue*, Dakar, 1962, Chapter 6.

55. Brathwaite, *Development*, 168; Higman, 22.

56. This impression is overwhelmingly clear from the evidence before the Graham Commission in 1832; *British Sessional Papers*, Reports, 1831-1832, 721.

Chapter 10

1. The key quotations from Bryan Edwards are very familiar: 'In countries where slavery is established, the leading principle on which the government is supported is fear, or a sense of that absolute coercive necessity, which leaving no choice of action, supersedes all questions of right . . . Yet that the slavery of some part of the human species, in a very abject degree, has existed in all ages of the world, among the most civilized, as well as the most barbarous nations, no man who has consulted the records of history disputes.' *History of the West Indies*, 1793, III, 13; II, 174. The earlier statement by Edward Long deserves to be better known: 'History evinces that, in all ages, there has been one set of persons uniting its efforts to enslave mankind; and another set, to oppose such attempts, and vindicate the cause of freedom. The accidental circumstances of man may, perhaps, occasion this difference: the rich are the natural enemies of the poor; and the poor of the rich; like the ingredients of a boiling cauldron, they seem to be in perpetual warfare, and struggle which shall be uppermost; yet if both parties could compose themselves, the faeces would remain peaceably at the bottom; and all the other particles range themselves in different strata, according to their quality, the most refined floating always to the top'. *History of Jamaica*, 1774, I, 25.

2. 'I agree that the slaves' resistance record was very impressive, but the bitter central fact about Caribbean slavery is that the planter class kept this vicious system going for nearly 200 years even though the slaves outnumbered them by ten to one.' Richard S. Dunn, review of Michael Craton, *Testing the Chains: Resistance to Slavery in the British West Indies*, Ithaca, Cornell University Press, 1982, *Journal of Interdisciplinary History*, XV, Summer 1984, 173-175.

3. O. Nigel Bolland, 'Systems of Domination After Slavery: The Control of Land and Labor in the British West Indies after 1838', *Comparative Studies in Society and History*, 23, 4, 1981, 591-619; Eric Foner, *Reconstruction: America's Unfinished Revolution*, New York, Harper, 1988.

4. Recorded first in the conference of the New York Academy of Sciences entitled 'Comparative Perspectives on Slavery in New World Plantation Societies', New York, May 6, 1976. A beguiling parallel conception, derived from ecological anthropology, is that of slaves establishing social 'niches', argued recently by Robert Dirks, *The Black Saturnalia: Conflict and Its Ritual Expression on British West Indies Slave Plantations*, University Press of Florida, 1987.

5. M. Moreau de Saint-Méry, *Description . . . de la partie française de l'Isle Saint-Domingue*, 1779, I, 123.

6. For example, Richard Ligon, *History of Barbadoes*, 1657, 46: '. . . and seeing the mustering of our men, and hearing their gun-shot

(than which nothing is more terrible to them) their spirits are subjugated to so low a condition, as they dare not look up to any bold attempt'.

7. Dirks, 'Slaves' Holiday', *Natural History*, 84, 10, 1975, 84-90; *Black Saturnalia*, 1- 8, 185-190.

8. See Petition of Barbados Assembly to the Regent over the Registry Bill, dated January 17, 1816, Public Record Office, London, CO 28/85, quoted in Craton, *op. cit.*, 256.

9. David Barry Gaspar, *Bondmen & Rebels: A Study of Master-Slave Relations in Antigua*, Baltimore, Johns Hopkins, 1985; Craton, *op. cit.*, 115-124.

10. Richard Price, ed., *Maroon Societies: Rebel Slave Communities in the Americas*, New York, Doubleday, 1973; Gaspar, *Bondmen & Rebels*, 173-214; C. G. A. Oldendorp, *A Caribbean Mission*, translated by A. R. High-field and V. Barac, Ann Arbor, Karoma, 1987, 1770, 233-237; Michael Craton, 'Seeking A Life of Their Own: Aspects of Slave Resistance in the Bahamas', paper presented at the International Slavery Congress, São Paolo, Brazil, June 1988, published in *The Indian Historical Review*, XV, 1-2, July 1988 and January 1989, 96-115.

11. Gordon K. Lewis, *Main Currents in Caribbean Thought: The Historical Evolution of Caribbean Society in Its Ideological Aspects*, 1492-1900, Baltimore, Johns Hopkins, 1983, 178-179.

12. Edward Long, *History of Jamaica*, II, 405, quoted *ibid.*, 179-180.

13. This argument is developed in Michael Craton, 'From Caribs to Black Caribs: The Amerindian Roots of Servile Resistance in the Caribbean', in Gary Y. Okihiro, (ed.), *In Resistance: Studies in African, Caribbean and Afro-American History*, Amherst, MA, 96-116.

14. Troy S. Floyd, *The Columbian Dynasty in the Caribbean, 1492-1526*, Albuquerque, New Mexico, 1973, 95-105.

15. Craton, *Testing the Chains*, 62-63, footnote 6; Richard Price *op. cit.*, 1-30.

16. Craton, *Testing the Chains*, 145-153, 204-207; Nancie L. Gonzalez, *Sojourners of the Caribbean: Ethnogenesis and Ethnohistory of the Garifuna*, Urbana, IL, 1988.

17. *Law and Diplomacy*, New York, Oxford, 1987.

18. Eugene D. Genovese, *From Rebellion to Revolution: Afro-American Slave Revolts in*

the Making of the Modern World*, Baton Rouge, La, 1979; Craton, *Testing the Chains*, 99-139.

19. Pierre J. Pannet, *Report on the Execrable Conspiracy Carried Out by the Amina Negroes on the Danish Island of St. Jan in America, 1733*, Aimery Caron and Arnold Highfield, St Croix, Antilles Press, 1984; Oldendorp, *Caribbean Mission*, 235-237; John L. Anderson, *Night of the Silent Drums: A Narrative of Slave Rebellion in the Virgin Islands*, New York, Scribners, 1975; Karen Fog Olwig, *Cultural Adaptation and Resistance on St. John: Three Centuries of Afro-Caribbean Life*, Gainesville, FL, 1985.

20. Craton, *Testing the Chains*, 67-96; H. Orlando Patterson, 'Slavery and Slave Revolts: A Socio-Historical Analysis of the First Maroon War, Jamaica, 1655-1740', *Social and Economic Studies*, 19, 1970, 289-335; Barbara Klamon Kopytoff, 'The Maroons of Jamaica: An Ethnohistorical Study of Incomplete Polities, 1655-1905', PhD dissertation, University of Pennsylvania, 1973.

21. John Gabriel Stedman, *Narrative of a Five Years' Expedition against the Revolted Negroes of Surinam in Guiana on the Wild Coast of South America from the years 1772-1777*, London, 1792; Richard Price, *op. cit.*, *The Guiana Maroons: A Historical and Bibliographical Introduction*, Baltimore, Johns Hopkins, 1976; *First Time*, Baltimore, Johns Hopkins, 1984; *Alabi's World*, Baltimore, Johns Hopkins, 1990.

22. J. J. Hartsinck, 'The Story of the Slave Rebellion in Berbice', *Journal of the British Guiana Museum and Zoo*, 20, 1958, III, 7-8, quoted by Lewis, *Main Currents in Caribbean Thought*, 226.

23. Craton, *Testing the Chains*, 270-272.

24. Jean Fouchard, *The Haitian Maroons: Liberty or Death*, New York, Blyden Press, 1981; Leslie F. Manigat, 'The Relationship Between Marronage and Slave Revolts and Revolution in St. Domingue-Haiti', in Vera Rubin and Arthur Tudent (eds), *Comparative Perspectives on Slavery in New World Plantation Societies*, Academy of Sciences, New York, 1977, 420-438.

25. Craton, *Testing the Chains*, 161-238; Genovese, *Rebellion to Revolution*; Roger Norman Buckley, *Slaves in Red Coats: The British West India Regiments, 1795-1815*, Yale, New Haven, 1979.

26. Craton, 'Seeking A Life of Their Own', *op. cit.* Gaspar, 'Amelioration or Oppression: The Abolition of the Slaves' Sunday Markets in Antigua, 1831', paper presented at the Twentieth Conference of Caribbean Historians, St Thomas, March 1988.

27. Craton, *Testing the Chains*, 241-321; Mary Turner, *Slaves and Missionaries: The Disintegration of Jamaican Slave Society, 1787-1834*, Urbana, IL, 1982.

28. Craton, 'Proto-Peasant Revolts? The Late Slave Rebellions in the British West Indies, 1816-1832', *Past and Present*, 85, November 1979, 99 - 125; 'The Passion to Exist: Slave Rebellions in the British West Indies, 1650-1832', *Journal of Caribbean History*, 13, Summer 1980, 1-20; *Testing the Chains*, 241-253.

29. Mary Turner, 'The Baptist War and Abolition'. *Jamaican Historical Review*, XIII, 1982, 31-41; Craton, 'Emancipation from Below? The Role of the British West Indian Slaves in the Emancipation Movement, 1815-1834' in Jack Hayward (ed.), *Abolition and After*, London, Frank Cass, 1985, 110-131; 'What and Who, to Whom and What: The Significance of Slave Resistance', in Barbara Solow and Stanley Engerman (eds), *British Capitalism and Caribbean Slavery: The Legacy of Eric Williams*, Cambridge University Press, 1987, 259-282.

30. Richard Hart, *Slaves Who Abolished Slavery*, London, Bogle-L'Overture, 1978, republished as *Esclavos que abolieron esclavitud*, Habana, Casa de las Americas, 1980; Eric Williams, *Capitalism and Slavery*, London, Andre Deutsch, 1964, 197-208.

31. Van Scholten's Proclamation rivals the Brazilian *Lei Aurea* of 1888 for succinctness, but is more carefully programmatic:

   1 All unfree in the Danish West India Islands are from today free.
   2 The estate Negroes retain for three months from this date the use of the houses and provision grounds of which they have hitherto been possessed.
   3 Labour is in future to be paid for by agreement, but allowance of food to cease.
   4 The maintenance of the old and infirm, who are not able to work, is, until further determined, to be furnished by the late owners.

Quoted by Eric Williams, *From Columbus to Castro: The History of the Caribbean, 1492-1969*, London, Andre Deutsch, 1970, 327. For the best account of Buddoe's rebellion and its aftermath, see Neville, A. T. Hall, 'The Post-Emancipation Court Martial in Fredericksted, St. Croix, July-August 1848: An Account and An Analysis', paper presented to the Thirteenth Conference of Caribbean Historians, Guadeloupe, 1981.

32. Eric Williams, *From Columbus to Castro*, 326; Henri Qangou, *La Guadeloupe, 1492-1848*, Paris, 1962.

33. Gerald Newton, *The Netherlands: An Historical and Cultural Survey, 1795-1977*, London, Benn, 1978, 174; R. A. J. Van Lier, *Frontier Society*, The Hague, 1971, 75.

34. Luis M. Díaz Soler, *Historia de la Esclavitud Negra en Puerto Rico*, Rio Piedras, Editorial Universitaria, 1974, Chapter IX, 201-224.

35. *Ibid.*, Chapter XII, 289-314; Eric Williams, *op. cit.*, 291-292. See also Franklin W. Knight, *Slave Society in Cuba during the Nineteenth Century*, Madison, WI, 1970, 77-84; Knight includes an interesting account of the slave revolt in Matanzas in March 1866 in which the slaves from several estates 'simultaneously withheld their labour, claiming that they had been declared free by the Cortes in Spain. The Negroes demanded that they be paid for their services. Although there was no report of any violence by the slaves, a large number of troops were deployed to force the men to go back to work'.

36. Rebecca J. Scott, *Slave Emancipation in Cuba: The Transition to Free Labour, 1860-1899*, Princeton, 1985, 58-62, 114-124.

37. Quoted in Scott, *op. cit.*, 118. See also 169-171.

38. Clarence H. Haring, *Empire in Brazil*, Cambridge, 1958; Reginald Coupland, *The British Anti-Slavery Movement*, London, 1933; G. R. Mellor, *British Imperial Trusteeship, 1783-1850*, Faber, London, 1951; Robert Brent Toplin, *The Abolition of Slavery in Brazil*, New York, Atheneum, 1972; Robert Edgar Conrad, *The Destruction of Brazilian Slavery, 1850-1888*, Berkeley, CA, 1972; *Children of God's Fire: A Documentary History of Black Slavery in Brazil*, Princeton, 1983.

39. Gilberto Freyre, *The Masters and the Slaves*, Knofp, New York, 1946; Frank Tannenbaum, *Slave and Citizen: The Negro in the Americas*, Vintage, New York, 1946. For a

short bibliography of traditionalist views, see Toplin, *op. cit.*, xii, footnote 1.

40. *Estudos Económicas*: IPE, University of São Paolo. Special issues on Slave Protest, 17, 18, 1987, 1988. Local Brazilian variants dealt within these essays include forms of slave resistance and protest in towns, mining and non-plantation rural areas, the phenomenon of slave-stealing and transfer with the slaves' own connivance, and of allegedly 'criminal' activity engaged in by slaves.

41. Toplin, *op. cit.*, 3-37, Conrad, *Destruction of Slavery*, 184-186, 268; *Children of God's Fire*, Part IX, 362-418; Stuart Schwartz, 'Resistance and Accommodation in Eighteenth-Century Brazil: The Slaves' View of Slavery', *Hispanic American Historical Review*, 57, 1977, 69-81.

42. Francisco Antonio Brandão Jr, *A escravatura no Brasil*, Brussels, 1865, quoted in Toplin, *op. cit.*, 32.

43. This position is argued at greater length in Craton, *Testing the Chains*, 323-334; 'Continuity Not Change: The Incidence of Unrest among Ex-Slaves in the British West Indies, 1838-1865', *Slavery and Abolition*, 1, Fall 1988, 144-170. See also O. Nigel Bolland, 'Systems on Domination', *op. cit.*, and the subsequent exchange between Bolland and William A. Green, *Comparative Studies in Society and History*, 23, 4, October 1981; 26, 1, January 1984.

Chapter 11

1. Contrast, for example, the approaches of Orlando Patterson, *The Sociology of Slavery: An Analysis of the Origins, Development and Structure of Negro Slave Society in Jamaica*, London, 1967, and Henry C. Wilkinson, *The Adventurers of Bermuda: A History of the Island from its Discovery and the Dissolution of the Somers Island Company in 1684*, London, 1933; *Bermuda in the Old Empire: A History of the Island from its Discovery and the Dissolution of the Somers Island Company until the end of the American Revolutionary War: 1684-1784*, London, 1950; and *Bermuda from Sail to Steam: The History of the Island from 1784 to 1901*, 2 vols, London, 1973. Remarkably, the most thorough comparative study remains James Stephen, *The Slavery of the British West India Colonies Delineated*, 2 vols, London, 1824, 1830, although cf. Frank Wesley Pitman. 'Slavery on British West Indian Plantations in the Eighteenth Century', *Journal of Negro History*, XI, 1926, 584-668; Lowell Joseph Ragatz, *The Fall of the Planter Class in the British Caribbean, 1763-1833: A Study in Social and Economic History*, New York, 1928, and Richard B. Sheridan, *Sugar and Slavery: An Economic History of the British West Indies, 1623-1775*, Barbados, 1974.

2. Michael Craton, 'Jamaican Slave Mortality: Fresh Light from Worthy Park, Longville and the Tharp Estates', *Journal of Caribbean History*, III, Nov. 1971, 1-27; *Sinews of Empire: A Short History of British Slavery*, New York, 1974, 187-199, 'Jamaican Slavery', in Stanley L. Engerman and Eugene D. Genovese (eds), *Race and Slavery in the Western Hemisphere: Quantitative Studies*, Princeton, NJ, 1975, 249-284; and *Searching for the Invisible Man: Slaves and Plantation Life in Jamaica*, Cambridge, 1977. B.W. Higman, 'Household Structure and Fertility on Jamaican Slave Plantations: A Nineteenth Century Example', *Population Studies*, XXVII, 1973, 527-550; 'The Slave Family and Household in British West Indies, 1800-1834, *Journal of Interdisciplinary History*, VI, 1975, 261-287; and *Slave Population and Economy in Jamaica, 1807-1834*, Cambridge, 1976.

3. The original Register is the Archives of the Bahamas, Nassau. I am grateful for the help accorded by the archivist of the Bahamas, Gail Saunders, who has made an important demographic study of the slave population of the Bahamas under the direction of Dr Barry Higman.

4. Craton, *Searching for the Invisible Man*, part 1, Chapters 3-6; Higman, 'Household Structure', *Population Studies*, XXVII, 1973, 527-550, and 'Slave Family', *Journal of Interdisciplinary History*, VI, 1975, 261-287.

5. The original Crown Lands grants are in the Bahamas Land Registry, Grant Book C, 1786-1879, Nassau. The Loyalist landholdings in Exuma in 1792 can be traced in a 'Plan of the Exumas and Hog Cay in the Bahamas etc. laid down by Actual Survey under the direction of Josiah Tattnall Esq. Surveyor General', C. O. 700/15, Public Record Office.

6. Michael Craton, *A History of the Bahamas*, London, 1962, 170, 180, 190 - 192.

7. *Dictionary of National Biography*, s.v. 'Rolle, John', John Lord Rolle (1750-1842), was chiefly famed as the subject, while MP for Devonshire, of the satirical anti-Pittite poem, *The Rolliad*, and for the fact that at the coronation of Queen Victoria (1837) he tripped over his robes while being presented to the young monarch.

8. In 1789, Governor Lord Dunmore testified that no African slaves had been imported into the Bahamas within living memory. Great Britain, *Parliamentary Papers*, 1789, XXVI (*Commons, Accounts and Papers*), Part III. Advertisements in the *Bahamas Gazette* (Nassau), however, indicate that some Africans were imported for the period 1790-1808. Of the 124 Africans owned by the 29 Exumian slaveowners other than Lord Rolle in 1822, no fewer than 80 were under 49-years-old and therefore almost certainly purchased after the move from Florida in 1784. Forty-three of the 124 were 38 and under in 1822 and these had to have been purchased after 1784. On the other hand, all 15 of Lord Rolle's African slaves in 1822 were over 49, and thus old enough to have been purchased before the migration from Florida.

9. The Bahamian Registration Act, passed in 1821, was even longer delayed than the Jamaican, which went into effect in 1817. Both registration systems called for triennial returns, the Jamaican running from 1817 to 1832 with six returns, and the Bahamian from 1822 to 1834 with five.

10. Carlo M. Cippola, 'Four Centuries of Italian Demographic Development' in D. V. Glass and D. E. C. Eversley (eds), *Population in History: Essays in Historical Demography*, Chicago, 1965, 570-587. The Worthy Park material used throughout this article is derived from the four sources cited at the beginning of Note 2 above.

11. Craton, *Searching for the Invisible Man*, Part I, Chapter 3. The rate indicated at Mesopotamia Estate, Jamaica (an unhealthy, low-lying plantation on the Cabarita flats of Westmoreland parish) was even lower than for Worthy Park, averaging 17.9 per 1,000 between 1753 and 1808 (Richard S. Dunn, 'A Tale of Two Plantations: Slave Life at Mesopotamia in Jamaica and Mount Airy in Virginia, 1799 to 1828', *William and Mary Quarterly*, 3rd series, 24, 1977, 32-65).

12. O. Andrew Collver, *Birth Rates In Latin America; New Estimates of Historical Trends and Fluctuations*, Berkeley, 1965, 101.

13. The average for 121 vessels carrying 41,625 slaves to Jamaica between 1764 and 1786 was 62.2 per cent males (Great Britain, *Parliamentary Papers*, 1789, XXVI [*Commons, Accounts and papers*], Part IV. Coincidentally, of the 143 African slaves on Exuma in 1822, 85 were males, or 59.4 per cent while the proportion of males among non-Rolle African slaves was 60.5 per cent .

14. At Worthy Park, the average fertility of African females between 1813 and 1817 was 82.4 per 1,000; for creole females, 176.5 per 1,000 (*Searching for the Invisible Man*, Part I, Chapter 3). At Montpelier and Shettlewood, the average fertility of African females aged 15-44 was 53 per 1,000 woman-years between 1817 and 1832; for creole females in the same age range over the same period, it was 85 per 1,000 woman-years (Higman, 'Household Structure', *Population Studies*, XXVII, 1973, Table 7, 549.

15. Higman, 'Slave Family', *Journal of Interdisciplinary History*, VI, 1975, 261-287; Edith Clarke, *My Mother Who Fathered Me: A Study of the Family in Three Selected Communities in Jamaica* . . . 2nd ed., London, 1966, (orig. Publ. 1957).

16. The distinction between 'housefuls', those living together and 'households', kin living together is made in Peter Laslett and Richard Wall (eds), *Household and Family in Past Time; Comparative Studies in the Size and Structure of the Domestic Group* . . . Cambridge, 1972. Those living together were listed by houses at Montpelier but, as in most Jamaican slave lists, consanguinity can only be traced with certainty through the female line. Higman recognised this deficiency in his 1973 paper but did not introduce the Laslett/Wall distinction until his 1975 paper.

17. Higman, 'Household Structure', *Population Studies*, XXVII, 1973, 548.

18. Higman has discovered polygynous households in both Jamaica and Trinidad but notes that, contrary to contemporary opinion, the polygynous family seems not to have been less fertile than the nuclear family. *Ibid.*, 539, 548; Higman, 'Slave Family', *Journal of Interdisciplinary History*, VI, 1975, 275. Philippe Ariès suggested in a 1973

seminar that West Africa was similar to 'pre-modern' Europe in respect of the comparatively low level of family organisation, and it is therefore tempting to suggest that family life emerged in West Indian society in much the same way as in Western Europe, although considerably later.

19. Precision, however, is impossible. Because parts of Eleuthera were in close contact with Nassau, there was considerable migration during the registration period, and families were often split up.

20. The terms used for slaves of mixed race had a precise meaning, at least in Jamaica. There, a mulatto was a person with one white and one black parent, a quadroon, with one white and one mulatto parent. Strictly defined, a sambo was a person with one mulatto and one black parent, although the term was loosely applied to any person of mixed race where neither parent was white. In the Bahamas, the distinctions seem to have been less precise and may have gone upon appearance rather than parentage.

21. Worthy Park Plantation Book, 1791–1811, No. 09777, Library of Congress.

22. There were 236 females disclosed in the 'pyramid' cohort data for 1794, of whom 131 were 15-49 and 126 were 15-44. Of the larger number, perhaps 90 were African and 41 creole. Of course, some of the women interviewed in 1795 would have been elderly, with grown children.

23. It is quite possible that these disastrous figures may have included deaths within the first nine days (the period during which African infants were regard as not yet fully part of the terrestrial world) and even induced abortions, as well as stillbirths.

24. For the spacing of children and lactation practices see, for example, Stanley L. Engerman, 'Some Economic and Demographic Comparisons of Slavery in the United States and the British West Indies', *Economic History Review*, 2nd series, XXXIX, 1976, 258-275.

25. For example, Ragatz, *Fall of the Planter class*, 33-36; Bryan Edwards, *The History , Civil and Commercial of the British Colonies in the West Indies*, 2nd ed., II, London, 1794, 147-154. For the best bibliography of antislavery writings see Lowell Joseph Ragatz, comp., *A Guide for the Study of British Caribbean History*, 1763-1834, *Including the Abolition and Emancipation Movement*, Washington DC, 1932.

26. J. M. Tanner, *Growth at Adolescence*, 2nd ed., London, 1962; C. Lefebvre, 'The Trend towards Earlier Menarche in London, Oslo, Copenhagen, the Netherlands and Hungary', *Nature*, CXXLIII, 1973, 95-96; J. M. Tanner, 'Growing Up', *Scientific American*, CCXXIX, Sept. 1973; 35-43. K. Bojlen and M. W. Bentzon, 'The Influence of Climate and Nutrition on Age at Menarche: A Historical Review and a Modern Hypothesis', *Human Biology*, XL, 1968, 69 - 85. All these items are cited in the important unpublished paper by James Trussell and Richard Steckel, 'The Estimation of the Mean Age of Female Slaves at the Time of Menarche and their First Birth', Harvard University Workshop in Economic History, Report 7677-11, March 1977.

27. Philip D. Curtin, 'Epidemiology and the Slave Trade', *Political Science Quarterly*, LXXXIII, 1968, 190-216.

28. Register of Slave Compensation Claims, 1834-1836, 960, Bahamas Archives.

29. Additional MSS 38346, fol. 57, British Library.

30. Edwards reckoned that £10 was 'the average value of the labour of each Negro, old and young', but that estates should obtain £25 profit each year for each 'able field Negro' (*History of the West Indies*, II, 132).

31. The peak year for Bahamian cotton seems to have been in 1791, when it was reported locally that 1,292,348 lb were exported. The total for Exuma was said to be 250,000 lb, of which probably one-third was produced on the Rolle Plantations. At that time, Exuma was, with Nassau, one of the two official Bahamian ports, with ships clearing out directly for Britain. For example, on December 25, 1791, Captain Wilson's ship *Minerva*, having arrived three weeks earlier with general trade goods, provisions and plantation supplies, left the island for London with 518 bales of cotton, weighing 26,333 lb. The barcadier was at the present site of George Town, though the township was to laid out until 1794.

32. An excellent example of such diversification, accompanied by an increasing degree of enforced self-sufficiency, can be derived from the journal of a resident slave-owner on San Salvador in slavery's last years: A.

Deans Peggs (ed.), *A Relic of Slavery: Far-quharson's Journal for 1831-32, copied from the original by Ormond J. McDonald, Assistant Resident Justice, Watling's Island*, 1903, Nassau, 1957.

33. D. Eltis, 'The Traffic in Slaves between the British West Indian Colonies, 1807-1833, *Economic History Review*, 2nd series, XXV, 1972, 55-64 modifies Eric Williams, 'The British West Indian Slave Trade after Its Abolition in 1807', *Journal of Negro History*, XXVII, 1942, 188-200.

34. See Governor Woodford to Wilmot Horton, Dec. 31, 1825, C.O. 295/67, 219, P.R.O.; Woodford to Lord Bathurst, Apr. 13, 1826, C.O. 295/71, 26; Col. Farquharson to Secretary of State, Oct. 12, 1828, C.O. 295/78, 233-236; Lord Rolle to Sir George Murray, June 10, 1828, C.O. 23/82, No. 45, P.R.O.

35. Of the slaves transferred to New Providence, 20 were in clearly defined families – simple nuclear families of seven, seven and four members, and one mother with child; 13 of the Rolle slaves in Grand Bahama were in two simple nuclear families of three and ten respectively; the four slaves in the Berry Islands consisted of a mother and her three children. Slave Registration Returns, V, 1834, Bahamas Archives.

36. Stephen, *Slavery of the British West India Colonies Delineated*, I, Appendix III, 454-474.

37. Report to Police Magistrate Nesbitt, enclosed in Governor Smyth to Murray, May 11, 1830, C.O. 23/82, No. 45.

38. This is the common belief; unfortunately, the actual deed does not appear to have survived. Quite possibly it was a verbal understanding, or even a clause in Rolle's will when he died in 1842. In any case, cynics might interpret Rolle's action as a mere gesture – granting his ex-slaves the right to unsaleable lands in reward for the numerical expansion that allowed him to be paid £7,200 or £20 a head for them by the Slave Compensation Board in 1837.

39. Lord Rolle to Murray, June 10, 1828, C.O. 23/82, No. 45.

40. *Caribbean Transformations*, Chicago, 1974, 151-152.

41. For the Grenadines, cf. Charles Shepherd's description of 1831: 'The Union Island contains two thousand one hundred and fifty acres, and is cultivated in cotton by one proprietor, it is very healthy, and the increase of the slaves is very great; this is the case in most of these islands, which may be attributed to the light work on cotton estates, the abundance of fish which they obtain with little trouble, and a compulsory sobriety, from the increased difficulty of obtaining rum,' (*An Historical Account of the Island of St Vincent*, London, 1831, 215). David Lowenthal and Colin G. Clarke, 'Slave-Breeding in Barbuda: The Past of a Negro Myth', in Vera Rubin and Arthur Tuden (eds), *Comparative Perspectives on Slavery in New World Plantation Societies*, New York Academy of Sciences, *Annals*, CCXCII, 1977, 510-535. For the 'slave breeding fallacy see, for example, Richard Sutch, 'The Breeding of Slaves for Sale and the Westward Expansion of Slavery, 1850-1860', in Engerman and Genovese (eds), *Race and Slavery*, 172-210.

42. Boston, 1974.

Chapter 12

1. John Quier, 'Report of the Jamaican House of Assembly on the Slave Issues', in Lt Governor Clarke's No. 92, Nov. 20, 1788; Public Record Office, London, C.O. 137/88, Appendix C.

2. Herbert G. Gutman, *The Black Family in Slavery and Freedom, 1750-1925*, New York, 1976, xxi.

3. Thomas S. Simey, *Welfare and Planning in the West Indies*, Oxford, 1946, 50-51, 79; Fernando Henriques, *Family and Colour in Jamaica*, London, 1953, 103; William J. Goode, 'Illegitimacy in the Caribbean Social Structure', *American Sociological Review*, XXV, 1960, 21-30; M. G. Smith, *The Plural Society in the British West Indies*, Berkeley, 1965, 109; H. Orlando Patterson, *The Sociology of Slavery*, London, 1967, 167.

4. Barry W. Higman, 'Household Structure and Fertility on Jamaican Slave Plantations: A Nineteenth-Century Example', *Population Studies*, XXVII, 1973, 527-550; idem, 'The Slave Family and Household in the British West Indies, 1800-1834', *Journal of Interdisciplinary History*, VI, 1975, 261-287; idem, *Slave Population and Economy in Jamaica, 1807-1834*, Cambridge, 1976. Higman's 'Family Property: The Slave Family in the British Caribbean in the Early Nine-

teenth Century', unpublished paper (1976) is now largely superseded by his 'African and Creole Slave Family Patterns in Trinidad', paper delivered at the Tenth Conference of Caribbean Historians, 1978. See ibid, 12.

5. James Stephens, *The Slavery of the British West India Colonies Delineated*, London, 1824, I, Appendix III, 454-474. The Bahamas, with almost exactly the same total land area as Jamaica (4,400 square miles), had approximately 10,000 slaves against 300,000 in Jamaica, Barbados, with only 166 square miles, had 65,000 slaves. In 1800, the ratio between blacks and whites in the Bahamas was about 4:1; in Barbados it was 8:1; in Jamaica 12:1.

6. David Eltis, 'The Traffic in Slaves between the British West Indian Colonies, 1807-1833', *Economic History Review*, XXV, 1972, 55-64. Perhaps through a misunderstanding, there was a partial census of Bahamian slaves in 1821. Most of these were relisted in 1822, but not all. The 1822 census book gives a grand total of 10,808 slaves, but this seems to omit the slaves listed in 1821 and not relisted in 1822. The intercolonial migration was at its peak between 1821 and 1822; its volume may never be known with complete accuracy.

7. Archives of the Bahamas, Nassau; Register of Returns of Slaves, Bahama Islands, 1821-1834. It was fortunate that the Bahamas Registration Act of 1821 required the listing of all slaves every three years, not just an initial census and subsequent triennial increases and decreases as in most other colonies. The act specified what information should be given but not the order of the lists. Despite this, there seems to have been a remarkable uniformity in the method used by those owners who chose to list their slaves in family and household groups. An absolutely certain distinction between family and household was scarcely possible, but a comparison of the data on slaves transferred from the Bahamas to Trinidad (where the registration returns gave fuller details), and corroboration between the triennial Bahamas censuses, suggested that although extended families were understated, the listings concentrated on families rather than mere cohabitation, and the groups listed were almost invariably cohabiting families, rarely mere 'housefuls'.

8. Michael Craton, 'Hobbesian or Panglossian? The Two Extremes of Slaves Conditions in the British Caribbean, 1783-1834', *William and Mary Quarterly*, 25, 1978, 324-356; idem, *Searching for the Invisible Man: Slaves and Plantation Life in Jamaica*, Cambridge, MA 1978, 60-118.

9. The proportions of African and coloured slaves in the 26 holdings in 1822 were remarkably close to those in the overall slave population, 20.0 and 6.9 per cent.

10. The average age of mothers at the birth of their first children given in Table 2, 22.37 years, is clearly overstated since the 479 mothers included many whose earlier children were old enough to have left the parental household, and were thus not recorded. When the 251 mothers aged 35 or more at the time of the census were excluded, the average age of the remaining 228 mothers at the birth of their first surviving child was 19.27 years. Of the females in the age range 15-49, 65.6 per cent were indicated as mothers. In all, the 479 mothers listed had 1,456 listed children, an average of 3.02 children each.

11. Of the 26 holdings analysed, 20 were established in the farther islands, with a total of 2,643 slaves, an average of 132 per holding. Six were established in New Providence and Eleuthera, with a total of 367 slaves, an average of 61. In 1834 (the only year for which figures have been tabulated), 481 of the 730 Bahamian holdings of five or fewer slaves, and 692 of the 1,088 of 20 or fewer, were in New Providence and Eleuthera (including Harbour Island), but only 26 of the 107 Bahamian holdings of more than 20 slaves. Archives of the Bahamas, Nassau; Register of Returns of Slaves, Bahama Islands, 1834. The 1834 tabulation has been made by Gail Saunders.

12. The figure for 1834 was 9.6 per cent, but by that date a considerable number had been manumitted.

13. Keith F. Otterbein, *The Andros Islanders: A Study of Family Organization in the Bahamas*, Lawrence, KS, 1966. There is as yet no scholarly study of family in New Providence, or of the huge migration that has concentrated more than half the Bahamian population in the capital. Gutman, *Black Family*, 444-445, 489-491.

14. In the 1822 sample of 26 holdings, five possible cases of polygyny occurred. One such

was Jack Stewart, a mulatto slave aged 66 belongings to James Moss at Acklin's Island, who appeared to live with Phoebe, an African aged 55, Kate, a creole aged 37, and 10 children aged between one and 15, all listed as mulattoes.

15. Permanent mates and their children generally shared a surname, but in female-headed families and transient unions a practice common later in the Bahamas may have been followed; children went by their mother's surname until they were 21 and then adopted their father's surname.

16. Craton, 'Hobbesian or Panglossian?', 19. Today there are thousands of Rolles in the Bahamas, including, it is said, two-thirds of the population of Exuma. Male children often had a prefix or suffix added, as with Young Bacchus, Jack Junior, Little Jim, or the African-sounding Jim Jim, son of Jim. Males were often named after their fathers, females more rarely after their mothers. Out of the 67 family units of the Williams group of slaves transferred to Trinidad there were 22 males named after their fathers and at least one after a grandfather; four females were named after their mothers, at least three after a grandmother, and one after a mother's sister.

17. In the population studied, 28 young mothers lived with their parents, their average ages being 18 years and 9 months. Only five were over 20-years-old, and the average age at the birth of their first children was 17 years and 8 months. Only one of the 28 had a second child.

18. Michael Craton, *A History of the Bahamas*, London, 1962, 173-174, 194-196.

19. William Wylly to President W. V. Munnings, Aug. 31, 1818, C.O. 23/67, 147.

20. *Regulations for the Government of the Slaves at Clifton and Tusculum in New Providence, Printed at the Office of the New Gazette*, 1815, enclosed in ibid.

21. Of Wylly's 67 slaves in 1821, as many as 53 lived in eight two-headed households (in two of which the family included a teenage single mother), with one female-headed family and a maximum of nine slaves living alone, averaging 49 years old and including six elderly Africans. Almost certainly, three of the household units at Clifton were the extended family of Jack, the African under-driver, and his wife Sue. Twenty of the 67 slaves were under the age of ten in 1821.

22. D. W. Rose, reporting on the slaves of Exuma, 1802; Craton, *History of the Bahamas*, 183.

23. Besides ten African couples, there were three holdings in which an African male headed the list with his creole mate. In these 13 holdings (half of the total) there were 187 Africans out of a total of 805 slaves or 23.2 per cent, not significantly more than the overall average, 18.8 per cent.

24. Act of 4 Geo. IV, c. 6; *Acts of the Assembly of the Bahama Islands*, Nassau, 1827, V, 227-228.

25. Archives of the Bahamas, Manumissions Index; Register of Returns of Slaves, 1825, 1828, 1831, 1834; Public Record Office, London; Register of Returns of Slaves, St Vincent, 1822, 1825. Craton, 'Hobbesian or Panglossian?' 19-20; C.O. 295/67, 219; 295/71, 26-35; 295/78, 233-265; Governor James Carmicheal Smyth to Lord Stanley, Oct. 27, 1830, C.O. 23/82, 368-420.

26. Evidence given on Jan. 18, 1825, C.O. 295/66, 53-59. A population of 107 increasing at the Rolle rate for 1822-34, 34.5 per thousand per year, would have reached 331 in the 34th year.

27.

		Men	Women	Boys	Girls	Infants	
July	1821	27	43	7	5	23	
February	1822	9	11	6	4	24	
July	1822	6	11	3	3	14	
March	1823	10	10	7	5	33	
June	1823	6	11	6	7	33	
Total		58	86	29	24	127	324

This compilation was made on Sept. 27, 1823. By that time, 19 children had been added to Williams' slaves by birth, and only seven of the total had been lost by death. This indicated a crude annual birth rate of 29 per thousand and a death rate around 11 per thousand. However, of 3,239 slaves imported into Trinidad from all sources between 1813 and 1822 (1,678 being males and 1,561 females), 232 males and 156 females had died, 388 in all, against only 236 births; C.O. 295/59, 252-255.

28. 'Return showing the number of Negroes imported into this Island by Burton Williams Esq.', enclosed in Governor Sir Ralph Woodford to William Huskisson, March 7, 1828, C.O. 295/77, 33-49.

29. C.O. 295/66, 57.

30. Craton, 'Hobbesian or Panglossian?' 19-21; Colin Clarke and David Lowenthal

'Barbuda; the Past of a Negro Myth', in Vera Rubin and Arthur Tuden (eds), *Comparative Perspectives on Slavery in New World Plantation Societies*, New York, 1977, 510-534.

31. The argument is proposed in Craton, 'Hobbesian or Panglossian?', which was first delivered at the conference on Comparative Perspectives in New World Plantation Societies, New York, 1976. Edith Clarke, *My Mother Who Fathered Me*, London, 1957.

Barbuda Household Types, 1851

Household Type	No. of Units	No. of Persons	Persons Per Unit	% total persons per unit type
1. Man, woman, children	76	425	5.59	67.57
2. Man and woman	14	28	2.00	4.45
3. Woman and children	12	50	4.17	7.95
4. Man and children	1	6	6.00	0.95
5. Three generations (ie two women and children	18	90	5.00	14.31 (95.23)
6. Men alone	7	7	1.00	1.11
7. Women alone	10	10	1.00	1.59
8. Women together	6	13	2.17	2.07 (4.77)
	144	629	4.73	100.00

Source: Colin Clarke and Lowenthal, private correspondence (Codrington records, Gloucester County Record Office, England).

32. What follows is the argument proposed by Higman, 'Family Property', now superseded by his 'Slave Family Patterns in Trinidad', 1977. The change was based on the analysis of the full 1813 slave population of 25,673 (a quarter of whom lived in Port-of-Spain), rather than the rural sample of 1,296 previously used.

33. Bryan Edwards, *The History, Civil and Commercial, of the British Colonies in the British West Indies*, London, 1801, II, 155.

34. Richard Ligon, *A True and Exact History of the Island of Barbadoes*, London, 1957, 47; Hans Sloane, *A Voyage to the Islands Madera, Barbados, Nieves, S. Christophers and Jamaica*, London, 1725, II, xlviii; Stanley L. Engerman, 'Some Economic and Demographic Comparisons of Slavery in the United States and the British West Indies', *Economic History Review*, XXIX, 1976, 258-275.

35. Quier, 'Report', 492; Lindsay, 'A Few Conjectural Considerations upon the Creation of the Human Race, Occasioned by the Present Quixotical Rage of setting the Slaves from Africa at Liberty', unpublished

ms. dated Spanish Town, July 23, 1788, British Museum, Additional Mss. 12439.

36. Higman, 'Slave Family Patterns in Trinidad', 14-18, 33-35. This strongly stressed the melding effect of the African slave trade to Trinidad. Only among the Ibo was there a recognisable transfer of specific African family patterns, and this was attributed to their high numbers and comparatively even sex ratio. When the African slaves were broken down by seven general regions of origin there were no really significant variations in the proportions of family types recreated in Trinidad.

37. Edwards, *British West Indies*, II, 155.

38. Sidney W. Mintz, *Caribbean Transformations*, Chicago, 1974, 151-152.

39. Peter J. Wilson, *Crab Antics: The Social Anthropology of English-Speaking Negro Societies of the Caribbean*, New Haven, 1973.

Chapter 13

1. Mrs A. C. Carmichael, *Domestic Manners and Social Condition of the White, Coloured and Negro Population of the West Indies*, 2 vols, 1834, vol 1, 246-247.

2. The debate over abolition and emancipation alone accounts for 170 pages of the monumental bibliography by Lowell J. Ragatz, *A Guide for the Study of British Caribbean History, 1763-1834*, Washington, Government Printing Office, 1932; Annual Report of the American Historical Association, 1930, 405-573. The key works were probably Granville Sharp, *A Repression of the Injustice and Dangerous Tendency of Tolerating Slavery . . . 1769*; Anthony Benezet, *Some Historical Account of Guinea*, Philadelphia, 1771; reissued 1787; Rev. John Wesley, *Thoughts on Slavery*, 1774, reissued 1784; John Ady et al., *The Case of Our Fellow Creatures, the Oppressed Africans*, 1783; Rev. James Ramsay, *An Essay on the Treatment and Conversion of African Slaves in the British Sugar Colonies*, 1784; Rev. John Newton, *Thoughts Upon the African Slave Trade*, 1788; Thomas Clarkson, *An Essay on the Slavery and Commerce of the Human Species, Particularly the African*, 1788; William Wilberforce, *The Speech on Wednesday, May 13, 1789, on the Question of the Abolition of the Slave Trade*, 1804; Zachary Macaulay, *Negro Slavery*, London, 1823; Rev. Thomas Cooper, *Facts Illustrative of the Condition of*

the Negro Slaves in Jamaica, 1824; James Stephen, The Slavery of the British West India Colonies Delineated, 2 vols, 1824, 1830; James Cropper, The Support of Slavery Investigated, 1834.

3. Ragatz, British Caribbean Guide, 1763-1834, parts 15 and 16, 391-404.

4. Matthew Gregory Lewis, The Journal of a West Indian Planter, 1834, 228.

5. Thomas Coke, A History of the West Indies, 3 vols, Liverpool, 1808-11 as quoted in Madeline Grant, 'Enemies to Caesar? Sectarian Missionaries in British West Indian Slave Society, 1754-1834', University of Waterloo, unpublished MA thesis, 1976, 79.

6. Rev. Hope Masterton Waddell, Twenty-Nine Years in the West Indies and Central Africa, Nelson, 1863, 37.

7. J. E. Hutton, A History of the Moravian Missions, Moravian Publications Office, 1872.

8. Coke, History of the West Indies, passim.

9. Michael Craton, A History of the Bahamas, Collins, 1962, 183 and 222; Rev. Edwin Angel Wallbridge, The Demerara Martyr: Memoirs of the Rev. John Smith, 1848.

10. F. A. Cox, History of the Baptist Missionary Society from 1792 to 1842, 1842; R. Lovett, History of the London Missionary Society, 2 vols, 1899.

11. Hutton, Moravian Missions, 177.

12. Quoted in Edinburgh Review, Mar. 1824, 244.

13. Rev. Elliott to LMS Directors, Dec. 7, 1808, quoted by Bernard Marshall, 'Missionaries and Slaves in the British Windward Islands', Association of Caribbean Historians, unpublished conference paper, Trinidad, 1980, 21.

14. Letter from Rev. Whitehouse to Wesleyan Missionary Society, July 1, 1829, in British Sessional Papers, Commons 1830-1, XVI, 91, as quoted in Grant, 'Enemies to Caesar?', 79; 'Copy of a Journal Containing Various Occurrences at Le Resouvenir, Demerara, Commenced in March 1817 by John Smith, Missionary', P.R.O., C.O. 111/46.

15. Grant, 'Enemies to Caesar?', 37 - 64.

16. British Sessional Papers, Commons, 1831 - 2, XLVII.

17. Quoted by Peter Duncan, A Narrative of the Wesleyan Mission to Jamaica, (1849), 312.

18. Grant, 'Enemies to Caesar?', Appendix II, 169-170.

19. Rev. John Lindsay, 'A Few Conjectural Considerations upon the Creation of the Human Race, Occasioned by the Present British Quixottical Rage of Setting the Salves from Africa at Liberty', BL, Add. MSS. 12439, footnote 258.

20. Rev. George W. Bridges, A Voice from Jamaica, 1823.

21. One thinks, in contrast, of the initial failure of the missionaries to make converts in Africa. For example, Livingstone, though usually regarded as the greatest of African missionaries, apparently made only one convert during his career, who later backslid. Tim Jeal, Livingstone, London, 1973.

22. See, for example, the witty interrogation of the missionaries by the village elders in Chinua Achebe, Things Fall Apart, New York, Fawcett Premier, ed., 1958, 134-137 and 164-167.

23. Quoted by Bernard Marshall, 'Missionaries and Slaves', p. 15.

24. Peter J. Wilson, Crab Antics: The Social Anthropology of English-Speaking Negro Societies of the Caribbean, New Haven, Yale University Press, 1973.

25. For example, see the way in which the Bahamian Baptist churches founded by the blacks, Prince Williams and Sharper Morris, divided on the coming of white missionaries in 1833-34. Michael Symonette and Antonia Canzanori, Baptists in the Bahamas: An Historical Review (Nassau, 1977) pp. 1-27.

26. Eugene D. Genovese, Roll, Jordan, Roll; The World the Slaves Made (New York: Pantheon, 1972) p. 7.

27. Robert Moore, 'Slave Rebellions in Guyana', in Papers Presented at the Third Conference of Caribbean Historians held at the University of Guyana, April 15-17, 1971, pp. 62-74.

28. Genovese, Roll, Jordan, Roll; p. 207.

29. C. F. Pascoe, Two Hundred Years of the SPG, 1701-1900 (1901).

30. Rev. John Clarke, Memorials of Baptist Missions to Jamaica (1869) pp. 9-31.

31. Ibid., p. 30.

32. Norman Cohn, The Pursuit of the Millenium; Revolutionary Millenarianism and Mystical Anarchists of the Middle Ages (1957) pp. 13-16.

33. Sidney Mintz and Douglas Hall, 'The Origins of the Jamaican Internal Marketing System', Yale University Publications in Anthropology, LVII (1960) pp. 1-26.

34. Memorial of Merchants and Planters interested in Dominica dated 5 Apr 1791, PRO, CO 71/19; Craton, *Testing the Chains*, ch. 17.

35. *Ibid.*, pt 6, ch.1

36. Governor Murray to Lord Bathurst, 24 Aug 1823, PRO, CO 111/39; Joshua Bryant, *Account of an Insurrection of the Negro Slaves in the Colony of Demerara* (Georgetown, 1824) p. 6; Craton, *Testing the Chains*, ch. 19.

37. Bryant, *Account*, p. 9.

38. Trial Proceedings for 5 Nov 1823, P.R.O C.O. 111/43, p. 295.

39. P.R.O., C.O. 28/86; Craton, *Testing the Chains*, ch. 18.

40. *Proceedings of a General Court Martial held at the Colony House in George Town, on Monday the 13th day of October 1823* (Hatchard, 1824); *Edinburgh Review*, XL (Mar-July 1824) 226-70; 'The Late Insurrection in Demerara and Riot in Barbados', P.R.O., C.O. 111/43; Craton *Testing the Chains*, ch. 19.

41. Cecil Northcott, *Slavery's Martyr; John Smith of Demerara and the Emancipation Movement, 1817-1824* (Epworth Press, 1976) pp. 110-12; Edwin Angel Wallbridge, *The Demerara Martyr; Memoirs of the Rev. John Smith, Missionary to Demerara* (1848 and Georgetown, 1943) Appendix V, pp. 257-309.

42. Northcott, *Slavery's Martyr*, p. 111.

43. Craton, *Testing the Chains*, ch. 21; Philip Wright, *Knibb 'The Notorious,' Slaves' Missionary, 1808-1845* (Sidgwick and Jackson, 1973) pp. 56-133.

44. Committee appointed 30 May 1832; evidence taken, 6 June-11 Aug. 1832; Report ordered to be printed, 11 Aug. 1832. *British Sessional Papers, Commons Accounts and Papers, 1831-2*, XLVII *(482)*.

45. Michael Craton, *Sinews of Empire; A Short History of British Slavery* (New York: Doubleday; Temple Smith, 1974) pp. 276-80.

46. Henry Bleby, *The Death Struggles of Slavery* (1853) p. 129.

Chapter 14

1. Edward Jordan, editorial in *The Watchman*, 1832.

2. Herbert Aptheker, commenting at the New York Academy of Sciences Conference, 'Comparative Perspectives on Slavery in New World Plantation Societies', New York, May 26, 1976.

3. Jean-Baptiste Labat, *Voyage aux isles d'Amerique*, 5 vols, Paris, 1693-1705, iv, 256.

4. For example, Mary Reckord Turner, 'The Jamaica Slave Rebellion of 1831', *Past and Present, 40, July* 1968, 108 - 125; H. Orlando Patterson, *The Sociology of Slavery: An Analysis of the Origins, Development and Structure of Negro Slave Society in Jamaica*, London, 1967, 265-283; H. Orlando Patterson, 'Slavery and Slave Revolts: A Socio-Historical Analysis of the First Maroon War, Jamaica, 1655-1740', *Social and Economic Studies*, xix, 1970, 289-325; Monica Schuler, 'Akan Slave Rebellions in the British Caribbean', *Savacou*, I, 1970, 8-31; Monica Schuler, 'Ethnic Slave Rebellions in the Caribbean and the Guianas', *Journal of Social History*, iii, 1970, 374-385; Richard Price, *Maroon Societies: Rebel Slave Communities in the Americas*, New York, 1973, Introduction, 1-30.

5. Michael Craton, *Sinews of Empire: A Short History of British Slavery*, London, 1974, 226-237.

6. Richard B. Sheridan, 'The Jamaican Slave Insurrection Scare of 1776 and the American Revolution', *Journal of Negro History*, lxi, 1976, 290-308.

7. Governor William Willoughby to Council of Trade and Plantations, July 9, 1668, writing of Barbados's population of 60,000, 'of which 40,000 blacks, whose different tongues and animosities have kept them from insurrection, but fears the Creolian generation now growing up and increasing may hereafter 'mancipate' their masters', *Calendar of State Papers, Colonial: America and the West Indies, 1661-8*, 1788, 586. See also Richard Ligon's comment in 1657: It has been accounted a strange thing, that the *Negroes*, being more than double the numbers of the Christians that are there, and they accounted a bloody people, where they think they have power or advantages; and the more bloody, by how much they are more fearful than others; that these should not commit some horrid massacre upon the Christians, thereby to infranchise themselves, and become Masters of the Island. But there are three reasons that take away this wonder, the one is, they are not suffered to touch or handle any weapons. The other, that they are held in such awe and slavery, as they are fearful to appear in

any daring act; and seeing the mustering of our men, and hearing their Gun-shot (than which nothing is more terrible to them) their spirits are subjugated to so low a condition, as they dare not look up to any bold attempt. Besides these, there is a third reason, which stops all designs of that kind, and that is, they are fetch'd from several parts of *Africa*, and speak several languages, and by that means one of them understands not another. Richard Ligon, *A True and Exact History of the Island of Barbados*, 2nd edn, London, 1673, 46.

8. Sir Robert Schomburgk, *The History of Barbados*, London, 1847, 267-400. The slave population of Barbados at the time of the first registration census in 1817 was 77,273, of whom 5,446 (or 7.1 per cent) were Africans, and 71,432 (or 92.9 per cent) were 'Barbadians', with 345 Creoles from other islands. In 1816 there were said to be 16,015 whites, or roughly 17.8 per cent of the total population, and 3.002 free coloureds, roughly 3.3 per cent; Public Record Office, P.R.O., C.O. 28/86.

9. Anon. *Remarks on the Insurrection in Barbados, and the Bill for the Registration of the Slaves*, London, 1816, 5.

10. According to the figures given in 1816 and 1817, the ratio was 6.7 to one in St Philip and 7.0 to one in St George, compared with an island average of 4.5 to one. In the four most affected parishes of St Philip, St George, Christchurch and St John, the ratio was 6.1 to one, compared with 3.6 to one for Bridgetown's St Michael parish. *Ibid.*

11. 'Such indeed was the Warfare pursued by those people, that in no position could I discover them in sufficient numbers for attack. Whenever I made my appearance they fled, but still pursued their system of devastation'; Colonel Codd to Governor Leith, Apr. 25, 1816; P.R.O., C.O. 28/84. 'The only plan I could then adopt', concluded Codd, 'was to destroy their Houses, in order to deprive them of some of their hiding places, and resources, and to recover their plunder.' *Ibid.*

12. 'Under the irritation of the Moment and exasperated at the atrocity of the Insurgents, some of the Militia of the Parishes in Insurrection were induced to use their Arms rather too indiscriminately in pursuit of the Fugitives.' *Ibid.* 'The Militia who could

not be restrained by the same discipline as the Troops put many Men, Women and Children to Death, I fear without much discrimination'; Rear Admiral Harvey of H.M.S. *Antelope* to J. W. Croker, Secretary of the Admiralty, Apr. 30, 1816; P.R.O., C.O. 28/84.

13. *The Report from a Select Committee of the House of Assembly of Jamaica, Appointed to Inquire into the Origin, Causes and progress of the Late Insurrection*, Barbados, 1818; hereafter *Report on the Insurrection in Barbados, 1816*, 37-63.

14. Evidence of Rev. J. H. Gittens, *Ibid.*, 37; Governor Leith to Lord Bathurst, Sept. 21, 1816; P.R.O., C.O. 28/84.

15. The *Report* was published on January 7, 1818 with only 250 copies to be circulated in Barbados and Britain; Schomburgk, *History of Barbados*, 397.

16. For example, 'Bussoe, the ranger; King Wiltshire, the carpenter; Dick Bailey, the mason; Johnny, the *standard bearer*; and Johnny Cooper, a Cooper; were the principal instigators of the Insurrection at Bailey's'; evidence of James Bowland, slave of The River plantation, *Report on the Insurrection in Barbados, 1816*, 33. A ranger was an élite slave whose job included looking after boundaries and fences, and matters of communication and business between estates.

17. Colonel Codd to Governor Leith, Apr. 25, 1816; P.R.O., C.O. 28/84.

18. *Ibid.*; see also *Report on the Insurrection in Barbados, 1816, passim.*

19. Colonel Codd to Governor Leith, Apr. 25, 1816; P.R.O., C.O. 28/84. The fear of a slave takeover was a perennial theme of descriptions of Barbadian slave revolts and plots. For example, the plot of 1676 was said to have included a plan to kill the white men, enslave their women and set up a black monarchy. It was to have been signalled by fires, but was betrayed by faithful slaves and savagely suppressed. Anon., *Great News from the Barbadoes, or a True and Faithful Account of the Grand Conspiracy of the Negroes against the English and the Happy Discovery of the Same. With the Number of Those that were Burned Alive, Beheaded, and Otherwise Executed for their Horrid Crimes. With a Short Description of that Plantation*, London, 1676, quoted in Schomburgk, *History of Barbados*, 296-298. Schomburgk de-

scribed similar themes for the upheavals of 1649, 1693 and 1702; *ibid.*, 267, 305, 309.

20. 'The Insurgents did not think our men would fight against black men but thank God were deceived . . . I assure you that the conduct of our Bourbon Blacks, particularly the light Company under Capt. Firth (an old Twelfth hand) has been the admiration of every body & deservedly', private letter from St Ann's Garrison, Barbados, Apr. 27, 1816; P.R.O., C.O. 28/84. For the Haitian rumours, see Schomburgk, *op. cit.*, 395.

21. Anon. Letter, June 6, 1816, P.R.O., C.O. 28/84.

22. Minutes of Assembly of Barbados, Aug. 6, 1816, P.R.O., C.O. 31/47.

23. In 1824, the population of the combined colonies of Demerara and Essequibo was said to be 77,000 slaves, 3,500 whites and 2,500 'free people of colour'. In 1817, the slaves in Demerara and Essequibo were 55 per cent African-born. Review of *Proceedings of a General Court Martial held at the Colony House in George Town on Monday the 13th Day of October 1823*, London, 1824, in *Edinburgh Review*, xl, 1824, 227; 'Returns of the Population of the Different Slave Colonies . . . [of Demerary and Essequibo, of the Colony of British Guiana]', in *Slave Populations (Slave Registries)* Parliamentary Papers, (hereafter P.P.), 1833, 700, xxvi.

24. Review of *Proceedings of a General Court Martial, 1823*, 243-245.

25. *Ibid.* 245-246. The harsh conditions in the Demerara plantations are most poignantly described in 'A Journal, Containing Various Occurrences at Le Resouvenir, Demerary. Commenced in March 1817, by John Smith, Missionary', P.R.O., C.O. 111/46. This has not yet been published in full, though it was generously excerpted in of *Proceedings of a General Court Martial, 1823*, 251-255.

26. 'Since I last wrote you I was on a Bush expedition for twelve days in search of Quammina (of Pln Success) & other ringleaders in the late insurrection, on the Morning of the fourth day we fell in with an immense Camp they had made – Corn & Rice were beginning to spring all around it – they fled long before we reached having a large swamp area to cross they seen us – we destroyed everything & came back to the back of Pln Mon-Repos & renewed our search the next day – when we fell in with

him & six more – We shot him & took him – the other, Richard – a head ringleader got away & is not yet taken. We gibbeted Quammina in front of Success Estate - all the others have since been hanged'; Hugh McCalmont to his namesake, Nov. 28, 1823, unpublished private letter in author's possession. Jack made a clearly ghost-written act of contribution at his trial, exculpating the planters and blaming the missionaries for misleading the slaves; Review of *Proceedings of a General Court Martial, 1823*, pp. 266 - 267.

27. Governor John Murray to Lord Bathurst, Aug. 24, 1823; P.R.O., C.O. 111/39; Captain Thomas Cochrane to J. W. Croker, H.M.S. *Forte* off Demerara, Sept. 23, 1823; P.R.O., C.O. 111/43; Resolutions of 'A General Meeting of the British Guyana Association, held at the Thatched House, on Thursday, 23rd October 1823, James Baillie Esqre., in the Chair'; P.R.O., C.O. 111/43.

28. Review of *Proceedings of a General Court Martial, 1823*, 268-269.

29. See, for example, Review of *Eighteenth Report of the Directors of the African Institution*, London, 1824, *et. al.*, in *Edinburgh Review*, xli, 1824-25, 210-211.

30. Although the population of whites and free coloureds is difficult to estimate exactly, in 1832, when there were 312,876 slaves in Jamaica, there were about 25,000 whites and 35,000 free coloureds and free blacks. For the best demographic and socioeconomic account of Jamaica in 1831, see B. W. Higman, *Slave Population and Economy in Jamaica, 1807-1834*, Cambridge, 1976.

31. This was a copy of a circular proclamation issued in 1824. Sent by Lord Gooderich to all West Indian governors on June 3, 1831, it was issued in modified form in Jamaica at the end of July 1831, at a time when the whites were meeting angrily in the parishes to discuss developments in London; *West India Colonies: Slave Insurrection*, P.P., 1831-32, 285, xvii, 3-5.

32. 'Report of a Committee of the House of Assembly of Jamaica, Appointed to Inquire into the Cause of, and Injury Sustained by, the Recent Rebellion in that Colony, together with the Examinations on Oath, Confessions and Other Documents Annexed to the Report', in *Jamaica: Slave Insurrection*, P.P., 1831-32, 561, xivii.

33. Details of the military campaigns are given in *West India Colonies: Slave Insurrection*; the originals of many of these papers are in P.R.O., C.O. 137/81.

34. For an objective review of the courts martial, see 'Abstracts of Trials by Courts Martials during the Continuance of Martial Law in Jamaica. Earliest Trial, 3rd Jany, Lates, 7th Feb. 1832', P.R.O., C.O. 137/185.

35. The itemised totals for losses returned for each of the parishes were: St James, £606,250; Hanover, £425,818; Westmoreland, £47,092; Manchester, £46, 270; St Elizabeth, £22,146; Trelawny, £4,960; St Thomas-in-the-East, £1,280; Portland, £772; a grand total of £1,154,588. 'Report of a Committee of the House of Assembly of Jamaica, Appointed to Inquire into . . . the Recent Rebellion', in *Jamaica: Slave Insurrection*, 39-45.

36. For example, of 81 slaves convicted before civil courts in St James parish, 43 were field slaves, 14 drivers and 24 craftsmen. This information is derived from P.R.O., C.O. 137/185, which gives detailed accounts of all trials under military and civil law in all parishes.

37. In all, only 14 free persons were tried and convicted after the rebellion, of whom at least three were free blacks. Only one of the 14 was executed for certain, most being flogged and transported; P.R.O., C.O. 137/185. For the role of the Moravians, see the documents relating to the trial of Pastor Henry Gottlieb Pfeiffer, Jan. 12-19, 1832, in *Jamaica: Slave Insurrection*, [ii], P.P., 1831-32, 482, xlvii, 13-20; J. H. Buchner, *The Moravians in Jamaica*, London, 1854. For the Wesleyans, see Rev. Henry Bleby, *Death Struggles of Slavery*, 3rd end, London, 1849. For the Presbyterians, see H. M. Waddell, *Twenty-Nine Years in the West Indies and Central Africa*, London, 1865. For the role of the free coloureds, especially the equivocal editor of *The Watchman*, see Mavis C. Campbell, *The Dynamics of Change in a Slave Society: A Sociopolitical History of the Free Coloureds of Jamaica, 1800-1865*, Rutherford, NJ, 1976.

38. Bleby, *op. cit.*, 129. The evidence of Sharpe's trial is in P.R.O., C.O. 137/185, 304-313.

39. For the last stages of the metropolitan debate, see *Memoirs of Sir Thomas Fowell Buxton*, Charles Buxton, London, 1848; J. H.

Hinton, *Memoir of William Knibb, Missionary in Jamaica*, London, 1847.

40. Apparently there was a single Wesleyan chapel in Bridgetown but in 1816 no minister. When the Demerara rebellion occurred, the Bridgetown chapel was wrecked and the missionary, Shrewsbury, forced to flee for his life. Anon. *The Late Insurrection in Demerara and Riot in Barbados*, London, 1823; P.R.O., C.O. 111/43.

41. 'In countries where slavery is established, the leading principle on which the government is supported is fear; or a sense of that absolute coercive necessity which, leaving no choice of action, supersedes all questions of right. It is vain to deny that such actually is, and necessarily must be, the case in all countries where slavery is allowed', Bryan Edwards, *The History, Civil and Commercial, of the British Colonies in the West Indies*, 3rd edn, 3 vols, London, 1801, iii, 36.

42. This is the essence of Eric Williams's famous attack on capitalistic imperialism, continuing through emancipation and even the ending of formal colonisation, though Williams overstresses the decline in sugar plantations before emancipation, underplaying the switch to Guyana and his own Trinidad. Eric Williams, *Capitalism and Slavery*, London, 1964; Eric Williams, *From Columbus to Castro*, London, 1970, but cf. Seymour Drescher, *A Case of Econocide*, Pittsburgh, 1977; Michael Craton, *Searching for the Invisible Man: Slaves and Plantation Life in Jamaica*, Cambridge, MA, 1978.

43. Crane Brinton, *The Anatomy of Revolution*, New York, 1965 edn.

44. David Brion Davis, *The Problem of Slavery in the Age of Revolution, 1770 - 1823*, Ithaca, NY, 1975, 349 - 62; Eugene D. Genovese, *In Red and Black: Marxian Explorations in Southern and Afro-American History*, New York, 1971, 407; *Selections from the Prison Notebooks of Antonio Gramsci*, Quentin Hoare and Geoffrey N. Smith (eds), London, 1971, 12.

45. Norman Cohn, *The Pursuit of the Millennium*, London, 1957.

46. P.R.O., C.O. 137/185, 304 - 313.

47. Governor Murray to Lord Bathurst, Oct. 21, 1823; P.R.O., C.O. 111/39.

48. *Report on the Insurrection in Barbados, 1816*, 29 - 31.

49. Colonel Codd to Governor Leith, Apr. 25, 1816; P.R.O., C.O. 28/84; Lieutenant-

Colonel Leahy's evidence, Nov. 5, 1823; P.R.O., C.O. 111/42; Sir Willoughby Cotton to Governor Lord Belmore, Jan. 2-4, 1823, in *West India Colonies: Slave Insurrection*, 20, 25, 27, 29-30, 33-35.

50. Matthew Gregory Lewis, *Journal of a West India Proprietor, Kept during a Residence in the Island of Jamaica*, London, 1834, 228. The verse, transcribed by one clearly unfamiliar with Jamaican creole, comes in Lewis account (March 22, 1816) of the trial at Black River of those implicated in an Ibo slave plot hatched on Lyndhurst Pen, St Elizabeth. The two chief instigators were said to be 'a *black* ascertained to have stolen over into the island of St Domingo, and a *brown* Anabaptist missionary'. In the same entry Lewis recorded a rumour current in Montego Bay that 'in consequence of my over-indulgence to my negroes, a song has been made at Cornwall [his estate] declaring that I was come over to set them all free, and that this was now circulating through the neighbouring parishes'. *Ibid.*, 226-229.

51. Craton, *Searching for the Invisible Man*, 319-322.

52. Sidney W. Mintz and Douglas G. Hall, 'The Origins of the Jamaican Internal Marketing System', *Yale University Publication in Anthropology*, 57, 1960, 3-26.

53. In Jamaica the connection between the Spanish and English usages was a direct one. The earliest of all references were to the 'pelincos' of Juan de Bolas and his fellow 'Spanish Negroes' deep in the interior beyond the English settlements, at Lluidas Vale, in 1660. *Calendar of Street Papers, Colonial: America and West Indies, Addenda, 1574-1660*, 132, 331; Michael Craton and James Walvin, *A Jamaican Plantation: The History of Worthy Park, 1670-1970*, London, 1970, 9, 15-16, 36-37.

54. 'They have *Saturdays* in the Afternoon, and *Sundays*, with *Christmas* Holidays, Easter called little or *Piganinny*, Christmas, and some other great Feasts allow'd them for the Culture of their own Plantations to feed themselves from Potatoes, Yams and Plantains, etc., which they plant in Ground allow'd them by their Masters, beside a small Plantain-Walk they have by themselves,' Hans Sloane, *A Journey to the Islands, Madeira, Barbados, Nieves, St Christophers and Jamaica*, 2 vols, London,

1707-25, I, 52, quoted in Mintz and Hall *op. cit.*, 12. For the best of all contemporary accounts of the slave provision grounds, see William Beckford, *A Descriptive Account of the Island of Jamaica*, 2 vols, London, 1790, I, 256, and ii, 129-187.

55. Bryan Edwards, *The History, Civil and Commercial, of the British Colonies in the West Indies*, 2 vols, London, 1793, ii, 133, quoted in Mintz and Hall, *op. cit.*, 21.

56. Edith Clarke, *My Mother Who Fathered Me*, London, 1957, 33-72; David Lowenthal, *West Indian Societies*, Oxford, 1972, 100-110.

57. There are numerous references, but see for example, Beckford, *op. cit.*, ii, 151-187; Sir Rose Price, *Pledges on Colonial Slavery, to Candidates for Seats in Parliament, Rightly Considered*, Penzance, 1823, 8-9; B.M. Senior, *Jamaica, as it was, as it is, and as it may be*, London, 1835, 40-41.

58. Evidence of William Taylor, *Report from Select Committee on the Extinction of Slavery throughout the British Dominions*. P.P. 1831-32 (721), xx, *Minutes of Evidence*, Session of June 6, 1823, 7-21.

59. P.R.O., C.O. 137/185, 304-313.

60. Proceedings, Nov. 5, 1823; P.R.O., C.O. 111/43, 293-298.

61. *Report on the Insurrection in Barbados, 1816*, 50-51.

62. *Ibid.*, 42 - 44.

63. Colonel Codd to Governor Leith, Apr. 25, 1816, P.R.O., C.O. 28/84; see note 20 above.

64. Anon., *A second Letter from Legion to His Grace the Duke of Richmond*, London, 1833, 101. It was in 1976 that Samuel Sharpe was designated the sixth official Hero of Jamaica by the P.N.P. government of Michael Manley, which in 1979 seemed to be leading Jamaica inexorably towards the status of a socialist republic within the British Commonwealth.

65. John Fowles, *The Ebony Tower*, London, 1975, 102.

Chapter 15

1. Eric Williams, *Capitalism and Slavery*, London, 1964, 197.

2. *Ibid*, 208.

3. *Ibid.*, 197-201.

4. *Ibid.*, 201.

5. *Ibid.*,201-206.

6. *Ibid.*,204-207. For the alleged revolt in British Guiana in 1808, Williams cited Governor Nicholson to Lord Castlereagh, June 6, 1808, C.O. 111/8, which clearly refers to a plot rather than an actual outbreak.

7. Henry Lord Boughtam, *Speeches on Social and Political Subjects*, 2 vols, London, 1857, II, 93-190.

8. 'Economic change, the decline of the monopolists, the development of capitalism, the humanitarian agitation in British churches, contending perorations in the halls of Parliament, had now reached their completion in the determination of the slaves themselves to be free.' Williams, *Capitalism and Slavery*, 208.

9. Bryan Edwards, *The History, Civil and Commercial, of the British Colonies in the West Indies*, 3 vols, London, 1793, III, 36.

10. *Parliamentary Debates*, XXIX, 1055-1158, Commons, April 2, 1792, excerpted in Eric Williams (ed.), *The British West Indies at Westminster, Part I, 1789-1823*, Port-of-Spain, 1954, 23. The fact that Eric Williams selected this and the subsequently quoted speeches by Grenville, Howick, Wilberforce and Palmer in his 1954 anthology might indicate that he himself saw the need to augment and refine the material in *Capitalism and Slavery*, originally published in 1944.

11. *Ibid.*,23.

12. *Ibid.*,24.

13. *Parliamentary Debates*, VII, 657-661, Lords, February 5, 1807, in Williams, *British West Indies at Westminster*, 35.

14. *Parliamentary Debates*, VII, 946-994, Commons, February 23, 1807, *Ibid.*,41.

15. *Parliamentary Debates*, XXXI, 772-785, Commons, June 13, 1815, *Ibid.*,71.

16. Michael Craton, *Testing the Chains: Resistance to Slavery in the British West Indies*, Ithaca, NY, 1982, 254-266.

17. Codd to Leith, April 25, 1816, in Leith to Bathurst, April 30, 1816, C.O. 28/85.

18. The Registry Bill had got as far as a first reading in 1815, but was withdrawn for that session. See Robert I. Wilberforce and Samuel Wilberforce. *The Life of William Wilberforce*, 5 vols, London, 1838, IV, 282-286.

19. *Parliamentary Debates*, XXIV, 1154-1220, Commons, June 19, 1816, in Williams, *British West Indies at Westminster*, 78.

20. *Ibid.*, 79

21. Matthew Gregory Lewis, *Journal of a Residence Among the Negro in the West Indies*, London, 1845 ed., 114-116. The rumoured conjunction between Wilberforce's campaign and political unrest among British slaves was not new in 1816; this was merely the most convincing case to date. As early as December 1791, the attorney Thomas Barritt wrote to his absentee employer about the fears of disturbances among the Jamaican slaves 'in consequence of what has happened in Hispaniola etc', 'These fears are not groundless', he added, 'for some weeks ago (say 5) a body of Negroes in Spanish Town who call themselves the Cat Club, had assembled drinking King Wilberforce's health out of a Cat's skull by way of a cup, and swearing secrecy to each other. Some of them were taken up and put into the workhouse, but will not divulge the business. In Trelawney or thereabouts, some Negroes have been detected making the Cartridges and firearms found in their houses, so that my Dear Sir, you see the Effects likely to take place in the West Indies by our Worthies at home.' Thomas Barritt to Nathaniel Phillips, St Thomas in the East, Jamaica, December 8, 1791, National Library of Wales, Aberystwyth, quoted in Clare Taylor (ed.), *West Indian Planter Attitudes to the American and French Revolutions*, Aberystwyth, 1977, n.p. Slebech Papers MS 8386.

22. Wilberforce and Wilberforce, *Wilberforce*, IV, 286-307; Sir George Stephen, *Anti-Slavery Recollections, in a Series of Letters addressed to Mrs Beecher Stowe*, London, 1854, 26.

23. Robin Furneaux, *William Wilberforce*, London, 1974, 358-383. What must have been particularly distressing to Wilberforce was the involvement of the Jamaican 'Black' Davidson in the Cato Street conspiracy in 1819, and the activities of other blacks in the radical underground in Britain, such as Robert Wedderburn, pastor of a 'Christian Diabolist' church and plotter of a Haitian-style revolution in Jamaica. See Iain McCalman, 'A Radical Underworld in Early Nineteenth Century London: Thomas Evans, Robert Wedderburn, George Cannon and their Circle, 1800-1830', unpublished PhD dissertation, University of Melbourne, 1983.

24. This is the position developed, with specific reference to Frederic Harrison in 1866, in Michael Craton, *Sinews of Empire: A Short History of British Slavery*, London and New York, 1974, 315-316.

25. Lord Bathurst to Colonial Governors, Downing Street, July 9, 1823, *Parliamentary Papers*, 1824, XXIV, quoted in Michael Craton, James Walvin and David Wright, *Slavery, Abolition, and Emancipation, A Thematic Documentary*, London, 1976, 300-303.

26. Craton, *Testing the Chains*, 267-290.

27. Governor Murray to Lord Bathurst, August 24, 1823, C.O. 111/39; *Ibid*, 283.

28. *Ibid.*, 288-289. Smith died of galloping consumption in Georgetown, just a week before George IV, in London, signed a reprieve with an order for deportation.

29. Zachary Macaulay to William Wilberforce, November 11, 1823, in Wilberforce and Wilberforce, *Wilberforce*, V., 202. Macaulay was countering the reported remark of Chinnery, private secretary to Canning, that the Demerara revolt was instigated by 'Wilberforce, Buxton and Co'.

30. Charles Buxton (ed.), *Memoirs of Thomas Fowell Buxton, Bart.*, London, 1849, 78; Brougham, *Speeches*, II, 113-190.

31. Wilberforce and Wilberforce, *Wilberforce*, V., 203.

32. Sehon S. Goodridge, *Facing the Challenge of Emancipation: A Study of the Ministry of William Hart Coleridge, First Bishop of Barbados, 1824-1842*, Bridgetown, Barbados, 1981, 5-6.

33. William Law Mathieson, *British Slavery and its Abolition, 1823-1838*, London, 1926; Anti-Slavery Thoughts, *Mississippi Valley Historical Review*, XLIX, 1962, 209-230.

34. Craton, *Testing the Chains*, 291-321.

35. *Ibid*, 241-253.

36. Henry Bleby, *The Death Struggles of Slavery*, London, 1853, 128-129; Craton, *Testing the Chains*, 300.

37. *Ibid.*, 316-319.

38. Graham Wallas, *The Life of Francis Place, 1771-1854*, London, 1928, 295-313. For the interaction between the anti-slavery movement and the general process of reform, see Seymour Drescher and Christine Bolt (eds), *Anti-Slavery, Religion, and Reform*, Folkestone, and Hamden, UK, 1980; David Eltis and James Walvin (eds), *The Abolition of the Atlantic Slave Trade*, Madison, West Indies, 1981; James Walvin (ed.), *Slavery and British Society, 1776 - 1846*, London, 1982. The best work on the direct relationship between the Jamaican revolt and the political process in the metropolis is now Mary Turner, 'The Baptist War and Abolition', *Jamaican Historical Review*, XIII, 1982, 31-41.

39. David J. Murray, *The West Indies and the Development of Colonial Government, 1801 - 1834*, Oxford, 1965, 191; Buxton, *Memoirs*, 238.

40. *Parliamentary Debates*, 3rd Series, x, March 7, 1832.

41. *Ibid.*, XI, March 23, 1832.

42. Mathieson, *British Slavery and its Abolition*, 223 - 224; George Spater, *William Cobbett: The Poor Man's Friend*, 2 vols, Cambridge, 1982, II, 496 - 499. The wording of the 1823 resolution was, perhaps, significant; emancipation 'at the earliest period that shall be compatible with the well-being of the slaves themselves, with the safety of the colonies and with a fair and equitable consideration of the interests of private property', Public Record Office, London, C.O., 320/1, 209.

43. *Parliamentary Debates*, 3rd series, XIII, May 24, 1832; Buxton, *Memoirs*, 245 - 246; Craton, *Testing the Chains*, 323. Buxton's wording can be significantly compared with that in the Canning resolutions of 1823, cited above.

44. *Parliamentary Debates*, 3rd series, XIII, May 24, 1832. See also Buxton, *Memoirs*, 201; Mary Turner, 'Baptist War and Abolition', 40 - 41.

45. Buxton to Mr East, October 15, 1832, Buxton Papers, III, 31 - 32, quoted in David Brion Davis, *Slavery and Human Progress*, New York, 1984, 203.

46. For detailed descriptions of the final emancipation debates, see Lowell J. Ragatz, *The Fall of the Planter Class in the British Caribbean, 1763-1883*, New York, 1928, 149-152; W.L. Burn, *Emancipation and Apprenticeship in the British West Indies*, London, 1937; Murray, *Colonial Government*, 193-202; Craton, *Sinews of Empire*, 227-280; William A. Green, *British Slave Emancipation: The Sugar Colonies and the Great Experiment, 1830-1865*, Oxford, 1976, 112-125; Davis, *Slavery and Human Progress*, 160-217.

47. Karl Marx, *Grundise*, London, Penguin Edition, 1973, 471-514; *Pre-Capital Economic Formations*, J. Cohen (ed.), London, 1964.

48. On this, compare *Testing the Chains*, 161-171, 241-253, with Eugene Genovese,

From Rebellion to Revolution: Afro-American Slave Revolts in the Making of the Modern World, Baton Rouge, 1, 1979.

49. Richard Fraucht, "A Caribbean Social Type: Neither 'Peasant' nor 'Proletarian' ", Social and Economic Studies, XIII, 1967, 295-300.

50. Antonio Gramsci, Selections from the Prison Notebooks, Quintin Hoare and Geoffrey Nowell Smith (eds), London, 1971, 161, 188-189, 365-366.

51. Williams, Capitalism and Slavery, 197-208; From Columbus to Castro: The History of the Caribbean, 1492-1969, London, 1970, 328-515; Inward Hunger: The Education of a Prime Minister, London, 1969, 338-343.

Chapter 16

1. This essay is a substantial extension of a section in the Epilogue of Testing the Chains: Resistance to Slavery in the British West Indies, Ithaca, Cornell University Press, 1982, 323-330.

2. Lorna E. Simmonds, 'Riots and Disturbances in Jamaica, 1838-1865', unpublished MA dissertation, University of Waterloo, 1982. See also Swithin Wilmot, 'Emancipation in Action: Workers and Wage Conflicts in Jamaica, 1838-1848', paper presented at Sixteenth Annual Conference of Caribbean Historians, Barbados, 1984.

3. The Guyana, Jamaica and Barbados episodes, however, were simply the most outstanding and best documented examples. Comparable outbreaks occurred at least in Dominica (1844, 1884, 1893), St Lucia (1849), Tortola (1853, 1885), Antigua (1856), St Vincent (1862) and Tobago (1876). Parallels are doubtless awaiting rediscovery in almost every colony and even some of the above await detailed analysis. However, see the following fine articles: Russell E. Chace Jr, "Protest in Post-Emancipation Dominica: The 'Guerre Nègre' of 1844", paper presented at Fifteenth Conference of Caribbean Historians, Jamaica, 1983; "Religion, Taxes and Popular Protest in Tortola: The Road Town 'Riots' of 1853", paper presented to the South-South Conference, Montreal, May 1984; Woodville Marshall, " 'Vox Populi': The St Vincent Riots and Distur-

bances of 1862', in B.W. Higman (ed.), Trade, Government and Society in Caribbean History: Essays Presented to Douglas Hall, Kingston, Caribbean Universities Press, 1983, 85 - 115; Bridget Brereton, 'Post-Emancipation Protest in the Caribbean: The "Belmana Riots" in Tobago, 1876', Caribbean Quarterly, V, 30, 1984, 110 - 123. For the general question of the formation of Caribbean peasantries and peasant responses to post-emancipation conditions, see Sidney W. Mintz, 'Slavery and the Rise of Peasantries', and the subsequent Commentary by Woodville Marshall in Michael Craton (ed.,) Roots and Branches: Current Directions in Slave Studies, Toronto, Pergamon Press, 1979, 213-248; O. Nigel Bolland, 'Systems of Domination after Slavery: The Control of Land and Labor in the British West Indies after 1838', Comparative Studies in Society and History, 23, 4, October 1981, 591-619; Russell E. Chace Jr, 'The Emergence and Development of an Estate-Based Peasantry in Dominica', unpublished manuscript, 1986.

4. Craton, Testing the Chains, Chapter 21. The fullest contemporary account was Joshua Bryant, Account of an Insurrection of the Negro Slaves in the Colony of Demerara, Georgetown, Guiana Chronicle, 1824. See also Edwin A. Wallbridge, The Demerara Martyr, Memoirs of Rev. John Smith, Missionary to Demerara, London, 1848; James Rodway, The History of British Guiana, 3 vols, Georgetown, 1891-94, II, 75-81; Cecil Northcott, Slavery's Martyr: John Smith of Demerara and the Emancipation Movement, 1817-1824, London, Epworth Press, 1976.

5. For the post-emancipation condition of Guyana see Alan H. Adamson, Sugar without Slaves: The Political Economy of British Guiana, 1838-1904, New Haven, Yale University Press, 1972; Jay R. Mandle, The Plantation Economy: Population and Economic Change in Guyana, 1838-1960, Baltimore, Johns Hopkins University Press, 1981.

6. The phrase is from a report by Rev. William Woodson, General Superintendent of Wesleyan Missions in British Guiana, dated March 7, 1856, enclosed in Governor Wodehouse to Colonial Secretary, March 10, 1856, P.R.O., London, C.O., 111/30. Woodson, who referred to 'the large number of Vile and Abandoned Women in these Riots and I regret to add

of *wild, rude and half savage children*', specifically advocated 'putting villagers more
firmly under Government', and compulsory work for three days, 'whether on their
own provision grounds or on the Estates',
as well as three days' schooling for all 'wild
children'.

7. Wodehouse to Colonial Secretary,
March 10, 1856, *Ibid.*

8. See the transcript of Smith's journal,
1817-1823, C.O. 111/46.

9. Rodway, *British Guiana*, III, 114.

10. C.O. 111/309. Orr's rhetoric still has
power. In one memorable phrase he
referred to the militiamen come to arrest
him as 'Glazed hatted dogs of war'. *Ibid.*

11. Wodehouse to Colonial Secretary, Feb. 24,
1856; C.O. 111/309.

12. *Ibid.*

13. *Ibid.*

14. Wodehouse to Colonial Secretary,
March 10, 1856; C.O. 111/309.

15. *Ibid.*

16. *Ibid.*

17. Wodehouse to Colonial Secretary,
March 25, 1856; C.O. 111/309.

18. Annotation by Permanent Undersecretary
H. M. Taylor following Wodehouse to Colonial Secretary, Feb. 24, 1856; C.O. 111/309.

19. *Ibid.*

20. Wodehouse to Colonial Secretary, May 9,
1856; C.O. 111/311.

21. Wodehouse to Colonial Secretary, March
10, 1856; C.O. 111/310.

22. Local Ordinances were initiated by the
Governor in Council, endorsed by the
Court of Policy and approved, or disap-
proved, in due course, by the Colonial Office. In practical terms they could therefore
be even more arbitrary than Acts passed by
Assemblies in self-legislating colonies. The
key Ordinances here were Numbers 20 and
21 of 1856, enclosed in Wodehouse to Colonial Secretary, Feb. 24, 1856; C.O. 111/309.

23. Ordinances Numbers 28 and 29; C.O.
111/312, 313.

24. Rodway, *British Guiana*, 130.

25. *Ibid.*, 135-136. One of the most interesting co-
incidences between 1856 and 1823 was that
John Sayers Orr and the ordinary black Guyanese were defended in the local press by Rev.
Edmund Wallbridge, a
Nonconformist missionary who had written
the biography of Rev. John Smith, 'The
Demerara Martyr', in 1848. For his pains,
Wallbridge earned an outpouring of obloquy
from the planters and praise from British Nonconformists to rival that accorded his hero 33
years before, and was forced to leave the colony. *Ibid.*

26. Craton, *Testing the Chains*, Chapter 22.
The most detailed of the many contempo-
rary accounts, from opposite sides, were
Bernard Martin, Sr, *Jamaica, As it was, as it
is, and as it may be*, London, 1835, and Rev.
Henry Bleby, *The Death Struggles of Slav-
ery*, London, 1853. For modern analyses
see Mary Reckord, 'The Jamaican Slave
Rebellion of 1831', *Past and Present*, 40 July
1968, 108-125; Stiv Jakobson, *Am I Not a
Man and a Brother? British Missions and the
Abolition of the Slave Trade and Slavery in
West Africa and the West Indies, 1786-1838*,
Uppsala, Gleerup, 1972; Philip Wright,
*Knibb 'The Notorious, 'Slaves' Missionary,
1803-1845*, London, Sidgwick and Jackson,
1973, 56 - 133. Edward K. Brathwaite,
Wars of Respect, Kingston, *Savacou*, 1979;
Mary Turner, *Slaves and Missionaries: The
Disintegration of Jamaican Slave Society,
1787 - 1834*, Urbana, University of Illinois
Press, 1982.

27. Committee appointed, May 30, 1832;
evidence taken, June 8-Aug 11, 1832;
report ordered to be printed, Aug. 11,
1832. Samuel Sharpe was hanged on May
23, 1832. The first Emancipation Act was
passed on July 31, 1833.

28. For the condition of Jamaica between 1834
and 1865, see Philip D. Curtin, *Two
Jamaicas: The Role of Ideas in a Tropical
Colony*, Cambridge, Harvard University
Press, 1955; Douglas G. Hall, *Free Jamaica:
1838-1865; An Economic History*, New
Haven, Yale University Press, 1959; Mavis
C. Campbell, *The Dynamics of Change in a
Slave Society: A Sociopolitical History of the
Free Coloreds in Jamaica, 1800-1865*,
Rutherford, Fairleigh Dickinson University
Press, 1976; Gad J. Heuman, *Between Black
and White; Race Politics, and the Free Coloreds
in Jamaica, 1792-1865*, Westport,
Greenwood, 1981.

29. Professor Douglas G. Hall at Association
of Caribbean Historians Conference,
Guadeloupe, 1981.

30. Monica Schuler, *Alas, Alas, Kongo; A Social
History of the Liberated African Immigration
into Jamaica, 1841-1865*, Baltimore, Johns
Hopkins University Press, 1980.

31. Edward Cardwell to Governor Eyre, June 14, 1865; C.O. 137/391.

32. For Governor Edward Eyre, see Sydney H. Olivier, *The Myth of Governor Eyre*, London, Hogarth Press, 1933; Geoffrey Dutton, *The Hero as a Murderer: The Life of Edward John Eyre, Australian Explorer and Governor of Jamaica, 1815-1901*, London, Collins, 1967.

33. Poster by Gordon to people of St Thomas-in-the-East, Aug. 11, 1865, quoted in *Report of the Jamaican Royal Commission, Part I, British Sessional Papers, Reports 1866, XXX*, 489-531.

34. *Ibid*.

35. *Ibid*.

36. *Ibid*. The letter was delivered to Governor Eyre in Spanish Town on the morning of Oct. 11, 1865, when the revolt was irreversibly underway.

37. *Ibid*., Geoffrey Dutton quotes a similar letter signed by Bogle and four others and allegedly found at Stony Gut: 'Blow your shells! Roule your drums! House to house; take out every man; march them down to Stony Gut; any that you find take them in the way; take them down with their arms; war is at my black skin; war is at hand ... Every black man must turn out at once, for the oppression is too great.'; Dutton, *Hero as a Murderer*, 275.

38. *Ibid*., 286.

39. *Report of the Jamaica Royal Commission (1866), Part I, B.S.P., Reports, 1866, XXX*, 490.

40. *Ibid*., 529.

41. Bernard Semmel, *Jamaican Blood and Victorian Conscience*, Cambridge, Houghton Mifflin, 1962; Gertrude Himmelfarb, *On Liberty and Liberalism; The Case of John Stuart Mill*, New York, 1974.

42. Michael Craton, *Sinews of Empire: A Short History of British Slavery*, New York, Doubleday, 1974, 315, quoting Frederic Harrison: 'The precise issue we raise in this is that throughout our empire the British rule shall be the rule of law; that every British citizen, white, brown or black in skin, shall be subject to definite, and not to indefinite powers ...'

43. Victor S. Reid, *New Day*, London, 1973, 1955; Sidney H. Olivier, *Jamaica the Blessed Island*, London, Faber & Faber, 1936; Samuel J. Hurwitz and Edith Hurwitz, Jamaica; A Historical Portrait, London, 1971.

44.

Craton, *Testing the Chains*, Chapter 20. The fullest contemporary account, although heavily biased was *The Report of the Select Committee of the House of Assembly appointed to inquire into the Origin, Causes, and Progress of the Late Insurrection*, Barbados, 1818. But see also, Sir Robert Schomburgk, *The History of Barbados*, London, Longman, 1847; Karl Watson, *The Civilised Island; Barbados, A Social History, 1750-1816*, Barbados, 1979; Hillary Beckles, *Black Rebellion in Barbados: The Struggle Against Slavery, 1627-1838*, Barbados, Carib Research and Publications Inc., 1987.

45. *Report from a Select Committee*, 25-34.

46. *Ibid*, 28-29.

47. *Ibid*, 34-57; Governor Leith to Lord Bathurst, Sept. 21, 1816, C.O. 28/85; Spooner to Bathurst, Feb. 4, 1817, C.O. 28/86.

48. Claude Levy, *Emancipation, Sugar and Federalism; Barbados and the West Indies, 1833-1876*, Gainesville, University of Florida Press, 1980.

49. See, for example, the petition of black freeholders of Carrington's Village, St Thomas parish, dated Aug. 7, 1876; C.O. 321/10, 473 sqq. The petitioners, who claimed to have held land since 1838, chiefly blamed absentee proprietors and the financial depression in general for crippling 'the emergence of our skilled and industrious peasantry', but pointed out that the island's great increase in sugar production had been achieved by labourers drawn from their own class, who were yet paid wages 'no more than affords the necessaries of life notwithstanding that food and the articles in general consumption are, at this time, plentiful and cheap'. They stated that many of them would have emigrated but for their attachment to their land and the fact that conditions in other islands were even worse, and begged the government to put up capital for small producers as had the Danish Government in St Croix, where estates were 'not even paying expenses'.

50. The population at the time of emancipation had been 101,000, of whom 82,000 had been slaves. In 1874, the total population was 162,000, of whom 66.4 per cent were blacks, 24.4 per cent coloureds and 10.2 per cent whites. The 'agricultural population' totalled 42,000. There were said to be 27,000 'seamstresses, laundresses and domestics', 29,500 schoolchildren and

40,000 unemployed, the latter being 'nearly all children under the age of 15'. Of the 42,000 agricultural labourers, 36,500 were over 15 years of age, 16,000 males and 20,500 females. Levy, *Emancipation, Sugar and Federalism*, 134, 80-83, 101, 135.

51. The essential evidence is to be found in three relevant Command Papers, C. 1539 and C. 1559 of 1876 and C. 1687 of 1877; B.S.P., *Accounts & Papers 1876, LIII* and *1877, LXI*.

52. This was succinctly described in Governor Pope Hennessy to Colonial Secretary, May 3, 1876 in C. 1559 of 1876, and memorably criticised by Samuel Jackman Prescod, the black editor and Assemblyman, in *The Liberal* newspaper of Sept. 25, 1858 – enclosed in Governor Hincks to Colonial Secretary, Sept. 25, 1858.

53. Pope Hennessy to Colonial Secretary, May 16, 1876, C.O. 321/9.

54. Pope Hennessy to Colonial Secretary, July 11, 1876, C.O. 321/10. Canefield arson had also steadily increased in recent years. In a speech in March 1876, the governor quoted the following figures: 1873, 116; 1875, 141; *Barbados People*, March 28, 1876, enclosed in Pope Hennessy to Colonial Secretary, March 28, 1876, C.O. 321/9.

55. Despatch of Jan 25, 1963, May 1, 1876. C.O. 321/9.

56. Unpublished manuscript quoted by Pope Hennessy to Colonial Secretary, May 8, 1876, C.O. 321/9. The anonymous person was probably a Rev. Chester.

57. *Ibid.* In the same despatch, Pope Hennessy quoted Governor Rawson (1869-75) assaying that the Barbadian whites would rather have had no troops at all than to have the black West India Regiment in garrison, and the Rev. Chester to the effect that the whites believed that if all white troops were removed from the West India Regiment soldiers would fraternise with the 'creole negroes' and a general massacre of whites ensure. This was 25 years after emancipation.

58. Bruce Hamilton, *Barbados and the Confederation Question, 1871-1885*, London, Brown Agents for Overseas Governments and Administrations, 1956. But see also Levy, *op. cit.*

59. James Pope Hennessy, *Verandah; Some Episodes in the Crown Colonies, 1867-1889*, London, Allen & Unwin, 1964. Also Hamilton, Levy, *op. cit.*

60. Then called Long Bay Castle. Governor Pope Hennessy also spent some time at Blackman's in St Joseph's parish. After a disorderly meeting on the Federation question in St John's on March 23, 1876, the plantocratic Barbados *Times* claimed that the trouble had been caused by 'some liberated persons and some of the dwellers near Long Bay Castle in St Philip', and noted that 'by looking at the Map, we find St John comes between the two last places where Mr. Hennessy had been residing, at Long Bay Castle and Blackman's'; *Times*, March 25, 1876, enclosed in Governor Hennessy to Colonial Office, March 28, 1876, C.O. 321/9.

61. This was after Pope Hennessy's outspoken speech to both houses of the legislature on March 3, 1876; Hamilton, *Confederation Question*, 54 - 57.

62. Quoted in *C. 1559* of 1876, 67.

63. Enclosed in Pope Hennessy to Colonial Secretary, May 30, 1876, *Ibid.*, 168-169. The Rev. T. Clarke was also quoted as having heard of a black countryman saying: 'De gubnor say de Queen gib de res of Gubnor's money fou help we, but dey no gib we. He gwine gib we, and gib we land too.'; Hamilton, *Confederation Question*, 46.

64. Fullest details enclosed in Pope Hennessy to Colonial Office, April 7, 1876. C.O. 321/9; Hamilton *Confederation Question*, 64.

65. Voluminous details in Pope Hennessy to Colonial Secretary, May 16, 1876, C.O. 321/9; and in *C. 1539* and *C. 1559* of 1876; Hamilton, *Confederation Question*, 71-74.

66. Pope Hennessy to Colonial Secretary, 1, May 14, 1876, *C. 1559*.

67. Pope Hennessy to Colonial Secretary, May 16, 1876, C.O. 321/9; Hamilton, *Confederation Question*, 71.

68. Major Tatton Brown to C. C. Sergeant, April 28, 1876, *C. 1559*.

69. *C. 1559*, 190 sqq.

70. There was an excellent full account of the trials, including the humane summing up by Judge Lushington Phillips in the London *Times*, Nov. 15, 1876, a copy of which was interleaved in C.O. 32/111.

71. Hamilton, *Confederation Question*, 93-95; Pope Hennessy, *Verandah*, 180-182.

72. Barbados Defence Association to Colonial Secretary, Aug. 9, 1876, *C. 1687*.

73. Michael Craton, 'Proto-Peasant Revolts? The Late Slave Rebellions in the British

West Indies, 1816-1832', *Past & Present*, 85, Nov. 1979, 199-125; 'The Passion to Exist; Slave Rebellions in the British West Indies, 1650-1832', *Journal of Caribbean History*, 13, Summer 1980, 1-20; *Testing the Chains*, Chapters 19-22, 239-321.

74. Noel Deerr, *The History of Sugar*, 2 vols, London, Chapman and Hall, 1949, 1950, II, 194-203; Eric Williams *From Columbus to Castro: The History of the Caribbean, 1492-1969*, London, Andre Deutsch, 1970, 39-40, 366-373; Levy, *Emancipation, Sugar and Federalism*, 57, 93, 107.

75. W. L. Burn, *Emancipation and Apprenticeship in the British West Indies*, London, Cape, 1937; Woodville Marshall (ed.), *The Colthurst Journal, 1835-1845*, Barbados, Caribbean Universities Press, 1979.

76. In each of the major outbursts, whites reported cases where the local constables stood on the sidelines or actually sided with the rioters.

77. There is not yet the work needed to relate the West Indies to the process of modernisation in general, along the lines of Immanuel Wallerstein's study of the whole world in an earlier period, *The Modern World-System: Capitalist Agriculture and the Origins of the European World-Economy in the Sixteenth Century*, New York and London, Academic Press, 1974; or Walter Rodney's *How Europe Underdeveloped Africa*, London, Bogle L'Overture Publications, 1972. Perhaps the closest so far is George Beckford, *Persistent Poverty: Underdevelopment in Plantation Economies of the Third world*, Oxford, Oxford University Press, 1972.

78. See, for example, Cecilia Karch, 'The Role of the Barbados Mutual Life Assurance Society during the International Sugar Crisis of the Late Nineteenth Century', paper presented at the Twelfth Annual Conference of Caribbean Historians, Trinidad, 1980. For the slight relaxation that came in the early twentieth century, see Woodville Marshal *et al.*, 'The Establishment of a Peasantry in Barbados, 1840-1920', paper presented at the Sixth Annual Conference of Caribbean Historians, Puerto Rico, 1974.

79. Report of Jamaica Royal Commission, *B.S.P., Reports, 1866, XXX*, 495.

80. This philanthropic/liberal stance, culminating in Reginald Coupland's *Wilberforce*, Oxford, Oxford University Press, 1923; W. L. Mathieson's, *British Slave Emancipation,* *1838-1849*, London, Longman, 1932 and G.R. Mellor's *British Imperial Trusteeship, 1783-1850* was notably pilloried by Eric Williams in *British Historians and the West Indies*, London, Andre Deutsch, 1966. Echoes of the older 'imperialist' tradition linger in William A. Green, *British Slave Emancipation: The Sugar Colonies and the Great Experiment, 1830-1865*, Oxford, Oxford University Press, 1976, which sparked off a memorable exchange between Green and Nigel Bolland, *Comparative Studies in Society and History*, 26, 1, Jan. 1984.

81. The series prefixed simply 'C.' began in 1861. When it reached 10,000 in 1900 it was superseded by the 'Cd.' series. The 'Cmd.' series began in 1930, and 'Cmnd.' in 1950.

82. *Report of the West Indies Royal Commission, 1989*, C. 8655, Norman Commission; *Report of the Hon. E.F.L. Wood M.P. on his visit to the West Indies and British Guiana, 1922*, Cd. 1679; *Report of the West Indies Sugar Commission, 1930*, Cmd. 3517, (Olivier-Semple Report); *Report on Labour Conditions in the West Indies, 1939*, Cmd. 6070 (Orde Browne Report); *Report of the West Indies Royal Commission, 1945*, Cmd. 6607 (Moyne Commission). See also Margaret Olivier (ed.), *Sydney Olivier: Letters and Selected Writings*, London, Allen & Unwin, 1948, 181-182.

83. Hamilton, *Confederation Question*, Appendix A, 141.

84. The original position was that of Eric Williams's, *From Columbus to Castro*. The present view is that of the numerous West Indian critics of Williams. See, for example, Gordon Rohlehr, 'History as Absurdity', in Orde Coombs (ed.), *Massa Day Dead*, New York, Doubleday Anchor, 1974, 69-108.

Chapter 18

1. This essay complements a rather more bibliographic study of the transition throughout the entire Caribbean given at the LASA annual meeting in Washington, April 1991, which follows in the present collection.

2. Ligon 1657; Leslie 1740; Belgrove 1755; Martin 1756; Long 1774; Luffman 1788; Dickson 1789; Beckford 1790; Moreton 1790; Edwards 1793; Pinckard 1806; Roughley 1823; Barclay 1826; M'Mahon

1838; Abrahams & Szwed 1983; Turner 1988 and 1991; and Morgan 1991.

3. See Beckles & Downes 1987; Beckles & Watson 1987; Beckles 1989a and b, and 1990.

4. British Sessional Papers (hereafter B.S.P.) 1832, XX, 721, 385 and 261.

5. As Sidney Mintz (1979, 225, 240-241) has generously pointed out, credit for the recognition of the phenomena associated with the 'peasant breach' should perhaps go to George Cumper, for an article published in 1959.

6. This, of course, was the reality behind the myth of intentional slave breeding, the stuff of sensational novelists such as Kyle Onstott, afforded near respectability by Richard Sutch (1975), but deflated in one alleged Caribbean case by David Lowenthal & Colin Clarke (1977).

7. In her recent study of Vere parish, Jamaica, Mary Turner (1991, 102-103) has argued that the jobbing gang system increased in reverse correlation to declining planters' fortunes, following the 'debt crisis' initiated in the 1760s; that it involved opportunistic upwardly mobile whites (who later tended to be pen-keepers rather than planters); and that the interest of owners of jobbing slaves to fulfil seasonal labour shortages neatly coincided with the interests of established plantation slaves to perform less work and 'negotiate' the terms of their labour by different forms of 'resistance'.

8. Laws of Antigua 1757, Act No. 212, November 25, 1757, clause 9; quoted in Gaspar (1985, 160-162).

9. Hamilton College, New York, Beinecke Collection, Antigua Plantation Papers n.d.

10. B.S.P. 1831-32, 18-21.

11. Like the Bahamian slaves, those of Belize were allowed to carry guns, and the lumber cutting crews had much the same practical freedom as black Bahamian mariners. Although timber extraction left little spare time for provision ground cultivation throughout the year, those Belizean slaves who could, marketed their surplus produce. As reported by Henderson in 1809, not only were timber crews allocated work by tasks, but when employed by their owners on their Saturday off-day, were paid 'the established rate' of three shillings and fourpence a day, in either cash or kind (Bolland 1991, 13).

12.

An official letter from the Commissioners of Correspondence of the Bahama Islands, Nassau, 1823; quoted in Higman (1984, 179) Craton & Saunders (1992, 258-259).

13. Colonial Office (hereafter C.O.) 23/87, Smyth to Goderich, August 9, 1832, 302, 377-378. See also Craton and Saunders (1992, 377-378) and Johnson (1991, 5).

14. C.O. 23/82, Smyth to Murray, March 8, 1830, 6; see also Johnson (1991, 6). The practice of slaves earning a share as mariners on privateering ships dated at least from 1748, when it was noted by Governor Tinker. At that time, he complained, no one wished to till the soil, 'especially in these times when a Common Seaman, nay a Negroe Slave, shall step on board a Privateer and in a Six Week Cruise return often with a Booty of a hundred pound sterling to his share' (Craton and Saunders 1992, 147).

15. B.S.P. 1816, 32 and Higman (1984, 245).

16. C.O. 23/86, Smyth to Goderich, August 2, 1832; see also Johnson (1991, 10).

17. *Bahama Gazette*, June 23, 1799; Craton and Saunders (1992, 378-384).

18. Smith 1776; Williams 1944; Craton 1974; Drescher 1977 and 1987; Davis 1984; Blackburn 1988; Ward 1988; Carrington 1988.

19. Green 1976 and 1984; Bolland 1981, 1988, 1989, 1990, 1991; Riviere 1972; Levy 1980; Moore 1987; Holt 1992.

20. The problems and possible value of Christianising slaves were both neatly encapsulated in a proclamation by Sir John Heydon, Governor of Bermuda, as early as 1669: 'Masters and Servants are hereby advised, and in the kings name required to live in peace, mutual love and respect to each other. Servants submitting to the condition wherein God hath placed them. And such Negroes as formerlie, or lately bin baptized by several Ministers, should not thereby think themselves free from their Masters and Owners, but rather, by the means of their Christian profession, obliged to a more strict bond of fidelity and service' (Lefroy 1877-79, II, 293-294).

21. Although founded in 1799, the Anglican Church Missionary Society did little active proselytising until the 1820s. The most energetic baptiser of slaves (at two shillings and sixpence a head) was Rev. G. W. Bridges, notorious as founder of the Colonial Church Union, under the auspices of which Jamaican Anglicans persecuted black

Jamaican sectarians, especially Baptists (Craton 1982; Turner 1982).

22. The spirit of missionary teaching was captured by Rev. John Wray, of the London Missionary Society in Demerara in 1827: 'A religious education only can prepare the negroes for a state of freedom and the general diffusion of true Christianity and good laws to encouraging Industry.' Wray also utilised a socialising catechism for his charges which included the following questions and answers: "Q.5: Suppose a servant or slave meets with an unfeeling master, does this lessen the duty of respect? A: By no means, for it is the command of God, I Peter 2: 18-19, 'Servants shall be subject to your masters with all fear, not only to the good and gentle, but also to the forward. . .' Q. 8: What is the duty of servants as to the property of their masters? A: To keep from and watch against the sin of theft, waste and negligence, and to be as careful of their master's property as if it were their own." Council for World Missions Archives (formerly L.M.S. Papers), School of Oriental and African Studies, London, Rev. John Wray, Demerara, to London 1827, Incoming Letters, Boxes 1-11, 1807-94, 5.

23. The general study of liberated Africans in the British West Indies is a great work yet to be accomplished (Schuler 1986; Wood 1981).

24. C.O. 23/94, *Bahama Argus*, November 11, 1835. See also Craton and Saunders (forthcoming).

25. C.O. 23/76, Grant to Goderich, No. 9, September 26, 1827; 23/107, Cockburn to Russell, No. 20, April 6, 1840. See also Johnson (1991, 84-109).

26. Burn 1937; Hall 1953; Green 1969; Marshall 1971, 1985; Wilmot 1984a, 1984b.

27. Another index, of course, was the relative availability of land, normally measured by its price. This varied from £1 per acre in parts of British Guiana, to maxima of £13 in Trinidad, £25 in Jamaica and £200 in Barbados. Craton and Walvin 1970; Higman (1988, 286); Beckles (1990, 108-116); Marshall, Marshall & Gibbs (1975, 88-104); Levy 1980; Gibbs 1987; Chamberlain 1991.

28. *Royal Gazette*, April 6, 1835, Colebrooke to Sms Donald McLean and Hector Murro.

29. Weller 1968; Adamson 1972; Mandel 1973; Tinker 1974; Sohal 1979; Haraksingh 1981; Rodney 1981.

30. B.S.P. 1841, 39, 624, 559-560; Adamson 1972, 52-54.

31. See also B.S.P. 1859, 20, 31, 93 and 1871, 20, 393, 118.

32. One of Adamson's (1972, 263) underlying themes is well-expressed in his statement, 'A fear of the masses . . . lies at the heart of Victorian liberalism and of Victorian colonial policy.'

33. This access stemmed largely from the planters' manipulation of the head right and quit rent system to their own advantage, and led to the establishment of land title registries long in advance of Britain.

34. *Morning Journal* (Jamaica) September 15, 1865, Letter to Her Majesty from the Poor People of St Ann, Jamaica; C.O. 137/222, 1865 The Queen's Advice, Dispatch from Cardwell to Eyre, Printed in Underhill 1866.

35. Eisner (1961, 220); Satchell (1990, 7-8, 125-127); Satchell 1991; Holt (1992, 403-406).

36. Newton 1973, 1977, 1984, 1987; History Task Force 1979; Petras 1988; Richardson 1983, 1985, 1989.

37. B.S.P. Reports 1866, XXX, Report of the Jamaican Royal Commission, Olivier 1933; Hall 1959; Semmel 1962; Dutton 1967; Campbell 1976; Schuler 1980; Heuman 1981; Simmonds 1982; Chace 1984, 1986, 1989; Brereton 1984.

38. The book, however, is as Walter Rodney planned it. The manuscript was delivered to Johns Hopkins University Press a few months, and revised in prison a few weeks, before Rodney was blown up in his car in June 1980. Published in 1981, it received the triennial Elsa Goveia Memorial Prize of the Association of Caribbean Historians (ACH) in April 1983.

39. Lobdell 1988; Hart 1988; Rich 1988; Trouillot 1989. As readers will doubtless have noted, this paper (unlike the general essay referred to in Note 1) does not adequately discuss the relationship between changing technology and labour systems. A useful range of papers on this topic, derived from the panel 'Changing Technology and the Labour Nexus' at the Americanists' Congress in Amsterdam in July 1988, was published in a special edition of the *Nieuwe West-Indische Gids* (Spring 1990). Of these, particularly valuable for present purposes are the position papers by the convenors, Peter Boomgaard and Gert Oostindie, and the contribution by Richard B. Sheridan.

Chapter 19

1. This essay was originally presented at the XIV International Congress of the Latin American Studies Association held in Crystal City, Virginia, on April 4-6, 1991, in a session including papers by Ciro Flamarion S. Cardoso and Nancy Priscilla Naro on Brazil, and by Ira Berlin on the USA.

2. Eugene D. Genovese, *From Rebellion to Revolution: Afro-American Slave Revolts in the Making of the Modern World*, Baton Rouge, Louisiana State University Press, 1979, Preface; C. L. R. James, *The Black Jacobins: Toussaint l'Ouverture and the San Domingo Revolution*, London, Secker and Warburg, 1938; Herbert Aptheker, *American Negro Slave Revolts*, New York, Columbia University Press, 1943.

3. David Geggus, 'The French and Haitian Revolutions, and Resistance to Slavery in the Americas: An Overview', *Revue Francaise d'histoire d'outre-mer*, LXXVI, 1989, 107-124. See also his 'Slave Resistance Studies and the Saint Dominigue Slave Revolt: Some Preliminary Considerations', University of Florida Occasional Papers, 4, 1983; 'Haiti and the Abolitionists: Opinion, Propaganda and International Politics in Britain and France, 1804-1838', in David Richardson (ed.), *Abolition and its Aftermath: The Historical Context, 1790-1916*, London, Frank Cass, 1985, 113-140.

4. *Ibid*, 110-116; Michael Craton, *Testing the Chains: Resistance to Slavery in the British West Indies*, Ithaca, Cornell University Press, 1982, 180-238; Roger N. Buckley, *Slaves in Red Coats: The British West India Regiments, 1795-1815*, New Haven, Yale University Press, 1979.

5. Robin Blackburn, *The Overthrow of Colonial Slavery, 1776-1848*, London, Verso, 1988, 519-550 [520, 533].

6. Seymour Drescher, *Capitalism and Antislavery: British Mobilization in Comparative Perspective*, New York, Oxford University Press, 1987; Robert Paquette, 'The Economics, Politics, and Ideology of Antislavery', *Nieuw Westindische Gids*, 63, 3-4, 1989, 242-250; David Brion Davis, *Slavery and Human Progress*, New York, 1984; David Eltis, *Economic Growth and the Ending of the Transatlantic Slave Trade*, New York, Oxford University Press, 1987; Louis and Rosamund Billington, ' 'A Burning Zeal for

Righteousness': Women in the British Anti-slavery Movement', in Jane Randall (ed.), *Equal or Different: Women's Politics in Britain 1800-1914*, Oxford University Press, 1987; Richard Holmes, *Coleridge: Early Visions*, Oxford University Press, 1990.

7. Gordon K. Lewis, *Main Currents in Caribbean Thought*, Baltimore, Johns Hopkins University Press, 1983, 171-238. Lewis is particularly severe with David Brion Davis, along with Robert Fogel, Stanley Engerman, Stanley Elkins and William Styron. *Ibid*, 171-172. Boswell quoted the attack on the planters from *Taxation No Tyranny* (1775) and attributed the pro-rebel toast to a bibulous occasion among 'some very grave men at Oxford' – before going on to an unusual attack on his hero's anti-slavery ideas. This section incudes the notorious passage 'To abolish a *status* which in all ages GOD has sanctioned, and man has continued, would not only be *robbery* to an innumerable class of our fellow subjects; but it would be extreme cruelty to the African Savages, a portion of whom it saves from massacre, or intolerable bondage in their own country, and introduces into a much happier state of life.' James Boswell, *The Life of Samuel Johnson LLD*, 2 vols, London, Dent, 1906 [1791], II, 146-148.

8. *Ibid*. Richard Hart, *Slaves who Abolished Slavery*, Vol. I, *Blacks in Bondage*, Kingston, 1980, republished as *Esclavos que abolicieron la esclavitud*, Havana, Collecion Nuestros Paises, Casa de las Americas, 1984. Despite the breadth and originality of Lewis's book, the relevant literature on the indigenous ideology of slave resistance is already large, and growing. Of works in English one particularly thinks of Sidney W. Mintz and Richard Price, *An Anthropological Approach to the Afro-American Past: A Caribbean Perspective*, Philadelphia, ISHI, 1976; Lucille Mathurin Mair, *The Rebel Woman in the British West Indies during Slavery*, Kingston, 1975; Edward Brathwaite, *Wars of Respect: Nanny, Sam Sharpe and the Struggle for People's Liberation*, Kingston, 1977; Monica Schuler, 'Afro-American Slave Culture', in Michael Craton (ed.), *Roots and Branches: Current Directions in Slave Studies*, Oxford, Pergamon, 1979, 121-155; Jean Fouchard, *The Haitian Maroons: Liberty or Death*, New York, 1981; Richard Price (ed.), *Maroon Societies: Rebel Slave Communities in the Ameri-*

cas, 2nd edn, Baltimore, Johns Hopkins University Press, 1979; David Barry Gaspar, *Bondmen & Rebels: A Study of Master-Slave Relations in Antigua, With Implications for Colonial British America*, Baltimore, Johns Hopkins University Press, 1985; Hilary Beckles, 'The 200 Years War: Slave Resistance in the British West Indies: An Overview of the Historiography', *Jamaican Historical Review*, 13, 1982, 1-10; *Black Rebellion in Barbados: The Struggle Against Slavery, 1627-1838*, Bridgetown, 1984; 'Caribbean Anti-Slavery: The Self-Liberation Ethos of Enslaved Blacks', *Journal of Caribbean History*, 22, 1&2, 1988, 1-19. This last item is of most interest to the present writer since it consists in part of a dissection of his own development as an analyst of slave resistance ideology in Michael Craton, *Sinews of Empire: A Short History of British Slavery*, New York, Doubleday, 1974; 'The Passion to Exist: Slave Rebellions in the British West Indies, 1650-1832', *Journal of Caribbean History*, 13, 1980, 1-20; 'Slave Culture, Resistance and the Achievement of Emancipation in the British West Indies, 1783-1838', in James Walvin (ed.), *Slavery and British Society, 1776-1846*, London, Macmillan, 1982, 100-122; *Testing the Chains* (1982).

9. Matthew Gregory Lewis, *Journal of West Indian Planter*, London, 1834, 228.

10. James, *Black Jacobins*, 1938, 66; Sidney W. Mintz and Douglas G. Hall, 'The Origins of the Jamaican Internal Marketing System', *Yale University Publications in Anthropology*, 57, 1960, 1-26, republished (with Mintz as sole author) in Sidney W. Mintz, *Caribbean Transformations*, Chicago, 1974; Richard Frucht, "A Caribbean Social Type: Neither 'Peasant' nor 'Proletarian' ", *Social and Economic Studies*, 16, 3, 1967, 295-300; Hilary Beckles, 'Slaves and the Internal Market Economy of Barbados: A Perspective on Non-Violent Resistance', unpublished paper, 20th Conference of Caribbean Historians, St Thomas, 1988; 'Slaves as Autonomous Cash Crop Producers and Retailers in Barbados, 1720-1826', in John Brewer and Susan Staves (eds), *The Property of Empire*, London, Routledge, 1992; Sidney W. Mintz, 'Slavery and the Rise of Peasantries', in Michael Craton (ed.), *Roots and Branches: Current Directions in Slave Studies*, Oxford, Pergamon, 1979 with

commentaries by Woodville Marshall, Mary Karasch and Richard Frucht, 213-253; Michael Craton, 'Proto-Peasant Revolts? The Late Slave Rebellions in the British West Indies, 1816-1832', *Past and Present*, 85, 1979, 99-125; Ciro Flamarion S. Cardoso, *Escravo ou Campones? O proto-campesinato negro nas Americas*, Sao Paulo, Editora Brasiliense, 1987.

11. Richard Hart, 'The Formation of a Caribbean Working Class', *The Black Liberator*, 22, 1973, 131-148; O. Nigel Bolland, 'The Politics of Freedom in the British Caribbean', unpublished paper, Conference, 'The Meaning of Freedom', University of Pittsburgh, 1988; 'The Extraction of Timber in the Slave Society of Belize', in Ira and Berlin and Philip Morgan (eds.), *Cultaration and Culture: Labor and the Shaping of Slave Life in the Americas*, Maryland, 1993; David Barry Gaspar, 'Amelioration or Oppression? The Abolition of the Slaves' Sunday Markets in Antigua (1831)', paper given at 20th Conference of Caribbean Historians, St Thomas, 1988; Mary Turner, 'Chattel Slaves into Wage Slaves: A Jamaican Case Study', in Malcolm Cross and Gad Heuman, *Labour in the Caribbean*, London, Macmillan, 1987; 'Slaves' Subsistence and Labour Negotiations', *Slavery and Abolition*, May 1991; Michael Craton and D. Gail Saunders, 'Seeking a Life of their Own: Aspects of Slave Resistance in the Bahamas', *Journal of Caribbean History*, 23, 2, 1991; *Islanders in the Stream: A History of the Bahamian People, Volume One, From Aboriginal Times to the End of Slavery*, Athens, Georgia University Press, 1992.

12. Philip Morgan, 'Task and Gang Systems: The Organization of Labor in New World Plantations', in Ian K. Steele and Stephen Innes (eds), *Work and Labor in Early America*, Chapel Hill, University of North Carolina, 1988, 189-220. For Jamaica, the levels of work established for all types of agricultural labour by apprentices in each parish were printed in the *Jamaica Almanacks* for 1835-38. These would repay a detailed analysis. Another general topic worth exploring is the hiring out of 'jobbing' slaves.

13. Eric Eustace Williams, *Capitalism and Slavery*, London, Deutsch, 1964, 197-208; Michael Craton, 'What and Who, to Whom and What: The Significance of Slave Resistance', in Barbara L. Sopow and Stanley L.

Engerman, *British Capitalism and Caribbean Slavery: The Legacy of Eric Williams*, Cambridge University Press, 1987, 259-282.

14. Hugh Tinker, *A New System of Slavery, The Export of Indian Labour Overseas*, Oxford University Press, 1974. The scholarly literature on the transformation of the slave work-force in the British West Indies into post-slavery forms is considerable, but the following, in chronological order, are particularly relevant: Douglas G. Hall, *Free Jamaica, 1838-1865: An Economic History*, New Haven, Yale University Press, 1959; Woodville Marshall, 'Métayage in the Sugar Industry of the British Windward Islands, 1838-1865', *Jamaican Historical Review*, 5, 1965, 28-55; Alan A. Adamson, *Sugar Without Slaves: The Political Economy of British Guiana, 1838-1904*, New Haven, Yale University Press, 1972; Jay Mandle, *The Plantation Economy: Population and Economic Change in Guyana, 1838-1960*, Philadelphia, Temple University Press, 1973; Michael Craton, *Sinews of Empire*, 1974, 293-312; 'The Transition to Free Wage Labour: The Case of Worthy Park, Jamaica, 1834-1846', in *Transactions of Seventh Caribbean Historian's Conference*, Kingston, Jamaica, 1976, later published as Chapter 12 of *Searching for the Invisible Man: Slaves and Plantation Life in Jamaica*, Cambridge, Harvard University Press, 1978, 274-315; Woodville Marshall, *The Colthurst Journal, 1835-1838*, Millwood, KTO, 1977; Douglas G. Hall, 'The Flight from the Estates Reconsidered: The British West Indies, 1838-42', *Journal of Caribbean History*, 10/11, 1978, 7-24; O. Nigel Bolland, 'Systems of Domination After Slavery: The Control of Land and Labor in the British West Indies after 1838', *Comparative Studies in Society and History*, 23, 4, 1981, 591-619; William A. Green, 'The Perils of Comparative History: Belize and the British Sugar Colonies after Slavery', ibid, 26, 1984 (with reply from Bolland), 112-125; Woodville Marshall, 'Apprenticeship and Labour Relations in Four Windward Islands', in Richardson, *Abolition and its Aftermath*, 1985; Swithin Wilmot, 'Emancipation in Action: Workers and Wage Conflict in Jamaica, 1838-1840', *Jamaica Journal*, 19, 3, 1986, 55-62; Russell E. Chace, 'The Emergence and Development of an Estate-Based Peasantry in Dominica',

unpublished conference paper, 1986; Woodville Marshall, 'Provision Ground and Plantation Labour: Competition for Resources', unpublished paper, 20th Conference of Caribbean Historians, St Thomas, 1988; O. Nigel Bolland, 'The Institutionalization of Planter Hegemony in the Colonial Polity of the British West Indies after 1838', 22nd Conference of Caribbean Historians, Trinidad, 1990; Susan Craig, 'The Popular Struggle to Possess the Land in Tobago, 1838-1855, ibid; Barry Higman, 'To Begin the World Anew: Responses to Emancipation at Friendship and Greenwich Estates, Jamaica', *ibid*; Roderick McDonald, 'The Journal of John Anderson, St. Vincent Special Magistrate, 1836-1839', *ibid*; Verene Shepherd, 'Livestock Farmers and Marginality in Jamaica's Sugar Plantation Society: A Tentative Analysis', *ibid*.

15. Russell E. Chace, "Protest in Post-Emancipation Dominica: The 'Guerre Nègre' of 1844", *Journal of Caribbean History*, 23, 2, 1989, 118, 41; Woodville Marshall, " 'Vox Populi': The St. Vincent Riots and Disturbances of 1862", in Barry W. Higman (ed.), *Trade, Government and Society in Caribbean History: Essays Presented to Douglas Hall*, Kingston, 1983, 85-115; Michael Craton, 'Continuity and Change: The Incidence of Unrest among Ex-slaves in the British West Indies, 1838-1876', *Slavery and Abolition*, 9, 2, 1988, 144-170; Bridget Brereton, "Post-Emancipation Protest in the Caribbean: the 'Belmana Riots' in Tobago, 1876", *Caribbean Quarterly*, V, 30, 1984; Swithin Wilmot, 'The Politics of Protest in Free Jamaica: The Kingston Christmas Riots, 1840 and 1841', 22nd Conference of Caribbean Historians, Trinidad, 1990; Walter Rodney, *A History of the Guyanese Working People, 1881-1905*, Baltimore, Johns Hopkins University Press, 1981.

16. Jaine Alexandre-Debray, *Schoelcher*, Paris, 1983, 68, quoted by Blackburn, *Overthrow of Colonial Slavery*, 493. For the most comprehensive survey of the process in the French Antilles, see Dale W. Tomich, *Slavery in the Circuit of Sugar: Martinique and the World Economy, 1830-1848*, Baltimore, Johns Hopkins University Press, 1990. Some of Tomich's conclusions, however, are challenged by a recent paper in which Seymour Drescher extends his

analysis of metropolitan abolitionism to the French case. Seymour Drescher, 'British Way, French Way: Opinion Building and Revolution in the Second French Emancipation', *American Historical Review*, 96, 3, June 1991, 709-734. Drescher, incidentally, appeared to be widening his distinctive perspective even further, advertising a paper on 'Dutch Capitalism and Antislavery' for a conference on the Lesser Antilles at Hamilton College in October 1992. Drescher later widened his perspective to include the Dutch empire. See Seymour Drescher, 'The Long Good-bye: Dutch Capitalism and Anti-slavery', in Robert Paquette and Stanley Engerman (eds) *The Lesser Antilles in the Age of European Expansion*, Gainesville, University Press of Florida, 1996, 345-367.

17. Blackburn, *Overthrow of Colonial Slavery*, 492, 498, 501-508; Neville A. Hall, 'The Post-Emancipation Court Martial in Frederiksted, St. Croix, July-August, 1848: An Account and an Analysis', 13th Conference of Caribbean Historians, Guadeloupe, 1981.

18. Michael Craton, 'Forms of Resistance to Slavery', in Franklin Knight, *The Slave Societies of the Caribbean*, Volume 3 of UNESCO History of the Caribbean, 1994.

19. *Ibid.* Luis M. Díaz Soler, *Historia de la esclavitud negra en Puerto Rico*, 3rd edn, Rio Piedras, 1970; Guillermo A. Barait, *Esclavos rebeldes: conspiraciones sublevaciones de esclavos en Puerto Rico, 1795-1873*, Rio Piedras, 1982.

20. Robert L. Paquette, *Sugar Is Made With Blood: The Conspiracy of La Escalera and the Conflict between Empires over Slavery in Cuba*, Middletown, Wesleyan University Press, 1988, 262.

21. Craton, 'Forms of Resistance to Slavery'; Rebecca J. Scott, *Slave Emancipation in Cuba: The Transition to Free Labor, 1860-1899*, Princeton University Press, 1985; 'Explaining Abolition: Contradiction, Adaptation, and Challenge in Cuban Slave Society, 1860-1886', in F. Moreno Fraginals, F. Moya Pons and Stanley L. Engerman, *Between Slavery and Free Labor: The Spanish Speaking Caribbean in the Nineteenth Century*, Baltimore, Johns Hopkins University Press, 1985, 25-53.

22. William Darity Jr, 'The Williams Abolition Thesis before Williams', *Slavery and Abolition*, 9, 1, 1988, 32-43; Howard Temperley, 'Eric Williams and Abolition: The Birth of a New Orthodoxy', in Engerman and Solow, *British Capitalism & Caribbean Slavery*, 1988, 229-257.

23. Engerman and Solow, *British Capitalism and Caribbean Slavery*, 1-23.

24. Most notable on the 'Williams' side have been Gunnar Myrdal, *An American Dilemma*, New York, 1994; Oscar and Mary F. Handlin, 'Origins of the Southern Labor System', *William and Mary Quarterly*, 3rd series, VII, 1950, 210-211; Kenneth M. Stampp, *The Peculiar Institution*, New York, 1956; Edmund S. Morgan, *American Slavery, American Freedom: The Ordeal of Colonial Virginia*, New York, 1975; T. H. Breen and Stephen Innes, *'Myne Owne Ground': Race and Freedom on Virginia's Eastern Shore, 1640-1676*, New York, 1980, and William McKee Evans, 'From the Land of Canaan to the Land of Guinea: The Strange Odyssey of the Sons of Ham', *American Historical Review*, 85, 1980, 45.

Arguing to the contrary have been Carl N. Degler, 'Slavery and the Generation of American Race Prejudice', *Comparative Studies in Society and History*, II, 1960, 48-66; Winthrop D. Jordan, *White over Black: American Attitudes Towards the Negro, 1550-1812*, Chapel Hill, 1968; Harry Hoetink, *Caribbean Race Relations: A Study of Two Variants*, Oxford, 1967, and Wesley Frank Craven, *White, Red, and Black: The Seventeenth Century Virginian*, Charlottesville, 1971. William A. Green, 'Race and Slavery: Considerations on the Williams Thesis', in Engerman and Solow, *British Capitalism and Caribbean Slavery*, 25-49.

25. Hilary Beckles, *White Servitude and Black Slavery in Barbados, 1627-1715*, Knoxville, University Tennessee Press, 1989.

26. Kenneth F. Kiple, *The Caribbean Slave: A Biological History*, Cambridge University Press, 1984.

27. These include Robert Paul Thomas, 'The Sugar Colonies of the Old Empire: Profit or Loss for Great Britain?', *Economic History Review*, XXI, 1, 1968, 30-45; Rogert Anstey, 'Capitalism and Slavery: A Critique', *Economic History Review*, XXI, 1968, 307-320; 'The Volume and Profitability of the British Slave Trade, 1761-1807', in Stanley Engerman and Eugene Genovese (eds), *Race and Slavery in the Western Hemisphere: Quantitative Studies*, Princeton, 1975; *The Atlantic Slave Trade and British*

Abolition, 1760-1810, New York, 1975; Stanley L. Engerman, 'The Slave Trade and British Capital Formation in the Eighteenth Century: A Comment on the Williams Thesis', *Business History Review*, 46, 1972, 431, and David Richardson, 'The Slave Trade, Sugar and British Economic Growth, 1748-1776', in Engerman and Solow, *British Capitalism and Caribbean Slavery*, 103-133. More supportive of Williams have been Richard B. Sheridan, 'The Wealth of Jamaica in the Eighteenth Century', *Economic History Review*, XVIII, 1965, 292-311; *Sugar and Slavery: An Economic history of the British West Indies, 1623-1775*, Barbados, 1974; Barbara Solow, 'Capitalism and Slavery in the Exceedingly Long Run', in Engerman and Solow, British Capitalism and Caribbean Slavery, 51-77, and Joseph E. Inikori, 'Slavery and the Development of Industrial Capital in England', *ibid*, 79-101.

28. Lowell J. Ragatz, *The Fall of the Planter Class in the British Caribbean, 1763-1833*, New York, 1928; Darity, 'The Williams Abolition Thesis Before Williams', 32-43.

29. G. R. Mellor, *British Imperial Trusteeship, 1783-1850*, London, Faber, 1951; Roger Anstey, *The Atlantic Slave Trade and British Abolition, 1760-1810*, London, 1975; Seymour Drescher, *Econocide: British Slavery in the Era of Abolition*, Pittsburgh University Press, 1977; 'The Decline Thesis of British Slavery Since Econocide', *Slavery and Abolition*, 7, 1, 1986; 'Paradigms Tossed: Capitalism and the Political Sources of Abolition', in Solow and Engerman, *British Capitalism and Caribbean Slavery*, 1988, 191-208; John R. Ward, *British West Indian Slavery, 1750-1834: The Process of Amelioration*, Oxford, Clarendon Press, 1988; Eltis, *Economic Growth and the Ending of the Transatlantic Slave Trade*, 1988.

30. Selwyn H.H. Carrington, 'Econocide – Myth or Reality: the Question of West Indian Decline, 1783-1806', *Boletin de Estudios Latinamericanos y del Caribe*, 36, 1984; 'The American Revolution and the British West Indies Economy', in Solow and Engerman, *British Capitalism and Caribbean Slavery*, 135-162; 'The State of the Debate on the Role of Capitalism in the Ending of the Slave System', *Journal of Caribbean History*, 22, 1&2, 1988, 20-41.

31. For the demographic aspects of the anti-slavery debate, Barry W. Higman, *Slave Population and Economy in Jamaica, 1807-1834*, Cambridge University Press, 1976; *Slave Population of the British Caribbean, 1807-1834*, Baltimore, Johns Hopkins University Press, 1984.

32. Craton, *Sinews of Empire*, 256-257. Above pages [5-6]. 'The callousness of the trading interest beyond the sea to the distresses of the kidnapped servitors and the miseries of the slave trade, gradually roused a philanthropic sentiment, which was eventually to exercise a powerful influence on the condition of labour at home . . . Comparative little progress was made till the philanthropic agitation was reinforced by political and economic reasons for abandoning the trade as detrimental.' William Cunningham, *The Growth of English Industry and Commerce in Modern Times*, Cambridge, 1907, 607, quoted in Selwyn Carrington, 'The State of the Debate on the Role of Capitalism in the Ending of the Slave System', *Journal of Caribbean History*, 22, 1&2, 1988, 20-41.

33. Francisco Moreno Fraginals, *The Sugarmill: The Socioeconomic Complex of Sugar in Cuba*, New York, Monthly Review Press, 1976; *El Ingenio: complejo económico social cubano del azúcar*, 2nd edn, 3 vols, Havana, Editorial del Ciencias Sociales, 1978; 'Plantations in the Caribbean: Cuba, Puerto Rico, and the Dominican Republic in the Late Nineteenth Century', in Moreno Fraginals, Moya Pons and Engerman, Between Slavery and Free Labor, 1985, 3-23.

34. Oscar Zanetti and Alejandro Garcia, *Caminos para el azúcar*, Havana, Editiones Ciencias Sociales, 1987; Jean Stubbs, *Tobacco on the Periphery: A Case Study in Cuban Labour History, 1860-1958*, Cambridge University Press, 1985; Andrés Ramos Mattei, *La Hacienda Azucarera: Su crecimiento y crisis en Puerto Rico (siglo XIX)*, San Juan, Centro de Estudios Puertorriquena, 1981; 'Technical Innovations and Social Change in the Sugar Industry of Puerto Rico, 1870-1880', in Moreno Fraginals, Moya Pons and Engerman, *Between Slavery and Free Labor*, 158-179; Benjamin Nistal-Moret, 'Problems in the Social Structure of Slavery in Puerto Rico during the Process of Abolition, 1872', *ibid*,141-156; Frank Moya Pons, 'The Land Question in Haiti and Santo Domingo: The Sociopolitical Context of the Tran-

sition from Slavery to Free Wage Labor, 1801-1843', *ibid*, 181-213; Francisco Scarano, *Sugar and Slavery in Puerto Rico: The Plantation Economy of Ponce, 1800-1850*, Madison, University of Wisconsin, 1984; 'Explaining Slavery: Peasants, Bureaucrats, and the Failure of Labour Control in Puerto Rico, 1750-1820', unpublished paper, Amsterdam, 1988; Laird W. Bergad, *Coffee and the Growth of Agrarian Capitalism in Nineteenth Century Puerto Rico*, Princeton, 1983; Astrid Cubano, 'Trade and Sugar Monoculture in Puerto Rico: The Sugar Crisis in the Arecibo Region, 1878-1898', 20th Conference of Cari-bbean Historians, St Thomas, 1988; Pedro San Miguel, *El mundo que creó el azúcar: las haciendas en Vega Baja, 1800-1873*, Rio Piedras, 1989; Michiel Baud, 'The First World Regional Change', *ibid*; Anon. (History Task Force, Centro de Estudios Puertorriquenos), *Labor Migration under Capitalism: The Puerto Rican Experience*, New York, Monthly Review Press, 1979; Peter Boomgaard and Gert Oostindie (eds), 'Changing Sugar Technology and the Labour Nexus', *Nieuwe Westindische Gids*, 1989.

35. Rebecca J. Scott, *Slave Emancipation in Cuba*, 1985; 'Explaining Abolition: Contradiction, Adaptation and Challenge in Cuban Slave Society, 1860-1886', *Comparative Studies in Society and History*, XXVI, 1984, 83-111 and in Moreno Fraginals, Moya Pons and Engerman, *Between Slavery and Free Labor*, 1985, 25-52.

36. Michael Craton, 'Commentary: The Search for a Unified Field Theory', in Boomgaard and Oostindie, 'Changing Sugar Technology and the Labour Nexus', 1989, 135-142; John Ward, 'The Amelioration of British West Indian Slavery, 1750-1834: Technical Change and the Plough', *ibid*; Richard B. Sheridan, 'Changing Sugar Technology and the Labour Nexus in the British Caribbean, 1750-1900, with Special Reference to Barbados and Jamaica', *ibid*; Alex van Stipriaan, 'Changing Sugar Technology and the Labour Nexus, Surinam, 1750-1900', *ibid*; Dale Tomich, 'Sugar Technology and Slave Labor in Martinique, 1830-1848' *ibid*.

37. Craton, 'Unified Field Theory', 1989, 135-140. My overall conclusion was: 'Change (including technological change) was ultimately driven by the quest for profit in the face of the world sugar price. Change, however, was limited not so much by the availability of capital or labour as by the availability of plentiful, cheap, fertile and politically unencumbered *land* – since both capital and labour would readily migrate or become available in such areas, and *only* to such areas'; *ibid*, 140-141.

38. See, for example, Bonham C. Richardson, 'Freedom and Migration in the Leeward Caribbean, 1838-1848', *Journal of Historical Geography*, 6, 1980, 395-405; *Caribbean Migrants: Environment and Human Survival on St. Kitts and Nevis*, Knoxville, University of Tennessee Press, 1983; *Panama Money in Barbados, 1900-1920*, Knoxville, University of Tennessee Press, 1985; Elizabeth McLean Petras, *Jamaican Labor Migration: White Capital and Black Labor, 1850-1930*, Boulder, Westview, 1988; Cecelia Karch, 'The Role of the Barbados Mutual Life Assurance Society during the International Sugar Crisis of the Late Nineteenth Century', 12th Conference of Caribbean Historians, Trinidad, 1980; 'The Growth of the Corporate Economy in Barbados: Class or Race Factors, 1890-1977', in Susan Craig, *The Contemporary Caribbean: A Sociological Reader*, 1, Port of Spain, 1982.

39. O. Nigel Bolland, 'Systems of Domination after Slavery: The Control of Land and Labor in the British West Indies after 1838', *Comparative Studies in Society and History*, 26, 1, 1981, 591-619; 'The Politics of Freedom in the British Caribbean', in Seymour Drescher and Frank McGlynn, *The Meaning of Freedom: The Dynamics of Race and Class in Post-Slavery Societies in the New World*, University of Pittsburgh Press forthcoming; Michael Baud, 'Sugar and Unfree Labour: Reflections on Labour Recruiting in the Dominican Republic, 1870-1940', Amsterdam, 1988; Elizabeth Fox-Genovese and Eugene D. Genovese, *Fruits of Merchant Capital: Slavery and Bourgeois Property in the Rise and Expansion of Capitalism*, Oxford University Press, 1983; Rosemarijn Hoefte, 'Plantation Labor after the Abolition of Slavery, Suriname, 1880-1930', *ibid*; Howard Johnson, 'A Modified Form of Slavery: The Credit and Truck Systems in the Bahamas in the Nineteenth and Early Twentieth Centuries', *Comparative Studies in the Society and History*, 28, 4, 1986, 726-758.

Chapter 20

1. My unsatisfactory attempt to achieve a better understanding of island and regional identities in the British West Indies is justified perhaps by the title of the series in which is given. The life and work of Elsa Goveia in fact epitomises the search for West Indian identity. Elsa herself – a Guyanese of Afro-Portuguese descent, working mainly in Jamaica and writing her most famous book on the Leeward Islands – was also, as Gordon Lewis reminds us, a pioneer explorer of West Indian identity, in her comparative studies of slave laws and, above all, in her pathbreaking first published book, entitled *A Study on the Historiography of the British West Indies to the End of the Nineteenth Century*, Mexico City, Pan-American Institute, 1956; reprint, Washington, DC, Howard University Press, 1980.

2. Peter Gzowski, in an address to the University of Waterloo History Society on Canadian Identity, March 14, 1991, also provided me with the concept of identity as concentric circles, developed below. For a valuable recent symposium on the concept of home, see *Home: a Place in the World*, *Social Research* 58, 1, Special Issue, Spring 1991, which incudes an especially relevant essay by Orlando Patterson in the section entitled 'Slavery, alienation and the female discovery of personal freedom'.

3. Edward Kamau Brathwaite, *Mother Poem*, Oxford, Oxford University Press, 1977; Derek Walcott, *Omeros*, New York; Farrar Straus, Giroux, 1990.

4. In a typically brilliant essay, Simon Schama dates the discovery of precision in landscape, with its implications for belonging and ownership, to a specific artist and a significant moment in European history. For him, the prototypical work was the series of drawings of the countryside near Haarlem produced by the Dutch artist, Hendrik Goltzius, in 1603. For Schama, though, this signified the emergence of a patriotic concept of 'homeland' against a smothering Spanish Imperialism, occurring at the end of the first phase of the Dutch War of Independence, rather than the genesis of bourgeois possessiveness, soon to spread to Britain and France. Schama's thesis seems to ignore that the Dutch, once free, were immediately imperialists themselves (if of a different sort from the Spanish), with their new colonial possessions intimately recorded by professional artists, including cartographers – a tradition soon emulated by the British and the French. Simon Schama, 'Homelands', in *Social Research* 58, 1, Spring 1991, 11-30.

5. A. A. Milne, *When We Were Very Young*, London, Mathuen, 1924, 36-37.

6. George Lamming, *In the Castle of My Skin*, London, Macmillan 1953; Wole Soyinka, *Aké: the Years of Childhood*, London, Collins, 1981.

7. Michael Craton, 'White law and black custom: the evolution of Bahamian land tenures', in *Land and Development in the Caribbean*, Jean Besson and Janet Momsen (eds), London, Macmillan Caribbean, 1987.

8. Walcott, *Omeros*, III, iii, 19.

9. Francis A. MacNutt (ed.), *De Orbe Novo: the Eight Decades o Peter Martyr D'Anghera*, 2 vols, 1912; reprint, New York, Franklin, 1970, II, 270; Fred Olson, *On the Trail of the Arawaks*, Norman, Oklahoma University Press, 1974, 89-120, 215-224.

10. MacNutt, *De Orbe Novo*, II, 252.

11. John R. Seeley, *The Expansion of England*, 1883, quoted by Frank W. Pitman in *The Development of the British West Indies, 1700-1763*, 1917, 2.

12. Elsa V. Goveia, *Slave Society in the British Leeward Islands at the End of the Eighteenth Century*, New Haven, Yale University Press, 1965; Edward K. Brathwaite, *The Development of Creole Society in Jamaica, 1770-1820*, Oxford, Clarendon Press, 1971.

13. Douglas G. Hall (ed.) *In Miserable Slavery: Thomas Thistlewood in Jamaica, 1750-1786*, London, Macmillan Caribbean, 1989.

14. 'The Negroes from some countries think they return to their own countries when they die in Jamaica, and therefore regard death but little, imagining they shall change their conditions, by that means, from servile to free, and so for this reason often cut their own throats. Whether they die thus, or naturally, their country people make great lamentations, mournings, and howlings about their expiring, and at funeral throw in rum and victuals into their graves, to serve them in the other world. Sometimes they bury it in gourds, at other times spill it on the graves'. Hans Sloane, *A Journey to the islands Madera, Barbados, Nieves, St Christophers and Jamaica . . .*, London, 1707, 1725, I, II.

15. This, of course, is not to deny completely the continuing emotional pull of Mother Africa. As Handler and Lange have shown, Barbadian slaves buried by their kin as late as 1800 were interred with their bodies aligned towards the east – although it should be noted, this was pointing in the direction of the Christian Holy Land (and even Britain) as well as back to the African heartland. See Handler and Lange, *Plantation Slavery in Barbados: an Archaeological and Historical Investigation*, Cambridge, Harvard University Press, 1978, 103-215.

16. Bruce Hamilton, *Barbados and the Confederation Question, 1871-1885*, London, Crown Agents, 1956; Robin W. Winks, *Canadian-West Indian Union: a Forty-Year Minuet*, London, 1968; Hilary Beckles provides me with an even more telling anecdote about the Barbadian blacks' patriotism. After Bussa's 1816 rebellion, 124 attainted slaves were transported to Honduras, with the survivors being shipped onwards to Sierra Leone in West Africa in 1819. More than 20 years later, they almost all 'loyally' petitioned Queen Victoria to be allowed to return to Barbados, 'the land of [their] nativity'. They were first offered Jamaica, but this they rejected, 'being totally ignorant of the manner and customs of that place'. In September 1841, on the strength of a positive evaluation of the exiles' orderly conduct by the acting governor of Sierra Leone, the colonial secretary, Lord John Russell, wrote that there were no objections to their return, although as yet there is no certain evidence that any of them achieved their aim. 'Humble Memorial of your Majesty's most dutiful Barbadian subjects being inhabitants of the colony of Sierra Leone', May 13, 1841; John Car, acting governor, Sierra Leone, to Lord John Russell, July 5, 1841, and Russell's reply, September 30, 1841, London, Public Record Office, C.O. 267/164.

17. Michael Craton, 'Reluctant Creoles: the planters' world in the British West Indies', in *Strangers Within the Realm*, Bernard Bailyn and Philip Morgan (eds), Chapel Hill, North Carolina, 1991.

18. Brathwaite, 'Horse weebles', in *Mother Poem*, 39-40.

19. Vidia S. Naipaul, *The Middle Passage: the Caribbean Revisited*, London, Andre Deutsch, 1962, 29.

20. Derek Walcott, 'Homecoming: Anse La Raye [for Garth St Omer], in *The Gulf and Other Poems*, London, Cape, 1969; and *Collected Poems, 1948-1984*, New York, Farrar, Straus & Giroux, 1986, 127-128.

21. '. . . and O was the conch-shell's invocation, mer was both mother and sea in our Antillean patois, os, a grey bone, and the white surf as it crashes and speaks its sibilant collar on a lace shore . . .' (Walcott, *Omeros*, II, iii, 14).

22. Michael Craton and Gail Saunders, *Islanders in the Stream: a History of the Bahamian People. Vol. One: From Aboriginal Times to the End of Slavery*, Athens, Georgia University Press, 1992.

23. Rosemary Brana-Shute (compiler and editor), with the assistance of Rosemarijn Hoefte, *A Bibliography of Caribbean Migration and Caribbean Immigrant Communities*, Gainesville, Center for Latin American Studies, University of Florida, 1983.

24. Dawn I. Marshall, 'The history of Caribbean migrations: the case of the West Indies', *Caribbean Review*, 11, I, Winter 1982, 6-9, 52-53; 'A history of West Indian migrations: overseas opportunities and 'safety-valve' policies', in *The Caribbean Exodus*, Barry B. Levine (ed.), New York, Praeger, 1987, 15-31; Elizabeth Thomas-Hope, 'The establishment of a migration tradition: British West Indian movements to the Hispanic Caribbean in the century after emancipation', in *Caribbean Social Relations*, Colin G. Clarke (ed.), Liverpool, Centre for Latin American Studies, 1978; Peter D. Fraser, 'Nineteenth-century West Indian migration to Britain', in *In Search of a Better Life: Perspectives on Migration from the Caribbean*, Ransford W. Palmer (ed.), New York, Praeger, 1990, 19-37; Olive Senior, 'The Colón people', and 'The Panama railway', *Jamaica Journal*, 1978-80, 41, 62-71; 42, 88-103; 44, 67-77; Lancelot S. Lewis, *The West Indian in Panama: Black Labor in Panama, 1850-1914*, Jamaica, Institute of Social and Economic Research, 1984; Bonham C. Richardson, *Panama Money in Barbados, 1900-1920*, Knoxville, Tennessee University Press, 1985.

25. Gordon K. Lewis, *Main Currents in Caribbean Thought*, Baltimore: Johns Hopkins, 1983.

Index